Rival Jerusalems

This pioneering book results from a major project funded by the Leverhulme Trust and the ESRC. It is based upon very extensive analysis of the famous 1851 *Census of Religious Worship* and earlier sources such as the 1676 Compton Census. Its scope and modern analytical methods eclipse all previous British work on its subject, and it is a major step forward in the study of religious history.

The book stresses contextual and regional understanding of religion. Among the subjects covered for all of England and Wales are the geography of the Church of England, Roman Catholicism, the old and new dissenting denominations, the spatial complementarity of denominations, and their importance for political history. A range of further questions are then analysed in even greater detail, using massive parish datasets of religious, socio-economic and demographic data for 2,443 English and Welsh parishes. Among the issues treated are regional continuities in religion, the growth of religious pluralism, Sundajy schools and child labour during industrialisation, free and appropriated church sittings, landownership and religion, and urbanisation and regional 'secularisation'. Regional contrasts between denominations, and between Wales and England, are persistent themes. The long-term importance of the geography of religion is stressed, for it bears on many crucial modern questions of regional cultures and national identities.

This book's advanced methods and findings will have far-reaching influence within the disciplines of history, historical and cultural geography, religious sociology, religious studies, and in the social science community in general.

K. D. M. Snell is Reader in Regional Cultures in the Department of English Local History, University of Leicester.

Paul S. Ell is Director of the Centre for Data Digitisation and Analysis, School of Sociology and Social Policy, The Queen's University of Belfast.

Rival Jerusalems

The Geography of Victorian Religion

K. D. M. Snell
and Paul S. Ell

PUBLISHED BY THE PRESS SYNDICATE OF THE UNIVERSITY OF CAMBRIDGE
The Pitt Building, Trumpington Street, Cambridge, United Kingdom

CAMBRIDGE UNIVERSITY PRESS
The Edinburgh Building, Cambridge CB2 2RU, UK http://www.cup.cam.ac.uk
40 West 20th Street, New York, NY 10011–4211, USA http://www.cup.org
10 Stamford Road, Oakleigh, Melbourne 3166, Australia
Ruiz de Alarcón 13, 28014 Madrid, Spain

First published 2000

Printed in the United Kingdom at the University Press, Cambridge

Typeface Trump Mediaeval 9.75/13.5 pt. *System* QuarkXPress™ [SE]

A catalogue record for this book is available from the British Library

Library of Congress Cataloging in Publication data

Snell, K. D. M.
Rival Jerusalems: the Geography of Victorian Religion
/ K. D. M. Snell and Paul S. Ell
p. cm.
Includes bibliographical references and index.
ISBN 0 521 77155 2
1. England – Church history – 19th century. 2. Sociology, Christian – England – History – 19th century. 3. Wales – Church history – 19th century. 4. Sociology, Christian – Wales – History – 19th century. I. Ell, Paul S. II. Title.
BR759.S54 2000
274.2′081 – dc21 99-37794 CIP

ISBN 0 521 77155 2

Scarcely anything, indeed, is more curious or puzzling, than the attempt to trace the causes why particular doctrines or religious parties should find one soil favourable and another adverse to their propagation and success. But, at all events, as far as facts are concerned, England furnishes a striking picture of sects and creeds almost supreme in one part and absolutely unknown in another.

HORACE MANN, 'On the statistical position of religious bodies in England and Wales', *Journal of the Statistical Society*, 18 (1855), p. 155.

Even people whose lives have been made various by learning, sometimes find it hard to keep a fast hold on their habitual views of life, on their faith in the Invisible . . . when they are suddenly transported to a new land, where the beings around them know nothing of their history, and share none of their ideas . . . in which the past becomes dreamy because its symbols have all vanished, and the present too is dreamy because it is linked with no memories. But even *their* experience may hardly enable them thoroughly to imagine what was the effect on a simple weaver like Silas Marner, when he left his own country and people and came to settle in Raveloe. Nothing could be more unlike his native town, set within sight of the widespread hillsides, than this low, wooded region, where he felt hidden even from the heavens by the screening trees and hedgerows. There was nothing here, when he rose in the deep morning quiet and looked out on the dewy brambles and rank tufted grass, that seemed to have any relation with that life centring in Lantern Yard, which had once been to him the altar-place of high dispensations. The white-washed walls; the little pews where well-known figures entered with a subdued rustling, and where first one well-known voice and then another, pitched in a peculiar key of petition, uttered phrases at once occult and familiar, like the amulet worn on the heart; the pulpit where the minister delivered unquestioned doctrine, and swayed to and fro, and handled the book in a long-accustomed manner; the very pauses between the couplets of the hymn, as it was given out, and the recurrent swell of voices in song: these things had been the channel of divine influences to Marner – they were the fostering home of his religious emotions – they were Christianity and God's kingdom upon earth . . .

And what could be more unlike that Lantern Yard world than the world in Raveloe? – orchards looking lazy with neglected plenty; the large church in the wide churchyard, which men gazed at lounging at their own doors in service-time . . . There were no lips in Raveloe from which a word could fall that would stir Silas Marner's benumbed faith to a sense of pain. In the early ages of the world, we know, it was believed that each territory was inhabited and ruled by its own divinities, so that a man could cross the bordering heights and be out of the reach of his native gods, whose presence was confined to the streams and the groves and the hills among which he had lived from his birth. And poor Silas was vaguely conscious of something not unlike the feeling of primitive men, when they fled thus, in fear or in sullenness, from the face of an unpropitious deity. It seemed to him that the Power he had vainly trusted in among the streets and at the prayer-meetings, was very far away from this land in which he had taken refuge, where men lived in careless abundance, knowing and needing nothing of that trust, which, for him, had been turned to bitterness. The little light he possessed spread its beams so narrowly, that frustrated belief was a curtain broad enough to create for him the blackness of night.

GEORGE ELIOT, *Silas Marner* (1861, Harmondsworth, 1969 edn), ch. 2, pp. 62–4.

Contents

List of figures *page* ix
List of tables xi
Preface and acknowledgements xv

Introduction 1

Part 1 Religious geographies: the districts of England and Wales
Paul S. Ell and K. D. M. Snell

1 The 1851 *Census of Religious Worship* 23

2 The Church of England 54

3 Old dissent: the Presbyterians, Independents, Baptists, Quakers and Unitarians 93

4 The geographies of new dissent 121

5 Roman Catholicism and Irish immigration 173

6 Denominational co-existence, reciprocity or exclusion? 185

Part 2 Religion and locality: parish-level explorations
K. D. M. Snell

7 A prospect of fifteen counties 201

8 From Henry Compton to Horace Mann: stability or relocation in Catholicism and Nonconformity, and the growth of religious pluralism (*with A. Crockett*) 232

9 The Sunday school movement: child labour, denominational control and working-class culture 274

10 Free or appropriated sittings: the Anglican Church in perspective 321

11 Conformity, dissent and the influence of landownership 364
12 Urbanisation and regional secularisation 395

Technical appendices

A Denominational statistics 423
B The correction of census data 425
C The religious measures 431
D Computer cartographic methods 438
E Landownership and the *Imperial Gazetteer* 440
F An 1861 Census of Religious Worship? 449

Bibliography 453
Index 483

Figures

2.1. Church of England percentage share of sittings in 1851 *page* 56

2.2. Church of England place of worship density in 1851 61

2.3. People per place of worship for the Church of England in 1851 63

2.4. Church of England index of occupancy in 1851 68

2.5. Church of England index of sittings in 1851 70

2.6. Church of England index of attendances in 1851 72

2.7. Church of England 'core' areas in 1851 73

3.1. United Presbyterian Church index of attendances in 1851 96

3.2. Independent index of attendances in 1851 100

3.3. Baptist index of attendances in 1851 105

3.4. Quaker index of attendances in 1851 110

3.5. Unitarian index of attendances in 1851 117

3.6. Old dissent index of attendances in 1851 119

4.1. Wesleyan Methodist Original Connexion index of attendances in 1851 125

4.2. Wesleyan Methodist Original Connexion index of occupancy in 1851 128

4.3. Wesleyan Methodist New Connexion index of attendances in 1851 134

4.4. Primitive Methodist index of attendances in 1851 138

4.5. Primitive Methodist index of occupancy in 1851 140

4.6. Wesleyan Methodist Association index of attendances in 1851 145

4.7. Wesleyan Reformer index of attendances in 1851 148

4.8. Bible Christian index of attendances in 1851 152

4.9. Calvinistic Methodist index of attendances in 1851 156

4.10. Countess of Huntingdon's Connexion index of attendances in 1851 161

4.11. Latter Day Saints index of attendances in 1851 165

4.12. New dissent index of attendances in 1851 168

5.1. Roman Catholic index of attendances in 1851 176

7.1. The registration counties for which parish-level data were compiled 202

8.1. Papists as a percentage of total 'inhabitants' in Monmouthshire in 1676 247

8.2. Roman Catholic percentage share of total attendances (all denominations) in Monmouthshire in 1851 248

8.3. Papists as a percentage of total 'inhabitants' in Leicestershire in 1676 251

8.4. Roman Catholic percentage share of total attendances (all denominations) in Leicestershire in 1851 252

8.5. Papists as a percentage of total 'inhabitants' in the East Riding in 1676 254

8.6. Roman Catholic percentage share of total attendances (all denominations) in the East Riding in 1851 255

8.7. Nonconformists as a percentage of total 'inhabitants' in Leicestershire in 1676 261

8.8. Old-dissent percentage share of total attendances (all denominations) in Leicestershire in 1851 262

9.1. Sunday school attendances in 1851 as a percentage of registration-district population 291

9.2. Sunday school enrolment and child labour in 1851 292

12.1. Index of total sittings (all denominations) in 1851 406

12.2. Index of total attendances (all denominations) in 1851 408

12.3. Population density in 1851 410

12.4. Persons per place of worship for all denominations in 1851 412

12.5. Index of occupancy for all denominations in 1851 413

Tables

1.1. Spearman (rank) correlation coefficients between denominations' total available sittings and the numbers at their highest attended services on Census Sunday, 1851. Parish-level data for all parishes in fifteen English and Welsh registration counties *page* 47

2.1. Percentages of parishes without clerical housing, and average values of parish livings: fifteen counties 86

2.2. Values of English and Welsh parish livings (the 15 counties), calculated for those with and without clerical accommodation 89

3.1. The strength of old dissent 94

4.1. The strength of the new denominations 122

6.1. Spearman (rank) correlation coefficients between major denominations, using their indexes of attendances, by registration districts 190

6.2. Spearman (rank) correlation coefficients between major denominations, using their indexes of attendances, distinguishing between English regions, by registration districts 195

7.1. Selected demographic characteristics of the fifteen counties 223

7.2. Percentage distribution of landownership categories by county 225

7.3. Socio-economic features of the fifteen counties 226

7.4. Families in agriculture, occupiers and agricultural labourers in 1831 228

7.5. Indexes of attendances for major denominations, and total index of attendances for all 1851 denominations, excluding Sunday scholars 230

8.1. Average parish percentages of Papists and Nonconformists in the Compton Census by county, and the percentage of parishes in 1676 containing Papists and/or Nonconformists 241

8.2. Continuity of Compton Nonconformity to old dissent in 1851, and Compton Papism to Roman Catholicism in 1851 – a parish-level analysis of 12 counties 242

8.3(a). Kruskal–Wallis test on grouped Compton Papist data against 1851 percentage share of Catholic attendances (of total attendances for all denominations) 244

8.3(b). Kruskal–Wallis test on grouped Compton Nonconformist data against 1851 percentage share of 'old dissent' attendances (of total attendances for all denominations) 244

8.4. Mean annual population growth rates (1811–51) and the continuity of Catholicism 264

8.5(a). Test for Papist strength decreasing in the presence of Nonconformity 267

8.5(b). Test for Nonconformist strength decreasing in the presence of Papism 267

9.1. English county-level analysis of the determinants of Sunday school pupils as a percentage of total population on census day, 1851 (stepwise multiple regression) 295

9.2. Total maximum-figure Sunday school attendance for selected denominations, as a percentage of total maximum-figure Sunday school attendance for all denominations, in each county 298

9.3. The percentage of denominational churches or chapels (by parish) which had any Sunday schools 300

9.4. Ratios of the total of each denomination's maximum Sunday school attendance to the denomination's maximum religious attendance 301

9.5. Church of England Sunday school index of maximum attendance, by categories of landownership 305

9.6. Total old dissent Sunday school index of maximum attendance, by categories of landownership 306

9.7. Total Methodist Sunday school index of maximum attendance, by categories of landownership 306

9.8. Welsh Calvinistic Methodist Sunday school index of maximum attendance, by categories of landownership 307

9.9. Total denominational Sunday school maximum attendance, by categories of landownership 308

9.10. Parish-level analysis of the total maximum Sunday school index of attendance, for all denominations combined (stepwise multiple regression) 311

10.1. County percentages of free sittings by denomination 347

10.2. Free and appropriated sittings, by denomination, for the fifteen counties and nationally 348

11.1. Landownership category and the size of parishes 371

11.2. Landownership and the Church of England's index of sittings 373

11.3. Landownership and the total dissenting index of sittings 375

11.4. Landownership and religious diversity 377

11.5. Mean denominational index of total attendances by landownership category 379

11.6. County mean 'religious diversity' measures, by landownership category 381

11.7. Values of the Anglican living and landownership 385

11.8. Average property values, population growth rates, acres per person and poor relief by landownership 387

11.9. Landownership categories and average parish employment of families (1831 occupational census) 390

11.10. Landownership categories and average parish percentages of the occupied population (1831) in different occupational categories 391

12.1. Spearman (rank) correlation coefficients between denominational indexes of attendance and population per square kilometre, at registration-district level for all of England and Wales; at parish level for all parishes in the fifteen counties; and at parish level between indexes of attendance and population growth rates, 1811–51 397

12.2. Categories of 'urbanisation', and their corresponding average index of total attendances for all denominations, at registration-district and parish levels 400

12.3. Spearman (rank) correlation coefficients between 'urbanisation' and indexes of attendances for all denominations, at registration-district and parish levels 402

12.4. Indexes of total religious attendance (all denominations) for the English border districts, the London districts, all Wales, all England, and English urban/industrial districts in the west midlands, the north-east and the north-west 415

A.1. Summary statistics for the major denominations, England and Wales 423

E.1. Landownership categories and source coverage by county 442

E.2. Number of owners in Leicestershire in 1832, by categories of landownership 445

E.3. Median test on Leicestershire landownership 446

Preface and acknowledgements

This project started in the mid-1980s, as part of a study of the cultural regions of the British Isles (which extended also to the regional novel). It grew out of concern over political centralisation and a widely felt need to know more about the history and persistence of British regional cultures. Religion, like the regional novel, is only one of many cultural elements – but it is essential to an historical understanding of regional cultures.

The necessary religious data collection, reading, collaboration and related work meant that this book has been a long time coming to fulfilment. After initial research, the project gained a two-year grant from the Leverhulme Trust (1992–4) which funded Paul Ell as a Research Associate. It was then awarded a three-year grant from the ESRC (1994–7) which funded Alasdair Crockett as a Research Associate. The grants were directed by K. D. M. Snell in the Department of English Local History, University of Leicester. We are particularly grateful to the Leverhulme Trust and the ESRC for their valuable support. K. D. M. Snell is grateful also to the Research Board of the University of Leicester for financial assistance, and to the University of Leicester for generous provision of computing equipment.

This book comprises something over half of this research on religious history, and it is due to be followed by a second work on 'Secularisation' by Alasdair Crockett. That study is now being pursued at Nuffield College Oxford, and will be published in the near future. For much of the project, it was planned to publish all the research as one very large book, by three authors, but limitations on book length made it impossible to pursue this. Alasdair's contribution to this book has been considerable, including the co-authorship of chapter 8, and we owe him a large debt of gratitude.

Responsibility for the chapters and appendices of this book is as follows. The introduction, chapters 6, 7, 9, 10, 11, 12 and appendices

A, E and F, were written by K. D. M. Snell. Chapters 1–5 and appendices B, C and D, were written by Paul Ell and K. D. M. Snell. Chapter 8 was written by Alasdair Crockett and K. D. M. Snell.

Computerised analysis of the registration-district data used Minitab and SPSS, and for the parish-level data we used mainframe and Windows versions of SPSS. Geographical analysis and computerised cartography were conducted with GIMMS, Arc/Info and Arc/View. The registration-district and parish-level data that this research project created and analysed are being deposited with the ESRC Data Archive at Essex University.

We would like to thank Louise Blodwell, Tony Cooper, Jillian Draper, Sean Hendy, Ralph Weedon and Simon Wilson for their help in data collection and computerisation. Margery Tranter of the Department of English Local History kindly provided the religious data for Derbyshire, and her knowledge of the local history of religion has been of considerable value. The staff of the Public Record Office, the Leicestershire County Record Office, and the National Library of Wales in Aberystwyth have been most helpful. In addition, for their advice on different aspects of this work, we express gratitude to Rod Ambler, John Beckett of the University of Leicester Computer Centre, Alan Everitt, Clive Field, Harold Fox, Robin Gill, Ieuan Gwynedd Jones, Kevin Lee, Gareth Lewis, Jo North, David Parsons, Charles Phythian-Adams, David Postles, Mohammed Quraishi, Revd Frank Rinaldi, Paul Ryan, Terry Slater, Margaret Spufford and Anne Whiteman.

Earlier versions of chapters 8 and 9 were published respectively in *Rural History*, 8:1 (1997), and *Past and Present*, 164 (1999), and permission for re-publication is gratefully acknowledged here.

Introduction

The state of the historiography

When George Eliot wrote *Silas Marner*, she was acutely aware of the regional differences in religious cultures through which Silas moved. Even people 'whose lives have been made various by learning', she wrote, find it hard to maintain their beliefs when they are transported into a new region, 'where the beings around them know nothing of their history, and share none of their ideas . . . in which the past becomes dreamy because its symbols have all vanished'. In Silas' move from a northern, strongly Nonconformist chapel setting – its familiar phrases like an 'amulet worn on the heart . . . the fostering home of his religious emotions' – to the large Anglican church of Raveloe and its associated culture, Eliot captured one of the fundamental regional contrasts of her time. Silas, she wrote, was vaguely conscious that 'each territory was inhabited and ruled by its own divinities': by its own 'native gods', whose influence was locally contained and not transferable. In the consequent disassociation of Silas from religious belief, a response to this regional transition and confrontation with people of differing views, she defined a fundamental cause of religious disillusionment.[1]

This was a subtle and sensitive lesson from a novelist of great intuition. We shall need to keep it in mind. For in her preoccupation with these themes, and in her awareness of regional contrasts and their effects, George Eliot was articulating thoughts which are now remote from the minds of many historians. It is often customary to begin academic books by stating the scholarly gaps that one's work tries to fill, and it is appropriate to do that here, albeit in a more austere style than that penned by George Eliot. This academic problem is easily stated. By comparison with many other countries, particularly with France

[1] George Eliot, *Silas Marner* (1861, Harmondsworth 1969 edn), ch. 2, pp. 62–4. The quotation is given more fully on p. v of this book.

and America, the understanding of English and Welsh religious regions is often crude and limited.[2] The major religious denominations in England have been described at a basic county level, but they have not been analysed in a more detailed way for the whole of England and Wales.[3] There have been many regional historical studies; but in these a well-judged national picture of religion has been forgone in the usual closeness of local focus. The major religious sources that lend themselves to such analysis have not been studied in any nationally comprehensive way.

Inadequate understanding of spatial patterns of religion has constrained many areas of knowledge, and has lost us many of the insights which were visible to George Eliot. Some of these should be mentioned. Assessments of the role of religion in politics, for example, have not paid much attention to region, despite the acknowledged primacy of religious influences upon political parties

[2] For examples of the many French and American studies on this subject, see G. le Bras, *Etudes de Sociologie Religieuse* (Paris, 1956), 2 vols.; F. Boulard and G. le Bras, *Carte Religieuse de la Rurale* (Paris, 1952); F. Boulard, *An Introduction to Religious Sociology* (1960); X. de Planhol and P. Claval, *An Historical Geography of France* (Cambridge, 1994); P. Deffontaines, *Géographie et Religions* (Paris, 1948); R. D. Gastil, *Cultural Regions of the United States* (Washington, 1975); E. S. Gaustad, *Historical Atlas of Religion in America* (New York, 1976); J. R. Shortridge, 'Religion', in J. F. Rooney, W. Zelinsky and D. R. Louder (eds.), *This Remarkable Continent: an Atlas of United States and Canadian Society and Cultures* (Texas, 1982). A sense of the scope of this subject in other countries can be gleaned from the huge bibliography in C. R. Park, *Sacred Worlds: an Introduction to Geography and Religion* (1994), pp. 288–312; G. J. Levine, 'On the geography of religion', *Transactions of the Institute of British Geographers*, 11 (1986), 428–40.

[3] The most notable discussion has been J. D. Gay, *The Geography of Religion in England* (1971). Our national work differs from his in a number of ways. Computerised methods were not available to him, and this limited what he could achieve. He did not include Wales. With a few exceptions (e.g. Lancashire), his data were described at county level, and therefore his maps were much less detailed than our own. Nevertheless, there is much of enduring value in his work, notably on broadly drawn geographical patterns. He also used more modern data, like the Newman Demographic Survey (which collected Mass attendance figures for 1958–62), or denominational marriage data for the early 1960s. *Ibid.*, pp. 95, 284, maps 19–20. He covered groups like the Jews, and 'quasi-Christian groups and eastern religions'. *Ibid.*, chs. 10–11. In our opening chapters, the aim is to complement his findings with much greater resolution, rather than re-tread ground that he covered; while in later chapters this book's approach becomes very different. There are also some maps of 1851 data in H. McLeod, *Religion and Society in England, 1850–1914* (1996), pp. 29, 33, 63; and his 'Religion', in J. Langton and R. J. Morris (eds.), *Atlas of Industrializing Britain, 1780–1914* (1986), pp. 213–15. See also Park, *Sacred Worlds*, pp. 70–5, as based on Gay. For a more regional study, the approach of which prefigures this book, see K. D. M. Snell, *Church and Chapel in*

and elections prior to the early twentieth century.[4] Compared with many other European countries, the cartography of electoral sociology in the nineteenth century has almost never been related to that of the religious denominations.

There have been renowned debates about the effects of Methodism on political behaviour, from Halévy to Eric Hobsbawm, E. P. Thompson and others,[5] or the roles of religion in fostering innovation, entrepreneurship and industrialisation.[6] These ought to have had an analytically regional focus, relating political action or entrepreneurship closely to patterns of religious affiliation. Yet such debates proceeded with little spatial or geographical sense of where the denominations were sited, or of how strong they were in applicable areas.

There is in Britain poor spatial understanding of popular religion, 'zones' of religious practice, areas of 'dechristianisation', and of cultural and political 'frontiers' defined via religion.[7] Nor has study of regional or occupational cultures connected much with regional patterns of religion, except at the most local of levels. Questions about

the North Midlands: Religious Observance in the Nineteenth Century (Leicester, 1991).

4 See for example K. D. Wald, *Crosses on the Ballot: Patterns of British Voter Alignment since 1885* (Princeton, 1983), pp. 10–18. Such a statement is most pertinent to historiography on the period before about 1885, although some would apply it later too.

5 E. Halévy, *A History of the English People in the Nineteenth Century: vol. 1: England in 1815* (1913, 1970 edn); E. J. Hobsbawm, 'Methodism and the threat of revolution', *History Today*, 7 (1957), also in his *Labouring Men* (1964); E. P. Thompson, *The Making of the English Working Class* (1963, Harmondsworth, 1975 edn), ch. 11. Hobsbawm pointed in general terms to the regional coexistence of Methodism with political radicalism, but this historiography did not much advance understanding of how local geographies of Methodist denominations related to regional socio-economic and political conditions. Compare D. Hempton, *Methodism and Politics in British Society, 1750–1850* (1984, 1987 edn), p. 236: 'The most satisfactory way of analysing the relationship between Methodism and politics in English society c. 1750–1850 is to root Methodism as firmly as possible in its religious, social, geographical and chronological context.'

6 One summary was M. W. Flinn, *The Origins of the Industrial Revolution* (1966, 1976 edn), pp. 81–90, a text that took up some of the ideas of Tawney, T. S. Ashton, Hagen, McClelland or Kindleberger, to review possible links between certain Nonconformist denominations and industrialisation. This remains among the best treatments of the theme in economic historiography. Even so, Flinn's discussion of possible educational and attitudinal influences of dissenters upon economic growth lacked geographical specificity. A similar point could be made about many works which discuss the possible economic influences of Puritanism.

7 Compare M. Vovelle, *Ideologies and Mentalities* (Cambridge, 1990), pp. 113, 159–62, on France.

the longer-term continuity of such cultural regions and patterns are not often raised.[8] The important issue of whether industrialisation fragmented and diversified the range and cohesiveness of regional cultures is poorly addressed in general,[9] and lacks connection with religious history. This is despite the marked proliferation of denominations during industrialisation, and the strongly regional identities of Roman Catholicism, Wesleyan and Primitive Methodism, Bible Christianity and many others. It is also despite the obvious relevance of this issue, like that of occupational cultures, to arguments about 'the making of the English working class'.

Requisite economic histories of the Anglican and other churches might have made much clearer the regional strengths and weaknesses of the respective churches. Yet the modern economic history of religion remains almost non-existent as a subject: most economic historians studying the period after about 1660 have an avid propensity to ignore anything religious, and the disciplinary allure of economics rather than history has brought little profit in this quarter.[10]

Such neglect is less apparent in demographic study – so distinguished in recent English historiography. This subject has had to consider religious contexts. Nonconformity had a major effect upon parish registration, especially after about 1780. Parochial Non-

[8] One exception here (on a rather earlier period) has been M. Spufford (ed.), *The World of Rural Dissenters, 1520–1725* (Cambridge, 1995).

[9] For discussion of this issue, see J. Langton, 'The Industrial Revolution and the regional geography of England', *Transactions of the Institute of British Geographers*, 9 (1984), 145–67; K. D. M. Snell (ed.), *The Regional Novel in Britain and Ireland, 1800–1990* (Cambridge, 1998), ch. 1, and K. D. M. Snell, *The Bibliography of Regional Fiction in Britain and Ireland, 1800–2000* (forthcoming), introduction.

[10] This neglect is remarkable when one considers the resourcefulness of historians on so many other issues. Aspects of the economic history of the church in the eighteenth and nineteenth centuries are covered in a few books like G. F. A. Best, *Temporal Pillars: Queen Anne's Bounty, the Ecclesiastical Commissioners and the Church of England* (Cambridge, 1964); E. J. Evans, *The Contentious Tithe: the Tithe Problem and English Agriculture, 1750–1850* (1976); F. Heal and R. O'Day (eds.), *Princes and Paupers in the English Church, 1500–1800* (Leicester, 1981); R. J. P. Kain and H. C. Prince, *The Tithe Surveys of England and Wales* (Cambridge, 1985); P. Virgin, *The Church in an Age of Negligence* (1988); and (for an earlier period) C. Hill, *Economic Problems of the Church* (Oxford, 1956). There are a number of usually very local articles, especially on tithe, often written from standpoints within agricultural history. This historiographical oversight contrasts markedly with voluminous contemporary evidence and publications, and is despite the many subjects open to study: such as tithe, charities, ecclesiastical landowning, enclosure and the clergy, glebe farming, pew rents, clerical fees, the economic effects of church building, Queen Anne's Bounty, or the Ecclesiastical Commission and financial reorganisation.

conformity, and its wider geography, have evident relevance for demographic sources. It is less often observed, however, that parish registers are an *Anglican* source. Their quality is likely to be highest where there was strong Anglican control or monopoly, rather than in regions where Nonconformity was more influential. We shall see that certain regions, and types of parishes, favoured the Anglican Church (southern and south midland counties, lowland areas, nucleated parishes, those with concentrated landownership, perhaps those with low demographic growth, and so on). Rather different regions and parishes often proved more hospitable to Nonconformity, especially to 'new dissent' (upland settlements, industrial areas, those which were 'open' in settlement, with scattered landownership, often with rapid population growth rates, areas of reclaimed or marginal agricultural land, and the like). Demographers who apply searching criteria to choose the best parish registers may easily alight upon Anglican monopolised parishes and areas to study, running a risk of becoming victims of their own assiduity and care. Such areas may share certain socio-economic, demographic and other historical attributes favourable to the Anglican Church, but these were not necessarily representative of other important regions, notably those which had fostered strong Nonconformity. Such possible connections need to be suggested, even though they almost certainly do not unsettle results from the widely distributed parishes used by leading English historical demographers. For those parishes frequently contained more Nonconformists than was ideal for the purposes of vital registration and family reconstitution; they had wide regional representativeness; the demographically reconstituted parishes were larger than average; the Anglican church comprised the major part of the population during the parish-registration era; and the Anglican data were reassuringly tested in many ways against figures from early civil registration.[11] Other such considerations could be added in defence of the Cambridge demographic findings, but the import of religious regions for this most advanced field of English historiography should be clear.

Within religious history itself, the geography of religion should be

[11] The main English parishes studied by the Cambridge demographers are mapped in E. A. Wrigley and R. S. Schofield, *The Population History of England, 1541–1871: a Reconstruction* (1981), pp. 40–2, and E. A. Wrigley, R. S. Davies, J. E. Oeppen and R. S. Schofield, *English Population History from Family Reconstitution, 1580–1837* (Cambridge, 1997), p. 31.

fundamental to understanding issues like church governance, schism and denominational formation, church and chapel building and the spread of architectural styles, religious education, charity and welfare, the evolution and influence of circuit systems, the biographies of religious leaders, regional cultural influences and biases affecting religious doctrine, popular religion, the urban or rural bases of denominations, and many other such matters. However, one often finds such subjects discussed with limited awareness of regional location. And denominational histories frequently prefer to imply wide affiliation and to concentrate on mobile personalities; an understandable stress is sometimes placed on expansive universality rather than the local church, and this is commonly linked with theological universalism. From such historical writing, converting the particular to the general, regional structures can often emerge in an impressionistic form only.

Issues of religious geography therefore occur across many areas of historical enquiry. These go well beyond the immediate history of religion itself, where they bear on virtually all aspects of denominational history. Despite this, it appears that secularised academic minds, limited spatial thinking, a predilection for national rather than regional or local description, and the fragmentation of historical specialisms have minimised awareness of religious regions and their importance. We are in danger of losing the sensitive regional knowledge and sense of difference that structured books like *Silas Marner*.

If we lean back from such reflections, and think instead of technical expertise and method, another point would be widely acknowledged. As far as method is concerned, historical studies of religion linger behind many other areas of social scientific and historical enquiry. There are salient exceptions,[12] but as a specialism amenable to quan-

[12] R. Currie, *Methodism Divided: a Study in the Sociology of Ecumenicalism* (1968); Gay, *Geography of Religion*; A. Everitt, *The Pattern of Rural Dissent: the Nineteenth Century* (Leicester, 1972); A. D. Gilbert, *Religion and Society in Industrial England: Church, Chapel and Social Change, 1740–1914* (1976, Harlow, 1984 edn); H. McLeod, *Class and Religion in the Late Victorian City* (1974); R. Currie, A. D. Gilbert and L. Horsley, *Churches and Churchgoers: Patterns of Church Growth in the British Isles since 1700* (Oxford, 1977); N. Yates, 'Urban church attendance and the use of statistical evidence, 1850–1900', in D. Baker (ed.), *Studies in Church History, 16: the Church in Town and Countryside* (Oxford, 1979); B. I. Coleman, *The Church of England in the Mid-Nineteenth Century: a Social Geography* (1980); A. M. Urdank, *Religion and Society in a Cotswold Vale: Nailsworth, Gloucestershire, 1780–1865* (Berkeley, 1990); Snell, *Church and Chapel in the North Midlands*. There has been

titative and related methods this large subject seems diffident and undeveloped. Orthodoxies have been little examined and refined by such methods. This is despite the fact that the historiography of religion overflows with arguments and views, expressed through literary or impressionistic statements, that are nevertheless of an essentially quantitative nature. Methodological innovation has slipped between the disciplinary isolation of a few interested geographers, and the scepticism of some religiously committed historians towards the secular bias of religious sociology and its methods. Quantitative approaches in much religious historiography have been limited, definitional precision has often been lacking, and variables have sometimes been inadequately constructed or handled. What some measures may indicate about the nature of religious provision or attendance has sometimes been insufficiently explained. The historiography contains many articles and editorial introductions providing valuable assessments of major sources *as sources* (those of 1676, 1715, 1829, 1851 and so on). But there have not been the intensive ensuing research projects and analyses that are plainly justified. Three decades ago, one author commented critically that 'The history of the empirical investigation into religion in this country over the last hundred years is littered with examples of dogmatic and general conclusions based on very shaky evidence.'[13] One would not word this in such strong terms now, but the sentiment might still be endorsed.

Research aims and methods of this book

Seeing the historiography from such perspectives, and with these points in mind, it seemed that the most creative way forward was to adopt the following main priorities:

(i) To computerise the published 1851 *Census of Religious Worship*, correct those registration-district data for omissions, test their reliability, develop further measures of denominational strength from the data, and map those comprehensively

growing use of quantifiable evidence in religious history, producing fascinating work like Urdank's book; but the generalisations made by R. A. Soloway back in 1972 remain valid: this has still not developed into any significant broader analytical advance. R. A. Soloway, 'Church and society; recent trends in nineteenth-century religious history', *Journal of British Studies*, 11 (1972), 152.

13 Gay, *Geography of Religion*, p. 22.

for England and Wales.[14] This would allow far more refined cartographic understanding and analysis of religious regions, and would permit many questions and debates about the extent, siting and reciprocity of denominations to be resolved.

(ii) To construct a series of closely related parish-level datasets, allowing analysis and mapping via computer cartography, of the 1851 *Census of Religious Worship* data on denominational provision, free and appropriated sittings, attendances, Sunday school attendances and related information. Even with a small team of researchers this was evidently too large a task to be done for the entire country. It was decided instead that fifteen counties would be selected as representing certain key features of the national geography of religion, informed by the registration-district analyses.

(iii) To compare the 1851 data with earlier sources, particularly the Compton Census of 1676, and (by way of a check on the mid nineteenth-century data) with the 1829 returns of non-Anglican places of worship. Much data from those earlier sources would also need to be computerised. This was likely to be a complex matter, given evidential and design differences between the historical sources. So a further aim was to create methodologies that enabled longitudinal and latitudinal study of these data.

(iv) To relate the religious and cultural data of 1676 and 1851 to many socio-economic variables, to answer questions about the local contexts, influences and regional cultures affecting denominational geographies and religious 'pluralism'. This was clearly best done at parish level.

(v) To analyse in their own right the socio-economic data that was being used, and to develop arguments or models of local/regional contexts and parochial divisions, incorporating cultural, religious, demographic and economic characteristics. The need here was not to advance deterministic arguments for their own sake, but rather to explore the adequacy of deterministic and contextual considerations affecting religious strength and siting, and to show precisely how significant or

14 Coverage was considered of Scotland as well, but (as discussed in chapter 1) the survival of the Scottish data is poor compared with England and Wales. For this reason Scotland was omitted.

> insignificant they may have been in different areas. The potential contribution of a more quantitative approach to such on-going debates was self-evident, allowing many historical questions to be resolved with much more precision.

Foremost among a very large set of research questions, it was hoped to assess how durable over time the geography of the major denominations had been, how they reciprocated or undercut each other regionally, what was the role of Sunday schools, what was the denominational significance of 'free and appropriated' sittings, and how important were social controls as exercised particularly through landowning patterns. A related aim was to consider where and how 'secularisation' (defined by falling church attendances) became apparent, and what its regional dimensions were. It was hoped to test and develop some of the rather ahistorical theories of religion in the social sciences, notably theories of 'secularisation', using the rich veins of computed data being created.

In short, a firmer sense of the regional features of religious history was felt necessary to extend the historiography of religion, to augment historical awareness of cultural regions (and the role of religion in their origins and persistence), and to enhance understanding of the importance of religion for related issues. We hope that this book, and the huge datasets constructed over many years for it (now made available to the research community),[15] will address these research priorities and extend understanding of these subjects.

As will become clear, this research has been conducted in a technically more sophisticated way than previous British studies. This will bring the history of religion to the fore of current techniques and methods. No closed or tight definition of the 'geography of religion' is adopted in this book, for the self-containment of disciplinary areas is most unhelpful. The approach is inter-disciplinary: very historical, and 'geographical' in its quantification and stress on spatial and regional understanding in the history of religion. Some readers from particular disciplines may encounter unfamiliar approaches and methods; but they can be reassured that many steps were taken to keep the text approachable, readable, and within reach of any modern student trained in history or the social sciences.

15 The data collected for this book are being deposited with the ESRC Data Archive at the University of Essex.

There are gains and losses in pushing ahead in this way. A priority for this research is the view that many features of the religious and cultural regions of the Victorian period have yet to be disclosed in an objective manner. There is also a growing sense that the many research subjects that bear on 'cultural regions' – dialect, the English, Welsh and Gaelic languages, political behaviour, patterns of folklore, regional fiction, surname distributions, migration fields, vernacular architecture and the like – should in due course be inter-related via broader syntheses, if not via group projects. This requires careful work within each field that lays an appropriate groundwork for this; and, to aid objectivity and comparison, much of that groundwork needs to be of a quantitative and geographical character. As public discussion focuses ever more intently upon the distinctiveness of parts of the British Isles, upon national and regional assemblies, upon regional voting patterns, upon the real or supposed identities of different areas, upon the evolution and drawing of cultural boundaries, and other such questions, it is crucial for modern British 'society' (if decentralisation is to mean anything positive) that the historical subjects be properly researched. The writing of religious history has sometimes been thought a reclusive and self-indulgent pursuit of dwindling contemporary significance – but the study of religious geographies, and the cultural and political regions associated with them, now have an increasingly obvious relevance for very prominent modern issues.

Such research is probably best conducted via the relatively impartial quantitative methods adopted here. There are losses involved in making less use of the rich literary evidence that has traditionally attracted religious historians, even though such omissions can be justified by pointing to the profusion of excellent and highly readable work already based upon such documentation. No historians would claim that the approaches adopted in this book are sufficient in themselves. However, given the priorities outlined above, few would dispute that there are considerable gains in taking religious historiography along this way in a more thorough manner.

Accordingly, the religious data for twenty-seven denominations from all 624 registration districts of the published 1851 Religious Census for England and Wales were computerised. Those data were corrected for omissions (as described in appendix B), new measures were formed to describe denominational coverage (see appendix C), and these were mapped with computer cartography (as outlined in appendix D). Over 500 variables were created for all English and Welsh registration districts, incorporating cultural, religious, demographic and geographical base variables. This comprises the first such religious cartography at registration-district level for these two countries.

To supplement those district data at *parish* level, fifteen census counties were investigated, with all their parish-level data being computerised. These were the Welsh counties of Anglesey, Caernarvonshire, Cardiganshire and Monmouthshire, and the English ones of Bedfordshire, Cambridgeshire, Derbyshire, Dorset, the East Riding, Lancashire, Leicestershire, Northumberland, Rutland, Suffolk and Sussex. As described in chapter 7, the counties were chosen primarily because they each represented distinctive regional features of the national geography of religion, as perceived from the registration-district level analyses, and because of their diverse social, economic and political characteristics.

The parish data were collected from the Public Record Office, from County Record Offices and from the published 1851 returns for Bedfordshire, Sussex and Wales.[16] All such 1851 religious data were computerised, excepting the figures on the income and endowments of the Anglican Church, which were inconsistently returned. The 1676 Compton Census data were computerised for all possible parishes in these counties (as outlined in chapter 8), and the 1829 returns of non-Anglican places of worship for Leicestershire were used as a further compelling test of the reliability of the 1851 data.

In addition to these religious and related parochial variables, we systematically collected and computerised parish-level social and economic data, to relate such data to the statistics and varying geographies established by the religious measures. The socio-economic data include all the 1831 occupational data; the 1811, 1831, 1841 and 1851 population data, with sex ratios, housing and so on; acreages as supplied at different dates; poor-relief expenditures for 1832–6, as published in the Annual Reports of the Poor Law Commissioners; rateable and real property values; data from the *Imperial Gazetteer* on values of the clerical livings, the nature of livings (rectory, vicarage, perpetual curacy), and availability of clerical housing; landownership

16 See the bibliography for details of religious data sources.

details as supplied by the *Imperial Gazetteer*, and (for Leicestershire) as obtained from land tax returns; and a number of related variables. These comprised base variables from which very many further ratio and ancillary measures were formed, utilising also the 1851 religious and Sunday school data.

At parish level this provided a total of 2,443 parishes, containing 4,645,702 people in 1851. Each of these 2,443 parishes had about 2,500 original and transformed religious and other variables. The resulting dataset of over 6 million observations was analysed on the University of Leicester mainframe computer, and then on personal computers as they became more powerful. For most of the counties all parish boundaries were digitised, entering the coordinate data into computer cartographic packages.[17] This allowed the computerised mapping of any variable. This was also done for the registration-district boundaries of England and Wales. While only a minute proportion of such maps can be published, given strict publishing constraints, such mapping is an invaluable aid to supplement quantitative analysis. This work inevitably led to advances in the handling and analysis of religious data, to the creation of more complex measures of religious strength and diversity, while also suggesting more sophisticated ways of testing the Compton Census, and the 1829 and 1851 data. These advances should prove useful to scholars of religion in other periods and countries.

Summary of the book

The opening chapter appraises the huge 1851 *Census of Religious Worship*, which is our main computerised religious source, although similar use is also made of the Compton Census and the 1829 returns. The next chapter provides a more precise geography for the Church of England than is currently available, followed by three chapters that do the same for Roman Catholicism, 'old dissent', and 'new dissent'. This is followed by an analysis of the extent of denominational complementarity or geographical affinity, addressing issues connected with 'the Tillyard thesis'. For these opening chapters, comprising the first section of this book, the national religious patterns for the

[17] Data were analysed on the mainframe computer with SPSS, SAS, GIMMS and Arc/Info, and on personal computers with SPSS for Windows. The data were mapped via GIMMS, ARC/INFO and ARCVIEW.

Anglican Church and for the main denominations are described, and explanations advanced. This is done with much higher cartographical and quantitative resolution than hitherto in the literature.

Among the results are the striking southern and midland geography of the Church of England and of 'old dissent', and the more northern and south-western geography of the Methodist denominations. Wales emerges as very distinctive in religious terms compared with England. The differences between Wales and England were persistent findings, repeated in many connections, like Sunday school education, or the effects of landownership. The ways in which the major denominations overlapped with or complemented each other regionally are shown, alongside the implications of this for denominational success or failure. Clear north–south and west–east divisions of the country emerge, and these have evidently had many enduring cultural and political ramifications. The 1851 geography of the Anglican Church, for example, was very similar indeed to the regions of electoral strength of the modern Conservative Party. Subsequent electoral geographies can be predicted with considerable precision from the 1851 Anglican and Nonconformist data.

In the second part of the book the resolution shifts down to parish level, for the chosen fifteen counties. These counties are described in chapter 7, prior to detailed analysis. An assessment of the extent of parochial religious continuity between 1676 and 1851 is then undertaken. The results are very surprising. It is usually thought that there was much continuity of local patterns of religious adherence. However, while there is some limited truth in this for Roman Catholicism, it was not so at parish level for Protestant Nonconformity. The latter dissenting denominations were much more mobile and transient than many have believed possible, particularly before the nineteenth century. The Catholics were relatively stable, at least until the post-famine Irish diaspora. The reasons for that, and the role of the Catholic landed families, are discussed.

The importance of Sunday schools (for example in the survival of denominations) is shown in chapter 9, although reservations are expressed about the historiographical thesis that they were independent agencies of 'the working class'. The highest Sunday school indexes of attendance were in fact found in Anglican dominated parishes of a 'closed' landed nature. This raises questions about the role of these schools in inculcating 'working-class' attitudes, and suggests that the importance of the Anglican Church in fostering this early and crucial form of 'mass education' has been understated by historians. In addition, the most crucial determinant of Sunday schools is shown to have been the regional incidence of child labour.

Analysis of 'free' and 'appropriated' seating in places of worship (chapter 10) indicates that the Anglican Church was often rather more open in the availability of its sittings than many other denominations. This modifies the views of contemporaries and historians who argued that proprietorial attitudes to Anglican pews, and the resulting exclusion of many inhabitants, played a significant part in causing anti-establishment resentment and dissent. As with Sunday school provision, in this and other regards the historical role of the Anglican Church emerges from this work with more credit than some might have anticipated.

In chapter 11 the discussion concentrates on the very strong associations between religious conformity and 'closed' or estate villages, where landownership was in few hands. It is shown how more varied occupational and landed characteristics were associated with religious dissent, and such contexts and their regional variations are specified with more precision than hitherto. This chapter extends a fuller cultural understanding to historical debates about the nature of parish divisions, and to typologies of 'open' and 'close' parishes.

Finally, in chapter 12, the issue of 'secularisation' is addressed, looking at the regionality of high or low church attendance, and exploring the question of whether urbanisation induced declining religious attendances. It is argued that cultural pluralism and inadequate church provision brought about lower church attendance – both in the larger cities and in the English rural borderlands. The chapter points towards the associated and fuller study of 'secularisation' due to be published by Alasdair Crockett.

The stress throughout is on the contextual understanding of religion. This may vary between the inter-denominational, geographical and more broadly socio-economic contexts of religion. Wickham once wrote that 'Unfortunately, "Church history", with few great exceptions, is invariably about the Church abstracted from society, about ecclesiastical institutions, personalities or movements, in which the world in which they are set seems quite incidental.'[18] This book does

[18] E. R. Wickham, *Church and People in an Industrial City* (1957, 1969 edn), p. 12.

not cover institutions and personalities to the extent that some would like (for reasons of space rather than academic principle); but the approach is certainly to discuss religion within its socio-economic and regional settings, especially at parish level, to place clearly ascertained limits on contextual influences, and to show how different strands of deterministic thinking may be held in control and assessed through quantitative methods. Once the extent of socio-economic contextual influences are defined, the field is then open for others to fill in the more rounded and holistic picture, taking account of the spatial and situational accounts given here.

A book like this, analysing such huge datasets, could focus on a great many issues, and limitations on length have prevented some of these from being fully explored. While the cartographical patterns of the main denominations are outlined in chapters 2 to 5, laying a groundwork relevant for many further subjects, many quantitative features of each denomination have not been shown. Some such descriptive statistics are easily accessible from the official census volume. While those figures were slight compared to what can now be generated, that census volume is still commendable in its thoughtfulness and accuracy.[19] Some descriptive statistics from the census for each denomination are printed in appendix A, and interested readers can make further calculations from those if required. Many more measures can be obtained by further analysis of the computerised data. As a rule, this book tries to avoid publishing work that overlaps with other material in print. The themes and arguments in part 2 of the book were chosen partly with this in mind.

It is common for reviewers to discuss what a book does *not* cover, and what they feel it might have done. It is in the nature of very large data analyses like this that many incidental issues which could have been explored become neglected, partly to maintain thematic coherency, partly to save space, and partly so as not to repeat what has been written elsewhere. One of the significant omissions here is the Jews. We analysed and mapped the data on them in the Religious Census, but it became clear that the Jews had already been admirably treated by others. There was little to add to previous research on Anglo-Jewry, at least from our perspectives. Such earlier work used

[19] In testing the published figures against the computerised data, one is repeatedly struck by the accuracy of Horace Mann's work.

the 1851 religious returns in conjunction with other sources like the *Jewish Chronicle* (particularly of 23 July 1847, which gave the numbers of *Ba'ale Batim* outside London, using returns to a detailed questionnaire issued by the Chief Rabbi to all congregations in Britain and the colonies), as well as the impressive data that the Board of Deputies collected from 1848. There were a number of problems with the published Jewish returns to the 1851 Religious Census, for they gave as Jewish congregations non-Jewish 'Israelites' at Bury, Lutterworth and Haslingden, and there was further confusion in Leeds and Sheffield. The distributions of Jewish congregations are well known from earlier research, being concentrated in London (especially in the registration districts of the City of London, St George Southwark, Marylebone, Stepney and St James Westminster), the seaports (e.g. Southampton, Dover, Yarmouth, Plymouth, Bristol, Liverpool, Hull, Newcastle or Sunderland) and a few inland centres (that is, in cities or towns like Leeds, Manchester, Merthyr Tydfil, Nottingham and Birmingham). We mapped all these for 1851, but the results were fairly predictable and did little to augment current scholarly understanding.[20]

It was initially planned to discuss 'secularisation' more fully, assessing the theory associated with this term via our data, and considering regional dimensions in the shifts towards a more secular society. However, it became clear that this extensive subject, with all the light that the Compton and 1851 Religious Censuses could shed on it, was one that required a separate volume. Alasdair Crockett is exploring the complex issues involved here, and his work on 'secular-

[20] For detailed examinations, see the thorough account in V. D. Lipman, 'A survey of Anglo-Jewry in 1851', *Transactions of the Jewish Historical Society of England*, 17 (1951–2), 171–88, especially his appendix on Jewish returns to the Religious Census (which for the Jews covered Friday evening to Saturday afternoon, 28–29 March); V. D. Lipman, *Social History of the Jews in England, 1850–1950* (1954); and the even more impressive discussions and closely researched local data from many sources in A. N. Newman (ed.), *Provincial Jewry in Victorian Britain* (Jewish Historical Society of England, 1975). This excellent work gives the fullest account of Victorian Jewish communities, and contains wide-ranging bibliographical references. Other discussions relevant to the early or mid-nineteenth century have included Gay, *Geography of Religion*, ch. 11; T. M. Endelman, *The Jews of Georgian England, 1714–1830* (Philadelphia, 1979); G. Williams, *The Making of Manchester Jewry, 1740–1875* (Manchester, 1976); A. Gilam, *The Emancipation of the Jews in England, 1830–1860* (New York, 1982); A. Weinberg, *Portsmouth Jewry* (Portsmouth, 1985); and A. N. Newman, *The Board of Deputies of British Jews, 1760–1985: a Brief Survey* (1987).

isation' with these data will be forthcoming as a separate book. This has influenced the present book in many ways, and it will comprise a logical extension of these chapters. In briefest summary, his work shows that the most rapid processes of 'secularisation' extended *first* in the direction of greater religious pluralism, in which faiths abounded and more openly competed against each other, and that this process of denominational competition, where it occurred most vigorously, *in turn* brought about disillusionment with formal religion, and itself hastened 'secularisation'. Where such denominational competition was weak (that is, in parishes where there were no dissenters in 1676), one later found relatively high levels of religious adherence, manifest in higher indices of attendance in 1851. But the greater the intensity of religious pluralism in 1676, the lower the levels of religious practice in 1851. Furthermore, the mapped geography of religious 'secularisation' across England and Wales indicated strongly regional dimensions. The secularising effects of religious pluralism discovered for England and Wales between 1676 and 1851 contrasted sharply with arguments proposed (notably for America) that religious pluralism fosters high religious adherence in all contexts. This is to summarise a complex argument, which must await subsequent publication.

The local and national research questions to which these data lend themselves, and the ways in which they may be cross-related to other data, are enormous. They are relevant both to local studies as well as to national research programmes involving religion. The data can be analysed further in conjunction with other earlier and later religious sources. This book stopped short, for example, of using the Evans list (1715), the Thompson list (1772) and (for quantitative purposes) visitation returns, although some other limited use is made of the latter. We did not relate the data to the 1989 English Church Census.[21] We did not map the Compton Census data at national level, despite persuasion from some scholars, although such cartography was undertaken at parish level for certain counties. This last omission was partly for reasons of time, partly for technical reasons, but mainly because the 1676 data are much inferior to the 1851 religious returns, and raise many problems of interpretation.

21 See P. Brierley (M.A.R.C. Europe), *Christian England: What the 1989 English Church Census Reveals* (1991).

The nineteenth-century data have considerable relevance to electoral statistics and study, bearing as they do on issues of religious or class influence upon voting patterns, and the debated change in emphasis from one to the other. The relevance of religious geographies for political analysis is touched upon in a number of chapters here, and while it was beyond the remit of this book to develop this, a foundation has been laid for others to examine these regional connections further.

Our socio-economic and demographic data alone (collected for their relevance to religious adherence) are open to a great many research questions. For example, many debates hinge around the relationships between factors like demographic growth, sex ratios, occupational structures, poor relief expenditure, agricultural structures, landownership, property values and parochial capital formation. These and other variables are included in the data, at an unprecedented scale of parochial coverage, and we have had occasion to broach inter-connections that go beyond the subject of religion. There is no need to predict the ways in which these data might be used by historians and social scientists, except to underline how diverse these are, whether for the religious issues covered in the forthcoming pages, or for issues of a non-religious nature.

Finally, Wales emerges from this research as distinctive in very many ways, having religious characteristics which often set it apart from England. The uneven celebration of the established church, or the divergence of Calvinistic and Arminian Methodism, were only two of the key contrasts here. Welsh socio-economic features as judged from quantitative measures were also frequently unique. These national differences – but also their internal regional elements – have been long enduring in both countries. The Welsh referendum in September 1997, on a separate political assembly for Wales, like previous referenda in the country (for example on Sunday opening), provided yet another breakdown of Wales into the broad regions that were prefigured by the religious data of 1851. However, as *The Times* commented on the 1997 referendum, 'Whatever its internal divisions, Wales has a political and cultural identity altogether more pronounced and separate than any recognisable English region.'[22] This is

[22] 'Lesson from Llanelli', editorial in *The Times* (20 Sept. 1997). See R. Williams, 'Are we becoming more divided?', *Radical Wales*, 23 (Autumn, 1989), 8–9, on the divisions between south Wales, the rural north and west Wales, and the border country.

a theme addressed on a number of occasions in this book. In any cultural, linguistic and demographic history of Wales, the distinguishing nature of Welsh religious geography should undoubtedly assume considerable prominence. It is not the intention here to argue for or against Welsh devolution: that is not the historian's role. However, these chapters do at many points try to shed light on what, in religious terms, Wales and England had in common historically, and what separated them.

Part 1

Religious geographies: the districts of England and Wales

1

The 1851 *Census of Religious Worship*

Introduction

On Sunday 30 March 1851, for the first (and last) time as part of the decennial population census, questions were asked about the religious composition of Great Britain.

Despite the unique importance of the resulting *Census of Religious Worship*, it has received remarkably little sustained analysis. Quite a number of articles, and edited works on particular counties, have assessed its reliability and used it to describe basic patterns of worship, but this book is the first to enter into thorough investigation of it.[1] A number of considerations have inhibited prior analysis.

[1] Among the main publications on the source are K. S. Inglis, 'Patterns of religious worship in 1851', *Journal of Ecclesiastical History*, 11 (1960), 74–86; J. Rogan, 'The Religious Census of 1851', *Theology* (1963), 11–15; D. M. Thompson, 'The 1851 Religious Census: problems and possibilities', *Victorian Studies*, 11 (1967), 87–97; W. S. F. Pickering, 'The 1851 Religious Census – a useless experiment?', *British Journal of Sociology*, 18 (1967), 382–407; R. M. Goodridge, 'The religious condition of the West Country in 1851', *Social Compass*, 14 (1967), 285–96; W. T. R. Pryce, 'The 1851 Census of Religious Worship: Denbighshire', *Trans. of the Denbighshire Historical Society*, 23 (1974), 147–92; R. W. Ambler, 'The 1851 Census of Religious Worship', *Local Historian*, 11 (1975), 375–81; D. W. Bushby (ed.), *Bedfordshire Ecclesiastical Census, 1851*, Bedfordshire Historical Record Society, vol. 54 (1975); I. G. Jones and D. Williams (eds.), *The Religious Census of 1851: a Calendar of the Returns Relating to Wales, vol. 1: South Wales* (Cardiff, 1976); D. M. Thompson, 'The Religious Census of 1851', in R. Lawton (ed.), *The Census and Social Structure: an Interpretative Guide to Nineteenth-Century Censuses for England and Wales* (1978); C. D. Field, 'The 1851 Religious Census: a select bibliography', *Proceedings of the Wesley Historical Society*, 41 (1978); R. W. Ambler (ed.), *Lincolnshire Returns of the Census of Religious Worship, 1851*, Lincolnshire Record Society, 72 (1979); B. I. Coleman, *The Church of England in the Mid Nineteenth Century: a Social Geography* (1980); I. G. Jones (ed.), *The Religious Census of 1851: a Calendar of the Returns Relating to Wales, vol. 2: North Wales* (Cardiff, 1981); B. I. Coleman, 'Southern England in the Census of Religious Worship, 1851', *Southern History*, 5 (1983); K. Tiller (ed.), *Church and Chapel in Oxfordshire, 1851*, Oxfordshire Record Society, 55 (1987); M. Seaborne, 'The Religious Census of 1851 and early chapel building in North Wales', *National Library of Wales Journal*, 26 (1990); E. Legg (ed.), *Buckinghamshire Returns of the Census of Religious Worship, 1851* (1991); K. D. M. Snell, *Church and Chapel in the*

Foremost among these have been the awesome scope of the source, its highly quantitative nature, and the inter-disciplinary skills and facilities necessary to undertake such a study. There have also been problems concerning the measures needed for the source, and doubts have sometimes been expressed about the accuracy of some of its details. Religious studies as a subject has been slow to adopt the quantitative methods necessary to analyse the census. And linked to this has been a feeling that its data are of limited relevance for studies of religion which concentrate on belief and faith, rather than external action and attendance at services.

However, for the most part objections and hindrances of these kinds can now be overcome. The 1851 data can be checked via internal statistical tests and managed in ways which surmount doubts about their accuracy. There is enormous scope for religious history to advance methodologically, in ways long accepted within the social sciences, without losing sight of many of its long-standing arguments and themes. For the latter have often been essentially quantitative rather than qualitative in nature. And, towering above all other sources for the modern history of English and Welsh religion, the 1851 *Census of Religious Worship* stands as a supreme endeavour of its period, a source ripe for close scrutiny and historical analysis.

This chapter appraises the Religious Census as a source of statistical information on worshipping patterns. It examines the context in which it was undertaken, the ways in which the data were gathered, the nature of those data at different spatial levels, their reliability and limitations, and how any such limitations may be dealt with. When we have assessed the source, and become more familiar with it, we can move in subsequent chapters to a survey and analysis of the huge body of data it contained.

Horace Mann made clear much of the purpose of the Religious Census when he wrote that 'it would be difficult to over-estimate the importance of authentic facts upon this subject [religion]; since, for

Footnote 1 (*cont.*)
North Midlands: Religious Observance in the Nineteenth Century (Leicester, 1991); J. A. Vickers (ed.), *The Religious Census of Hampshire, 1851* (Hampshire Record Series, Winchester, 1993); M. Tranter (ed.), *The Derbyshire Returns to the 1851 Religious Census* (Derbyshire Record Society, vol. 23, Chesterfield, 1995). An admirable bibliographical survey is C. D. Field, 'The 1851 Religious Census of Great Britain: a bibliographical guide for local and regional historians', *The Local Historian*, 27:4 (1997), 194–217.

many reasons, the religion of a nation must be a matter of extreme solicitude to many minds. Whether we regard a people merely in their secular capacity, as partners in a great association for promoting the stability, the opulence, the peaceful glory of a state; or view them in their loftier character, as subjects of a higher kingdom, – swift and momentary travellers towards a never-ending destiny; in either aspect, the degree and direction of religious sentiment in a community are subjects of the weightiest impact: in the one case to the temporal guardians of a nation – to its spiritual teachers in the other.'[2] The first half of the nineteenth century brought growing concern that Britain, as a Christian country, was failing to meet the moral standards demanded by such a premise. The period was one of significant religious change and development, illustrated for example by the Evangelical Revival, the Oxford Movement, the growth and divisions within Methodism, the substantial expansion of Nonconformity generally, and the spread of agnosticism and secularisation. Dramatic economic, industrial, urban and demographic changes put severe strains upon the churches, presenting them with major problems of adaptation and reform. There was particular concern that religious provision was failing to keep pace with the growth and changing distribution of population. Coupled with this was a pervasive fear among many commentators that the voluble working classes were increasingly falling outside the scope of organised religion, or were gravitating towards anti-establishment denominations. As Rawding commented: 'Religious belief was often central to the lives of labouring men, and so the control of the religious environment by the ruling classes had an importance which can easily be missed today.'[3] Contemporaries were faced with pressing issues that required an assessment of the strength of Nonconformity, and there were many who hoped that a Census of Religious Worship would demonstrate the continuing predominance of the Church of England.

We need to remember that it was not unusual for the government or political parties to be deeply engaged with religious issues. As Blake pointed out, the Tory Party was closely associated with the interests

2 *Census of Great Britain, 1851: Religious Worship, England and Wales, Report and Tables*, LXXXIX (1852–3), p. viii. Henceforth this census volume will be referred to simply as *Census of Religious Worship*.

3 C. Rawding, 'The iconography of churches: a case study of landownership and power in nineteenth-century Lincolnshire', *Journal of Historical Geography*, 16 (1990), 158.

of 'Anglican exclusivity',[4] and we will see how closely linked that party was with the geographical strongholds of the established church. Government involvement in religious matters was much more conspicuous than it is today, and the Anglican Church and Nonconformist denominations were far more politically active. This was true with regard to education, slavery, disestablishment, the Marriage Act (1836), Test and Corporation Act repeal, Catholic emancipation and the Irish question, the Church Reform Act (1836), tithe commutation, pluralities (1838, 1850), licensing, municipal cemeteries, dissenters' burial services and much else. Earlier in the nineteenth century, there had been Lord Sidmouth's concerns over the political consequences of religious itinerancy (concerns shared by many in the established church), his bill in May 1811 to restrict it, and the opposition against that bill from groups like the Protestant Society for the Protection of Religious Liberty, and the Methodist Committee of Privileges.[5] The licensing of dissenting chapels under the Toleration Act was of course politically motivated, and closely monitored by Sidmouth and many others.[6] In 1818 Parliament voted £1,000,000 for Anglican church building, followed by a further £500,000 six years later.[7] In 1834 Peel appointed a commission to examine the state of the established church in England and Wales, its report largely responsible for the creation of the sees of Ripon and Manchester, and for further diocesan reorganisation. Religious issues had been very prominent indeed during the agitation for the 1832 Reform Act.[8] After that Act, dissenters probably comprised about a fifth of the electorate;[9] a point not lost on Melbourne's ministers as

[4] R. Blake, *The Conservative Party from Peel to Churchill* (1972), p. 11.

[5] The best discussion is D. W. Lovegrove, *Established Church, Sectarian People: Itinerancy and the Transformation of Dissent, 1780–1830* (Cambridge, 1988).

[6] See for example Sidmouth's demands for an account of the number of licences issued each year at Quarter Sessions from 1809 to the end of 1820, under Wm. & Mary c. 18 and 19 Geo. III, c. 44. Letter to the Clerk of the Peace, Leicestershire, November 1821: Leics. C.R.O., QS 95/1/3/3.

[7] See M. H. Port, *Six Hundred New Churches: a Study of the Church Building Commission, 1818–1856, and its Church Building Activities* (1961), and the Church Building Acts, notably those of 1818–19, 1822, 1843, 1856.

[8] R. Cowherd, *The Politics of English Dissent, 1815–1848* (1956); R. Brent, *Liberal Anglican Politics: Whiggery, Religion and Reform, 1830–1841* (Oxford, 1987); J. A. Phillips, *The Great Reform Bill in the Boroughs: English Electoral Behaviour, 1818–1841* (Oxford, 1992).

[9] R. Anstey, 'Religion and British slave emancipation', in D. Eltis and J. Walvin (eds.), *The Abolition of the Atlantic Slave Trade* (Madison, Wisconsin, 1981), pp. 51–3.

they tried to gain dissenting support on marriage law, the universities issue, civil registration, church rates and so on. 'The Church in Danger' was a major issue during the 1841 election, as it was to be in 1868. Church rates were the subject for open confrontation over an extended period.[10] The Anti-State Church Association, connected with Edward Miall, which in 1853 became the Liberation Society, aimed to separate the Church of England from the state and establish the 'voluntary principle', and so end many advantages and privileges of the Anglican Church. It gained strength noticeably from the 1840s.[11] The highly political appointment of bishops was always contentious, particularly in the early nineteenth century.[12] Throughout the nineteenth century, it is hard to find political issues that were *not* overlaid and influenced by religious debate, and nobody could be in any doubt that religious conformism or dissent carried as their corollaries strong voting predispositions.[13] The political importance of the *Census of Religious Worship* was manifest to all, and its politicised

[10] R. Brent, 'The Whigs and Protestant Dissent in the decade of reform: the case of the Church Rates, 1833–1841', *English Historical Review*, 102 (1987); O. Anderson, 'Gladstone's abolition of compulsory church rates: a minor political myth and its historiographical career', *Journal of Ecclesiastical History*, 25 (1974). After a campaign of over thirty years, their payment became voluntary with the Compulsory Church Rate Abolition Act of 1868.

[11] D. W. Bebbington, *The Nonconformist Conscience: Chapel and Politics, 1870–1914* (1982), pp. 22–30.

[12] In 1816 for example, Herbert Marsh was appointed to Llandaff, it would appear largely as a result of his services as an economic advisor during the Napoleonic Wars. W. Gibson, 'The Tories and church patronage: 1812–30', *Journal of Ecclesiastical History*, 41 (1990), 266–7.

[13] See for example T. J. Nossiter, 'Aspects of electoral behaviour in English constituencies, 1832–1868', in E. Allardt and S. Rokkan (eds.), *Mass Politics: Studies in Political Sociology* (New York, 1970), p. 180, on the political implications of dissenting or Anglican affiliation; or see his 'Voting behaviour, 1832–1872', *Political Studies*, 18 (1970), 385; P. F. Clarke, 'Electoral sociology of modern England', *History*, 57 (1972); D. W. Bebbington, 'Nonconformity and electoral sociology, 1867–1918', *Historical Journal*, 27 (1984), 633–56; D. Beales, 'The electorate before and after 1832: the right to vote, and the opportunity', *Parliamentary History*, 11:1 (1992). See also H. Faulkner, *Chartism and the Churches: a Study in Democracy* (1916, 1970 edn); G. I. T. Machin, *Politics and the Churches in Great Britain, 1832–1868* (Oxford, 1977). There is a very large literature on religion and politics after 1851, and notable among such studies have been H. Pelling, *Social Geography of British Elections, 1885–1910* (1967), e.g. pp. 3–4, 74, 97, 101, 107–8, 122, 127, 226, 420–34, 433; K. D. Wald, *Crosses on the Ballot: Patterns of British Voter Alignment since 1885* (Princeton, 1983); G. I. T. Machin, *Politics and the Churches in Great Britain, 1869–1921* (Oxford, 1987); E. F. Biagini, *Liberty, Retrenchment and Reform: Popular Liberalism in the Age of Gladstone, 1860–1880* (Cambridge, 1992).

interpretation echoed through the years after 1851. Given the political quandaries and religious rivalries that it aroused, it is small wonder that the exercise was never repeated.[14]

There was also a considerable thirst for quantitative data during this period, which was crucial for a more rigorous, empirically grounded and factual understanding of regional societies, religious cultures and economic life. Such figures appealed 'to the heart of a generation which . . . had a veritable passion for "facts"', as J. F. C. Harrison has written.[15] In 1847 G. R. Porter published a new edition of his *Progress of the Nation, in its Various Social and Economical Relations, from the Beginning of the Nineteenth Century*. He argued that it would almost seem to be a duty to gather such 'well-authenticated facts'.[16] Something of that attitude pervades the parliamentary debates on the Religious Census. It is also clear that comparable religious censuses in very many other advanced countries were on British legislators' minds, and there was a distinct sense that Britain should also conduct one.[17] The public appetite was revealed by the remarkable fact that 21,000 copies of the *Census of Religious Worship* were sold almost as soon as it was published.[18] The data collection of the Religious Census was a logical outcome in a Christian age of the concerns that had already brought so much poor-law, welfare, industrial, demographic and agricultural data into the public domain, via a formidable and completely unprecedented array of Select Committee and other investigative reports.

The organisation of the Religious Census

George Graham, the Registrar General for the 1851 Population Census, had expressed concern about the lack of accurate statistics on

14 For further discussion of this point, see appendix F.

15 J. F. C. Harrison, *The Early Victorians, 1832–51* (1971), p. 9.

16 Summarised in *ibid.*, pp. 8–9.

17 Comparable religious censuses were held around this time for Austria, Bavaria, Belgium, Denmark, France, Prussia, Saxony, Sweden, and Württemberg. Ireland had such a census in 1834. In Spain, such information was obtained through the civil administration. Religious censuses were also taken in some British colonies, although in some such cases – like Australia – there were doubts as to their accuracy. See the speech by Sir George Lewis, in *Hansard's Parliamentary Debates*, CLIX (11 July 1860), 1703–6. On the unsatisfactory Australian religious census, see M. H. Marsh, in *ibid.*, 1720–1. America conducted counts of churches and sittings: see Sir John Trelawny's speech in *ibid.*, 1728.

18 *Hansard's Parliamentary Debates*, CXXXV (11 July 1854), 32.

religious worship. He suggested that the 1851 census should include sections on both religion and education, arguing that there was a need for such information, and that any attendant costs would be minimal.[19] He pointed out that the existing administration used to gather statistics for the population census could be employed in gathering the additional data. Graham's enthusiasm for a religious census was matched by the eagerness of Lord John Russell's government. Although the planned Census of Religious Worship was not included in the original Census Act,[20] the Secretary of State was empowered under that Act to make any additional enquiries that he thought necessary. On this authority, Graham initiated planning for a census of religion.

The Registrar General appointed as his agent Horace Mann, a 28-year-old barrister, making him responsible for organising the census. It was Mann's view that 'There are two methods of pursuing a statistical inquiry with respect to the religion of a people. You may either ask each individual, directly, what particular form of religion he professes; or, you may collect such information as to the religious acts of individuals as will equally, though indirectly, lead to the same result. The former method was adopted, some few years ago, in Ireland, and is generally followed in the continental states when such investigations as the present are pursued. At the recent Census, it was thought advisable to take the latter course; partly because it had a less inquisitorial aspect, – but especially because it was considered that the outward conduct of persons furnishes a better guide to their religious state than can be gained by merely vague professions.'[21]

[19] In fact the total cost of the population, religious and educational censuses of 1851 appears to have been well in excess of £100,000. This was subsequently cited as part of an argument against having another educational census in 1861, although it seems not to have been part of any case then against a repeated religious census. See *Hansard's Parliamentary Debates*, CLIX (11 July 1860), 1739–40. It is worth bearing in mind also that in 1851 the high proportion (about 70 per cent) of census costs hitherto carried by the parishes (covering enumeration) were to be paid by a grant from Parliament, so that the whole expense of the 1851 census fell for the first time upon the national exchequer, rather than falling heavily on local funds. The Treasury had hitherto only paid for the central office. See G. C. Lewis' speech in *Hansard's Parliamentary Debates*, CXI (6 June 1850), 870–1. This appears to have given the government more leeway in the range of census questions it felt able to ask in 1851. On the enumeration and other census allowances payable, see *Census of Great Britain: Instructions to Enumerators*, XLIII (1851), pp. 4, 39.

[20] 13 & 14 Vic. c. 53.

[21] *Census of Religious Worship*, p. cxix. This was later cited at fuller length in the House of Commons by E. Baines in 1860, when he argued in its favour, and for the 'perfect success' of the 1851 Religious Census. *Hansard's Parliamentary Debates*, CLIX (11 July 1860), 1700–1.

Accordingly, it was decided to hold a census of religion based upon attendances rather than stated profession. As Mann argued, a census of profession would probably have gone beyond the accepted role of the British state at that time.[22] For the historian of religion, a census of religious actions is certainly far more valuable than a census of profession. In the nineteenth century it is likely that there would have been such a stigma attached to atheism and agnosticism that the vast majority of those who rarely, or never, attended worship would have professed allegiance to the established church. This would have dramatically and unrealistically inflated its actual strength. In addition, the often complex patterns of attendance, with some worshippers attending both established church services and Nonconformist services, would have been completely lost. As we shall see, such multi-attendance remains a problematical area in the interpretation of the Religious Census. But there can be little doubt that attendance rates, associated as they were by contemporaries with faith and a desire to practise that faith, provide the most satisfactory outcome for the historian.[23]

The stated purpose of the census was to discover how far the means of religious instruction had kept up with the growing population over the previous half century, and to what extent the spiritual needs of the population were being met. It aimed to provide information on the number of places of worship belonging to each denomination, and their numbers of attendances and sittings. These were considered the most essential matters, although there were many lesser questions. Originally it was planned to make completion of the religious returns compulsory, with any failure to complete the returns being an offence. Queries were raised about this however, for example about whether the clergy should have to disclose their incomes,[24] and other matters which might 'excite needless alarm'.[25] Having taken legal advice, the government felt that as a census of religion was not specifically prescribed in the Census Act, penalties could not be imposed on those failing to make returns. Nor did the government wish to act in an 'inquisitorial manner'.[26] Lord Brougham and others indicated that questions posed which were not compulsory would still yield 'information of considerable value' and

[22] On this issue, see appendix F.

[23] R. M. Goodridge, 'The religious condition of the West Country in 1851', *Social Compass*, 14 (1967), 287.

[24] *Hansard's Parliamentary Debates*, CXIV (14 March 1851), 1316–17.

[25] *Hansard's Parliamentary Debates*, CXV (18 March 1851), 113.

[26] *Hansard's Parliamentary Debates*, CXIV (14 March 1851), 1308.

'great utility'.[27] A voluntary system in connection with the religious returns was therefore introduced, although this may not have been made entirely clear by enumerators to those making the returns. Sir George Grey was among those who took the view that even without strict compulsion, all clergy would still 'give full information on such important matters as the amount of provision for education and religious worship in their respective districts'.[28]

Returns were requested from every place of worship in Britain, and they contain an enormous body of statistical information. Three different returning forms were devised by Horace Mann.[29] The established-church form, to be completed by clergy of the Church of England, had more questions than those addressed to ministers of dissenting chapels. It requested the date of construction of the church or chapel of ease, if erected after 1800; the number of sittings contained in the building, with a distinction being made between free and other (or appropriated) sittings; the number of people at morning, afternoon and evening services on Sunday 30 March 1851; the number of Sunday scholars present at the same times; and the average attendances over a stated period for both general congregation attendances and Sunday school scholars. There were also questions referring to church endowments and sources of income like pew rents, fees, dues or Easter offerings.[30] The Nonconformist

27 *Hansard's Parliamentary Debates*, CXIV (14 March 1851), 1308–10.

28 *Hansard's Parliamentary Debates*, CXV (18 March 1851), 114.

29 The Church of England form was blue, the general Nonconformist form was blue and red, and the Quaker form was black and white to avoid confusion. See for example E. Legg (ed.), *Buckinghamshire Returns of the Census of Religious Worship, 1851* (1991), p. vii.

30 The information on Anglican income provided by the census was very extensive indeed, but for this book it was decided not to analyse it. The subject is extremely complex, given the varied sources of income then available to the Anglican Church: tithe (with all the complexity of that, given parochial differences in commutation, rent charges, etc.), glebe, land and property rents, fees, other dues, Easter offerings, pew rents, bishops' augmentations, endowments, annuities, and the like. Some incumbents declined to submit such details, a few clearly taking offence at the request that they do so. More commonly, they submitted differing personal assessments of their income that were not standardised across parishes, and many were evidently in some confusion as to what they ought to be returning. There was some puzzlement over whether net or gross income should be returned, and how these ought to be defined. A few rather self-defensive clergy submitted detailed lists of their expenditure and costs as well, like curate charges, rates, property and land taxes, buildings repair, insurance and so on. The census information on all this is extensive (and supplements that in other sources, like the data on values of the living in the *Imperial Gazetteer*, computerised at parish level for the second half of this book). The subject of nineteenth-century clerical income has long deserved a book in its own right.

return was comparable, except that information on income was not requested, and it was asked whether the building was used exclusively as a place of worship. A separate return was sent to Quaker meeting houses requesting similar details, the measurements of the building (as a guide to standing room), and the estimated number of persons capable of being seated. All forms permitted further remarks to be made by the informant if he wished, and these supply a fascinating additional range of information, covering as they do issues like rivalries between denominations, the Welsh language at services, endowments and income, the condition of the place of worship, pew rents, Sunday scholars, special conditions operating on that Sunday, and other observations.

The published *Census of Religious Worship*

The Religious Census, and a report by Horace Mann, was published on 3 January 1854.[31] It was divided into several sections. In a fairly substantial discussion, Mann deliberated on the origins and growth of the key denominations and sects. He then examined spiritual provision and destitution, considering in turn accommodation and attendance, although placing more emphasis on the former. He calculated that accommodation was required for 58 per cent of the population, and discussed areas where an appropriate level of accommodation had not been reached. This drew him into differentials between urban and rural seating provision. Accommodation was clearly insufficient in general terms to house an 'ideal' worshipping community. In the remainder of this section of his report, Mann concentrated upon the alleged absence of the working classes from worship. Finally, he examined the disparate levels of accommodation provided by denominations. His account of attendance was less extensive. Here Mann attempted to calculate what would be an acceptable figure for attendances.[32] We shall discuss these further features of his report in the context of the historiography on the Census of Religious Worship.

Several tables showing these and related subjects, organised at various spatial levels, were included in the census volume. Summary data were recorded for the whole of England and Wales, for the 11

[31] The Scottish Report and Census was published later, in March 1854.

[32] For Scotland the report was far briefer. Mann stated here that there was insufficient time to prepare as detailed a report as that for England and Wales.

registration divisions,[33] for the 28 dioceses, for the 43 English registration counties and North and South Wales, for 73 large towns (including 9 London boroughs), and for 624 registration districts in a large sub-section marked 'Detailed Tables'.

The opening sections of this book analyse the published data for the 624 registration districts of England and Wales.[34] At this level published information is available for each denomination on the number of sittings, both free and appropriated, the total number of attendances (including Sunday scholars) at services in the morning, afternoon and evening, and the number of places of worship in each district. In Scotland, although the same data are available, they are arranged at a different and less convenient spatial level,[35] that is, for counties and for burghs (or parishes which contain burghs).[36] There was no Scottish administrative unit equivalent to the registration district – burghs being confined to urban areas only.[37] The lack of Scottish registration-district data, or data published for similarly specified areas, is one reason why this book does not cover Scotland. Analysis of the Scottish data is further circumscribed because the original returns, as available

[33] These registration divisions were London, the South Eastern Counties, the South Midland Counties, the Eastern Counties, the South Western Counties, the West Midland Counties, the North Midland Counties, the North Western Counties, Yorkshire, the Northern Counties, and the Welsh Counties.

[34] In the detailed registration-district tables all registration districts are numbered. Anglesey, the final district, is numbered 623 and almost all researchers have assumed, therefore, that there were only 623 registration districts. This is not the case as Pontefract District was numbered 504(a) in the census and Hemsworth District 504(b), making the total number of Registration Districts 624.

[35] *1851 Census Great Britain: Report and Tables on Religious Worship and Education, Scotland*, LIX (1854, Shannon, 1970 edn), p. xii.

[36] *Ibid.*, pp. 22–34, but beware of the note on p. xii.

[37] Mann wrote of the Scottish published returns that 'the particulars respecting these returns are not presented in minuter subdivisions of the country than *Counties*. This course was rendered necessary by a pledge, which was deemed essential to the success of the inquiry, that no individual return should be made public. It was found, when preparing the Tables, which at one time it was intended to give, of *Parishes*, that this could not be done without virtually violating the condition upon which, it may be reasonably held, the request for information was complied with.' *Ibid.*, p. xii. Hume, in one of the earliest commentaries on the census wrote: 'In 1851, a "Census of Religious Worship" was compiled for each of the two sections of Great Britain. That for Scotland was published separately, and at a comparatively early period after the receipt of the detailed information. It had been anxiously looked for: and was therefore issued with somewhat less care than was bestowed on the publication for South Britain.' A. Hume, *Remarks on the Census of Religious Worship for England and Wales, with Suggestions for an Improved Census in 1861, and a Map, Illustrating the Religious Condition of the Country* (1860), p. 5.

for England and Wales, have been lost north of the border. The rate of return was also poorer than for England and Wales, the voluntary aspect of the census being for various reasons more problematical in Scotland. In addition, the distinctive and unique nature of the Scottish denominations, which usually lacked direct English or Welsh counterparts of any comparable strength, make it appropriate for an examination along these lines of Scottish religion to be conducted separately by other historians.

The collection of Religious Census data

In assessing the thoroughness of the Religious Census, the process by which returns were collected needs to be described. Some weeks before Census Sunday, local enumerators were appointed and instructed by Mann to collect the names and addresses of ministers in their district to whom census forms should be sent. It was permissible to provide, if the incumbent was unavailable, the name and address of a responsible nominee of the denomination. These details were forwarded to the local registrars – of which there were 2,190 in England and Wales – who sent the forms out for the nominated official's completion.[38] The enumerators involved in the collection of the Religious Census (30 March) were also involved in the collection of the population census data the next day. Each enumerator was either already, or was instructed to become, very familiar with his district. There were 30,610 of these districts or sections, which were generally very small – each enumerator was responsible for an area comprising an average of about 100 houses.[39] Completed schedules were collected by the enumerators on 31 March. The enumerators were instructed to check the returns for completeness and endeavour to complete any missing replies, sometimes sending further forms to incumbents and returning officials. On or before 8 April the schedules were to be delivered to the local registrars, who checked the returns again for completeness and accuracy. If information was missing an Inform-

[38] As well as the normal census forms, and the forms for the Religious Census, there were also forms for all heads or keepers of Day Schools, Sunday Schools, Evening Schools for Adults, and Literary and Scientific Institutions. *1851 Census Great Britain: Report and Tables on Education, England and Wales*, XC (1852–3), p. xciv.

[39] *1851 Census Great Britain: Report and Tables on Education, England and Wales*, XC (1852–3), p. xciv.

ant's Form was sent to the enumerator requesting information. Finally, 'when made as perfect as was possible',[40] the forms were sent on to Horace Mann in London, to arrive by 22 April. Further checks and communications with local officers then ensued, to obtain as complete coverage as possible. These measures taken for the collection of data appear to have been very thorough indeed.[41]

Criticisms of the Religious Census

Despite this process, the accuracy of the Religious Census has been much debated, with far more discussion of the source *as a source*, than systematic attempts to analyse it comprehensively. The historiography of the census clearly demonstrates this, and this has hitherto been appropriate.[42] It is important to consider both contemporary concerns about the Religious Census as well as the limitations assessed by historians.

Criticisms fall into several headings. First, it has been argued that the enquiry itself was defective in the way it was envisaged and framed. There had been much debate about the form it should take. Where comparable religious enquiries had been made in other countries, the preference had often been to proceed with an examination of stated or perceived profession. However, this carried an intrinsic advantage for the established church, one felt likely to convey a completely unrealistic picture, and it was thought that an investigation that aimed to assess personal acts of religious adherence was preferable. Mann ably summarised the objections to a census of profession, claiming that such a census 'would produce results utterly untrustworthy; since numbers of people, who have not the slightest connection with any religious communion, would, from the mere shame of openly avowing practical atheism, enrol themselves as members of some church, most probably the Church of England'.[43]

40 *1851 Census Great Britain: Report and Tables on Education, England and Wales*, XC (1852–3), p. xciv.

41 See also *Census of Great Britain: Instructions to Enumerators*, XLIII (1851, Shannon edn, 1970), pp. 29–31; *Census Great Britain: Tables of the Population and Housing*, XLIII (1851, Shannon edn, 1970), pp. xi–xvi.

42 For example Ambler, 'The 1851 Census of Religious Worship'; Thompson, 'The 1851 Religious Census: problems and possibilities'. Both are appraisals of the source.

43 H. Mann, 'On the statistical position of religious bodies in England and Wales', *Journal of the Statistical Society*, 18 (1856), 142.

As the census returns were not compulsory, it has been argued that the census was inaccurate through insufficient returns being made. In Scotland, as Mann admitted, non-completion of returns was a problem: 'the statistics are not complete; and . . . no means are in your [the Registrar General's] possession of computing the extent of the deficiency. The effect of the instruction given to enumerators – that the inquiry was a *voluntary* measure – was much more awkward in Scotland than in England; the enumerators were less careful, after this announcement, to deliver forms, and parties were less willing to supply the information. The absence, likewise, of a staff of local officers within the sphere of your own influence (as are the Registrars in England) prevented any attempt, like that made here, to supply, by subsequent inquiries, such deficiencies as really became apparent.'[44] Of the 3,395 places of worship recorded in Scotland, 481 (14 per cent) failed to provide both sittings and attendance data.[45] This was a far higher proportion than for England and Wales. Some places of worship in Scotland were apparently not even issued with a return. The Scottish data have resulting limitations, although much useful work may be still done with them.[46]

For England and Wales however, the returns were of a far higher quality. We have seen that their method of collection was exacting. The published data show that, after all lines of enquiry were exhausted, 2,524 of the returns contained no sittings data and 1,394 lacked data concerning attendances. In many such cases, there were good reasons for such omissions – for example, no service having been held on that day. Of the 34,467 returns in England and Wales only 390 (or 1.1 per cent) lacked information on both sittings and attendances. Some such places of worship were clearly dilapidated or derelict.

44 *1851 Census Great Britain: Report and Tables on Religious Worship and Education, Scotland*, LIX (1854, Shannon, 1970 edn), p. ix, and see G. Graham's letter to Viscount Palmerston, 20 March 1854, *ibid.*, p. vii.

45 There were no Scottish attendance returns from 32 per cent of Established churches, 12 per cent of Free churches, and 10 per cent of United Presbyterian churches. See C. G. Brown, *The Social History of Religion in Scotland since 1730* (1987), p. 59.

46 Unfortunately, as the Scottish returns have not survived, places of worship not furnishing a return cannot be identified. For detailed analysis this renders under-completion much more serious than it was for England and Wales. The Scottish religious census is ably discussed in Brown, *Social History of Religion in Scotland*, pp. 59–63, 72–5, 77–83; A. A. MacLaren, *Religion and Social Class: the Disruption Years in Aberdeen* (1974), pp. 31–49, 46; see also C. A. Piggott, 'A geography of religion in Scotland', *Scottish Geographical Magazine*, 96 (1980), 130–40.

Where enumerators were unable to furnish returns they advised the local registrar rather than invent figures themselves. It would, indeed, be a cause for concern if all returns had been completed.

Finally, the form of enquiry was criticised for providing details of attendances rather than attendants. Mann made clear that the Census was not concerned with actual attendants: 'The inquiry undertaken in 1851 related to the provision for religious worship and the extent to which the means provided were made use of. It was not an enumeration of professed adherents to the different sects.'[47] He did attempt to estimate the true size of worshipping communities, by formulating an equation for calculating attendants, one that he had little faith in, and which has been sceptically received by almost all historians. We will consider this later when discussing the measures that can be created from the data. There has been much interest in calculating the number of worshippers in 1851, but there is no reliable way of obtaining such a figure. David Thompson was entirely correct when he argued that 'It is impossible to discover how many people went to church on 30 March 1851',[48] although this need not be a serious limitation if the census is used with care, for example to consider the relative strengths of denominations.

A second criticism of the census suggests that faulty initial enquiries may render some of its statistics defective. Denominations claimed that some of their places of worship were omitted from the census.[49] Certainly there was a weakness in the method of enquiry adopted by Mann. As already mentioned, a few days before the census, enumerators were instructed to record every place of worship in their district together with the name and address of 'a responsible official'. If, at this stage, a Nonconformist place of worship was omitted from the list there was little chance of the error being detected later and of that place of worship receiving an enumeration form. However, this problem is not as prominent as it may seem. In the case of the established church, returns for each church and chapel of ease were checked against the Clergy List and, where there was a discrepancy, further enquiries were made. It is also very unlikely that any Nonconformist minister was

47 *The Times*, 22 July 1870, p. 4.

48 Thompson, 'The 1851 Religious Census: problems and possibilities', 91.

49 See for example J. Kennedy, 'On the census returns respecting Congregational worship', *The Congregational Yearbook* (1855), p. 35. Here it was suggested that omissions occurred particularly when places of worship were not separate buildings.

unaware of the Religious Census and, if he did not receive an enumeration form, it seems probable that he would have made this known to the enumerator. Local studies appear to confirm these views.[50] Even if it was accepted that substantial numbers of churches and chapels were omitted in 1851, there is no evidence to suggest that this occurred more in some English and Welsh divisions than others. When one is comparing denominational support across registration districts, rather than dealing with absolute numbers, errors in the census that are regionally specific are the main concern. One historian has covered this point well: 'Even if the degree of error is not inconsiderable, it can be assumed that the errors were equally distributed over the country – a reasonable assumption in the light of no contrary evidence – and therefore the results are of value in determining relative levels of church attendance in various regions, for example, between county and county, and between town and countryside.'[51]

In some cases confusion seems to have arisen over what constituted a 'place of worship', for a plethora of places could serve as such. This was not only a matter of poorer congregations making do with barns, shop floors and the like, as it extended to workhouses and schools in which Anglican services were held. Such returns usually bolstered the following of the established church, causing raised eyebrows in some Nonconformist circles. However, the main denominational charge ran the other way, for many dissenting places of worship did not match Anglican expectations, and were criticised accordingly. One sees this for example in occasional, and rather triumphal, complaints from Anglican authorities and parliamentarians that some dissenting attendances exceeded their stated numbers of sittings. However, the conclusion they wanted to draw – that these dissenting attendance figures were therefore fabrications – is not persuasive. In poorer places of worship, many used to stand. This was commented on for Roman Catholic churches by Edward Baines (MP for Leeds).[52]

50 For example, A. Rogers, 'The 1851 Religious Census returns for the City of Nottingham', *Transactions of the Thoroton Society of Nottingham*, 76 (1972), 75. He found that all places of worship in contemporary local trade directories were also included in the Religious Census. Other evidence on places of worship also tends to confirm the comprehensive nature of the census.

51 Pickering, 'The 1851 Religious Census – a useless experiment?', 387.

52 *Hansard's Parliamentary Debates*, CLIX (11 July 1860), 1700. He also pointed out that Catholic services were held several times during the morning. On the handling of this, see *Census of Great Britain: Instructions to Enumerators*, XLIII (1851), p. 12.

Indeed, in countering such a criticism of the census, the MP Frank Crossley made the telling point that attendances could easily exceed sittings, just as in the House of Commons, where there were 'sittings for about 200', but where there were '650 members', who crowded in during important debates.[53] In some places, congregations even overspilled to ground outside the chapel, especially when people had come to hear a popular preacher. Whatever the steam stoked up over these issues at the time, in an atmosphere of denominational charge and counter-charge, to the historian these details seem minor when aggregated at registration-district level. At that level, fine questions of data accuracy, occasionally expressed as inter-denominational accusation, can have only the most negligible effect upon quantitative analysis. They matter more at the parochial level, but there they are more visible and open to judgement when one inspects the enumerators' forms.

At the time criticism was focused in particular upon the attendance figures which – unlike sittings – were less readily checked by independent viewers. A number of objections were made in Parliament about the census, with fears voiced over the accuracy of this information.[54] For obvious reasons in Parliament, but outside it as well, such fears came overwhelmingly from the established church rather than from the dissenting bodies. Before the census, Bishop Wilberforce of Oxford presented a petition to the House of Lords from the Deanery of Newbury, complaining that some replies would not be made; that some replies 'must necessarily be vague and incorrect'; and that the general result would propagate error rather than truth. He felt that 'the incorrect information thus obtained would be made available to the prejudice of the great interests over which the ministers of the Church were bound to watch'. The bishop pointed out that answering the queries was not compulsory. He felt that 'authentic information was only attainable when demanded under a penalty'. Prior to the next census, he thought that it should be made imperative that clergy and others answer the questions. His instinct was to advise his own clergy not to respond, although he did not wish to place himself in an antagonistic position towards the government.

53 *Hansard's Parliamentary Debates*, CLIX (11 July 1860), 1727. See also Ambler, *Lincolnshire Returns of the Census of Religious Worship, 1851*, p. xvi.

54 The following account is from *Hansard's Parliamentary Debates*, CXV (27 March 1851), 629–34.

Earl Granville, the Bishop of Salisbury, Earl Fitzwilliam and the Marquess of Breadalbane all made further, and less critical, points in the House of Lords. It was conceded by Earl Granville that the question about the endowments of the benefices of the Church of England might have to be withdrawn. But it would be a great disappointment to the public if no efforts were made by the government to ascertain statistics on the spiritual and secular education of the people. He believed that the returns would be 'of a generally accurate and ample character', and that it was 'important to ascertain whether the spiritual instruction afforded had kept pace with the increased wants of the population of 1851'. He felt that, while other religious bodies were willing to co-operate with the government, 'it could not but redound greatly to the disadvantage of the ministers of the Established Church if they were, on this occasion, to persist in their disinclination to make these important returns in reference to the position and circumstances of their own Church throughout the country'. This was a point reinforced by the Bishop of Salisbury, who indicated that 'if the ministers of the Established Church declined making these returns, they would stand in a position disadvantageous as contrasted with the conduct of ministers of other Churches'. The Church of England, he claimed, had 'no reason to shrink from the closest examination'; but he felt that these particular returns would necessarily be incomplete and imperfect, and that 'unjust, mischievous, and dangerous' inferences would be drawn from the results.

The Marquess of Breadalbane had little time for these prelates' views, although unlike some contemporaries he did not accuse them of a rearguard defence of Anglican political advantage. 'That the returns, in many cases, would be incomplete, might be true; but that was no reason why they should ask for no information at all.' And he added, in a forthright manner, that 'The ministers of Dissenting denominations had not intimated any unwillingness to make the required returns; and he could not attribute it to anything but laziness to find this opposition on the part of clergymen of the Established Church.' Needless to say, this was a position that the Bishop of Oxford objected to, one that he found to be 'not very fair'.

The levels of completed returns cited earlier suggest that little heed was taken of anyone who advocated non-compliance. Nor is there evidence to indicate that Anglican attendance figures were deliberately falsified. The Anglican clergy were widely used by the state to gather quantitative and qualitative information throughout the nineteenth century and earlier. For example, in 1800 the government had requested bishops to ask their clergy to answer four questions relating to the state of agriculture and food supply in their area.[55] In 1801 the clergy acted as enumerators for the first population census. Place names on the first Ordnance Survey maps were moderated by them together with local landowners.[56] There was a long tradition of clergy responding to episcopal enquiries. In the light of so many similar precedents, it would be almost incomprehensible if clergymen of the established church, linked as they were to the state and its enquiries, systematically failed to provide fairly accurate attendance and seating information. Most clergy would probably have felt themselves to be seriously in breach of their duties if they had not provided the required information.[57]

Some churches and chapels may have included Sunday school scholars in their attendance figures. The census forms very clearly requested details of Sunday scholars to be given separately from the 'general congregation' attending services – they were to be entered in a row below the latter, with another row provided for the total figure. It was thus hard to avoid doing this, but it was probably not universally followed, for in some returns only a total figure was given. This may have been partly because the presence or absence of Sunday school classes, or the numbers of scholars in them, reflected upon the incumbent, minister or congregation. Where the matter was thus avoided, one suspects that no Sunday schools had been held, or that the numbers attending them had been embarrassingly small. When Mann compiled the statistical tables which he published in the census, he added the Sunday scholars to the general congregation attendances for the same period of the day. Perhaps one should not criticise him for taking this approach. Mann was very far removed

55 W. E. Minchinton, 'Agricultural returns and the government during the Napoleonic Wars', *Agricultural History Review*, 1 (1953), 38–9; *A Century of Agricultural Statistics: Great Britain, 1866–1966* (HMSO, 1968), p. iii.

56 J. B. Harley, 'Place-names on the early Ordnance Survey maps of England and Wales', *Journal of the British Cartographic Society* (1971), 93.

57 They were also subject to extremely flattering approaches from the Registrar General. On 13 March 1851 they were written to as clergy 'so eminently qualified by position, character, and office, to exercise . . . a beneficial influence on the minds of [your] less educated neighbours'. This letter asking for their help was signed: 'Your faithful Servant, George Graham'. *Census of Great Britain: Instructions to Enumerators*, XLIII (1851, Shannon edn, 1970), p. 41.

from modern data handling capabilities and, given the resources open to him, what he achieved was phenomenal enough without historians asking for more. He had limited space and wished to communicate information in an accessible manner. He was aware that the Sunday scholars generally represented current and many future supporters of each denomination. The age structure of the overall population was relatively low, and Sunday scholars were normally aged between 5 and 16. For Mann, it would have seemed mistaken to omit such pupils where they were entered on the forms as requested, but run a risk of some such scholars being included within figures for general attendances where only totals had been returned. His solution therefore seems legitimate. The inclusion of these scholars within the published attendance figures does not raise serious problems, and historians have little option but to analyse the published registration-district totals of attendances as given. Nevertheless, for the parish-level work in part 2 of this book, using the original returns, the approach adopted has been to keep Sunday scholars separate, which facilitates greater analytical precision, allows them to be added to total attendances if necessary, and permits them to be studied in their own right.[58]

After the census, the Registrar General's Office was widely praised, even by the Bishop of Oxford.[59] However, there were claims, again particularly by this bishop, that Nonconformists had deliberately exaggerated their attendance figures. In a statement that may not have endeared him to Nonconformists, the bishop pointed out that 'Many of their ministers were not often in the same rank of life as the clergy of the Established Church.'[60] He allowed that 'in large Dissenting chapels in large towns the ministers were men of education', and no doubt their returns were honestly made. But in 'very little places . . . small licensed rooms in remote villages', served by 'men who had not the advantages of education – and who were not the objects of general view and observation', he had 'no hesitation in saying there was continually a misrepresentation in point of fact as to the relative numbers of the Established Church and of the

[58] For further discussion, see appendix C, pp. 431–2.

[59] *Hansard's Parliamentary Debates*, CXXXV (11 July 1854), 24. Earl Granville praised the Registrar General's conduct of the Religious Census for showing 'great powers of administration and great care for the public interest in every possible way'. *Ibid.*, 33.

[60] For the bishop's 1854 speech, see *ibid.*, 23–8.

Dissenters'.[61] A number of points were then relayed by him, from Anglicans complaining of particular malpractices on census day among their dissenting neighbours. Such complaints included matters like deliberately trying to swell numbers on that day, for example by having special sermons preached; cross-attendance at different dissenting services; exaggeration of dissenting numbers; averages not being fairly given; double attendances at dissenting services, and so on. Furthermore, unfavourable weather 'had kept many persons who lived at a distance from attending at church'. In some areas – and particularly among Baptists and Independents – the census had clearly been seen as a 'trial of strength between the Church and the Dissenters, and the congregations were to muster in strength'. The clergy had sometimes viewed the questions as 'impertinent or intrusive', and had neglected to answer them. By comparison, 'the Dissenters were wide awake on the occasion'. One wonders how awake the bishop was, for his speech ended in a rather foggy style, although his fears and hopes were evident enough: 'Whatever the truth was on this subject it ought to be told, and there should not go forth to the public, on mistaken facts, a statement as to the relations of the different religious bodies in this land. It should go forth, except it was true, that it was an episcopal figure of speech to say what he said – that, thank God, the great majority of the people of this country do still belong to the Established Church.'

The House of Lords was hardly a venue in which Nonconformist

61 Patronising inter-denominational charges of dishonesty were common. The Bishop of St Davids argued (against another census) that 'It was unfair to the Dissenters themselves . . . to expose them to the temptations of making such misrepresentations'. *Ibid.*, 30. Or the Revd Hoskins, Rector of Blaby (Leicestershire), wrote in his parish book of how the Baptist superintendent 'says by opening the School . . . they can accommodate 80 to 100 more!! As to this & other following Statement – Ludat [sic] Judeus!!!' On the Wesleyan figures for his parish he was equally scathing: 'Even suppose this Statement to be correct – it was their *Opening* Day & many came from Leicester . . . I fear that the return from the Dissenters both as to congregation & Scholars has been greatly exaggerated – They gave notice on the previous Sunday for every one to attend – was this fair??' He commented remorsefully that he had omitted to mention the gallery and chancel in his own return, 'by accident'. See Leics. C.R.O., DE 3352/86 (9 April 1851). However, it seems more than likely that many Anglican incumbents also gave notice for everyone to attend.

For at least one subsequent local religious census, that for Bath on 6 November 1881 (conducted by enumerators employed by *Keene's Bath Journal*), notice was not given in advance, to avoid this criticism that had been made by some in 1851. See J. Eades, I. Duffy and B. Crofts, 'Methodism in the 19th century', in B. Crofts (ed.), *At Satan's Throne: the Story of Methodism in Bath over 250 Years* (Bristol, 1990), pp. 95–7.

counter-arguments had much airing. It does seem very unlikely, however, that returns were falsified in a way that systematically favoured the dissenters rather than the established church. Encouragement of members of each faith to attend may have taken place over the whole country, and this probably has little influence on comparative denominational analysis. Indeed, the established church was much better positioned to 'bully' people into attending – had it so wished – than were its rivals. A doubt might also go forth, more than merely an academic figure of speech, as to whether the fullest education produced the most *honest* returns. It is evident that many of the examples given by the bishop – like service times arranged to allow people to attend across different parishes and thus be double counted – can only have had a significant influence upon Nonconformist returns if they occurred on a large scale, and indeed if they comprised a national or at the very least a regional conspiracy. There is no evidence for this, even at a very localised level. Multiple attendance was hardly a phenomenon restricted to Nonconformists. Adverse weather conditions may have affected dissenters more than Anglicans, for dissenters often had to walk longer distances to worship, although attendance at the established church could involve lengthy distances in larger parishes.

As the returns were to be aggregated, local detail was elusive and some felt that this might allow abuses to be hidden. Such were the comprehensive methods used to collect data, however, that Mann claimed that falsifications could readily be detected. It was surely unlikely that a minister, whatever his denomination, being aware that there were 30,000 enumerators each responsible for a handful of places of worship, would deliberately falsify figures. Each returning official also had to pledge for the accuracy of his return, stating on the form 'I certify the foregoing to be a true and correct Return to the best of my belief. Witness my hand this day . . .'[62] It would take an exceptionally cynical view of nineteenth-century ministers and clergy to suggest that deliberate manipulation occurred on any widespread scale. There is no evidence which supports any allegation of considerable, deliberate falsification.

A number of other factors may also have had an effect on the figures, so as to raise questions about them. 30 March was mid-Lent,

[62] *Census of Religious Worship*, p. clxxii.

or Mothering Sunday, and some potential worshippers visited their parents rather than attending church. Ambler suggested that Mothering Sunday may have had a particular impact in Lancashire, Cheshire and several midland counties, although little cultural history has been written on regional observances of this kind.[63] There were also reports on some census returns of bad weather and illness reducing attendances; although one is not surprised to find that there were no reports of larger than expected congregations due to good weather and a healthy population. In the east midlands there was apparently an outbreak of influenza in Leicester, of measles in Nottingham, and a thunderstorm in southern Leicestershire.[64] More generally, it has been suggested that the weather was poor in the north and west, although the weather seems not to have been abnormal for that time of year. Ambler has also pointed out that agricultural work, especially in pastoral areas during the lambing season, may have reduced attendances. Further, some rural churches held services on alternate Sundays and so may not have made a return for attendances on Census Sunday. Pickering is probably correct in his judgement that such factors are unlikely to have been so specific geographically as to vitiate regional comparisons between denominations.[65] And in mid nineteenth-century England and Wales, it would be hard to think of *any* seasonal moment not open to suggestions like these. In the 'remarks' made on the returns, one can find such occasional comments for all regions, and there is little reason to believe that they detract much from the general accuracy of the data.

David Thompson has written that 'the figures given for accommodation are probably the most accurate of any in the Census'.[66] This is clearly correct, although there are some difficulties with the seating data. As noted above, some churches had higher maximum attendances than sittings, probably because they had not been able to supply seating commensurate to demand. In such cases, and where it was normal to stand, the attendance data may be preferable. One needs also to note that returning officials occasionally

63 Ambler, 'The 1851 Census of Religious Worship', 379; and see his (ed.), *Lincolnshire Returns*, p. xxxi.

64 Thompson, 'The 1851 Religious Census: problems and possibilities', 87–97.

65 Pickering, 'The 1851 Religious Census', 386.

66 Thompson, 'The Religious Census of 1851', in Lawton (ed.), *The Census and Social Structure*, p. 248.

recorded the number of pews in their church or chapel rather than the number of individual sittings. This was easily identified by local enumerators, and was resolved either through contacting the incumbent or using a multiplier to extrapolate from pews to sittings, the latter being a task the historian infrequently has to perform. In some cases the distinction between free and appropriated sittings was misinterpreted, a matter raised in chapter 10. Where discussion focuses on seating this book will usually be dealing with total sittings, and so the distinction between types of seating does not arise.

Testing the Religious Census

We have dwelt in some detail on criticism of the Religious Census, and seen that the attendance figures have attracted more doubts than those for sittings. The latter were also easily verified by other observers after the census. It is possible now to test these data for their internal consistency, by examining the relation between sittings and attendances for the major denominations in England and Wales.

Inspection of the data in this way, especially graphically and at parish level, allows dubious returns to be observed and more closely investigated. For each denomination, regional plots and identification of deviant cases can shed much light upon the relations between sittings and attendances, and the regional historical circumstances that underlie such relations. This is a complex area of investigation that will not be expounded at length here.[67] But in general terms it is worth explaining what the relationships were between sittings and attendances, and how denominations compared. Such tests are an excellent way of verifying the accuracy of the census, by assessing the internal consistency of its data. Table 1.1 gives the results – over fifteen English and Welsh counties – of rank correlations between the total sittings in 2,443 parishes and the maximum attendances for the denomination in question (that is, the maximum figure out of the morning, afternoon or evening attendances).

Correlations of this kind can be performed in a variety of other

[67] In a rudimentary way, at least one contemporary was aware of such possibilities. Looking at the ratios between attendances and sittings, Edward Baines argued that there is 'internal evidence of the most decisive kind of the honesty and substantial accuracy of those who made these returns'. *Hansard's Parliamentary Debates*, CLIX (11 July 1960), 1700.

Table 1.1. *Spearman (rank) correlation coefficients between denominations' total available sittings and the numbers at their highest attended services on Census Sunday, 1851. Parish-level data for all parishes in fifteen English and Welsh registration counties*[68]

Denomination	Correlation coefficients	N. of parishes	Significance
Church of England	0.666	2,101	.000
Church of Scotland	0.244	11	.469
United Presbyterian Synod	0.817	18	.000
Presbyterian Church in England	0.741	42	.000
Independents	0.800	498	.000
General Baptists	0.792	80	.000
Particular Baptists	0.764	163	.000
New Connexion General Baptists	0.881	12	.000
Baptists (unspecified)	0.679	289	.000
Society of Friends	0.424	60	.001
Unitarians	0.712	47	.000
Moravians	0.600	4	.400
Wesleyan Methodist	0.832	771	.000
Methodist New Connexion	0.707	35	.000
Primitive Methodist	0.814	393	.000
Bible Christian	0.667	21	.001
Wesleyan Methodist Association	0.915	73	.000
Independent Methodist	0.765	29	.000
Wesleyan Reformers	0.813	57	.000
Welsh Calvinistic Methodists	0.813	163	.000
Countess of Huntingdon	0.646	11	.032
New Church	0.843	15	.000
Brethren	0.850	8	.007
Other Isolated Congregations	0.651	98	.000
Roman Catholics	0.842	100	.000
Catholic & Apostolic Church	0.888	30	.000
Mormons	0.393	45	.008

68 The parish-level data used for this table are from fifteen English and Welsh registration counties, described in much fuller detail in part 2 of this book. The counties chosen for parochial analysis were Anglesey, Bedfordshire, Caernarvonshire, Cambridgeshire, Cardiganshire, Derbyshire, Dorset, the East Riding, Lancashire, Leicestershire, Monmouthshire, Northumberland, Rutland, Suffolk and Sussex. All 2,443 parishes for these registration counties were used. The column headed 'No. of parishes' in table 1.1 gives the total number of parishes for which the denomination in question was present and holding an attended service. For earlier checking of the census along these lines, at registration-district level, see Snell, *Church and Chapel in the North Midlands*, pp. 12–14.

ways, for example by using total attendances for each denomination. The results stay very much the same. The maximum attendances for every denomination have been used for table 1.1, because they are the most logical adjunct and point of comparison to the denomination's total sittings in each parish. Several points emerge clearly. There is a clear relationship between sittings and attendances: the correlations being strongly positive (i.e. when sittings increase so do attendances). The correlation coefficients are almost all very high. In the few instances where they are less strong, one is dealing with minority denominations in a small number of parishes. In the case of the Quakers special conditions applied, with their often movable seats and an emphasis on standing room. This was recognised by Horace Mann when he devised a different returning form specifically for them, and when he later commented on their returns.[69]

For those denominations that had been in existence longest, the coefficients in table 1.1 tend to be lower: their sittings had normally been in place long before 1851, and sittings in some cases were out of line with the attendances they had in 1851. This was most obviously true for the Church of England, despite some ecclesiological reforms which were underway. William Cobbett repeatedly observed in his *Rural Rides* that many Anglican churches were catering for parish populations much smaller than was implied by their seating capacities, and he thought that population must have declined in these parishes.[70] While one does not endorse the anti-Malthusian arguments that he felt were justified by his observation, one can certainly find many large Anglican churches – in Dorset, Suffolk, Rutland, east Leicestershire and elsewhere – left stranded in settlements that had experienced population decline, for example because of changes from arable to pasture farming, or because of local de-industrialisation. To a lesser extent, some similar mismatch between sittings and attendances also held for most old dissenting denominations. It is noticeable in table 1.1 how the New Connexion General Baptists (formed in 1770) stand apart from their older counterparts. The Roman Catholics have a very high coefficient, and this is because the 1851 Religious Census was beginning to reflect the cultural impact of the 1845–9 Irish famine. Irish immigration was leading to very considerable

[69] Mann's comments on the Quakers are in *Census of Religious Worship*, p. clvii.
[70] W. Cobbett, *Rural Rides* (1830, Harmondsworth, 1967 edn), for example pp. 463–7.

reorientation of Catholic worshipping capacity and seating, with the recent establishment of many new places of Catholic worship, a process that was to continue in a striking manner after 1851.

By comparison with old dissent, denominations like the Wesleyan Methodists, Primitive Methodists, New Church, Welsh Calvinistic Methodists, or Wesleyan Reformers had higher coefficients. The newest denominations (particularly the Wesleyan Methodist Association, founded in 1835) tended to have the highest correlation results. As one would expect, the more proximate to 1851 the denomination's origins, the more its sittings were in alignment with its 1851 attendances. These are interesting and historically significant denominational nuances. But the main conclusion from table 1.1 is the generally very high correlations between the two types of data in the census. The results are statistically very significant indeed, as seen in the fourth column of table 1.1. This close match between sittings and attendances at the parish level is highly reassuring as a test for the reliability of the source.

These correlations were also performed for the 624 registration districts of England and Wales. The resulting coefficients were even higher, in the large majority of cases being above 0.900, with the same kind of denominational variations as outlined above. The Quakers (0.687), the Church of England (0.883), or the Church of Scotland (0.786) had among the weakest associations between sittings and attendances (although these coefficients are still high); while denominations like the Welsh Calvinistic Methodists (0.981), the Wesleyan Methodists (0.951) or the Bible Christians (0.950) had among the highest.[71] Coefficients of such magnitude indicate exceptionally tight 'fits' between the two variables.

The Religious Census was a unique endeavour, and nothing like it occurred before or after. It is thus hard to match it with other chronologically proximate sources. However, the 1851 parish returns were compared with the 1829 returns of non-Anglican places of worship for Leicestershire. Despite the time that had elapsed between these, the results showed exceptionally close correspondence between the two sources, with parish-level correlations for all

[71] Calculations were only performed for registration districts where the denomination in question was present. The published registration-district data can be less precise than the unpublished enumerators' returns, notably because they do not distinguish between different Baptist denominations.

Nonconformity of 0.95 between the two dates, and cartographic results that were virtually interchangeable.[72] Another exercise (in the field of political sociology) has related the 1851 returns to *per capita* clergy distributions in 1891. This forty-year gap of course allows considerable change over time to interfere with the comparison. However, the results of relating the 1851 data to those for 1891 were very reassuring indeed, producing coefficients of between 0.73 and 0.81 for the established church and Nonconformists respectively. Kenneth Wald described such results as 'spectacular'. It certainly adds reassurance to the 1851 data, once more showing the Religious Census to be very reliable.[73]

Where congregations were large in 1851, rounded estimation of attendances by returning officials was probably more likely to occur. This takes the form of the rounding of some attendance numbers to the nearest 10, 50 or 100. Methods of counting attendances varied. As Inglis suggested, some incumbents counted worshippers as they entered or left the church or chapel.[74] Others clearly estimated attendances. In one Welsh case, objections were made to actually counting such people on the Sabbath![75] It seems plausible to suppose that

[72] This is discussed further in chapter 8.

[73] K. D. Wald, *Crosses on the Ballot*, pp. 130–6. These results are aggregated at a broader level than our data, focused by the author on voting patterns and constituencies, the denominations being grouped as Anglican, Roman Catholic or Nonconformist. The resulting coefficient for the Roman Catholics was 0.48, lower than for the two Protestant groups, but that was only to be expected given the huge post-famine impact on Catholicism of Irish immigration (*ibid.*, p. 130). Another religious measure was derived in the following way. Under the 1870 Education Act, control over the municipal system of elementary education was vested in elective school boards, the elections to which were contested between denominations. In 1902, the school boards' responsibilities were transferred to local governing authority committees, members being appointed proportional to party strength on the authority. Denominational competition was thus switched to the local councils, giving a further indication of religious strength. The 1851 data showed strong correlations with such local education authority membership, c. 1902 (*ibid.*, pp. 129–31). For our purposes however, the considerable time lag (1851 to 1902) and different entities being measured here make this comparison one of incidental interest. Our parish data lend themselves to study of local religion and political voting patterns, but that would be a separate project.

[74] Inglis, 'Patterns of religious worship', 76.

[75] W. Williams, Rector of Llanfair-Mathafarn-Eithaf Parochial Chapelry in Anglesey, remarked: 'I give the general estimated average rather than be a party to have the congregation *counted* on the Sabbath' (his emphasis). Jones, *Religious Census of 1851: North Wales*, p. 396. The rector of Bradwell (Suffolk) was equally difficult, claiming that he could not count when he was 'employed in the spiritual Duties of my office as Minister of the Gospel of Christ'. P.R.O., HO 129/227/37.

rounded estimates were more likely when attendances were large, and perhaps this entailed a tendency to round slightly upwards. There is little evidence to indicate that where estimation took place the returns exaggerated the number of attendants. In scattergrams this would reveal itself in a tendency for the ratio of attendances to sittings to increase, with a clear upward curve developing in the plotted data. This was examined for each major denomination at registration-district and parish levels. For the most part the relationships are clearly linear. Some slightly non-linear associations emerge at parish level, but these show no consistent pattern across denominations. It may have been tempting for those making returns to estimate their congregations rather generously, but the evidence demonstrates that this did not usually happen. Nor is there much reason to think that a proclivity to estimate had a geographical bias. These tests all show the source to be accurate, more so than one might have dared to expect.

Conclusion

This survey has shown that the Religious Census data were collected with commendable rigour and care. It may be the case that the sittings data are more reliable than those for attendances; but there are strongly supportive quantitative associations between the two resulting variables, pointing to their mutual reliability. Tests of this sort, like comparison of the returns with other sources of religious data – and there is further confirmatory discussion along these lines in the chapters ahead – leave one in no doubt that this huge source is one of remarkable value to the historian, historical geographer and sociologist.

This basic accuracy of the source was accepted by many contemporaries and increasingly is accepted by almost all historians. In an address to the Statistical Society, Horace Mann stated that 'on an entire review of all these various objections, to the plan of the inquiry, to the authenticity of the returns, and to the value of the inferences, I am really unable to arrive at any other conclusion, than that the general facts and totals of the census are substantially correct. Isolated errors, doubtless, may be pointed out, but not such a number of errors as would cause a noticeable alteration in the aggregate.'[76]

[76] Mann, 'On the statistical position of religious bodies', 147.

Mann defended the census against many accusations which he thought were simply careless, saying that those accusations 'are ludicrously false'.[77] In this he was supported by one of the most famous of Nonconformist MPs, Edward Baines, who thought the census had been a 'perfect success',[78] who praised the 'very able Report' of 1851, and who tried hard to have exactly the same exercise repeated in 1861.[79] The view that the 1851 returns were unfair to the Church of England was, Baines claimed, 'destitute of all real substance . . . there was no unfairness whatever'.[80] Frank Crossley reiterated such views, once more wishing to have a similar census in 1861.[81] The High Church *Christian Remembrancer* felt that 'on the whole the Church of England may accept the general results [of the census] as not a very untrue picture.'[82] Sir Morton Peto claimed in Parliament that the Religious Census was 'substantially correct'.[83] Even its greatest critic, the Bishop of Oxford, stated in his charge to his clergy in 1854 that 'he was perfectly satisfied of the accuracy of the census so far as his diocese was concerned'.[84]

Whatever the limitations of the source, particularly the problem of calculating precise numbers of attendants, it is unquestionably the most comprehensive source for nineteenth-century religion, and probably for British religion in any period. It was never repeated.[85] Almost all scholars now agree with Coleman that 'The methodology for using the census evidence in both its printed and primary forms has been given considerable attention by historians, as has the reliability of the data. Though the limitations of the latter become clear when small locations like individual parishes are considered, for larger areas there is no doubt that it provides a picture that is both generally reliable and extremely revealing.'[86] Milburn wrote that 'the

77 As reported by Bernal Osborne in *Hansard's Parliamentary Debates*, CLIX (11 July 1860), 1718.

78 *Hansard's Parliamentary Debates*, CLIX (11 July 1860), 1700.

79 *Hansard's Parliamentary Debates*, CLIX (11 July 1860), 1701–2, 1741.

80 *Hansard's Parliamentary Debates*, CLIX (11 July 1860), 1699.

81 *Hansard's Parliamentary Debates*, CLIX (11 July 1860), 1727–8. For further discussion of the 1860 debates on whether there should be another Religious Census in 1861, see appendix F of this book.

82 *The Christian Remembrancer* (April 1851), n.p.

83 *Hansard's Parliamentary Debates*, CLIX (11 July 1860), 1726.

84 Reported by Bernal Osborne in *Hansard's Parliamentary Debates*, CLIX (11 July 1860), 1718.

85 The reasons why the Religious Census was not repeated in 1861 or later are discussed in appendix F.

86 Coleman, *The Church of England in the Mid-Nineteenth Century*, p. 6; and see the verdict in Ambler, *Lincolnshire Returns*, p. xxii.

Census is unique . . . we have nothing like it for any other period. It was taken at an important moment in the evolution of English society and at a time when religion was one of the prime social forces . . . it stands as a magnificent piece of evidence for a fuller understanding of the strength and deployment of the churches in mid-Victorian England.'[87] The final assessments should remain those of David Thompson, who wrote of how 'There is no other collection of statistical material which is as complete for comparing varying practice from place to place and from denomination to denomination.'[88] 'Since 1851 there have been a number of unofficial censuses of religious worship conducted with varying degrees of rigour. None has the national coverage of the 1851 census, however, and in no other is there the same opportunity to link religious practice with other demographic information collected at the same time. For this reason the 1851 Religious Census, despite its manifest deficiencies, is likely to remain an important source for nineteenth century social history.'[89] It 'stands out as a fascinating revelation of the religious state of Britain in the middle of the century'.[90]

[87] G. E. Milburn, 'The Census of Worship of 1851', *Durham County Local History Society*, 17 (1974), 11.

[88] Thompson, 'The 1851 Religious Census: problems and possibilities', 97.

[89] Thompson, 'The Religious Census of 1851', 262.

[90] *Ibid.*, 241.

2

The Church of England

Introduction

The Church of England was numerically by far the most important denomination in 1851. Its central position as the established church warrants treatment in its own right in this chapter, where our aim is to describe and (in general terms) account for its distribution in 1851. In doing this, we have used nearly the full range of possible Anglican variables, partly to indicate their mutually reinforcing character, and partly to familiarise readers with the variables and their distinctive qualities. These were produced and mapped for every denomination, but we will not provide such detail for other denominations in later chapters. The concentration there will usually be on the index of attendances. As outlined earlier, the analysis in these opening chapters focuses on the 624 registration districts of England and Wales.

In dealing separately with the Church of England, an important preamble should be made, for it is one that bears on comparisons between denominations. The Anglican Church is routinely criticised for its 'inflexibility' and failure to adapt to industrialising circumstances. We will see examples of this in the following pages, and this is a line that historians have readily adopted. However, one needs to bear in mind that compared to its rival denominations the Church was severely hampered by its long history: by earlier geographies of settlement that were becoming anachronistic, by estate churches built by landowners for their own convenience, and later made more public, by emoluments, fees and advowsons which were regarded as perquisites and which could be legitimately traded, by parliamentary constraints (e.g. over boundary changes), by canon law, by impropriations (leading to low levels of clerical income), by common incumbencies until death, by parson's freehold, by clerical responsibility for dilapidations on their houses, and so on. In short, the Church was faced with inherent, fundamental problems of an historical and legal nature – and these were not applicable to any form of dissent. Within the frameworks of the mid nineteenth century, many of these problems were insurmountable. Certainly they coloured in many ways the geographical situation that the Church found itself in.

'Proportion share' measures for the Anglican Church

The Religious Census permits three 'proportion share' measures to be calculated, based on sittings, attendances and numbers of places of worship. Such measures are very reliable, but have received little discussion in the historiography. We shall consider them initially, and then turn to other measures. The Anglican shares of all denominational sittings, attendances and places of worship measure its share of religious provision (in terms of sittings, attendances or churches). They do not take account of varying levels of apparent 'religiosity' across England and Wales. The Anglican 'percentage share of sittings' is its percentage share of all sittings in each registration district. This is shown in figure 2.1.[1]

The data mapped here show marked regional variations, with high values in a number of well-dispersed areas, all but one of them south of a line from the Dee estuary to the Wash. There were two most prominent regions. The larger of these covered much of west Sussex and Surrey, east Hampshire, some Berkshire districts, and parts of south and west London. It included all but the far west of the Diocese of Winchester and all districts in the western portion of the Diocese of Chichester. These were areas where settlements were predominantly nuclear, and parishes small. Some of the highest results for the denomination were found in five districts in Sussex: Steyning, Petworth, Thakeham, Westhampnett and Westbourne (all well over 80 per cent). Many south Downs parishes were conspicuous, where a lack of available surface water had restricted settlement and population growth. Almost as high figures were found in Catherington and

[1] Our adopted method to select map class breaks is based on 'quantiles'. This places equal numbers of observations into each legend division, excluding observations with a zero value. Thus if there were five class categories, with the exception of one for zero values, and 100 observations, class breaks would be calculated to place 20 observations in each category. This has the advantage that class breaks, which can significantly alter the interpretation of maps, are objectively derived rather than being based on varying *ad hoc* judgement.

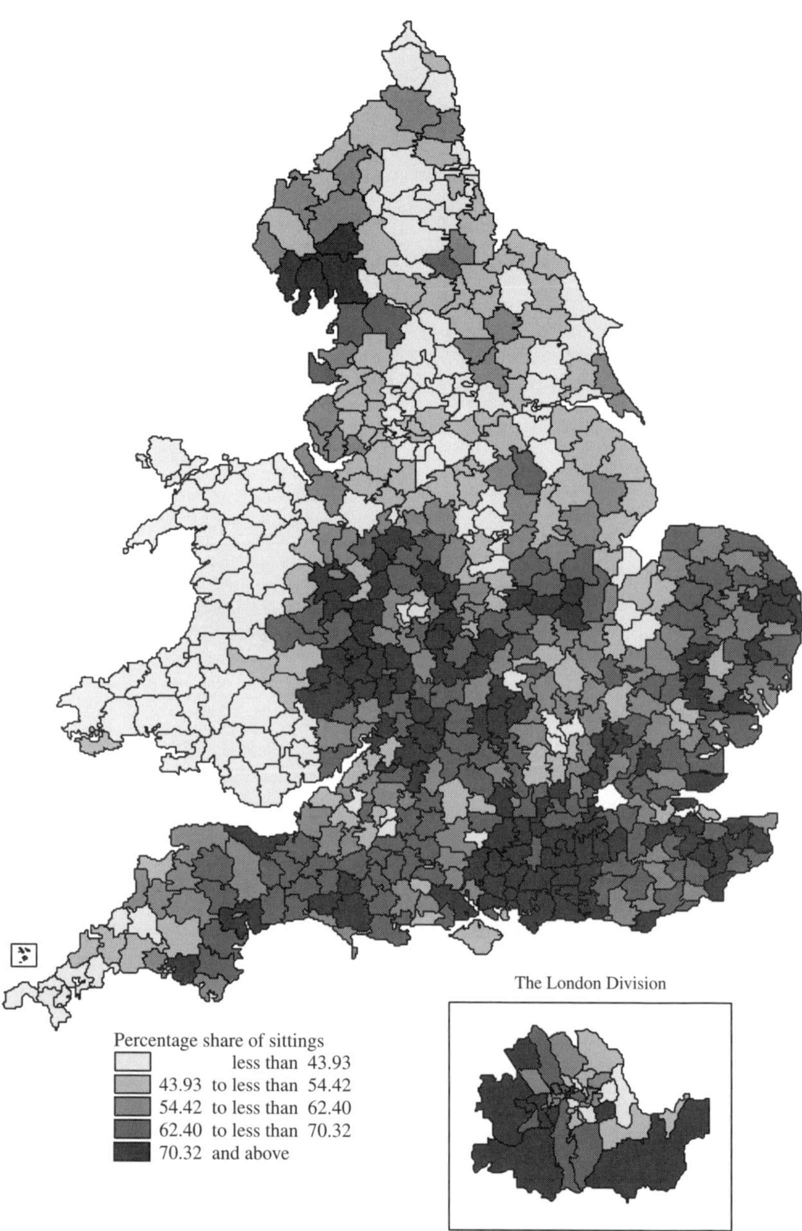

Figure 2.1. Church of England percentage share of sittings in 1851

Petersfield in Hampshire, and Farnborough and Godstone in Surrey.[2] Within this broad region a few exceptions are worth mentioning. The highly urbanised Portsea Island was one such, and so was the rural Isle of Wight. In London too, high values were limited to the south and west, with low values in the north-eastern quarter.

The second major Anglican area, rather less clearly demarcated, was in the west midlands: in Herefordshire, Worcestershire, north Gloucestershire, and parts of Shropshire, with two linear extensions, running along Staffordshire's western and northern border, and skirting Birmingham and the Black Country into felden Warwickshire and east Staffordshire. The established church was strong throughout this region away from urban areas, its figures being slightly less than in central southern England. There were, however, a number of high values in country-town based districts, including Ledbury and Weobly in Herefordshire, Church Stretton, Cleobury Mortimer and Bridgnorth in Shropshire, and Pershore in Worcestershire. The figures were almost as high in the Gloucestershire Cotswold districts of Cirencester, Northleach and Stow on the Wold. As in the south, there were exceptions to the general pattern. Much lower values were found in some urban areas, including the old-established county towns of Shrewsbury and Worcester, the coal and iron-ore rich Black Country, and districts around Birmingham (together with one or two in north Warwickshire). A second island of rather lower values included the east Shropshire coalfield areas of Madeley and Wellington, and lower figures distinguished Coventry and the east Warwickshire coalfield.

In the rest of England high percentage shares of sittings for the Church of England were less clustered. Districts with highest quantile figures were found fairly widely in southern and central England. They included districts around the Exe estuary in Devon, and a number in west Dorset and west Somerset. There were a sizeable number in mid and east Kent, comprising much of the Canterbury diocese. In the midlands, one sees districts around Oxford, areas of the north midlands centred upon Stamford and Oakham, and further east Thingoe, Sudbury and Samford in Suffolk, and a number of districts surrounding (but not including) Yarmouth. Only one region north of

[2] For the most part, we have adopted census spellings and usage of registration-district names. Some of these differ from modern use, as for example Yarmouth rather than Great Yarmouth.

the Dee–Wash line had returns in the highest quantile, and this comprised Ulverstone in the far north of Lancashire, Bootle in the south of Cumberland and Westmorland's two western districts.

One of the most striking features of the geography of the Church of England was the weakness of the Church through so much of the north and west of England, and in Wales. The largest area of low Anglican percentage-share values was in Wales. There was a dramatic decline of values along the southern part of the English–Welsh border, between the dioceses of Hereford and St David. The lowest value for England and Wales – coal and iron dominated Merthyr Tydfil – lay on the Welsh side of this region. Other very low values nearby included Abergavenny, Newport, Neath and Crickhowell, all of these being under 20 per cent. Of the total of Wales' 48 registration districts, about half of them had Anglican percentage shares of sittings of under 30 per cent. This marked Wales off very significantly from most of England.

Much of the census northern division, Yorkshire, and the north-west division, had low or very low Anglican values. These were lowest in the industrial belt of Yorkshire, in northern Derbyshire, and along much of Yorkshire's north-east coast. The Church of England was not only weak north of the Dee–Wash line. There were other weak regions in the south: most of Cornwall (similar to Wales in its scattered settlements and Celtic heritage); an area following a south-westerly line from Lincolnshire, alongside the Wash through Cambridgeshire, and into the Vale of Aylesbury; and an area around Christchurch and Weymouth on the south coast extending into Dorset.

Another percentage-share measure is a denomination's share of total attendances. For the Church of England this reveals very similar patterns to those just described, the measures being very highly correlated with each other. Their congruence is such that we shall not describe the latter measure in any detail.[3] Some historiography sees attendance measures as being of limited reliability; but such a tight match here adds further reassurance to an evaluation of the Religious

[3] The mean Anglican percentage share of attendances was 53 per cent, and the median 54 per cent. The lowest figures were for Merthyr Tydfil (6.2%), Bala (7.8%) and Pwllheli (8.9%). The fourteen lowest districts were all Welsh. The highest were for West London (99.2%), Thakeham in Sussex (96%), Droxford in Hampshire (94.5%) and Alresford in Hampshire (90.3%).

Census. The 1851 sittings data are usually thought to be the most dependable, but such confidence can be extended to the attendance figures.

There is also the percentage share of places of worship. This was slightly different to the other measures.[4] Anglican churches tended to be larger than those of any other denomination, without a myriad of very small churches and chapels. Comparison of the average sizes of denominations' seating capacity shows the Anglican Church differing from its rivals, which affects this measure. Even so, the geography of this variable remains broadly similar to the other proportional share measures. The most obvious differences were in the east of England, where much of Lincolnshire, East Anglia and Essex had figures in the two upper quantiles of the data. These are regions renowned for their large number of medieval churches and chapels, which were among the most economically prosperous parts of medieval England.[5] In general terms these three percentage share indicators reveal the same spatial pattern of Anglicanism relative to other denominations.[6] The north–south difference, with the established church achieving its greatest comparative strength in south, central and eastern England, is a very clear result.

Anglican place of worship density

Three additional measures can be calculated from the number of places of worship. The first is place of worship density, defined as the density of places of worship per 10 square kilometres.[7] This is shown

4 The Anglican Church's maximum percentage share of churches was 90 per cent (West London), and in only four districts was this 80 per cent or higher (West London, Thakeham, Ongar and Henstead). In three districts the share was under 15 per cent (Todmorden, Tynemouth and Merthyr Tydfil, the latter being the lowest at 14.1%).

5 Hence they have high Anglican percentage shares of churches, moderately high Anglican percentage shares of sittings (since many of those medieval churches were large), but moderate or low Anglican percentage shares of attendances since there were proportionately few worshippers in 1851. In contrast, in Wealden parts of Kent, Surrey and Sussex the Church of England was proportionately worse off in terms of churches than many other denominations, but not in terms of attendances at those churches.

6 This is confirmed by Pearson's correlation, which shows highly significant coefficients between these measures. The Anglican percentage share of churches correlates with the Anglican percentage share of attendances at 0.794 ($p = .000$), while between the Anglican percentage shares of sittings and attendances, $r = 0.938$.

7 This measure was strongly skewed towards zero with a mean of 4.6, but a median of only 1.0.

in figure 2.2. The minimum was 0.11 in Rothbury, Northumberland, rising to over 330 in the City of London district.

With this measure very high values were associated with urban areas. In London all 36 districts had values in the highest quantile. Throughout Wales and England only six districts had values over 100, all being in London: City of London, St James, Westminster, Strand, Holborn, East London and West London. Outside London, urban districts in the top quantile included Newcastle upon Tyne, Sunderland, Gateshead, Liverpool, West Derby, several around Manchester, Bradford, Dewsbury, Hunslet, Leeds, Shrewsbury, Wolstanton, Stoke-on-Trent, Birmingham and its environs, Coventry, Leicester, Derby, Cambridge, Reading, Hastings, Brighton, Portsea Island and Exeter. Such greater provision of churches was to be anticipated. Less predictable are those regions with high place of worship density which were not heavily urbanised.

Central and eastern Norfolk and Suffolk had been highly populated in medieval times, given the major textile industries that had so often financed their church-building activities, and it is not surprising that small parish sizes had emerged, producing high place of worship densities. Other areas like this included a large tract running from central Lincolnshire south-westward into south Nottinghamshire and Derbyshire, including much of Leicestershire and central Northamptonshire. A rather less clearly defined area included parts of Herefordshire, Worcestershire and Gloucestershire. One may also find this south of Bath and Bradford-on-Avon to the English Channel at Weymouth, in parts of east Kent, in a fringe just outside London, and on the south coast from Westhampnett to Brighton.

On the other hand, this measure was below average in much of northern and south-western England, the Fens, and almost all of Wales. In the north, away from industrial Lancashire, Yorkshire and Tyneside, values were almost invariably low. Parts of Cumberland and Northumberland were among the lowest for England and Wales. In the south-west, districts with low values included Cornwall, central and north Devon, and upland areas of west Somerset. One or two other, usually lowly populated, areas of England had low place of worship densities, including much of the central Weald, the Fenlands and Fen edge, parts of Shropshire, and the New Forest in Hampshire.

The established church therefore had its highest concentration of places of worship in urban areas, although of course this measure

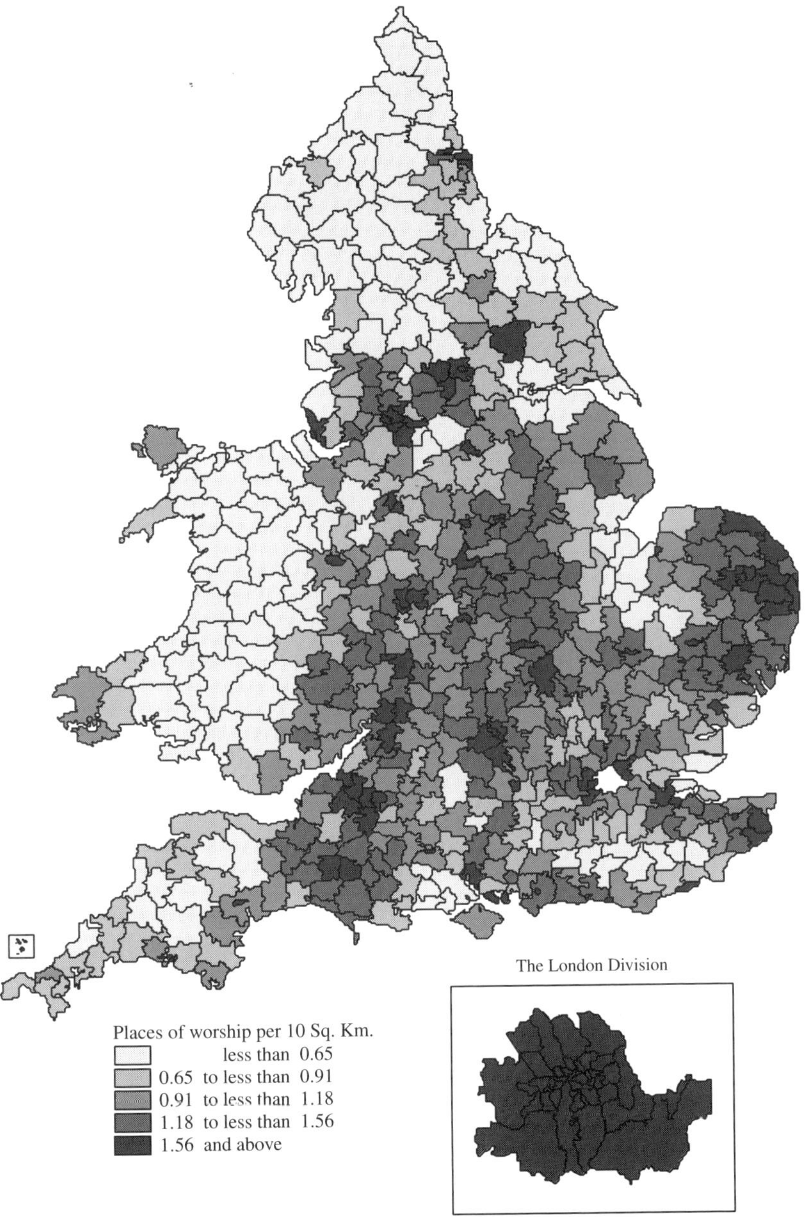

Figure 2.2. Church of England place of worship density in 1851

pays no attention to the larger urban population sizes, and possible demand. Viewed in the light of that urban demography, the Church was still relatively weak in the towns. The measure bears testimony to Anglican efforts to adjust to demographic growth, industrialisation and urban migration. The historical legacy of the Church and its attendant problems were still very apparent though. Its provision in East Anglia remained very high. This measure alone cannot show how successful the Church's response to socio-economic change was. For that it is necessary to look at other measures.

People per place of worship for the Church of England

One such further measure is people per place of worship. (This takes each district's population, and divides it by the number of places of worship for the denomination.) The result indicates the number of people in a district that each place of worship nominally served, and this is mapped for the established church in figure 2.3. The measure offers a better indication of how well the population was catered for, although it does not take account of the size (in sittings) of each place of worship. Persons per place of worship ranged from a low of 219 at Billesdon in Leicestershire (an area of much historical out-migration, and of enclosure that changed open-field arable to pasture, where Anglican provision on this measure was at its greatest), to a maximum of 13,514 at St Luke in north-central London (where established church provision was weakest).[8]

The Church of England was clearly most inadequate in a number of urban areas, most notably in London. Here, all but two districts fell into the highest quantile of this measure. Only five districts in England and Wales had values over 10,000, all of them in London. A second set of high values included much of southern Lancashire and parts of the more proximate West Riding. All Lancashire's industrial towns were included here, as were those in Yorkshire as far east as Leeds and Barnsley. The highest values in this region were in Lancashire, with figures in excess of 7,000 for Manchester, Liverpool and Chorlton. A number of rather smaller areas with high numbers of people to Anglican churches are found, like Birmingham, much of Tyneside, Hull and its suburbs, the Medway towns, some of the south

[8] The distribution of values for this measure was skewed away from zero. Its mean was 1,657, and the median 925, showing the effect of some very high values.

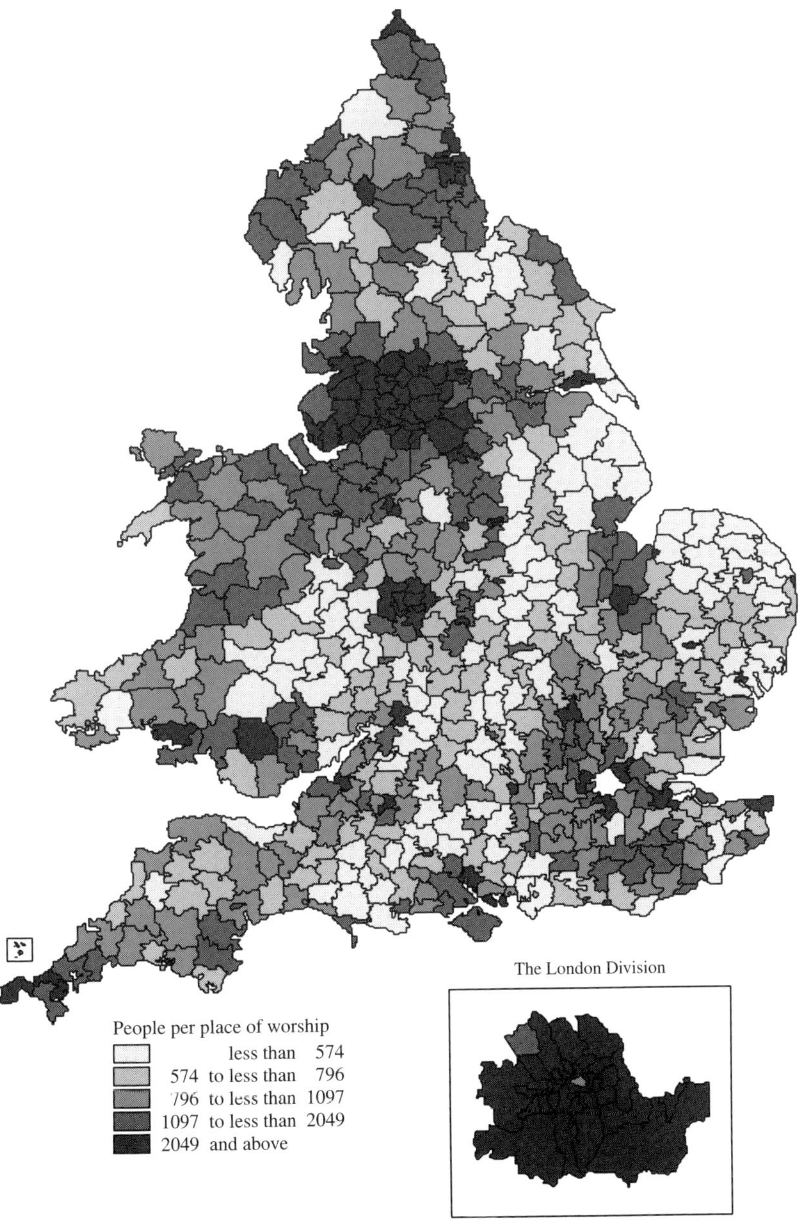

Figure 2.3. People per place of worship for the Church of England in 1851

Welsh valleys, and towns like Coventry, Reading, Bristol and Stoke-on-Trent. The measure was high in urban areas generally, compared to their hinterlands.

In some rural areas also, this measure of people per Anglican Church was fairly high. This was true in many northern districts, as throughout county Durham, north Northumberland (including Berwick-upon-Tweed, Glendale, Belford and Alnwick), north-west Cumberland along the Scottish border, Cheshire and Flint. Further south in England one sees something similar around the Wash, in the central Weald and the Isle of Thanet, the New Forest, the Isle of Wight, the far tip of Cornwall, and a rather less clearly defined area around London. In all of north Wales this measure was around or above average and, although usually making rather better provision in south Wales, the established church was weak in central western Wales and in the southern mining and industrial areas.

This confirms the strengths of the Church in much of the midlands and central southern England, East Anglia, Lincolnshire, the eastern portions of Yorkshire, extending into a few (increasingly English-speaking) rural areas of south and mid Wales. The lowest values were in some North Riding districts, an area covering much of Lincolnshire, the Trent Valley, Leicestershire, south Warwickshire, the Welsh Marches up to south Shropshire, parts of East Anglia, and in districts around, but not including, Southampton. Some of the lowest values in England and Wales were in Norfolk (where place of worship density was correspondingly high). Like Lincolnshire, Norfolk was a rural county of low population density, exceptionally well endowed with medieval churches. A. W. N. Pugin, ashore from his sailing expeditions, was struck by the 'half ruined and almost deserted churches along the Norfolk coast . . . complete mines of carved and beautiful ornament'.[9] Norfolk had over 900 Anglican churches, one for every three square miles, as W. G. Hoskins said when discussing church isolation and desertion in the county.[10] This relative excess of Anglican churches has become ever more apparent in the twentieth century, when so many of them have been deemed redundant.[11]

9 A. W. N. Pugin, *Contrasts* (1836, Leicester, 1969 edn), pp. 17–18.

10 W. G. Hoskins, 'Landscapes of England: Marsh and Sea' (BBC programme, 1975).

11 See e.g. Redundant Churches Fund, *Churches in Retirement; a Gazetteer* (HMSO, 1990), pp. 76–84, 88–99. This fund was established in 1969 following the Bridges Commission. The redundancy of Lincolnshire churches in the twentieth century is a

The sizes of Anglican churches

One factor which might alleviate small numbers of churches relative to population would be the space available in them. We therefore calculated the mean sizes of churches for each district, by dividing total sittings (both free and appropriated) by the number of churches. This variable for the established church shows a fairly large variation, with registration-district average church sizes ranging from 139 to 2,009.[12]

There was a high correspondence between this and people per place of worship. Average church sizes were largest in London, and a number of adjoining areas. Around two-thirds of the twenty highest values were found there, from 1,111 in Islington up to 1,625 in St Luke (in north-central London). Then much of southern Lancashire and the south-west West Riding, places like Liverpool, Manchester and Sheffield, showed strongly. In general the measure was associated with urban areas, most particularly industrialised towns like those of Lancashire and Yorkshire, as well as Birmingham, Wolverhampton, Tyneside, Hull and its immediate hinterland, Bristol, Coventry, the Potteries, Nottingham, Derby, Leicester, Reading and Plymouth.[13]

Sizes of Anglican churches were low in most of Wales, parts of Herefordshire, Gloucestershire, Wiltshire, and Berkshire, in central and eastern England, together with inland areas of northern England. They were very low through much of eastern England from Bellingham on Northumberland's Scottish border down through western county Durham, inland North Riding, some parts of the West Riding, much of Lincolnshire, Nottinghamshire and Leicestershire, and into Norfolk and Suffolk.

These three place-of-worship derived measures show strong connection between average church sizes and population density. The Church of England's building of larger churches in newly-industrialising and expanding towns is most apparent in London, in the cotton

persistent feature of N. Pevsner, J. Harris and N. Antram, *The Buildings of England: Lincolnshire* (1964, Harmondsworth, 1990 edn), e.g. pp. 184, 201–2, 205, 220, 226–7, 234, 245, 309, 580–1, 599, 619–20, 608, 754, 776, 807–8. Much the same picture emerges from N. Pevsner, *The Buildings of England: North-West and South Norfolk* (1962, Harmondsworth, 1990 edn), e.g. pp. 75, 84, 89, 90, 93, 106, 154, 161, 168, 178. See also W. Rodwell, 'Archaeology and the Church', *Antiquity*, 49, no. 193 (1975), 37.

12 The mean was 430, and the median 345.

13 Pearson's correlation coefficient between mean church size and population density was 0.506.

and woollen towns of Lancashire and Yorkshire, in Birmingham and the Black Country, and on Tyneside. Not only were Anglican churches and chapels larger in these industrial areas than elsewhere, but in some cases the density of places of worship was greater.[14] Despite this observed responsiveness to changing concentrations of population, the Church's reaction was still clearly insufficient.[15] In urban areas churches were larger, but then there were well above average numbers of people living in the vicinity of each church.[16]

These three measures are in close agreement. The Church was very weak throughout Wales, particularly in north Wales. Provision was also poor over much of northern England and in parts of the south-west. Other smaller zones of weakness are consistently identifiable. These include an area around the Wash, and parts of the Weald. On the other hand, the Anglican Church was usually strong in the south, was particularly prominent in much of East Anglia, and in a broad band of districts (akin to the Jurassic escarpment) stretching from the north Lincolnshire coast to the Dorset–Hampshire border.

Anglican levels of occupancy

We turn now to the question of demand for these churches. We need to see whether, in areas where provision was limited, there was pressure on the Church's resources, or if provision was meagre because there was no requirement. An index of occupancy, calculated by dividing each denomination's total attendances by its total sittings, offers an indication of pressure on churches. For the Church of England this index ranged from a low of 24 (Pwllheli in north Wales) to a high of 247 (for Leicester).[17]

[14] Pearson's correlation coefficient between population density and place of worship density is 0.773.

[15] The question arises as to whether the size of the church or the provision of opportunities to worship was more important. It is possible that some compensation for this urban situation might have been sought via greater numbers of services, if that could be demonstrated to have occurred.

[16] Pearson's correlation coefficient was 0.603 between population density and people per place of worship.

[17] The Leicester figures for the Church of England have been questioned by some researchers, and this value should be regarded with some caution. The next highest index of occupancy value was 206 in Salisbury. The registration-district mean was 99, and the median 97.

A clear spatial pattern is evident from figure 2.4, showing this index of occupancy. The ratio of attendances to sittings was particularly high throughout much of southern and eastern England south of a line from the Severn to the Wash. It was very high in many parts of London (excepting the north-east), and in a broad band of districts stretching from the Fens south-west to the Solent. Beyond this area, one finds high values on the border of Devon with Somerset and Dorset, parts of west Hampshire and bordering districts. Further north high values were much rarer, tending to be restricted to large towns. These included parts of south Lancashire, Newcastle upon Tyne, Chester-le-Street, Durham, Shrewsbury, Birmingham and Bromsgrove and, in the east midlands, Derby and Leicester. Further east, one finds high figures for places like Yarmouth, King's Lynn and Colchester.

The figures were very low in northern England generally, excepting the towns just mentioned, in almost all of Wales, and in Cornwall. They were lowest in central and northern Wales, central Cornwall, the north Pennines, the North York Moors, Holderness, north Lincolnshire and north-east Norfolk.

This index of occupancy confirms that the services of the established church were most sought after or accessible in the south. In the north and west, where later in the nineteenth century the Church endeavoured to increase its coverage, there seems not to have been very much demand outside the southern Lancashire towns – existing provision of churches appears to have been adequate, despite the north being where Anglican provision was most patchy. In some newly-industrialised areas the picture could be more complex, but often in such areas demand was not that strong, despite the high population densities and relative dearth of Anglican churches. In the industrial West Riding the index of occupancy was little above the Welsh–English average. This was also true for much of the Black Country, and parts of Tyneside. Accommodation was felt to be inadequate by the Church in such areas, but here there was little pressure on Anglican sittings, only about as much as in some old established and well-endowed county towns like Shrewsbury, Worcester or Bury St Edmunds.

Anglican indexes of sittings and attendances

We have deliberately used measures so far that are not usually constructed by historians. The historiography mainly discusses indexes

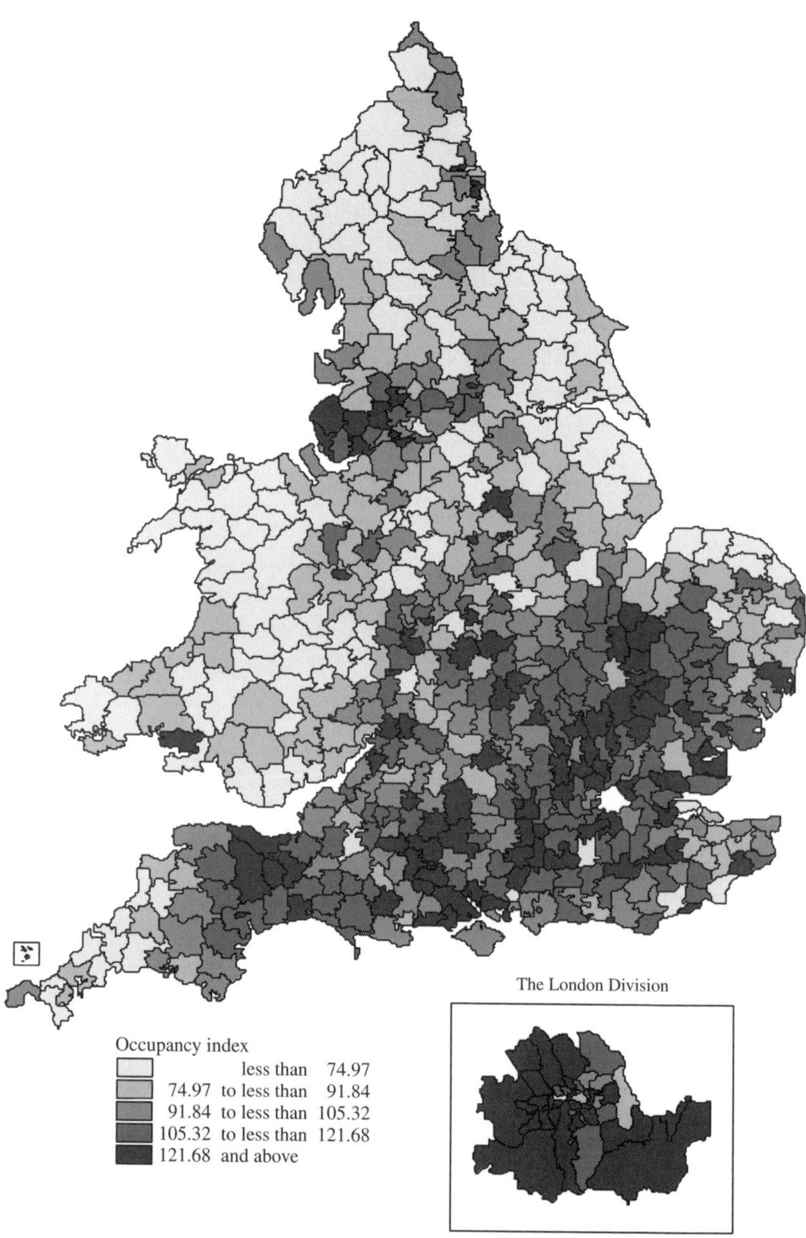

Figure 2.4. Church of England index of occupancy in 1851

of attendance or sittings, but one can note the differently focused possibilities available. We will look now at the more conventional measures, to see how they compare with the patterns of Anglican provision and worship so far established.[18]

The index of sittings is shown in figure 2.5. It shows the Church to be relatively strong everywhere if the range of values is compared with that for other denominations, as we shall see in subsequent chapters.[19] Its geography conforms broadly to the earlier variables. It was most prominent in counties along the south coast (excepting Cornwall, the New Forest, and the High Weald of Sussex), throughout the English midlands (leaving aside Birmingham and the Black Country), and in East Anglia. These strongholds were divided by a tract of districts with lower values, coming south from the Wash to London, and spreading east and west along the Thames valley. Further north the Church of England had far fewer high figures.[20] There was, however, a band of fairly high values stretching from south-west Cumberland through Westmorland, into the North Riding, and from this point southwards along much of the east coast of Yorkshire and Lincolnshire. The Church was weak in Cornwall, in much of Wales, northwards into Cheshire and south Lancashire, and through much of Northumberland and Durham.

The index of attendances was very similar, but with a few

18 The index of sittings is expressed as a denomination's total sittings in each registration district divided by the registration-district population, multiplied by 100. Thus an index of sittings of 100 would indicate that the whole population could be accommodated by the denomination at any one service. The index of attendances is derived in a similar way, by taking total recorded attendances on Census Sunday. For further information, see appendix C.

19 The mean and median Anglican indexes of sittings were 36 and 37 respectively. The largest number of observations (around 170) were between 40 and 50. When other denominational maps are presented, readers should pay attention to the dividing figures they are based on. For technical and presentational reasons these have had to be specific to each denomination's map, rather than being universal across all denominations. Thus a darkest shaded area for, let us say, the Primitive Methodists, will represent a much weaker status for that denomination compared to an equally darkly shaded area for the Anglican Church.

20 Some of the north–south contrasts can readily be seen from Table G of the *Census of Religious Worship*, pp. cclxxiv–cclxxxv, which calculated a measure (with slightly differing premises from us) that one would term an 'index of sittings'. In the north, one finds examples of Anglican indexes like Lancashire (19.1), Northumberland (18.1), the West Riding (21.7), or Durham (17.6). Contrasting southern figures were Dorset (51.1), Rutland (58.1), Suffolk (47.9), Wiltshire (46.1). Middlesex was 18.7, Westmorland was 42.5, but those aside, the southern Anglican indexes were almost all much higher than the northern ones.

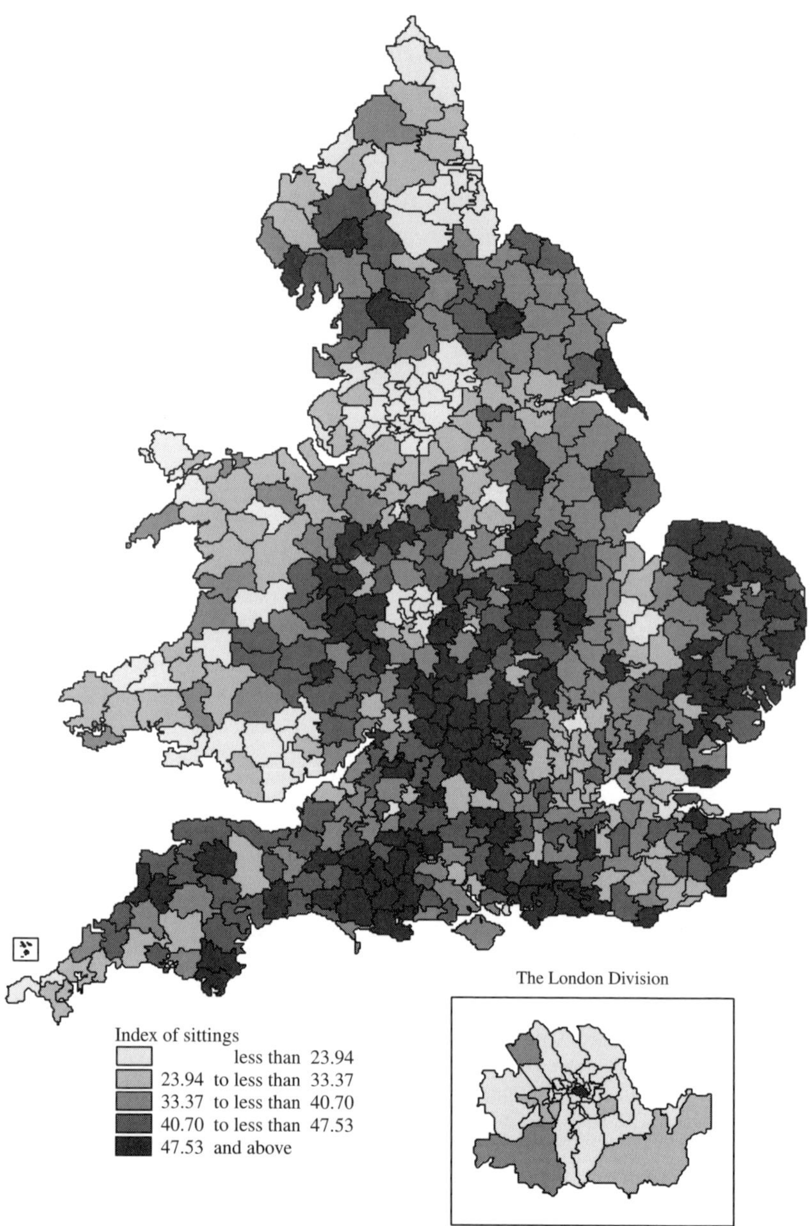

Figure 2.5. Church of England index of sittings in 1851

significant variations. Figure 2.6 shows the same striking division north and south of the Severn–Wash line, as seen in all the maps. The Church's Welsh and northern deficiencies are very apparent. Once again in the south it was weak in Cornwall, the Weald, the Wash, and in London, but also in the Thames marshes and an area around Bristol. There is little need to describe these more conventional measures more fully, as they reinforce the geographical patterns described above.

The Anglican heartlands

Of all the denominations, only the Church of England was present in all 624 registration districts in England and Wales. Its minimum share of sittings was 9.5 per cent, and its minimum share of attendances was 6.2 per cent (both for Merthyr Tydfil) – low figures, but not as low as the equivalent minima for other denominations. One needs to be aware that several of the more minor denominations failed to obtain such levels of support even in their strongest areas. Although the Anglican Church was omnipresent it was not omnipotent, its strength clearly varying significantly by region. There were dramatic regional variations in its patterns of worship, which are consistently shown by the different variables considered.

If we describe the heartlands or 'core' areas of strength of the Anglican Church, in an exercise that uses a quantitative combination and threshold level of five different measures, the picture in figure 2.7 emerges.[21] The first 'core' area covered parts of east Hampshire, west Sussex, and much of Surrey. A second ran through parts of east Devon, central and west Somerset, and most of Dorset. A third included a number of districts in east Kent. Further north another encompassed much of Herefordshire, parts of west Worcestershire and south Shropshire and, a little away from this group, some districts immediately east of Leicester. A number of the variables suggested that the Church of England was strong in parts of East Anglia, but close inspection reveals that these tended not to concur exactly. A summary would be that the Church was particularly strong to the east of

[21] The 'core' measure is constructed by taking the unweighted mean values for the percentage share of sittings, percentage share of attendances, percentage share of places of worship, the index of sittings and the index of attendances, and for the map plotting registration-district values in the top 20 per cent of the resulting distribution.

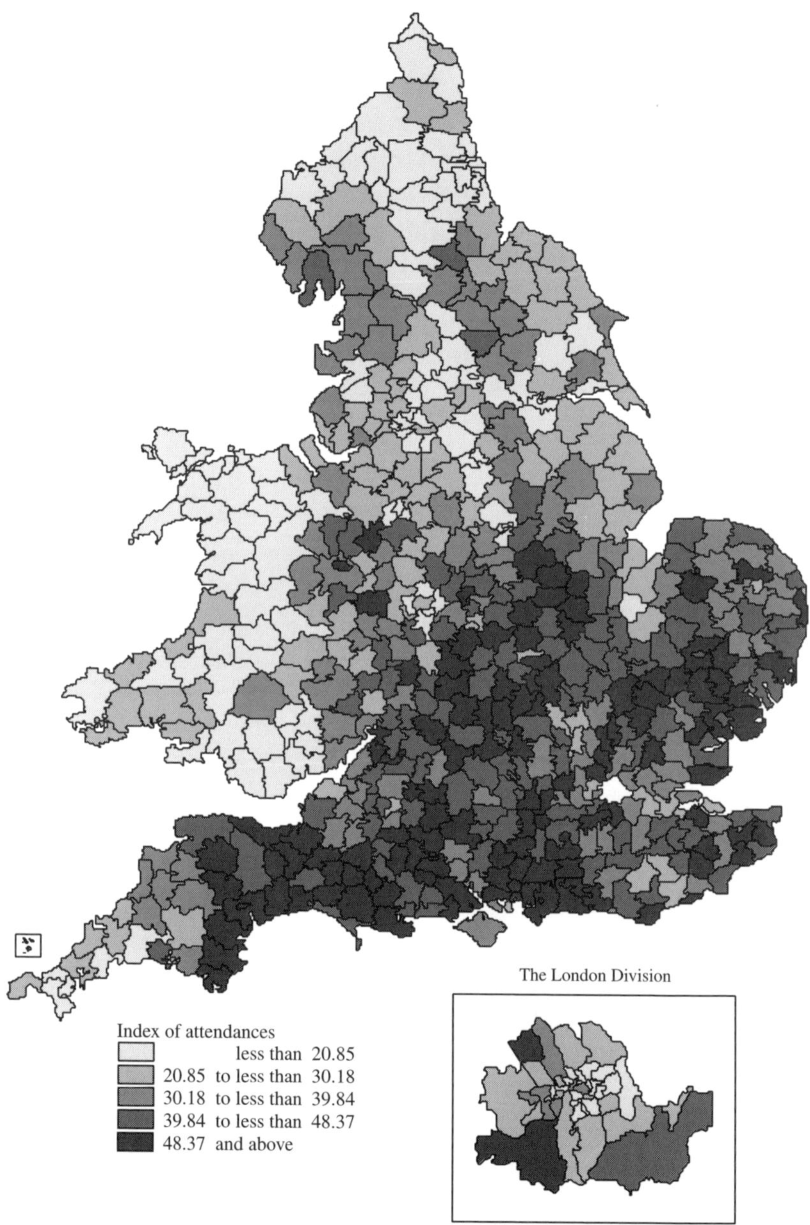

Figure 2.6. Church of England index of attendances in 1851

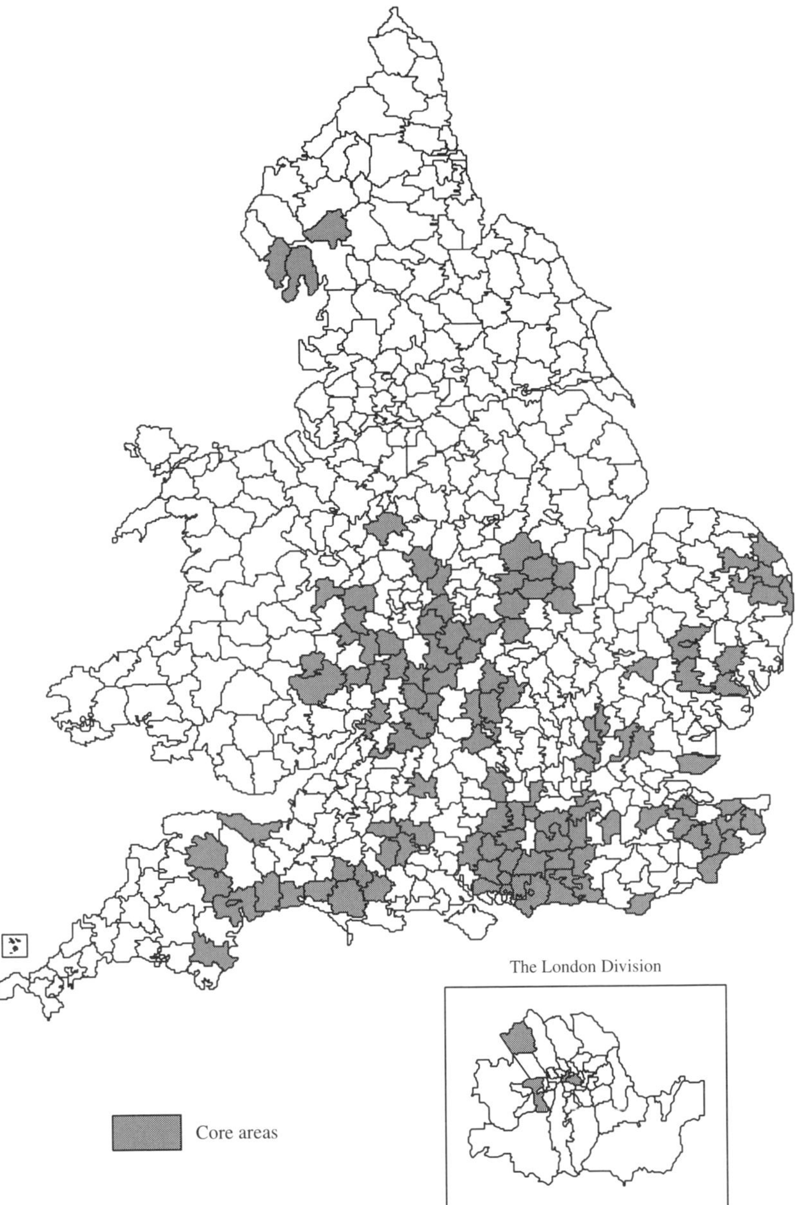

Figure 2.7. Church of England 'core' areas in 1851

Norwich, around and to the south-west of Bury St Edmunds, and in three Essex districts. In northern England only three districts could be identified within these same parameters as core areas of strength: Ulverstone in north Lancashire, Whitehaven in Cumberland and West Ward in Westmorland. Not a single such 'core' area emerges in Wales.

The Anglican Church and the geography of Conservatism

Political historians will see in these maps some striking resemblances to Tory or Conservative voting patterns. In broaching this subject, we need to remind ourselves that any discussion of the political propensities of religious groups is a matter of *tendencies*.[22] As Phillips has rightly said, 'religion was only one of many group interests that affected electoral behaviour'.[23] There were also manifold social and political orientations within the Anglican Church (notably in the 1840s and 1850s), as within the larger plethora of interests encompassed by Roman Catholicism and Nonconformity.[24] These are important caveats. Nevertheless, all historians are agreed that political parties had strong religious allegiances. On issues like Test and Corporation Act repeal, religious disabilities, electoral reform, opening of universities to dissenters, church rates, education, licensing and temperance, the Irish question, or disestablishment, contemporaries associated the parties with different policies. Anglican clergymen had strong Tory voting preferences, which contrasted sharply with the Whig/Liberal dispositions of Catholic, Independent, Baptist, Unitarian, Presbyterian and increasingly (after 1832) Methodist ministers. Some studies have demonstrated how remarkably strong these denominational divisions were.[25] Few political

[22] K. D. Wald, *Crosses on the Ballot: Patterns of British Voter Alignment since 1885* (Princeton, 1983), p. 59.

[23] J. A. Phillips, *The Great Reform Bill in the Boroughs: English Electoral Behaviour, 1818–1841* (Oxford, 1992), p. 277.

[24] Phillips stressed that 'Nonconformity may have meant very different things to different people, a problem aggravated by the variety of Nonconformist denominations, but the "meaning" of subscribing to the Established Church, at least nominally, is too nebulous to be addressed behaviourally. Agreement would never be reached about who the Anglicans were, much less what it meant to call them that.' *Ibid.*, p. 285.

[25] Phillips, *Great Reform Bill*, pp. 278–83; J. R. Vincent, *Pollbooks: How Victorians Voted* (Cambridge, 1967), pp. 67ff.

issues did not have a strongly religious tenor. In the late twentieth century, the Church of England has only to murmur sentiments of political partiality and it is shrilly accused of 'playing at politics'. However, in the age of 'Victorian values' such ecclesiastical political involvement was taken for granted. After all, it was elemental to a prominent role for the churches, the decline of which some politicians now lament.

One certainly should not reduce something as complex as electoral interpretation to religious geography. Furthermore, in drawing attention to this political dimension we need to bear in mind the limited suffrage eligibility of the mid nineteenth century (excluding very many working-class men and all women), the complications raised by plural and non-resident voting, and the socio-economic influences affecting denominational support. Bearing such caveats in mind however, the political historiography suggests that in the mid nineteenth century religion was more vital in voting than the question of class,[26] the latter emerging strongly (according to different historians) from 1906, or in 1910, or during and after the First World War.[27] The arguments about this later chronology do not concern us here, and unfortunately the literature on this issue often tends to ignore geographical dimensions. However, it is very clear that during the eighteenth and nineteenth centuries the Whigs or Liberals were concerned

26 D. E. D. Beales, *The Political Parties of Nineteenth-century England* (1971), pp. 21–2; Phillips, *Great Reform Bill*, p. 302. Many of the denominations were socially distinctive, one's religion suggesting much about one's class, as many historians have said, and it needs to be stressed that analytical distinctions between 'class' and 'religion' as factors in nineteenth- and early twentieth-century voting can be rather simplistic. Methodism itself had quite different emphases in class terms, as for example between Wesleyan and Primitive Methodism. K. D. M. Snell, *Church and Chapel in the North Midlands: Religious Observance in the Nineteenth Century* (Leicester, 1991), ch. 5; Phillips, *Great Reform Bill*, pp. 292–3.

27 For this important debate on the later electoral significance of religion, see H. Pelling, *Social Geography of British Elections, 1885–1910* (1967); D. Butler and D. Stokes, *Political Change in Britain* (1969, 1974 edn), pp. 130, 155, 160–7; P. F. Clarke, 'Electoral sociology of modern England', *History*, 57 (1972); N. Blewett, *The Peers, the Parties and the People: the General Elections of 1910* (1972); W. Miller and G. Raab, 'The religious alignment at English elections between 1918 and 1970', *Political Studies*, 25 (1977), 227–51; J. P. D. Dunbabin, 'British elections in the nineteenth and twentieth centuries: a regional approach', *English Historical Review*, 95 (1980); Wald, *Crosses on the Ballot*; D. W. Bebbington, 'Nonconformity and electoral sociology, 1867–1918', *Historical Journal*, 27:3 (1984), 633–56; G. I. T. Machin, *Politics and the Churches in Great Britain, 1869–1921* (Oxford, 1987); Phillips, *Great Reform Bill*, ch. 8.

to remove Nonconformist disabilities, and in many other ways they promoted dissenting interests. This may even have increased after the 1832 Reform Act. (We will see later how areas of Liberal strength related to those of Nonconformity.) The Tories by comparison had sought to perpetuate religious disabilities. Over a long period they were strongly associated with the interests of the established church, the church that Macaulay termed 'the Tory party at prayers'. As was clear during the debates over disestablishment, many saw these two as being like faithful twins. Peel's Tory Party had been especially pledged to the defence of the Church of England.

Political parties were highly regional in their allegiances, and thus very susceptible to local religious influences.[28] Indeed, local religious issues often brought forward candidates, further regionalising political parties. The religious and political traditions of different areas were seen as closely connected by contemporaries. While the spatial aspects of religious–political links are often neglected in this country,[29] the electoral geography itself is very clear. As M. Hirst wrote, 'there was a tendency for a larger proportion of boroughs to be conservative in the east and south of England, the areas of strongest Anglican support'.[30] By the time of the 1874 election, the line from the Humber to the Exe had become even more a division between Liberal and Tory boroughs.[31] Our distributions of greatest Anglican regional strengths closely resemble the most solid areas of Conservative electoral support, manifest for example in those areas infrequently or never voting Liberal between 1885 and 1910. In most elections, the major regional strengths of the Liberal Party in its

[28] T. J. Nossiter, *Influence, Opinion and Political Idioms in Reformed England: Case Studies from the North-east, 1832–74* (Brighton, 1975), p. 2: 'Politics was still highly local . . . Constituencies, generally, sought – often in vain – for local representatives of local interests in preference to tried party men . . . General elections involved public opinion but it was seldom nation-wide in character, but rather the simultaneous expression of a variety of public opinions represented by individual constituencies . . . Each election involved the weighing of local issues, local candidates and thirdly, local feeling on such issues as appeared to be at stake in the national dissolution.' Or see Wald, *Crosses on the Ballot*, p. 160, on the importance of 'local' factors.

[29] This neglect contrasts with the situation in France, where there has been a long tradition of relating the geography of religion to the spatial aspects and electoral sociology of political allegiance. See for example M. Vovelle, *Ideologies and Mentalities* (Cambridge, 1990), pp. 157–8.

[30] M. Hirst, 'The electoral system', in J. Langton and R. J. Morris (eds.), *Atlas of Industrializing Britain, 1780–1914* (1986), p. 218.

[31] *Ibid.*, p. 224, and see his maps on pp. 221, 223, 226–7.

heyday,[32] and later of the Labour Party, fell outside the 'core' Anglican districts.[33]

Well into recent decades, the safest majorities for the Conservatives have overlapped with Anglican strongholds in 1851. One thinks for example of the southern rural constituencies the Conservatives were reduced to in the 1997 General Election. Conservative ideology changed in very many ways; the political issues were different; the pervasiveness of Anglican justification in Conservative politics abated, or even claimed Methodist influence at the highest level from the late 1970s; the religious ambience of the early Victorian era became transmuted into a more secular politicised form. Yet it is an extraordinary example of structural continuity that this basic regional divide – which had earlier comprised the most Anglican regions of the south and midlands, as against what we will see as the surrounding arc of dissenting regions in the north (let alone Scotland), in Wales, and in the south-west – has persisted largely intact, having been translated into the regional political forms of north and south, or of Scottish, Welsh and Cornish nationalism, that we are familiar with in our own lifetimes.

Interpretation and conclusions

By 1851 the Church of England had lost much of its earlier outright dominance. The long-term changes are plain to see. A succession of enactments after the 1689 Act of Toleration had reduced the restrictions on dissenters, and (as will be shown) by 1851 the Religious Census bore witness to Nonconformist strength. Despite Anglican economic gains through enclosure, in many other ways the Church had long since lost much control over its wealth, notably with impropriation after monastic dissolutions and the passing of many

32 On Liberal strengths up to 1880, see Nossiter, *Influence, Opinion and Political Idioms*, maps on pp. 205–7.

33 Even in 1945 and 1997, large areas of the rural south, the south midlands, and parts of the west midlands stayed Conservative. Particularly from 1885, these 'Anglican' areas have usually been overwhelmingly Conservative, as for example in 1885, 1886, 1929, 1955, 1966 or 1979. For detailed electoral maps, see M. Kinnear, *The British Voter: an Atlas and Survey since 1885* (1968, 1981 edn). By contrast, not a single Conservative MP was returned for Wales (or Scotland) in 1997. The identification of Nonconformist heartlands with Whig/Liberal and later Labour heartlands will become clear in chapters 3 and 4.

benefices and tithes into lay hands.[34] It was gradually losing political influence, although this was to be a long-term erosion, and what remained was still very substantial. Even so, the determination of the state to support the established church and religious exclusivity had weakened. An anti-clerical movement to disestablish the Church of England, to remove its advantages and assert 'the voluntary principle', was gathering pace in 1851, particularly with the Anti-State Church Association from the 1840s, which was to become the Liberation Society. This achieved disestablishment in Ireland in 1869, and in Wales in 1912 (effective from 1920). The movement had very major political influence in the 1860s, '70s and '80s, strongly affecting Liberal policy, as with the abolition of compulsory church rates in 1868, or in the 1885 election.

The effects of this declining political endorsement were compounded by the regional inadequacy of Anglican administrative and organisational structures. The parochial system had already been partially by-passed for important secular business, as with the 1834 Poor Law Amendment Act, or the 1836 Act for Registering Births, Deaths and Marriages in England, both of which were of crucial administrative significance. In northern counties permissive legislation like the 1662 Settlement Act had allowed the option of displacing the parish by township administration for some purposes, accepting *de facto* practice in many areas. In administrative, religious and wider cultural terms, it was clear that the older parochial structures sometimes had grave difficulties in coping with demographic growth, mobility and urban industrialisation.[35]

Until 1818, the parish and diocesan structure of the established church had changed little since Henry VIII's reign. The rate of new ecclesiastical parish formation increased considerably only from about 1835, and notably after 1845.[36] The dioceses adapted very slowly to changing circumstances. They were not helped by being

[34] The Church's wealth was to be further eroded by the late nineteenth-century agricultural depression, and its effect on land values, although perhaps that helped to reduce agitation in England for disestablishment.

[35] The point has been made by many historians, among them A. D. Gilbert, *Religion and Society in Industrial England: Church, Chapel and Social Change, 1740–1914* (1976, Harlow, 1984 edn), e.g. pp. 94–7, 110–13.

[36] As brought about through the 1818 and later Acts by the Commissioners for Building New Churches (under 58 Geo. III, c. 45); by the Ecclesiastical Commissioners (under 6 & 7 Wm. IV, c. 77); and by the actions of bishops (under 1 & 2 Wm. IV, c. 38).

hamstrung by the controlling hand of Parliament. Only in the decades immediately preceding the Religious Census had their reform commenced. In 1836 for example, following recommendations from the Ecclesiastical Commission, the Diocese of Ripon was created, followed by the Diocese of Manchester in 1847.[37]

In nucleated village settlements, such as those predominating in the English rural south, the organisational structure of the Church was adapted to local needs, and (to many Anglican minds at least) substantial agrarian and demographic changes had still not harmed the inherited parochial patchwork. For many scattered settlements and out-townships in the north however – often with relatively poor agriculture, cottage-industrial by-employment, and prior to higher capitalised water and steam power – the parish as a phenomenon was outspread and less locally significant compared to the south. Parishes had evolved which were large in acreage, often encompassing a significant number of townships and hamlets, some of which were distant from church or chapel.[38] In many such areas townships had historically been small, scattered, their tithes and agrarian clerical assets often unable to maintain a minister. Through much of the eighteenth century, sparseness of population meant that this weakness was not much acknowledged, and its ecclesiastical results (made so visible in 1851) had often been shrugged off as matters of small consequence.

It is interesting to observe here that industrialisation progressed in settlements and towns that were frequently ill-adjusted to parochial structures, in circumstances that could be far from any Anglican parochial archetype. Midland and northern cottage industries often located themselves in relatively neglected districts of waste and common, areas of inter-commoning, extra-parochial places, or areas of ill-defined boundaries and ambiguous administration. The need for by-employments of an industrial nature commonly arose in precisely those localities which the Church of England (mindful of the need for tithe and profitable glebe) had decided were not worth sustained

[37] Anomalies existed in the south too. For example, until 1836 Dorset had been an isolated part of the Diocese of Bristol. See G. Hill, *English Dioceses: a History of their Limits from the Earliest Times to the Present Day* (1900), chs. 10–11, for more detail on diocesan boundary changes.

[38] On the regionally comparative sizes of parishes, see Gilbert, *Religion and Society*, pp. 100–1.

attention. These were areas of high clerical non-residency, perhaps ministered to by curates, often comprising part of a pluralist's benefices. As a consequence, they were frequently grounds onto which dissent had gravitated, making the most of such openings. Readers will see this in later chapters. This is not the place to enter into the important questions of cultural or denominational values underpinning economic development; although as Ashton and others observed, it seems likely that a preparedness to question religious orthodoxy could readily be extended to doubts about traditional economic behaviour.[39] However, it should not surprise us that so many early entrepreneurs (in counties like Glamorgan, Monmouthshire, Lancashire, Yorkshire, Derbyshire or Staffordshire) were dissenters. This need not necessarily involve links between theological outlook amd economic *mentalité*. From a *spatial* point of view, it was entirely logical and expected that such regional entrepreneurs should often have been Nonconformists. After all, the local need for inventive employment beyond agriculture, and the conditions for the success of Nonconformity, went hand in hand geographically, affected as they were by the same contexts.[40]

All the religious measures show the established church doing less well in urban areas, particularly in growing industrial towns. Many historians have commented on the tardiness with which the Anglican parochial system adapted to urbanisation, often adducing this as the key to its failures.[41] It is sometimes suggested that traditional parish

[39] T. S. Ashton, *The Industrial Revolution, 1760–1830* (Oxford, 1948), pp. 17–19.

[40] This brings together three areas of historiography: the findings here on religious geography, the literature on cottage industrial or 'proto-industrial' location, and historical discussion of the links between Nonconformity and industrial entrepreneurship. Among a very large historiography, see M. W. Flinn, *The Origins of the Industrial Revolution* (1966), pp. 6–7, 81–90, 102; E. E. Hagen, *On the Theory of Social Change: How Economic Growth Begins* (Cambridge, Mass., 1962); J. Thirsk, 'Industries in the countryside', in F. J. Fisher (ed.), *Essays in the Economic and Social History of Tudor and Stuart England* (Cambridge, 1961); P. Kriedte, H. Medick and J. Schlumbohm, *Industrialisation Before Industrialisation: Rural Industry in the Genesis of Capitalism* (Cambridge, 1981); R. Houston and K. D. M. Snell, 'Proto-industrialisation? Cottage industry, social change and the Industrial Revolution', *Historical Journal*, 27 (1984), 473–92; P. K. O'Brien and R. Quinault (eds.), *The Industrial Revolution and British Society* (Cambridge, 1993); P. Hudson (ed.), *Regions and Industries: a Perspective on the Industrial Revolution in Britain* (Cambridge, 1989); P. Hudson, *The Industrial Revolution* (1992, 1996 edn), p. 22.

[41] For example, J. D. Gay, *The Geography of Religion in England* (1971), pp. 73–4. As he comments, the clergy themselves were mainly rurally situated, and not prone to appreciate or remonstrate about the urban predicament that was emerging for their Church.

structures were poorly suited to urban areas, where alternative senses of place, occupational affiliations, class segregation and ghettoes emerged that paid little heed to parish boundaries. Townspeople also often lacked the ties of vulnerable deference to Anglican employers or landlords that kept many agricultural labourers and tenants to the Church. Even in the countryside such restraints could be weakened by out-migration, or when economic circumstances strengthened the hands of tenants.[42] It was also harder to establish relationships between urban incumbent and prospective worshipper. This was especially true for those denominations (like the Church of England) which had large urban churches, and which (unlike the Roman Catholics or the Jews) lacked an almost ethnic sense of concord and solidarity among many followers. The move to urban inhabitancy was very marked indeed in England and Wales compared with other European countries, but we still know little about what 'the parish' meant to people in nineteenth-century towns, about how this essentially rural Anglican construct translated and was adapted to the newer urban environments, and was thought about there. As a structural consideration however, it would certainly appear that a dawning sense of parochial ineffectiveness and redundancy was one reason for Anglican weakness in the industrialising districts.

The creation of new parishes was a complex process requiring parliamentary consent, one that occurred slowly until about 1825. Thereafter significant improvements began, hastened by the 1843 Act 'to make better provision for the spiritual needs of populous parishes'.[43] However, local clergy often opposed the formation of new

[42] Machin, *Politics and the Churches*, p. 7. The agricultural unions (so often themselves led by Methodist lay preachers like Arch, Sage or Edwards) were to encourage out-migration or emigration in the interests of higher wages, better material conditions and greater freedom from employer manipulation among those rural workers who remained on the land.

[43] 6 & & Vic. c. 37. See also 19 & 20 Vic. c. 104 (1856). These measures facilitated parochial sub-division by the Ecclesiastical Commissioners and consequent erection of new churches. This was an important stage in the organisational reform of the Church of England. Many urban parishes, in places like Leeds, were subdivided into districts (later termed 'Peel districts'), each with a small church and with stipends provided for a minister. The patron and incumbent of the mother church had simply the right to comment, although of course the approval of the bishop was required. Such urban church extension appears to have owed something to Peel and Graham's concern over Chartist agitation in industrial towns. See M. H. Port, *Six Hundred New Churches: a Study of the Church Building Commission, 1818–1856, and its Church Building Activities* (1961), p. 117; G. F. A. Best, *Temporal Pillars: Queen Anne's Bounty, the*

subdivided parishes, partly because in many marginal or upland areas this could have adverse effects on the value of their livings. These were often the areas where Nonconformity was gaining ground.

Changes in ecclesiastical provision in medieval southern and midland England appear to have been closely related to population changes,[44] but this responsiveness probably became less flexible thereafter. Certainly there were few new churches built during the eighteenth century, indeed until the Million Act in 1818, an Act which also made it easier to alter parish boundaries.[45] However, population doubled over that time. The Church was sometimes slow to construct new buildings in response to demographic change and early industrialisation, and the ratio of population to Anglican places of worship increased steadily. The Religious Census did not attempt to give the dates of construction for churches erected before 1801; but it does show considerable increase in building thereafter: 55 churches in the 1800s, 97 in the 1810s, 276 in the 1820s, rising to 667 in the 1830s and 1,197 in the 1840s.[46]

In 1818 John Bowdler organised a petition pressing for more churches. Such efforts resulted in the founding of the 'Society for Promoting the Enlargement, Building and Repair of Anglican Churches and Chapels in England and Wales', which was incorporated by parliamentary Act a decade later. Its purpose was to 'remedy the deficiencies of places set aside for Public Worship in our towns and cities'. Between 1818 and 1824 the Society received grants from government totalling £1.5 million, and it raised a further £4.5 million in personal subscriptions. The local results of this are evident in

Footnote 43 (*cont.*)
Ecclesiastical Commissioners and the Church of England (Cambridge, 1964), pp. 195–6, 408; R. E. Rodes, *Law and Modernization in the Church of England: Charles II to the Welfare State* (Notre Dame, Indiana, 1991), p. 168. Partly as a consequence, the number of parish livings rose by nearly 3,000 from c. 1825–75. M. J. D. Roberts, 'Private patronage and the Church of England, 1800–1900', *Journal of Ecclesiastical History*, 32 (1981), 207. See also K. D. M. Snell, *Parish and Belonging in England and Wales, 1660–1914* (forthcoming).

44 L. J. Proudfoot, 'The extension of parish churches in medieval Warwickshire', *Journal of Historical Geography*, 9 (1983), 231–46.

45 This provided £1 million of government money to build new churches, and set up the Church Building Commissioners to manage the fund. Other Acts and grants followed in the 1820s and later.

46 Dates were not given for 2,118 churches, and 9,667 were said to pre-date 1801. In 1831 the ratio of population to places of worship was 1 to 1,175. By 1851 this had risen to 1 to 1,296. *Census of Religious Worship*, pp. xxxviii–xl.

Religious Census returns, and it contributed to raise the average size of churches, and their numbers in the towns. There remained many more people to each urban church than elsewhere, and in that sense this response seems to have been inadequate. However, this matter is shown to be rather more complex by our 'index of occupancy', which suggests that in many areas where Church of England provision was limited, there was in fact little demand for such churches and sittings. This was particularly the case in north-east London, and in the industrial West Riding.[47] Urban areas were showing a predisposition among large segments of the population to worship as Nonconformists (occasionally persuaded by employers like Titus Salt or the Strutts), and religious indifference was apparent in some town districts, although that should not be exaggerated. Urban population density was high and increasing, with rapid in-migration, particularly among younger people. Many of these were migrants from Ireland, Scotland and Wales. If these were inclined to worship anywhere it would most likely be with denominations they had known in their home areas. The worshipping communities of such churches identified with these migrants and helped them adapt to town life. The religious groups benefiting in this regard were ones like the Presbyterian denominations, the Welsh Calvinistic Methodists,[48] and of course the Roman Catholics.

Although the established church did respond to inadequate provision, its reaction fell short of what was needed. The Church's weaknesses in northern England, Cornwall, and around the Wash were probably due mainly to a combination of large parishes, poor livings and subsidiary settlements. Hostile over a long period to Methodism, the Church failed to appreciate the benefits in such areas of Methodist organisation. By contrast, tighter manorial controls and a narrow structure of landownership worked in the Anglican Church's favour, as is seen in a later chapter.[49] With one or a few Anglican landholders,

[47] In the London Division there was much variation in Church of England support. Areas of Anglican strength were associated with the more affluent areas of the capital and the expanding suburbs.

[48] In districts like Liverpool, Manchester, Salford, Bristol, Wolverhampton, Birmingham, Merthyr Tydfil, Westminster or Southwark.

[49] Chapter 11. See also A. Everitt, 'Nonconformity in country parishes', supplement to *Agricultural History Review*, 18 (1970), 189–91; A. Everitt, *The Pattern of Rural Dissent: the Nineteenth Century* (Leicester, 1972); B. I. Coleman, *The Church of England in the Mid-Nineteenth Century: a Social Geography* (1980), , pp. 17–19.

the population could be closely controlled and encouraged to attend the established church. This was facilitated by small parishes with one settlement, allowing greater ease of access to church, while also lacking variety of employment and the means for independency. Such areas were often agriculturally wealthy, rich in tithe, having high valued livings and resident clergymen. These were abundant in the rich dioceses of Winchester, Salisbury, Chichester, Hereford and Worcester. Where there were larger numbers of cottagers, owner occupiers, semi-independent artisans or industrial workers, taking advantage of less deferential forms of employment, the Church was less easily placed. For example, the Church was fairly weak in Lincolnshire, but it was especially vulnerable and threatened by Methodism in the larger 'open' parishes, rather than in the estate villages.[50]

A related factor had been the incidence of clerical absenteeism or non-residence, a problem long associated with parishes in which livings were poor. Some of these had been augmented by Queen Anne's Bounty, to provide residences and to purchase or annex land to augment incomes. Considerable improvements occurred in this regard during the nineteenth century; but often Nonconformity, atheism or indifference had already taken hold, in part because of eighteenth-century neglect. Gay pointed out that 'In 1743 out of a total of 836 parishes in the diocese of York, 393 had non-resident incumbents and a further 335 were held by pluralists.'[51] An Act to promote the residence of parish clergy had been passed in 1777, 'making provision for the more speedy and effectual building of houses' for their residence, and while one can find much archival evidence of clerical accommodation being improved under this enactment, it seems to have had only a limited effect on non-residence.[52] In 1812 a parliamentary enquiry had found that there were 4,813 incum-

50 C. Rawding, 'The iconography of churches: a case study of landownership and power in nineteenth-century Lincolnshire', *Journal of Historical Geography*, 16 (1990), 160–1. During the second half of the century, the Anglican Church in north Lincolnshire revived somewhat, partly because of a reduction in pluralism and absenteeism, once characteristic of areas like the Wolds.

51 Gay, *Geography of Religion*, p. 71.

52 17 Geo. III, c. 53. For examples of house improvements under the Act, see Leics. C.R.O., ID 41/18/21 (visitation returns, 1777–8, e.g. Leir, Knipton and Sproxton), pp. 118, 262, 278. The Act appears to have been taken seriously, for many references of this kind may be found.

bents who were non-resident, and only 3,694 curates served their parishes. Six years later, only 40 per cent of parishes had resident clergy. Substantial reforms had taken place by 1850, but still well over a thousand beneficed clergy were non-resident.[53]

In bishop's licences allowing non-residency, a number of reasons habitually crop up, foremost among them ill-health, the lack of clerical housing, and the minister being resident in the neighbourhood but not in the parish, the distance sometimes being mentioned. In Oadby (Leicestershire) it was because of 'the Vicarage house being a small mean cottage, unfit for your residence'.[54] Other such reasons for other parishes in this county included 'no house of residence'; 'your being engaged in duty elsewhere';[55] 'your advanced age, ill health, and inability to perform the duty';[56] 'the small value of your said Benefice';[57] 'infirmity of your wife',[58] and so on. One finds also reasons like 'being the licensed Master of the Free Grammar School at Ashbourn', or being a 'licensed lecturer' in a Collegiate Church elsewhere;[59] or in one sad case 'on account of your being utterly incapacitated from performing any clerical duty whatever'.[60]

Licences for absence were usually granted for a limited duration, one or two years, although some were periodically renewed. A curate could be appointed to perform the duties instead, with a salary of about £70 per annum in Leicestershire in the 1820s and '30s. Some historiography on this subject, like many contemporary critics, would have us believe in a myth of avaricious and idle clergymen milking their benefice revenues from afar. One can find a few examples of something akin to this, although a case was sometimes made for the health-giving qualities of the Mediterranean air. However, an uncynical reading of visitation returns, glebe terriers and bishops' licences suggests that there were often real problems over housing and clerical ill-health. Whatever one's verdict on this, there is no

53 R. Brown, *Church and State in Modern Britain, 1700–1850* (1991), pp. 98, 427. 47 per cent of the 10,261 beneficed clergy were non-resident in 1810. See Gilbert, *Religion and Society*, p. 131 and note 2, who shows the marked amelioration of this thereafter.

54 Leics. C.R.O., ID 41/32/1–124 (no. 1, 1827): licences issued by the Bishop of Lincoln to incumbents who had applied with good cause to be absent from their parishes, arranged by parish. These licences cover 1827–52. Other examples of unfit housing may be found in nos. 9, 15, or 83. See also 57 Geo. III, c. 99, a copy of the licence having to be given to churchwardens.

55 Leics. C.R.O., ID 41/32/1–124, no. 41.

56 *Ibid.*, no. 5.

57 *Ibid.*, no. 8.

58 *Ibid.*, no. 10.

59 *Ibid.*, no. 4.

60 *Ibid.*, no. 109. In Leicestershire there were a number of cases pleading 'advanced age, ill health and inability to perform the duty' (e.g. *ibid.*, no. 5).

Table 2.1. *Percentages of parishes without clerical housing, and average values of parish livings: fifteen counties*

	% of livings without housing	N. of parishes providing housing data	Mean value (£) of parish livings	Median value (£) of parish livings	N. of parishes providing data on value of living
Ang.	72.4	76	353	296	38
Beds.	19.0	121	283	248	112
Caerns.	57.4	61	260	225	45
Cambs.	25.7	140	510	300	140
Cards.	71.3	94	148	123	82
Derbs.	26.4	87	374	269	99
Dors.	34.5	264	282	251	229
Lancs.	23.8	21	1,380	783	76
Leics.	24.4	213	362	300	210
Mon.	55.0	120	192	170	103
N'umb.	18.4	87	388	300	82
Rut.	22.4	49	338	300	48
Suff.	24.4	426	351	311	422
Suss.	32.9	292	332	277	281
York, E.Rid.	35.4	161	309	250	161
Total	33.3	2,212	367	273	2,128

Source: Imperial Gazetteer.

doubt that many northern, south-western and Welsh parishes experienced such clerical absence well into the nineteenth century. Non-residency seems to have been much less of a problem in those areas where we documented the Anglican Church performing best.

The issue of Anglican non-residency may be examined for the parishes in the fifteen counties that will be used later for detailed parish analysis. The second column of table 2.1 shows for each county the percentage of parish livings stated as being without clerical accommodation in the *Imperial Gazetteer*. This source documents the 1860s, a few decades later than our discussion above, and certainly in that earlier period the percentage would have been higher. A lack of clerical accommodation did not necessarily mean that the clergyman was non-resident, but it is a good indication. It points in a telling way to the adequacy of Anglican provision. There are strikingly high percentages of parishes without adequate accommodation in Anglesey,

Caernarvonshire, Cardiganshire and Monmouth. All these had a majority of parishes without clerical accommodation. The Welsh counties differ very noticeably from the English.[61] However, even for English counties, at this late date, there are some surprisingly high figures, as for the East Riding, Sussex and Derbyshire, where the Anglican Church was relatively weak.

The Church's wealth was very uneven regionally, and poor livings help to explain absenteeism. In the early nineteenth century the Church's total income was around £7 million, and it had about 16,000 clergy. Moorman rightly suggested that this should have been sufficient to allow a reasonable living for each clergyman, 'but in fact the division of the Church's income was so inequitable that a few favoured individuals were in enjoyment of considerable fortunes while many of the clergy were in want'.[62] In the 1830s about a third of clergy were at, or below, what might be termed a contemporary 'poverty line'.[63] This uneven division of wealth continued in the second half of the century, with for example livings in Cumberland being so poor that it was difficult to obtain graduates for them.[64] The rich and strongly Anglican south midland counties were also most affected by parliamentary enclosure, concentrated as it was in the triangle between Dorchester, Norwich and York. This brought major economic benefits to clergy, augmenting livings which were already relatively high in value.[65]

61 The percentage of livings without accommodation in the 351 documented Welsh parishes was 63.5, while for the 1861 English parishes it was 27.6.

62 J. R. H. Moorman, *A History of the Church of England* (1973), p. 332.

63 E. J. Evans, 'Some reasons for the growth of English rural anti-clericalism, c.1750–c.1830', *Past and Present*, 66 (1975), 100.

64 Pelling, *Social Geography*, p. 321.

65 The geography of parliamentary enclosure coincides to some extent with our Anglican cartography, notably to the north of an Oxford–Cambridge line. (There are obvious southern exceptions, like the long-enclosed counties of Essex, Kent and Sussex.) The Church benefited considerably from this land re-allocation, also gaining from tithe commutation and from having its fencing and ditching done at others' expense. By contrast, more western and northern long-enclosed areas were often ones of scattered settlement, lacking the nucleated village structures that favoured the Church of England in central and southern England. For the distribution in England of commutation of tithes under enclosure Acts, 1757–1835, see R. J. P. Kain and H. C. Prince, *The Tithe Surveys of England and Wales* (Cambridge, 1985), p. 24. For the distribution of enclosure by Act, see M. E. Turner, *English Parliamentary Enclosure* (Folkestone, 1980), p. 59, or M. E. Turner, *Enclosures in Britain, 1750–1830* (1984), p. 25; M. Overton, 'Agriculture', in J. Langton and R. J. Morris (eds.), *Atlas of Industrializing Britain, 1780–1914* (1986), p. 45 on parliamentary enclosure. One

Queen Anne's Bounty had been used with mixed success from 1704 to augment poor livings. The Bounty had had much influence in Wales over previous decades, where a large number of livings had been less than £50, but small livings often did not qualify for aid, because of the need for a patron's benefactions to match Bounty augmentation. The Bounty paid much respect to private patronage and generosity, which was very unevenly located. It also failed to raise significantly the value of urban and industrial parishes, where many employers were dissenters and thus not inclined to initiate aid for the Church of England. Nor did it do much to build parsonage houses.[66] The data we have seen on the values of livings, and the cartography of the Church of England, bear witness to this background of regional historical neglect, stemming essentially from the failures of the bishops who managed the Bounty. From 1809 the Church of England began with greater determination to address the problem of poor livings, particularly in the north. From that date eleven annual grants of £1 million were secured from government to supplement Queen Anne's Bounty. In 1836 the Church Pastoral Aid Society was formed to help resolve the poor-livings issue.

Our own work on values of clerical livings, using parish figures in the *Imperial Gazetteer*, shows how extreme regional disparities of Anglican living values were.[67] Mean and median values are shown in table 2.1, for the parishes in fifteen Welsh and English counties. Once

Footnote 65 (*cont.*)
should note also Overton's map (p. 45) of the ratio of labourers to occupiers not employing labour, as the southern, eastern and south midland high ratios of labourers to such occupiers overlap significantly with Anglican strongholds. This hints at the cultural effects of agrarian waged employment dependency, and contrasts with areas where a fuller degree of economic independence seems to have permitted greater religious independence of mind.

[66] On Queen Anne's Bounty, see *Census of Religious Worship* (1851), p. xxxviii; C. H. Hodgson, *An Account of the Augmentation of Small Livings by the Governors of the Bounty of Queen Anne* (1826, 2nd edn, 1845); *Select Committee on First Fruits and Tenths, and Administration of Queen Anne's Bounty*, XIV (1837); Best, *Temporal Pillars*; M. R. Austin, 'Queen Anne's Bounty and the poor livings of Derbyshire', *Derbyshire Archaeological Journal*, 92 (1973), 75–89; I. Green, 'The first five years of Queen Anne's Bounty', in R. O'Day and F. Heal (eds.), *Princes and Paupers in the English Church, 1500–1800* (Leicester, 1981); S. Harratt, 'Queen Anne's Bounty and the augmentation of Leicestershire livings in the age of reform', *Leicestershire Archaeological and Historical Society*, 61 (1987), 8–23.

[67] The parish-level analyses will be described in fuller detail later. Figures on the values of livings are taken from J. M. Wilson, *The Imperial Gazetteer of England and Wales*, 6 volumes (Edinburgh, n.d., c. 1870–2).

Table 2.2. *Values of English and Welsh parish livings (the 15 counties), calculated for those with and without clerical accommodation*

	English parishes			Welsh parishes		
	English average value of living (£)	Standard deviation	N. English parishes	Welsh average value of living (£)	Standard deviation	N. Welsh parishes
Without accommodation	213	192	450	154	118	142
With accommodation	390	349	1,337	279	164	126
Total	345	326	1,787	213	154	268

Notes:

ANOVA test on English parishes:
F ratio: 105.0
probability: .0000

ANOVA test on Welsh parishes:
F ratio: 52.3
probability: .0000

more, the Welsh figures are noticeably lower than the English. The average for 268 Welsh parishes was £213. For 1,787 English parishes it was £345. These findings can be elaborated further by table 2.2, which shows the results of calculating English and Welsh average living values for parishes with clerical accommodation, and for those without. (This can only be done for those parishes provided with both headings of data in *The Imperial Gazetteer.*) In both countries, the clerical livings with habitable housing were very significantly wealthier than those without, being worth nearly twice as much. In addition, the two groups of English livings tended to be considerably richer than their Welsh equivalents. It is evident that the problem of poor livings was intimately tied to the issue of clerical housing and non-residence, the two problems for the Church going hand in hand, each compounding the effects of the other. These factors must have had a considerable impact on the regional effectiveness of the established church, and they tie in well with our cartographic findings.

Other factors compounded the Church of England's administrative and structural weaknesses. In certain areas Anglican ministers were deeply unpopular. Probably the greatest bone of contention concerned tithes. Over a long period farmers protested that, compared to merchants and industrialists, they were bearing too heavy a burden of taxation, and they objected to paying 10 per cent of their income to the clergy. Ill-feeling over tithes was particularly acute during periods of agricultural depression, notably after the Napoleonic Wars. Enclosure provided an opportunity to end tithe payment in its traditional form, but the resulting rent payments were almost as unpopular, coupled as they were by the accurate impression that the clergy were major beneficiaries of enclosure. Both the labouring poor, themselves losing many rights upon enclosure,[68] and many of their farmer employers, were further alienated from the Anglican Church as a consequence. General commutation of tithes in 1836 did not necessarily lessen protests as the clergy were widely given land in lieu of their tithe. Church rates levied upon dissenters as well as Anglicans were a long-running cause of dissension. There was widespread concern that the cost of church restoration, or of new and larger churches, would be paid for by increasing the rate. There was a long succession of failed bills after 1834, and it was not until Gladstone's Act of 1868 that church rates were made voluntary.[69] A further reason for anti-clericalism was that so many Anglican clergy were also magistrates. Evans estimated for 1761 that 11 per cent of Anglican ministers were magistrates, and that this percentage had increased to 22 per cent by 1831.[70] They were increasingly required to enforce the new and widely unpopular poor law, the game laws, and other scorned aspects of the penal code. The distribution of clerical magistrates was uneven, and larger numbers filling this unpopular role may help account for lower Anglican attendances. For example, Lincolnshire (a county of strong Methodism) had as many as 47 per cent of its clergy also serving as magistrates.[71]

The Anglican reforms of the first half of the century were certainly significant. As well as parochial and diocesan reorganisation, affecting structures, boundaries, church building, revenues and funding, these reforms encompassed issues like nepotism, pluralities and non-

[68] K. D. M. Snell, *Annals of the Labouring Poor: Social Change and Agrarian England, 1660–1900* (Cambridge, 1985), ch. 4; J. M. Neeson, *Commoners: Common Right, Enclosure and Social Change in England, 1700–1820* (Cambridge, 1993).

[69] 31 & 32 Vic. c. 109. Towns had often moved in this way already. See O. Chadwick, *The Victorian Church* (1970, 1980 edn), vol. 2, p. 195.

[70] Evans, 'Some reasons', 101.

[71] In Cambridgeshire it was 45 per cent, in Bedfordshire 41 per cent, in Northamptonshire 39.5 per cent, and 36 per cent in Warwickshire. See Evans, 'Some reasons', 104.

residence, cathedral establishments, tithe, payments to curates, access to seating, repair of new chapels, and the like. As Gilbert and others suggested, such improvements certainly had considerable effect, and they were preconditions for a revitalised church. Even so, an argument could still be made that these efforts came too late, and that establishment inertia over a long period had compounded increasingly glaring structural weaknesses.

If this was so in many regions of England, it was even more applicable to Wales. We have seen how Welsh livings were exceptionally poor, with clerical housing grossly inadequate. Many churches were badly dilapidated. Average parish sizes were well above those of southern England. Habitations or settlements were often scattered, distant from church, lacking possibilities for social control. To be sure, there were 'estate villages' in Wales, often ones (like those of Lord Penryn) that industrialised and attracted large numbers of migrants; but the connotations of the English 'close' village had much less applicability in the Welsh countryside. The class demarcations of Victorian English agriculture were far less pronounced in Welsh rural society, where close kinship ties, inter-change of labour between farms and upward mobility from servant to small tenant were common experiences.[72] In Wales farm servants comprised much higher proportions of rural workers than in England, and the ratio of labourers to farmers was very low.[73] As the southern and mid-Wales Rebecca riots in the 1840s revealed only too clearly, distinctions between rural classes were indistinct, blurred by a shared sense of purpose that owed much to language, kinship and senses of place. Urban attendance at the established church could be very socially selective, and for the most part rural migrants to the Welsh towns were not inclined to abandon their earlier religious affiliations.

Ieuan Gwynedd Jones has written of the differences between the settled border-country villages, and the extended valleys of central and west Wales or the scattered pastoral settlements of the north. As the leaders of the Anglican reform movement were aware, it was in

[72] I. G. Jones, *Communities: Essays in the Social History of Victorian Wales* (Llandysul, 1987), p. 224; D. W. Howell, *Land and People in Nineteenth-century Wales* (1977); A. D. Rees, *Life in a Welsh Countryside: a Social Study of Llanfihangel yng Ngwynfa* (1950); K. D. M. Snell, 'Deferential bitterness; the social outlook of the rural proletariat in eighteenth- and nineteenth-century England and Wales', in M. L. Bush (ed.), *Social Orders and Social Classes in Europe since 1500: Studies in Social Stratification* (1992), pp. 158–84.

[73] Snell, *Annals of the Labouring Poor*, pp. 96–7.

the west and north in particular that 'endowments were inadequate or alienated into the pockets of lay-men or distant corporations, and . . . clergy therefore were poverty-stricken, ill-educated and demoralized'.[74] Gwyn Williams reminds us that many clergy were dedicated men,[75] but given such conditions it is not surprising that pluralism and absenteeism were common. Welsh-speaking congregations quite properly had little time for incumbents who could not even speak their language at services, a failure often attested to in returns for the Religious Census. The anglicisation of the Church in Wales effectively turned it into a foreign institution. Between 1715 and 1870, not a single bishop in Wales was Welsh.[76] Welsh visitation returns can make for sorry reading, and in the worst cases one sees lonely monolingual Englishmen confiding their problems to their English bishop, sometimes attacking dissenters in disdainful and insulting terms, speaking of church keys taken from them, of social ostracism, of the force of Nonconformist rivalry.[77] That rivalry had been mounting in a formidable manner. Between 1801 and 1851, it has been estimated that a chapel was completed in Wales every eight days, resulting in 2,813 chapels by 1851.[78] We have seen that there was considerable regional diversity in the operation of the established church in England, but this distinction between Wales and England will emerge as even more fundamental in the following chapters.

[74] Jones, *Communities*, p. 220.

[75] G. A. Williams, *When Was Wales? A History of the Welsh* (Harmondsworth, 1985), pp. 150, 204.

[76] Pelling, *Social Geography*, pp. 348–50.

[77] See e.g. National Library of Wales, B/QA/22, vol. 1 (1814, Diocese of Bangor), Penmachno: 'many dissenters . . . of the very lowest order, a disorderly rabble . . . '; N.L.W., B/QA/22, vol. 1 (1814, Diocese of Bangor), Rhiw, for a much more offensive and alienated statement; N.L.W., SD/QA/17 (1845, Archdeaconry of Cardigan), Troedyraur: 'the Rebecca riots drove away most of the English . . . I have no English attendants. I have not been able to get the Child.n of Dissenters to come to Church at all'.

[78] J. Davies, *A History of Wales* (1990, Harmondsworth, 1993 edn), p. 359.

3

Old dissent: the Presbyterians, Independents, Baptists, Quakers and Unitarians

This chapter discusses the geography of old dissenting and related denominations, that is the Presbyterian Church in England, the United Presbyterian Church, the Church of Scotland, the Independents (or Congregationalists), the Baptists, the Quakers and the Unitarians. One has reservations about any such grouping which are worth mentioning. 'Old' and 'new' dissent are terms of historical convenience, like the 'industrial revolution' and so many others used by historians. Though categories of this sort are useful in many ways, and have a basic chronological justification, one needs to be aware that many 'old dissenting' denominations benefited enormously from the evangelical revival of the eighteenth century, which itself originated within the Anglican Church. This was particularly true for the Congregationalists, the Particular Baptists and the New Connexion General Baptists. Methodist innovations like itinerancy were also shared by some older denominations. There were many contemporaries who commented upon these denominations as a whole, and who would have had some sympathy with Gilbert's view that such denominations were 'linked in a single, if multiform, social and religious phenomenon'.[1] Denominational spread was affected in a host of ways by affinities, as well as by inter-denominational hostilities; and such affinities underlay similar growth patterns, as well as the comparable or complementary dispersion of denominations shown here.

A more detailed reservation has to do with source coverage. The registration-district tables of the 1851 Religious Census failed to divide Baptists into the Particular Baptists, General or Arminian Baptists, and (from 1770) the General Baptists of the New Connexion. This was largely because of large numbers of undefined Baptist returns. Ideally

[1] A. D. Gilbert, *Religion and Society in Industrial England: Church, Chapel and Social Change, 1740–1914* (1976), p. 51; E. Halévy, *A History of the English People in the Nineteenth Century: vol. 1, England in 1815* (1913, 1970 edn), pp. 410, 419, 422.

Table 3.1. *The strength of old dissent*

	Index of attendances (mean)	Index of sittings (mean)	Index of occupancy (mean)	N. of registration districts providing sittings
Independents	8.0	7.0	111.6	579
Baptists	6.7	5.4	121.1	541
Quakers	0.3	1.4	22.8	265
Unitarians	0.8	1.2	76.0	152
Presbyterian Church in England	2.0	2.8	91.9	45
United Presbyterian Church	3.2	3.5	85.1	34
Church of Scotland	2.5	2.5	94.1	15

the Calvinistic Particular Baptists would be included as an old dissenting denomination and the General Baptists as 'new dissent', but one cannot do this with the published census figures. The Baptists have therefore been grouped together here. (They will later be separated more readily with parish-level data.) Lesser problems of a comparable sort also affect other denominations. In particular, the 'Independents' included a wide range of doctrinal beliefs, which makes their categorisation difficult. For example, certain Independent congregations came close to Presbyterianism, while others had more in common with Methodist evangelicalism, in some cases being Independent Methodists.[2] 'Independents' are of course normally thought of as an old dissenting denomination, and this has been followed here, despite the heterogeneity of beliefs that this label can entail.

The strength of these denominations across the districts of England and Wales is seen in table 3.1.[3] The Independents and the Baptists were certainly the strongest, both in spatial coverage, and with regard to indexes of attendances and sittings. The Presbyterian denominations – the Church of Scotland, Presbyterian Church in England, and United Presbyterian Church – were weakest in extent. Although the Quakers were in many more districts than the Presbyterian denomi-

[2] And see D. M. Thompson, 'The Religious Census of 1851', in R. Lawton (ed.), *The Census and Social Structure: an Interpretative Guide to Nineteenth Century Censuses for England and Wales* (1978), p. 250.

[3] In each case, figures are calculated only for those districts in which the denomination had sittings.

nations, more than the Unitarians indeed, they were the weakest when one considers these measures. The Quakers also had an exceptionally low index of occupancy – that is, their attendances were extremely low relative to their sittings, a point we will return to. The average index of attendances shows that even in those districts where these older denominations were present, they were all fairly weak, particularly if one leaves aside the Independents and Baptists.

Presbyterianism

There were few Presbyterian congregations in England and Wales, although Presbyterianism had enjoyed an important past. In the nineteenth century it continued to dominate the religious geography of Scotland. The denomination had its origins in the work of Calvin in Geneva and his attempts to establish a church government based on New Testament teachings. This resulted in no hierarchical priesthood, but rather a class of ministers, putting stress on government by both ministers and the laity, or elders. Presbyterianism was predestinarian in doctrine, and it promoted simple 'dignified' services.[4] In 1643, during the English Civil War, the parliamentarians had turned to Scotland for armed assistance, and subsequently, under the Solemn League and Covenant, Presbyterianism had become established doctrine.[5] Following the Restoration, and the re-establishment of the episcopal system, Presbyterianism in England and Wales began a decline from which it never recovered. In the 1662 Act of Uniformity it was listed as a dissenting group. Further, in 1719 a dispute between Calvinistic and Arminian doctrines within Presbyterianism resulted in a major split, leading to a movement of Arminian-minded congregations towards Unitarianism, and further shifts of Calvinistical ones towards Independency, although some Congregationalists subscribed to Unitarianism too.[6] By 1851 few of the 'old' congregations still identified themselves as Presbyterian, much of the Presbyterian presence in England being associated with recent Scottish and Ulster immigrants.

[4] F. L. Cross, *The Oxford Dictionary of the Christian Church* (1957), pp. 1101–2.

[5] J. D. Gay, *The Geography of Religion in England* (1971), pp. 124–9.

[6] For a more detailed discussion see C. G. Bolam, J. Goring, H. L. Short and R. Thomas, *The English Presbyterians: from Elizabethan Puritanism to Modern Unitarianism* (1968), esp. chs. 4–6.

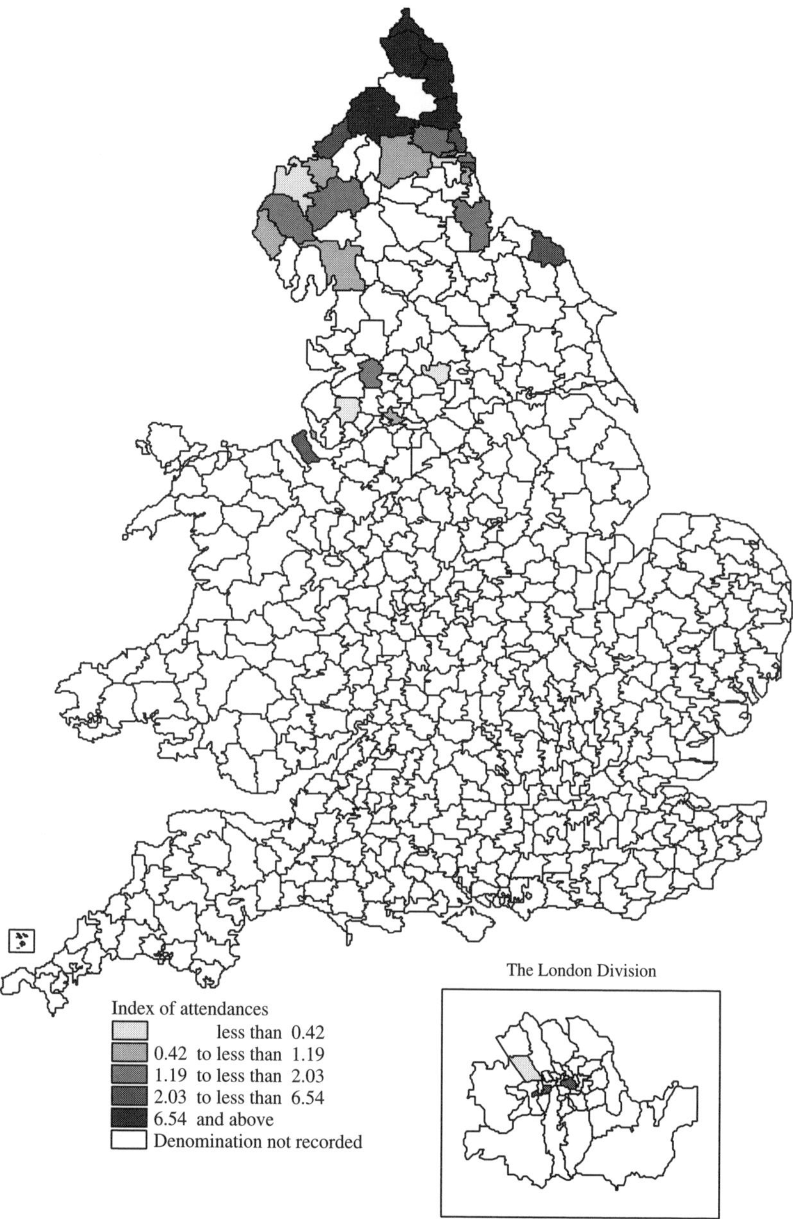

Figure 3.1. United Presbyterian Church index of attendances in 1851

The least common Presbyterian denomination in England and Wales was the Church of Scotland, present in only 15 of the 624 registration districts. It was found in three main areas: in six districts near the Scottish border, in a few districts in London, and around Manchester.[7] It was strongest around Berwick-upon-Tweed, and in London in St Martin-in-the-Fields and neighbouring St James, Westminster. Even in such areas, however, it was weak compared with other denominations. Its index of occupancy (with a mean of 94) suggests that the very limited level of Church of Scotland provision was sufficient to cope with demand.

The United Presbyterian Church was more widely distributed than the Church of Scotland,[8] but was not as common as the Presbyterian Church in England. The denomination was found in just over 5 per cent of all districts. The spatial patterns of worship for the United Presbyterian Church were similar to those of the Church of Scotland. This denomination was present in the most northerly districts of England, particularly Northumberland.[9] It was found in three London districts and in a scattered collection of localities stretching from the Wirral in Cheshire eastward to Bradford. The Presbyterian Church in England had the greatest spatial coverage of the three Presbyterian denominations, and had more presence in London than the others. Like the other Presbyterian groups, it was strongest in Northumberland.[10]

These three denominations tended to exist alongside each other, and the index of attendances map for the United Presbyterian Church (figure 3.1) illustrates the pattern well. Only in those areas where all the Presbyterian denominations were at their maximum strength were they likely to have had much impact on the religious character of the district. Such places included Berwick-upon-Tweed, Bellingham, Belford, Glendale and Rothbury, where indexes of sittings and attendances were in the twenties and low thirties.

7 In 1851 it had three presbyteries in England: London (having 5 congregations), Liverpool and Manchester (with 3 congregations), and the north of England (8 congregations).

8 It had 5 presbyteries in England, containing 62 congregations on the English side of the border.

9 On Northumberland, see R. Gill, *Competing Convictions* (1989).

10 M. R. Watts, *The Dissenters. Vol. 1: From the Reformation to the French Revolution* (Oxford, 1978), p. 277, points to the inadequate parochial structure and large parish sizes in this northerly region as the major factor ensuring Presbyterian survival there after 1662.

By 1851 many of the earlier Presbyterian congregations were listed as Independent or 'other isolated congregations', and one may therefore take this distribution of Presbyterianism as reflecting Scottish settlement in England.[11] All three Presbyterian groups looked in various ways to Scotland and the majority of their worshippers may well have been Scottish, particularly in the Church of Scotland and the Presbyterian Church in England. Pelling quotes Hamilton, Archdeacon of Lindisfarne, at the Church Congress of 1881: 'In the rural parishes of Northumberland the agricultural population for two centuries has been constantly recruited from the neighbouring kingdom of Scotland, and hence we have a strong Presbyterian element pervading the whole of the working classes.'[12] In Lancashire and the West Riding, and in London too, Presbyterianism was affected by an influx of Irish Presbyterians from Ulster, as well as of Scots seeking work. Only a few isolated congregations elsewhere had survived from the seventeenth-century heyday of Presbyterianism.

The Independents

The Independents (or Congregationalists) were found much more widely than the Presbyterians. The denomination was absent in only 45 districts. Originally the Independents came from the radical wing of the Puritan movement in Elizabethan England. For a time they worked within the established church, but were slowly driven out. Many of the sect's early leaders were suspended Anglican clergy. The principles of Independency were first set out by Robert Browne in Norwich in 1581: hence the term 'Brownists'. Cross writes that 'Congregationalism is that form of Church polity which rests on the independence and autonomy of each local church. It professes to represent the principle of democracy in Church government, a polity which is held to follow from its fundamental belief in Christ as the sole head of His Church.'[13] Mann summarised their system by saying that 'Every individual church . . . is held to be complete within itself,

[11] Gay, *Geography of Religion*, p. 128.

[12] H. Pelling, *Social Geography of British Elections 1885–1910* (1967), p. 322, citing *Church Congress Report* (1889), p. 141. Many enumerators' returns to the Religious Census bear this out. For example, 'The inhabitants of Falstone are mainly Presbyterian, the parish is situated on the border of Scotland.' Or 'Ingram is a parish at the foot of the Cheviots composed chiefly of Presbyterians.' P.R.O., HO 129, 552–63 (Falstone and Ingram).

[13] Cross, *Christian Church*, p. 329.

not wanting nor admitting any interference on the part of other churches or of representative assemblages or synods.'[14] He suggested that 'The doctrines of the Congregational churches are almost identical with those embodied in the Articles of the Established Church, interpreted according to their Calvinistic meaning.'[15]

After the sect was formed, it suffered from religious persecution culminating in the execution of three of its leaders in 1593. As a result the Norwich congregation broke up and Independent activity moved to the Netherlands. From there, in the early seventeenth century, clandestine congregations were established in East Anglia. The sect gained much ground during the English Civil War and Commonwealth period, being particularly strong in the army, and it had Cromwell's close sympathy. With its independent structure and its lack of a centralised religious hierarchy, it was relatively well-placed to survive the persecution that came with the Restoration. It also gained considerably from the coalescence with Presbyterianism following the Act of Uniformity.

Independent congregations were largely self-governing and supporting, and so disparate views were contained within the movement. Often congregations had rather different forms of worship, and we are not dealing with an entirely coherent denomination. However, by 1851 a degree of fusion within the movement was apparent. Gay wrote that 'Co-operation between one group and another became increasingly necessary. Associations of ministers were formed to discuss the evangelization of their areas and many wished these County Associations to be federated into a national union.'[16] In 1832 this pressure resulted in the formation of the Congregational Union of England and Wales.

With regard to the religious geography of the Independents, the measures all reflect similar patterns. Their index of attendances can be seen in figure 3.2. They were strongest in almost all of Wales, and virtually the whole of Essex and parts of Suffolk. Wales had the highest measures, especially south Wales, with districts like Newcastle-in-Emlyn and neighbouring Lampeter having notably high figures. Further north in Wales the Independents were weaker, particularly in a narrow band of districts across Wales from Aberystwyth.

[14] *Census of Religious Worship*, p. li. [15] *Ibid.*, p. liii.
[16] Gay, *Geography of Religion*, p. 137.

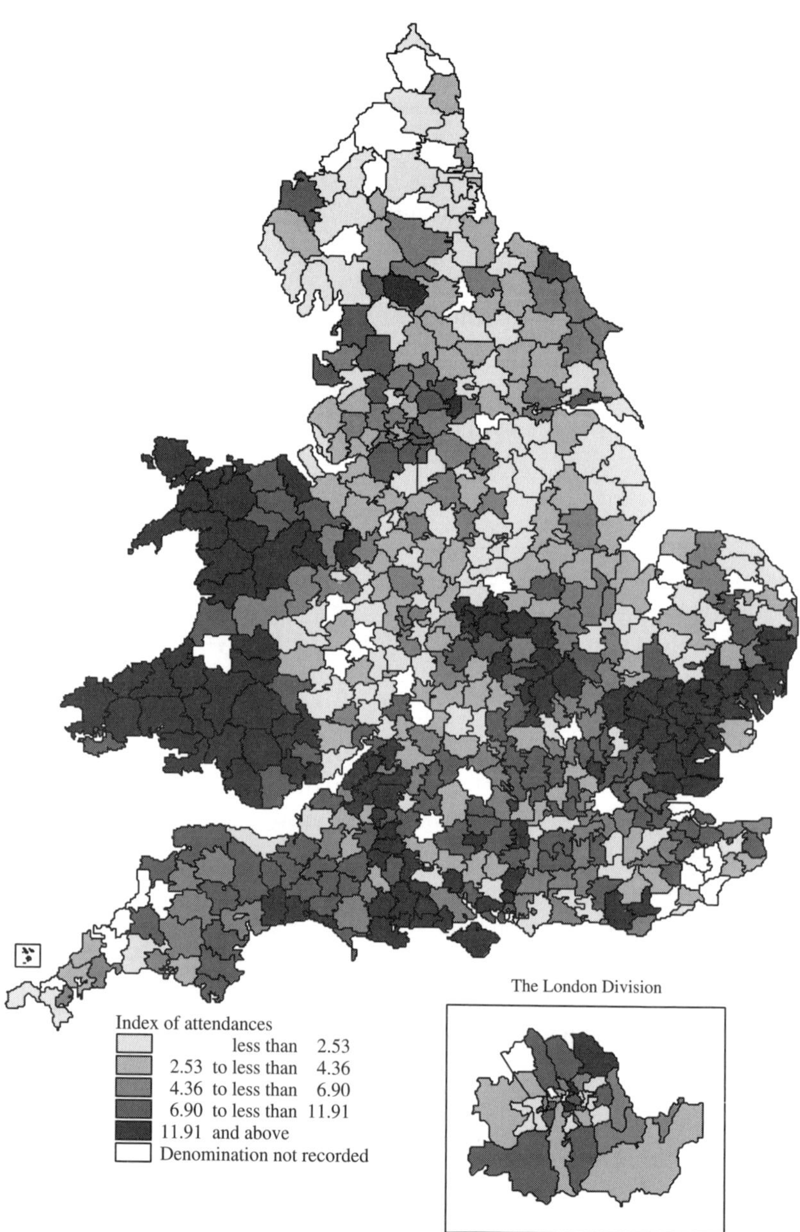

Figure 3.2. Independent index of attendances in 1851

Another area of Independent strength covered almost all of Essex, bordering districts of Suffolk, and extended into north-east London. This is a good example of urban religious allegiance being heavily influenced by its rural hinterland, and the origins of urban migrants. There were other patches of strength, more generally across southern England to central Devon, around (but not including) Poole in Dorset, on the Devon–Dorset border, in Gloucestershire, and in three districts to the north and east of Brighton. In the remainder of England there were one or two other areas of high values, as in south Leicestershire into neighbouring Warwickshire and Northamptonshire.[17]

The denomination was weakest in the far north, where there were several districts in which no Independents were recorded. This area covered much of Northumberland, the North Riding, parts of Lancashire, Derbyshire, Nottinghamshire, Lincolnshire, and it encompassed also central and north Leicestershire, and parts of Norfolk. In the Fens and Brecklands the Independents were mostly absent. (These northern, north-eastern and eastern regions were to be where Wesleyan and Primitive Methodism became strong.) Other smaller areas of below average Independency included Cornwall, parts of Kent, south Shropshire, almost all of Herefordshire and Worcestershire, and south Warwickshire.

The index of occupancy allows one to relate these strengths and weaknesses to demand. There was a very limited relationship between the Independents' index of occupancy and areas of strength as judged by other measures, and in this regard they were quite dissimilar to some other denominations, like the Church of England. In other words, where they were strongest – in sittings, attendances and chapel numbers – they were not actually under much pressure. The exception to this was in parts of Essex. Nor was there great demand for urban sittings. Their index of occupancy was high in some parts of London, but low in the centre of the capital. In the Lancashire–Yorkshire industrial belt their occupancy values were not particularly high, and were even lower in the Black Country. Where the Independents were weak, low occupancy figures were generally found, implying that in such areas even limited Independent provision adequately met demand. This was

17 There was a fairly clear association for the Independents between place of worship size and areas of high population density. Their places of worship were above average size in many urban areas. The census shows that the Independents responded well to the pressures of a large population by building more, and larger, places of worship.

true in almost all of the most northern counties, and generally throughout eastern England south or east of the Wash.

Several considerations help account for these patterns. The first Congregational Church has been traced to Norwich, and exiled Congregationalists spread their creed from the Netherlands.[18] The strength of the Independents in Essex and south Suffolk is related to this. The Compton Census suggests that Essex was the strongest Nonconformist county in the province of Canterbury.[19] In 1851 this region of old dissenting strength was still apparent. Much of Essex was forested in the medieval period, and later comprised areas of dispersed and scattered settlement. In other words, it was the kind of area where the Anglican parochial system did not always function effectively, and where dissent could more readily gain footholds. Indeed, there seems to be some wider association between Independent strength and forested areas of late settlement. The best example of this is the area of Independents from south Gloucestershire to the Dorset coast.

East Anglia had been one of the strongest Presbyterian areas, but after the Restoration, persecution led to decline in the Presbyterian system of organisation. Many of these congregations eventually became Independents. Furthermore, the textile employment of Suffolk and Essex seems to have imparted a degree of religious freedom to industrial workers. This was also the case in the textile regions of Gloucestershire and Wiltshire and in the hosiery districts of the east midlands, other areas of Independent strength.

In Wales the figures may be misleading to some extent. It is possible that Anglo-centric classifications were applied to what were essentially Welsh sects. In many ways the Welsh Independents were very different from their English namesakes. The denomination, as defined in the census, was strongest in areas that were still Welsh-speaking in 1851. The Independents were less strong in the industrial valleys, attracting English as well as Welsh labour, in south Pembroke where English-speaking farmers were long established, and in the Marches.[20]

The Baptists

The Baptists were the second most common old dissenting denomination after the Independents, located in 541 out of the 624 districts.

18 R. W. Dale, *History of English Congregationalism* (1907).

19 *Victoria County History, Essex*, vol. 2, p. 71.

20 Pelling, *Social Geography*, p. 348.

They were spatially more limited and, on almost all measures, weaker than the Independents. The first Baptists came to Britain in the 1530s, when a number of Dutch Baptists left the Netherlands as a result of religious persecution and established chapels in East Anglia. The Baptists had little initial success in winning English converts, until the founding by Smyth of a Baptist congregation in Lincoln in 1603. Smyth emigrated to Amsterdam and died in 1612. In that year some of his converts returned from the Netherlands and established a Baptist chapel at Pinners Hall in London.[21] In a separate development, a Baptist group of Calvinistic doctrine was begun in England in 1633. It was not until the Civil War that Baptists of either disposition won significant numbers of converts, and they established themselves during the religious freedom of that period.[22]

At the close of the seventeenth century there were two fairly strong Baptist denominations – the Arminian General Baptists and the Calvinistic Particular Baptists. The eighteenth century saw a steady decline in the General Baptists, some of whose supporters were won over by a new Baptist group, the General Baptists of the New Connexion, whose first congregation met in 1770 at Donington Park in Leicestershire.[23] Horace Mann identified five separate Baptist denominations in 1851.[24] Unfortunately these denominations were not specified separately in the registration-district data of the Religious Census, all being included under a general Baptist classification. It is therefore not possible to examine at this level individual Baptist denominations, although the original enumerators' forms allow this at parish level in later chapters.[25] In 1813 a combined body for all Baptist denominations (the Baptist Union) was formed, aiming to combine General and Particular Baptists. As within Presbyterianism, there was a relaxation of Calvinistic tenets among the Particular Baptists before and during the nineteenth century, older Calvinistic beliefs and 'closed' communion being preserved in the separation of the Strict and Particular Baptists. As these developments suggest, by

21 E. Routley, *English Religious Dissent* (Cambridge, 1960), pp. 77–8.

22 Gay, *Geography of Religion*, pp. 118–22.

23 A. C. Underwood, *A History of the English Baptists* (1947), p. 149.

24 The Particular Baptists, General (New Connexion) Baptists, General (Unitarian) Baptists, Scotch Baptists, Seventh Day Baptists, and there were also undefined Baptists in the returns. *Census of Religious Worship*, pp. lviii–lxii.

25 1,042 Baptist places of worship did not clearly define what branch they belonged to (assuming that most were able to do so), being some 32 per cent of the total.

1851 some of the earlier distinctions between Calvinistic and Arminian Baptists were less marked.[26]

The main difference between Baptist and Independent doctrine lay in the Baptist view that religious belief could only be accepted by profession. It could not be conferred to an individual by another, as through child baptism. Hence baptism should not take place until the individual could profess belief in adulthood. Baptists also believed that baptism should take place by total immersion. Organisationally the Baptist denominations were similar to the Independents. Congregations were largely autonomous. They could elect their own ministers, and control entry. Each Baptist denomination did, however, have county associations and an annual conference, to which each church could send a representative.

The Baptists' index of attendances is shown in figure 3.3. The highest values were in a broad band of districts running south-westward from Holbeach on the Wash, becoming more discontinuous through to Somerset. Particularly high values were found in Huntingdonshire, Cambridgeshire, south Buckinghamshire and west Hertfordshire, in and to the north of the Chilterns. This region extended also from Huntingdonshire through central Northamptonshire into west Leicestershire, south Derbyshire and Nottinghamshire. The second major area of Baptist strength was in south Wales. Some high values were found here, although they tended not to be quite as strong as in the south-east midlands. The largest area covered the south Welsh valleys, reaching up to Hay-on-Wye and as far west as Swansea. A second Welsh area was in the far south-west, while another included Rhayader and Newtown. Lesser areas of Baptist strength were the Lancashire–West Riding border, east Norfolk and Suffolk, parts of Sussex and Kent, north-east Devon, neighbouring parts of Somerset, and one or two districts in north Wales.

The Baptists shared regions of weakness with the Independents. These included north and north-east England, much of Yorkshire, Cheshire, Staffordshire, parts of Shropshire, Herefordshire, Lincolnshire, Derbyshire, north Norfolk, as well as several seaboard districts from Cornwall's north Atlantic coast to west Sussex. These are regions where we shall see the greatest strengths of Methodism, which complemented old dissent in this regional way.

[26] Cross, *Christian Church*, pp. 127–9.

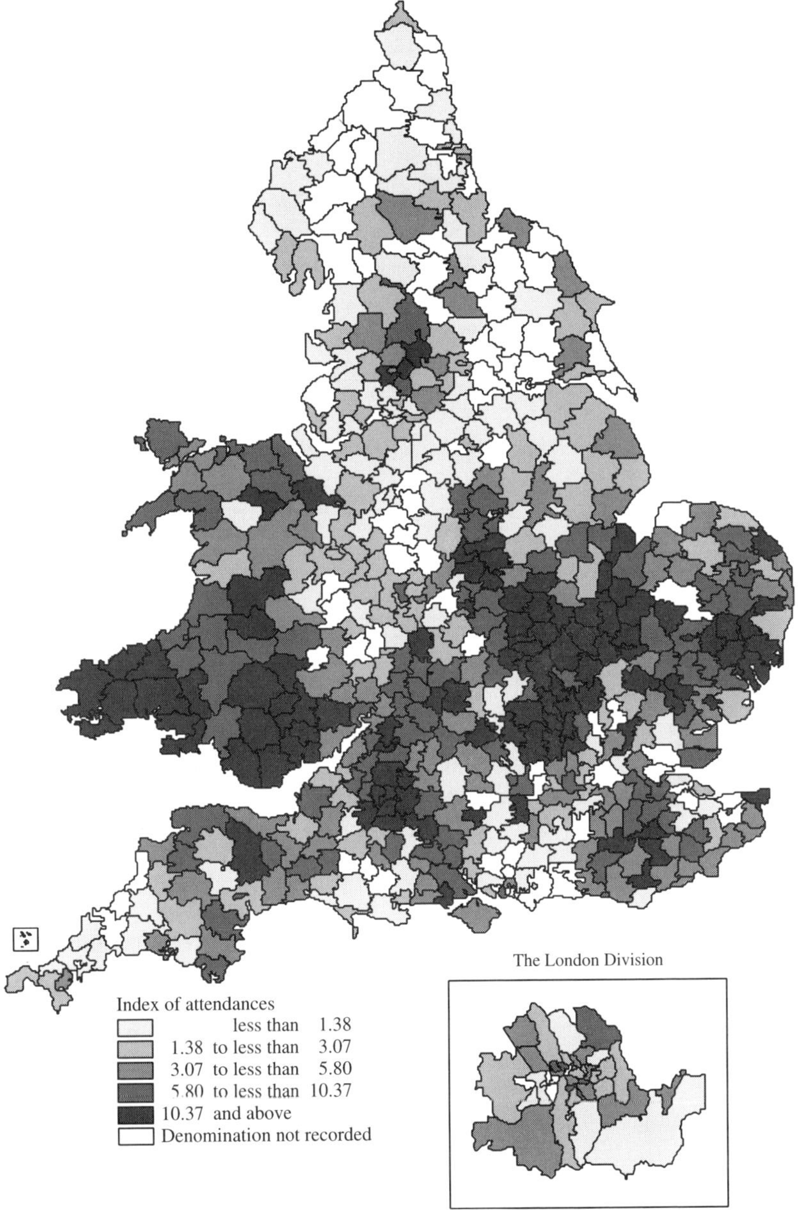

Figure 3.3. Baptist index of attendances in 1851

The Baptist index of occupancy showed pressure upon existing provision, more so than the other older denominations. The index was highest in the strongest Baptist areas, where provision was still inadequate relative to demand. The largest area of high occupancy values (ranging above 150), covered much of the Baptist heartland south of the Wash: Cambridgeshire, Huntingdonshire, Bedfordshire, Buckinghamshire, Suffolk and Essex.[27] There were many pockets of high occupancy figures in the other main areas where one finds Baptist strength, but these were less conspicuous than in the region just described.[28] As one would expect, in many areas where the Baptists were weak their index of occupancy was also low, as in the most northern counties. It would appear that where Baptist provision was limited in 1851 this was largely through lack of demand.

The aggregation of Baptists in the registration-district data makes it difficult to explain these patterns. In Wales Baptist strength was largely due to the presence of the Particular Baptists. In England the General Baptists of the New Connexion were of much greater significance. The Baptist regions in 1851 overlay their regions of strength in the seventeenth century. E. D. Bebb suggested, using licences resulting from the 1672 Declaration of Indulgence, that their main areas were in Kent, Lincolnshire, Somerset and Wiltshire.[29] Further late seventeenth-century evidence from the minutes of the Association of the General Baptists suggests that they were strongest 'in Kent, and that they were also numerous in Buckinghamshire, Leicestershire, Lincolnshire, and Sussex – these five counties possessed two-thirds of the total number of the General Baptist churches'.[30] The Particular Baptists 'were most numerous in the

27 The Baptist mean index of occupancy was higher than any other old dissenting denomination, much higher in some cases. (See table 3.1.) In other words, this was a denomination that was regionally well adjusted to its actual and prospective followers, one that under this way of thinking showed a readiness for further expansion in the areas where it was best equipped to do so. The Independents shared some similarities, but the contrast with the Quakers is very striking.

28 There was no correlation in spatial patterns between districts with high Baptist index of occupancy values and those with high population densities. In areas where population had expanded most, Baptist provision remained adequate, although parts of London were an exception.

29 E. D. Bebb, *Nonconformity and Social and Economic Life* (1935), ch. 2.

30 Gay, *Geography of Religion*, p. 119. General Baptist chapels are very numerous in Leicestershire, often springing from the society at Barton in the Beans. C. Stell, *An Inventory of Nonconformist Chapels and Meeting-houses in Central England* (1986), p. 117.

group of counties formed by Devon, Somerset, Gloucestershire, Wiltshire and Berkshire, and also in London. Elsewhere congregations were few and far between.'[31] Pelling suggested that dissent in the south-east was strongest 'on the high ground of the Chilterns and the Weald – on old forest or common land, beyond the reach of the squires and parsons of the settlement'.[32] He went on to argue that in the sixteenth and seventeenth centuries, Baptists became a powerful force in areas like Suffolk, Essex, the old textile districts of Wiltshire, and in framework knitting parishes in Leicestershire.[33] These were then industrial centres, and in that sense there is a parallel to the later growth of Methodism in many industrialising areas of the late eighteenth century. In Wales the Baptists responded quickly to the rapidly increasing population in Carmarthen, Glamorgan and Monmouthshire, which arose through coal mining, metal working and related industries. In 1797 for example, Cardiff had under 2,000 inhabitants and no Baptist place of worship. A century later its population was 164,000, and it had over twenty Baptist churches.[34] The Baptists were also more successful than other denominations in adapting to the linguistic situation in Wales, winning over both English and Welsh speakers, pragmatically using whatever language most suited local people.[35]

There is debate as to how successful the Baptists were in the towns and cities of the industrial revolution in England. Underwood suggested that the remarkable expansion of the number of Baptist places of worship, from 652 in 1801 to 2,789 by 1851, was 'specially marked in the new industrial districts'.[36] Others like Whitley have disagreed, arguing that the Baptists 'lost touch with the workers, they saw no problem in the rise of cities. In Lancashire and the West Riding it is true that the spinners and weavers were influenced, but elsewhere there seemed to be a loss of touch, so that men were allowed to drift away from religion.'[37] In fact, there was no clear pattern of Baptist

31 Gay, *Geography of Religion*, p. 119, and see his county maps on pp. 290–1. Gay's study was restricted to England and did not cover the Particular Baptists in Wales.

32 Pelling, *British Elections*, p. 62. There is excellent coverage of the contexts of religious dissent in the Chilterns in M. Spufford (ed.), *The World of the Rural Dissenters, 1520–1725* (Cambridge, 1995), *passim*.

33 Pelling, *Social Geography*, pp. 89–90, 143, 206.

34 W. T. Whitley, *A History of British Baptists* (1923), p. 299.

35 P. N. Jones, 'Baptist chapels as an index of cultural transition in the South Wales coalfield before 1914', *Journal of Historical Geography*, 2 (1976), 350.

36 Underwood, *English Baptists*, p. 201.

37 Whitley, *British Baptists*, p. 303.

strength in urban areas, and much depended on where the towns were located. The denomination was strong, as Whitley intimates, in a few Lancashire and West Riding districts, but also in cities as far apart as Leicester, Bristol, and some parts of London. All of these were in, or near, core regions of Baptist strength. The Baptists were weak in towns which were situated in unimportant regions for the denomination – Tyneside for instance. To a considerable extent, the urban presence of the Baptists reflected the religious geography of a town's hinterland.[38]

The Quakers

After the Presbyterian denominations, the Quakers were the least common old dissenters. They had sittings in 265 of the 624 districts in England and Wales (42 per cent). However, this does not make apparent the weakness of the denomination by 1851, for in districts where the Quakers were found they were much less numerous than the other denominations discussed here. As seen in table 3.1, Quaker measures were well below those for the Independents and Baptists, and were even below corresponding figures for each of the Presbyterian groups, although those denominations were less widely dispersed. Attendance figures for the Quakers were especially low, and this was a matter of some concern at the time within the denomination.

The Quakers, or Seekers, arose through the initiative of George Fox during the religious upheavals of the Civil War. Fox, a Leicestershire-born apprentice shoemaker, brought 'convincement' to a group at Swarthmore Hall in Lancashire in 1652.[39] The denomination became known as the Quakers, initially as a nickname, as they 'tremble at the Word of the Lord.'[40] They were characterised by a lack of formality and ritual. Fox felt that other denominations placed too much

[38] This mixed urban situation shows itself in weak correlation coefficients. Where there were Baptists present, the Spearman coefficient between population density and the Baptist index of sittings was −0.102, between population density and the index of attendances −0.043, and between population density and the index of occupancy 0.115. No clear linear patterns are evident, and so one needs to be wary of any attempt to generalise on the issue of the Baptists and urbanisation.

[39] S. E. Ahlstrom, *A Religious History of the American People* (1972, New Haven, 1974 edn), pp. 176–8.

[40] Cross, *Christian Church*, p. 1130.

reliance on ceremonies and a priesthood. It was not possible, he argued, to preach with conviction through intellect and learning, but rather through divine instruction. Their radical Protestant background led them to the view that it was unnecessary, even harmful, to have a paid ministry, and they rejected marriage by a priest. There was relatively little organisation of worship within the denomination.[41] This was a religion 'in which intensely individualistic and spiritual motifs became predominant'.[42] Central to their beliefs was a conviction in the 'Inner Light' expressed by God working through the soul.[43] Anyone, through good actions, could discern and respond to the 'Inner Light', or the Immanence of God, and thus Calvinistic principles were rejected. Quaker adherents were marked by their speech and dress. Frivolous activities involving art, music and dance were rebuffed. Communion with God was not to be tied to a place, a priestly caste or sacraments, nor to the Bible, although that was a good guide. For a long period they were a very exclusive group compared to others, rejecting mixed (inter-denominational) marriages until as late as 1860. However, they became one of the most reformist of denominations, engaging in many philanthropic pursuits, like the abolition of slavery, or famine relief in Ireland.[44] They were often found in urban trading occupations that allowed them to work in a way that was consistent with a resolute opposition to tithe payment.[45]

Their geographical presence can be seen in figure 3.4, which shows their index of attendances. They were fairly influential in only a few districts. Notable among these were Sedbergh in the West Riding of Yorkshire, where there were four Quaker chapels with space for 540

41 *Census of Religious Worship*, pp. lxii–lxvii.

42 Ahlstrom, *American People*, p. 176.

43 Routley, *Religious Dissent*, pp. 96–7.

44 See K. D. M. Snell (ed.), *Letters from Ireland During the Famine of 1847* by A. Somerville (Dublin, 1994), pp. 50, 64.

45 Quakers resisted tithe payment (which Christ was said to have ended), and repudiated any among them who paid tithe. They also opposed church rates, military service and refused to take oaths, like the Oath of Allegiance in 1660–1. The tithe factor probably had the greatest influence upon their locations. See A. W. Braithwaite, 'Early tithe prosecutions: friends as outlaws', *Journal of the Friends' Historical Society*, 49 (1960), 148–56; E. J. Evans, '"Our faithful testimony": the Society of Friends and tithe payments, 1690–1730', *Journal of the Friends' Historical Society*, 52 (1969), 106–21; B. Reay, 'Quaker opposition to tithes, 1652–1660', *Past and Present*, 86 (1980), 98–120; N. J. Smelser, *Social Paralysis and Social Change: British Working-class Education in the Nineteenth Century* (Berkeley, 1991), p. 68, cites Lord Petty (the Chancellor of the Exchequer) in 1807 as saying that 'he never knew of an agricultural Quaker'.

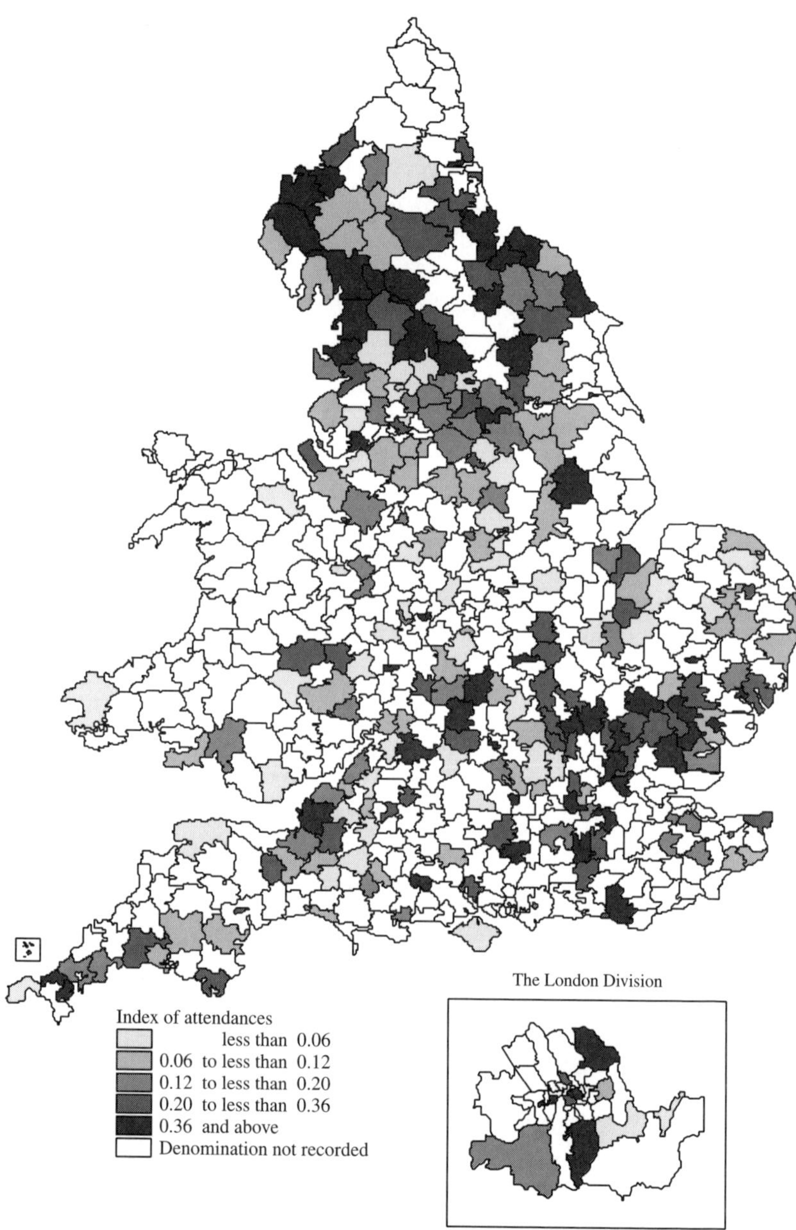

Figure 3.4. Quaker index of attendances in 1851

worshippers, Hemsworth (also in the West Riding), Witham in Essex, Dorking in Surrey, Wigton in Cumberland, and Askrigg in Yorkshire's North Riding. The Quakers were strongest in northern England, in almost all of Cumberland,[46] the western parts of Westmorland, north Lancashire,[47] the north-western parts of the North and West Ridings, and from Darlington and Stockton to eastern parts of the North Riding.

A number of other smaller areas show high values for Quakers. Most significant of these were several districts in Essex, where other old dissenting denominations were prevalent. There was a smaller group of districts in south Warwickshire and north-west Oxfordshire, and more on the Sussex–Surrey border. Other isolated examples can be found. They were more frequently in urban districts than rural ones, in towns like London, Leicester, Birmingham, Worcester, Norwich and Newcastle.[48] The denomination was absent in 359 districts. It was almost completely unrepresented in Wales, largely missing in Northumberland, from the Lincolnshire coast south-westward to the Severn estuary, and from Kent to north Cornwall, including many of the most southerly regions of England.

There were remarkable mismatches between total sittings and total attendances for the Quakers. For example, in Penzance there were two Quaker places of worship with sufficient accommodation for 280, but on Census Sunday they recorded a collective total of only 6 worshippers, a ratio of sittings to attendances of around 47 to 1. Other examples of this phenomenon could be mentioned, in some localities giving an impression of a denomination from which considerable leakage of membership had occurred. The index of attendance values were significantly lower than those for the index of sittings. When one examines attendance data, it is worth emphasising that, compared to other denominations with a similar geographical coverage, the Quakers were very weak almost everywhere. Their systems of certification may have helped to obviate this, by fostering movement

46 On the role of Quakers in the late acceptance of the Reformation in Cumbria, see M. Clark, 'Northern light? Parochial life in a 'dark corner' of Tudor England', in K. L. French, G. G. Gibbs and B. A. Kümin (eds.), *The Parish in English Life, 1400–1600* (Manchester, 1997), pp. 70, 73.

47 On Lancashire Quakerism, see B. G. Blackwood, 'Agrarian unrest and the early Lancashire Quakers', *Journal of the Friends' Historical Society*, 51 (1966), 72–6.

48 See also Watts, *Dissenters*, vol. 1, p. 286.

between Quaker communities.[49] However, historians have frequently described how the denomination was in decline by the mid eighteenth century, and there are many signs of this in the census figures.[50]

The index of occupancy (see table 3.1) shows this mismatch between Quaker sittings and attendances very clearly indeed. Although a maximum of 191 was recorded at Lincoln, the lowest was only 1.2 at Amersham, Buckinghamshire, where there were two Quaker chapels with accommodation for 430, but only 5 attendances on Census Sunday. The mean and median values of this index were only 22.8 and 16.0 respectively, values that were far lower than for any other old dissenting denomination.[51] Total attendances on Census Sunday rarely exceeded sittings for the Quakers, and it is evident that the denomination's provision was not under much pressure anywhere.

The disparity between sittings and attendances, and the low level of support for Quakerism even in its strongest areas, make these spatial patterns of worship hard to explain. Some Quakers seem to have been almost indifferent to visible signs of support, expressed in terms of attendances, giving priority to an individual's spiritual receptivity. As

49 The Quakers had a very efficient system of 'notes of removal', or 'removal certificates', which were carried as passport-like testimonials when they moved from one Monthly Meeting to the compass of another. Many of these survive, particularly for counties like Lancashire. These certificates bore testimony to the credentials of the Quaker, and helped the person to be absorbed into the Quaker body of a new area. Prospective grooms from outside the local society were often asked to supply a certificate of commendation. Some other denominations had similar forms of certification, like the Methodists after 1765, or like the Welsh letter of recommendation, *llythyr canmoliaeth*, carried between chapels, and these had parallels in the eighteenth-century poor-law settlement certificate system. Among denominations, such a system was certainly most advanced within Quakerism. It may have obviated some of the weaknesses of their local congregations, facilitating movement and inter-change between these. And for a denomination so insistent upon endogamy it helped widen the choice of marriage partners.

50 N. Yates, R. Hume and P. Hastings, *Religion and Society in Kent, 1640–1914* (Woodbridge, 1994), p. 17; M. Humphreys, *The Crisis of Community: Montgomeryshire, 1680–1815* (Cardiff, 1996), p. 174; A. M. Urdank, *Religion and Society in a Cotswold Vale: Nailsworth, Gloucestershire, 1780–1865* (Berkeley, 1990), pp. 250–2; but see also S. Wright, *Friends in York: the Dynamics of Quaker Revival, 1780–1860* (Keele, 1995). Many Quakers had emigrated to America, for example with William Penn's emigration schemes of the 1680s.

51 What is more, this index of occupancy uses *total* attendances over three possible service times, and expresses these as a ratio to fixed sittings. In other words, well under one in five seats were being occupied in the Quaker churches, surely a dire situation for the denomination.

such, for members of this denomination, perhaps census data like these are of limited relevance.

'Most Quakers were from the rural and urban *petite bourgeoisie*: very few members were drawn from the proletariat.' Gay and a number of other authors have made this point.[52] Among the most successful Quakers were industrialists, some of whom sponsored Quaker accommodation. Well-known examples included the Cadbury family at Bournville in Birmingham, the Fry family in Bristol, or the Rowntrees in York.[53] There was also an early association between Quaker industrialists and the cloth trade – particularly in East Anglia and the south Lancashire cotton towns – and this might account for the consistent presence, if not strength, of Quakers in those areas.[54] It has been suggested that during Fox's lifetime the denomination was particularly strong in Cumberland.[55] In both this county and in north Lancashire religious openings certainly existed, with less denominational competition than elsewhere, and probably with lesser enforcement of anti-Quaker restrictions. This may have allowed the Quakers to attain the presence there shown in figure 3.4. Some of these northern areas harboured the survival of native Catholicism too. In Wales by contrast, where religious attendances were high, an intense rivalry may not have enabled the Quakers to gain much of a foothold at all. They appear to have been 'squeezed out

52 Gay, *Geography of Religion*, p. 178; W. A. Cole, 'The social origins of the early Friends', *Journal of the Friends' Historical Society*, 48 (1957); R. T. Vann, 'Quakerism and the social structure in the Interregnum', *Past and Present*, 43 (1969); R. T. Vann, *The Social Development of Early Quakerism, 1655–1755* (Cambridge, Mass., 1969); B. Reay, 'The social origins of early Quakerism', *Journal of Interdisciplinary History*, 11 (1980); Urdank, *Religion and Society*, pp. 250–3, who shows also artisans like broadweavers, and waged clothworkers, as a small minority of Quakers.

53 Other Quaker industrialists included the Darby family at Coalbrookdale, Barclays, Lloyds, the Peases and Gurneys (banking), Clarks (shoes), Reckitts (starch), Allen and Hanburys (medicine), Huntley and Palmers (biscuits), Bryant and Mays (matches), Swan Hunter (shipbuilding), Price Waterhouse (accounting). Extensive Quaker networks, trust and honour within the denomination, tight self-regulation, and familiarity with a diversity of regional opportunities appear to have conduced to this remarkable commercial success. See H. Davies, *The English Free Churches* (1952, Oxford, 1963 edn), p. 111; M. W. Flinn, *The Origins of the Industrial Revolution* (1966), p. 89; J. Walvin, *The Quakers: Money and Morals* (1997). Such industrial power gave them considerable influence in areas like the north-east, especially in Darlington (where they were frequently mayors) and the Tees Valley.

54 The cloth towns (of Essex, Lancashire, Yorkshire, west Suffolk, Gloucestershire, Wiltshire, Nottinghamshire and Norfolk) were more widely associated with old dissent. See Watts, *Dissenters*, vol. 1, pp. 354–5.

55 *Victoria County History, Cumberland*, vol. 2, p. 95.

of existence' by Methodist theology, and by the adoption of that theology by Independents and Baptists.[56] This situation was aggravated in Wales by the way in which the Quakers used the English language, for this made them unattractive to the Welsh, and caused them to be seen as an English importation.[57] The Quakers were a non-proselytising denomination, unlike the Wesleyan Methodists and many others. Seeing themselves as a distinct people, with a priesthood of all believers, they regulated themselves strictly, and were quick to expel members. They relied heavily on internal recruitment, made little use of Sunday schools, and they could also be remarkably mobile. Thus in the face of determined competition they did not readily sustain themselves. They had little role to play in the Evangelical Revival, not sharing in the gains made by some other old dissenting denominations.[58] Such considerations help to explain the significant disparities between their sittings and attendances, although further study of Quaker practice at inter-parish level is needed to explain their regional strengths.[59]

The Unitarians

Unitarians believed in the personal unity of God, that is, in God as one person only, and this led to their rejection of the Trinity, and thus of the divinity of Christ – views that had resulted in their exclusion from the Act of Toleration. They held that Jesus brought a new moral dispensation, yet he was felt to be like other men. The Bible was a source of inspiration, but no more. They did not believe in

56 I. C. Peate, *Tradition and Folk Life: a Welsh View* (1972), p. 84.

57 Humphreys, *Crisis of Community: Montgomeryshire*, p. 174.

58 Routley, *Religious Dissent*, p. 151.

59 A fine local study is Urdank, *Religion and Society*, ch. 8. For many further insights into Quaker local development or decline, see W. C. Braithwaite, *The Beginnings of Quakerism* (1912, Cambridge, 1955 edn); J. Sykes, *The Quakers* (1958); E. Isichei, 'From sect to denomination in English Quakerism', *British Journal of Sociology*, 15 (1964), and her *Victorian Quakers* (Oxford, 1970); D. H. Pratt, *English Quakers and the First Industrial Revolution: a Study of the Quaker Community in Four Industrial Counties, Lancashire, York, Warwick and Gloucester, 1750–1830* (New York, 1985); B. Reay, *The Quakers and the English Revolution* (1985); S. Davies, *Quakerism in Lincolnshire: an Informal Study* (1989); R. T. Vann and D. Eversley, *Friends in Life and Death; the British and Irish Quakers in the Demographic Transition* (Cambridge, 1992). With the other referenced works, these provide detailed accounts of Quaker history, often in particular areas, although they rarely explain the regionally varied levels of Quaker support.

eternal punishment, the personality of the devil, nor in fallen spirits, and their services and sermons were based on rational rather than emotive thought. A belief in science among Unitarians led many into industry. There was in fact considerable diversity of views within this denomination, and some confusion still existed in 1851 between Unitarians, General Baptists, Presbyterians and Congregationalists. Many Presbyterian chapels and endowments had come into their hands during the early eighteenth century,[60] and this background affected their nineteenth-century geography, particularly in the older Devon and Somerset areas of Presbyterianism. Their church government was essentially congregational, property being controlled by local trustees, and congregations appointing their own ministers and ruling themselves without regard to courts or synods. 237 such Welsh and English churches made returns to the Religious Census.

The Unitarians' geographical spread is indicated by the well-known presence of so many leading personalities associated with the denomination, like Joseph Priestley in Birmingham, the founder of modern Unitarianism, followed in the same city by the Chamberlains, or in Leicester by figures like John and William Biggs, who were among the many Unitarians dominant in political life following the Municipal Reform Act.[61] Or one thinks of people like Thomas Belsham, James Hill, Joseph Dare, Octavia Hill, Mrs Gaskell, Kay-Shuttleworth, Morgan Williams, Walter Coffin, Harriet and James Martineau, Samuel Courtauld, the Strutts, John Fielden, Frances Power Cobbe and many other notable figures.[62] They were often middle-class, sometimes part of political elites, usually Liberal in politics, concentrated in cities like Manchester, Liverpool, Hull, Birmingham and Cardiff, particularly in south Lancashire, north-east Cheshire, the West Riding, north Derbyshire, and to a limited extent the Black Country. They were much involved in corn-law repeal, and to a somewhat lesser extent the church-rate issue, favouring free trade, frequently inter-marrying among themselves and forming

[60] *Religious Census*, p. lxviii.

[61] Leicester's Unitarian Great Meeting Chapel became known as the 'Mayors Nest'. After 1835 half the town's magistrates were Unitarian, and over half the aldermen. Many were connected with the hosiery trade. Leicester's Unitarians included Fielding Johnson, the banking family of the Pagets, Josiah Gimson, and many others of repute.

[62] R. V. Holt, *The Unitarian Contribution to Social Progress in England* (1938, 1952 edn); R. Watts, *Gender, Power and the Unitarians in England, 1760–1860* (1998).

significant economic alliances between towns like Manchester, Liverpool, Birmingham and Leicester. Unitarianism also had followers in London and along the southern English coast.[63] As Gay says, there is 'no doubt about the overwhelming dominance of Lancashire, Cheshire and the West Riding within Unitarianism', and this pattern was accentuated in the twentieth century as the denomination became even more focused around Manchester.[64]

Figure 3.5 is a map of the Unitarian index of attendances. It shows clearly the importance of Lancashire and parts of the West Riding for the denomination. In addition, there were important centres around Lampeter, in many midland and East Anglian towns, and in a surprisingly large number of districts along the south coast, partly due to the Presbyterian inheritance. The very highest total attendances for the Unitarians were (in descending order) Birmingham, Manchester, Liverpool, Bolton, Ashton-under-Lyne, Bristol, Sheffield, Bury, Haslingden, Kidderminister, Dudley and Brighton. If one looks at their index of attendances, other areas show up as well. These included Tenterden, Ringwood, Ipswich, Bridport, Kidderminster, and particularly Newcastle in Emlyn, Lampeter and Aberayron. This Lampeter area, known to some Anglicans as '*y spottyn du*' (the black spot), had a number of Unitarian chapels.[65] There were Unitarians also in places like Merthyr and Aberdare, and in these and other areas they often had a reputation for Chartist politics. Wales' first working-class newspaper, *Y Gweithiwr/The Worker*, was edited by Unitarians,[66] and the country's first Nonconformist MP, Walter Coffin, who took Cardiff in 1852, was a Unitarian. Their reputation as leaders in dissent was well established in the 1830s and '40s, although they lost some of this renown to the Baptists and Independents in the second half of the century.

[63] Gay, *Geography of Religion* pp. 181–3, 228, 317, who also gives figures for Unitarian marriages in 1952. [64] *Ibid.*, p. 183.

[65] I. G. Jones, 'Ecclesiastical economy: aspects of church building in Victorian Wales', in R. R. Davies *et al.* (eds.), *Welsh Society and Nationhood: Historical Essays Presented to Glanmor Williams* (Cardiff, 1984), p. 229; Peate, *Tradition and Folk Life*, p. 85. Lampeter's Unitarian index of attendance was easily the highest in Wales and England, at 6.1, followed by Aberayron (3.9) and Newcastle in Emlyn (3.5). The highest such figure in England was Ringwood (3.5).

[66] G. A. Williams, *When Was Wales? A History of the Welsh* (Harmondsworth, 1985). p. 190.

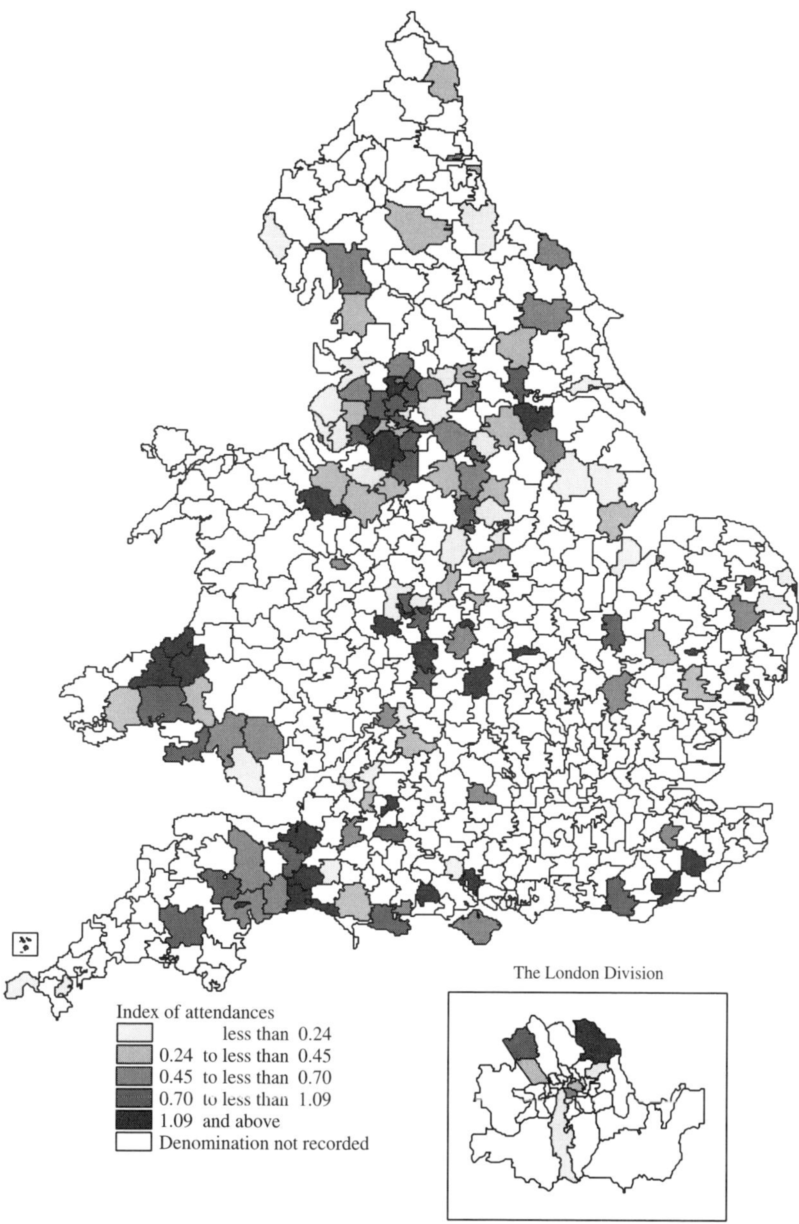

Figure 3.5. Unitarian index of attendances in 1851

Conclusion: 'old dissent' as a whole

There has been an interest in much historiography to examine old dissent in its entirety. To relate our findings to that approach, we can briefly examine the geography of combined old dissent, using the denominations of this chapter. The combined index of attendances can be seen in figure 3.6. 'Old dissent' was prominent in three main regions of England and Wales. It was strongest of all in south Wales, being fairly conspicuous in Wales generally, mainly due to the Independents and Baptists, notably the Particular Baptists.[67] The second major area included much of the south midlands (notably Buckinghamshire and Northamptonshire), Essex, Hertfordshire, south Suffolk, parts of the north midlands and north-east London. (These were earlier Puritan areas, like parts of Surrey, Sussex and Gloucestershire.)[68] Towards the north of this English region, old dissenting strength was primarily due to Baptist predominance, while further south it owed more to Independency. In this area the Quakers were fairly strong but, even when most influential, they can have had only a limited impact. The third main area included several districts near the Scottish border, due to the three Presbyterian denominations.

Smaller pockets of old dissenting strength included some districts south of the Severn (mainly due to the strong presence of Baptists), the old west country woollen industrial area, some districts on the fringe of the New Forest around Bournemouth (mainly because of Independency), a small number of districts around Brighton, and finally on the West Riding–south Lancashire border.

These denominations were particularly weak in much of eastern England from the Tees to the Wash, and across Norfolk. Away from districts bordering Scotland, they were inconsiderable through almost all of the extreme north, in the East and North Ridings, in Lincolnshire, Nottinghamshire, east Leicestershire and most of Norfolk. A second major tract of weakness ran from central Cheshire, through the west midlands to the Severn. Other areas where old dissent was insubstantial included Cornwall, central Kent, west

[67] For further discussion see E. T. Davies, *Religion in the Industrial Revolution in South Wales* (Cardiff, 1965).

[68] F. Tillyard, 'The distribution of the Free Churches in England', *Sociological Review* 27 (1935), 17.

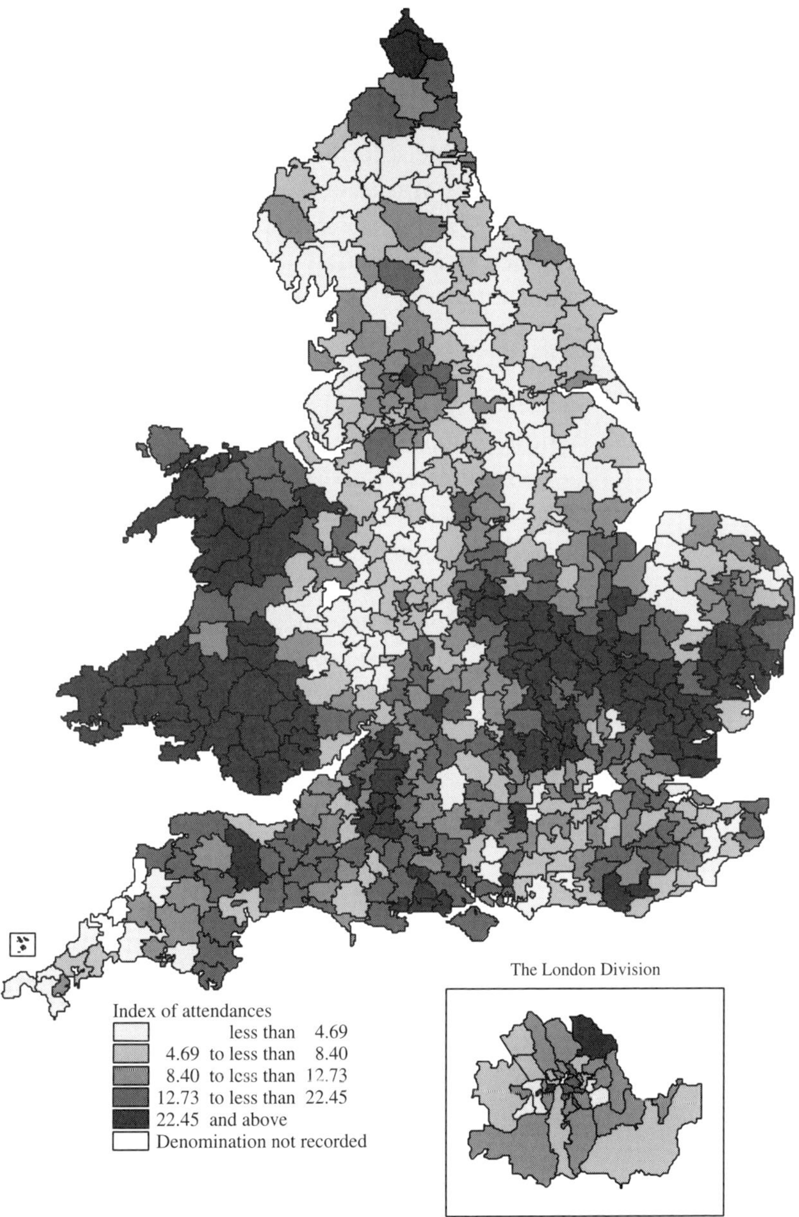

Figure 3.6. Old dissent index of attendances in 1851

Sussex, north from the Solent into Berkshire, and some districts in London. Many of these areas lacked the presence of one or more of the main older denominations.

We have not used the full range of religious measures, because they are almost always in tight mutual agreement. The picture shown is of a complex pattern of religious observance, with marked differences between each of the old dissenting denominations. This underlines the need to consider each denomination in turn rather than 'old dissent' as a unitary phenomenon, as so often in the historiography. However, when one does consider 'old dissent' as a whole, large regions become apparent as lacking or having very limited presence of such dissent. We will see very clearly in the following chapter how the leading new dissenting groups stepped into those areas, and developed in them, their orientations often being influenced not so much by the prior hold of the Church of England as by opportunities offered to complement regionally the old dissenters. It will then become apparent how new and old dissent complemented each other: how their denominations – usually seen non-spatially as theological and organisational alternatives – ought also to be defined and analysed in regional terms.

4

The geographies of new dissent

The century or more after the 1730s saw not only old dissent and Roman Catholicism developing in unexpected ways, but witnessed the origins and expansion of the new dissenting denominations, usually unfurling from the Evangelical Revival within the Anglican Church and from Wesleyan Methodism. The mid eighteenth century is often said to have been a time of lassitude within old dissent, of widespread religious indifference and scepticism, of physical decay of churches, and of growing anachronism and complacency within the established church. Whatever the questionable basis of claims like these,[1] there seems little doubt that new dissent in many ways intensified spiritual and social consciousness, making religious education more available, reaching to many among the labouring poor, and popularising spiritual issues through such means as open evangelism, increased numbers of chapels, and popular hymnology. Further, in the wake of the French Revolution, the reform movements and their enlightened radicalism came quickly to question the conservative part played by the Church of England, and this impetus gave additional motive and mission to religious dissenters as they adopted stances on political issues.

This chapter elaborates the spatial patterns of the new dissenting denominations which developed after the 1730s to be recorded in 1851.[2] Table 4.1 shows some summary figures describing these,[3] and

[1] There are some reasons to question them. See for example W. M. Jacob, *Lay People and Religion in the Early Eighteenth Century* (Cambridge, 1996), *passim*; H. D. Rack, *Reasonable Enthusiast: John Wesley and the Rise of Methodism* (1989, 1992 edn), p. 224.

[2] 'New dissent' in 1851 is taken here as the Wesleyan Methodist Original Connexion, the Wesleyan Methodist New Connexion, the Primitive Methodists, the Calvinistic Methodists, Lady Huntingdon's Connexion, the Wesleyan Methodist Association, the Wesleyan Reformers, the Bible Christians, the Independent Methodists and the New Church. The Latter Day Saints are discussed in this chapter, although they are not included in summary calculations for 'new dissent' as a whole. We have not included other 'isolated congregations', many of which were Methodist inspired, because of the

Table 4.1. *The strength of the new denominations*

	Index of attendances (mean)	Index of sittings (mean)	Index of occupancy (mean)	N. of registration districts providing sittings
Wesleyan Methodists	9.8	9.2	110.8	599
Wesleyan Methodist New Connexion	2.2	2.2	105.7	83
Primitive Methodists	4.7	3.8	131.7	441
Wesleyan Methodist Association	2.3	2.4	103.7	116
Wesleyan Reformers	2.2	1.6	141.8	108
Bible Christians	4.2	3.7	118.9	86
Calvinistic Methodists	16.5	13.3	117.6	72
Lady Huntingdon's Connexion	1.8	1.8	108.5	55
Independent Methodists	2.2	1.7	160.6	7
Moravians	1.3	1.2	116.2	22
New Church	0.4	0.5	84.7	37
Latter Day Saints	0.7	0.5	151.2	129

interested readers will find further detail in appendix A. We will pay most attention to the Wesleyan and Primitive Methodists, which were evidently the most dominant. Of lesser importance, but still very significant, were the Wesleyan Methodist New Connexion, the Wesleyan Methodist Association and the Wesleyan Reformers. It is appropriate also to consider denominations which, while having a less extensive coverage, were of great significance in certain localities. The most striking examples were the Calvinistic Methodists in

Footnote 2 and 3 (*cont.*)
impossibility of distinguishing sects within this grouping in the published census tables. See *Census of Religious Worship*, p. clxxx. Nor have we included Sandamanians (e.g. in Liverpool and West Ward), Southcottians (e.g. in Stockport and Warrington) or Inghamites (e.g. in Burnley and Clitheroe), as they were present in such few districts. The Moravians are detailed in table 4.1, and although they are normally viewed as 'new dissent' we have not otherwise covered them. Their main centres were (in descending order of total attendances) districts like Bedford (1,430 attendances), Bradford, St Neots, Ashton-under-Lyne, Dewsbury, Oldham, Bath, Otley, Stoke Damerel, Bristol, Shardlow and Chepstow (280 attendances). They were very weak or non-existent in London, East Anglia, the south-west, the north-east and far north, and were absent in Wales outside Chepstow.

3 Figures are calculated only for those districts in which the denomination had sittings.

Wales, and the Bible Christians in south-west England. Remaining denominations like the Independent Methodists were much less widespread, but are worth the further discussion we will give them.

The Wesleyan Methodist Original Connexion

The Wesleyan Methodist Original Connexion was the most important new dissenting denomination. It was absent from only 25 districts, and its strength on almost all measures exceeded the other denominations in this chapter, with the exception of the Calvinistic Methodists in Wales. It was stronger also than any old dissenting faith. This was despite the numerous schisms affecting Wesleyanism, including around the time of the census, from which emanated the other Methodist denominations.

The origins of the Original Connexion lay in John Wesley's conversion experience in 1738. This occurred in London during a reading of Luther's preface to the Epistle to the Romans, in which Wesley felt himself to receive an assurance of salvation. During the 1740s the main tenets of Methodism were established; but throughout his life Wesley remained a clergyman in the Church of England and maintained that the role of Methodism was to complement the established church, a mission that inevitably had a strongly regional dimension. The Wesleyan Methodists did not give sacraments until 1795, under the Plan of Pacification which followed Wesley's death in 1791.[4]

The doctrines held by the Wesleyans accorded substantially with the articles of the established church, interpreted in their Arminian sense. The Wesleyans offered alternatives to Anglican organisation, and worshipped with more enthusiasm, but they did not initially question the principle of church establishment. Nor did they share a sense of themselves as being fully dissenters, and this set them apart from other Nonconformists. Many Wesleyan Methodists in the eighteenth century (and even later) worshipped with the Anglican Church.[5] Despite this doctrinal affinity, they were very different indeed in objectives and organisation, and this alone made a parting of the ways almost inevitable. Rather than relying on the parochial system, commonly with a church and minister in each parish,

[4] R. Watson, *A Biblical and Theological Dictionary* (1832), pp. 684–8.

[5] See for example M. J. L. Wickes (ed.), *Devon in the Religious Census of 1851: a Transcript of the Devon Section of the 1851 Church Census* (1990), p. 9.

Wesleyan Methodism functioned within circuits. As Horace Mann perceived, this organisational system was highly efficient: 'a circuit comprising perhaps twenty preaching places is adequately served with from two to four regular itinerants, assisted by the local preachers, and at an expense proportionably small when compared with any system having a fixed minister for each congregation'.[6] By 1851 there were 428 Wesleyan circuits in England and Wales, and these were continually reorganised and newly defined to suit circumstances and opportunities.

Wesleyan Methodism was composed of societies, a collection of which formed a congregation, and a group of congregations formed a circuit. Circuits were joined together into districts. The highest Wesleyan Methodist authority was the Conference. Initially, John Wesley and his brother had been the ultimate authority in the Connexion, Wesley being 'the fount of all Methodist orders'.[7] The Conference was established to take over this responsibility upon their deaths, and much power was concentrated there. For example, no chapel could be built without Conference's agreement, and the Conference had the final say on whether a proposed minister was suitable. Conference was composed solely of ministers, and lay members of the Connexion had no representation in it. It was probably this, above all, and the power that it exercised, which explains the schisms that later racked the Connexion.[8]

In view of Wesley's aim to complement the established church (borne out in his travels to places like Kingswood, the Black Country, Tyneside, Gwennap, Sheffield or Leeds, as documented in his *Journals*),[9] it is most interesting to view the geographical patterns of provision and worship that resulted. The index of attendances for this denomination is mapped in figure 4.1, and we shall refer to this and the index of occupancy, making occasional mention of other measures. The Wesleyan Methodists were strongest in a very broad region that covered much of north-east England from central Northumberland as far south as north Leicestershire and south Lincolnshire. This stretched also to all of Derbyshire and eastern Cheshire. Particularly

[6] *Census of Religious Worship*, p. lxxv. For further discussion of parish and circuit, see K. D. M. Snell, *Parish and Belonging in England and Wales, 1660–1914* (forthcoming).

[7] R. Currie, *Methodism Divided: a Study in the Sociology of Ecumenicalism* (1968), p. 25.

[8] *Census of Religious Worship*, pp. lxxv–lxxvii.

[9] Such travels are well discussed in Rack, *Reasonable Enthusiast*, e.g. pp. 190–1, 214, 216, 220–1, 229, 236.

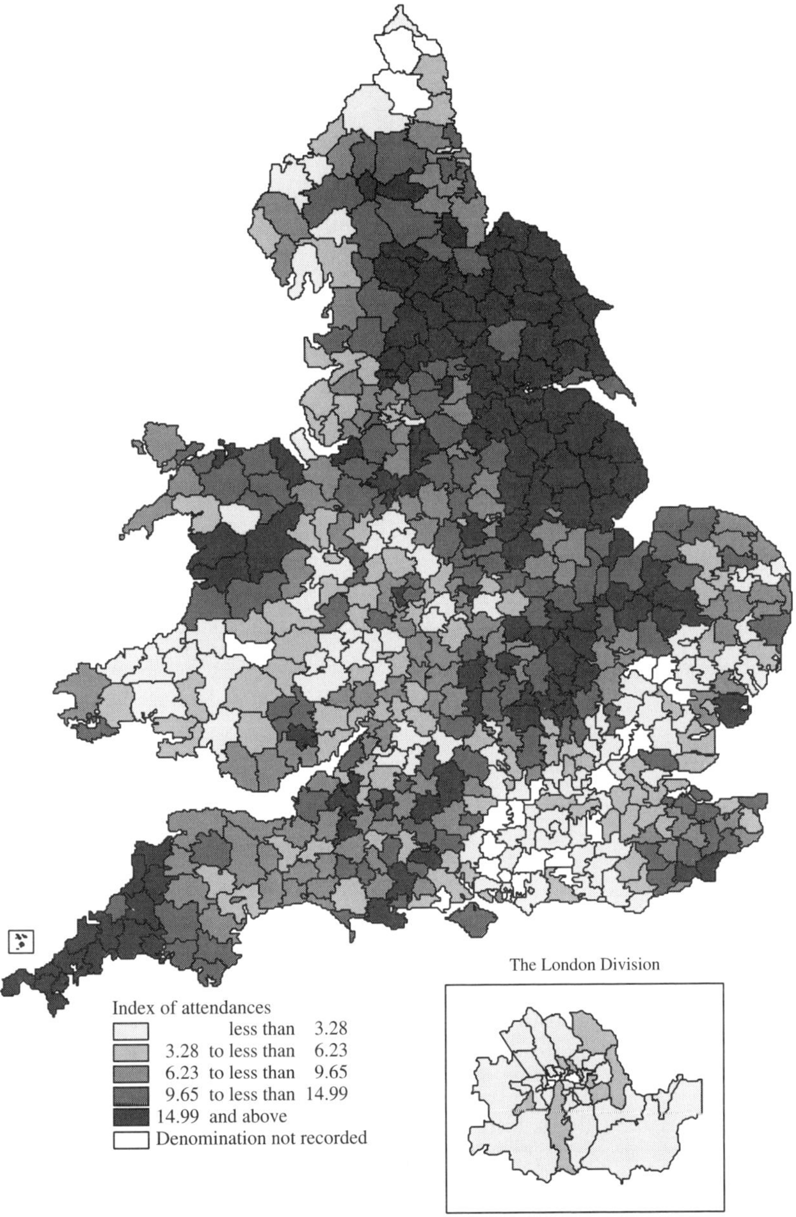

Figure 4.1. Wesleyan Methodist Original Connexion index of attendances in 1851

high figures were recorded to the north of the West Riding and in the west of the North Riding. Throughout this large area percentage-share measures of attendances show Wesleyan Methodists in excess of 23 per cent. The district of Reeth in the North Riding recorded the highest measures in England and Wales, with indexes of sittings and attendances at over 44 per cent. The denomination was clearly at its most influential along much of the North Sea coast, from south Northumberland to Norfolk, including the Wash and the Fens. There were relatively few other areas of comparable Wesleyan strength. The most significant of these was in Cornwall, most noticeably in the west of the county. Districts like Redruth and Truro were especially notable. The denomination was strong also along the Sussex–Kent border, in south Gloucestershire and north Somerset near to the Bristol Channel, in parts of the Black Country, and in a few scattered locations in north and central Wales.

By comparison the denomination had low figures in a broad swathe of districts from south Norfolk to the English Channel between Lymington in Hampshire and Eastbourne in Sussex, and this included London. In many of these districts Wesleyan Methodism was not represented at all. Such weakness extended also to south Wales, to much of the west midlands, Somerset and Devon, to most districts bordering Scotland, and to one or two coastal districts in the north-west. Despite its influence in Cornwall, the decline of the denomination's fortunes across the Cornish border in Devon was remarkable, and probably owes much to the older dissent established in Devon before 1740.[10]

Smaller areas of Wesleyan weakness were most commonly associated with high and rapidly expanding populations. The largest of these (outside London) included south Lancashire and industrial parts of the West Riding. The denomination was weak in many urban areas, like Exeter, Derby, Nottingham, Leicester, Newcastle upon Tyne, Hull, Norwich, King's Lynn and Bristol. The Wesleyan Methodists were rather slower to construct chapels in response to population changes in such areas than is sometimes asserted, and the numbers of townspeople to each chapel could be very large, despite the sizes of the urban chapels.[11]

[10] R. Brown, *Church and State in Modern Britain, 1700–1850* (1991), p. 460.

[11] Persons per place of worship ranged from 402 at Helmsley in the North Riding of Yorkshire to 79,759 in Whitechapel. The vast majority of districts had values in the

The 'index of occupancy' provides the best measure of where the denomination had over-provided, and where it was under pressure with attendances far exceeding sittings.[12] This index for the Wesleyans is shown in figure 4.2. High indices indicate high attendances relative to sittings, and therefore high pressure on Wesleyan provision. Low indices indicate lack of demand for existing sittings, and thus over-supply by the denomination. The measure ranged from 25 at Bellingham in Northumberland up to 645 in Billericay, Essex. In a small number of districts the index was very high indeed, indicating a severe lack of seating provision relative to demand. There was one large band of high values where pressure on Wesleyan provision was obvious. This stretched from just south of the Wash through the south midlands and on south-westward through Wiltshire and Dorset, to Poole Harbour and Purbeck. This band was broadest in its northern parts and here included districts in south Cambridgeshire, north Hertfordshire, all of Bedfordshire, Buckinghamshire, Huntingdonshire and east Oxfordshire. Further south-west, the greatest concentration of high values was in Wiltshire and along the Dorset–Hampshire border. This zone of above-average indices also spread further west from Poole Harbour to Falmouth. Other high index of occupancy values included a number of coastal, or near coastal, districts in the census eastern division,[13] and a larger group in Kent. There were high values in a few north Welsh districts (where Calvinistic Methodism dominated), in parts of the industrial West Riding, and in and around Birmingham. In some London districts, but by no means the majority, the figures were also above average.

In other words, all these areas were ones where there would have been scope for Wesleyan Methodism to have expanded provision, to its probable advantage. These districts often overlapped with 'core' areas for the Anglican Church and old dissent. Despite the obvious demand for Wesleyan Methodism in these areas (which must have been clear in more rudimentary ways to mobile preachers with a sense of comparison), the denomination failed in (or desisted from) building sufficient chapels to meet it. Although Wesleyan Methodist

range up to 5,000. The average sizes of Wesleyan chapels were largest in the south Lancashire–West Riding industrial belt, the south Wales valleys, the Black Country, mining areas of Cornwall, and on Tyneside, as well as London and some less industrial county towns. [12] See appendix C for a definition and discussion of this measure.

[13] Norfolk, Suffolk and Essex.

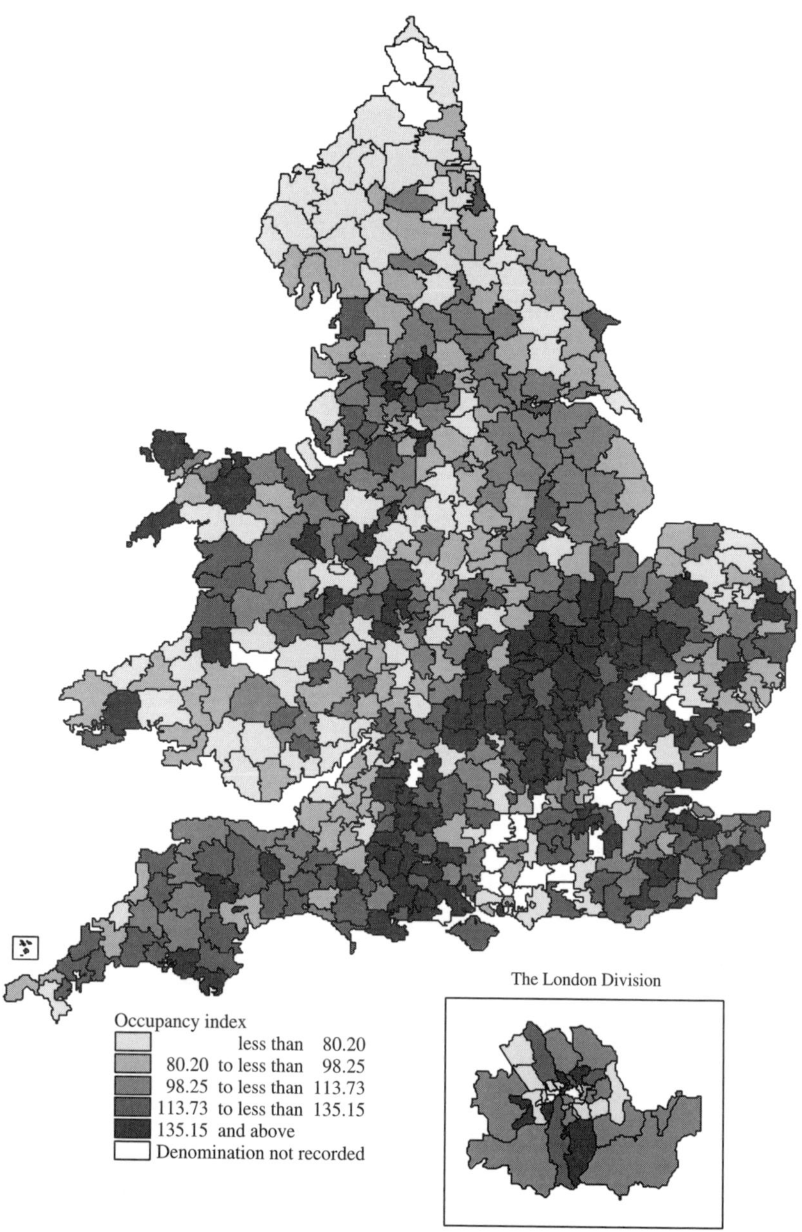

Figure 4.2. Wesleyan Methodist Original Connexion index of occupancy in 1851

indices of attendances were high in some such areas (like south Norfolk to Oxfordshire), there seems to have been some reluctance to tread further on other denominations' ground.

By contrast, this index of occupancy was low in many northern districts, particularly the most northerly areas.[14] The same can be said for much of the North Riding, south Wales, west Sussex, and parts of Essex. In the west and north midlands the pattern was more complex, but the figures were low in the Vale of Evesham, in north and east Staffordshire, and in much of Derbyshire and Nottinghamshire.

One can therefore summarise demand relative to supply as follows. In the largest area of Wesleyan Methodist strength, in the north down to the north midlands,[15] denominational provision was not usually under any real pressure. Through the whole of these regions the Wesleyan supply of chapels and sittings was adequate and, in more northerly areas, provision far exceeded demand. In other Wesleyan Methodist areas, however, the ratio of attendances to sittings was rather higher. This was true in Cornwall, but was much more so in those districts extending from Norfolk to Weymouth. The interesting question to ask here is why the denomination did not take advantage of this. One answer seems to be the prior strength of other denominations. Where the denomination was at its weakest, this did not seem to be because of lack of provision. In south Wales, for example, the index of occupancy was well below average. It is worth pointing out that this measure for the Wesleyan Methodists was far lower in many urban areas than was true for many other denominations, and this shows a relative lack of pressure on Wesleyan urban chapels.

It was originally Wesley's intention not to rival the Church of England, but rather to reinforce it where it was failing. This would certainly suggest an association between Anglican weakness and the key areas of Wesleyan Methodism. At first sight this appears to be borne out, and the northern over-supply just discussed would further reinforce this. One thinks of the large and scattered parishes in many parts of Yorkshire and the north, as well as Cornwall or north Wales. The internal organisation of Wesleyan Methodism, with its circuit systems, lay preachers and field preaching, meant

[14] And see R. Currie, 'A micro-theory of Methodist growth', *Proceedings of the Wesleyan Historical Society*, 36 (1967), 73.

[15] The North Midland division was taken by the census as Leicestershire, Rutland, Nottinghamshire, Derbyshire and Lincolnshire.

that people in scattered or neglected settlements could be very effectively serviced. We have shown how the Church of England was also weak in newly-industrialised areas, and here too Wesleyan Methodism was often (but certainly not always) to the fore. One thinks for example of the Black Country and Birmingham, and the south-eastern Welsh valleys.

At this point it is worth returning to the historiography. Gay argued that the distribution of Methodism in the nineteenth century 'was largely determined by the geographical variations in the Church of England's ability to maintain a proper pastoral oversight of the people in the 18th century . . . John Wesley saw his own work as complementing and reinforcing the work of the Established Church in areas where the Church was weak. Where the Church was running efficiently and catering for the needs of the local community, Wesley left well alone.'[16] Gay added that this was especially true in Cornwall. The spread of Methodism in that county was, he felt, impossible to explain without close reference to the established church.[17] He consistently interpreted the spread of Wesleyan Methodism with reference to Anglican weaknesses. There is clearly much truth in this. An added consideration is that Methodism gained from anti-clerical sentiments in those rural areas where the established church had been so successful in recent land reorganisations. In some rural areas (Gay noted Lincolnshire and Yorkshire, but one can go much wider than that),[18] judgement between Anglican and Wesleyan merits were swayed by the experience of enclosures, tithe and/or its commutation, and the other changes affecting rural livelihoods.[19] There is an obvious overlap between many areas of Wesleyan attendances (and especially pressure on Wesleyan chapels) and the map of parliamentary enclosure.[20] Many historians have documented how the wider agrarian changes often conduced to ill-feeling against the established church, and gains for Methodism. In many such regions Methodism adopted a class-conscious form: 'the chapel became a symbol of revolt against the squire and the vicar, and a centre where the agricultural labourer could gain his self-respect and his indepen-

[16] J. D. Gay, *The Geography of Religion in England* (1971), p. 145.

[17] *Ibid.*, p. 159. Brown, *Church and State in Modern Britain*, p. 121, sees Methodism as 'virtually the established religion' in Cornwall, as in areas like Kingswood or Newcastle.

[18] Gay, *Geography of Religion*, p. 162.

[19] K. D. M. Snell, *Annals of the Labouring Poor: Social Change and Agrarian England, 1660–1900* (Cambridge, 1985), chs. 1–4.

[20] M. E. Turner, *English Parliamentary Enclosure* (Folkestone, 1980), pp. 35, 59.

dence'.[21] As will be seen below, such arguments are even more persuasive when applied to Primitive Methodism.

The progress of Methodism in the face of weak alternative denominations has been stressed by a number of historians. Some have indicated that Methodism made headway in industrial areas because older denominations were fairly well established in the countryside.[22] Pelling supported this argument, making reference for example to Yorkshire, and notably to the West Riding.[23] These arguments are backed up by impressionistic viewing of the maps. However, it is possible to exaggerate them. It will be seen in chapter 6 that quantitative testing sustains them, but not very strongly. There were reasonably persistent inverse spatial relationships between the Anglican Church and the Wesleyans, but these results were rather weak, and probably weaker than statements like those by Machin, Pelling or Gay imply.

We have stressed how flexible Wesleyan Methodist organisation was compared to the established church, and how (over its first century or so) it could more readily adapt provision to demand. It was evident to Mann and many others that 'The practice of the Wesleyan Methodists is, not to preach long in any place unless they succeed in forming a "society".'[24] Where they were unsuccessful, they moved on, concentrating their resources where there were receptive congregations, and where the established church had insufficient support to muster effective opposition.[25] Their patterns of provision

21 Gay, *Geography of Religion*, p. 163. Among many possible references, see E. J. Evans, 'Some reasons for the growth of English rural anti-clericalism, c.1750–c.1830', *Past and Present*, 66 (1975); A. Howkins, *Poor Labouring Men: Rural Radicalism in Norfolk, 1870–1923* (1985), pp. 39–56; J. Obelkevich, *Religion and Rural Society: South Lindsey, 1825–1875* (Oxford, 1976), pp. 213–56; W. Cobbett, *Rural Rides* (1830, Harmondsworth, 1967 edn), pp. 106, 180.

22 For example, G. I. T. Machin, *Politics and the Churches in Great Britain, 1832–1868* (1977), p. 8.

23 H. Pelling, *Social Geography of British Elections, 1885–1910* (1967), pp. 289–90.

24 *Census of Religious Worship*, p. lxxv.

25 Anglican opposition to Methodism cannot be underestimated, and played a significant part in determining the eventual locations of Methodism. See for example N. Ratcliff (ed.), *The Journal of John Wesley, 1735–1790* (1940), pp. 131, 155–61, 164–7, 168, 172–6, 188–9, 191, 196–5, 230–1; J. Walsh, 'Methodism and the mob in the eighteenth century', in G. J. Cuming and D. Baker (eds.), *Studies in Church History: Popular Belief and Practice* (Cambridge, 1972), pp. 213–17; A. D. Gilbert, *Religion and Society in Industrial England: Church, Chapel and Social Change, 1740–1914* (1976), pp. 78–9; J. Ritson, *The Romance of Primitive Methodism* (1909), pp. 161–73; A. W. Davison, *Derby: its Rise and Progress* (Wakefield, 1970), p. 118; K. D. M. Snell, *Church and Chapel in the North Midlands: Religious Observance in the Nineteenth Century* (Leicester, 1991), pp. 71–2, n. 9.

reflect this to some extent, although one drawback to the ease with which they built chapels in the north was a tendency there to over-express themselves in bricks and mortar. Whatever the initial hopes they may have had, our figures suggest that the scale on which they did this was often superfluous.[26]

Finally, the geography of the Wesleyan Methodists bears witness also to the numerous schisms that the denomination faced from the 1790s onwards. In 1797 the New Connexion was formed; in 1810 the Primitive Methodists left the Original Connexion; they were followed by the Wesleyan Methodist Association in 1827; and shortly before the Religious Census, in 1849, the Wesleyan Reformers began further to swell the dissentient Methodist groups. Each successive schism had regional aspects to it. There were many lesser schisms, like that of the Independent Methodists, and some such egress was very local indeed. These various off-shoots from Wesleyan Methodism often attained significant regional followings, bearing distinctive relations to the parent organisation. Sometimes schism took on a colouring of social class, but in all cases these Methodist secessions limited the amplitude of the Original Connexion, especially as congregations breaking away often took their chapels with them. It is to these other Methodist denominations that we now turn.

The Wesleyan Methodist New Connexion

The Wesleyan Methodist New Connexion was the oldest of the denominations to split from the Original Connexion. In 1797, when the Wesleyan Methodist Original Connexion formally left the Church of England, Alexander Kilham, the New Connexion leader, refused to sign the Plan of Pacification and the New Connexion was born. Kilham had long been lobbying for more democracy within the movement, for wider control by local congregations and chapel trustees, and for the right of Methodism to give its own sacraments. He felt that the Wesleyan leadership wielded too much power, and he wished to see lay responsibility enlarged. In terms of theological

[26] Over-provision of churches by this and other denominations is a central theme in R. Gill, *The Myth of the Empty Church* (1993). See also S. J. D. Green, *Religion in the Age of Decline: Organisation and Experience in Industrial Yorkshire, 1870–1920* (Cambridge, 1996), p. 89, on 'the Victorian notion of sacred progress measured in ecclesiastical bricks and mortar'.

belief the Original and New Connexions were similar; but they stood for very different levels of centralised control, democracy and distributed power within their organisations.[27] The New Connexion was indeed called the 'Tom Paine Methodists' in Huddersfield, and E. P. Thompson saw it as draining the 'more democratic and intellectual elements' of Methodism.[28]

This denomination was found in just 83 registration districts – 13 per cent of the total. Its index of attendances is mapped in figure 4.3. It was unrepresented in East Anglia (with the exception of Yarmouth) and in the south-east. It was only present in one Cornish district, in Weymouth in the south-west, and in only two districts in the far north-east of Wales. It was more common in the north and west midlands, in Yorkshire, and in the extreme north-east, being 'essentially a phenomenon of the Midlands and the North'.[29] However, it was absent from Cumberland, Westmorland, the North Riding and Rutland; and in several other counties it was present in only one or two districts. This makes it weaker in coverage than either the Wesleyan Methodist Association or the Wesleyan Reformers; but where it was found it was generally as strong as the former and rather stronger than the Wesleyan Reformers.

The distribution of the New Connexion was quite complex, without any large regions of high values, but rather several small groups of scattered districts.[30] The largest of these was on the Derbyshire–West Riding border. Others included Gateshead and Tynemouth, Hayfield, Chesterfield, Wortley, Barnsley, and Ecclesall-Bierlow along the Yorkshire and north midlands border. In the west midlands, there were one or two districts in north Staffordshire and around the Forest of Arden. The denomination was fairly strong throughout industrial north Staffordshire, and in parts of Cheshire and Lancashire – particularly along the Yorkshire border, around Tyneside, and on the Derbyshire–Nottinghamshire border.

These patterns fill out in a westerly direction some of the midland

[27] Gay, *Geography of Religion*, pp. 149–50; Currie, *Methodism Divided*, pp. 27–28, 58–60; Rev. A. Kilham, *The Life of the Rev. Alexander Kilham . . . One of the Founders of the Methodist New Connexion in the Year 1797. Including a Full Account of the Disputes which Occasioned the Separation* (1838), pp. 214–15.

[28] E. P. Thompson, *The Making of the English Working Class* (1963, Harmondsworth, 1975 edn), pp. 49–50.

[29] Gay, *Geography of Religion*, p. 150.

[30] The indexes of sittings and attendances never reached high levels, at the most between about 7 and 10 in Stoke on Trent, Dudley and Stourbridge.

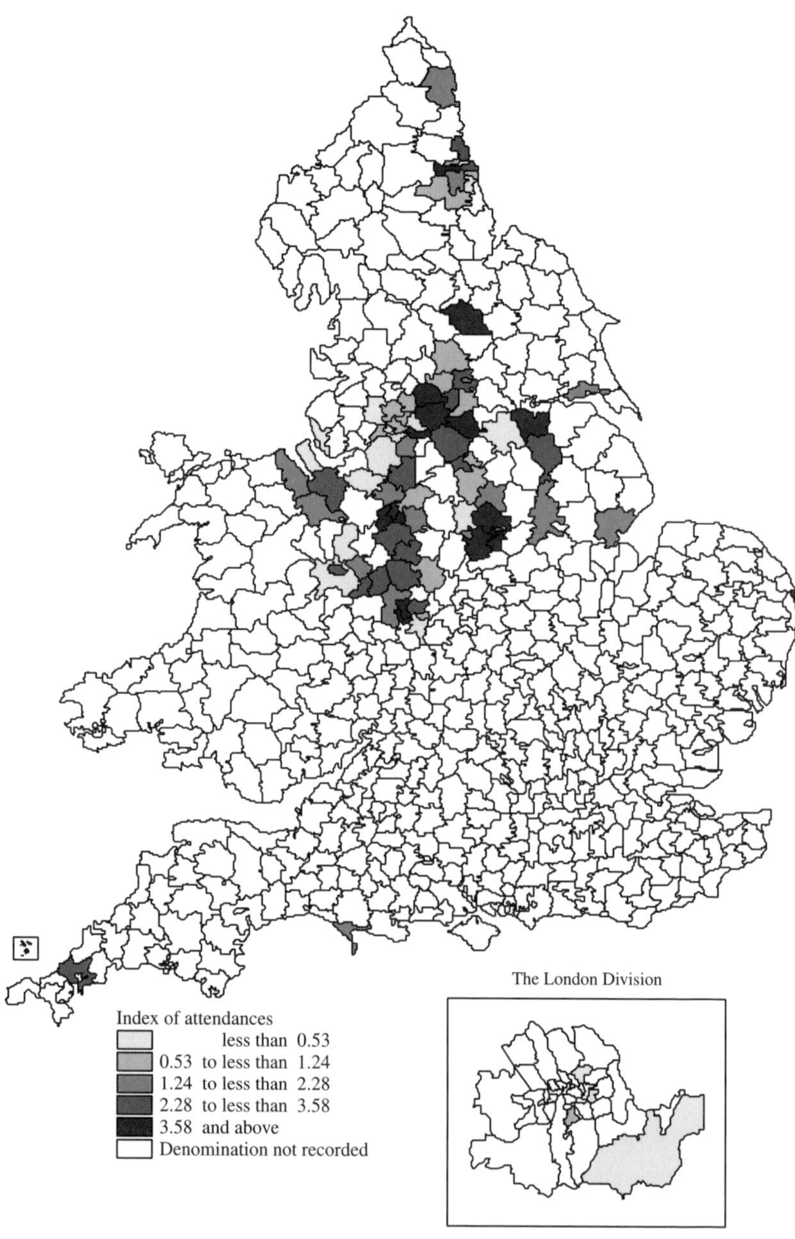

Figure 4.3. Wesleyan Methodist New Connexion index of attendances in 1851

and north-eastern Wesleyan Methodist areas, extending as they do into the more radical textile and pottery manufacturing districts. Given theological similarities between the New and Original Connexions, it was to be expected that they might win converts in similar areas; but the more questioning stance of the New Connexion on secular issues, and its stress on 'the rights of Englishmen', clearly appealed more to many industrial workers in counties like Staffordshire, Nottinghamshire and the West Riding, and in towns like Sheffield and its surrounding hamlets.[31] The New Connexion was particularly successful in securing new members when the Original Connexion suffered local disputes. For example, during the Cornish revival of 1813–14 there was dissension within the Original Connexion over the division of responsibility between ministers and laity. The New Connexion developed as a result in the Falmouth district, which included Ladock chapel where the dispute was centred. Similar conflicts and outcomes took place in London during 1816 and 1817.[32] Currie wrote that 'New Connexionists tried to offset the disadvantage of their speedy expulsion from Wesleyanism by actively proselytizing that denomination with New Connexion propaganda',[33] and such efforts continued during the first half of the nineteenth century. The New Connexion frequently invoked the spirit of John Wesley in its own defence and in criticisms of the Original Connexion.

Primitive Methodism

After Wesleyan Methodism, Primitive Methodism was the most important Methodist denomination in terms of coverage. It was present in over 70 per cent of districts in England and Wales. In terms of places of worship, sittings and attendances, the Primitive Methodists were second only to the Original Connexion. The denomination had 2,871 places of worship compared to the Original Connexion's 6,579, a total of 414,030 sittings compared to 1,446,580, and 511,195 attendances compared to 1,544,528 for the Original Connexion.[34]

Primitive Methodism was formed by Hugh Bourne and William

31 'They remained in touch with the industrial workers and were not unsympathetic to the radical cause.' P. B. Cliff, *The Rise and Development of the Sunday School Movement in England, 1780–1980* (Redhill, 1986), p. 105.

32 Currie, *Methodism Divided*, pp. 61–2.

33 *Ibid.*, pp. 59–60.

34 *Census of Religious Worship*, pp. clxxxi–clxxxii. These figures incorporate Horace Mann's estimates for defective returns.

Clowes in Tunstall and Burslem in north Staffordshire in 1810–12, following an evangelistic movement over the previous decade.[35] Both men had originally been Wesleyan Methodist ministers. The denomination arose as a result of the perceived increasing conservatism of the Original Connexion, which appeared to be stagnating, becoming worldly, intent on appeasing a suspicious government, and failing to win over further converts and the working classes.[36] The Wesleyan Methodist leadership itself was attempting to restrict field preaching and 'Camp Meetings' – several days of outdoor singing, praying and preaching – which Bourne, Clowes and others organised, under the influence of the American Methodist Lorenzo Dow. While in doctrinal terms (belief in grace and spiritual equality), as well as in many features of organisation,[37] the Primitive Methodists differed little from the Original Connexion, they sought to recover a vitality which they felt was dwindling in Wesleyan Methodism. One of their historians has written of how 'the simplicity and spiritual fervour of the Primitives seemed like the renaissance of a Methodist golden age that had apparently died with John Wesley'.[38] The Connexion had a straightforward approach to preaching which emphasised the importance of the gospel: 'They preached the "three R's: ruin, repentance, and redemption"; the appropriate style was "plain, pithy, pointed, and practical". Conversions were the aim, as many and as quickly as possible.'[39] Camp meetings and lovefeasts were held regularly by the Connexion.

In organisation, like the Original Connexion, the Primitive Methodists were composed into classes, societies, circuits and districts. In conference, however, laymen had more influence than was the case for the Original Connexion.[40] Individual circuits had much

[35] Among its best histories are L. Petty, *The History of the Primitive Methodist Connexion* (1864, 1880 edn); H. B. Kendall, *The Origin and History of the Primitive Methodist Church*, 2 vols. (n.d., c. 1905); Ritson, *Romance of Primitive Methodism*; J. S. Werner, *The Primitive Methodist Connexion: its Background and Early History* (1984).

[36] *Census of Religious Worship*, p. lxxxi; Werner, *Primitive Methodist Connexion*, p. 15; H. McLeod, *Religion and the Working Class in Nineteenth-Century Britain* (1984), pp. 26–30.

[37] H. B. Kendall, *Handbook of Primitive Methodist Church Principles and Polity* (1913), pp. 61–2.

[38] Werner, *Primitive Methodist Connexion*, pp. 14–15.

[39] Obelkevich, *Religion and Rural Society*, pp. 223–4.

[40] Their first conference was held in 1820. This was followed by very rapid expansion, especially in 1820–4. R. Currie, A. D. Gilbert and L. Horsley, *Churches and Churchgoers: Patterns of Church Growth in the British Isles since 1700* (Oxford, 1977), pp. 70, 82.

more power. It has been pointed out that the Connexion was in its early decades composed of independent circuits. By the mid nineteenth century these had amalgamated into semi-independent districts, being from 1849 under stricter central authority, with binding rules and procedures, a structure that led to the formal emergence of a unified church.[41]

The main areas of Primitive Methodist strength may be viewed in figure 4.4, and show many similarities to those of the Wesleyans. They included, along the east coast, districts in south-west Northumberland and west county Durham, parts of the North and East Ridings, most of north Lincolnshire, and much of Norfolk.[42] The Primitive Methodists were also strong on the English side of the Welsh border, in north Staffordshire and the pottery towns, Derbyshire, Nottinghamshire, and on the Hampshire–Berkshire border. Much the same picture emerged from their percentage-share values, which were high in central and northern England. Such areas included the Northumberland–Durham border, a larger area from Pickering in the North Riding through most of the East Riding and north Lincolnshire, parts of Staffordshire, Derbyshire and Nottinghamshire and a region extending from Cheshire and Shropshire down the English side of the Welsh border. In some of these regions the denomination was of very considerable significance. For example, at Weardale in county Durham it had 2,735 sittings (after correction) compared to 2,720 for the Church of England, and in Alston it also had more sittings than the Anglican Church. Even in an area like the Clun district (Shropshire), it had 21 places of worship while the Church of England had 19 churches, although it could not match the Anglican sittings or attendances there.[43]

Primitive Methodist places of worship were small, and (allowing for

[41] Kendall, *Origin and History of the Primitive Methodist Church*, vol. 1, pp. 159–61; Werner, *Primitive Methodist Connexion*, pp. 136–40; R. Colls, *The Pitmen of the Northern Coalfield: Work, Culture and Protest, 1790–1850* (Manchester, 1987), pp. 178–9.

[42] See also Rev. H. Woodcock, *Piety among the Peasantry: being Sketches of Primitive Methodism in the Yorkshire Wolds* (1889); W. M. Patterson, *Northern Primitive Methodism* (1909); E. J. Hobsbawm, *Primitive Rebels: Studies in Archaic Forms of Social Movement in the Nineteenth and Twentieth Centuries* (Manchester, 1959, 1963 edn), pp. 136–7.

[43] The Primitive Methodist index of attendance was over 20 in Alston and Gainsborough, coming just below that in districts like Walsingham, Pickering, Whitchurch, Cricklade, Downham, Glanford Brigg, Goole or Wayland.

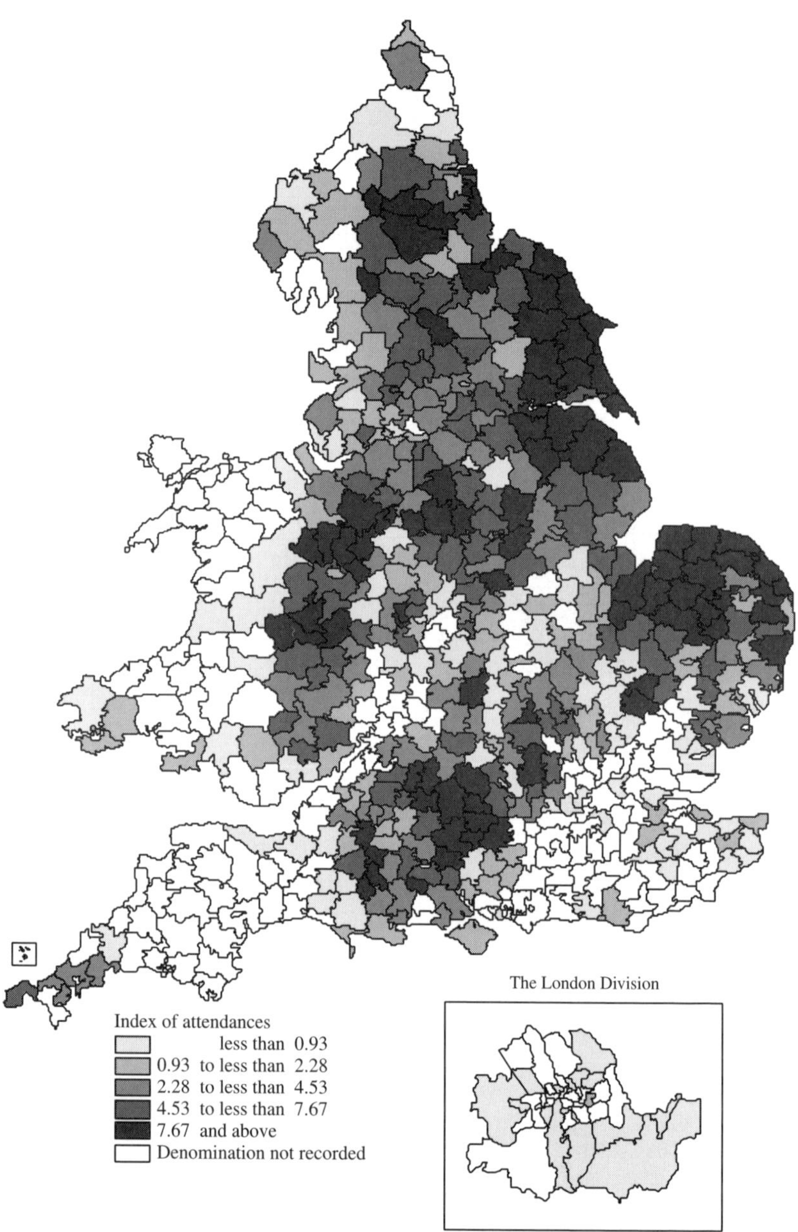

Figure 4.4. Primitive Methodist index of attendances in 1851

general strength) there tended to be more of them relative to some other denominations. This can affect figures based on places of worship in various ways, showing them to have a strong percentage share of churches compared to other denominations. For example, if one compares mean and median chapel sizes for the Primitive and Wesleyan Methodists, the former were 154 and 124 (sittings) respectively, while the Wesleyans were 243 and 178. This may have rendered Primitive Methodism a less visually impressive denomination compared to some others, but it probably both appealed to lower social classes, and helped to avoid inflexibly high costs of maintenance and administration. Such smaller buildings were also consistent with a more participatory and democratic church.

The Primitive Methodists were almost completely absent from much of Wales, from many areas in the south-west and especially east Cornwall, Devon,[44] much of Somerset, and many areas of south-east England, like Sussex, most of Surrey, parts of Kent, and all but the north-east of Essex. They also had no presence in a scattered band of districts from the Wash to the Severn estuary, in parts of north Lancashire and in some areas bordering Scotland. They were weak in much of southern and central England south of the Severn–Wash line, with the important exceptions of Norfolk, adjoining parts of Cambridgeshire and Suffolk, and a large area of Wiltshire, Hampshire and Berkshire. In London, indexes of sittings and attendances were very low, where the denomination was present.

The index of occupancy for the Primitive Methodists (see figure 4.5) ranged from a low of 4 at Morpeth in Northumberland,[45] to a high of 359 at Cleobury-Mortimer in Shropshire (where there were 4 places of worship with sittings totalling 128 and total attendances of 460). The largest group of above-average values was from East Anglia to Dorset and east Somerset, a pattern shared with Wesleyan Methodism. South-east of this line, where the denomination was present, a few high values were also recorded, and this was so also in Birmingham, the Black Country and in north Lancashire.

As with Wesleyan Methodism, their index of occupancy was below average in the most northerly districts (except an area around Newcastle upon Tyne), in parts of the North and East Ridings, in most

[44] And see Currie, *Methodism Divided*, pp. 101–2.

[45] Here the two Primitive Methodist chapels contained, after data correction, 472 sittings, but attendances of only 20 were recorded on Census Sunday.

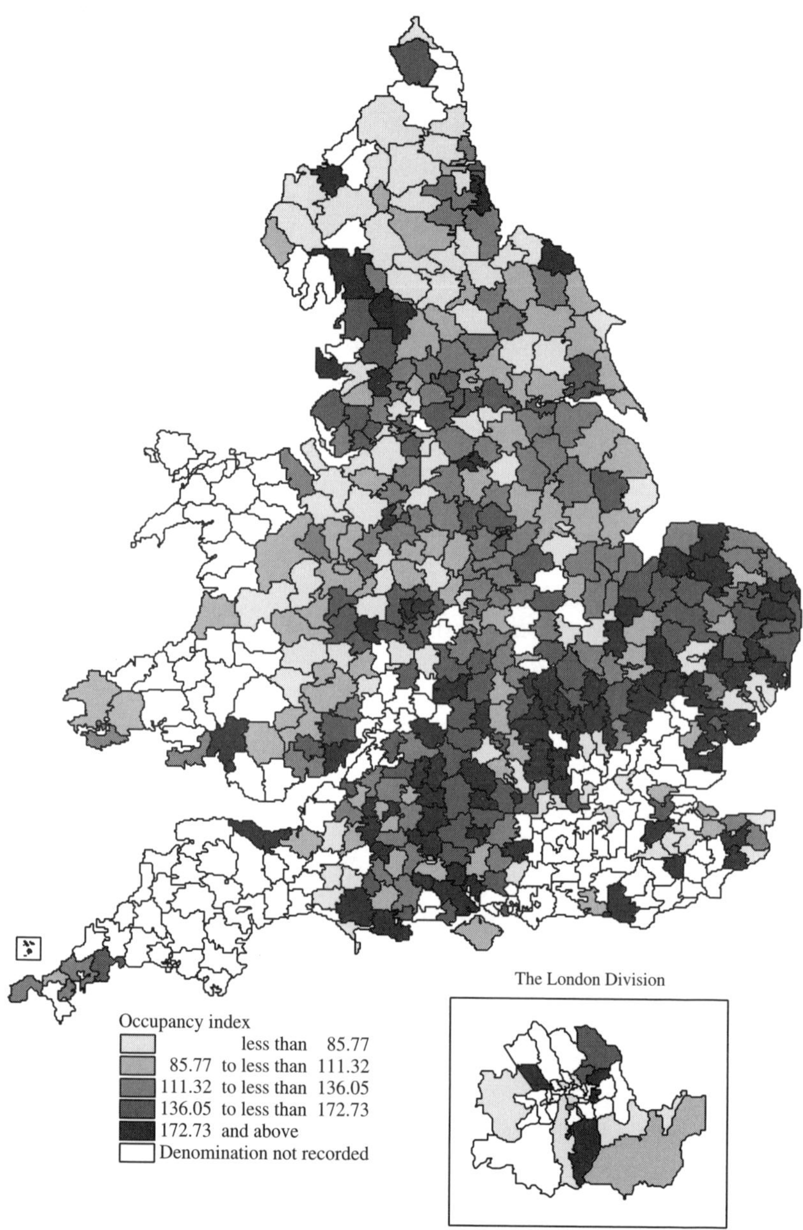

Figure 4.5. Primitive Methodist index of occupancy in 1851

of Wales and adjoining English districts, and in the west and north midlands more generally. The generally poor correspondence between the index of attendance and the index of occupancy suggests that provision of places of worship and sittings did not have a major effect on this denomination. It was after all flexible, adaptable, still often very humble in its places of worship (using barns, shops and other such buildings as well as formally designated chapels), and so perhaps this is a result that was to be expected.

Primitive Methodism therefore tended to coincide regionally with Wesleyan Methodism, 'clinging to its skirts', as Kendall put it.[46] In some ways the two denominations were similar and predisposed to gain converts in the same areas. Primitive Methodism had after all broken away from the Original Connexion. The Primitive Methodists had their original support around the Staffordshire Potteries, where William Clowes' father was a Burslem potter, a trade William had been apprenticed to. A process of diffusion accounts for the denomination's outgoing success from this region and in nearby Derbyshire, Shropshire, and along the central Welsh borderlands. Kendall and others have described also the zeal with which the sect spread north-east along the Trent.[47] Its followers were often from lower status occupational groups like agricultural workers and miners: for example the Durham miners, fishermen in East Anglia,[48] or railway workers in Swindon and Didcot.[49] In south Lindsey a significant proportion of Primitive Methodists were farm labourers,[50] and much the same was true of Norfolk and the East Riding.[51] Earlier work on baptism registers in the north midlands showed how Primitive Methodism differed in social and occupational terms from Wesleyan Methodism, and supported

46 Pearson's correlation coefficient between the Wesleyan Methodist and Primitive Methodist index of sittings was 0.483. (See chapter 6 for further measures of this sort.) Kendall, *Origin and History of the Primitive Methodist Church*, vol. 1, p. 117. While this generalisation certainly holds, some of its best ventures were nevertheless in localities by-passed by the Wesleyan Methodists, like parts of north Staffordshire. D. M. Valenze, *Prophetic Sons and Daughters: Female Preaching and Popular Religion in Industrial England* (Princeton, 1985), p. 82.

47 Kendall, *Origin and History of the Primitive Methodist Church*, vol. 1, p. 29. Mow Cop, a place of such significance for the Primitives, was near the source of the Trent, and the river assumed great symbolic importance in some accounts of the gushing flow of the denomination.

48 A. H. Patterson, *From Hayloft to Temple: Primitive Methodism in Yarmouth* (Norwich, 1903).

49 Gay, *Geography of Religion*, p. 151.

50 Obelkevich, *Religion and Rural Society*, p. 220.

51 Pelling, *Social Geography*, pp. 90, 290.

Kendall's claim that his denomination had an attraction for lower social classes and manual workers.[52] As Mann wrote of the Connexion: 'Its sphere of operations is . . . much more exclusively among the poor; numbers of whom, no doubt, who probably would never venture to the formal meetings of the other sects, are found attending the out-door preaching or engaging in the cottage service conducted by the Primitive Methodists.'[53] Such class comparisons between these leading Methodist denominations suggest why they were found in similar regions, and why the Primitives did well among labourers in the arable eastern counties as well as in some areas of heavy industry that were drawing in rural migrants.

It is often suggested that Primitive Methodism was strongly rural as a phenomenon, although there were important exceptions like the potteries and the Durham and Northumberland mining communities.[54] The agricultural union leader Joseph Arch was after all a Primitive Methodist lay preacher, as were many of his associates.[55]

[52] Snell, *Church and Chapel in the North Midlands*, ch. 5. Analysis of any Primitive Methodist baptism register indicates very large numbers of labourers. See for example the records of the Scotter circuit: Lincs. C.R.O.: Meth. B/Brigg/33/1 (1825–37), where 59 per cent of entries had labourer fathers. Or see Lincs. C.R.O., Meth. B/Alford/33/1; Meth. B/Boston/33/1; Meth. B/Sleaford/45/1; Meth. B/Grimsby/33/1; Horncastle District Marriage Book, 5TP/2/2/1–2; Leics. C.R.O.: Whitwick and Coleorton, N/M/73/48 (where miners outnumber labourers); Hinckley and Barwell, N/M/142/75 (where framework knitters outnumber labourers); or George Street, Leicester, MF/15/3; Derbs. C.R.O.: Ilkeston, RG/4/33, where again the dominant occupations were coalminer, framework knitter and labourer; these were rivalled by 'naylors' in Duffield, RG/4/565. See also E. D. Steele, *Palmerston and Liberalism, 1855–1865* (Cambridge, 1991), p. 167: 'a small but authoritative middle-class element, varied in size between the major sects, strongest among Baptists and Congregationalists, weakest in Primitive Methodism'; T. J. Nossiter, *Influence, Opinion and Political Idioms in Reformed England: Case Studies from the North-east, 1832–74* (Brighton, 1975), pp. 17–19: 'overall the social gulf between the worshippers in a wesleyan and a primitive chapel was a real one. The wesleyans were respectable middle and lower middle class shopkeepers, tradespeople and merchants'; McLeod, *Religion and the Working Class*, pp. 26–30; Currie, *Methodism Divided*, pp. 100–1, 206–7.

[53] *Census of Religious Worship*, p. lxxxiii.

[54] Hobsbawm, *Primitive Rebels*, pp. 137–8; R. Colls, *The Colliers Rant* (1977), pp. 76–101; and his *Pitmen of the Northern Coalfield*, pp. 118–203.

[55] P. Horn, *Joseph Arch* (1971). Primitive Methodist preachers were active union leaders in mining also – very many examples could be given, like Jonas Hooper of the South Derbyshire branch of the D.N.M.A. See C. Griffin, *The Leicestershire and South Derbyshire Miners, vol. 1, 1840–1914* (Coalville, 1981), p. 122; Colls, *Colliers Rant*, pp. 78, 98–9, 100, 115; Colls, *Pitmen of the Northern Coalfield*, esp. ch. 12. As Ritson wrote, 'this Church was almost without rival in the colliery villages'. Ritson, *Romance of Primitive Methodism*, pp. 278–84.

The denomination was found in many rural 'open' parishes, as will be seen later, tending to be excluded from estate villages or 'closed' parishes, as for example in south Lindsey.[56] The changes in patterns of rural life during the 1820s and 1830s, the seeming failures of rural protest in 1816, 1821–2 and particularly of Captain Swing in 1830–1, the antagonisms caused by the new poor law and the rural constabulary, the relinquishing of earlier paternalistic responsibilities among many rural elites and their stress on 'independence' among the labouring poor, were all considerations that tended to foster sectarian brands of rural religion. On small obtainable pieces of ground in many parts of arable England, Primitive Methodist chapels began to be erected in increasing numbers after 1830–1, and then at the same time as the union workhouses were being built.[57] For the next half century this was often to be the faith that 'Hodge' and his family alighted upon as they struggled for basic human recognition.[58] The literary evidence for this is overwhelming, although Wesleyan Methodism, the Baptists and (in the south-west) the Bible Christians also had a very large role to play here.[59] From a quantitative angle we can confirm that the denomination was strongly associated with districts of low population density, that is, with the more rural areas. Among Methodist denominations, the Welsh Calvinistic Methodists and then the Bible Christians were certainly the most rural in provenance; but they were

56 Obelkevich, *Religion and Rural Society*, p. 238; R. W. Ambler, *Ranters, Revivalists and Reformers: Primitive Methodism and Rural Society, South Lincolnshire, 1817–1875* (Hull, 1989), pp. 56–7.

57 This is clear from dates of the erection of chapels on the enumerators' forms. Primitive Methodist membership more than doubled between 1831 and 1841. Gilbert, *Religion and Society*, p. 31. See also E. J. Hobsbawm and G. Rudé, *Captain Swing* (1969, Harmondsworth, 1973 edn), pp. 248–51, where the stress is laid on the bitter aftermath of the Swing unrest; Colls, *Pitmen of the Northern Coalfield*, pp. 151–61, who rightly draws attention (among other factors) to the effects of cholera in 1831–2.

58 Gay, *Geography of Religion*, p. 151; Obelkevich, *Religion and Rural Society*, p. 256; Hobsbawm, *Primitive Rebels*, pp. 129, 135–42, 148, 190; H. Gurden, 'Primitive Methodism and agricultural trade unionism in Warwickshire, 1872–5', *Bulletin of the Society for the Study of Labour History*, 33 (1976); Ambler, *Ranters, Revivalists and Reformers*; Howkins, *Poor Labouring Men*, ch. 3. It was also a faith in which women could play a crucial role. See Valenze, *Prophetic Sons and Daughters*.

59 Beyond the above references, see J. E. Coulson, *The Peasant Preacher: Memorials of Mr. Charles Richardson* (n.d., 2nd edn, 1866). The way in which travelling Methodist preachers fitted into the interstices of rural communities in Sussex and Kent was explored, in a roundabout way, by S. Kaye-Smith's novel, *The Tramping Methodist* (1908, 1924 edn).

followed by Primitive Methodism.[60] Such results are what one would expect in the light of the latter's major distribution through counties like the East Riding, Lincolnshire and Norfolk, as well as parts of Wiltshire, Hampshire, Dorset and Berkshire.

The Wesleyan Methodist Association

Following Wesleyan and Primitive Methodism, the Wesleyan Methodist Association and the Wesleyan Reformers were the most extensive Methodist denominations, being found in similar numbers of registration districts: 116 and 108 out of 624 in England and Wales. And in other ways these two were broadly equal in strength. The origins of the Wesleyan Methodist Association go back to a seemingly slight argument over the provision of an organ in a Leeds Wesleyan Methodist chapel.[61] Yet the resulting dispute, over Conference power and what was felt to be an artificiality of worship in the Original Connexion, was symptomatic of many other confrontations between Conference and laity. Following the consequent rift in 1827, the Protestant Methodists were formed, headed by Matthew Johnson and James Sigston.[62] This group later merged with the Methodists led by Samuel Warren to form the Wesleyan Methodist Association, which held its first Assembly in 1836.[63]

A few districts aside, the Wesleyan Methodist Association could not compare in adherents to the Original Connexion or Primitive Methodism. Nor was it comparable in size to the major old dissenting denominations. Figure 4.6 shows that it was almost completely absent from large parts of the country, including Wales, East Anglia, the south-east, the south midlands, and the west and north midlands.

60 Spearman correlation coefficients between 1851 population density (people per square kilometre at registration-district level) and the main Methodist denominations' index of attendances (taking districts where each was present) were as follows: Calvinistic Methodism, −0.703; Bible Christianity, −0.442; Primitive Methodism, −0.288; Wesleyan Methodist Association, −0.239; Wesleyan Methodism, −0.215; the Wesleyan Reformers, −0.128; and the New Connexion, −0.127. In other words, they all tended to be inversely associated with urbanisation, and to be more associated with rural areas, the first three denominations most so.

61 Gay, *Geography of Religion*, pp. 154–5.

62 Currie, *Methodism Divided*, pp. 218–19.

63 The Wesleyan Methodist Association joined the Wesleyan Methodist Reformers in 1857 to form the United Free Methodist Church, which had almost 40,000 members and James Everett as its first president. In 1907 this amalgamated with the Bible Christians and the New Connexion to produce the United Methodist Church.

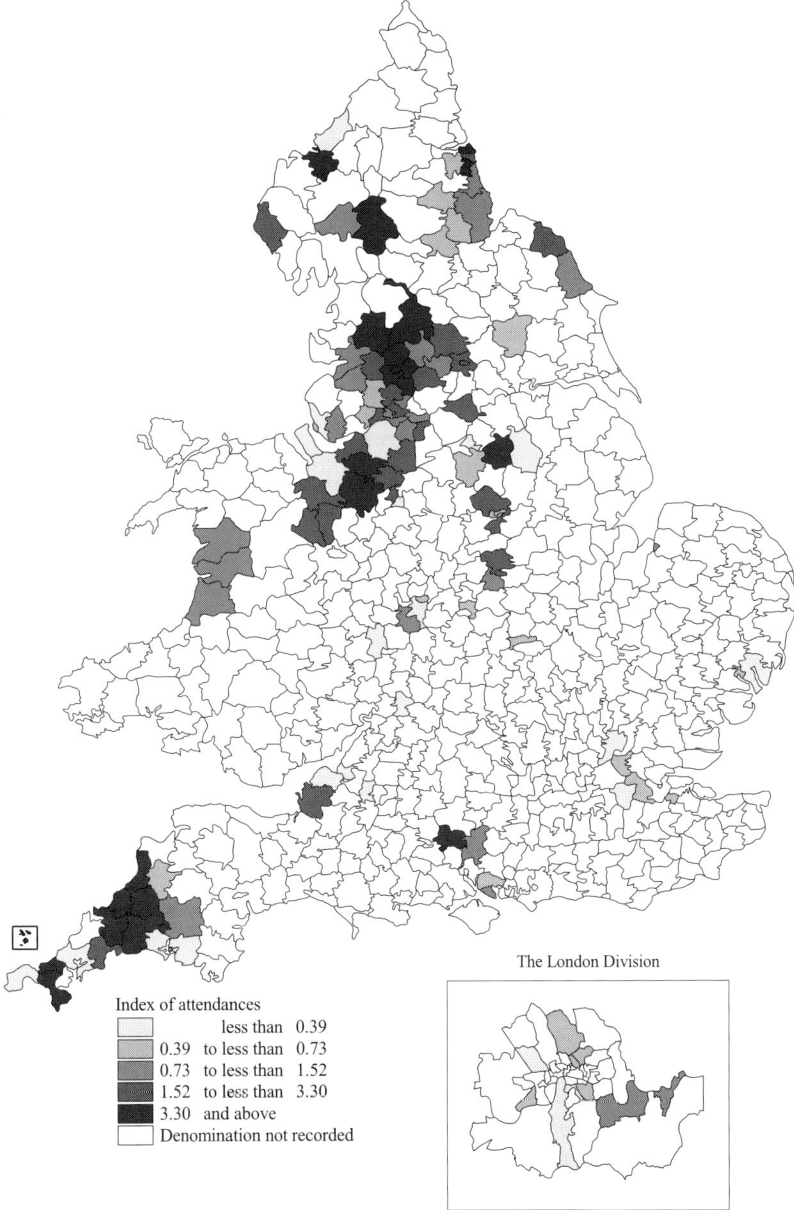

Figure 4.6. Wesleyan Methodist Association index of attendances in 1851

It was also unrepresented in the registration counties of Dorset, Wiltshire and Northumberland. The denomination was slightly stronger in terms of percentage share of places of worship than in its shares of sittings or attendances. This has been observed for other small denominations, and reflects the very small size of many places of worship (which were often not purpose-built buildings) compared to larger faiths.

The denomination was relatively conspicuous in a few districts, like Camelford and Bodmin in Cornwall. In these the Wesleyan Methodist Association secured percentage shares (however calculated) in excess of 20 per cent. It was particularly strong in Bodmin, where it had 19 places of worship and 3,902 sittings. The Association had in excess of 20 per cent of places of worship in a number of other districts, including Helston in Cornwall, Rochdale in Lancashire, and Carlisle in Cumberland. Other areas included five districts in eastern Cornwall, several in a discontinuous line from Skipton in the West Riding as far south as Nantwich in Cheshire, and isolated districts in Cumberland, Nottinghamshire and Hampshire. The denomination was also found in parts of London and surrounding areas, and between the Tyne and the Tees.

The Wesleyan Association coincided with the Original Connexion in Cornwall, and in some northern areas, but elsewhere not as much as one would expect. In the main strongholds of the Original Connexion this very strength seemed to preclude the Association. In some parts of England, most notably in Lancashire and Cheshire, where the Association did well, the Original Connexion appears correspondingly weaker, probably as a result of its societies losing support to the Association. About 6 per cent of Wesleyan members went over to the Association.[64] The denomination also made the most of the weaknesses of the established church. In Cornwall for example, large parishes, scattered settlements, fishing and semi-industrial communities, and a distinctive cultural identity sometimes still expressed in the Cornish language had weighed against the Church of England, and the Association clearly gained both from this, and from the lack of a strong tradition of Cornish old dissent compared to Devon. This inverse relation between the Anglican Church and the Association also held in industrial Lancashire and Yorkshire, in many ports, by the Solent and

[64] Currie, *Methodism Divided*, p. 65.

in the New Forest, in Woodbridge near Ipswich, in Bedminster and Axbridge, around Aberystwyth, and on Tyneside. Some such districts were industrial, and this provided a context also for the denomination in parts of London, Birmingham, Leicester and Nottingham.

The Wesleyan Reformers

The Wesleyan Reformers were formed only two years before the census was taken, following disagreement between James Everett and the head of the Original Connexion. Everett, William Griffith and Samuel Dunn were accused of complicity in publishing the 'Fly sheets' which criticised the Methodist establishment and leadership. Although this was the immediate cause of their expulsion by Conference in August 1849, there were underlying factors that were more important. It was felt that Jabez Bunting (called by some Reformers 'the Pope of Methodism') and his supporters had turned Conference into an oppressive metropolitan clique, that the domination of ministers in the Original Connexion was excessive, and that few opportunities in church governance and initiative remained open to lay members.[65] Sympathisers of the three men expelled were themselves either forced to resign or were ejected from the Connexion, and the episode caused intense ill-feeling in many areas. These expulsions and resignations were at their height at the time of the Religious Census, and indeed continued thereafter for some years, so the picture of the denomination that the census is able to provide is a fairly transitional one.[66]

Like the Wesleyan Methodist Association, the Wesleyan Reformers were not found in most of England and Wales. As seen in figure 4.7, they were very rarely present in the south-east and in Wales, the west midlands, the north-west and the far north. There were two main regions where the Reformers were successful, along with some smaller

[65] O. A. Beckerlegge, *The United Methodist Free Churches* (1957), pp. 30–9; W. H. Jones, *History of the Wesleyan Reform Union* (1952), p. 17; Obelkevich, *Religion and Rural Society*, pp. 184–6; R. Chew, *James Everett: a Biography* (1875). Bunting retained control of the Original Connexion until his death in 1858.

[66] It is also worth bearing in mind that some Wesleyan Reform chapels returned their census forms by still calling themselves 'Wesleyans', and this may cause underestimation of their numbers. It takes considerable local information to unravel such details, and so we have instead analysed the figures as published by Mann without making any changes to them.

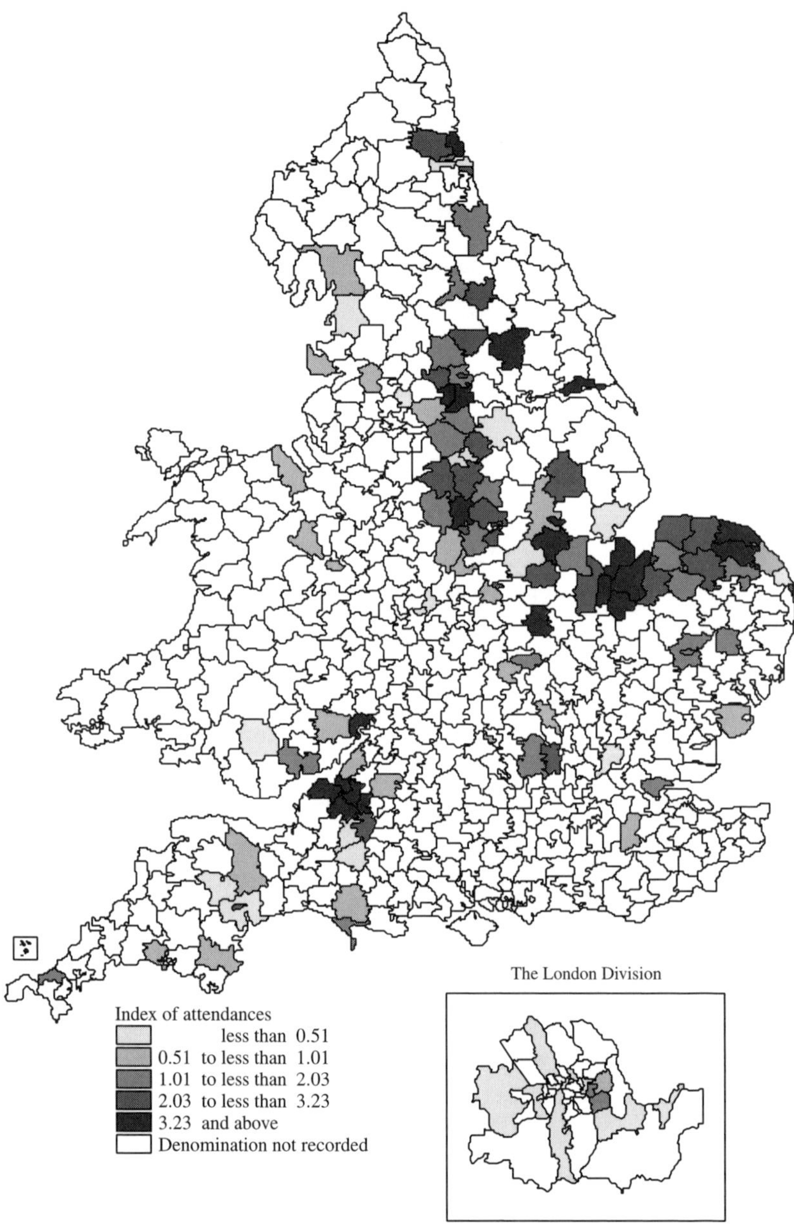

Figure 4.7. Wesleyan Reformer index of attendances in 1851

areas, and these show a striking tendency to complement the Wesleyan Methodist Association. The first region stretched from Oakham in Rutland, up to Grantham, through the Fens and across north Norfolk. Here the Wesleyan Reformers were most conspicuous in Wisbech, North Witchford and Holbeach, and further east in an area of north-east Norfolk centred on Aylsham. The second region was from north-west Leicestershire through much of Derbyshire (and bordering Nottinghamshire) into the West Riding. This continued as far as Castle Ward in Northumberland although the denomination was unrepresented in a number of these more northerly districts.[67] The Wesleyan Reformers were well above average strength in central and northern Derbyshire, in and north of Belper, in north Staffordshire, in the central West Riding (especially Wakefield), to the south of Sheffield and in Tynemouth and Castle Ward in Northumberland. The denomination was also particularly strong in north-east Somerset and in the far south-west of Gloucestershire. It was present (although not in any great strength) in parts of London, in three or four districts in south Lancashire, in the south Welsh valleys, and in five districts in Devon. However, if a 'core' area is to be identified for the Wesleyan Reformers it would be south of the Wash and in north Norfolk – particularly around Erpingham, Aylsham, Mitford, Walsingham, Docking and King's Lynn.[68]

The Religious Census affords a picture of the denomination at an early stage. Like the Primitives, it was found near the Original Connexion, comprising as it did many resigned or expelled members of the parent organisation. In 1851 the denomination had had little time to proselytise and win new members beyond those from the Wesleyan Methodists. In north Norfolk, Lincolnshire, Derbyshire and the West Riding the Wesleyan Reformers had clearly taken significant numbers from the Wesleyan Methodists.[69] It was to take many

[67] The highest percentage-share values were in Dewsbury in the West Riding, Aylsham in Norfolk, and Dursley in Gloucestershire, while districts like Keysham, Bristol or Westbury-on-Severn were also high on other measures.

[68] The index of sittings for the Wesleyan Reformers ranged up to 7.2, while the index of attendances went up to 10.8. The two variables' mean values were 1.6 and 2.0 respectively (where the denomination was present). In other words, where the Reformers were found they tended to be quite weak.

[69] In the Lincoln, Louth and Market Rasen circuits there were 'disastrous secessions; over half the rural membership in these circuits was lost, never to be regained'. Obelkevich, *Religion and Rural Society*, p. 184. See also R. W. Ambler (ed.), *Lincolnshire Returns of the Census of Religious Worship, 1851* (Lincolnshire Record Society, vol. 72, 1979), p. lv.

more. Currie pointed out that 'The Fly Sheets controversy damaged Wesleyanism in Derbyshire more severely than anywhere else in the country except Norfolk: Derbyshire Wesleyanism lost more than half its members in 1850–5.'[70] This concentration of Wesleyan Reformer strength in Derbyshire was due in part to the connections of the ministers initially expelled from the Original Connexion. Griffith was superintendent of the Ripley Circuit, Dunn was superintendent of the Nottingham Circuit nearby, and Everett had worked in the county earlier in his career.[71] The spatial distribution of the Wesleyan Reformers was often dependent on the character of ministers in Original Connexion circuits. Where these ministers were conciliatory, the Reformers tended not to appear at all; but where Wesleyan Reformer ideas were received in a hostile manner the schism was often most severe.[72]

The Bible Christians

Two Methodist denominations were present in relatively few districts, but were highly concentrated in particular regions, where they were widely found, and where they made a very important contribution to local culture and religion. These were the Bible Christians and the (Welsh) Calvinistic Methodists.

The Bible Christian Church was formed in 1815 at Shebbear in north Devon. Its first circuit was along the Devon–Cornwall border. The denomination, led by William O'Bryan (and sometimes called Bryanites), was unlike other small Methodist denominations in that it did not originate from a schism with the Original Connexion, but was formed separately.[73] During its early years its members were

[70] Currie, *Methodism Divided*, pp. 204–5, see also p. 75; M. Tranter (ed.), *The Derbyshire Returns to the 1851 Religious Census* (Derbyshire Record Society, vol. 23, Chesterfield, 1995), pp. lxxiv–lxxvi, for a detailed assessment of losses due to the controversy in Derbyshire. The acrimony spilled over into some returns. See e.g. *ibid.*, pp. 74, 85–6, 46, for an attack on the 'proceedings of the Wesleyan Conference which hath caused the very extencive agatation in the conexion and the arbatrary conduct of the preachers in the Ilkeston circuit in expelling a number of righteous men without charge or trial the number of worshippers has greatly decreased the last twelve months . . . '

[71] Chew, *James Everett*; D. A. Barton, 'William Griffith (1806–83): the Hercules of the Reform movement', *Proceedings of the Wesley Historical Society*, 43 (1982).

[72] Obelkevich, *Religion and Rural Society*, p. 186.

[73] F. W. Bourne, *The Bible Christians: their Origin and History, 1815–1900* (1905), pp. 13–23.

simply called Methodists.[74] In 1817 O'Bryan and Thorne, his deputy and later a leader of the denomination, drew up the first set of Rules of Society. Thorne claimed that 'We kept as close as possible to Mr. Wesley's Rules, and resolved in making them agreeable with the Bible.'[75] Such were these similarities that the Bible Christians applied for membership of the Methodist Church, an application that was rejected. The denomination cooperated with the Primitive Methodists, with whom they shared many similarities.[76] In organisational terms the Bible Christians resembled other Methodist denominations, for example relying heavily on the circuit system, itinerancy and lay preachers.

Where they were found, the Bible Christians were a significant force, often of equal, or greater, strength than all but the Original Connexion and the Primitive Methodists. They were strongest (see figure 4.8) in the districts from Tiverton on Devon's border with Somerset to Helston and Penzance in south-west Cornwall. This included almost all of Cornwall (with the exception of an area around Plymouth), and much of central and north Devon. The denomination was strongest of all in the central parts of this region. In the district of Holsworthy in west Devon, for example, the Bible Christians had 19 places of worship with accommodation for 2,515 and total attendances on Census Sunday of 3,168 – some 35.9 per cent of all religious attendances.[77] At St Columb in Cornwall the equivalent percentage share was 22. In a number of districts in this region they had more places of worship than the Anglican Church. Such high values were less consistently observed in west Cornwall and east Devon, but Bible Christianity was still a characteristic feature of those areas.

Further east in Somerset, and in south Devon too, Bible Christianity progressively declined, and here the denomination was sometimes not found at all. Further east in Dorset and Wiltshire Bible Christianity was completely absent. However, the sect was not confined solely to the south-western peninsula, but extended to a few other areas. It was strong on the Isle of Wight, and was found in a group of districts across the Solent around Southampton, and north from Portsea Island along Hampshire's border with Sussex. Further east, Bible Christianity had established itself in central Kent and

[74] T. Shaw, *The Bible Christians, 1815–1907* (1965), p. 22.

[75] Shaw, *Bible Christians*, pp. 22–3.

[76] Gay, *Geography of Religion*, pp. 152–4.

[77] These figures are after correction of the original data.

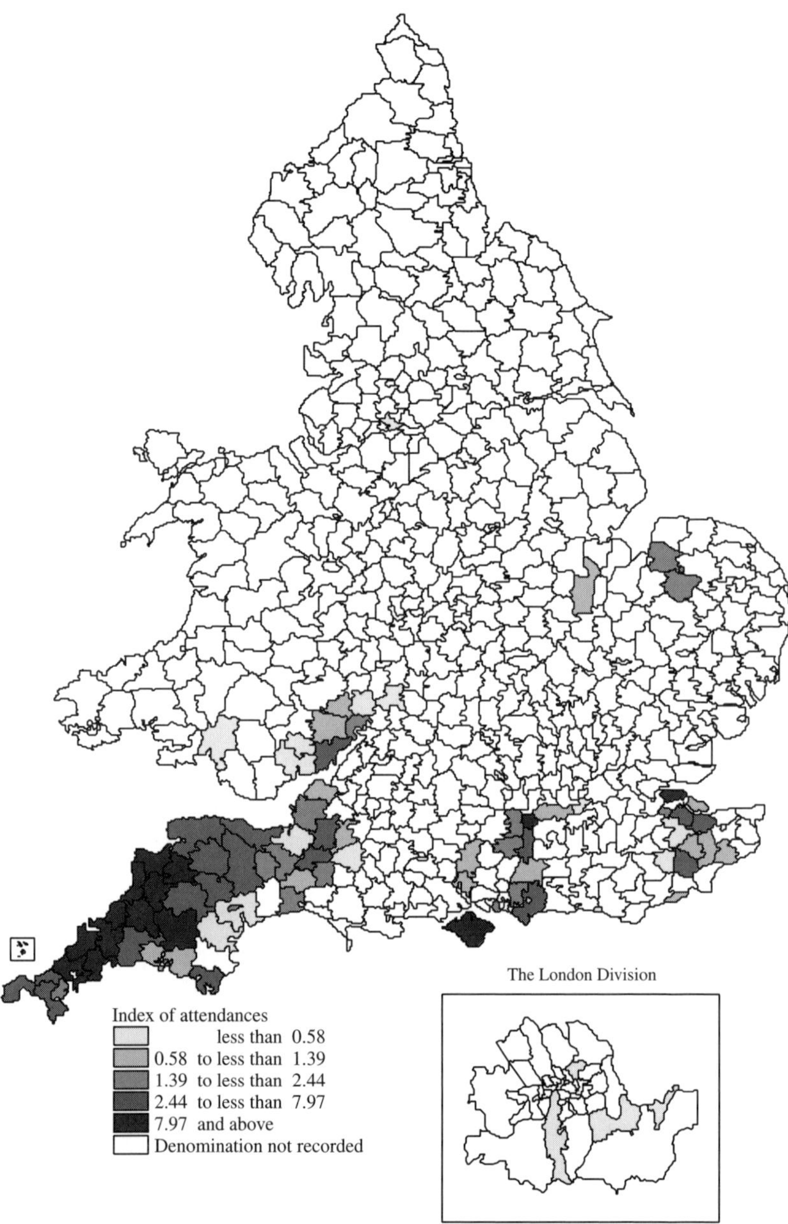

Figure 4.8. Bible Christian index of attendances in 1851

around the Medway estuary, and in a few London districts. Finally, it was also found across the Bristol Channel in south-east Wales and the Forest of Dean, and in a few districts near the Wash.

The Bible Christians were thus highly concentrated in Devon and Cornwall with a few outposts of support elsewhere. They had clung to the area of their original formation, and their support diffused out from its centre in east Devon as circuits expanded and divided. Shaw described this process well: 'In the face of all their difficulties the work of the Connexion went steadily forward, constantly reaching out from each new base to another area. From the north of Devon the preachers were invited to Dulverton in Somerset at the end of 1820; from the Weare circuit which they founded there they went forward to Monmouthshire. Mary Ann Werrey . . . was appointed to the Scilly Isles in 1821, and in 1823 she was working on the Channel Islands.'[78] The denomination had considerable emotional and ideological appeal to farmers, labourers and other rural workers, in small family-farm contexts. Both its theology and anti-clerical socio-economic beliefs were much less attractive or relevant in urban areas. These were characteristics, like its democratic government and camp-meeting methods, which it shared with Primitive Methodism.

The spread of the denomination away from the south-west, in Hampshire, the Isle of Wight, Kent and London was largely through evangelism in the 1820s.[79] Shaw described how in 1821 the society sent missions 'into the dark and destitute parts of the United Kingdom'.[80] The most successful of these was to the Isle of Wight. By 1851 the Bible Christians had 26 places of worship on the Island, second only to the Church of England. Here the denomination could accommodate 3,157 people and, on Census Sunday, registered 4,545 attendances (after correction). However, two factors probably limited the spread of the denomination out of the south-west. The Bible Christians were culturally tied to the rural and maritime peoples of Devon and Cornwall, and had little appeal outside these counties. They formed, as Wickes and Gay both wrote, a west country denomination;[81] and Gay added that 'Even where Bible Christian congregations were established in the North of England, in nearly all cases the members were found to be migrants from Devon and

[78] Shaw, *Bible Christians*, p. 29. [79] Gay, *Geography of Religion*, p. 153.

[80] Shaw, *Bible Christians*, p. 33.

[81] Wickes, *Devon in the Religious Census*, p. 9; Gay, *Geography of Religion*, p. 152.

Cornwall.'[82] Further, the Bible Christians were so similar to the Primitive Methodists that there was little to be gained in their competing in the same areas. The Primitives were the largest Methodist seceding denomination, with remarkable and trenchant working-class influence in many areas, and yet they had no congregations in Devon, and were only found in the far west of Cornwall. Whether by courtesy, design or natural competitive exclusion, a situation of reciprocal advantage was arrived at surprisingly early by these two denominations, creating a distinctive religious division in the south-west that is clearly visible in the 1851 evidence.

The Calvinistic Methodists

The Calvinistic Methodists, or Welsh Calvinistic Methodists as they were occasionally referred to in the Religious Census, were found almost exclusively in Wales. They were Presbyterian in government, with ministers elected by the people, but their ordination was an act of the Presbytery. In doctrine they believed in predestination, contrary to the Arminian tenets of the Original Connexion. Their foundation dated back to 1736, at Trevecca by Howel Harris, and their first Association was held in 1743. As with the Original Connexion, the Calvinistic Methodists originally intended to complement the Church of England, assisting it in areas where it was less effective. Like the Original Connexion too, 'the process of formation into a separate body was . . . gradual and slow',[83] growing out of a nexus of small communities or 'societies' in the north and west.[84] They did not build their first chapel until 1747, and ministers were not appointed or sacraments administered until 1811, which marks their establishment as a denomination. Among the Calvinistic Methodists the circuit system was used, although their circuits were called counties. Itinerant preachers were common, and much power was vested in the Quarterly Association, an equivalent to the Wesleyan Methodist Conference.[85]

Some caution is needed in the interpretation of the published census figures for this denomination. In the census summary tables

[82] Gay, *Geography of Religion*, p. 153.

[83] *Census of Religious Worship*, p. xci.

[84] I. G. Jones, *Communities: Essays in the Social History of Victorian Wales* (Llandysul, 1987), p. 224; A. H. Dodd, *A History of Caernarvonshire, 1284–1900* (1990), p. 263.

[85] *Census of Religious Worship*, pp. xci–xciii.

the terms 'Calvinistic Methodists', 'Welsh Calvinistic Methodists', and 'Lady Huntingdon's Connexion' may in some cases relate to similar religious bodies, and are occasionally used almost interchangeably. Nor do the registration-district tables and the county summary tables always match each other quite as one would expect, although Mann adjusted the latter to cover the historical county. The term 'Calvinistic Methodist' may sometimes have been used instead of, or as well as, the term 'Lady Huntingdon's Connexion' in the registration-district tables. An entry marked as 'Lady Huntingdon's Connexion' has been recorded by us under that heading, and an entry of either 'Calvinistic Methodist' or 'Welsh Calvinistic Methodist' has been added to the Calvinistic Methodist total with which this section deals.[86]

The Calvinistic Methodists were found in just 72 districts, almost 12 per cent of the total for England and Wales. If we take these districts and compare the corresponding values for the Wesleyan and Primitive Methodists (in districts where those were found), the Calvinistic Methodists emerge stronger than the Primitives, and generally as strong, or stronger, than the Wesleyan Methodists. In some districts they were by far the dominant religious force. If we look at percentage share of sittings figures, for example, a number of districts had values which exceeded 20 per cent, with 12 districts exceeding 30 per cent – over 15 per cent of Calvinistic Methodist districts.

All measures reveal remarkably similar geographies of worship and provision, and these are well indicated by figure 4.9. The highest figures stretched through a tapering band of districts which was at its broadest in north Wales, where it extended from Anglesey to Ruthin, coming to its narrowest around Tregaron. In this area, the Calvinistic Methodists in a number of districts were not only far more important than any other dissenting denomination, but were stronger than the Church of England, no matter what measure one takes. For example, at Bala their index of sittings was 50.5 and their percentage share of total attendances was 64.2 per cent. At Pwllheli the corresponding

[86] Even if Calvinistic Methodist, Welsh Calvinistic Methodist, and Lady Huntingdon's Connexion figures were combined, it would make little difference to the patterns shown here. The joint denomination would be found in a few more districts in England, but the overriding picture would still be of a faith that was markedly strong in Wales, and Wales alone.

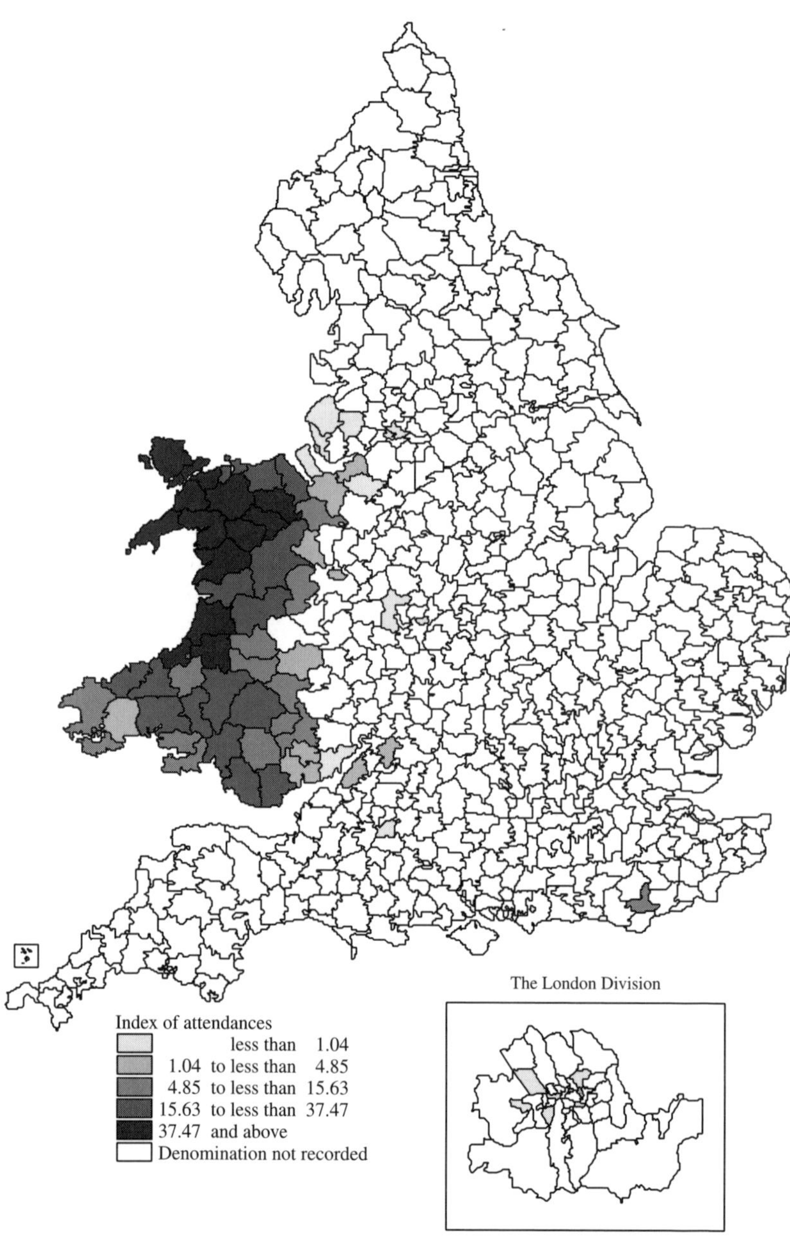

Figure 4.9. Calvinistic Methodist index of attendances in 1851

figures were 43.4 and 57.6, at Festiniog 41.2 and 53.0, and at Llanrwst 40.2 and 56.5. Observations in the second highest quantile were spread more widely through Wales. These included virtually all districts in north Wales which did not fall into the highest quantile – apart from a few on the English border – and a number of districts in southern central Wales, particularly those running westward from Pembroke, Newcastle in Emlyn, and Carmarthen to Brecknock. Even in these districts the Calvinistic Methodists were still a significant force. The second highest quantile for their index of attendances, for example, ranged from 15.6 up to 37.5, and for their percentage share of churches from 17.0 per cent to 29.3 per cent. The corresponding national figures for Wesleyan Methodism were respectively 9.7 to 15.0, and 19.7 to 27.6. Taken within its own region therefore, such comparative figures show just how important Calvinistic Methodism was.

The Calvinistic Methodists were weakest in districts along the English border, and they were also relatively weak in south-east and south-west Wales. We have seen by contrast how the Independents, Baptists and to some extent the Unitarians succeeded in south Wales. The borderline between the Calvinistic Methodists and in particular the Baptists was most certainly not watertight, but it does seem to indicate a loose cultural frontier within Wales, one that has been described many times and via many criteria.[87] In the more industrial southern areas, Calvinistic Methodist attendances were well below average, particularly in districts like Pontypool and Newport and, nearer the English border, Chepstow and Monmouth. Monmouthshire divided between its western and eastern sections as far as Calvinistic Methodism was concerned, with migrants from rural Wales bringing the faith with them as they entered parishes like Bedwelty.[88] The denomination was almost totally absent in east Monmouthshire. In addition, average, or below average, values were fairly consistently observed in Haverfordwest, Pembroke and Narbeth. In the few areas outside Wales where the Calvinistic Methodists were found (mainly in Cheshire, Lancashire and London), they were consistently weak or very weak. Liverpool became the

[87] See for example J. G. Lewis, 'The middle borderland', in E. G. Bowen (ed.), *Wales: a Physical, Historical and Regional Geography* (1957), p. 484.

[88] The Abergavenny district had 13 Calvinistic Methodist chapels. The Monmouth district had none.

exception to this, where their presence expanded considerably until the early twentieth century, focused on the 'cathedral' in Princes Road and many smaller chapels.

Calvinistic Methodism was thus overwhelmingly a Welsh denomination, and its services and Sunday schools were more commonly held in Welsh than was so for other denominations, although it made efforts also to reach English speakers.[89] It is no coincidence that the denomination was so prominent where the speaking of Welsh was normal. Other denominations also found it difficult to prosper if they proselytised in English, and the Religious Census provides much evidence of the use of Welsh by various denominations.[90] Wesleyan Methodism found a place in the bilingual zone of cultural transition in north-east Wales, and in the Rhiwabon coalfield, as in the southern industrial valleys. But as Pryce says, it had little role further west, where it 'was fraught with linguistic difficulties to such an extent that its early pioneers virtually handed Welsh-speaking Wales over to Hywel Harris and his Calvinistic followers'.[91] Comparison of the geography of their spiritual descendants shown here with maps of the nineteenth-century Welsh language clearly shows this.[92] The alien nature of English in these areas was accompanied by an often inconsequential presence of the Anglican Church, which was frequently viewed with suspicion in the large and scattered settlements of rural Wales.[93] This was a suspicion that many Methodist preachers did

[89] Jones, *Communities*, pp. 178, 232–3.

[90] Even in industrial centres like Merthyr, according to the *Morning Chronicle* correspondent, among the 'four most popular sects in twenty-five out of twenty-nine of their meeting houses the Welsh language alone is used'. The dissenting elders and authorities 'recognized the predilection of the people for their own vernacular tongue'. J. Ginswick (ed.), *Labour and the Poor in England and Wales, 1849–1851, vol. 3: the Mining and Manufacturing Districts of South Wales and North Wales* (1983), pp. 72–3.

[91] W. T. R. Pryce, 'Migration and the evolution of culture areas: cultural and linguistic frontiers in north-east Wales, 1750 and 1851', *Transactions of the Institute of British Geographers*, 65 (1975), 99–100. Wesley frequently illustrated the problems that his Connexion had in Wales by referring to the Old Testament story of a Babel of Tongues.

[92] For example, the mapped division between the distinctive cultural provinces of *Cymru Gymraeg* (Welsh Wales) and *Cymru ddi-Gymraeg* (Anglicised Wales) in Pryce, 'Migration and the evolution of culture areas', 81; or see J. W. Aitchison and H. Carter, 'Rural Wales and the Welsh language', *Rural History*, 2:1 (1991), 63, 67.

[93] G. J. Lewis, 'The geography of religion in the middle borderlands of Wales in 1851', *Transactions of the Honourable Society of Cymmrodorion* (1980), 141: 'Everything associated with English was regarded as alien'; Pryce, 'Migration and the evolution of culture areas', 101. G. A. Williams, *When Was Wales? A History of the Welsh*

little to dispel. As Lewis argued, 'the districts where Calvinistic Methodism predominated were sparsely populated hill areas, occupied by an overwhelmingly Welsh-speaking population. Beyond this zone, Calvinistic Methodism lacked any significant hold, thus emphasising a close association between this denomination and the Welsh language.'[94] These and related features of Welsh Calvinistic Methodism will occupy us in more detail when we assess the parish-level census data, in the second part of this book.

The other Methodist denominations

Two other Methodist denominations were covered in the published census. These were Lady Huntingdon's Connexion and the Independent Methodists. Neither was pronounced in terms of its spatial spread, or any intensity of following in particular localities, but they require brief discussion.

Lady Huntingdon's Connexion was found in just 55 districts in England and Wales, being about 9 per cent of the total. It was almost always weak compared to most other denominations.[95] In 1746 George Whitefield, who was a close associate of the Wesleys although Calvinistic in theology, met Selina, the Countess of Huntingdon. By 1750 she was acting as Whitefield's patron, assisting him to spread his beliefs through her network of aristocratic friends. Her college at Trevecca was formed in 1768 to train ministers for the Church of England. In 1783, following a dispute with an Anglican incumbent over parochial interference, she formally seceded from the church. By her death in 1791, her ministers were serving between fifty-five and eighty chapels, many of which later moved into Independency.[96]

The Religious Census reveals a dispersed pattern of worship for her

(Harmondsworth, 1985), pp. 150, 204, argues that the Anglican clergy were over-abused by Nonconformists (despite undoubted earlier problems of pluralism, non-residence and nepotism), and that many were committed to popular religious instruction, the eisteddfod movement, involved in Welsh nationalism, and subscribed heavily to the University at Aberystwyth. Such a view is supported also by D. Parry-Jones, *My Own Folk* (Llandysul, 1972), pp. 58–9, who stresses links between Nonconformity and the Anglican Church in Carmarthenshire.

94 Lewis, 'Geography of religion in the middle borderlands of Wales', 141.

95 Identification of the Lady Huntingdon's Connexion in the registration-district census tables can be questionable, for the reasons outlined above in connection with Calvinistic Methodism.

96 Gay, *Geography of Religion*, pp. 148–9; Rack, *Reasonable Enthusiast*, pp. 283–6.

Connexion, shown in figure 4.10. It was entirely absent from Yorkshire and more northerly counties, and in the south-west and Wales was present in only one or two districts. It was most frequently found in south Lancashire and on the English side of the Welsh border, especially in the Worcester area. Over the rest of England the Connexion seems to have been rather randomly located, owing much to her contacts. The locations in Lancashire and on England's Welsh border could in fact owe something to imprecise census distinctions between Calvinistic Methodists, Welsh Calvinistic Methodists, and Lady Huntingdon's Connexion, and some of these congregations may have been (Welsh) Calvinistic Methodists.

The Independent Methodists were formed after 1806, led by Peter Phillips, a Quaker Methodist, and they were, as Currie wrote, 'a strange congeries of diverse chapels'.[97] As their name suggests, they believed in the autonomy of each congregation. Although an annual conference was held, this had no power over individual congregations; its sole purpose was to debate ideas. Independent Methodists had sittings in only seven registration districts out of the full 624, mainly in the English midlands and southern England.[98] Even in these they did not attract much support, their maximum index of attendance being 3.2 in Atherstone, and their maximum percentage share of attendances being 3.6 per cent. They arose in different areas largely as a result of local disputes between ministers and either the circuit or conference, and factors such as personality clashes seem largely to have influenced where such localised schisms occurred.[99]

The New Church

The New Church (or Swedenborgians) had its origins in the voluminous writings of the Swede Emanuel Swedenborg. While Swedenborg himself did not form or minister in a church, nor probably want a sect formed upon his doctrines,[100] his work was influential,[101] and it led in

[97] Currie, *Methodism Divided*, p. 57.

[98] Warminster had 451 sittings, followed (in descending order) by Nuneaton, Bingham, Leicester, Twakeham, Atherstone and Fareham.

[99] See Werner, *Primitive Methodist Connexion*, pp. 25–8, for details of these schisms in Manchester, Stockport, Macclesfield and Warrington.

[100] S. E. Ahlstrom, *A Religious History of the American People* (1972, New Haven, 1974 edn), p. 485, and see pp. 483–8.

[101] For example, it had a strong influence on William Blake, who attended the first general conference of the church in April 1789.

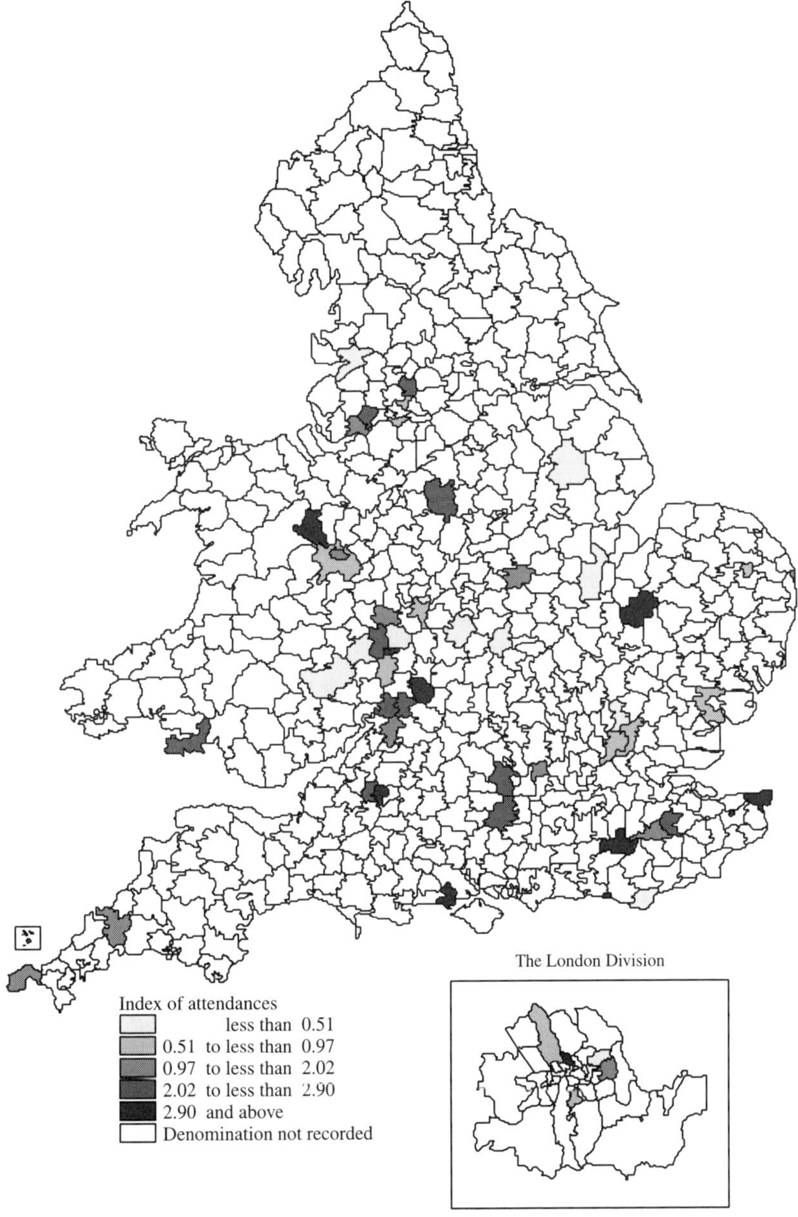

Figure 4.10. Countess of Huntingdon's Connexion index of attendances in 1851

1787 to the formation of this denomination. His writings were best received in England (and then America), being adopted by two Anglican ministers in the 1780s – John Clowes, Vicar of St Johns in Manchester, and Thomas Hartley of Winwick in south-west Lancashire. The sect held its initial congregation at Great Eastwick in 1788, and in 1791 the first conference met. Swedenborg combined elements of theosophy and pantheism, and on some issues the New Church was doctrinally quite different from other churches.[102] Its members believed that the scriptures held hidden meanings which were revealed only to members of their Church. In terms of government, ultimate responsibility was in the hands of a conference composed of both ministers and laymen.[103]

The New Church was established in 37 districts in England and Wales, and when present its strength was very limited. Its maximum index of attendances was only 2.7 (in Colchester), and its maximum percentage share of attendances only 2.9. The New Church was found close to its Lancashire origins, being strongest in Bolton, Bury and Haslingden, and some nearby areas of the West Riding.[104] It extended to the north midland coalfield between Derby and Nottingham, and also to three districts in and around Colchester. Elsewhere the New Church was even weaker, as in London, Birmingham, Norwich and Newcastle.

The Latter Day Saints

Although not normally considered as 'new dissent', and not included in the amalgamated totals for new dissent in the final section of this chapter, we include a brief discussion of the Latter Day Saints (or Mormons) here. The sect arose in the United States as a result of a series of visions experienced by Joseph Smith after 1822, which resulted in his proclaimed discovery, buried in a hillside, of engraven records giving the fullest account of the gospel. His translation of these texts (which were in 'Egyptian characters . . . exhibiting many

[102] Watson, *Biblical and Theological Dictionary*, pp. 935–7.

[103] *Census of Religious Worship*, pp. xcv–xcviii.

[104] Its highest total attendances were in Bury (1,028 in four chapels, which must have comprised well over 600 attendants), followed by Bolton, Haslingden, Manchester, Liverpool, Huddersfield, Colchester, Holborn, Blackburn and Birmingham. H. McLeod comments that it was 'quite strong in Manchester and Salford' in *Religion and the Working Class*, p. 47.

marks of antiquity') resulted in the *Book of Mormon*, published in 1830. Smith wanted this addition to the Bible to be taken literally. The subsequent movement, which originated in Manchester (in the state of New York), tried to establish itself in a succession of places mainly in Missouri, Illinois and finally Utah, facing considerable hostility. The adverse reaction to Mormonism had a number of causes, and it was intensified by the leaders' polygamy, which became an open issue from 1852. This did little for their reputation in many parts of England and Wales either, where it was open to irreverent remark. Joseph Smith and (after his murder at the hands of a mob in 1844) his successor Brigham Young, claimed that Christ's Kingdom on earth was soon to be created, first at Nauvoo and subsequently, after the Saints were driven out, at Salt Lake City in Utah.[105] It was the duty of every Christian to journey to Nauvoo (and later Salt Lake City) in preparation for the event.

This American denomination did not appear in England and Wales until 1837 when seven missionaries landed in Liverpool. From Liverpool they travelled north to Preston, where their first converts were baptised in the river Ribble. After this successful mission another followed in 1840, led by Young. They had reached a membership of about 33,000 by 1851.[106] To help their converts reach Nauvoo, an emigration system was organised from English ports, particularly Liverpool.[107] Mormon statistics indicate that, by 1851, nearly 17,000 converts had left England and Wales for America, and persistent emigration depleted numbers this side of the Atlantic.[108]

By 1851 the Latter Day Saints had established congregations in 129 registration districts – a little over 20 per cent. Although in spatial terms this was most impressive, and indeed comparable to some second-rank Methodist denominations, in terms of other measures

105 For the Mormons' move to Salt Lake City, see R. H. Jackson, 'The Mormon experience: the plains as Sinai, the Great Salt Lake as the Dead Sea, and the Great Basin as desert-cum-promised land', *Journal of Historical Geography*, 18 (1992), 41–58.

106 J. F. C. Harrison, *The Second Coming: Popular Millenarianism, 1780–1850* (1979), p. 189.

107 P. A. M. Taylor, *Expectations Westward: the Mormons and the Emigration of their British Converts in the Nineteenth Century* (1965); J. B. Allen and M. R. Thorp, 'The mission of the Twelve to England, 1840–41: Mormon Apostles and the working classes', *Brigham Young University Studies*, 15:4 (1975).

108 *Census of Religious Worship*, pp. cvi–cxii; Gay, *Geography of Religion*, pp. 191–2; Harrison, *Second Coming*, p. 189.

the denomination was less striking. In these 129 districts, the Latter Day Saints had 182 places of worship, that is, usually only one in each district.[109] In very few cases, therefore, did they have a significant impact on the religious character of an area. In all but 16 districts, their index of sittings was less than one. Most districts which contained them had a Mormon index of sittings between 0.01 and 0.6.

The regional distribution of the denomination was complex, and as J. F. C. Harrison wrote, 'it would be hazardous to generalize confidently about the geographical, religious, and social origins of the British Mormons'.[110] Their index of attendances is mapped in figure 4.11. There were few consolidated areas for the Latter Day Saints, nor were there many regions in which they were consistently strong or weak. They were largely unrepresented in the south-west, being completely absent from Cornwall. Only occasionally were they present in the southern counties of Kent, Sussex, Berkshire, Essex and Suffolk. In central Wales, and in northern England too, the movement was rare. For example, there were no congregations in Westmorland or the North Riding, and congregations were sparse indeed in Northumberland, Durham, Cumberland and in much of the rest of Yorkshire.

The 1851 data suggest that the Latter Day Saints were found most often in Cheshire and south Lancashire. They were also quite widespread in the south Welsh mining valleys,[111] in parts of London, in an area of the north midland coalfield, parts of west Hertfordshire and adjoining counties, and an area to the west of Norwich. In midland and southern England they were often found in large towns, cities and their hinterlands, like Birmingham, Coventry, Shrewsbury and

[109] This feature makes it hard for us to correct missing values for the Latter Day Saints. If there was only one Mormon church in a district, and this failed to provide information, it is difficult to compensate for such omission via consistent use of our methods, which rely on an interpolation of mean values for the denomination in that district. In five of the seven Cheshire registration districts in which Mormons were reported, sittings data were not provided for any place of worship. We did not use 'special-case' methods to deal specifically with this denomination; but the result is a tendency to under-represent their presence.

[110] Harrison, *Second Coming*, p. 189.

[111] There were 32 Mormon congregations in Wales in 1851. Many Welsh Mormons were recruited by Daniel Jones in and around Merthyr, and once in America they tried to set up Welsh communities, like Brynffynnon in Tennessee. Many ended up in Utah.

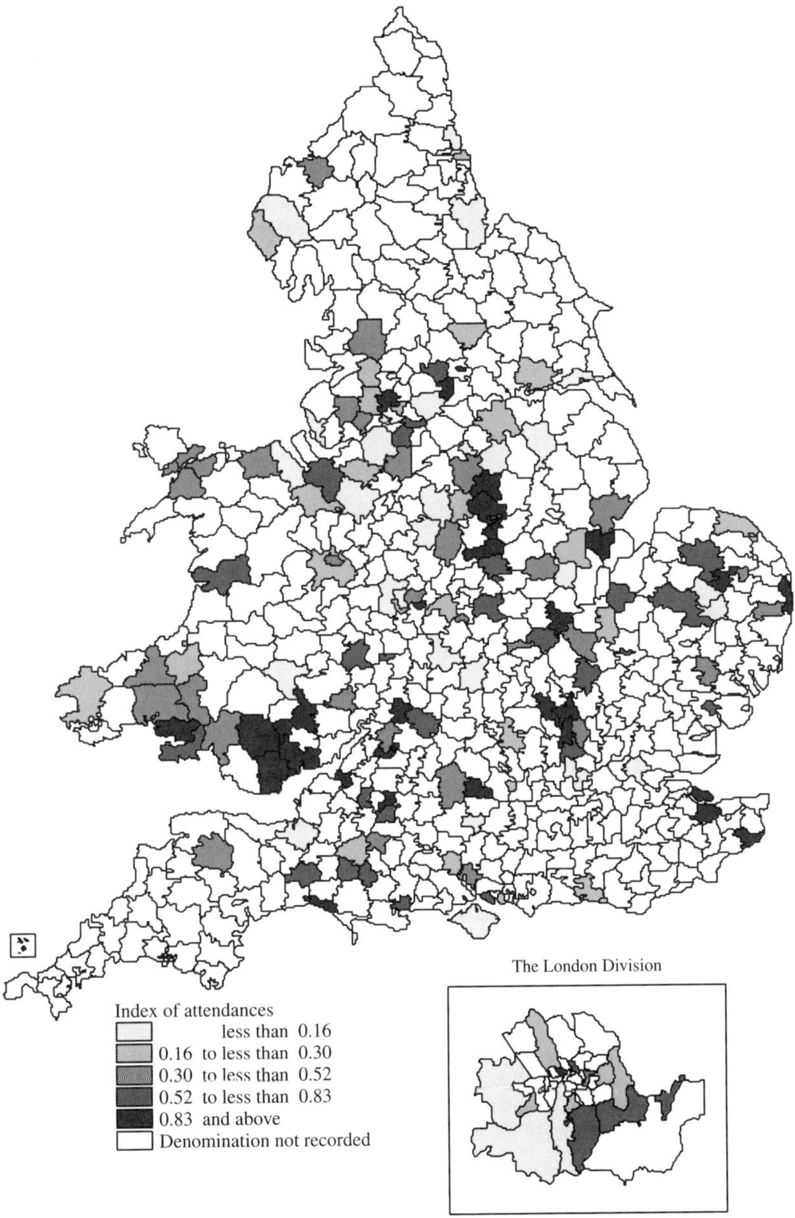

Figure 4.11. Latter Day Saints index of attendances in 1851

Cambridge, while also being present in ports like Liverpool, Hull, Tyneside, Newport, Bristol, Southampton and Dover.[112]

The stress on emigration to a Promised Land, coupled with an efficient emigration service, inevitably concentrated significant numbers in the ports. Places of worship in 1851 like the 'Mariner's Bethel' at the bottom of Southampton's High Street bear witness to this.[113] Figure 4.11 shows that it is possible to exaggerate a connection with ports; but Gay was surely correct in writing that 'Many of the English converts emigrated . . . It was inevitable therefore that those English ports which maintained regular services to and from the eastern seaboard of America should become centres of Mormon activity.'[114] As the main aim of the Latter Day Saints was to send converts to America, there was little point for them to develop a complex network of chapels in remote rural areas which their own mission would quickly make redundant. The Latter Day Saints were most successful in securing working-class converts through the simple and compulsive nature of their religion, and their promise of an imminent second coming and a much improved life, which fed into a long tradition of popular religious aspiration and millenarianism.[115] 'As Nauvoo was . . . built up to sound like a contemporary Garden of Eden, it is small wonder that many of the English converts to Mormonism, most of whom were poor, gladly responded to the call.'[116]

Conclusion

The denominations considered here had spatial patterns of worship that varied considerably. One or more of these faiths were present in 615 of the 624 registration districts in England and Wales, about 99

[112] Harrison wrote that their initial successes were 'in Lancashire, Yorkshire, the Staffordshire Potteries, the Black Country, Herefordshire and Gloucestershire; with extensions into Scotland, Wales and "the great Babylon", London . . . These seem to have remained the strongholds of Mormonism during the next decade . . . they also made headway in rural parts of the West Midlands.' See his *Second Coming*, pp. 189–90, 258–9, n. 68, giving membership figures for the main Mormon conferences in 1850, as centred upon English cities and Wales.

[113] J. A. Vickers (ed.), *The Religious Census of Hampshire, 1851* (Hampshire Record Series, Winchester, 1993), p. 97.

[114] Gay, *Geography of Religion*, pp. 193, 195. He points out that large Mormon followings persisted in Liverpool, Hull, Bristol, Southampton and Plymouth as late as the 1960s.

[115] *Census of Religious Worship*, pp. cxi–cxii; Harrison, *Second Coming*, pp. 176–92.

[116] Gay, *Geography of Religion*, p. 192.

per cent of the total. In some areas, our main religious variables indicate that new dissent *in toto* was a very potent force indeed, sometimes being supported by very many more people than the Church of England. In 64 districts, it had percentage shares of attendances in excess of 50 per cent, and there were nine districts in excess of 70 per cent.[117] Its maximum index of attendances was 83.0 in Aberystwyth, followed in descending order by Llanrwst (68), the Scilly Isles (66), Pwllheli (65), Bangor (63), Machynlleth (62) and Bala (61).[118] In many other districts of course new dissent had much less impact upon local religious culture, and in nine it was non-existent.[119] The distribution for 'new dissent' combined together is mapped in figure 4.12, using the overall index of attendances. All of our descriptive variables bear out this pattern, and (as for individual denominations) there are very strong correlations indeed between the various possible measures.[120]

Clearly, the largest area of strength for new dissent stretched from central Northumberland south to Leicestershire and north Norfolk, being particularly strong in county Durham, Yorkshire, Derbyshire and north Lincolnshire.[121] In these counties almost all Methodist denominations were found in strength, excepting the Calvinistic Methodists and Bible Christians. The second major area for new dissent included much of north and central Wales, where some of their highest percentage shares were gained. In north Wales this was largely due to the Calvinistic Methodists and, to a far lesser extent, the Wesleyan Methodists. Then there was Cornwall, highly associated with the Bible Christians and the Original Connexion. Other

117 These were Camelford, St Austell, Redruth, Wolstanton, Paterley Bridge, Goole, Reeth, Weardale and Alston, interestingly none of them in Wales, where old dissent remained so strong.

118 Aberystwyth was also the only district whose total dissenting index of attendances (i.e. for *all* non-Anglican faiths) exceeded 100, standing as it did at 104. It was followed by Machynlleth (92), Dolgclly (90), Bangor, Cardigan, Pwllheli and Crickhowell (89). The top eighteen districts on the measure of total dissenting index of attendances were all Welsh, before one reaches English districts (among many more Welsh) like Leighton Buzzard, Melksham, Luton, Westbury, St Ives, Dursley, the Scilly Isles, Royston, Amersham, Braintree or Launceston.

119 St Martin in the Fields, London City, Reigate, Petworth, Ongar, Catherington, Halstead, Belford and Rothbury.

120 In this case, the correlation coefficients between all possible variables describing new dissent ranged from 0.761 to 0.961, confirming the accuracy, and to some extent the interchangeability, of those variables for historical use.

121 There is striking resemblance here to the counties of the Danelaw, although any cultural connection seems unfathomable.

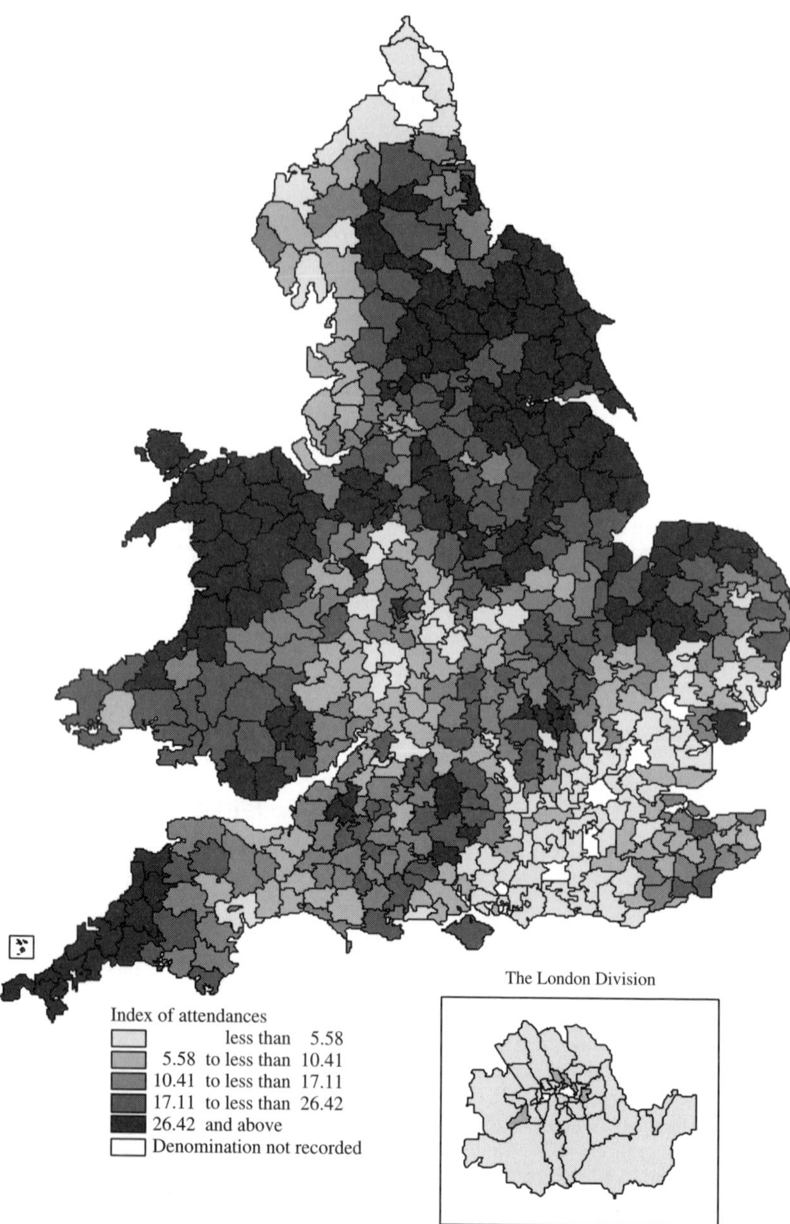

Figure 4.12. New dissent index of attendances in 1851

rather lesser areas of new dissent were the Black Country, the Bristol area, and around Leighton Buzzard and Luton in south Bedfordshire.

New dissent had much less presence in central and southern England, and in south Wales. It was weakest of all in south Leicestershire,[122] Northamptonshire, a large band of districts from east Norfolk south-westwards through London down to the New Forest, in south-west Wales, on Lancashire's seaboard, and in northern Northumberland. As we have seen, such areas were often ones where old dissent was earlier established, and of course the Anglican Church was on its firmest foundations in the southern counties.

Wesleyan Methodism had implanted best in areas where parishes were least cohesive and tightly knit, where itinerant evangelism, the circuit system, voluntary auxiliaries and the connexional principle worked to greatest advantage. In rural areas it was often associated with the more traditional, often upland (but also fenland) regions of small farms, and surviving farm service, where more isolated farmsteads and small local groups required modest economy and flexibility of provision. There was overlap here with the eastern arable regions, but where Methodism co-existed with high labour proletarianisation in agriculture (in Norfolk, or parts of the East Riding and Lincolnshire) it often adopted its most confrontational social forms.[123] It is a noteworthy feature of the maps that Primitive Methodism had a more eastern (i.e. arable) basis than Wesleyan Methodism. Denominations breaking away from the Original Connexion were at their most visible near their origins, often near the Original Connexion, the institutional consolidation of which they objected to. Wesley might have been dismayed by some of the political views later expressed (and the conditions that roused them); but his aim from the 1730s not to challenge the Church of England, but to complement and extend it, seems to have been realised to striking effect. The maps pay a considerable tribute to the way in which he and his helpers were able to put one of his maxims into practice not only in class terms, but also at a regional level: 'go always, not only to those that want you, but to those that want you most'.[124]

122 Snell, *Church and Chapel in the North Midlands*, pp. 15–24.

123 At county level, Wesleyan Methodism was positively correlated with the survival in 1851 of farm service (at 0.374), and negatively with high male labour-to-farmer ratios (at −0.356). For discussion of the strictly agrarian contrasts, see Snell, *Annals of the Labouring Poor*, pp. 94–7.

124 Revd J. Wesley, 'Rules for a helper' (1744), in *The Works of the Rev. John Wesley*, 6 (1810), p. 350.

One striking point emerges from figure 4.12, when it is compared to the earlier maps. This is the way in which the Methodists complemented each other. They formed an overarching containment or encirclement of the Anglican (and to some extent old dissenting) heartland. This was achieved mainly through the combined presence of Wesleyan and Primitive Methodism, Welsh Calvinistic Methodism, and Bible Christianity. Each of these laid hold of major regions to the north and west of the Anglican 'core' areas, and this pattern was buttressed (and its interstices to some extent filled) by the other breakaway Methodist denominations. With reference to the main north–south and west–east divisions of the country taken as a whole, to Welsh identity (whether defined mainly by the Welsh border or in the discourse of *Cymru Gymraeg*), and plainly with regard to enduring political cleavages of the nation, these divisions were fundamental and of great historical and cultural significance.

The associations between Liberal and Labour politics and the prior regional foundation of old dissent were mentioned earlier. Such continuities and political ramifications are even more striking when one examines new dissent, and it is worth ending on this note. There is long-standing debate about how conservative Methodism was in political terms, and how associated it may have been with anti-establishment politics. The arguments on this issue, and the charges laid at the door of Methodism, are well known and do not need much rehearsing here. Modifying the views of Cobbett, Halévy, E. P. Thompson and others (notably on Wesleyan Methodism), a number of historians like Eric Hobsbawm have argued that Methodism was strongest in those parts of the country most associated with political radicalism, like the West Riding or the north midlands.[125] Furthermore, historians of the rural labour movement have pointed repeatedly to the key role played by Methodism in agricultural unionism in the English midlands and eastern counties, just as others have stressed how important it was to very many groups like the

[125] W. Cobbett, *Rural Rides* (1830, Harmondsworth, 1967 edn), pp. 137, 181–2, 187–8; I. Dyck, *William Cobbett and Rural Popular Culture* (Cambridge, 1992), pp. 96–100; E. Halévy, *A History of the English People in the Nineteenth Century: vol. 1: England in 1815* (1913, 1970 edn); Thompson, *Making of the English Working Class*, ch. 11; E. J. Hobsbawm, 'Methodism and the threat of revolution in Britain', in his *Labouring Men* (1964). Or see E. Gaskell, *The Life of Charlotte Brontë* (1857, Harmondsworth, 1983 edn), pp. 139–40.

Cornish or north-eastern miners, or the slate workers of north Wales.[126]

What is now abundantly clear at the national level is the strong regional coincidence between Methodism and those areas that developed Liberal or Labour voting preferences after 1851. The discussion of Anglican strength in chapter 2 showed how closely the Church of England was regionally linked to subsequent Conservative voting. By contrast, the encircling patterns of north midland, northern and western Methodist strengths shown here overlap significantly with any cartography of Liberal and Labour voting after 1851. Indeed, one can use the parameters of Anglican, old dissenting and Methodist strength in 1851 to predict much later voting patterns with very considerable precision.[127] In the second half of the nineteenth century, and perhaps beyond, Nonconformity 'was generally the most potent predictor of the vote'.[128] Nonconformity 'comprised the backbone of the Liberal party'.[129] As Edward Baines (the Liberal MP for Leeds) said in Parliament, the five million or so dissenters of England and Wales 'formed the great strength of his own party'.[130] Anti-Conservative sentiment was certainly most apparent outside south-eastern and midland England: in 'peripheral English counties', in the north, in Wales, and the Celtic fringe generally, that is, in many of the Methodist regions.[131]

126 N. Scotland, *Methodism and the Revolt of the Field* (Gloucester, 1981); Howkins, *Poor Labouring Men*, chs. 3–5; P. Horn, 'Methodism and agricultural trade unionism in Oxfordshire: the 1870s', *Proceedings of the Wesley Historical Society*, 37 (1969); J. G. Rule, 'The Labouring Miner in Cornwall, c.1740–1870' (unpublished Ph.D thesis, University of Warwick, 1971); J. C. C. Probert, *The Sociology of Cornish Methodism to the Present Day* (Redruth, 1971); Colls, *Pitmen of the Northern Coalfield*; R. M. Jones, *The North Wales Quarrymen, 1874–1922* (Cardiff, 1981).

127 This is shown well in as yet unpublished work by Alasdair Crockett.

128 K. D. Wald, *Crosses on the Ballot: Patterns of British Voter Alignment since 1885* (Princeton, 1983), pp. 150, 157, 163–5. 'Nonconformity was a strong, significant, negative predictor of Conservatism.' Over 90 per cent of Nonconformist candidates at elections ran as Liberal or Labour in 1900, 1906 and 1910, a tendency most true for Baptists (1885, 1892, 1900–10), then Congregationalists, and then Methodists, although all leaned this way. *Ibid.*, pp. 197, 200.

129 M. Barker, *Gladstone and Radicalism: the Reconstruction of Liberal Policy in Britain, 1885–94* (Hassocks, 1975), pp. 12, 208.

130 *Hansard's Parliamentary Debates*, CLIX (11 July 1860), 1737.

131 Wald, *Crosses on the Ballot*, pp. 138–9, 151–9, and as he says, peripheral nationalism in Wales, Scotland and outer England was expressed via Nonconformity, a view shared by M. Hechter, *Internal Colonialism: the Celtic Fringe in British National Development, 1536–1966* (1975).

One can think of exceptions to this in mid century, as in the more anti-Catholic parts of Lancashire,[132] and in 1887 nearly a third of leading lay Wesleyans were said to be unionist.[133] Yet the religious traditions in many Methodist regions ensured subsequent reversion to Liberalism, as after the 1902 Education Act. There was, as Bebbington has written, 'striking consistency over time in the regional strength of anti-conservative voting . . . political cleavages based on the religious communities persisted well into the twentieth century'.[134] The historically predictive quality of mid nineteenth-century religious geography becomes very precise indeed in many cases – as with the regional connection between Welsh Calvinistic Methodism and the support for Plaid Cymru, or for Welsh devolution, or a separate Welsh assembly. Much the same is true of English Methodism in the south-west and southern Liberal voting.

A whole range of further questions is thus thrown up for political scientists and historians: about the changing links between regional religion and political tradition; about whether Methodism itself was the key instrument in the definition of political stances, or whether it simply fitted more neutrally but acceptably into pre-existing areas of on-going anti-establishment perspective (and indeed into industrialising areas where such political positions may have been most likely to develop); about the regional chronologies of the shifts from essentially religio-political issues to more secular (if still highly moral) political ones; about the enduring attitudinal connections (in some areas but less in others) between religion and political views; about whether 'Methodism' (in its great variety of forms and ways) dampened or invigorated radical politics at different times in what became the Liberal or Labour voting areas. This is not the place to enter into such discussions, and on some of these questions the geography of religion connects with a fascinating political historiography already in existence. But in addressing the distribution of new dissent we hope that this chapter demonstrates the value of a strongly *regional* approach to the history of religion, and indicates how relevant this can be for many cultural and political issues that concern us today.

132 M. Kinnear, *The British Voter: an Atlas and Survey since 1885* (1968, 1981 edn), p. 14.

133 D. W. Bebbington, 'Nonconformity and electoral sociology, 1867–1918', *Historical Journal*, 27 (1984), 645.

134 Bebbington, 'Nonconformity and electoral sociology', 655. In areas like south-west Norfolk this lasted into the 1960s or later.

5

Roman Catholicism and Irish immigration

The presence of Roman Catholicism in the Religious Census is of particular interest, for the census was taken only six years after the onset of the Irish famine. Any account and mapping of the Catholic census data cannot but illuminate the tragic aftermath of that catastrophe, reflecting as it does much of the Irish diaspora in England and Wales that resulted. Cartographic analysis of the patterns of Catholicism from this source are among the ways in which post-famine settlement can be observed, a process of settlement that had a profound effect on regional cultures and religion in some parts of the British Isles. There had been earlier famines in Ireland, and there was a long history of Irish settlement in the towns and cities of England and Wales. Yet prior to the great famine of 1845–9 Irish migration had very often been short-term, or seasonal, working as harvesters, construction workers, in the armed forces and the like – particularly to arable, market-gardening or fruit-growing rural areas where the harvest earnings were high.[1] The earnings enabled conacre and other rents to be paid in Ireland. After the famine however, this seasonal migration tended to decline and Irish migrants settled in a more permanent way. From the distressed regions particularly of western and southern Ireland, they came across the water to parishes of long-standing Catholic allegiance, occasionally to rural parishes, but much more often to the English textile and heavy industrial areas, and to districts of transport employment. There had been a significant Catholic (and to some extent Irish) presence in English towns throughout the eighteenth

[1] On the Irish famine see C. O'Grada, *The Great Irish Famine* (1989); C. Woodham-Smith, *The Great Hunger: Ireland, 1845–1849* (1962); K. D. M. Snell (ed.), *Letters from Ireland During the Famine of 1847*, by A. Somerville (Dublin, 1994). On Irish harvest migration, J. H. Johnson, 'Harvest migration from nineteenth-century Ireland', *Transactions of the Institute of British Geographers*, 41 (1967); B. M. Kerr, 'Irish seasonal migration to Great Britain, 1800–1838', *Irish Historical Studies*, 3 (1942–3); A. O'Dowd, *Spalpeens and Tattie Hokers: History and Folklore of the Irish Migratory Agricultural Worker in Ireland and Britain* (Dublin, 1991).

century, especially in London and the Diocese of Chester.[2] Irish Catholic settlement after the famine was to be even more heavily concentrated in such urban environments.

Before we describe the cartography of this transforming Catholic presence, we need to be aware of a feature of Catholic attendance behaviour. Horace Mann commented on how it 'will be observed, that in the morning the number of attendants was more than the number of sittings: this is explained by the fact that in many Roman Catholic chapels there is more than one morning service, attended by different individuals'.[3] We have seen that Roman Catholicism had a high association between its sittings and attendances, higher indeed than most other denominations.[4] This was related to its high 'index of occupancy' figures: as Mann pointed out, its attendances were large relative to its sittings.[5] Compared to other denominations, there were more multiple Catholic services in the morning. As a result of these, a larger population could be accommodated by the denomination than the figures for sittings might suggest. The same was true for other denominations, but for the different reason of multiple attendance during the day. An unknown proportion of attendances for other denominations comprised those attending church or chapel more than once. In the Roman Catholic Church, however, it was unusual for people to attend more than one mass on Sunday. We may therefore be seeing in the Catholic figures a closer representation of attenders rather than attendances, compared with many other denominations.

This point needs to be borne in mind. We scrutinised the data to see

[2] M. Rowlands, *Catholics of Parish and Town, 1558–1778* (1999).

[3] *Census of Religious Worship*, p. cii.

[4] See table 1.1 on the association between sittings and attendances in chapter 1.

[5] The 'index of occupancy' is a denomination's attendances, divided by its total sittings, multiplied by 100. An 'index of morning occupancy' uses only the morning attendances for this calculation. The median Roman Catholic indexes of occupancy at registration-district level are generally above the median figures for other denominations, but do not differ much from the Primitive Methodists, the Latter Day Saints, the Welsh Calvinistic Methodists, the Baptists or the Independent Methodists. A few very high cases for the Catholics at registration-district level raise their mean and standard deviation when using this measure. At the parish level, using the fifteen-county data for 2,443 parishes, the Catholic median figure for this measure was lower than the Welsh Calvinistic Methodists and Latter Day Saints, and not dissimilar to the Primitive Methodists. However, the median figure for the Catholic index of *morning* occupancy (at parish level) was notably higher than for the other denominations. This suggests the use of Catholic measures based on total attendances or sittings (rather than morning- or afternoon-specific measures) as being most comparable with other denominations.

if there were any adverse repercussions for the analysis of Catholic figures, and concluded that there were not. Analysis of all the possible statistical measures of Roman Catholicism shows very close associations between them, which are typical of other denominations, and this inspires confidence in their data. All variables derived from the published Catholic census data were mapped and closely inspected, and they confirm the same geographical patterns. The same conclusions emerged from analysis of the parish-level data. All the Catholic measures appear to be valid and highly informative. We need to recall that many persons stood by custom in Roman Catholic worship, and a use of sittings-based measures will not take account of this. The practice was not conspicuous in enumerators' returns, and probably did not vary much regionally. It seems appropriate therefore to ground our contours of Catholicism mainly on religious attendances, taking the index of total attendances as being among the most revealing indicators. Figure 5.1 shows this mapped for England and Wales.

The map shows that Roman Catholicism in England was weak, or absent, in very many districts south of a line from the Wash to the Bristol Channel, and in a band running from Cumberland south along the Pennines. Making due allowance for London, always a major Catholic centre, Gay earlier referred to 'the dichotomy between the Catholic North, and the non-Catholic South' in 1851.[6] As one can see from the map, this was an English division that certainly existed across the Wash–Severn axis, despite small exceptions in pockets of the south. The southern regions were where the penal laws had been most rigorously enforced, and their effectiveness there is borne out in the 1851 distribution of the denomination.[7] In addition, it was almost completely absent in central and northern Wales, indeed being weak throughout Wales except for some southern heavy industrial areas. In 1780, Joseph Berington had written that in many counties, 'particularly in the West, in South Wales, and in some of the Midland counties, there is scarcely a Catholic to be found'.[8] This

6 J. D. Gay, *The Geography of Religion in England* (1971), p. 95.

7 The main change after 1851, notably in the twentieth century, has been the penetration in ever larger numbers of Catholics into the midlands and south-east of England, as their members rose in social status, as more immigrated, as prejudicial measures against them diminished, and as their geography became more representative of the general population. Gay, *Geography of Religion*, pp. 88, 92, 96–7.

8 Cited in Dom B. Hemphill, *The Early Vicars Apostolic of England, 1685–1750* (1954), pp. 103–4.

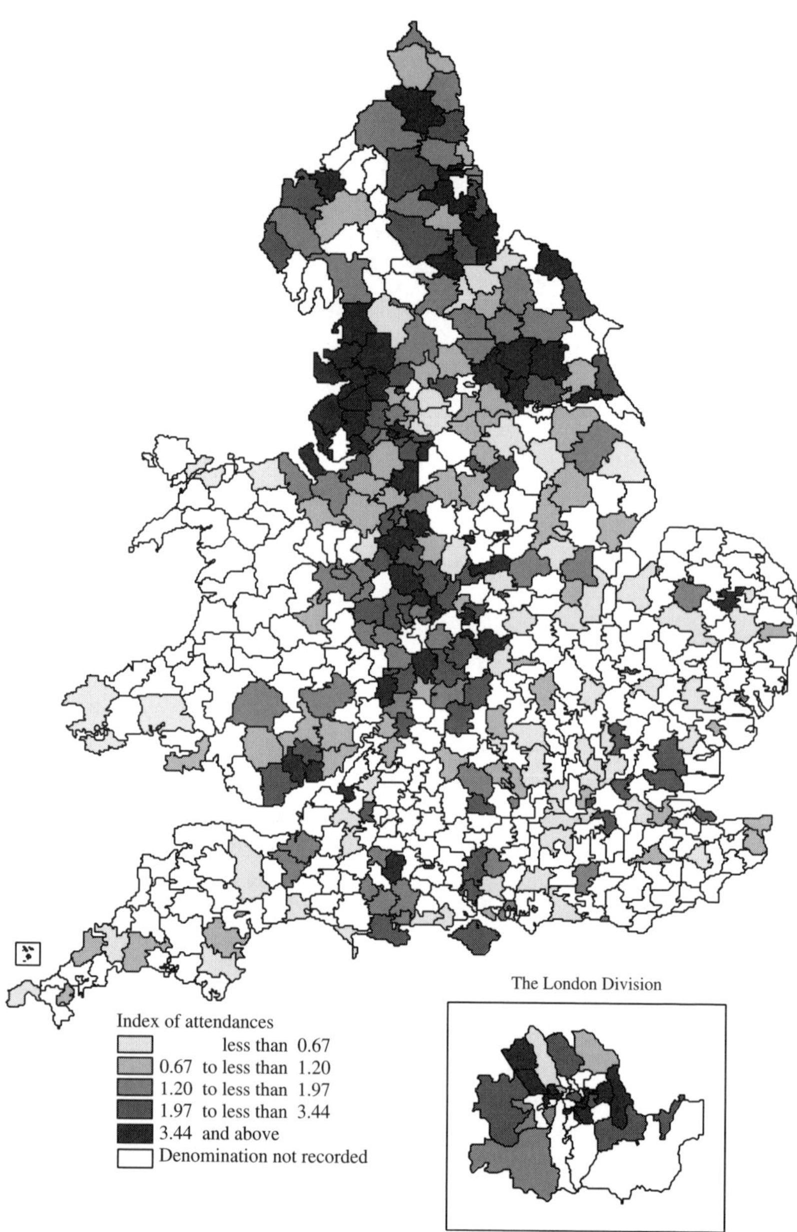

Figure 5.1. Roman Catholic index of attendances in 1851

situation had changed by 1851, giving much less cause for his general pessimism, but one can certainly see traces of his description remaining valid.

Catholicism was above average strength in essentially five regions. The first, a very clearly defined zone, included all of Lancashire's central and western districts. Lancashire Catholics survived the Reformation in greater numbers than elsewhere, being well away from the most heavily Protestantised south-eastern regions of the country.[9] They were later considerably augmented by Irish migrants, placing the county among the most striking areas of Catholic strength. It was recognised as such by Berington in 1780, for he saw London and Lancashire as having the largest numbers of Catholics.[10] The county had 114 places of Catholic worship, 20 per cent of the total in England and Wales.[11] The district of Liverpool exhibited extreme values for Catholics. It had nine Catholic churches with accommodation for 8,806, and showed 27,650 attendances in the morning, and a total of 40,300 attendances over all three times of the day.[12] Manchester had 21,771 total attendances, West Derby 18,102, Preston 12,771, and Wigan 7,927. Such districts had many Catholic places of worship. These were particularly high figures, but many other north-western districts had high numbers of attendances, such as Chorley, Clitheroe, Chorlton, Salford, Blackburn and Ormskirk. Indeed, for many years prior to 1851, one part of Manchester had been known as 'Little Ireland'; it was documented as such by commentators like Engels, J. P. Kay, G. C. Lewis and Angus Bethune Reach. Other parts of Lancashire had similar reputations. This band of high Catholic presence stretched from the Kendal district through much of the little industrialised north of Lancashire down to Liverpool, Wirrall, Manchester and some of the mill towns near the Cheshire border. The cultural and political repercussions of this west-central Lancashire Catholic presence, and its Protestant, Tory-voting

9 R. Hutton, *The Rise and Fall of Merry England: the Ritual Year, 1400–1700* (1994, Oxford, 1996 edn), pp. 96, 106–7, 140–1.

10 Hemphill, *Early Vicars Apostolic*, p. 103. The 1841 census gave a figure of 105,916 Irish in Lancashire, 34,300 of them in Manchester and 49,639 in Liverpool. *1841 Population Census*, preface, pp. 14–17.

11 *Census of Religious Worship*, pp. cxlvi–cxlvii.

12 These figures are for the Liverpool registration district. *Census of Religious Worship*, p. 92, no. 461. The figures for the city of Liverpool can be found in *ibid.*, p. cxlvii.

counterpart further east, were as striking to contemporaries as they have been to historians.[13]

Beyond Lancashire, relatively high attendance measures were found in parts of Yorkshire, like Bradford, Selby, Tadcaster and some adjoining districts. Further north, in a discontinuous band of districts in the north-east, Catholics were readily found in northern Northumberland and were numerous in the seaboard districts of county Durham. These included Rothbury, Durham district, Newcastle upon Tyne,[14] and districts like Stockton, Darlington and Teesdale. As Hemphill commented, the north 'had all along been the most Catholic part of the country'.[15]

Next there was a group of districts in the west midlands, where index figures were fairly high in south and central Staffordshire, like Penkridge, Walsall, Stafford and Tamworth, but extending to the Severn in the south, Nottingham in the east, and Cheadle in the north. Total numbers of attendances were highest in Nottingham, Wolverhampton and Birmingham (between 3,277 and 4,672). Further east in the midlands, the denomination was present in significant numbers in urban areas like Beeston, Derby and Loughborough. In the majority of registration districts in London where it had places of worship, it was of average or above average strength. The districts of Bermondsey, St Olave Southwark, Strand and St George Southwark had the highest percentage share of Catholics in London, the latter

[13] R. Halley, *Lancashire: its Puritanism and Nonconformity* (Manchester, 1869); F. O. Blundell, *Old Catholic Lancashire* (1925); A. H. Birch, *Small-Town Politics: a Study of Political Life in Glossop* (Oxford, 1959), pp. 20–2, 175–7; G. F. A. Best, 'Popular Protestantism in Victorian Britain', in R. Robson (ed.), *Ideas and Institutions of Victorian Britain* (1967); J. Vincent, 'The effect of the Second Reform Act in Lancashire', *Historical Journal*, 11 (1968), 84–94; E. R. Norman (ed.), *Anti-Catholicism in Victorian England* (1968); K. T. Hoppen, 'Tories, Catholics and the General Election of 1859', *Historical Journal*, 13 (1970); E. D. Steele, 'The Irish presence in the north of England, 1850–1914', *Northern History*, 12 (1976); J. A. Hilton, *Catholic Lancashire* (1981); J. A. Hilton, *The Lancastrian Catholic Heritage: a Historical Guide* (Wigan, 1984); P. F. Clarke, *Lancashire and the New Liberalism* (Cambridge, 1971); P. Joyce, *Visions of the People: Industrial England and the Question of Class, 1848–1914* (Cambridge, 1991), pp. 125–6.

[14] The returns for St Andrews Catholic Chapel in Newcastle commented: 'There are 10,000 Roman Catholics in Newcastle, 6000 of whom are served by one Roman Catholic priest, attached to this chapel. About 1000 labourers having families in Ireland attend this chapel'. P.R.O., HO 129, 552–563 (Newcastle St Andrew). This is cited here for general impression, rather than strict accuracy. There was a total of 4,893 Catholic attendances in the district of Newcastle upon Tyne.

[15] Hemphill, *Early Vicars Apostolic*, p. 104.

two districts being the most notable in a ranking of London Catholic indexes of attendance. The London numbers of total attendances were highest (in descending order) in the districts of Marylebone, St George Southwark, Strand, Bermondsey, Stepney, St Giles, Kensington and Islington.[16]

There were other less concentrated areas of strength. Catholic shares of all religious sittings were above average in some south Welsh valleys, notably in industrial and coastal Monmouthshire and the adjoining parts of Glamorgan. There were also a few individual districts, sometimes remote from other areas of Catholic strength, in which the denomination was relatively conspicuous. The Isle of Wight, parts of Dorset, Billericay and Chelmsford in Essex, Thanet in Kent, Bourn and Boston in Lincolnshire, Tisbury in Wiltshire, and East Stonehouse (centred on the Plymouth docks) were the main examples of these.

The 'index of occupancy' measure (which relates attendances to available sittings) suggests where there was a high demand for Catholic provision and a failure as yet to respond adequately to that demand. It is clear that this pressure upon available seating prevailed in many urban areas, very strikingly so in the registration districts of

[16] Marylebone had 7,800 total attendances, the others listed here were all over 3,000. For discussion of the London Irish, see J. Hickey, *Urban Catholics: Urban Catholicism in England and Wales from 1829 to the Present Day* (1967); L. H. Lees, 'Patterns of lower-class life: Irish slum communities in nineteenth-century London', in S. Thernstrom and R. Sennett (eds.), *Nineteenth-century Cities* (New Haven, 1969), 365–83; L. H. Lees, *Exiles of Erin: Irish Migrants in Victorian London* (Manchester, 1979); R. Swift and S. Gilley, *The Irish Presence in the Victorian City* (1985); J. C. H. Aveling, *The Handle and the Axe: the Catholic Recusants in England from the Reformation to Emancipation* (1976), pp. 303–4, on the Irish Catholic areas in Holborn, Wapping, Bermondsey, Whitechapel, Soho and Southwark by the 1770s. Middle-class Catholics were to be found especially in St Patrick's, Soho. One must also recall anti-Catholic prejudice, particularly in London. Catholics and their mass houses had been targeted during the five days of Gordon riots in 1780 – protests mainly in London, ostensibly against the Relief Act of 1778. There were to be many further expressions of anti-Catholic sentiment in the city. Catholics were long maligned by the English cockney, and treated as recalcitrant interlopers by the trade societies. Anti-Catholic mobs remained a problem in London and elsewhere shortly before and at the time of the Religious Census. Prime Minister Lord John Russell's public denunciation of the Catholic Church's supposed 'pretension of supremacy over the realm of England', fears for the safety of Faber and the London Oratory Church, and the Evangelical Alliance's organised antagonism against Roman Catholics, all contributed to anti-Popery riots, and to attacks on priests and buildings. 1851 ended with the start of Giacinto Achilli's libel case against John Henry Newman, which became a focus for anti-Catholicism.

Runcorn, Whitechapel, Sunderland and Bradford.[17] Other districts with high ratios of attendances to sittings were those of London and Middlesex: notably, in descending order, Whitechapel, St Giles, West Ham (Essex), St Olave Southwark, Stepney, Poplar, Strand, St George in the East, Islington, Mary-le-Bone and Bermondsey. In most of these cases, one is seeing the disproportion between Irish famine immigration and prior Catholic provision. Outside London, taking districts again in descending order, there were very high index of occupancy measures for Darlington, Gravesend, Whitehaven, Great Boughton, Liverpool, Malton, Barton-upon-Irwell, Durham, Manchester, Medway and Salford.[18] As for the London areas, these districts had high figures on this occupancy measure because of the unprecedented religious demands inaugurated locally by Irish immigration and settlement. Many of these districts were to experience steady or dramatic growth in Catholic provision after 1851, and it is easy to see why.

On the other hand, one can find in the 1851 data some areas where even total Catholic attendances for all services on Census Sunday fell below the sittings available for them. These were often districts in which Irish immigration was slight, in some cases where an older Catholic presence had not been much augmented by mid century. Among them were the districts of Worthing, Chichester, Guildford, Kingston, Midhurst, Dartford, Thanet, Eastry, Windsor, Tunbridge, Newbury, Bicester, Chipping Norton, Chelmsford and Hereford. A few northern districts were in this group, like Barnsley, Ashton-under-Lyne, Easingwold or Doncaster; but, as one might expect, the occurrence of such districts tended to be in the south or midlands.

Several main causes account for the patterns in Roman Catholic geography. There was the survival, in fairly limited areas, of Catholic communities whose origins usually dated from before the Reformation. These were normally situated some distance from London and centres of power, and as will be seen in chapter 8, they had sometimes been dependent upon the sympathy of local recusant gentry.[19] The total number of Catholics involved in such cases was

17 In all these the index was over 1,000.

18 In all of these districts the index was over 350.

19 After the Reformation some local settlements remained almost entirely Catholic, and examples of this may be found in Lancashire, Northumberland, Yorkshire, Lincolnshire, the Welsh marches, Cornwall or south Norfolk. For a common view of

small, especially compared with the towns, even if (at parish level) they could achieve very high indexes of attendances.[20] Such Catholic gentry in the countryside help to explain the scattered survival of rural Catholicism even today. In some localities gentry families had survived the period of penal legislation, and the anti-Catholic prejudice that accompanied it,[21] even though they suffered from double land taxes, fines, difficulties in purchasing lands, claims on their estates by Protestant relatives (as under the 1699 Act for 'further preventing the growth of Popery'),[22] shortages of lucrative civil and military offices under the Test and Corporation Acts, inability to practise law, or benefit from advowsons, and other problems. The peers for example (like the Dukes of Norfolk) were excused the Oath of Supremacy. Following the 1778–9 and 1791 extensions of toleration to Catholics, and Catholic emancipation in 1829, such long-established families more openly maintained places of worship, providing a base for missions and priests, and encouraging their local community and employees to worship in the Catholic church.[23] There were significant Catholic-owned estates in Northumberland, Durham, north Lancashire, and smaller numbers in Yorkshire (particularly in

the role of Catholic gentry, see Gay, *Geography of Religion*, pp. 85–6: 'Catholicism in England became inextricably linked with the Catholic squires and nobility. If we could plot the distribution of all the Catholic county families in 18th-century England, we would have a good distribution map of Catholicism.' This view now seems exaggerated: compare Rowlands, *Catholics of Parish and Town*, who places much more stress on urban Catholicism. Moreover in some rural areas, like Egton (north Yorkshire), Catholic survival occurred outside of any seigneurial community, its character being more dispersed, various and humble in affiliation, accommodating well to Protestant neighbours. W. J. Sheils, 'Catholics and their neighbours in a rural community: Egton Chapelry, 1590–1780', *Northern History*, 34 (1998); D. E. Fox, 'Families, Farming and Faith' (unpub. M.Phil thesis, University of Leicester, 1998).

20 The most remarkable example of this was the parish of Everingham (East Riding), which recorded a Roman Catholic index of attendances of 136.

21 This is recalled in a number of returns to the 1851 Religious Census. For example, at Hathersage the Catholic priest, Benjamin Hulme, remarked: 'one of the oldest chapels in England – once unroofed by a gang of Ruffians – urged on by their no-popery zeal – something like what at present animates the soul of Lord John Russell'. M. Tranter (ed.), *The Derbyshire Returns to the 1851 Religious Census* (Derbyshire Record Society, 23, Chesterfield, 1995), p. 195.

22 See for example Leics. C.R.O., QS 45/5/1 (1749).

23 Leading Catholic families could have dependants changing to their faith, like servants, gamekeepers, shopkeepers and other village inhabitants, as at Biddlestone or Callaly in Northumberland. Tenants also might often be Catholic, this even being in some cases a condition of tenancy. J. Bossy, 'Four Catholic congregations in rural Northumberland, 1750–1850', *Recusant History*, 9 (1967), 93–7. He rightly notes exceptions to this however, as at Hesleyside.

the North Riding), Monmouthshire and the midlands. Their influence can often be traced in 1851. For example, in the north-eastern districts of Hexham, Rothbury, Teesdale and Morpeth (where the denomination was found in some strength) there were the Catholic estates of Minsteracres, Felton, Hesleyside and Croxdale.[24]

Locally important though such families could be, their agrarian bias meant that they were not as significant by the mid eighteenth century as the urban Catholics in London, many Lancashire towns, and (in lesser numbers) in some older county towns like York, Durham, Norwich, Worcester or Winchester. Overlaid upon these earlier patterns, sometimes with a different occupational composition and geography, were the Irish Catholic immigrants of the early nineteenth century and famine years. Irish immigration, like Irish seasonal migration, occurred throughout the first half of the nineteenth century. It was facilitated by the growing numbers of regular and cheap steamships operating between English, Welsh, Scottish and Irish ports.[25] Much of this immigration was due to the less researched earlier years of Irish famine, like those of 1821–2; but it reached its tragic height with the potato crop failures of 1845–50. As a consequence of indigenous Catholic growth after 1778, 1791 and 1829, and Irish immigration, the numbers of Catholic churches in England and Wales almost doubled between 1824 and 1853.[26] In 1841 there were 300,000 Irish-born residents in England and Wales. By the 1851 census that had

[24] Gay, *Geography of Religion*, p. 94.

[25] F. Engels, *The Condition of the Working Class in England* (1845, Glasgow, 1984 edn), p. 123, the passage costing fourpence; A. Redford, *Labour Migration in England, 1800–1850* (1926, Manchester, 1976 edn), chs. 8–9; R. Lawton, 'Irish immigration to England and Wales in the mid-nineteenth century', *Irish Geography*, 4 (1959); S. Gilley, 'The Roman Catholic mission to the Irish in London, 1840–1860', *Recusant History*, 10 (1969), 125; Lees, *Exiles of Erin*, pp. 45–8.

[26] They grew from 346 in 1824, to 616 in 1853. The rate of growth was fairly sustained, but most brisk in 1824–6, and after 1838. This was more rapid than for the combined Protestant churches. *Census of Religious Worship*, pp. ci and cxlvii–cxlviii. For the growing numbers of religious houses and priests (1841–53), see *ibid.*, p. cii, table B. This was a remarkable invigoration compared to the rather depressed condition of English and Welsh Catholicism in much of the eighteenth century. For earlier figures, from sources like the Reports of the Vicars Apostolic to Rome, giving numbers of Catholics, priests and missions (for 1706, 1773, 1780 and 1803), see T. G. Holt, 'A note on some eighteenth century statistics', *Recusant History*, 10 (1969), 3–10. He documents large increases from c. 1800. For London's Catholic population, which far outnumbered the seats available in the city's Roman Catholic churches, in places like Deptford, Poplar or Hackney, see Gilley, 'The Roman Catholic mission', 124–5, 130; W. G. Lumley, 'The statistics of the Roman Catholic Church in England and Wales', *Journal of the Statistical Society of London*, 27 (1964).

reached 519,959.[27] Huge numbers landed at Liverpool and worked in the industrial north-west. Many others arrived in places like Newport, Tyneside and London, either settling in coastal vicinities or moving on to other industrial areas like the west midlands. A large Roman Catholic presence in Plymouth was linked to its role as a port of departure for the New World, and other ports shared this function. An 1850 Directory commented that there were 320 poor Irish in Plymouth waiting for emigration ships.[28] In naval ports like Portsmouth the Irish presence had grown since their involvement as troops, seamen and dockers during the Napoleonic Wars. In addition, the priests who left France after the Civil Constitution of 1791 had often resided in coastal towns like Falmouth, Poole, Christchurch, Plymouth, Portsmouth or Whitby, and they made a considerable contribution to the local cause of Catholicism.[29]

Such urban provenance was a striking feature of Catholicism, and it conferred long-term advantages which many other denominations lacked. As Norman commented: 'The missionary nature of the Church at the end of the eighteenth century . . . well adapted it to face the social dislocations of the new industrial concentrations. It had no ancient structure of parochial administration or out-moded diocesan finance, as the State Church had, to encumber its approach to the new population.'[30] He estimated that 'by the 1850s, something like eighty per cent of its Catholic congregations were Irish and working-class'.[31] As this indicates, the Catholic Church over the coming decades was to have a strongly urban and proletarian allegiance, much more so than in the seventeenth or even eighteenth century; and this support and Catholic identity were naturally fortified by the persisting indigenous hostility against Irish labouring immigrants.[32]

[27] P. Hughes, 'The English Catholics in 1850', in G. A. Beck (ed.), *The English Catholics, 1850–1950* (1950), 44–5. There were probably between 800,000 and a million Catholics in England by 1851, that is between 4.5 and 5.5 per cent of the population. Gay, *Geography of Religion*, pp. 89, 97.

[28] W. White, *History, Gazetteer and Directory of Devonshire* (Sheffield, 1850), p. 634.

[29] D. Bellenger, 'The English Catholics and the French exiled clergy', *Recusant History*, 15 (1979–81).

[30] E. Norman, *The English Catholic Church in the Nineteenth Century* (Oxford, 1984), p. 7.

[31] *Ibid.*, p. 7.

[32] H. McLeod, *Class and Religion in the Late Victorian City* (1974), p. 35; H. McLeod, *Religion and the Working Class in Nineteenth-Century Britain* (1984), p. 38; S. Gilley, 'Protestant London, No-Popery and the Irish poor, 1830–60', *Recusant History*, 10 (1970); S. Gilley, 'Papists, Protestants and the Irish in London', in G. J. Cuming and D. Baker (eds.), *Studies in Church History: Popular Belief and Practice* (Cambridge, 1972).

In 1851 the Roman Catholic Church in England and Wales had certainly not reached its nineteenth-century apogee, for the poverty of the recently arrived Irish held back the institutional expansion of facilities that subsequently emerged. (Nor perhaps should one assume that the Irish had been as regular church attenders in Ireland, or upon arrival, as they were later to become.) Lynn Hollen Lees has pointed out that 'In 1851 there were not enough priests and churches to accommodate any more Catholics. Almost 20 per cent of the Irish-born in London lived in census districts without any sort of Catholic chapel, and Catholic Churches in heavily settled Irish areas were filled to capacity. The lack of space helps to explain the low Catholic attendance record.'[33] It is clear from the occupancy measures we derive from the Religious Census that the Catholic Church was under most pressure in the urban and highly populated areas,[34] where its indexes of attendance were high, and where it was to build large churches. Its growth after 1851 was to be focused in those areas. That expansion was certainly to become one of the most striking success stories of post-1851 religion.[35]

33 Lees, *Exiles of Erin*, pp. 181–2.

34 At registration-district level, for 299 districts where Catholics were present, the index of occupancy was correlated at 0.343 with population density, and at 0.320 with population size in 1851. The index of occupancy was also correlated at 0.339 with its index of attendances ($p = .000$ in all cases).

35 R. Currie, A. D. Gilbert and L. Horsley, *Churches and Churchgoers: Patterns of Church Growth in the British Isles since 1700* (Oxford, 1977), p. 153; Norman, *English Catholic Church*, pp. 205–6; M. P. Hornsby-Smith, 'An unsecular America', in S. Bruce (ed.), *Religion and Modernization: Sociologists and Historians Debate the Secularization Thesis* (Oxford, 1992), p. 127.

6

Denominational co-existence, reciprocity or exclusion?

Introducing the historiography

This chapter aims to resolve certain long-standing debates about the regional reciprocity or proximity of the major denominations. Some of the most widely found and important hypotheses in nineteenth-century religious historiography have been concerned with how Wesleyan Methodism and its various offshoots were related to the strengths and weaknesses of the Church of England, and secondly to the regional presence of the old dissenting denominations. The conclusions reached on these matters have a number of significant implications for further issues, bearing as they do on religious rivalries and the reasons for denominational success or failure, the regional political influence of denominations, and the extent to which they acted in union with or in antagonism against each other. In handling such issues historians have adopted different regions for study, and varied units for analysis: sometimes the county, sometimes the registration district, occasionally the parish, or township. Some religious scholars have been vague about what units of analysis they are using, or indeed what regions they are discussing, and many have couched their arguments in rather impressionistic terms. The data and methods here allow some further understanding of these issues. For the purpose of this chapter, analysis will be of the registration-district data mapped earlier in this book, for this is best tailored to study the whole compass of Wales and England.

The major arguments to consider may be summarised. Tillyard published an article as long ago as 1935, one that quickly attained the status of 'the Tillyard thesis', arguing that the English counties in which the Methodist churches became strong were noticeably distinct and separate from the regions of old dissent in the form of the

Congregationalists, Baptists and Presbyterians.[1] His data for the early twentieth century were of the number of full-time ministers in each county, and the number of people to each minister. Using county rankings based on these figures, he argued that 'A comparison of the two lists shows how complementary to the other denominations the work of the Methodists has been. Not one of the first twelve counties of the first list appears among the first twelve in the second list. Much the same thing applies to the end of the list. Of the ten counties at the bottom of the first list not one appears in the ten counties at the bottom of the second list.'[2]

A number of historians have elaborated or qualified this argument for the complementary nature of old and new dissent, often basing their views on Tillyard's figures. However, it has been shown elsewhere that Tillyard's own data, when tested statistically, yield very low correlation coefficients that do not support his arguments in a convincing way.[3] In fact, his figures indicated almost no relationship of any sort between old and new dissent in England, and on the basis of such figures it is surprising that historians gave any credibility to the Tillyard thesis. There may well be a relationship of the sort he argued for – and the national maps hint strongly at such regional complementarity – but such an association is not adequately demonstrated by Tillyard.

Views like those of Tillyard have been presented by other authors. One well-respected argument to similar effect was made by Robert Currie, modestly offered 'as a possible starting point for inquiry'.[4] His research led him to the view that 'whilst the older dissent generally grew strong where the Church of England was strong, deriving (at least historically) much of its membership directly from the Church of England, Methodism grew strong where the Church of England was weak, and recruited from those sections of the population that Anglicanism failed to reach . . . the bulk of Wesleyan membership and

1 F. Tillyard, 'The distribution of the Free Churches in England', *Sociological Review*, 27 (1935), 1–18. He used figures for the new Methodist Church, comprising Wesleyan and Primitive Methodism, and the United Methodists. 2 *Ibid.*, 11.

3 K. D. M. Snell, *Church and Chapel in the North Midlands: Religious Observance in the Nineteenth Century* (Leicester, 1991), pp. 3–4. Spearman's rank correlation between Tillyard's figures for old and new dissent was only −0.080, showing an almost complete absence of relationship between the figures on which he based his thesis, and which subsequent historians have widely referred to.

4 R. Currie, 'A micro-theory of Methodist growth', *Proceedings of the Wesleyan Historical Society*, 36 (1967), 73.

the greatest sustained Wesleyan growth occurred in precisely the areas where the Church of England was weakest'.[5] In judgements like this, the Church of England is seen as having had the pivotal role, and its regional strengths or weaknesses are held to have had a prime influence upon the other denominations. Some authors view Nonconformity of almost any kind as tending to occupy ground that the established church had neglected. Other arguments interpret previous Anglican strength as having a predominant effect mainly upon Methodist development.

Some historians have taken a different, and sometimes a more sceptical, position on these issues. Coleman, for example, in one of the most detailed examinations of the 1851 religious data for the south of England, suggested that there was 'no firm inverse relationship between levels of Anglican practice and levels of Nonconformity. In some areas, both did well; in other areas, both badly.'[6] It has also been shown elsewhere that analyses of such relationships using *county-level* data and large religious groupings can point to the same conclusions: that there is little correspondence of any sort between the Anglican Church and Protestant dissent in 1851.[7] As was clear from such earlier work, what is needed is analysis of data taken from more refined geographical units than the county, making finer denominational distinctions, and supplying an overview of all England and Wales, against which regional diversities and separate experiences may then be set and explained.

In what probably best summarises most historians' judgements to date, Gilbert argued that Nonconformity was generally successful 'only where the Church was either too weak or too negligent to defend its traditional monopoly of English religious practice. There was an important inverse relationship, in short, between the decline of "Church" religiosity and the proliferation of "Chapel" communities

[5] Currie, 'Micro-theory of Methodist growth', 68.

[6] B. I. Coleman, *The Church of England in the Mid-nineteenth Century: a Social Geography* (1980), p. 9. See also his 'Southern England in the Census of Religious Worship, 1851', *Southern History*, 5 (1983). For an important regional study assessing these issues, and reaching rather different conclusions, see D. G. Hey, 'The pattern of Nonconformity in south Yorkshire', *Northern History*, 8 (1973).

[7] Snell, *Church and Chapel*, pp. 6–8. In that exercise, prior to more conspicuous results with registration-district analysis in *ibid.*, pp. 28–38, there was little correspondence between Welsh and English county figures for Anglican and Protestant dissenting attendances. The same was true for North Midland registration-district indexes of sittings.

in the period preceding the Anglican reforms of the 1830s.'[8] He stressed that 'The demographic and economic revolutions damaged the parochial system, and enlarged the context for Nonconformist growth, not by creating but by proliferating the kinds of situations in which the machinery of the religious Establishment broke down.'[9] As is clear from previous chapters, this is a persuasive summary. Situations like these included a host of growing towns and cities, many rural dispersed or multi-nucleated settlements in the north, but also in parts of the south and midlands too, upland regions like the Lake District, newly drained fenlands, or the many outworking, mining, quarrying and related industrial communities, with their increasingly non-agricultural workforces, which expanded so markedly during the eighteenth and nineteenth centuries.

A feature of much historiography has been a tendency to separate 'church' and 'chapel', and to assess these questions by means of such a dichotomy, using it as the main explanatory framework. In Alan Everitt's pioneering work on these issues, one of the main preoccupations was to isolate the local conditions that fostered religious dissent, the latter again usually taken in its entirety. Everitt had much of value to say about varieties of dissent, which he handled with

[8] A. D. Gilbert, *Religion and Society in Industrial England: Church, Chapel and Social Change, 1740–1914* (1976, Harlow, 1984 edn), p. 94; A. D. Gilbert, 'Religion and political stability in early industrial England', in P. K. O'Brien and R. Quinault (eds.), *The Industrial Revolution and British Society* (Cambridge, 1993), p. 89; H. McCleod, *Religion and the Working Class in Nineteenth-century Britain* (1984), p. 22: 'chapels sprang up where the Established Churches were weak: in new communities without their own parish church, in outlying hamlets, in working-class neighbourhoods of cities. It is evident that groups such as the Methodists were filling a vacuum left by the failure of the Established Churches'; H. D. Rack, *Reasonable Enthusiast: John Wesley and the Rise of Methodism* (1989, 1992 edn), pp. 179, 214–15, 220–1, 236, 271; C. Brooks, 'Introduction', in C. Brooks and A. Saint (eds.), *The Victorian Church: Architecture and Society* (Manchester, 1995), p. 4; J. Davies, *A History of Wales* (1990, Harmondsworth, 1993 edn), p. 360. Or see J. D. Gay, *The Geography of Religion in England* (1971), pp. 109, 145, 147–8, 159: 'The distribution pattern of Methodism which emerged in the 19th century was largely determined by the geographical variations in the Church of England's ability to maintain a proper pastoral oversight of the people in the 18th century. As a faithful member of the Church of England John Wesley saw his own work as complementing and reinforcing the work of the Established Church in areas where the Church was weak. Where the Church was running efficiently and catering for the needs of the local community, Wesley left well alone . . . Methodism was to become most influential in the areas where the Church of England had failed to provide for the pastoral needs of the people – in Cornwall, the Black Country, the north-east and the new industrial areas in Lancashire and Yorkshire.'

[9] Gilbert, *Religion and Society*, p. 110.

characteristic sensitivity and discernment, but his writing on this subject was mainly concerned with the fundamental dichotomy of the Anglican Church or Nonconformity. He was interested in isolating the types of parish where the former could maintain its congregations, as compared with those other parishes where a variety of local conditions favoured the establishment of chapels and allowed dissent to thrive.[10] Many contemporaries thought in similar terms too, which was inevitable given the context of an established church – some indeed spoke of dissenters in one breath as though they were all 'Methodists', or some such breed.[11]

A church and chapel dichotomy has enabled many most illuminating interpretations to be presented by historians, and it has much enhanced the quality of local religious history. Many further examples of Nonconformist success could be discussed in relation to the varying topographies and socio-economic contexts in which they occurred, and these differed in many ways. However, the main aim in this chapter is to clinch the arguments at the level of broad generalisation, on the national scale, and to do this one needs developments of method, as well as to keep the interesting local examples and literary evidence under firm and balanced control within a quantitative overview. It is necessary also to digress beyond the relationship between the Church of England and 'Nonconformity', to explore quantitative associations between the main strands of Nonconformity itself. For there is little doubt that many contemporaries found these latter divisions, particularly those within Methodism, as being most fundamental to their religious experiences.[12] There are good reasons for thinking also that perceptions about such divisions may often have had as important an influence upon denominational location as perceptions about the regional dominance or deficiencies of the established church.

Analysis of the registration-district data

In religious historiography, very few authors have examined the arguments presented by Tillyard, Currie, Gilbert or Everitt via the

[10] A. Everitt, *The Pattern of Rural Dissent: the Nineteenth Century* (Leicester, 1972); and his 'Nonconformity in country parishes', in J. Thirsk (ed.), *Land, Church and People: Essays Presented to Professor H. P. R. Finberg* (Reading, 1970).

[11] See for example Squire Lavington in C. Kingsley, *Yeast* (1851, 1902 edn), p. 90.

[12] R. Currie, *Methodism Divided: a Study in the Sociology of Ecumenicalism* (1968).

Table 6.1. *Spearman (rank) correlation coefficients between major denominations, using their indexes of attendances, by registration districts*

	England (576 districts)	Wales (48 districts)	England & Wales (624 districts)
Church of England & Baptists	0.271*	−0.002	0.144*
Church of England & Independents	0.300*	−0.269	0.141*
Church of England & Wesleyan Methodists	−0.203*	−0.090	−0.174*
Church of England & Primitive Methodists	−0.194*	0.296	−0.099
Church of England & all old dissent	0.300*	−0.188	0.137*
Church of England & all new dissent	−0.265*	−0.352	−0.339*
Wesleyan Methodism & Baptists	−0.007	−0.157	−0.013
Wesleyan Methodists & Independents	−0.184*	−0.321	−0.167*
Wesleyan Methodism & Primitive Methodists	0.427*	0.130	0.404*
Wesleyan Methodism & all old dissent	−0.145*	−0.346	−0.136*
All new dissent & all old dissent	−0.191*	−0.257	−0.070
Primitive Methodists & Baptists	−0.043	0.116	−0.083
Primitive Methodists & Independents	−0.159*	−0.401	−0.219*
Baptists & Independents	0.256*	0.207	0.318*

Note: * = significant at .001

quantitative methods that would be appropriate to test them. This is despite the quasi-quantitative terminology in which these arguments are often expressed. If the Tillyard or Currie theses are correct, one would expect to find significant negative correlations between the Anglican Church and the Methodist denominations, and between old and new dissent, over all the registration districts. To test this, table 6.1 gives the Spearman (rank) correlation coefficients for the major denominations, showing the relationships between their index of attendances for England and Wales separately, and then for England and Wales combined in the final column. The analysis was conducted in a variety of ways, using Pearson's correlation also, and using the index of sittings as well as attendances. In all these exercises the results were very similar indeed, and so this table is presented as best illustrating the inter-relationships between the major denominations and religious groups.

The findings in this table are statistically strongest for England, rather than Wales, given the larger numbers of English districts being examined. If one starts with the 576 English districts, the table shows clearly that the Church of England was associated on the ground with the old dissenters, taking the predominant Baptists and Independents. The coefficients were invariably positive here, and overall (using these and all other old dissenting denominations) the association was positive ($r = 0.300$). To generalise therefore, old dissent and the Church of England were co-associated, tending to be strong in the same regions. This confirms many impressions gained from the maps in previous chapters. Even so, while the coefficients are very significant statistically (given such a large number of districts), they are not that high, and so one should not exaggerate the co-association between the established church and old dissent.[13]

This contrasts with the relation between the established church and the two largest Methodist denominations. Here one finds negative associations: in other words, Methodism tended to develop in areas where the established church was weak. There was almost no difference in this between Wesleyan and Primitive Methodism. The Church of England was even more negatively associated with 'new dissent' when these and all the other new dissenting denominations are grouped together ($r = -0.265$).

The relationships between the dissenting denominations are also intriguing, and these can be as historically revealing as those involving the Church of England. It is very clear from the English correlations that Wesleyan and Primitive Methodism went hand in hand regionally – this relation was the strongest result of this analysis. It has been argued elsewhere, for the North Midlands, that Primitive Methodism as a breakaway group was one that appealed to lower social classes, in similar regions to those in which Wesleyan Methodism gained hold.[14]

[13] The Quakers were inversely associated with the Anglican Church ($r = -0.102$), as one would expect for such a persecuted faith, and also with Wesleyan Methodism ($r = -0.135$, $p = .001$). They were positively associated with Primitive Methodism ($r = 0.129$, $p = .001$). This analysis shows little relation of Quakerism to any other denomination.

[14] Snell, *Church and Chapel*, ch. 5, esp. pp. 41–5. This argument was based on occupational data in Nonconformist baptism registers for Leicestershire, Lincolnshire and Derbyshire.

The national coefficients here reinforce the view of regional similarity between these two denominations, which is what their respective histories would lead us to expect.[15] By comparison, old and new dissent were negatively associated, more significantly so for England than was shown in Tillyard's data, although perhaps not as strongly as one might presume. The Roman Catholics (not in the table) tended to be strongest in areas separate from the old dissenting regions (−0.191), especially away from the Baptists (−0.231), and away from the most Anglican areas (−0.237).[16] All these results were confirmed by a variety of different analyses for England, using different statistical procedures and religious measures. In most cases the correlations are not that striking, and of course a great many other considerations must be taken into account when interpreting the regionality of denominations. However, there are fairly clear dispositions within the data. At the level of broad generalisation about England, there is no doubt that these conclusions are valid, and that Tillyard and Currie were correct in the arguments they made.[17]

The Welsh situation had some similarities with the English, although there were exceptions. Independency (and to a much lesser extent the Baptists) in Wales was negatively associated with the established church, contrary to the pattern in England. The same inverse relation held between combined 'old dissent' and the established church. It is interesting that Welsh 'new dissent' when amalgamated was more inversely associated with the established church than in England, and evidently there were religiously contrasted regions in Wales underlying this, involving in particular the heartlands of Welsh Calvinistic Methodism.[18] In Wales, Wesleyan Methodism was strongly disassociated with the Independents and

[15] This is quite unlike the relation between Bible Christianity and Primitive Methodism in England, two denominations that in some respects appealed to comparable groups among the lower-middle and working classes ($r = -0.342$, $p = .000$). Such a result shows how well these two denominations reciprocated each other regionally: the Primitives in the midlands, the north-east and eastern counties, the Bible Christians in the south-west.

[16] These Roman Catholic coefficients are all significant at .001.

[17] A rather similar point was in fact made by Sir John Pakington (MP for Droitwich) in the parliamentary debates over whether there should be another Religious Census in 1861. He spoke of how 'our Dissenting brethren' had 'filled up that vacancy which exists in the means and administration of the Church of England'. *Hansard's Parliamentary Debates*, CLIX (11 July 1860), 1730.

[18] Welsh Calvinistic Methodism is not shown in table 6.1, given its specificity to Wales. Within Wales, its Spearman correlation coefficients with the following main denominations were as follows: Church of England −0.362; Independents 0.149; Baptists −0.390; all old dissent −0.120; Wesleyan Methodists 0.132; Primitive

with 'old dissent' combined, more so than in England. Old and new dissent in general terms were more regionally separate, mainly because of the disassociation between the Baptists and Welsh Calvinistic Methodists, which was plainly visible in the maps. As in England, the Baptists and Independents tended to be co-associated, but old dissent tended to be inversely related to the presence of the established church.[19] In all such generalisations broad tendencies are being described in the entire Welsh data, and more localised studies would throw up a finer assortment of patterns.

The overall English and Welsh picture is of course broadly similar to that described for England alone, given the numerical predominance of English districts. There was a weak disposition for old dissent to be strongest in similar regions as the Church of England. There were rather more striking negative relationships between the established church and Methodism or new dissent, although compared with Wesleyan Methodism the probably more assertive Primitive Methodists must have found themselves frequently jostling the established church in similar regions, for there was almost no inverse association between them ($r=-0.099$). These two major new dissenting denominations tended to share regions of strength, and the same was true for the two main old dissenting faiths. In both cases, this similarity of regional coverage between the Baptists and Independents ($r=0.318$) and between Wesleyan and Primitive Methodists ($r=0.404$) provide the strongest results in the last column of table 6.1. Finally, there was a tendency for old and new dissenting denominations to be negatively correlated, which once more reinforces the religious geographies seen earlier in the maps.[20]

Methodists −0.704. (Only the last result is significant at .001. The Baptist result is significant at .01.)

19 None of these Welsh findings is significant at the .001 level, because of the much smaller numbers of registration districts in Wales providing data compared with England. The analyses do however cover the whole of Wales, and in this sense the conclusions are definitive.

20 It is possible that some of these bivariate correlations are affected by the prior effect of the Church of England on the denominations concerned, and it is helpful to 'remove' statistically such a background influence. The Church of England needs 'to be held constant' as it pre-dates the others. Accordingly a number of the key denominational associations were explored via partial correlation, a procedure suitable for such a problem. Taking account of the Anglican Church in this manner tended slightly to weaken the coefficients between the Baptists and Independents, between Wesleyan and Primitive Methodism, and between old and new dissent, but it did not have much effect on them. The relation between Wesleyan Methodism and old dissent stayed the same.

Regional differences in England

There are English regional differences within this picture that are worth mentioning.[21] Table 6.2 shows some broad comparisons. Besides the connection between the Wesleyan and Primitive Methodists, the denominations show little association between each other at this level in the London, south-east and eastern census divisions. It is interesting that in this region, in or proximate to the metropolis, denominations were more random with regard to each other. This kind of relative heterogeneity is hard to make tangible to the historical imagination, but it must have marked off experience around the metropolis from that in other more distant regions, which seem to have had either greater polarisations of religious adherence, or a more marked propensity for certain denominations to share common ground while neglecting other areas within their broad region. For in those other regions (beyond the south-east) the quantitative patterns become more striking. The established church was negatively associated with the two main Methodist denominations and all new dissent – for the Primitives this was most notable in the midland counties, and for the Wesleyans in the south-west. There was striking disassociation between new dissent and the Church of England in the south-west, and between old and new dissent in the same region. Primitive Methodism had little influence in the south-west, but there was a significant relationship between Wesleyan Methodism and Bible Christianity there.[22] In most of these regions there were positive correlations between the established church and the old dissenting faiths. The three most northern divisions show the most striking correlation within Methodism, and a tendency for old and new dissent to be disassociated geographically. Otherwise many of the relationships are weak in the north.

Much of this picture supplements in a predictable way the national patterns of table 6.1. However, it is a lesson of table 6.2 that regional co-associations can differ from any national picture. While the regions tend towards consistent results, this is by no means always the case, and groups of census divisions can readily be found that run counter to the general picture. Further analytical fragmentation of the

[21] The 48 registration districts in Wales do not allow much scope for regional subdivision at this level when using rank correlation, so this section is restricted to England.

[22] r = 0.325 (sig. = .003).

Table 6.2. *Spearman (rank) correlation coefficients between major denominations, using their indexes of attendances, distinguishing between English regions, by registration districts*

	London, South-east & Eastern divisions (187 districts)	South-midland, North-midland, & West-midland divisions (185 districts)	South-west division (79 districts)	North-west, Yorkshire & Northern divisions (125 districts)
Church of England & Baptists	−0.033	0.211	0.143	0.023
Church of England & Independents	0.104	0.344*	0.379*	0.040
Church of England & Wesleyan Methodists	−0.081	−0.175	−0.451*	0.131
Church of England & Primitive Methodists	0.122	−0.410*	0.046	−0.075
Church of England & all old dissent	0.013	0.326*	0.373*	−0.106
Church of England & all new dissent	0.012	−0.372*	−0.544*	0.053
Wesleyan Methodism & Baptists	0.147	0.214	−0.264	−0.011
Wesleyan Methodism & Independents	−0.192	−0.135	−0.359*	0.149
Wesleyan Methodism & Primitive Methodists	0.356*	0.404*	0.003	0.682
Wesleyan Methodists & all old dissent	−0.066	0.104	−0.362*	−0.184
All old dissent & all new dissent	−0.052	0.008	−0.439*	−0.162
Primitive Methodists & Baptists	0.209	−0.136	0.075	0.034
Primitive Methodists & Independents	−0.018	−0.228	0.099	0.021
Baptists & Independents	0.112	0.264*	0.205	0.246

Note: * = significant at .001

country produces greater variety still. In Norfolk, Suffolk and Essex for example (the census Eastern Division), there were much stronger inverse relationships between old and new dissent than was found nationally, and many further examples like this could be mentioned. When generalising about these issues, historians will need to be keenly aware of such differences. As was written elsewhere, 'it is frequently incorrect to argue in the hard and fast historiographical manner for particular patterns of association as generally applying'.[23]

Conclusion

These mid nineteenth-century results are fairly conspicuous at the national level, despite the regional variations. They reinforce the impressions from religious cartography. There were many regional variations in these inter-relationships, but emphasis has been placed on the overall patterns. Religious geographies in 1851 were of considerable stability, with the exception mainly of some features of Catholicism. Even though religious adherence weakened into the next century, it would be extraordinary indeed if any other data sources in the nineteenth century altered in a significant way the national picture given here. Pre-1851 data are hard to use for such analyses, because such data often lack precise denominational specificity (as with the 1676 Compton Census), or lack completeness on the 1851 scale. Other nineteenth-century data, like the 1829 religious returns, show very tight matches indeed with the 1851 returns, as will be seen in chapter 8. It will be shown there that one certainly should not overstate the case for local religious continuities between 1676 and 1851, and in the seventeenth and eighteenth centuries it remains possible that such co-associations may differ in a number of ways from those in 1851. However, for the mid nineteenth century, epitomising as it does something close to the final fruition that many of these denominations achieved, this chapter's conclusions and the previous cartography should at last have resolved the Tillyard and related debates at this registration-district level of analysis.

The implications of this for religious historiography are of much interest, and here one anticipates greater study and appreciation of the contrasting experiences of different regions, and the ways in which the 'national' patterns of association may have influenced the

[23] Snell, *Church and Chapel*, p. 35.

more tangible and political aspects of religious history that can be uncovered through more conventional literary sources. The relationships between denominations – using the word 'relationship' in its everyday meaning – must have been coloured in many ways by the quantitative realities and juxtapositions discussed, and by the relative regional intensities of them. A statistical relationship on the ground between two or more denominations is evidently a different matter to a social, theological or political relationship, and nobody would wish to deduce the latter in any simple manner from the former. Yet the two are certainly connected and may influence each other in many ways. Strengths, associations and regional structures that can be described quantitatively affect the form and intensity of denominational conflict. Relations between church and chapel varied considerably, according to the regional contexts. In some regions dissent was hardly likely to be viewed as a threatening anti-establishment entity; in other more Anglican regions it manifestly was. This depended partly on the regional strengths and congruity of denominations, and on the rivalry between local personalities. Rivalry and proximity (say of old dissent and the established church in many southern and midland regions) had quite different effects from those found where dissent gained ground in a vacuum of religious provision. The Church of England (a complex and eclectic body at any time, not least in 1851) was itself affected by these disparate regional realities, which contributed to the diversity of political and moral stances emanating from it. Anglican–Methodist frictions were far more regionally varied than much written history describes, just as they also varied over time, ranging for example from Wesley's conservative declarations, to the Primitive Methodism of many agricultural union leaders. Much the same was true of the little-discussed relationships between old dissent and Methodism. Historians need to make much more sense of the conflicting localised evidence of mutual tolerance or outright antagonism. To do so they will need above all to be comparatively regional, having a more refined sense of denominations' locations and of how these fit into the national frame.[24]

[24] The necessity for a regional (and indeed cartographical) understanding relates to many general arguments. See for example the influential work by H. Perkin, *The Origins of Modern English Society, 1780–1880* (1969, 1976 edn), e.g. pp. 34–7, arguing for old and new dissent as being akin to layers of filling in a 'sandwich'-like social structure, attracting different social affiliations. Whatever the empirical value of such a view, it seems compromised by showing little awareness of the regional dimensions of religious support.

Some religious historians may balk at the quantitative methods used here. They will prefer to generalise from parochial examples, or from literary impressions, or from intimately understood local case studies. It is entirely appropriate that a variety of methods be practised. One advantage of quantification is that it contributes to define problems and historical questions that can then prompt further refocusing of traditional research with literary evidence, facilitating a branching into other paths. There is of course a risk that conclusions reached through the social statistics might remain isolated from the more conventional religious historiography; but one can surely trust that the systematising skills of historians will allow them to meld in original ways such different approaches. It will be necessary in due course to progress much beyond the statistical verification of generalisations current in religious historiography, which has been the concern in this chapter. The historical quantitative approach to religion, or the historical sociology or geography of religion, has barely commenced as a subject – the fresh approaches open to it are immense – and one hopes that the questions asked will refine and extend conventional religious history, rather than becoming yet another rarefied and isolated sub-specialism.

The national picture is now clearer, and the cartography has portrayed in a more approachable way the regional dimensions. Within an understanding of that national framework, one can now appreciate more fully the distinctiveness of regional experiences, and the understanding of those regional histories can have a greater sense of what was special about them, and of what they lent to the national panorama. As the most renowned English historical demographers were aware, one needs to understand the overall complex before one can come to terms in a balanced way with the regional or local. The second part of this book will shift its analytical terms of reference considerably. Having described the national geographies, from now on the attention shifts to *parishes* from fifteen counties, rather than registration districts. This parish-level data will allow the coverage of further themes in the more tightly focused and regionally subtle way that they warrant.

Part 2

Religion and locality: parish-level explorations

7

A prospect of fifteen counties

The fifteen registration-district counties chosen for parish-level analysis were the Welsh ones of Anglesey, Caernarvonshire, Cardiganshire and Monmouthshire, and for England Bedfordshire, Cambridgeshire, Derbyshire, Dorset, the East Riding, Lancashire, Leicestershire, Northumberland, Rutland, Suffolk and Sussex. They provide a total of 2,443 parishes. These parishes contained 4,645,702 people in 1851, or 26 per cent of the population of England and Wales. The counties were selected primarily because they each represent distinctive regional features of the national geography of English and Welsh religion, and because of their diverse social, economic and political characteristics. The diversity of English and Welsh regions has often been downplayed in historical writing, and so it is important to describe these counties in a comparative way. This will provide a framework for later discussion.[1]

The Welsh counties

Let me start with the counties in Wales, where distinctive religious patterns were central to Welsh identities. Anglesey and Caernarvonshire, the north-western counties of 'Welsh Wales', and the western county of Cardiganshire, are remaining centres of the Welsh language today. They were even more dominated by Welsh culture and language in 1851.[2] Even so, by 1851 *Cymru Gymraeg*, Welsh Wales, had been shrinking for over a century. Rural out-migration, and industrial development in the more anglicised and increasingly English-speaking areas

1 Some mention is made of religious features in this chapter, but for further comparison readers should refer to appendix A.

2 On regional aspects of the Welsh language, see J. W. Aitchison and H. Carter, 'Rural Wales and the Welsh language', *Rural History*, 2 (1991); J. W. Aitchison and H. Carter, *The Welsh Language 1961–81: an Interpretative Atlas* (Cardiff, 1985). As late as 1921, 87 per cent of the population in Anglesey spoke Welsh: K. O. Morgan, *Rebirth of a Nation: Wales, 1880–1980* (Oxford, 1981, 1988 edn), p. 243.

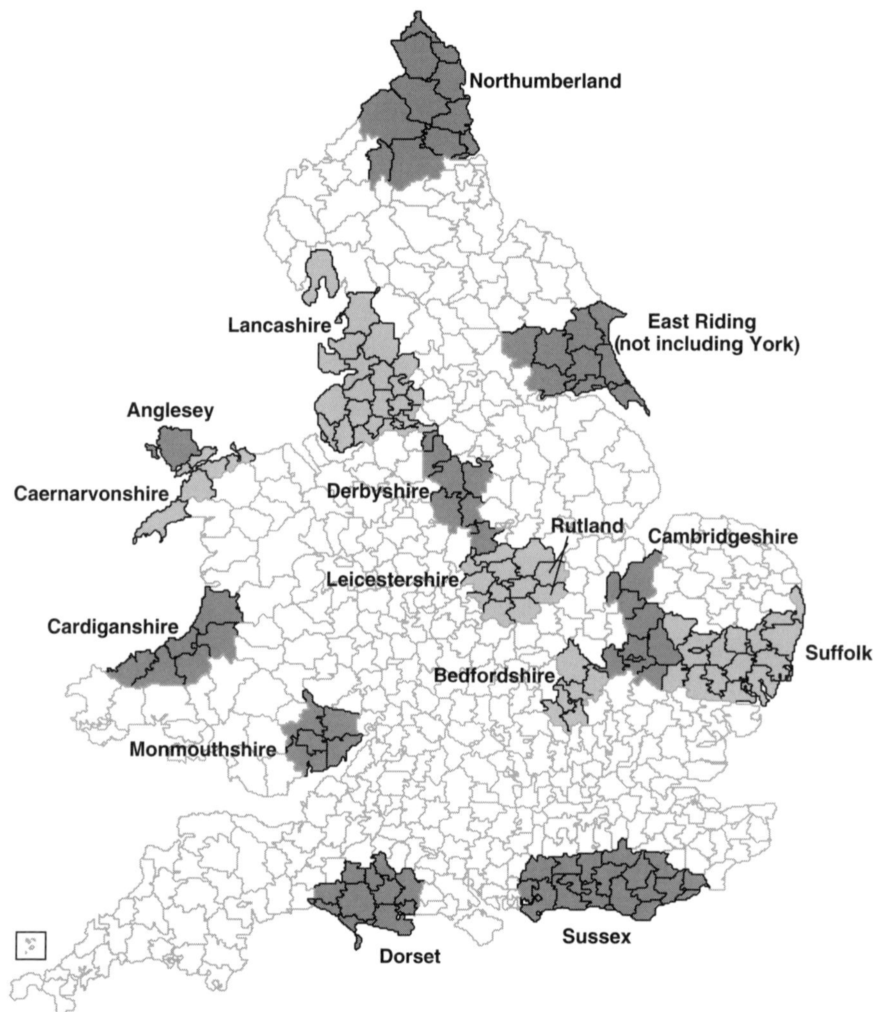

Figure 7.1. The registration counties for which parish-level data were compiled

of south-east Wales, were concentrating population elsewhere. The linguistic boundary was gradually creeping westwards.[3] In 1851 this process had not encroached much on these three Welsh counties, where religion and language epitomised what many see as the most salient features of Welsh culture.

Like Caernarvonshire, Anglesey was dominated by very large estates. The so-called New Doomsday Survey of 1873, and its amended later editions, established that about 67 per cent of Caernarvonshire (and 61 per cent of Anglesey) lay in estates of over 3,000 acres. These were the highest percentages in Wales. Half of Caernarvonshire was owned by six landlords, whose estates averaged over 25,000 acres each.[4] These figures are for a period slightly later than 1851, and for the historical county area, but there was considerable continuity until the late nineteenth century of this pattern, and of the dominant landed families. Such estates were vast sheep walks, and the two counties were also renowned cattle-rearing areas.[5] Western Anglesey, the western tip of Lleyn, and the lowlands around Aber, were more arable-based. The *Imperial Gazetteer* commented on Anglesey that 'The farm buildings and the cottages are generally poor and mean', adding that oats, barley, rye and potatoes were the chief crops. These, it described for Caernarvonshire, were sometimes very precarious, adding that 'Husbandry, in general, is rude; yet has been much improved'.[6]

Tenants on the north-west Welsh estates operated small-scale farms, some of them developing other livelihoods. Some small farmers depended on occasional work in the slate quarries, and the scattered nature of the slate workings made such dual occupations possible. There were important slate operations at Penrhyn, Bethesda

3 J. Rhys and D. Brynmor-Jones, *The Welsh People* (1923, New York, 1969 edn), pp. 543–50; W. T. R. Pryce, 'Migration and the evolution of culture areas: cultural and linguistic frontiers in north-east Wales, 1750 and 1851', *Transactions of the Institute of British Geographers*, 65 (1975), 79–107; W. T. R. Pryce, 'Welsh and English in Wales, 1750–1971: a spatial analysis based on the linguistic affiliation of parochial communities', *Bulletin of the Board of Celtic Studies*, 28 (1978), 1–36; W. T. R. Pryce, 'Wales as a culture region: patterns of change, 1750–1971', *Transactions of the Honourable Society of Cymmrodorion* (1978); W. T. R. Pryce, 'The Welsh language, 1751–1961', in H. Carter and H. Griffiths (eds.), *The National Atlas of Wales* (Cardiff, 1981).

4 D. W. Howell, *Land and People in Nineteenth-century Wales* (1977), pp. 20–2.

5 *Ibid.*, p. 112.

6 J. M. Wilson, *The Imperial Gazetteer of England and Wales*, vol. 1 (Edinburgh, n.d., c. 1870–2), p. 373.

and Llanberis, the workforce often settled in surrounding parishes such as Llandysilio.[7] These two counties contained many other industries, like the copper mining on the western side of Parys Mountain, in decline by the mid nineteenth century, its labourers moving to railway and harbour works. The mining of sulphate of copper, and of lead and silver, had excavated the centre of this hill.[8] The industry promoted the growth of Amlwch, which had been an enchanting fishing hamlet of six houses in 1766. In this neighbourhood the ore was smelted, the miners housed, the copper and other products exported, and the surrounding area heavily polluted by sulphurous fumes. Indeed, the incensed vicar of Amlwch claimed a 'smoke trespass' of £15 a year for the discomfort he endured. One doubts that the town was thought to be a very propitious living by Anglican clergymen, whose position was further compromised by the fact that the parish church had been built by the Parys mining company.[9] Tobacco manufacturing, with alum and vitriol works, made a further contribution to the town's atmosphere.

In Caernarvonshire, copper, zinc and lead were major sources of work, alongside local industries exploiting mill-stone and ochre. Bangor turned slates into billiard tables, chimney-piers and the like. By 1851 it was already much visited by tourists. This development, to become so associated with the Caernarvonshire, Denbighshire and Flintshire coast, was in train also at Llandudno, where ownership of the coastal area by the Mostyn family led to rapid expansion of a carefully planned resort.[10] Small fishing villages were sprinkled around the coast.

The mid nineteenth-century years were crucial for the extension of railways into north Wales. The Chester–Holyhead route was constructed between 1844 and 1850, with its eye-catching bridges across the Conway and the Menai Straits. Many people thought that Holyhead would become a major Atlantic port. It had seen consider-

[7] J. O. Lindsay, *A History of the North Wales Slate Industry* (Newton Abbot, 1974); F. A. Barnes, 'Settlement and landscape changes in a Caernarvonshire slate quarrying parish', in R. H. Osborne, F. A. Barnes and J. Doornkamp (eds.), *Geographical Essays in Honour of K. C. Edwards* (Nottingham, 1970); M. Jones, 'Y chwarelwyr: the slate quarrymen of north Wales', in R. Samuel (ed.), *Miners, Quarrymen and Saltworkers* (1977).

[8] R. Millward and A. Robinson, *Landscapes of North Wales* (Newton Abbot, 1978), pp. 108–16; J. Rowlands, *Copper Mountain* (1966, Llangefni, 1981 edn).

[9] Millward and Robinson, *Landscapes of North Wales*, p. 113.

[10] *Ibid.*, pp. 132–3.

able harbour developments since 1809, and it had its own industries of ship-building, rope-making, with a large labour force of dockside workers, engineers and mechanics, drawn from local parishes like Llanfaethly. Further rail extensions by 1852 had connected the line to Bangor and Caernarvon, and had opened up the slate ports of Port Dinorwic and Port Penrhyn.

In both counties, Nonconformity in the form particularly of the Calvinistic Methodists – termed 'the Methodists', or *yr hen gorff* (the old body) – exercised a dominant hold. Anglesey was said to be the most Nonconformist county in Wales. Here, as in Caernarvonshire, Cardiganshire, and other north and west Welsh counties, preachers had a pervasive influence. Chapel attendance rates were extremely high, and indeed remain comparatively high even today.[11] Anglican clergy may have usually avoided the smoke of Amlwch, but a bleak and sometimes angry sense of cultural isolation seeps through many of their visitation returns from these counties, testimony to the strength of anti-Anglican sentiment. For there was resentment against alleged inequitable treatment at tithe commutation, and strong feeling against absentee impropriators. Chapel services and Sunday-school lessons were often held in Welsh, as the Religious Census attests. Much use was made of the Welsh Bible, that most crucial instrument in the transmission of Welsh. An emergent Welsh nationalism here focused on tithes, rents, tenant right and security of tenure, franchise reform, Welsh language and education, coupled with a deepening antagonism towards the anglicised gentry. All this was inextricably fused with Nonconformity.

Many of these characteristics were shared by Cardiganshire, that mid Welsh county whose coastline and beautiful but poorly productive hills straddle the flank of the Irish sea like a half moon, and which contains within it the sources of the Severn, the Wye and the Rheidol. It was '*par excellence* the county of upland parishes', as Ieuan Gwynedd Jones remarked.[12] Many of these were very large. Llanbadarn Fawr was nearly 53,000 acres, and others like Llandewi-Brefi, Llanfihangel Geneu'r Glyn, or Llanfihangel y Creuddyn came close to this. Such parish sizes had been largely dependent on topography, the

11 R. Gill, *The Myth of the Empty Church* (1993), pp. 53–4.

12 I. G. Jones, 'Ecclesiastical economy: aspects of church building in Victorian Wales', in R. R. Davies *et al.* (eds.), *Welsh Society and Nationhood: Historical Essays Presented to Glanmor Williams* (Cardiff, 1984), p. 222.

nature of settlement and the need to secure adequate resources for clerical incumbents. There was strong emphasis on sheep and cattle rearing, and farms were usually small, averaging about 50 acres. Barley and oats were the main crops. Woollen cloth and glove manufacturing sometimes went hand-in-hand with husbandry. Lead was mined, alongside zinc, copper and slate, with many mines to the north of the Rheidol, up to Plynlimon,[13] an area where Wesleyanism gained ground. Fishing villages like Llangranog were scattered along the coast. Cardiganshire was an isolated county, with high rural birth rates. It had much out-migration, often of a seasonal nature to the lowlands and to England. Isolation persisted for an extended period – the railway only reached Cardigan in 1880 – and yet large numbers of Cardiganshire workers were employed in dairying activities in London, bringing their religion across the Welsh hills, over the midland plain, and into the metropolis.

Ieuan Gwynedd Jones described Cardiganshire as 'in some important yet mysterious respects deeply religious. The contribution of Cardiganshire as a whole to the religious life of Britain has been enormous.'[14] Welsh Calvinistic Methodism was conspicuous. In Llanrhystud, an agricultural parish of 139 farmers, there were four Calvinistic Methodist chapels.[15] Llanbadarn Fawr had nine such chapels, while Llanfihangel Geneu'r Glyn and Llandewi-Brefi had five each. Llangeitho, in the south of the county, was an epicentre for Methodist revivals, and such revivals began in many other places too: at Tre'rddol and Ystumtuen, Bontgoch, Pontrhydygroes, or Yspyty Ystwyth. The religious culture of the county permeated its popular views and protest movements. It was the setting for 'the war of the Little Englishman' in the 1820s, on Mynydd Bach. 'Rebecca' took a firm hold in the 1840s, sometimes ejecting English residents. The incumbent of Troedyraur wrote of how 'I had at first here one whole English [service] the others wholly Welch but the Rebecca riots drove away most of the English since I have regularly Welch two services where I have no English attendants.'[16]

Cardiganshire was a recruiting ground for ministers who were to

[13] D. Bick and P. W. Davies, *Lewis Morris and the Cardiganshire Mines* (1994).

[14] I. G. Jones, *Communities: Essays in the Social History of Victorian Wales* (Llandysul, 1987), p. 35.

[15] *Ibid.*, p. 51.

[16] Visitation Returns: Archdeaconry of Cardigan, Queries and Answers, Clergy, 1845. National Library of Wales, SD/QA/17.

serve throughout Wales and beyond. Llangorwen saw the first Tractarian church in Wales. Yet such intense religious activity took place in a county with church buildings in a notoriously poor state, a county with few clerical rectors (a rector was entitled to the great or rectorial tithes), tithes commonly being alienated to laymen.[17] Such neglect was not universal, and families like the Lloyds of Bronwydd generously assisted both church and chapel. Some other estates too seem to have been prepared to provide land for the building of places of worship: estates like those owned by the Pryse, Powell and Lisburne families, from which MPs were traditionally elected, families well aware of the electoral significance of so many dissenting voters.[18]

Monmouthshire, the fourth Welsh county for this book, has been neglected by historians, probably because of its ambiguous position on the Welsh–English border. Yet in the period 1801–31 it had the fastest rates of demographic growth found in Britain and, like Glamorgan, it was a key county in heavy industrialisation. An 1811 population of 60,603 for the registration-district county had risen to 156,461 by 1851. This gives a rate of growth higher even than Lancashire. In the eighteenth century, upland areas in the north and north-west had been known as 'the Wilds of Monmouthshire'; but by 1851 this western region had been transformed by mining and iron-working. The Welsh migrants brought Calvinistic Methodism with them. The oats, barley, sheep and other products of Monmouthshire were commonly sent into the south Wales industrial regions.

In the forest areas, like the Forest of Dean, there were industries with a long and complex history. By 1821 there were at least eighteen water-wheels powering local iron-works in the immediate vicinity of Tintern.[19] Iron wire had been made here from about 1566.[20] The steep hillsides between Tintern and Chepstow, so appealing to the eyes of Wordsworth and Turner, were in fact very extensively quarried, the limestone transported down the Wye, and thence to centres like Bristol. Such quarrying also occurred in areas like Bedwas, Ifton,

[17] I. G. Jones points to families like the Chichesters from Devon, who owned the tithes of nine parishes, taking £5,411 annually in tithes, and paying nothing back to the parishes or their churches. See his *Communities*, p. 41.

[18] R. J. Colyer, 'The gentry and the county in nineteenth-century Cardiganshire', *Welsh History Review*, 10 (1980–1), 504–5.

[19] R. Howell, *A History of Gwent* (1988, Llandysul, Dyfed, 1989 edn), p. 141.

[20] H. A. Evans, *Monmouthshire* (1911), p. 58.

Risca, Machen or Newport. The woodland industries included the stripping of bark for tanning leather, chair-leg turning, hurdle and barrel-hoop manufacture. Many general-purpose saw-mills produced pit-props for the Welsh collieries.[21]

Major transport and port developments between 1790 and 1850 accompanied the expansion of heavy industry. Newport was a transport centre. Its level land and easy access to the interior had by 1820 made it the largest coal port in Britain, excepting only those of Tyne and Wear. The town was the destination for many Irish famine refugees, and some of them knew that they were coming to a county with long-standing Catholic families. This immigration helped expand iron manufacture and coal mining. Output in both rose greatly from about 1830, with massive increases of population in the coal-producing parishes during the next two decades, as in Glamorgan. In due course four-fifths of the population of Wales became located in these two counties.

Such industrial development was not without its darker aspects, and one thinks not only of the effects on the landscape. The secret colliers' organisation of the 'Scotch Cattle' had a fearful reputation in the industrial areas, providing a counterweight to many degenerate features of industrialism in the region: the widespread use of (illegal) truck, the 'long-pay' system of delayed wage payments, often in vouchers, the ruthless disregard for human welfare by many employers, and the anti-union tactics. There was widespread interest in setting up a south Wales Chartist state, and the Newport uprising of 1839 was perhaps the most notable expression in Britain of militant Chartism.

Little is as yet known of the role of the Welsh language in such unrest. Yet it is worth stressing how Welsh much of Monmouthshire still was. The county had been strongly Welsh-speaking in the seventeenth century, and chapel services were widely held in Welsh well into the nineteenth century. Even in Monmouth, on the far eastern side of the county, Welsh was still much spoken in the early 1780s. In west Monmouthshire, according to William Coxe, the English were spoken of as 'Saxons' in the early nineteenth century. In Blaenavon half the population spoke no English at all in 1815. Welsh was then spoken along the Wye, or in places like Trevethin parish church, and the *Monmouthshire Merlin* wrote in 1829 of the 'doggedness with

[21] A. M. Jones, *The Rural Industries of England and Wales, vol. 4: Wales* (1978), pp. 54–7.

which the lower class of inhabitants' stayed Welsh-speaking.[22] Just a few years before the 1851 Religious Census, the 1847 Educational Commissioners were forthright in their attacks on the supposed educational effects of the Welsh language in Monmouthshire. However, English and Irish immigration was re-shaping Welsh culture, and many churches were abandoning Welsh around the period of the Religious Census.

The class-based agrarian structures of many arable areas in England were less apparent in Monmouthshire, for it was a county of small farms, low labour-to-farmer ratios, and an extensive rural gradation of status. The nature of 'labour' itself was often different in rural Wales from lowland England.[23] The 'all-round' labourer, skilled in many tasks, less specialised than the English carters, shepherds, stockmen and their likes, was a common feature of the Welsh countryside. Older forms of farm service also survived, while Welsh rural technology looked old-fashioned to English observers. Traditional fluidity of occupations in rural Wales should be stressed. Many farm labourers shifted seasonally between mining, quarrying, building labour, ironworking and wood-cutting. These features need to be remembered, along with the family farms and rural social structures associated with them, when thinking about the religious and associated features of the Welsh counties.

The English counties

Moving into England, Dorset is an excellent example of a large southern agricultural region dominated by the Church of England. This was a county of chalk downs and sandy heaths, and it was largely non-industrial. The local exceptions to this included stone, marble and quarrying works in Portland and the Isle of Purbeck, the workers of which were thought to be most receptive to Nonconformity.[24] There

[22] Howell, *History of Gwent*, pp. 178–81; J. R. Guy, 'Eighteenth-century Gwent Catholics', *Recusant History*, 16 (1982–3), 78–9, on the persistence of the Welsh language in this county; G. J. Williams, *The Welsh Tradition of Gwent* (Cardiff, n.d.).

[23] K. D. M. Snell, 'Deferential bitterness: the social outlook of the rural proletariat in eighteenth- and nineteenth-century England and Wales', in M. L. Bush (ed.), *Social Orders and Social Classes in Europe since 1500: Studies in Social Stratification* (1992).

[24] M. Moore, 'Stone quarrying in the Isle of Purbeck: an oral history' (unpublished MA dissertation, Dept. of English Local History, University of Leicester, 1992).

was a significant fishing industry, mainly for mackerel, benefiting towns like Poole,[25] with an assortment of related industries such as ship-building, sail-making, net-making, thread, twine and cordage manufacture.[26] There were various other relatively small 'manufactories' in the county, like rope-making, sack-making at Beaminster, a declining or precarious cloth, woollen, hemp or flax industry in a few areas like Netherbury, Burton Bradstock, Chardstock, Lyme Regis, Dorchester or Fordington, button-making around Blandford, Shaftesbury and Sherborne, silk-working at Cerne Abbas and Sherborne, outwork lace-making in west Dorset, glove-making in Yetminster and other villages near Yeovil, paper in Witchampton and Wareham, and leather, boot and shoe manufacture in Wareham. These varied industries were usually ignored by commentators on Dorset. Their focus was upon agricultural workers said to be left behind by the march of progress, a perception that some exaggerated. However, diverse though these industries were, they were not usually sizeable employers of labour. They do not detract much from the agricultural nature of the county.

Dorset's rural labouring poor were certainly among the most impoverished, lowly paid and poorly educated in England and Wales. The events of 1834 in Tolpuddle imparted notoriety to the county. Rural living standards in 1851 were little better than a hundred years earlier. Cottage conditions, as Lord Shaftesbury (and his factory-district critics) complained, were often atrocious.[27] This was a county of sheep and corn husbandry, and dairying, and its growing specialisation on the latter was facilitated by the railway.[28] Sheep farming was especially significant on the extensive chalkland areas that run from north-east Dorset through to its central and southern parishes.

There were also expansive areas of wasteland and scattered population, notably in eastern parts of the county, as vividly depicted in *The Return of the Native*. Hardy commented that Sundays had little

[25] N. Pevsner and J. Newman, *The Buildings of England: Dorset* (1972, Harmondsworth, 1985 edn), p. 318. [26] G. Grigson, *Wessex* (1951), pp. 56–62.

[27] K. D. M. Snell (ed.), *The Whistler at the Plough*, by A. Somerville (Manchester, 1852, 1989 edn), pp. 27–9, 36–43, 48–66, 229–35, 333–8, 408–13; and K. D. M. Snell, *Annals of the Labouring Poor: Social Change and Agrarian England, 1660–1900* (Cambridge, 1985), ch. 8, on conditions in Dorset at this time, and the attitudes of rural labourers.

[28] P. J. Perry, 'Working-class isolation and mobility in rural Dorset, 1837–1936', *Transactions of the Institute of British Geographers*, 46 (1969); Snell, *Annals of the Labouring Poor*, ch. 8.

significance here: 'going to church, except to be married or buried, was exceptional at Egdon'.[29] In similar places like Cranborne, Lytchett-Minster, Stour Provost or Motcombe, contemporaries were often struck by the lack of religious provision and the opportunities thereby offered to dissenters. Cranborne, for example, was described as being 'vast . . . anything like a village does not exist, and scarcely three houses are found together'. This was said to foster a 'feeling of independence',[30] coupled with much irreligiosity. A recent Anglican clergyman familiar with the parish tells me that nothing has changed.

Nevertheless, Anglican landlord dominance loomed large. Dorset contained many country 'seats', in locations like Sherborne, Stalbridge, Parnham, or Edmondesham. Milton Abbas, said to be 'the best known of Dorset villages',[31] was only one example of a carefully planned estate village, its houses demolished and relocated, and its park landscaped by Capability Brown. Such an ethos took hold easily where there were comparatively few small landowners, and where ownership of large landed units was well above the national average. About 36 per cent of the land was in estates of over 10,000 acres, and there were many large farms.[32]

Dissent in Dorset was weak, concentrated in the coastal region, in towns like Bridport, Portland, Swanage or Wareham. Poole had long been a centre for Nonconformity. It had strong parliamentary sympathies during the Civil War, and the Act of Uniformity failed to dislodge its Presbyterian or Independent rector. It had been the headquarters of the parliamentary party in Dorset, its walls later being destroyed by Charles II.[33] The Congregationalists, and to a limited extent other old dissenters, had a number of strongholds. Their strength extended to villages like Stoke Abbott, Sturminster Marshall and Sydling St Nicholas. They ranked somewhat below the Wesleyan Methodists as the county's main dissenters in 1851, followed by the Primitive Methodists. Other denominations were very sparse. Early Methodism had been much persecuted in parts of Dorset, often with magisterial approval, as at Stalbridge or Shaftesbury.[34]

29 T. Hardy, *The Return of the Native* (1878, 1971 edn), p. 96.

30 W. Densham and J. Ogle, *The Story of the Congregational Churches of Dorset from their Foundation* (1899), pp. 108–9.

31 C. Taylor, *Dorset* (1970), pp. 152–3.

32 W. B. Stephens, *Education, Literacy and Society, 1830–1870: the Geography of Diversity in Provincial England* (Manchester, 1986), p. 208.

33 Densham and Ogle, *Story of the Congregational Churches of Dorset*, pp. 181–6.

34 B. J. Biggs, *The Wesleys and the Early Dorset Methodists* (Gillingham, Dorset, 1987).

Moving eastwards along the coast one comes to Sussex, a large registration county of 317 parishes, second in size only to Suffolk among the chosen fifteen counties. Here the Church of England was strongly dominant and, as in Dorset, its parochial structure functioned well, with generally small parishes containing one nucleated settlement. In many rural areas the Anglican Church completely monopolised worship. Old dissent, dating back to fifteenth- and sixteenth-century Lollardy, was stronger than new dissent in Sussex, and it had particular influence in the Weald and on the South Downs. Dissent was most conspicuous in the towns, like Brighton, Hastings, Rye or Shoreham.

Sussex had significant sub-regions, mutually dependent in fascinating ways. This long-enclosed county contained the coastal plain, the South Downs, the gault clay, the lower greensand, and the low and high Weald. Agricultural specialisation reflected this varied topography. In the thinly populated Weald the sandy or obdurate clay soils were poor, farms were small, isolated, lowly capitalised and often said to be backward. Brandon and Short have written of the long-term relative freedom of this area, where the people were poor, akin to frontier settlers, being independent, resourceful, and developing crafts like iron-making and textiles to redress their precarious subsistence from the land.[35] It is little surprise that dissenters were often found in the Weald.[36] This had long been an area of squatter encroachments and fragmented landownership. The later eighteenth century had seen an extension of arable cultivation here and some improvement of roads.[37] By the mid nineteenth century proximity to London had ensured that 'cockney boxes', or 'villadom', were bringing irreversible changes to Wealden communities.

As was true of these other southern counties, Cambridgeshire lay within the regions of greatest Anglican strength. However, the situation of old dissent in the eastern counties was shown earlier, and this county has been selected for parochial analysis mainly because of its high share of old dissenting congregations. There was strong presence

35 P. Brandon, *The Sussex Landscape* (1974), pp. 36–7; P. Brandon and B. Short, *The South East from A.D. 1000* (1990).

36 A. Everitt, *The Pattern of Rural Dissent: the Nineteenth Century* (Leicester, 1972), pp. 11, 59–60; E. Lord, 'Communities of common interest: the social landscape of south-east Surrey, 1750–1850', in C. Phythian-Adams (ed.), *Societies, Cultures and Kinship, 1580–1850: Cultural Provinces and English Local History* (Leicester, 1993), pp. 188–96.

37 Brandon, *Sussex Landscape*, p. 179.

of Baptists and Independents, and in 1851 the total places of worship for the older denominations outnumbered those for new dissent.[38] Cambridgeshire was very largely agricultural, although with distinctive northern and southern contrasts. The registration county was significantly larger than the administrative county, notably in the north-east, where it extended considerably into Norfolk. Its industries included the manufacture of white bricks, coarse pottery, baskets, reed-matting and straw-plait. Open-cast coprolite digging, along the fen edge east of Cambridge and in west Cambridgeshire, was expanding from mid century. Cambridgeshire farms were predominantly arable, interspersed with areas of meadow and pasture.[39] They tended to be small. Emparking and estate dominance characterised places like Wimpole, Madingley, Tetworth, Croxton or Chippenham, but the county was not one with conspicuous gentry presence. Rather it was one of small gentry and corporate landownership, with the roles of the Cambridge colleges very apparent in its rural history.[40]

James Caird in 1851 spoke of south Cambridgeshire as containing buildings that were 'chiefly wood and thatch, antique and inconvenient . . . very tempting and very subject to the fire of the incendiary', which he took to be 'almost a nightly occurrence'. Cambridge University fellows would have been surprised by Caird's view that their county was 'in a semi-barbarous state'; and they may also have known little about its very low wages.[41] These conditions have even eluded some modern historians. They provided the context for considerable opposition in Cambridgeshire to the 1834 Poor Law, under the Anglican leadership of the Reverend Maberley, and a year before the Religious Census they were the setting for a dramatic account of rural exploitation and unrest in Charles Kingsley's novel *Alton Locke*. He entitled one chapter 'The men who are eaten'. His work reminds one how very adverse rural conditions could be in south-eastern rural counties at this time.[42]

38 For fascinating discussion of old dissent in Cambridgeshire, see M. Spufford (ed.), *The World of Rural Dissenters, 1520–1725* (Cambridge, 1995).

39 C. Vancouver, *A General View of the Agriculture of the County of Cambridge* (1794); C. Taylor, *The Cambridgeshire Landscape: Cambridgeshire and the Southern Fens* (1973).

40 A. S. Bendall, *Maps, Land and Society: a History, with a Carto-bibliography of Cambridgeshire Estate Maps, c. 1600–1836* (Cambridge, 1992).

41 J. Caird, *English Agriculture in 1850–51* (1852, Farnborough, 1968 edn), pp. 467–8.

42 Charles Kingsley, *Alton Locke* (1850), vol. 2, ch. 7.

The other East Anglian county studied here is Suffolk, a huge county of nearly 500 parishes. In many Suffolk villages the Anglican Church faced little religious rivalry, even though clerical non-residence was said to be common.[43] In 1851 there were 519 Anglican places of worship – many of them outstanding buildings – as against about 192 places for old dissenting congregations, and around 166 for new dissenters. Like Cambridgeshire, Suffolk was another strongly arable county, with pastoral enclaves in east Suffolk. Agriculture was advanced and skilful, characterised by large farms. This was unfortunately a county of severe rural poverty and high poor rates, with a history of rural protest in years like 1816, 1822 and 1830–1, coupled with deficient rural education, and illiteracy rates which were above the national average.[44]

Manufacturing was not much advanced, although there were important works for making agricultural implements in places like Leiston and Peasenhall. Brewing, iron and brass-founding, rope-making, salt manufacture, boat-building, brick-making, paper-making, leather-working and other usually small-scale industries were in towns like Ipswich, Woodbridge, Bury St Edmunds and Lowestoft. Textile industries also survived, particularly on the Essex border.[45] Furthermore, and showing up in the 1831 census category of 'other families' not in agriculture or trade, there were the fishing villages and towns: places like Lowestoft, Kirkley, Gorleston, Woodbridge, Aldeburgh, Pakefield, Chelmondiston, Barking, Kessingland and Southwold. In short, as an arable, Anglican-dominated county, with notable old and new dissenting growth among both agricultural inhabitants and workers in other industries, the religious data for Suffolk invite close analysis.

At first sight Bedfordshire might not seem one of the most intriguing counties for detailed analysis of religion. It is little studied by historians. And yet it had surprising socio-economic characteristics. It contained the lowest proportion of 'persons of independent means' of any English county. It had a very high incidence of early marriages.[46] It had the highest illiteracy figures in England.[47] Its illegiti-

[43] Stephens, *Education, Literacy and Society*, p. 74. [44] *Ibid.*, pp. 80–1.

[45] D. C. Coleman, 'Growth and decay during the Industrial Revolution: the case of East Anglia', *Scandinavian Economic History Review*, 10 (1962), and his *Courtaulds: an Economic and Social History*, vol. 1 (Oxford, 1969).

[46] Stephens, *Education, Literacy and Society*, p. 350. [47] *Ibid.*, pp. 184–5.

macy rates were exceptionally high. It had higher rates of child labour (especially of girls) than any other county, including industrialised textile counties like Lancashire.[48] By the mid nineteenth century it was one of the leading areas for putting-out cottage industries. In 1873 over half of the county was owned by less than 50 people. And it had been more affected by parliamentary enclosure than virtually any other county.[49] Its religious attendance rates were higher than the rest of the English counties studied here – higher indeed than some of the Welsh counties. This was a county of very strong Anglican adherence; and yet among the fifteen counties it was also the one in which both the Baptists and the Wesleyan Methodists did best.

Bedfordshire was largely arable on the lower greensand, with associated problems of poor housing, low wages, gang labour on the larger farms, winter-time unemployment and high pauperism. Dairying and vegetable-growing were found in the south, producing for London. The easily worked soil around Sandy and in the Vale of Bedford had long been reputed for market-gardening. There were gentry and aristocratic seats especially in central and southern parts, with estates of the Russells, de Grey, St John, Crawley and Whitbread families. Brickyards in central Bedfordshire benefited from the advance of the railway in the 1840s,[50] and there were industries like malting. But the most significant industries were straw-hat manufacture and lace, both of which employed very large numbers of children. One tends to forget now that mid nineteenth-century Britain was an intensely hat- and bonnet-wearing culture compared with today. Many suggestive forms of headgear were produced to satisfy class snobbery, social nuances, working habits and very gendered deportment. Huge numbers of these hats, with much variety of names, were made in Bedfordshire. The industry flourished in small-scale units and cottage 'factories', with putting-out centres in towns like Luton, Dunstable, Ampthill, Biggleswade and Toddington. It had mushroomed in the first half of the nineteenth century, during a time of rapid population increase, when overseers and landlords were eager to install cottage industries which might reduce poor rates, and when some of the major London firms moved parts of their businesses to Bedfordshire. The most suitable straw for plaiting was found on the

[48] *Ibid.*, p. 168.

[49] M. E. Turner, *English Parliamentary Enclosure* (Folkestone, 1980), p. 180.

[50] P. Bigmore, *The Bedfordshire and Huntingdonshire Landscape* (1979), pp. 206–7.

chalklands of north Hertfordshire and south Bedfordshire. The lace industry complemented this regionally, being more situated in north Bedfordshire.[51] By 1851 these industries were associated with the highest proportions of employed child labour in the country,[52] which, as will be seen, had striking repercussions for the use of denominational Sunday schools. Contemporaries commented on girls walking about with their plait in hand. Impressed as they often were with such industriousness, they were less enamoured of the high illegitimacy and early marriages of plaiting districts, believing that children left national schools early, going to plaiting schools and thence into an early independent adulthood.[53] The industry was in its heyday around mid century, and was to decline from then as supplies of plait came in from the Far East. Even at that point, women still found employment in the hat trade, migrating to work in Luton and other towns.[54]

Further north in Rutland, one finds a small sparsely populated county, distinguished for its landlord-dominated parishes, many of them 'closed' or estate villages, a county with overwhelming Anglican supremacy. In 1873, 45 per cent of its acreage was owned by the aristocracy, and a further 26 per cent by commoners holding more than 10,000 acres.[55] W. G. Hoskins tells us that in the 1880s four great houses owned half of Rutland.[56] Such figures were far higher than for any other English county. Gentry seats and their influence were conspicuous at Exton, Normanton, Ketton, Morcott, Cottesmore, Burley-on-the-Hill and many other places. The county was politically

51 G. F. R. Spenceley, 'The origins of the English pillow lace industry', *Agricultural History Review*, 21 (1973); P. Horn, 'Child workers in the pillow lace and straw plait trades of Victorian Buckinghamshire and Bedfordshire', *Historical Journal*, 17 (1974); J. Bourke, '"I was always fond of my pillow": the handmade lace industry in the United Kingdom, 1870–1914', *Rural History*, 5 (1994).

52 Stephens, *Education, Literacy and Society*, pp. 21–2, 111. Nearly 17 per cent of 5–9-year-old males were 'occupied' in Bedfordshire in 1851, the kind of figures found in many third-world countries today.

53 P. Horn, *The Victorian Country Child* (1974, 1985 edn), pp. 122–7; P. Sharpe, 'The women's harvest: straw-plaiting and the representation of labouring women's employment, c. 1793–1885', *Rural History*, 5 (1994), 129–42.

54 Bigmore, *Bedfordshire and Huntingdonshire Landscape*, p. 186.

55 Figures from T. J. Nossiter, *Influence, Opinion and Political Idioms in Reformed England: Case Studies from the North-east, 1832–74* (Brighton, 1975), pp. 208–9, as adapted from J. Bateman, *The Great Landowners of Great Britain and Ireland* (1878, 1883 edn). (The figures exclude waste land.)

56 W. G. Hoskins, *Rutland* (Leicester, 1949), pp. 10–11; or see C. E. M. Joad, *The Untutored Townsman's Invasion of the Country* (1946), p. 107.

a very safe Conservative stronghold, with three families (Noel, Heathcote and Finch) virtually monopolising political life.[57] Nonconformity was weak: compared to 53 places of worship for the established church in 1851 in the administrative county, there were 6 places for the Independents, 12 for the Baptists, 1 for the Quakers, 17 for the Wesleyans, and 1 for the Primitive Methodists. Non-agricultural industries were few, although Rutland was well-endowed with a variety of locally quarried limestone. The architectural results are well-displayed in the villages and churches that enchanted Hoskins and so many other commentators.

Leicestershire was a county of more varied contrasts, notably between its eastern and western divisions. The east and south tended towards pasture, specialising in sheep and cattle, the sheep having the long-staple wool that was so interwoven with the hosiery industry of the county. Many parishes in the east experienced severe de-population in medieval times, and remaining open fields were enclosed early during parliamentary enclosure. Dairy farms were numerous around Melton Mowbray. By contrast, the west, south-west and north of the county, like the centrally located city of Leicester, were areas of growing population, of hosiery industry (in 1851 still based on the framework-knitting machine), and coal mining. Hosiery was a classic 'putting-out' industry, with its county centres in Leicester, Loughborough and Hinckley feeding dependent villages in a wide hinterland with raw materials, and the bag-hosiers and merchants taking back the worked materials. The industry, alongside hand-loom weaving further north, was a major casualty of the period. In 1845 it was the subject of a large and depressing select-committee investigation, revealing some of the worst excesses of petty-fogging industrial capitalism ever found in Britain. It was within this milieu that leaders like Thomas Cooper captivated large crowds by espousing physical-force Chartism. Besides being the centre of the hosiery industry, Leicester manufactured boots and shoes, lace, agricultural and other machinery. Coal mining centred around Ashby-de-la-Zouch, and the registration county of Leicestershire also encompassed some of the southern Derbyshire colliery villages. The county was notable for its old dissenting congregations, which were especially prominent in

[57] H. Pelling, *Social Geography of British Elections, 1885–1910* (1967), pp. 220–2; D. Reeder, *Landowners and Landholding in Leicestershire and Rutland, 1873–1941* (Leicester, 1994), pp. 3–4, 57.

southern, central and western areas.[58] Leicester, the most central of all English cities, was widely referred to in the nineteenth century as the 'Metropolis of Dissent'.

In Derbyshire contemporaries were struck by a very varied topography. One has the flat or undulating area of the south, the irregular regions of the mid and north-east, and the high upland Peak district of the west and north-west. Much of the latter was rough moorland pasture cut by gritstone edges and limestone scars, worked by farmers whose occupations often assimilated other small-scale industrial activity. This region contrasted both with the fertile alluvial soil of the Vale of Trent and the cold clays of the coal measures. Mineral springs at Buxton, Matlock and Bakewell drew large numbers of visitors each year. The picturesque nature of the county's scenery enhanced further the settings for its many stately homes, Chatsworth, Kedleston, Haddon, Hardwick and Sudbury among them. Coal was worked extensively in the south and especially in the east; and there were many industries mining or quarrying lead, zinc, manganese, barytes, marble, alabaster, limestone and fluorspar. The area around Ashover – one of strong Methodist influence – contained a highly developed lead industry and a fascinating associated culture, now largely disappeared, although the old workings are still clearly visible as small lunar-like craters and long rakes throughout the upland landscape. In addition there were silk, cotton and lace manufactures at centres like Belper, Derby, Glossop and Cromford, with textile work put out to surrounding villages, much hosiery and framework knitting, malting and brewing industries, pottery, tile and brickworks, and long-established iron foundries. This was a county of strong Wesleyan and Primitive Methodist allegiance, with significant presence also of the Independents and Baptists: one in which dissenting sittings in 1851 exceeded those for the Anglican Church.[59]

Despite their significance, the textile manufactures in Derbyshire have been overshadowed in reputation by those of Lancashire: the

[58] K. D. M. Snell, *Church and Chapel in the North Midlands: Religious Observance in the Nineteenth Century* (Leicester, 1991), ch. 3.

[59] M. R. Austin, 'Religion and society in Derbyshire in the Industrial Revolution', *Derbyshire Archaeological Journal*, 93 (1974); M. Tranter, 'Landlords, labourers, local preachers: rural nonconformity in Derbyshire, 1772–1851', *Derbyshire Archaeological Journal*, 101 (1981); M. Tranter (ed.), *The Derbyshire Returns to the 1851 Religious Census*, Derbyshire Record Society, vol. 23 (Chesterfield, 1995), esp. her introduction.

county that one most associates with the first phase of industrialisation. Its global prominence was based above all on steam power applied to key processes in the cotton industry, this innovation having a great effect upon many related industries. These changes have been extensively debated. It is clear that huge increases in output and profit were obtained in a first stage of technological applications taking effect from *circa* 1780, and then in particular from around 1820. Demographic growth, in-migration, urbanisation and its social consequences occurred at a pace that alarmed many commentators, like Engels, and efforts to understand what was happening in Lancashire had a profound effect on the evolution of nineteenth-century thought, religion and politics. In 1851, the county was still absorbing the huge influx of Irish refugees from the potato famine, a phenomenon that accentuated Lancashire's urban problems, and that was to impart Catholic and anti-Catholic reputations to many areas within it.

The Lancashire towns grew up in Anglican parish structures never designed for such urbanisation, and these were slow to adapt to administrative, religious and cultural challenges. The point can be underlined by noticing that the *parish* of Manchester had 213 places of worship in the 1851 Religious Census – and this figure, probably a slight underestimate, was over half that for all Cambridgeshire. Other urban areas experienced considerable religious diversity within their parochial bounds, albeit on a smaller scale: Ashton-under-Lyne, Blackburn, Bolton-le-Moors, Bury, Eccles, Lancaster, Liverpool, Prescot, Preston, Prestwich, Rochdale, Whalley and Wigan were the most noticeable. In parishes like these, with their many chapelries, hamlets and townships, religious organisation was very different to that further south.

Compared to Lancashire, the East Riding of Yorkshire was very agricultural. It was a leading area for Wesleyan and Primitive Methodism, especially in those lowland parishes with links to Hull, and this is why it was chosen for this book. It had low population density, and its landed property was concentrated in relatively few hands. In 1873 eleven men owned about 28 per cent of the land, and under a hundred families owned well over half the county.[60] It was much improved through enclosure, with considerable engrossing of farms, under-drainage or reclamation of land, the introduction of turnips allowing

[60] D. Hey, *Yorkshire from AD 1000* (1986), p. 287.

fattening of sheep and the associated change to more advanced husbandry rotations.[61] On the light-soil Wolds in particular, there had been a significant shift to arable and the Norfolk four-course system, accompanied by careful village and farmstead planning in many parishes, the re-siting of pantiled farm houses away from village centres, and restricted cottage building. Strongly traditional in some features of its rural institutions, the East Riding was a high-wage region compared to further south. Many of its farms were isolated, notably so on the Wolds. They were conservative in their relationships of employment, and unusually dependent upon male farm servants.[62] The Wolds also had many estate parishes; indeed, it has been suggested that 40 per cent of villages on the Wolds were of a 'closed' nature.[63] In the county at large, such 'closed' parishes included Boynton, owned by Sir George Strickland, a parish with neither a public house nor chapel,[64] Bugthorpe, Bishop Burton, Warter, Langton, Sledmere, and the emparked, estate village of Escrick near York.

Non-agricultural industries were centred above all at the major port of Hull, by now probably the third largest port in the country, importing timber, Baltic iron, grain, flax, linseed and rape-seed, with industries such as flour-milling, seed-crushing, herring-curing and ship-building. Local canal development promoted the growing tile and brick works at Newport. There were other key centres however, and these included Bridlington (a watering place from the later eighteenth century, but also a wood-importing port), Beverley (with its tanning, ship-building, iron-founding and light engineering, all of which gained from the opening of the railway in 1846), and Driffield (a market town which also contained corn mills, breweries, maltings and warehouses). There were a number of busy fishing ports, like those of Northumberland, and the expansion of the railways was starting to promote resort development.

Northumberland, the most northerly county in England, and the

[61] H. E. Strickland, *A General View of the Agriculture of the East Riding of Yorkshire* (1812); C. Howard, *A General View of the Agriculture of the East Riding of Yorkshire* (1835); G. Legard, 'Farming of the East Riding of Yorkshire', *Journal of the Royal Agricultural Society*, 9 (1848); O. Wilkinson, *The Agricultural Revolution in the East Riding of Yorkshire* (1956); A. Harris, *The Rural Landscape of the East Riding of Yorkshire, 1700–1850* (Oxford, 1961).

[62] S. Caunce, *Amongst Farm Horses: the Horselads of East Yorkshire* (Stroud, 1991).

[63] K. J. Allison, *The East Riding of Yorkshire Landscape* (1976), p. 193.

[64] *Ibid.*, p. 194.

fifth largest, has a varied, often rugged and barren landscape, rising from the coast to the ranges of the Cheviots on the borders of Scotland and Cumberland. Its wilder regions, like Redesdale, were slowly shedding their lawless reputations, even though their many defensive pele houses still stood testimony to the acrimonious feuds which had once riven this border district. Warkworth, Bamburgh, Alnwick, Norham, Newcastle, Berwick – the castles of these and many other such places bore witness to the same history. Scottish influence was especially noticeable in the western hills, was markedly evident in forms of speech, in the morphology of villages, and in religion. Presbyterians – 'the Scots in exile'[65] – outnumbered Anglicans in some northern areas, and provide one reason for examining this county. Emerging out of this earlier history were many proliferating industries, and a varied, sometimes very prosperous, agriculture. The county's industrial base was diverse. It was best known for the Durham–Northumberland coalfield, and the iron and other industries that grew up in close association with coal. The banks of the Tyne below Newburn formed one of the most densely populated tracts of land in the world; this contrasted markedly with the rural areas, which were largely destitute even of sizeable villages, and where farms and hamlets were few and far between. Many of the upland parishes were huge in size, large expanses of moorland and sheep pasture, sometimes of cattle grazing, providing livestock for the major animal fairs at places like Corbridge. Elsdon was described by Bulmer as 'a wild dreary waste'. At about 75,000 acres it was larger than many of the other moorland parishes, like Falston or Haltwhistle, but still half the size of Simonburn. The farms in such parishes were correspondingly large – in Glendale and Bamborough wards they were between 300 and 3,000 acres. Like Rutland, and to some extent Dorset, Northumberland had a high predominance of great estates, and it contained many model or estate villages, Belsay, Ford, East and West Matfen, Walton, Whitfield, Capheaton and Cambo among them.

As reported by Caird, the county's agricultural labourers were paid chiefly in corn, had a house and garden rent-free, potato ground, generally kept a cow, and received various other perquisites. Labourers were certainly better off than their counterparts in the

[65] Nossiter, *Influence, Opinion and Political Idioms*, p. 18. On Presbyterianism in north Northumberland, see Gill, *Myth of the Empty Church*, ch. 2.

south of England.[66] Farm servants, termed hinds, survived in this county, yearly contracts being negotiated at hiring fairs held in towns like Bellingham and Haltwhistle.[67] Cottages, as Caird wrote, were often very poor. The occupants were frequently bound to keep a girl or young boy to help with farm work, the so-called 'bondager system', that was soon to become a cause of labouring protest.[68]

Quantitative contrasts between the fifteen counties

These county descriptions have relied upon conventional literary description. Another comparative approach can be taken now, by using some of the quantitative data created for every parish in these counties. In due course these data will be combined in cultural and religious analyses.

Table 7.1 shows the counties to have markedly different demographic features. Rutland's population was the smallest, being only about one eighty-fourth that of Lancashire, which had over two million people in 1851. The other counties range between these two in size. Mean parish populations varied considerably, and this was related to the north–south topographical and administrative divisions that had created some huge northern parishes. The northern counties often based their poor-law administration on the township rather than the parish, partly in response to such contrasts in acreage, and this was a key administrative difference within England. Again the Rutland–Lancashire comparison brings this out well, indicating the two extremes in parochial size. Major repercussions ensued for local administration, for the Anglican Church (although many townships were either chapelries or linked with a chapelry), and for the success of Nonconformity. There were also large differences in county demographic growth. Lancashire's annual growth rate was 2.27 between 1811 and 1851, and even this was exceeded in Monmouthshire. For many other counties the rate was appreciably lower. The two most industrial counties had the highest growth, followed by Cambridge-

66 Caird, *English Agriculture in 1850–51*, p. 389.

67 T. F. Bulmer, *History, Topography, and Directory of Northumberland* (Manchester, 1886), pp. 566, 650.

68 The 'bondage' system has been well described by J. P. D. Dunbabin, *Rural Discontent in Nineteenth-century Britain* (1974), esp. chs. 7, 11.

Table 7.1. *Selected demographic characteristics of the fifteen counties*

County	1851 population	Mean parish population (1851)	County population growth rate, 1811–1851
Ang.	60,897	791	1.38
Beds.	129,668	1,046	1.45
Caerns.	77,020	1,242	1.42
Cambs.	192,864	1,294	1.64
Cards.	98,123	1,033	0.85
Derbs.	257,773	2,455	1.24
Dors.	184,073	648	0.99
Lancs.	2,056,736	26,368	2.27
Leics.	232,023	1,013	1.05
Mon.	156,461	1,304	2.40
N'umb.	302,632	3,326	1.27
Rut.	24,380	435	0.68
Suff.	327,191	677	0.91
Suss.	338,238	1,067	1.47
York, E. Rid.	207,623	1,214	1.28
All counties	4,645,702	1,903	1.67

shire, Sussex, Bedfordshire and Caernarvonshire, which had significant localised industry or in-migration to certain parts. Some of the agricultural counties also had high levels of population growth.[69]

County landownership patterns are of much significance in religious geography. Table 7.2 gives the percentages of parishes falling into the four landownership categories reported in the *Imperial Gazetteer*. That gazetteer classified parishes into four groups: those where land was held entirely (or almost entirely) in one hand; those in which land was held in few hands; those where property was subdivided; and those in which the property was much sub-divided. These *Imperial Gazetteer* classifications were used by Alan Everitt to argue that landownership had many ramifications for religious observance, and they have also been used here.[70] Table 7.2 supplies a

[69] See also P. Deane and W. A. Cole, *British Economic Growth, 1688–1959* (Cambridge, 1962, 1969 edn), pp. 108–9, 115, 118, 127, 131.

[70] Everitt, *Pattern of Rural Dissent*, e.g. pp. 70–1, 80–2, 88, 90.

county breakdown of the 'valid' percentages of each landownership category of parish.[71]

The highest percentages of wholly 'closed' parishes, where property was held by one family or person, appear to have been in Dorset, Rutland, Bedfordshire and Sussex. Dorset contained 25 such parishes.[72] In Rutland, parishes like Martinsthorpe, Stoke Dry and Wakerley had highly concentrated landownership, an attribute they shared with Leicestershire parishes such as Cranoe, Foston and West Leake. Similar features marked the Monmouthshire parishes of Bassaleg, Llanwern, Monkswood, Oldcastle, Portscuett, and St Pierre with Runstone. Percentages like those in the table are complicated by parishes which were not classified by the source: parishes which tended to be more sub-divided or urban ones. One simple way to handle this is guardedly to define 'closed' parishes as those in which property was held in one or a few hands, and express them as percentages of *all* parishes (including the missing ones). This is done in the final column of table 7.2. One observes the relatively large percentages of such parishes in Caernarvonshire, Monmouthshire, Anglesey, Dorset, Bedfordshire and Northumberland. At the other extreme were Lancashire, Derbyshire, Cambridgeshire and Leicestershire. These tended to be industrial, and/or counties with many small owners and tenants. For example, in Cambridgeshire property in the northern, late-enclosed fenland parishes was often heavily subdivided.

Further socio-economic features of the counties are illustrated in table 7.3. These are the numbers of parishes in each county, mean parish acreage, persons per acre in 1851, value of real property per acre and per inhabitant, *per capita* poor relief, and a final column showing

[71] Landed classifications were not given for some parishes in the *Imperial Gazetteer*. The number of parishes for which this information could be obtained is shown in the column headed 'valid cases', compared with the number 'missing' in the next column. ('All parishes' in the final column refers to valid and missing cases combined.) Omissions were more likely to occur for the most sub-divided or urban parishes, the source taking it as obvious that these were considerably 'sub-divided' in ownership. So the percentages in table 7.2 need to be treated cautiously. See appendix E for further discussion and for the numbers underlying table 7.2.

[72] Dorset parishes stated as having property concentrated almost entirely in one hand were Bloxworth, Bradford Abbas, Little Bredy, Chaldron Herring, Compton Vallence, Coombe Keynes, Fifehead Magdalen, Hamworthy, Haydon, Hinton Parva, Kimmeridge, East Lulworth, Melbury Sampford, Milton Abbas, Moore Critchell, Moreton, Nether Cerne, Over Compton, Pointington, Sutton Waldron, Up-Cerne, Warmwell, Winterbourne Came, Woodlands and Woodsford.

Table 7.2. *Percentage distribution of landownership categories by county*

County	Land in one family (% of valid cases)	Land in a few families (% of valid cases)	Land sub-divided (% of valid cases)	Land much subdivided (% of valid cases)	Valid cases (N. parishes with information)	N. missing parishes	'Closed parishes' (columns 1 + 2) as % of all parishes
Ang.	3.2	63.5	15.9	17.5	63	14	54.5
Beds.	11.9	52.4	25.0	10.7	84	40	43.5
Caerns.	4.2	75.0	8.3	12.5	48	14	61.3
Cambs.	2.5	54.4	11.4	31.6	79	70	30.2
Cards.	0.0	53.8	7.7	38.5	65	30	36.8
Derbs.	1.5	41.5	20.0	36.9	65	40	26.7
Dors.	14.9	60.1	7.7	17.3	168	116	44.4
Lancs.	0.0	16.7	26.2	57.1	42	36	9.0
Leics.	3.7	48.1	22.2	25.9	135	95	30.4
Mon.	5.7	58.5	16.0	19.8	106	14	56.7
N'umb.	1.8	64.3	17.9	16.1	56	35	40.7
Rut.	13.0	65.2	13.0	8.7	23	33	32.1
Suff.	4.2	54.4	20.4	21.1	285	199	34.5
Suss.	9.3	47.0	21.9	21.9	183	134	32.5
York, E.Rid.	1.6	52.5	22.1	23.8	122	49	38.6
All counties	5.8	53.5	17.8	22.9	1,524	919	37.0

Table 7.3. *Socio-economic features of the fifteen counties*

County	N. parishes	Mean parish acreage	People per acre 1851	Real property values per acre (£)	Real property values *per capita* (£)	Poor relief *per capita* 1832–6 (£)	Value of Anglican livings/value of real property
Ang.	77	2,817	0.33	1.41	4.23	0.32	0.05
Beds.	124	2,506	0.40	1.91	4.93	0.85	0.06
Caerns.	62	4,408	0.28	1.17	4.22	0.32	0.04
Cambs.	149	3,691	0.29	1.83	6.45	0.62	0.07
Cards.	95	6,313	0.16	0.51	3.12	0.27	0.04
Derbs.	105	5,463	0.38	1.87	4.60	0.23	0.03
Dors.	284	2,235	0.29	1.49	5.13	0.54	0.08
Lancs.	78	15,606	1.36	6.58	4.85	0.24	0.01
Leics.	230	2,343	0.33	2.20	6.58	0.62	0.07
Mon.	120	2,750	0.48	2.70	5.69	0.27	0.03
N'umb.	91	13,445	0.18	1.13	6.38	0.34	0.02
Rut.	56	1,909	0.23	1.76	7.73	0.58	0.10
Suff.	484	1,968	0.31	1.80	5.81	0.85	0.10
Suss.	317	3,187	0.35	1.99	6.12	1.11	0.05
York, E. Rid.	171	3,836	0.25	1.82	7.41	0.45	0.04
All counties	2,443	3,761	0.49	2.29	5.33	0.52	0.04

the total county value of Anglican livings expressed as a ratio of the counties' total real property values.[73]

One should note the counties' varying sizes. Rutland had only 56 parishes, while Suffolk had 484. The northern parishes tended to be much larger than the southern. Average parish acreages in Northumberland or Lancashire were seven to eight times greater than Rutland, and (as mentioned in earlier chapters) these north–south (and to some extent west–east) contrasts had profound implications for social, economic and religious life. With regard to population density, Cardiganshire and Northumberland were very thinly populated. Lancashire's density of population separated it markedly from all other counties, including Monmouthshire.

Property values per acre show striking differences.[74] Lancashire once more emerges conspicuously, by far the richest county at £6.58 per acre, followed by Monmouthshire, Leicestershire, Sussex and Derbyshire, with the more agricultural counties lower. Cardiganshire, with a property value per acre of only £0.51, was certainly the poorest. Another way to consider county wealth is to look at real property values *per capita*, and here a slightly different picture emerges. Rutland, the East Riding, Leicestershire, Cambridgeshire, Northumberland and Sussex feature relatively highly. Lancashire with its huge population was poorer on this measure than Dorset, but still not as poor as the western and northern Welsh counties. A related indicator is *per capita* poor relief, for the early–mid 1830s. The southern and eastern agricultural counties, where rural poverty and de-industrialisation were at their most chronic, and the semi-industrial county of Leicestershire, with its severe problems of depressed framework-knitting, have the highest figures. While this measure is a

[73] In this table, the number of parishes refers to registration counties in 1851. The real property values *per capita* relate 1851 populations to property values of the mid 1860s, taken from the *Imperial Gazetteer*. They should therefore be treated as approximate. The poor-relief *per capita* figures use 1831 population data in relation to the 1832–6 poor-relief data, as supplied in sequential Poor Law Commission Reports. (Those data were chosen rather than later expenditures because the later data are beset by problems arising from varied regional adoption of the New Poor Law. It was also desirable to use relief data from before the Religious Census.) The values of Anglican livings and real property values (for the final column) use parish data from the *Imperial Gazetteer*. These are later than the 1851 census, but they rarely misrepresent a longer-term parochial situation. Figures are from registration-county aggregations of the parish data.

[74] This is an average across all parishes in each county for which such values were available in the *Imperial Gazetteer*.

Table 7.4. *Families in agriculture, occupiers and agricultural labourers in 1831*

County	Families in agriculture as % of total families	Occupiers not employing labourers as % of total occupiers	N. of labourers in agriculture per occupier employing labourers
Ang.	41.9	58.5	3.1
Beds.	56.9	25.3	8.5
Caerns.	40.0	57.3	2.8
Cambs.	51.8	35.4	6.3
Cards.	55.1	49.9	2.5
Derbs.	24.6	59.4	3.2
Dors.	45.5	30.1	6.3
Lancs.	9.7	59.6	3.1
Leics.	30.5	42.0	4.0
Mon.	27.6	41.2	3.0
N'umb.	21.7	33.2	4.5
Rut.	55.0	50.8	4.4
Suff.	53.2	20.4	7.2
Suss.	42.3	29.4	8.2
York, E.Rid.	33.9	33.2	3.7
All counties	28.4	45.0	4.7

complex one, affected also by the relative generosity of relief payments, these findings support what is known about the geography of pauperism, and the unemployment and high poor-rate problems of the depressed agrarian south.[75] The last column of the table gives an interesting but crude indicator of the economic strength of the Church of England relative to real property values. The value of Anglican livings is not encompassed in any straightforward way by the measure of property values, as it includes fees, tithes and the like. But the higher ratios found in the southern rural counties of Rutland, Suffolk, Dorset and Cambridgeshire are noticeable, particularly in view of the national geography of the Church of England.

Table 7.4 describes aspects of landed employment, calculated from the 1831 census. The most agricultural counties, with highest percentages of families in agriculture, were Cardiganshire, Bedfordshire, Suffolk, Rutland and Cambridgeshire. Ratios between types of occu-

[75] F. Driver, *Power and Pauperism: the Workhouse System, 1834–1884* (Cambridge, 1993).

pier and labourers are also shown, relevant as they are to issues of rural deference or independence and their possible influences upon religious adherence. Occupiers not employing labourers as a percentage of total occupiers are shown in the third column. Welsh figures for this more traditional family farming are very high, but not as high as Lancashire and Derbyshire – and it is an interesting paradox of economic history that these two are among the most industrial counties. The Welsh counties had low numbers of labourers relative to employing occupiers (column four), and this was also true of Lancashire, Derbyshire and the East Riding.[76] This contrasts markedly with the most heavily proletarianised rural counties: Bedfordshire, Cambridgeshire, Dorset, Suffolk and Sussex all loom prominently here, just as they did with regard to *per capita* poor relief.

In conclusion, one can summarise the religious character of each county. Table 7.5 gives the overall index of attendances for major denominations.

For all counties together, the Anglican Church was easily the strongest denomination, followed by the Wesleyan Methodists, the Independents and the Baptists. Roman Catholicism was very weak even in counties associated with it, like Lancashire, Monmouthshire or Northumberland. The Church of England achieved its highest figures in southern and midland counties, like Dorset, Suffolk and Rutland. The Baptists and Independents did well in counties like Cambridgeshire, Cardiganshire, Bedfordshire or Monmouthshire. However, this table might be dedicated to the ministers and congregations of the Welsh Calvinistic Methodists, for in their strongholds their strength exceeded that of the Church of England in *any* region. In the most Welsh counties old dissent also completely overshadowed the established church. Wesleyan Methodism asserted itself strongly in Bedfordshire and the East Riding, and surprisingly also in Rutland and Dorset, while the Primitive Methodists had their greatest showing in Derbyshire, Cambridgeshire and the East Riding. 'Other Methodists', a varied group created for this table, had a noticeable presence in Northumberland, and also in Cardiganshire and Derbyshire.

If one casts one's eye along the row for Lancashire, or for Northumberland, other intriguing points emerge. These two counties' indexes were extraordinarily low. Lancashire was the most

[76] Snell, *Annals of the Labouring Poor*, pp. 96–7, gives further county figures.

Table 7.5. *Indexes of attendances for major denominations, and total index of attendances for all 1851 denominations, excluding Sunday scholars*

County	Roman Catholics	Church of England	Total Baptists	Independents	Calvinistic Methodists	Wesleyan Methodists	Primitive Methodists	Other Methodists*	Index of total attendances
Ang.	0.0	6.7	7.0	13.1	44.7	8.8	0.0	0.4	82.4
Beds.	0.1	23.9	19.1	7.2	0.0	19.6	4.4	0.3	76.7
Caerns.	0.2	4.5	3.8	10.3	36.2	7.0	0.0	0.0	62.3
Cambs.	0.2	26.2	14.5	4.3	0.0	8.6	5.0	1.7	61.6
Cards.	0.0	13.6	15.5	20.2	31.9	0.6	0.0	3.8	87.5
Derbs.	1.5	15.6	3.1	3.2	0.0	8.8	6.5	3.5	43.0
Dors.	0.3	34.6	1.2	8.8	0.0	9.0	2.2	0.3	57.8
Lancs.	3.2	13.3	1.3	2.8	0.4	3.9	1.0	1.6	32.1
Leics.	1.2	24.5	9.8	5.0	0.0	7.4	3.8	1.2	54.0
Mon.	1.9	12.2	16.5	9.9	4.5	8.7	2.0	0.9	57.9
N'umb.	2.1	13.2	1.0	1.5	0.0	0.6	2.5	6.3	36.1
Rut.	0.0	33.7	8.6	3.0	0.0	8.7	1.2	0.9	57.4
Suff.	0.2	33.3	10.3	10.7	0.0	3.5	2.8	0.7	62.1
Suss.	0.3	30.9	3.5	4.7	0.0	3.4	0.2	1.3	46.4
York, E. Rid.	1.5	15.7	0.9	3.5	0.0	15.3	7.8	1.3	47.7
All counties	1.9	18.3	4.6	4.9	2.3	5.7	2.2	1.8	44.8

Notes: * 'Other Methodists' comprise the Wesleyan Methodist New Connexion, Bible Christians, Wesleyan Methodist Association, Independent Methodists, Wesleyan Reformers and Lady Huntingdon's Connexion.

'secular' county, closely followed by the border county of Northumberland. Derbyshire, Sussex and the East Riding were also very low. Cardiganshire and Anglesey, and surprisingly Bedfordshire, were at the other extreme of this 'secular'–'religious' spectrum. Wales had higher attendance figures than England. The diversity of these figures underlines the contrasting regional levels of religious attendance. The Welsh–English differences, and the local contexts and influences that may have affected these religious features, are matters that will now be explored in further detail.

8

From Henry Compton to Horace Mann: stability or relocation in Catholicism and Nonconformity, and the growth of religious pluralism

The two major censuses of religion that have most preoccupied historians and cultural geographers have, without doubt, been the Compton Census of 1676 and the *Census of Religious Worship* of 1851. Over more than two centuries, probably indeed throughout British history, no other religious censuses were conducted to rival these two sources. The religious history of the intervening period has, however, been researched by using other documentation, including the Evans list of 1715, the returns of Papists in 1767 and 1780, selected visitation returns, and the 1829 religious returns.

The Compton Census has received growing scholarly attention in recent years, due very largely to the magisterial work of Anne Whiteman.[1] Named after Henry Compton, Bishop of London, this census comprised returns made by the Church of England's clergy, who were told to count inhabitants, Papists and dissenters. The latter two categories were intended to encompass those residents who were 'Popish Recusants or persons suspected for such Recusancy' and 'other Dissenters . . . in each parish (of what Sect soever) which either obstinately refuse or wholly absent themselves from the Communion of the Church of England at such times as by Law they are required'.[2] The census consisted of a problematical division into three groups, which did not distinguish between separate old dissenting denominations.

Perhaps the main difficulty with this 1676 source is the question of

1 Research on the Compton Census has been enormously advanced by A. Whiteman (ed.), *The Compton Census of 1676: a Critical Edition* (Oxford, 1986), with the assistance of M. Clapinson. This major and finely documented achievement leaves historians forever indebted to Whiteman, and this chapter makes heavy use of it. See also A. Whiteman, 'The Compton Census of 1676', in K. Schurer and T. Arkell (eds.), *Surveying the People* (Oxford, 1992), pp. 78–96; A. Whiteman and M. Clapinson, 'The use of the Compton Census for demographic purposes', *Local Population Studies*, 50 (1993), 61–6.

2 Whiteman, 'Compton Census', in Schurer and Arkell, *Surveying the People*, p. 81.

what was being counted by separate incumbents in different dioceses. It is certain that the many respondents interpreted the unclear (and to some extent regionally different) instructions given them in varying ways. The intention was to count numbers of males and females over sixteen falling into each of the three categories, and it is believed by most historians that this was the normal practice.[3] However, some respondents counted all heads of households, or all males, or all men and women, while others tallied the entire population, and still others may have adopted alternative criteria for inclusion. In some cases it is not clear either whether servants or lodgers were included.[4] To compound this, the first column of Compton data refers in some areas to inhabitants, in others to conformists. The Compton census is bedeviled with questions arising out of such confusion.[5]

[3] See Whiteman, *Compton Census*, p. lxiv, a conclusion she reaches after making comparisons with the Protestation returns of 1641–2. See also E. A. Wrigley and R. S. Schofield, *The Population History of England, 1541–1871: a Reconstruction* (1981), pp. 33–7, 570. They tested the 1676 data in various ways, using it to check the representativeness of their 404 parishes.

[4] Whiteman, *Compton Census*, p. lxxx, but she doubts that any serious omissions took place.

[5] For discussion of the Compton Census, see in particular Whiteman's work, noted above, and her select bibliography, *Compton Census*, pp. 647–55; J. C. Cox, 'A religious census of Derbyshire, 1676', *Journal of the Derbyshire Archaeological and Natural History Society*, 7 (1885), 31–6; W. G. D. Fletcher, 'Religious census in Leicestershire in 1676', *Transactions of the Leicestershire Architectural and Archaeological Society*, 6 (1887), 296–303; W. G. D. Fletcher, 'Religious census of Shropshire in 1676', *Transactions of the Shropshire Archaeological and Natural History Society*, 1 (1889), 75–92; W. Mooney, 'A religious census of Berkshire in 1676', *Berkshire, Buckinghamshire and Oxfordshire Archaeological Journal*, 4 (1889), 112–15, and 5 (1900), 55–9; J. H. Cooper, 'A religious census of Sussex in 1676', *Sussex Archaeological Collections*, 45 (1902), 142–8; A. S. Langley, 'A religious census of 1676, A.D.', *Lincolnshire Notes and Queries*, 16 (April, 1920), 33–51; E. L. Guilford, 'Nottinghamshire in 1676', *Transactions of the Thoroton Society*, 28 (1924), 106–13; T. Richards, 'The religious census of 1676: an inquiry into its historical value, mainly in reference to Wales', supplement to the *Transactions of the Hon. Society of Cymmrodorion* (1925–7), 14–30; S. A. Peyton, 'The religious census of 1676', *English Historical Review*, 48 (1933); F. G. James, 'The population of the diocese of Carlisle in 1676', *Transactions of the Cumberland and Westmorland Antiquarian and Archaeological Society*, 51 (1952), 137–41; W. B. Stephens 'A seventeenth century census', *Devon and Cornwall Notes and Queries*, 29 (1958); C. W. Chalkin (ed.), *The Compton Census of 1676: the Dioceses of Canterbury and Rochester*, Kent Archaeological Society Records, 17 (1960), 153–74; M. Spufford, 'The dissenting churches in Cambridgeshire from 1660–1700', *Proceedings of the Cambridgeshire Antiquarian Society*, 61 (1968), 67–95; A. Everitt, 'Nonconformity in country parishes', supplement to the *Agricultural History Review*, 18 (1970), 186–8; R. Stanes, 'The Compton Census for the Diocese of Exeter, 1676', *Devon Historian*, 9 (1974), 14–27, and 10 (1975), 4–16; D. Wykes, 'A reappraisal of the reliability of the 1676

Its use as a demographic source, which has been so tantalising for the late seventeenth century, has invited various ways of 'correcting' its data. This complicated approach has taken the form of applying 'multipliers', following assumptions as to what the incumbents' figures referred to, assumptions based partly on the 1811:1676 ratios of population, and also on close inspection of other local sources for the parishes in question. The Compton manuscript data are multiplied to obtain something that might approximate to a total 'population' for each settlement. Some quite detailed and ingenious work has been done in this regard, assessing what multipliers may be appropriate for each parish.[6]

In the very large majority of cases, the parish was the geographical settlement for the purposes of data collection in 1676. In a few cases, alternative areas of settlement may have been used, but this was very uncommon. While there was considerable general continuity of parish boundaries over extended periods, nevertheless in many instances the parishes of 1676 were not those of 1851, a point that one needs to bear in mind.

By contrast, we have seen how impressive and encompassing the 1851 *Census of Religious Worship* was. Its detail and specification far exceeds that of 1676. The Compton Census is 'a potential minefield' by comparison.[7] Compton estimates different phenomena, in an alternative way, to the 1851 source. And neither the original Compton figures, nor the attendance data of 1851, are direct counts of believers or separate attendants. While we know with some precision what the 1851 returns are (attendances, sittings, Sunday school attendances and so on), in many cases nobody is sure what the Compton figures refer to, nor indeed how people were selected as belonging to one religious category rather than another. It is partly for this reason that his-

Footnote 5 (*cont.*)
"Compton Census" with respect to Leicester', *Transactions of the Leicestershire Archaeological and Historical Society*, 60 (1980), 72–7; P. Jackson, 'Nonconformity and the Compton Census in late seventeenth-century Devon', in K. Schurer and T. Arkell (eds.), *Surveying the People* (Oxford, 1992), 117–129.

6 See Whiteman's general introduction and appendices to *Compton Census*, and her 'Compton Census'; T. Arkell, 'A method for estimating population totals from the Compton Census returns', in K. Schurer and T. Arkell (eds.), *Surveying the People* (Oxford, 1992), pp. 97–116; Jackson, 'Nonconformity and the Compton Census', also in Schurer and Arkell, *Surveying the People*, pp. 117–124.

7 'Introducing the documents' in Schurer and Arkell, *Surveying the People*, p. 34; Spufford, 'The dissenting churches in Cambridgeshire', 95.

torians have restrained themselves from making long-term comparisons between the sources, except in some cases for quite localised studies, where it has been possible to illuminate the Compton Census with extraneous data. This has included data obtained from the 1603 enquiry into communicants, Papists and non-communicants, the Protestation returns of 1641–2, Hearth Tax returns,[8] Easter books, pre-industrial listings of inhabitants like that of Clayworth, or indeed data from the much later 1811 population census.[9]

This reluctance to relate the religious sources to each other has been further compounded by the usual division of historians into 'early-modern' specialists, interested in the Compton Census and its period, and Victorian specialists who have normally treated the 1851 religious returns in isolation from much earlier documentation. The result has been that some of the most intriguing questions open to historians of English and Welsh religion have never been asked or resolved with any comprehensiveness. For example, what kinds of local continuities exist between Compton and 1851? How, if at all, can one measure them? What regional or county variations can be found in such continuities, and why? What do these tell us about the local stability or otherwise of dissent? Can the conclusions suggest anything about the adequacy of the Compton Census itself, and its use for demographic and religious studies?

These are important historical questions. To address them here, all parishes in twelve registration counties have been used, that is, those of our fifteen counties for which Compton data are available. These are Anglesey, Bedfordshire, Caernarvonshire, Cambridgeshire, Cardiganshire, Derbyshire, Leicestershire, Monmouthshire, Rutland, Suffolk, Sussex and the East Riding of Yorkshire.[10] All Compton data were computerised, reworking those 1676 data to the 1851 parochial units, to enable comparison between the two dates.

8 See Whiteman, *Compton Census*, pp. lix–lxxvi.

9 On Easter books, see S. Wright, 'Easter books and parish rate books: a new source for the urban historian', *Urban History Yearbook* (1985); and her 'A guide to Easter books and related parish listings', *Local Population Studies*, part 1, 42 (1989); and part 2, 43 (1989). On the demographic relation between 1676 and 1811, see Whiteman, 'Compton Census', p. 88; Wrigley and Schofield, *The Population History of England*, pp. 33–7. These historians were not concerned with appraising *religious* continuities from the seventeenth- and nineteenth-century sources.

10 The other three counties (Dorset, Lancashire and Northumberland) were omitted here because they lack adequate Compton data.

Ratios and the Compton Census

The 1676 returns are relatively problematical compared with those for 1851, and their use needs to be carefully judged. For the most part the concern here is not with the demographic potential of the Compton data. And on this parish-by-parish scale, using all parishes across twelve counties, it has not been possible to examine the returns in conjunction with other seventeenth-century sources, like the Hearth Tax, although this may be undertaken at a later date.[11] It appeared that the use of different multipliers, which had the effect of grossly altering the original 1676 data, produced final figures which reflected too much the assumptions behind the choice of multiplier. In some cases, detailed knowledge of the later seventeenth-century local demography and the history of a settlement suggested that multipliers (mainly based on 1811:1676 ratios) were questionable, and it is unsafe to assume that individual parish populations grew in line with national trends. Places like Llandudno, for example, reported to have 26 Conformists and 1 Papist in 1676, were indeed tiny settlements in the later seventeenth century, and in such cases one would need to be wary of extrapolating back through time and applying large multipliers to the 1676 data. It is easy to assume that such settlements, in the seventeenth century, replicated on a smaller scale the population size and functions that they had attained by the early or mid nineteenth century, and to apply multipliers producing such an effect, but clearly such assumptions are inherently risky.

After consideration of the census and possible multipliers, one method of handling the 1676 data was chosen: the use of ratio data rather than absolute figures. The one thing one *can* be certain about is that each incumbent would have applied the same criteria across the three categories he was returning figures for. In other words, the *ratios* between each figure, *for distinct parishes*, are likely to be very reliable as an indication of the relative levels of conformity or dissent. For example, if in one parish 10 per cent of the total parish figure was Papist, in principle this would enable a realistic comparison with another parish for which the figure was 1 per cent – even though the data in the first parish might refer to total population, while in the

[11] On the Hearth Tax data, see in particular N. Alldridge (ed.), *The Hearth Tax: Problems and Possibilities* (Hull, 1983); J. Patten, 'The Hearth Taxes, 1662–89', *Local Population Studies*, 7 (1971), 14–27.

second they might have referred to adult males only. In this sense, feasible comparisons between parishes and counties become possible using ratio or percentage data. This would be subject to much greater levels of assumption if one used any multiplier-dependent method that aimed for standardised *absolute* parish figures for each religious grouping. Accordingly, Whiteman's published data for each parish were computerised, adjusted after complex tests to deal with the problem of whether the first column represents 'conformists' or inhabitants, and internal ratios and percentages were calculated on a 'parish-by-parish' basis from those data. Many questions remain about the interpretation of partial conformity and related issues. But this procedure gives the best obtainable measure of the relative levels of dissent or conformity in each settlement in 1676, which permits comparison statistically and cartographically with a comparable handling of the 1851 data.

Another problem in comparing the Compton Census with the 1851 Religious Census concerns the spatial areas used to gather the data. Over time, there was considerable continuity of parish spatial areas, and significant parochial discontinuities between 1676 and 1851 probably do not affect more than about 5 per cent of the total parishes. In a few cases local data from 1676 have been amalgamated to build up to the areas of parishes in 1851, thus facilitating comparison between the two dates. In some urbanising districts, forming a separate parish in 1676, but subdivided into separate parishes by 1851, the data are less readily comparable across time, and in some cases the comparison has to be abandoned. There is no way one can divide settlement-specific 1676 data to deal with this kind of change, and it was not wished to depart from our resolve throughout to standardise the data to 1851 parish units. Again, the use of ratio data acts to minimise this problem. For instance, when one finds that a settlement in 1676 had a certain proportion of Papists, or Nonconformists, it seems historically reasonable to relate this figure to data for the same general locality in 1851, even though the local boundaries may not be exactly coterminous. If historians were trying to compare absolute populations in such a way more serious problems would arise. In addition, non-parametric techniques and cartographical analysis will be used to investigate continuities, and these methods with this kind of ratio data are not highly dependent upon identical geographical areas being compared in every case. In the very large majority of parishes, of course, no such difficulty exists.

Adjusting the Compton Census

Having decided to use this 'ratio method' as the basis for analysis, the task was first to adjust the Compton figures. One major problem in the interpretation of the 1676 data has been whether the first column of the Salt manuscript, as used by Whiteman, represented 'conformists' or 'inhabitants'. Whiteman devised some ingenious tests to help resolve this question for different dioceses and archdeaconries, tests which were based on the frequency of figures 'rounded' to the nearest ten in the first column, published under the often illusory heading 'conformists'. This allowed her to gauge whether the returned data had later been subtracted from to produce the figures for the other two columns, and thus whether column 1 of the Salt manuscript represented inhabitants or conformists.[12] To correct the published data where necessary, her example was followed, further elaborated here by conducting chi-squared tests to establish the significance of the differences between the actual number of percentages rounded and the 10 per cent one would expect by chance.[13]

These tests were made on parishes in the 1851 registration-district county areas, into which the parish-level data are arranged. All the chosen counties fall into distinctive dioceses with slight exceptions at certain boundaries, like that between the registration counties of Leicestershire and Warwickshire.[14] After experimentation with the data, and bearing in mind the uncertain nature of the adjustments being made, it became clear that the cases of boundary mismatch between diocese, historical county and registration county were completely insignificant for these quantitative methods, although they could well be important for more localised studies using smaller numbers of parishes.

The tests carried out involved the same initial premises as Whiteman's, namely that:

(i) in general it was inhabitants (whether they be all adults, males, or whatever) that were originally recorded by the incumbents, rather than 'conformists'.

12 See her discussion in *Compton Census*, pp. lii–liv, lxxxvi–lxci.

13 Additional tests were carried out to check for rounding based on multiples of twelve. The results were all negative (i.e. very close to the 8.3% expected by chance alone), confirming Whiteman's judgement on the possibility of this form of tabulation.

14 For maps of the dioceses and their relation to historical counties, see G. F. A. Best, *Temporal Pillars: Queen Anne's Bounty, the Ecclesiastical Commissioners, and the Church of England* (Cambridge, 1964), pp. 514–15, maps 1 and 2.

(ii) high levels of rounding in column 1 of the published data indicated that the figures had not been subsequently corrected (i.e. subtracted from), and therefore that column 1 may be taken to represent inhabitants.

(iii) that a high level of rounding for all three columns (conformists, dissenters and Papists) when added together is indicative of subsequent correction having taken place, and therefore that one should be inclined to believe that column 1 represents 'conformists'.

For each county, we calculated the percentage of rounding for column 1 using all parishes that had Compton data. We did a parallel calculation for the totals of columns 1, 2 and 3. We carried out a chi-square test to see how significantly the observed number of rounded returns differed from the expected number (which would be one in ten from random chance alone). The results suggested that inhabitants were recorded for Anglesey, Caernarvon, Cambridgeshire, Cardiganshire, Leicestershire, Rutland and the East Riding, that conformists were recorded for Derbyshire and Sussex, and that no clear result could be established for Bedfordshire, Suffolk and Monmouthshire.[15] In almost all cases these findings matched Whiteman's conclusions. Such tests cannot be relied upon in their entirety, and after careful deliberation with Whiteman, in which she raised issues relating in particular to the ambiguous returns for some of the Welsh counties, and clear documentary evidence for Leicestershire indicating alternative conclusions for that county, we opted to take column 1 of the published Compton Census as representing 'conformists' for Bedfordshire, Derbyshire, Leicestershire and Sussex, and 'inhabitants' for the remaining eight counties. The computerised parish data for these counties were then adjusted accordingly, preparatory to more detailed analysis.

Analysis of continuity between 1676 and 1851

For the subsequent analysis, the Compton figures for conformists, Nonconformists and Papists were expressed as a percentage of the adjusted total Compton figure, and the 1851 attendance data for

[15] This procedure and the tests are described in more detail in A. Crockett and K. D. M. Snell, 'From the 1676 Compton Census to the 1851 Census of Religious Worship: religious continuity or discontinuity?', *Rural History*, 8 (1997), 59–61.

equivalent denominations ('old dissent' and Catholicism) were expressed as the percentage share of total attendances for all denominations.[16] Thereby for both dates one is dealing with a comparable ratio figure. The 'old' dissenting denominations of 1851 that were used to compare with dissenters in 1676 were the General Baptists, Particular Baptists, unspecified Baptists, Quakers, Presbyterian Church in England, Unitarians, and Independents. Two main statistical methods were used to pursue the question of whether the geographical distributions of dissenters and Papists in 1676 bore any resemblances to those of the mid nineteenth century. Using parish-level data, Spearman's rank correlations of denominational data were undertaken for each county and for all counties combined,[17] and secondly, the Kruskal–Wallis non-parametric test was applied to the total data for all counties to give some overall tests of significance for any relationships between the 1676 and 1851 data.

It is interesting first to give a general picture of the relative strengths of Papism and Nonconformity in 1676, for there were considerable contrasts across counties. Table 8.1 gives the mean percentage (unweighted by parish) that was Papist and Nonconformist across the documented parishes.[18] The percentage Catholic was usually very low, but in Monmouthshire Papists were quite conspicuous. For the Nonconformists, Monmouthshire, Bedfordshire and the East Riding stand out as having the highest figures. The fourth column shows the percentage of parishes that had Papists and/or Nonconformists present. The Anglesey figure is suspiciously low, as perhaps are the other west and north Welsh counties, but otherwise Monmouthshire, Bedfordshire and the East Riding, with Leicestershire, stand out as being more dissenting than the others.

Following very many indications and suggestions in the religious and cultural historiography, considerable continuity in parochial geographical patterns was anticipated. The findings are perhaps surprising. Table 8.2 shows the results of correlating the Compton data for Papists and Nonconformists with the Roman Catholic and old dissent

[16] The index of total attendances was also used (as well as the percentage share), but the results were almost identical. For reasons of consistency with the Compton ratio measure, only the percentage-share measure is reported here.

[17] Rank correlation was the preferable method for this data, which is often non-normally distributed statistically.

[18] This is probably the best summary measure, given the lack of absolute comparability across all parishes of the Compton data.

Table 8.1. *Average parish percentages of Papists and Nonconformists in the Compton Census by county, and the percentage of parishes in 1676 containing Papists and/or Nonconformists*

	Mean % Papist	Mean % Nonconformist	% of Compton parishes with Papists and/or Nonconformists	N. (Compton parishes)
Ang.	0.03	0.15	8.1	62
Beds.	0.17	7.90	85.0	120
Caerns.	0.53	0.75	43.4	53
Cambs.	0.09	3.41	66.4	134
Cards.	0.00	2.13	45.3	75
Derbs.	1.44	1.48	67.8	87
Leics.	0.42	2.89	71.8	213
Mon.	8.05	12.0	92.7	82
Rut.	0.85	1.29	69.4	49
Suff.	0.92	3.17	63.1	195
Suss.	0.74	3.99	65.9	287
York, E. Rid.	2.05	5.02	82.9	105
All counties	1.09	3.89	66.6	1,462

percentage share of total attendances in 1851. We expected to find high positive coefficients when these relationships were examined in this way. However, if one looks at the fourth column, giving the results for Compton Nonconformity and old dissent in 1851, it can be seen that the coefficients are often quite low. Only those for Leicestershire, Monmouthshire, Sussex and the East Riding are statistically significant. For all counties combined, the coefficient of 0.105 is low, but highly significant because of the very large number (1,462) of parishes being used. For nearly half the counties, the parish-level data from 1676 and 1851 are almost random with regard to each other. The East Riding shows the clearest result, indicating some local continuity of Nonconformity in certain parishes, and its continued absence or low presence in others. But in few of the counties is there significant correlation between the data for these two dates. In the two northern Welsh counties the coefficients are even weakly negative. These are certainly unforeseen results. Some continuity is demonstrated; but it was very frequently the case that the presence of old dissenting Nonconformity in 1851 bore no relation to its local geography in 1676.

Table 8.2. *Continuity of Compton Nonconformity to old dissent in 1851, and Compton Papism to Roman Catholicism in 1851 – a parish-level analysis of 12 counties (Spearman's rank correlations)*

	Compton Papism & Roman Catholic % share of attendances, 1851	sig.	Compton Nonconformity & old dissent % share of attendances, 1851	sig.	N. parishes
Ang.	No Compton Papists		−0.022	.865	62
Beds.	−0.030	.741	0.073	.427	120
Caerns.	−0.070	.617	−0.071	.612	53
Cambs.	0.344**	.000	0.068	.436	134
Cards.	No Compton Papists		0.176	.130	75
Derbs.	0.310**	.003	0.142	.188	87
Leics.	0.268**	.000	0.213**	.002	213
Mon.	0.225*	.042	0.219*	.048	82
Rut.	No Catholics in 1851		0.021	.888	49
Suff.	0.148*	.039	0.119	.099	195
Suss.	0.116*	.050	0.156**	.008	287
York, E. Rid.	0.117	.236	0.337**	.000	105
All counties	0.209**	.000	0.105**	.000	1,462

Notes:
* = passes 95% level
** = passes 99% level

In addition to treating 'old dissent' *en masse*, by grouping the denominations together, we also conducted separate correlations against the 1676 Nonconformists using 1851 percentage share of attendance data for Quakers, General Baptists, Particular Baptists and Independents, taking each of these 1851 denominations separately. The same general conclusions of a lack of strong continuity emerged. There were connections traceable for the Quakers in Cambridgeshire, Suffolk, and the East Riding, for General Baptists in Leicestershire, and for Independents in the East Riding, but in all cases these were fairly weak. The overall picture was of a lack of connection between the data from the two dates, and in very many cases the associations were weakly negative.

We turn next to the Papists. Table 8.2 shows a higher degree of continuity for them. Over all the counties, the coefficient is 0.209, and over so many parishes this is highly significant statistically. There is little continuity demonstrated in Bedfordshire or Caernarvonshire, but in other counties the results are more in line with prior expectations. In Cambridgeshire, Derbyshire and Leicestershire there were high correlations between the Papists of 1676 and the Roman Catholics of 1851, and significant results are also shown for Monmouthshire, Suffolk and Sussex. The Roman Catholics would certainly appear to have maintained their local strongholds and allegiances to a greater extent than did the old dissenters. The details of this continuity can be explored further below, by looking at these issues from a cartographic angle.[19]

The hypothesis of religious continuity was further tested by using the non-parametric Kruskal–Wallis test. The results of this analysis are shown in table 8.3. For both sets of tests, for Papism and Nonconformity, the Compton data were split into four groups based on percentages of the denomination(s) – as shown in the left-hand columns of table 8.3.

The results of the Kruskal–Wallis test reinforce our interpretation of the correlations. The higher the levels of Compton Papism, the higher the levels of percentage share of Catholicism in 1851, as demonstrated both by the mean rank and the actual mean. The Kruskal–Wallis test statistic (which is basically a non-parametric form of one-way analysis of variance) was significant at all confidence levels ($p=.0000$), adding quantitative backing to the argument that, over all counties together, the higher the strength of Papism in 1676, the higher the Catholic share in 1851. In other words, it supplies strong evidence for local geographical continuity of Catholicism over time, and this will be discussed more fully below.

The results for Nonconformity are less definite. The overall test

[19] Spearman and Pearson correlations were also conducted for these religious groups using the 1851 index of attendances against the 1676 data, and the results were very similar to those reported here. In both these exercises, all Compton-documented parishes were included in the analysis, and this involved making use of many places which in 1676 had no Nonconformist or Papist presence. Correlations were also undertaken by only including parishes which had Compton figures greater than zero for Nonconformists or Papists. One could debate the methodology and historical interpretation of these differing methods, but the overall coefficients resulting were alike for all procedures.

Table 8.3. *(a). Kruskal–Wallis test on grouped Compton Papist data against 1851 percentage share of Catholic attendances (of total attendances for all denominations)*

Compton Papism (% of 'inhabitants')	1851 Catholicism (% share) mean	mean rank	n. of parishes (N. = 1462)
No Papists present	0.10	719.4	1,172
Up to 5% Papist	0.68	770.6	199
5% to 10% Papist	1.74	782.0	42
More than 10% Papist	6.88	818.0	4

Notes: Test result (corrected for ties): chi-square = 68.4, significant at the 99% confidence level (p = .0000).

Table 8.3. *(b). Kruskal–Wallis test on grouped Compton Nonconformist data against 1851 percentage share of 'old dissent' attendances (of total attendances for all denominations)*

Compton Nonconformity (% of 'inhabitants')	1851 'old dissent' (% share) mean	mean rank	n. of parishes (N. = 1462)
No Nonconformity present	13.7	684.5	576
Up to 5% Nonconformists	16.4	757.8	545
5% to 10% Nonconformists	17.8	748.2	174
More than 10% Nonconformists	19.9	790.1	167

Notes:
Test result (corrected for ties): chi-square = 16.9, significant at the 99% confidence level (p = .0007).
(Please note that although mean rank is used for the statistical test, the actual means are shown for greater interpretability.)

statistic passes the 99 per cent confidence level, and the strength of Nonconformity in 1851 rises in line with the grouped Compton data. However, the differences are not as strong as those for Catholicism, reinforcing the previous correlation findings that spatial continuity of old dissent is only weakly detectable and certainly should not be exaggerated.

The cartography of religious continuity

The statistical analysis has thus far proved successful in demonstrating some continuity of Catholicism from 1676 to 1851, and somewhat weaker continuity of old dissent over the same 175-year period. However since these quantitative results use all the documented parishes from each county, or all parishes from all counties combined, questions now arise as to the exact nature of the local continuities and discontinuities. A more geographically sensitive analysis is needed to illuminate many further features. To this end, therefore, we mapped the Papists and Nonconformists at the two dates at parish level.

In addition to the general attraction of a cartographically enriched analysis, mapping was also seen as beneficial for two more specific reasons, relating to some of the problems inherent in comparing the Compton census with 1851 data. Expressed simply, the data in 1676 refer to 'inhabitants' in a parish, while the attendance data of 1851 refer to places of worship and their attendances. This discrepancy between what the sources describe reduces the utility of parish-by-parish comparisons (such as the correlations and Kruskal–Wallis tests), since it tends spatially to 'concentrate' the 1851 data, which perforce is confined to particular places of worship. Unlike for the Church of England, it can be argued that this effect has particular bearing on Papists and dissenters, who in 1676 would have been recorded in their home parish, but who were recorded in 1851 in the parish where they attended worship. Journeys to church or chapel were not normally more than about three miles, indeed Gilbert suggested not more than about one mile.[20] Nevertheless, such travel could mean the difference

[20] A. D. Gilbert, *Religion and Society in Industrial England: Church, Chapel and Social Change, 1740–1914* (1976, Harlow, 1984 edn), p. 101, citing a parliamentary enquiry of 1852, which indicated that in many cases a mile was the limit people would consider travelling; R. Currie, A. D. Gilbert and L. Horsley, *Churches and Churchgoers: Patterns of Church Growth in the British Isles since 1700* (Oxford, 1977), p. 117. Instances of much longer distances can easily be found, but they were probably not usual. For examples and further discussion, see Public Record Office, HO 129/223/33 (Falkenham, Suffolk), or HO 129/226/22 (Bungay, Suffolk); W. M. Jacob, 'Evidence for dissent in Norfolk, 1711–1800, from the records of the Diocese of Norwich', in N. Virgoe and T. Williamson (eds.), *Religious Dissent in East Anglia: Historical Perspectives* (Norwich, 1993), p. 40; Everitt, *Pattern of Rural Dissent*, p. 8; R. W. Ambler, 'Social change and religious experience: aspects of rural society in South Lincolnshire, with specific reference to Primitive Methodism, 1815–75' (unpublished Ph.D thesis, University of Hull, 1984), p. 152; M. R. Watts, *The Dissenters. Vol. 1* (Oxford, 1978), p. 287; M. Kinnear, *The British Voter: an Atlas and Survey since 1885*

between dissenters being recorded in, say, four parishes in 1676, but only one (and at a higher level) in 1851. This is what we mean by describing the 1851 Religious Census as having a tendency spatially to concentrate population. In addition to this broader problem, it is also important to note that parish-by-parish comparisons over time cannot discriminate between very local adjustments, such as a chapel relocating across a parochial boundary into a neighbouring parish, major regional changes, such as the complete shift in the distribution of a denomination, and absolute growth or decline. All three sorts of change can reveal themselves in the same statistical effect, and so detailed cartography is required to overcome such problems.

To address these issues we mapped at parish level the key variables: percentage Papist and Nonconformist in 1676, and percentage shares for Catholics and old dissent in 1851. Maps for Anglesey, Caernarvon, Cambridgeshire, Derbyshire, Leicestershire, Monmouthshire, Sussex, Rutland and the East Riding were produced. These are amenable to very extended and localised interpretation, and for reasons of space only a very small selection of them will be discussed here, paying special attention to the question of Catholic persistence, which quantitative analysis has pointed to as being of significance. Some denominations were very weak in certain counties, like Catholicism in Anglesey, Caernarvonshire, Cambridgeshire and Rutland, and this has also affected the choice of counties discussed. The aim is to highlight common factors in the persistence or discontinuity of religious denominations. The cartographic focus will therefore be on Monmouthshire, Leicestershire and the East Riding: counties which are important in the history of Catholicism, and which also have a significant presence of old dissenters.

Certain common patterns emerge. In every county mapped, there was a clear tendency for a wider dispersal of Papists or old dissenters in 1676 to have narrowed considerably in the 1851 maps. By that date, Catholicism in particular was concentrated in certain parishes which, in 1676, had been surrounded by a Catholic presence. Figures 8.1 and 8.2 show this contrast very clearly for Monmouthshire, and the same can be seen for Leicestershire and the East Riding in figures 8.3 to 8.6.

Footnote 20 (*cont.*)

(1968, 1981 edn), p. 128. Tollpike roads were not usually an inhibition, as journeys to worship on Sundays were exempted from toll. See S. and B. Webb, *English Local Government, vol. 5: The Story of the King's Highway* (1913, 1963 edn), p. 137.

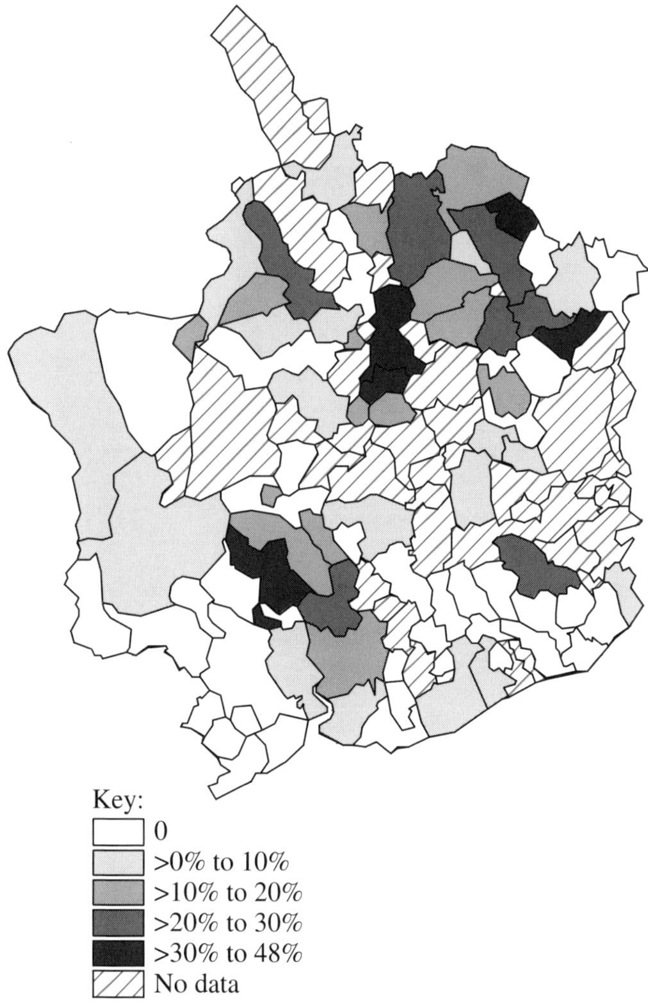

Figure 8.1. Papists as a percentage of total 'inhabitants' in Monmouthshire in 1676

The generalised, seemingly more dispersed nature of Papism, that pervades the Compton Census in every county, gives way to localised 'epicentres' of the denomination in 1851. One is seeing by that date religiously central parishes which, particularly after the 1791 Catholic Relief Act, provided services for their followers, some of whom were certainly coming from surrounding parishes which are not being documented in the 1851 census.

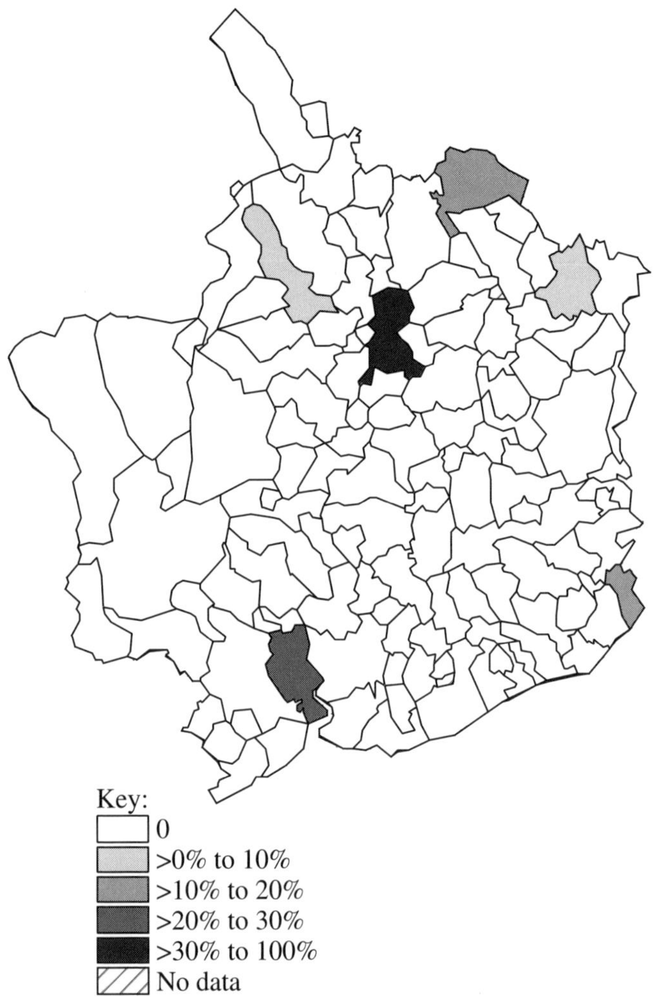

Figure 8.2. Roman Catholic percentage share of total attendances (all denominations) in Monmouthshire in 1851

Monmouthshire (figures 8.1 and 8.2), an important county in Catholic history, illustrates this apparent contraction. A widely diffused pattern of Papists in 1676, over 43 parishes in the north and south, gave way to only six parishes in which they were documented in the 1851 census. These later parishes were themselves clearly divided into three types: northern market towns (Abergavenny, Monmouth), agricultural, old Catholic-landowner parishes of the north (Llanarth, Skenfrith), and the southern port or industrial parishes of St Woollos (now in Newport) and Chepstow. In every Monmouthshire parish in which there were Papist congregations in 1851, there had been some Papists present in 1676. That said, the nature of Catholicism here in 1851, as in so many other counties, was divided between the older Catholic centres, like Monmouth, and those newer, fast-growing towns with Irish immigration. It is worth noting how the Irish seem to have gravitated towards urban districts that had a longer history of Papist presence.

Monmouthshire was a long-standing Catholic area, notably north Monmouthshire (like south Herefordshire), assisted earlier by such figures as the Marquis of Worcester at Raglan, and it had a Jesuit mission at Cwm and Franciscan missions at Abergavenny and Perthir. Abergavenny and Monmouth 'had been largely Catholic towns'.[21] The Monmouth Catholic church in St Mary's Street opened as early as 1793, while the Gothic Roman Catholic church in Welsh Street, Chepstow, was built only three years later. Monmouth, the county town, had long been known for its high Tory sympathies, its mass-house where people openly worshipped, and for its hostility towards visiting Methodist preachers. While some historians have stressed the virtual collapse of Catholicism in eighteenth-century Wales, and have drawn attention to the relative lack of Catholic patrons there,[22] it is clear that this county was something of an exception.[23] In 1773 Monmouthshire had 'one of the highest proportions of Catholics in the whole country'.[24] Such survival owed much to key Catholic families, like the Gunters and Crofts of Abergavenny, the Milbornes of Wonastow, the Berkeleys of Clytha, the Needhams of St Maughan's, the Powells and then the Lorymers of Perthir in Rockfield (where Bishop Prichard had lived in the early eighteenth century),[25] the Williamses of Llanfoist, the Scudamores of Skenfrith, the Jones family

21 P. Jenkins, '"A Welsh Lancashire"? Monmouthshire Catholics in the eighteenth century', *Recusant History*, 15 (1979–81), 176.

22 E. I. Watkin, *Roman Catholicism in England from the Reformation to 1950* (1957), p. 110.

23 See also D. Attwater, *The Catholic Church in Modern Wales* (1935); P. Howell, 'Church and chapel in Wales', in C. Brooks and A. Saint (eds.), *The Victorian Church: Architecture and Society* (Manchester, 1995), p. 128.

24 Jenkins, '"A Welsh Lancashire"?', 177.

25 Dom B. Hemphill, *The Early Vicars Apostolic of England, 1685–1750* (1954), pp. 143–5.

of Llanarth (a parish held in few hands, which was entirely monopolised by Catholicism in the 1851 census).[26] These were commonly resident families, with very strong traditions and senses of identity, with long-surviving patronymics, employing Catholic servants, renting to Catholic tenants, frequently dealing with tradesmen and lawyers who also shared their religion. The visitation returns speak time and again of these families' preference for Catholic servants, and of the 'perversion' of employees to their faith. In Llanvihangel by Usk, for example, the incumbent complained in 1848 of one labourer who 'has been lately perverted to Popery, – I believe through the influence of the Clytha family, in whose service he is'.[27] These households protected priests who ministered to a large surrounding area. They controlled ecclesiastical patronage in a way that was tolerant towards Catholics.[28] The relative isolation of Catholics in this part of the country, weakly linked also as they were to Rome, with the influence of such families, and with support reaching beyond their households to small independent craftsmen who were 'almost traditionally disaffected from the Establishment',[29] were all factors playing a major role in the survival of Catholicism here.

This was one of the best examples of Catholic survival, with Catholicism in Monmouthshire augmented by Irish migration to its industrial areas. Other counties shared a pattern of seeming geographical consolidation when one compares the 1851 data to the very differently assembled data of 1676. The survival of Catholicism elsewhere also owed much to key landed families, although their role was most evident in the countryside. In Leicestershire (figures 8.3 and 8.4), the persistence of the older faith can be seen in small rural parishes like

[26] And see J. H. Matthews, *The Vaughans of Courtfield* (1912), on another key family in north Monmouthshire.

[27] Or in Llanarth 'there are as near as I can guess 110 [?] Papists – consisting of poor & wealthy Inhabitants. There are occasional perversions: brought about I believe through the influence of the wealthy Proprietors.' For these and other similar cases, see National Library of Wales, Visitation Returns: Deaneries of Abergavenny and Monmouth. Clergy 1848. LL/QA/36. Or see Hemphill, *Early Vicars Apostolic*, pp. 103–4, quoting Joseph Berington in 1780: 'Excepting in the towns and out of Lancashire, the chief situation of Catholics is in the neighbourhood of the old families of that persuasion. They are the servants, or the children of servants who have married from those families.'

[28] J. R. Guy, 'The Anglican patronage of Monmouthshire recusants in the seventeenth and eighteenth centuries', *Recusant History*, 15 (1979–81), 453; and his 'Eighteenth-century Gwent Catholics', *Recusant History*, 16 (1982–3), 78–88.

[29] Guy, 'Anglican patronage', 82.

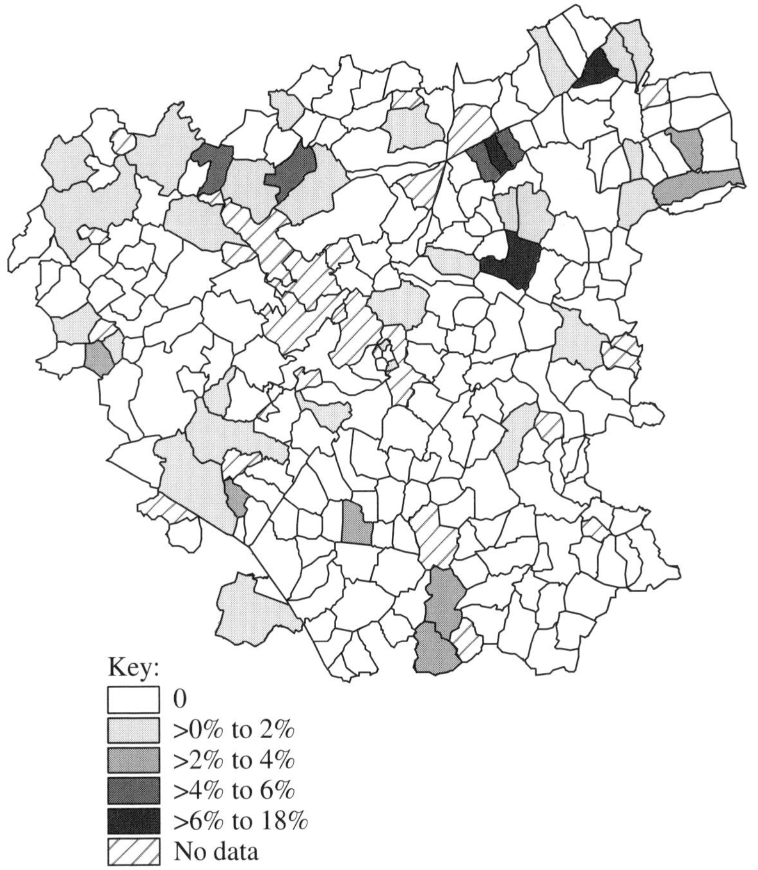

Figure 8.3. Papists as a percentage of total 'inhabitants' in Leicestershire in 1676

Husbands Bosworth, Eastwell, Monks Kirby, but also in the hosiery or mining towns of Shepshed, Whitwick, Loughborough or Hinckley, which all had Papists present in 1676. Very many other parishes which had Papists in 1676 displayed no Catholic congregation in 1851, and in some cases (Ashby Folville, Saxelby or Grimston) this seems to represent substantial change. The maps show a localised concentration of the earlier distributions, still serving the same general areas, but in 1851 consolidated into central foci where churches had been built. Some cases, like Melton Mowbray in the north-east of the county, a market town which in 1676 had no Papists, now served a surrounding rural district that had shown a fair scattering of Papists in 1676. A large

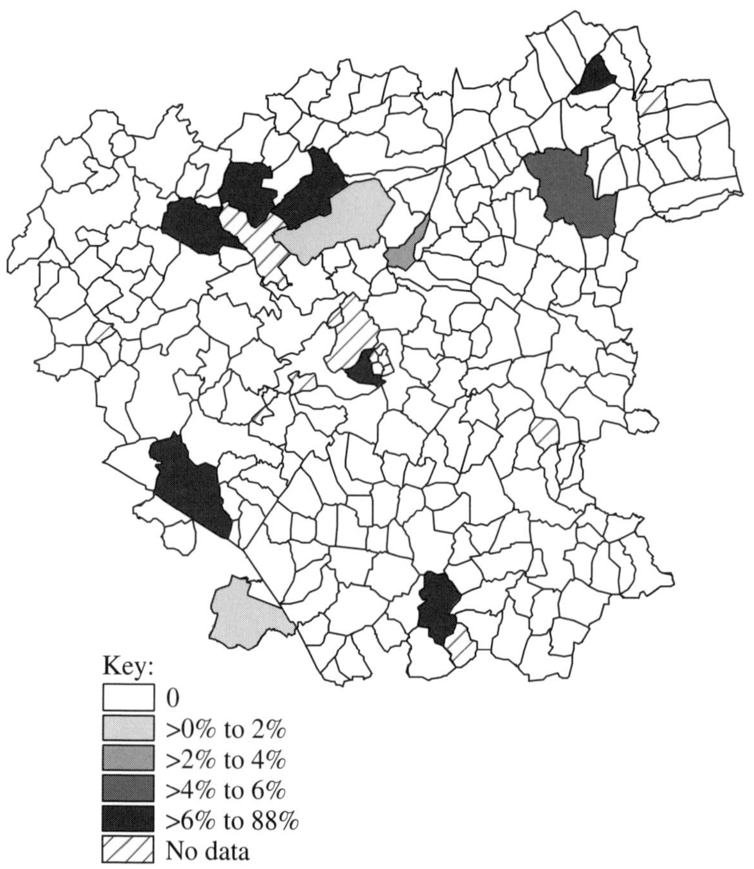

Figure 8.4. Roman Catholic percentage share of total attendances (all denominations) in Leicestershire in 1851

Irish settlement in St Mary's, Leicester had also developed (in the centre of the map), where in the later seventeenth-century source there had been no Papists documented. On the one hand, there was again the influence of dominant landowner families, like the Nevills of Nevill Holt (until shortly before 1851),[30] the Turville-Petres of

[30] B. Elliott, 'A Leicestershire recusant family: the Nevills of Nevill Holt', *Recusant History*, 1st part, 17 (1984), 173–80; 2nd part, *Recusant History*, 17 (1985), 374–85; 3rd part, *Recusant History*, 18 (1986), 220–4; B. Elliott, 'The history of Catholicism in Market Harborough', *Harborough Historian*, 2 (1985), 2–3; B. Elliott, 'An eighteenth century Leicestershire business woman: the Countess Mary Migliorucci of Nevill Holt', *Leicestershire Archaeological and Historical Society*, 61 (1987), 77–82; H. E. Broughton (ed.), *Nevill Holt: Studies of a Leicestershire Estate* (Leicester, 1985); G. Holt, *The English Jesuits, 1650–1829* (1984), p. 149.

Husbands Bosworth,[31] or the de Lisle family at Grace Dieu, a centre of Catholic liturgy and missionary work near Loughborough. Some of these were influential in urban as well as rural areas. This was coupled in Leicestershire with the outstanding and charitable example set by the Cistercians of Mount St Bernard in Charnwood Forest after 1837,[32] whose monks had come initially from Mount Melleray in Ireland, or by the Dominicans in Leicester and Hinckley.[33] On the other hand, there was the role of longer-standing urban Catholicism, and of Irish immigration both to older Catholic districts in the east Midlands, and notably to the industrial areas: places in west Leicestershire like Whitwick, beginning to transmute the geography of Catholicism by the sheer numbers involved.[34]

31 Husbands Bosworth was the seat of the Turville Constable Maxwell family. There was Catholic influence here from the early seventeenth century, well documented by family papers in Bosworth Hall Library. See Leics. C.R.O., Catalogue DG 39. 54 on the family MSS. See also Leics. C.R.O., QS 45/1/23; QS 45/3/2 (1748) (Papist estates). Resident Roman Catholic priests at the Hall were buried in the parish churchyard. The parish had 80 Catholic 'followers' recorded in 1829, the highest in Leicestershire. (Leics. C.R.O., QS 95/2/2). The Pugin-influenced Catholic church of St Mary was built in the grounds of Bosworth Hall in 1873–4. See also R. B. Pugh (ed.), *The Victoria County History of the Counties of England* (1964), vol. 5, p. 36.

32 B. Elliott, 'The return of the Cistercians to the Midlands', *Recusant History*, 16 (1982–3), 99–104; L. Jewitt, *Guide to the Abbey of Mount St Bernard* (4th edn, 1897); A. C. Lacey, *The Second Spring in Charnwood Forest* (Loughborough, 1985). The literature on their later reformatory covers aspects of their earlier history. See B. Elliott, 'Mount St Bernard's Reformatory, Leicestershire, 1856–81', *Recusant History*, 15 (1979), 15–22; his 'Mount St Bernard's Reformatory: a reply', *Recusant History*, 15 (1979–81), 302–4; J. L. G. Tucker, 'Mount St Bernard's Reformatory, 1856–81: a correction', *Recusant History*, 15 (1979–81), 213–17.

33 On the Dominican Order in Hinckley, see Leics. C.R.O., QS 45/8/1–4, giving the returns made under 10 Geo. IV, c. 7, ss. 28 and 30, and the oaths required under 31 Geo. III, c. 32. Catholicism is also documented in the town in Leics. C.R.O., QS 45/7/2 (1791, a chapel in a dwelling house); QS 45/7/3 (1793, a 'new erected building'); and QS 45/7/4 (1825). For declarations of loyalty to the Crown from Hinckley, Eastwell, Burbatch, Burbage and Eaton Catholic priests and residents, see Leics. C.R.O., QS 45/6/1. The named occupations were widow, gent, labourer, hosier and farmer.

34 The Leicestershire Catholic Baptism Registers suggest the extent and chronology of Irish immigration after the Famine. In some parishes which had earlier indicated a Catholic presence, the inflow of Irish surnames was small (e.g. Hinckley St Peter, Shepshed St Winifred, Melton Mowbray St John, and perhaps Measham St Charles, although there were evidently Irish there). But in the fast expanding mining town of Whitwick there was a huge increase in the Irish from the late 1840s, with well over 50 Irish surnames present by the early–mid 1850s which had not appeared earlier (Leics. C.R.O., Catholic Baptism Registers for the above churches, and for Whitwick Holy Cross, 1843–66). Mining rather than hosiery towns seem to have had greatest inflow. Other Irish are documented as on tramp near these settlements, Irish Catholic mothers bringing their children for baptism, 'of course *pro Deo*, they being deadly poor!!', one priest commented. (Leics. C.R.O., Melton Mowbray St John, Catholic Baptisms, 1843–97.)

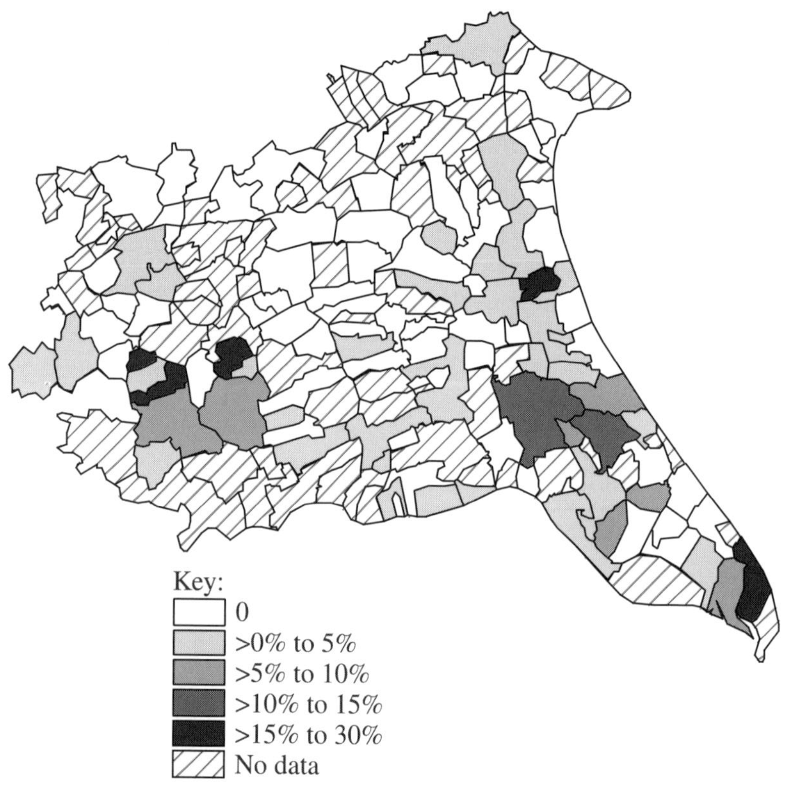

Figure 8.5. Papists as a percentage of total 'inhabitants' in the East Riding in 1676

In the East Riding of Yorkshire (figures 8.5 and 8.6), Catholicism was also much dependent upon family fortunes and survivals. Large Catholic gentry families during the penal times had been careful to give employment preference to fellow Catholics, partly for reasons of security. The survival of this faith in centres such as Holme-on-Spalding-Moor, Everingham or Swine, was largely due to these families. The Constable family at Everingham was one which endured, despite considerable trials and sequestrations, and the Italian-looking Chapel of the Virgin and St Everilda next to Everingham Hall, completed by Lord Herries in 1839, was, Pevsner wrote, 'a sign of Catholic confidence after the Act of Emancipation in 1829'.[35] Even so, earlier

[35] N. Pevsner, *The Buildings of England: Yorkshire: York and the East Riding* (Harmondsworth, 1972), p. 226. However, most Catholic architecture was the fashionable Gothic, by architects like Hansom and Pugin, as at Sicklinghall or Leeds.

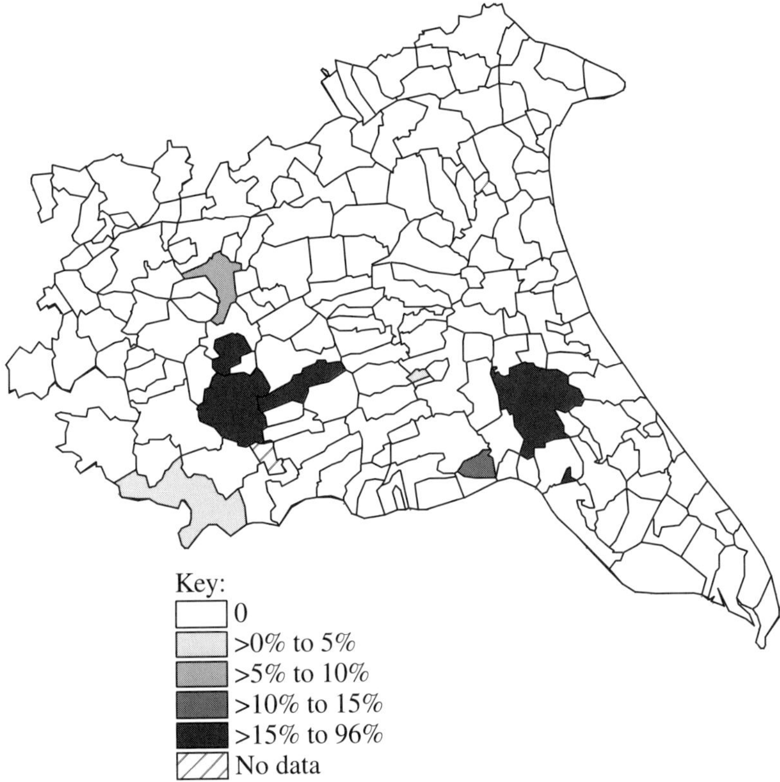

Figure 8.6. Roman Catholic percentage share of total attendances (all denominations) in the East Riding in 1851

persecution, double land taxes,[36] prohibitions on the receipt of legacies,[37] fines,[38] a lack of profitable offices for Catholics, the early eighteenth-century agricultural depression, or the lack of heirs through too few possible brides had hit other families badly, as at Howden or Spaldington. During the eighteenth century, it has been said that 'they felt a dying race', 'acutely aware that Catholicism depended straitly on the gentry and they were very visibly . . . vanishing'.[39] This

[36] As under the Land Tax Act of 1692, 4 Wm. & Mary, c.1, s. 34. See M. Rowlands, 'The iron age of double taxes', *Staffordshire Catholic History*, 3 (1963). A few Catholic landowners were however able to escape this by various means. [37] See 11 & 12 Wm. c. 4.

[38] For example, if they sent their children overseas for education.

[39] H. Aveling, *Post Reformation Catholicism in East Yorkshire, 1558–1790* (York, 1960), p. 47; R. W. Linker, 'English Catholics in the eighteenth century', *Church History*, 35 (1966); Hemphill, *Early Vicars Apostolic*, p. 83; Elliott, 'An eighteenth century Leicestershire business woman', 81.

overlooks the often buoyant numbers of urban Catholics; but it was true of many estates, like Welwick or Swine, even though the latter parish still had a Catholic congregation in 1851.

In other cases, conversions to Catholicism like that by Lord Langdale at Holme safeguarded the church.[40] It has been pointed out that successive archiepiscopal surveys indicate growing numbers of Catholics in the East Riding throughout the eighteenth century, despite their frequent pessimism, although this growth barely matched the general levels of demographic increase.[41] Only Beverley St Mary, Hedon and Sancton had Catholics at the later date but *not* in 1676. But then, of the 43 parishes for which Papists had been reported in 1676, only three had Catholic congregations in 1851. This is a remarkable contraction, even after one has taken into consideration the contrasted nature of the two sources. It reinforces accounts which have stressed the decline of Catholicism in many rural parishes, especially during the eighteenth century, and Catholic emancipation may have done little to reverse this in some such areas.[42] There were, as a

[40] K. M. Longley, *Heir of Two Traditions: the Catholic Church of St John the Baptist, Holme-on-Spalding-Moor, 1766–1966* (1966).

[41] Aveling, *Post Reformation Catholicism*, p. 46.

[42] J. C. H. Aveling, *The Handle and the Axe: the Catholic Recusants in England from the Reformation to Emancipation* (1976), p. 286, and pp. 301–2, where he points to the difficulties in holding the rural poor to Catholic rituals, Latin prayers and irregular masses, especially with the decline in resident Catholic gentry. The rural poor in eastern regions were often very anti-Irish, competing with them for work. There was by now little of that sense of loss which had characterised rural areas in earlier centuries, when the cycle of festivals and other Catholic attributes were abandoned.

Some of our other census counties, discussed in less detail here, show considerable discontinuities of Catholicism. In Rutland, a noticeable Catholic presence in 1676 was replaced by no documentation whatever of Catholics in 1851. In Anglesey and Caernarvonshire, a scattering of Papists in Llandudno, Eglwys Rhos and surrounding parishes in 1676, with a few others dispersed elsewhere, had given way to an 1851 congregation only in Bangor. In Suffolk, there was only one parochial example of continuity between the two sources (Stoke-by-Nayland), although there had been 39 parishes with Papists in 1676. None of the Suffolk parishes with over 10 per cent Papist in 1676 (Long Melford, Flempton, Bulmer, Stanningfield and Wetterden) had any Catholic places of worship in 1851. In Bedfordshire, hardly a Catholic stronghold, there was not a single case of continuity between the two dates. In Sussex, of 44 parishes with Papists in 1676, only two had a Catholic place of worship documented in 1851 (Arundel and Slindon). None of the Sussex parishes with over 10 per cent Papist in 1676 (Burton, Clapham, Coates, Midhurst, Racton, Shipley or Westfire) had Catholic places of worship in 1851. Derbyshire had six out of 38 parishes showing continuity between 1676 and 1851 (Bakewell, Chesterfield, Eckington, Glossop, Hathersage and Tideswell). Hathersage was very strongly Catholic at both dates, but

counter-balance, about 1,200 Catholics at mass on Census Sunday in Hull – nearly half the figure for Irish-born in the city – and Catholics were growing rapidly there. But the influx of Irish into Hull and certain other parts of the East Riding had lesser effects than in many other more industrial counties, notably Lancashire, where there had also been large numbers of urban Catholics for at least a century before 1851.

The role of dominant Catholic families, mainly in rural areas, could be described at length for the other counties. Doubts have sometimes been expressed about how crucial a role Catholic landowners played, and it has been pointed out that landowner superiority could be a disadvantage to a local Catholic community in some circumstances, especially if the gentry family did not take their responsibilities seriously.[43] In addition, urban Catholicism was almost certainly numerically more important than that in the countryside, and had probably been so for a considerable period.[44] Nevertheless, Hemphill had some justification in pointing to the way that Catholic gentry had sustained Catholic missions in many places.[45] Catholic mission centres frequently grew out of private chapels of recusant gentry, a Catholic parochial structure coming much later, from 1918. In our other counties there were the Huddlestones at Sawston Hall (Cambridgeshire),[46] the Duke of Devonshire in Derbyshire, the Haggerstons of Ellingham (Northumberland) – which Bossy discussed as 'a laboratory example of the construction of a seigneurial congregation'[47] – or Netherwitton

other parishes which had conspicuous Catholicism in 1676 (notably Carlton and West Hallam) had no Catholic venues in 1851.

43 J. Bossy, 'Four Catholic congregations in rural Northumberland, 1750–1850', *Recusant History*, 9 (1967), 110.

44 A view stressed in M. Rowlands, *Catholics of Parish and Town, 1558–1778* (1999).

45 Hemphill, *Early Vicars Apostolic*, p. 78; Watkin, *Roman Catholicism in England*, p. 115. For a good example of this in East Lulworth, Dorset, where a third of the inhabitants were Catholic in 1766, see B. J. Biggs, *The Wesleys and the Early Dorset Methodists* (Gillingham, Dorset, 1987), p. 18; P. Wright, *The Village That Died for England: the Strange Story of Tyneham* (1995, 1996 edn), pp. 18–22. With regard to the effects of charity, R. Southey dryly wrote that 'proselytes always abound in the neighbourhood of a wealthy Catholic family'. *Letters from England* (1807, Gloucester, 1984 edn), p. 157.

46 T. G. Holt, 'An eighteenth century chaplain: John Champion at Sawston Hall', *Recusant History*, 17 (1984), 181–7; N. Pevsner, *The Buildings of England: Cambridgeshire* (Harmondsworth, 1954), p. 368; *History, Gazetteer, and Directory of Cambridgeshire* (no author, Peterborough, 1851), p. 266. The Hall, with its secretive priest hole, had been burnt after Queen Mary spent a night there in 1553.

47 J. Bossy, 'More Northumbrian congregations', *Recusant History*, 10 (1969), 12–13.

or Berrington in the same county.[48] There were many other such examples. Additional important considerations could be mentioned to account for local survival: an evasion or weak enforcement of the penal legislation of 1688, 1696, 1700 or 1715; the economic successes of some of the key families, like the Constables at Everingham;[49] the role of 5,500 or so exiled French clergy by 1797, who were hospitably received in England, including in some of our parishes, and who contributed to the opening of many new churches;[50] the 1791 Catholic Relief Act and eventual emancipation, and so on.[51] Yet with regard to issues of localised continuity,[52] the cartographic work here reinforces Aveling's thesis that English Catholicism 'certainly has always had something about it which has made it the most doggedly parochial and local of Christian Churches. English Catholics have been always stubbornly devoted to particular sites, buildings, rituals.'[53] One can exaggerate this feature, as the quantitative analysis shows; but when one assesses local continuities it was this quality, partly due to landowner protection, which appears to have set English Catholicism apart from the more mobile, transient and peripatetic

[48] Bossy, 'More Northumbrian congregations', 24; and see his 'Four Catholic congregations'. [49] Aveling, *Post Reformation Catholicism*, p. 52.

[50] D. Bellenger, 'The English Catholics and the French exiled clergy', *Recusant History*, 15 (1979–81); D. Bellenger, *The Exiled French Clergy in the British Isles after 1789* (Bath, 1986); F. P. Isherwood, *Banished by the Revolution* (Jersey, 1972); Aveling, *Handle and the Axe*, pp. 308–18; Elliott, 'The return of the Cistercians', 99. The priests began to come over after the Civil Constitution of 1791, as did many English Catholics living in France. Robert Southey, no friend to Catholicism, commented on how 'The English clergy, trembling for their own benefices, welcomed the emigrant priests as brethren . . . the Catholic priests obtained access everywhere'. *Letters from England*, p. 155. Nearly 900 Catholic chapels opened between 1791 and 1814, notably in the north (Watkin, *Roman Catholicism in England*, p. 158). These priests certainly played a role in places like Arundel, Slindon, Abergavenny, or some of the coastal settlements of the East Riding, although their confident, state-centred style of Catholicism was very different to that found in England.

[51] In some rural parishes like Danby and Lythe in north Yorkshire, after strong gentry support earlier, Catholicism then survived from the late sixteenth century without any significant gentry aid: a survival due to geographical isolation, the persistence and tenacity of rather humbler inhabitants, and their proximity to the coast and thus to continental priests. See D. E. Fox, 'Families, Farming and Faith' (unpub. M.Phil thesis, University of Leicester, 1998), pp. 176, 210–11, 213.

[52] We are here concerned with issues of local continuity, not with sheer numbers in particular places. The largest numbers of Catholics were in urban areas: in London, Liverpool, Wigan, Preston and major county towns like York, Norwich, Durham or Chester. London contained a fifth of all English Catholics in the 1767 returns. Catholic gentry had little role in such long-term urban survival. See Rowlands, *Catholics of Parish and Town*. [53] Aveling, *Handle and the Axe*, pp. 358–9.

tendencies of many of the old dissenters, who lacked that fixity and longevity in particular sites that was more associated with the Catholics.

The changing location of old dissent can be illustrated cartographically and in further temporal depth for any of the chosen counties, and Leicestershire is a good example of this. The county warrants such treatment because it had the greatest overall continuity of Papism and Nonconformity (see table 8.2). It was appropriate also to test the reliability of the 1851 data, so we analysed the 1829 returns of non-Anglican places of worship which survive for this county, assessing them in relation to those of 1676 and 1851. The 1829 returns show a striking similarity to the 1851 parochial distributions, very strongly confirming the accuracy of the latter.[54] Correlation between the 1829 and 1851 parish data for all Nonconformist denominations gave a result of 0.95. This is an exceptionally close match, despite the twenty-two years between the two dates, the differences in the way

54 The 1829 returns originated from a resolution of the House of Commons on 19 June 1829 calling for 'A Return of the number of Places of Worship not of the Church of England in each Parish, distinguishing as far as possible of what sect or persuasion, and the total number of each sect in England and Wales'. Many of the returns were burnt in the 1834 conflagration at the Houses of Parliament, but copies survive for some counties in Quarter Session records. In effect they record places of worship and the numbers of 'followers', 'adherents' or 'members' reported by each parish, there being some doubt over the precise categories returned and how distinct those were. (The forms often used the term 'adherents'.) And so problems of comparability arise once again when one relates these returns to the other two sources. For example, for Leicestershire Catholicism in 1829 one has Husbands Bosworth (80), Eastwell (25), Eaton (4), Hinckley (40), Holt (48), Hose (5) and an unspecified figure for Leicester. Bracketed figures are for numbers of adherents (subject to the above doubt). This format is quite different to that of 1676 or 1851, but it still describes a Catholic picture immediately recognisable in 1851. The 1829 returns may be found in Leics. C.R.O., QS 95/2/2. For further documentation on their purpose and interpretation, see Leics. C.R.O., QS 95/2/3/4/2, and QS 95/2/3/1–2. Many of the returns (like Hose or Eaton above) document only a handful of adherents, and the numbers are in some cases so small that they must describe house meetings rather than chapels or purpose-built places of worship. It is unclear whether the numbered adherents were only of those resident in the returning parish, and there may be some parochial variation in this. On the 1829 returns, see R. W. Ambler, 'A lost source? The 1829 returns of non-Anglican places of worship', *The Local Historian*, 17 (1987), 483–9, and see his references; R. W. Ambler, 'Religious life in Kesteven – a return of the number of places of worship not of the Church of England, 1829', *Lincolnshire History and Archaeology*, 220 (1985), 59–64; Ambler, 'Social change and religious experience', pp. 148–53; N. Caplan, 'Sussex religious dissent, c. 1830', *Sussex Archaeological Collections*, 120 (1982), 193–203; M. Tranter, '"Many and diverse dissenters" – the 1829 religious returns for Derbyshire', *The Local Historian*, 18 (1988), 162–7; R. Gill, *The Myth of the Empty Church* (1993), pp. 96, 107.

the data were organised and collected, and the likelihood that some buildings were temporarily out of use in 1829 or 1851. It is a finding that is remarkable and reassuring.[55] In other words, one may rely very strongly indeed on the 1851 returns for Leicestershire (and probably for other counties too, as the accuracy of the Leicestershire 1851 data is probably typical). The longer-term disparities between the data for 1676 and 1851 cannot therefore be owing to possible inaccuracies in that for 1851. One can observe also that the central-point foci of the 1851 data – that is, centred upon places of worship to which some parochial outsiders migrated – seems not to affect adversely its comparability with the somewhat more ambiguous 1829 returns.

Further cartographic presentation is shown in figures 8.7 and 8.8. These indicate Leicestershire Protestant Nonconformity in 1676, and the later geography of the old dissenting denominations in 1851. There is no need to show an equivalent map of the 1829 data, for it is almost a mirror image of that for 1851. The long-term contrasts 'on the ground' are clear. The earlier seventeenth-century Nonconformist distributions, covering a large majority of parishes, had given way by 1851 to more concentrated patterns in the southern half of the county, and in the Charnwood, Shepshed and Loughborough areas of the north. Regularly spaced chapels in the southern parishes were serving surrounding parishes within travelling distance, as in Hinckley, Lutterworth and Misterton, Theddingworth, Market Harborough and proximate villages. Whereas in 1676 there had been little to choose between Nonconformist strength in the south and elsewhere, this was clearly not so by 1851. By then certain parts of the county, like some of the estate and other villages of the north-east, had virtually lost these denominations. Parts of Leicester, in the centre of the county, were further augmenting its nineteenth-century reputation as the 'Metropolis of Dissent'. Southern parishes like Broughton Astley or Whetstone, or Monks Kirby in the south-west,[56] showed continuity of dissenting tradition, but even in this area there

[55] The Mormons and the 1851 census category of 'other isolated congregations' were excluded from this calculation.

[56] This strongly dissenting parish was perched on the border, in the historical county of Warwickshire, but in the registration county of Leicestershire: an example perhaps of strategic use of the county boundary to help avoid local authorities' jurisdiction. On frontier settlements and dissent, see A. Everitt, 'Nonconformity in country parishes', in J. Thirsk (ed.), *Land, Church and People: Essays Presented to Professor H. P. R. Finberg* (Reading, 1970), pp. 193–7.

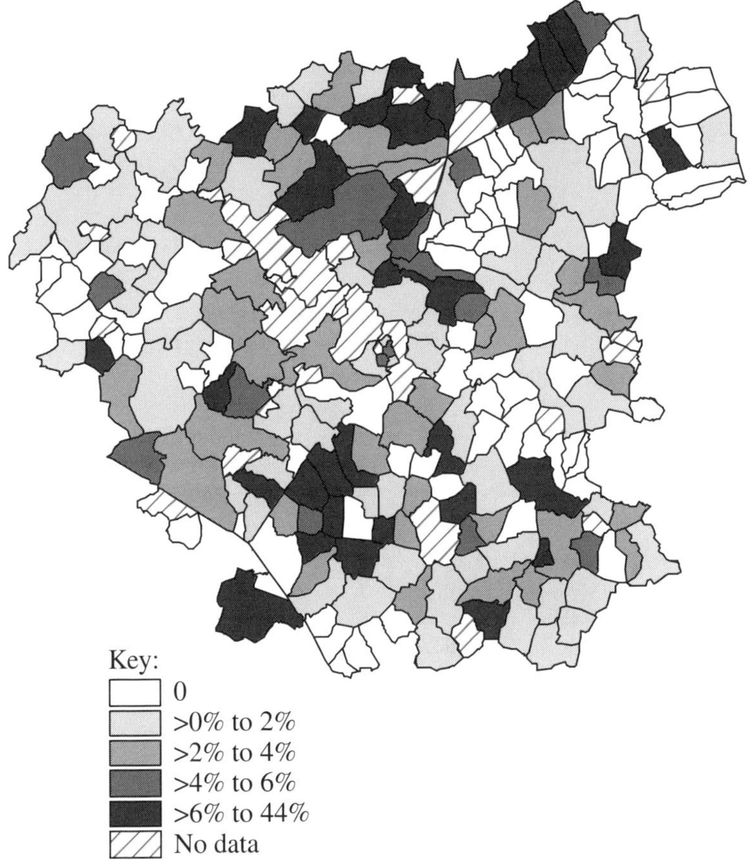

Figure 8.7. Nonconformists as a percentage of total 'inhabitants' in Leicestershire in 1676

was considerable localised difference over time in the parishes revealing dissenters.

Anglican dominance continued in two small areas: a group of parishes in the lowly populated pastoral area to the immediate east of Leicester (including Scraptoft, Thurnby, Houghton on the Hill, King's Norton, Ilston on the Hill, Shangton), and another group in the north-east of the county beyond Melton Mowbray,[57] where only Hose stayed in the strongest dissenting categories over the two dates. Very

[57] Parishes like Scalford, Goady Marwood, Waltham on the Wolds, Thorpe Arnold, Saltby, Sproxton, Coston, Edmondthorpe, Saxby or Wymondham.

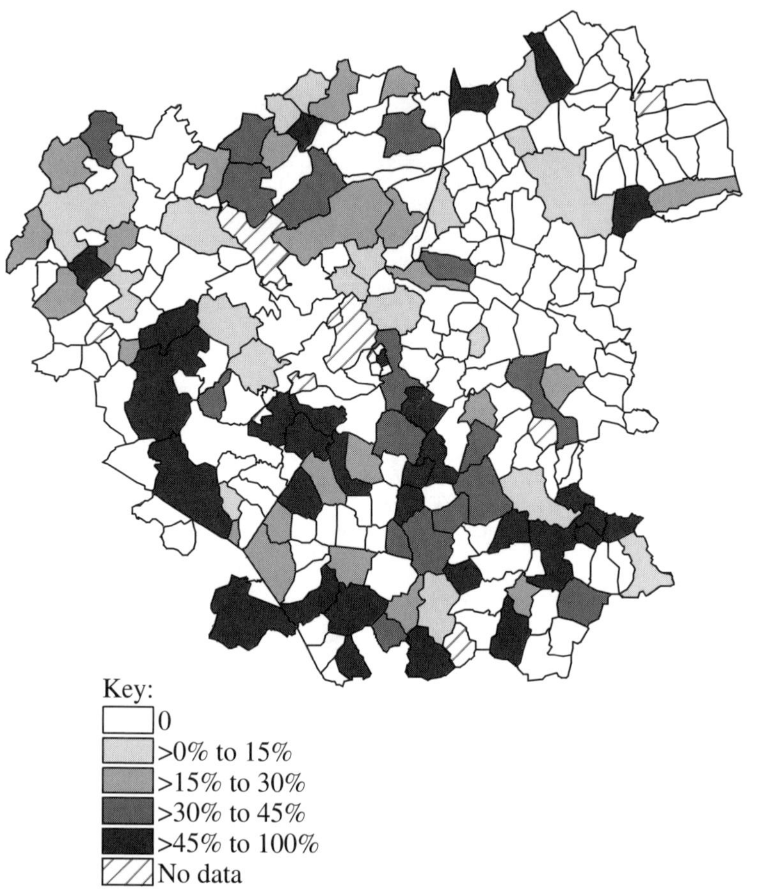

Figure 8.8. Old-dissent percentage share of total attendances (all denominations) in Leicestershire in 1851

many parishes which had been in the highest category for Nonconformity in 1676 had by 1851 no dissenting chapels whatever for the Anglican Church to contend with. Garthorpe, Pickwell, Nether Broughton (in the north-east), Saddington, Willoughby Waterless, Peatling Parva, Dunton Bassett, Cosby (in the south), Twycross or Wanlip were all examples of places that had moved in this way. Leicestershire was not exceptional in such discontinuity. Indeed, as seen in table 8.2, it is second only to the East Riding in its strength of continuity displayed by correlation. In mapping the other counties one is often even more struck by such evidence for localised discontinuities of old dissent.

The changing strength of Papism and Nonconformity

Following these detailed county studies, we can survey further changes indicated in the data as affecting Papism and Nonconformity between 1676 and 1851. Addressing Catholicism first, in the 1,462 parishes across the twelve counties with data for *both* 1676 and 1851, Catholics represented 0.8 per cent of the total 'inhabitants' in 1676, and 1.1 per cent of total attendances in 1851. In the 39 parishes with Catholics in 1851, the mean Catholic percentage share of attendances was quite high, at 17.0 per cent, with some very high and unique figures for Llanarth (Monmouthshire), Everingham (East Riding), and Eastwell (Leicestershire), all over 85 per cent.[58] Indeed, that 1851 figure of 17.0 per cent is over three times as high as the nearest equivalent figure for 1676: a mean of 5.5 per cent for Papists as a percentage of the total population, taking the 290 parishes with Papists. Overall though, this 'concentration' of Catholics into fewer parishes in 1851, but in greater proportions, seems to be overshadowed by absolute decline. Indeed, it is difficult to argue that the suggested increased strength of Papism, in the 27 parishes where it persisted and in its 12 'new' parishes, can in any way offset the massive shrinkage in its base: from 290 parishes in 1676 to 39 parishes by 1851.

As argued above, this narrowing is certainly due in part to the different coverage supplied by the two sources, which acts to produce spatial concentration. But it is also a sign of the absolute decline in Catholicism by 1851, a time just before the full effects of Irish immigration were felt on institutionalised religion. These two trends can be further elucidated with reference to socio-economic changes between 1676 and 1851, and more specifically to the demography and

[58] The parish of Eastwell had 17 per cent of its Compton population as Papist, and an exceptionally high percentage share for the Roman Catholics in 1851 of 87.8 per cent. A Catholic chapel had been built around 1806 (another source gives 1798), apparently in lieu of one at the Hall which had been destroyed. The parish had been owned by the Eyres from 1631, and was purchased by the Duke of Rutland in the very early nineteenth century. See *Kelly's Directory of Leicester and Rutland* (1922 edn), pp. 76–7; *Wright's Directory of Leicestershire and Rutland* (Leicester, 1896), p. 544; W. White, *History, Gazetteer, and Directory of Leicestershire* (Sheffield, 1846), pp. 233–4. The 1851 religious data suggest very ineffective Anglican competition in this parish. The Catholic traditions of Eastwell can be traced through the eighteenth century in the Leics. C.R.O. See QS 45/1/4, QS 45/1/15, QS 45/3/4 and QS 45/1/21 (1737, 1739, 1750 and 1752 registrations of Catholic estates by Roland Eyre of Eastwell Hall); QS 45/1/25/1 and QS 45/2/52 (1777); QS 45/1/26 and QS 45/2/53 (1785); and QS 45/7/1 (1791 registration of a chapel in a dwelling house, by Robert Beeston).

Table 8.4. *Mean annual population growth rates (1811–51) and the continuity of Catholicism*

	mean	median	n.
Parishes with Catholics in 1676 but *not* in 1851	0.78	0.72	263
Parishes with Catholics in 1676 *and* 1851	1.11	0.98	27
Parishes with Catholics in 1851 but *not* in 1676	1.59	1.29	12

nature of landholding in the parishes. The growth rates of parishes with regard to the presence of Catholics are examined in table 8.4. The parishes with long-term Catholic presence, over *both* sources, had higher mean population growth rates (1.11) in the first half of the nineteenth century than those parishes where Papists were present in 1676, but not in 1851. Catholic churches were most likely to have been built by 1851 in the faster growing parishes of earlier Papist presence. It is worth observing that Catholic-landlord dominated parishes were in some cases 'closed' or estate parishes, with low demographic growth rates. Those relatively few parishes with Catholics in 1851, but *not* in 1676, had the highest growth rates (1.59): these were commonly urban/industrial centres where urbanisation was coupled with Irish Catholic immigration.

Hitherto the role of traditional recusant families has been stressed for the survival of Catholicism, families which often dominated small rural parishes of a 'closed' character with inherently low growth rates. This could be both an advantage as well as a disadvantage for the wider history of British Catholicism, for such relatively stable parishes were not ones with a proclivity to rapid industrial and demographic growth. It is clear from table 8.4 that parishes with Catholics present *only* in the 1851 source were far outnumbered by the other two categories of parish (i.e. those with Catholics in 1676): in 1851 the poverty of refugees from the Great Famine was still too acute to allow the foundation of many new churches. But the table suggests how a new expansive situation was necessarily arising by 1851, in response to the needs of the Irish settlers, whose places of worship were going to assume such a dominant role in the subsequent growth of urban Catholicism in England and Wales.[59] For our concerns it is clear that

59 On the large increase of Catholics in England and Wales in the half century after 1851, from around 700,000 to over 1,500,000 by 1900, see Currie *et al.*, *Churches and*

Catholicism between 1676 and 1851 was marked by three processes: (i) the continuity of some archetypical Catholic estate parishes, (ii) an apparent spatial concentration of Catholicism, due in part to the differing nature of the two sources, and (iii) the emergence of larger urban Catholic communities as a result of Irish immigration.

What can be said of the changing *extent* of Protestant nonconformity over time? This is again a notoriously difficult matter to estimate, given the problematic comparability of the sources. 63.1 per cent of our parishes in 1851 had some degree of active Protestant nonconformity, as revealed in attendances at a place of worship, while in the late seventeenth century as many as 60.6 per cent of parishes had some Nonconformists. This is a high figure for the later seventeenth century. Once again one should stress the different sources being used, revealing different phenomena, with the 1851 census accounting Nonconformists from outside places who were coming in to the parish to worship, whatever the denomination. A more realistic comparison over time would be to say that 3.89 per cent of the total 'inhabitants' for 1676 were Protestant nonconformist. And yet by 1851, 60 per cent of total attendances were of a Nonconformist nature in these parishes, taking all possible Protestant nonconformists. This is a spectacular change. Even when one selects only the six denominations comprising 'old dissent', that 1676 figure still rises appreciably by 1851, with old dissent accounting for 11.5 per cent of attendances, a figure all the more remarkable in the face of strong Methodist and other rivalry.[60]

Examining the data from the perspective of the Anglican conformists, the fact that only 39 per cent of attendances were Anglican by 1851 (with 60 per cent Nonconformist and about 1 per cent Catholic),

Churchgoers, p. 153; E. Norman, *The English Catholic Church in the Nineteenth Century* (Oxford, 1984), pp. 205–6. On the urban impact of the Irish Catholics after the 1840s, see L. H. Lees, *Exiles of Erin: Irish Migrants in Victorian London* (Manchester, 1979); J. Hickey, *Urban Catholics: Urban Catholicism in England and Wales from 1829 to the Present Day* (1967); J. A. Jackson, *The Irish in Britain* (1963); M. A. G. Ò Tuathaigh, 'The Irish in nineteenth-century Britain: problems of integration', *Transactions of the Royal Historical Society*, 5th series, 3 (1981), 149–73; S. Gilley, 'The Roman Catholic mission to the Irish in London, 1840–1860', *Recusant History*, 10 (1969), 123–45.

60 All calculations in this section only use the 1,462 parishes which had data for 1676, so as to keep the parochial basis for comparison over time identical. However, if one takes *all* 1,990 parishes in the same counties for which data are available in 1851, the equivalent figure here would be even higher, at 19.3 per cent for 'old dissent'.

underlines the very radical and dramatic change that had occurred from the situation in the late seventeenth century (when just over 95 per cent of inhabitants were conformist), especially when one bears in mind the large numbers of people not attending *anywhere* in 1851. This growth of religious pluralism lay behind the turbulent response among contemporaries to the *Census of Religious Worship*. It certainly was a change of the utmost importance and consequence, surely one of the most dramatic shifts in British history. It will be argued elsewhere that this growth of religious pluralism should be seen as a key occurrence in the emergence of 'secularisation'.[61]

Toleration, persecution and religious regions

Papism and Nonconformity have been discussed so far largely in isolation from each other. It is, however, instructive to examine issues arising from the interactions between them, as evidenced by their relative spatial distributions in 1676.

Two broad arguments might apply to the relative distribution of Papists and Nonconformists. First, it might be argued that the two were found in close proximity in areas noted for religious tolerance. Second, it might be the case that hostilities between Nonconformity and Papism would act against them being located in the same parishes. (One thinks for example of the earlier harassment of recusants in areas of Puritan strength, as in north-east Norfolk, and the long-term antagonism of many Nonconformists against Roman Catholicism.) From the data we discovered that just over 60 per cent of the Compton-documented parishes contained Nonconformists. If there was no association between Nonconformity and Papism, one would expect the same percentage of parishes with Papists also to contain Nonconformists. In fact, virtually 70 per cent (202) of the 290 parishes with Papists also had Nonconformists. A chi-square test was carried out to test this difference for significance, and it proved positive at the 95 per cent confidence level.[62] There is therefore preliminary evidence for a certain degree of spatial association between the two groups.

Investigating this issue further, one can examine not just locational association in 1676 but also the relative strength of Nonconformity

[61] By Alasdair Crockett, in his forthcoming book on this subject. [62] $p = 0.027$.

Table 8.5. *(a). Test for Papist strength decreasing in the presence of Nonconformity*

	Strength of Papism (percentage of 'inhabitants')	
Parishes in 1676 with:	mean	mean rank
Papists *only* (n = 88)	7.6	176.7
Papists *and* Nonconformists (n = 202)	4.6	132.0

Notes:
Result: mean rank significantly different at the 99% confidence level and higher. z = −4.2 (p = .0000).
Hypothesis that Papist strength decreases in the presence of Nonconformity can be accepted.

Table 8.5. *(b). Test for Nonconformist strength decreasing in the presence of Papism*

	Strength of Nonconformity (percentage of 'inhabitants')	
Parishes in 1676 with:	mean	mean rank
Nonconformists *only* (n = 684)	6.6	450.2
Nonconformists *and* Papists (n = 202)	6.0	420.9

Notes:
Result: mean rank not significantly different at the 95% confidence level. z =−1.4 (p = .1532).
Hypothesis that Nonconformist strength decreases in the presence of Papism can be rejected.

and Papism in parishes where they co-existed. A series of Mann-Whitney 'U' tests were conducted to establish (i) whether the strength of Papism was lower in parishes where Nonconformity was also present than parishes with Papism alone, and (ii) whether the relative strength of Nonconformity was lower in parishes where Papists were also present than parishes solely with Nonconformists. The results are shown in table 8.5.

The table shows that whereas Papist strength was significantly weaker in parishes with Nonconformity present, the strength of Nonconformity was unaffected by the presence of Papism. When interpreted in the context of the previous chi-squared test, our overall conclusion is that while Papism and Nonconformity were often found in the same places, where such overlap occurred the strength of Papism was significantly lower. In other words, these quantitative results lend support to the argument that Papism and Nonconformity were often associated together geographically in religiously pluralistic parishes; but one should also qualify this, insofar as the presence of Nonconformity appeared to reduce Catholic strength. We presume that it did so through localised hostility and persecution, although this is a matter that deserves to be explored further through more complicated historical models of religious conflict, diversity and coexistence.

Interpretation and conclusions

Some of the findings of this chapter are subject to doubts and vagaries concerning the Compton Census of 1676. There is much less reason to doubt the accuracy of the 1851 census data, and tests of that source against the 1829 religious returns overwhelmingly validate it. We tested and adjusted the Compton Census in a manner appropriate for analyses on this scale. And by using the data in a ratio (rather than absolute) form, the most severe complications of the source were overcome, although this procedure does limit some questions that historians and demographers would like to pursue.[63] Certain problems remained, however, especially when comparing the Compton Census with the 1851 data, and these need to be summarised as caveats to our conclusions.

The 1676 figures for Papists were probably more accurate and unproblematical than those for Nonconformity; although we need to bear in mind the long-standing problem for incumbents of 'Church Papists', and in this, as in other sources, there may have been a reluctance to report as Catholic certain local landowners. On the overall distribution of Roman Catholics, Whiteman thought that the census 'is probably reasonably reliable', if perhaps tending to underestimate.

[63] For example, in considering the relation between population growth and denominations, we have not published research making use of demographic growth rates between 1676 and 1851, as calculated from these sources, although they gave similar results to those of table 8.4. We do not wish to preclude the demographic use of the 1676 data in any way, and some experts have suggested that those data are best suited for such purposes. See in particular Whiteman, *Compton Census*, p. lxxxii; Whiteman and Clapinson, 'The use of the Compton Census'.

There were many more difficulties at the time in deciding who ought to be included as Nonconformists however, especially given the definition provided. Quakers and Baptists would clearly have been regarded as Nonconformist. But in many cases Independents and Presbyterians may not have been seen as such, especially if they were partial attendants at the Anglican church while also sometimes frequenting a conventicle. Tolerant churchwardens may have concealed the religious proclivities of some of their parishioners, especially better-off ones. Indeed, in some cases the churchwardens themselves may even have been dissenters.[64] It seems that in some well-documented parishes, like Great Eversden in Cambridgeshire, the Compton Census was certainly in error.[65] We might suspect that an overall figure of about 4.7 per cent being Papist or Nonconformist is too low for 1676, and that such a figure would hardly have justified inaugurating the census, even if the purpose had been to assuage Royal anxiety. For reasons associated particularly with poor drafting and irregular circulation of the original questions, the problems of partial conformity, and the individual judgements of so many clergymen, Whiteman wrote that 'the [Compton] census figures, contributed by perplexed incumbents, can only give a very patchy and inconsistent body of evidence about the strength of Dissent in 1676'.[66]

The second problem that has faced this analysis of stability and relocation is the fact that the Compton Census measured people, whereas the 1851 census measured attendances (i.e. at specified places of worship). The 1851 data were in this sense more concentrated. This difference in the sources has a pervasive and statistically uncontrollable influence when measuring Papist and Nonconformist persistence, although it probably has almost no bearing on the main contrasts we have drawn between Papist and dissenting Protestant continuities, as both groups are subject to it. This kind of documentary difference is a classic example of a familiar problem in historical research: of the way in which the precise delineation of historical change is shrouded to the historian by a shift in the focus of

64 M. Spufford (ed.), *The World of Rural Dissenters, 1520–1725* (Cambridge, 1995), pp. 200–4. See also pp. 179–80.

65 Spufford, 'The dissenting churches in Cambridgeshire', 81.

66 Whiteman, 'Compton Census', p. 92. And see Spufford's view that 'great caution must be employed in using the census, and that it is a difficult or impossible source on which to base estimates of total population, even if not of dissenters' (Spufford, 'The dissenting churches in Cambridgeshire', 95).

sources, a shift *which itself* reflects in varying ways the historical changes that have occurred, and which one is trying to describe. In this case the change was from small-scale and often furtive worship (inviting controversial head counts of nominal adherents) to large church-based denominational gatherings (inviting a Census of Religious Worship focused on places of worship, their sittings and open acts of attendance). The cartographic methods used here help to handle these mismatches between sources, and to display the effects of each. Yet this documentary problem in varying guises confronts all efforts to analyse religion over time, both before and after 1851.[67] Some reasonably firm impressions can be gleaned by careful procedures, but it needs to be stressed that exact contrasts over time, involving absolute numbers and equivalent measures, will certainly remain elusive.

For Catholicism there was fairly strong evidence for selective continuity, although when one looks at subsequent changes affecting the 1676 distributions, most counties showed a characteristic pattern of decline down to a few 'core' parishes by 1851. This process was more than the parochial centring which inevitably occurs when surveying the 1851 source against the Compton Census. There was on the one hand continuity or decline in the 'old Catholic' parishes, and on the other hand reinvigoration through Irish immigration. 'Genuine' continuity tended to be in smaller rural parishes with dominant Catholic landlords, while from the 1840s the increasingly permanent Irish settlers gradually moved away from the areas of their traditional seasonal agricultural work, and now gravitated to industrial settlements, market towns, ports or cities.[68] Subsequent Catholic recruitment was to be overwhelmingly from the Irish, rather than from any wider indigenous populations.[69]

[67] Similar problems have much preoccupied historians of the period since 1851. See for example R. Gill, *Competing Convictions* (1989); Gill, *Myth of the Empty Church.*

[68] On the changes to traditional patterns of Irish migration, see B. M. Kerr, 'Irish seasonal migration to Great Britain, 1800–1838', *Irish Historical Studies*, 3 (1942–3), 365–80; R. Lawton, 'Irish immigration to England and Wales in the mid-nineteenth century', *Irish Geography*, 4 (1959); J. H. Johnson, 'Harvest migration from nineteenth-century Ireland', *Transactions of the Institute of British Geographers*, 41 (1967), 97–112; A. O'Dowd, *Spalpeens and Tattie Hokers: History and Folklore of the Irish Migratory Agricultural Worker in Ireland and Britain* (Dublin, 1991).

[69] C. Brooks and A. Saint (eds.), *The Victorian Church: Architecture and Society* (Manchester, 1995), p. 13. Even in 1851, almost two-thirds of Catholics in England had been born in Ireland. See Aveling, *Handle and the Axe*, p. 19.

In the case of Protestant nonconformity there is only slight evidence for parochial continuity. This has surprised both us and other historians of the subject. It runs contrary to many findings and presumptions from local historical studies, both in our period and covering an earlier time.[70] Continuity certainly existed in terms of larger regions, such as old dissent in Leicestershire, but at the level of the *parish* arguments for continuity are much more questionable. It is possible that this owes something to the points raised above about the adequacy of the Compton Census, like the problems associated with partial conformity, perhaps rendering the religious data 'imperfect and variable'.[71] However, a number of historians have compared the Compton data with other chronologically proximate sources, like church court records, visitation returns, or the 1669 Conventicles Return, and argued for its general reliability, especially as a guide to the geographical distribution of dissent.[72] In Kent for example, it has been argued that 'the census provides a reasonable guide to those parts of Kent in which Protestant nonconformity was a significant element in the local community'.[73]

Beyond arguments of this sort, that are intrinsic to the source, other points need to be taken into account. Some of the dissenters of 1676 were old people, surviving from a very different era, in small numbers in particular parishes, and perhaps one should not expect much continuity from such cases,[74] especially if parish population turnover, of their children, was as high at that time as Laslett suggested.[75] We

70 Most notably, see the emphases on earlier continuity of local dissenting traditions in the Chilterns and Cambridgeshire, in Spufford, *World of Rural Dissenters*, *passim*, and especially her ch. 1.

71 Whiteman, *Compton Census*, pp. lxxvi–lxxvii.

72 Whiteman pointed out with regard to the 1669 Conventicles Return that 'Once the distribution of Dissent has been put on a geographical basis, independent of parochial, archidiaconal and diocesan confines, the discrepancies between the 1669 and 1676 figures are much reduced', *Compton Census*, p. lxxviii. Or see the comments, made for south-east Cambridgeshire, on the 'close correspondence between the Compton Census and church court records', in E. Carlson, 'The origins, function, and status of the office of churchwarden, with particular reference to the diocese of Ely', in M. Spufford (ed.), *World of Rural Dissenters, 1520–1725* (Cambridge, 1995), pp. 178–9. Spufford argued elsewhere, with reference to parts of Cambridgeshire, that the Compton Census recorded more dissenters than the visitation returns nearest to it in date, and more indeed than 'impeccable' Nonconformist sources of the same time: Spufford, 'The dissenting churches in Cambridgeshire', 94.

73 N. Yates, R. Hume and P. Hastings, *Religion and Society in Kent, 1640–1914* (Woodbridge, 1994), p. 15.

74 Whiteman, *Compton Census*, p. lxxix.

75 P. Laslett, 'Clayworth and Cogenhoe', in his *Family Life and Illicit Love in Earlier Generations* (Cambridge, 1977).

need to recall also the covert, fugitive, persecuted nature of much dissent in the 1670s, and meetings frequently had to shift location, given the general environment in which dissenters found themselves. Nonconformists were usually slow to build permanent chapels, often renting rooms for worship in secular buildings, and this was inevitable when their numbers were usually still so small, and scattered across many localities. More permanent chapels began to be built from the 1680s, but in many cases these, and other formal structures for meetings, were put in place much later. From 1676 to 1851 (175 years) is a long time, and it is probable that if one took later sources like the Evans list firmer links to 1851 could be established.

Even so, most Nonconformists (with notable exceptions like the Quakers) did not experience the sustained levels of hostility that the Catholics endured, and the extent of Nonconformist continuity needs always to be considered with an eye also on the higher local perpetuation that the Catholics achieved, with their very different survival strategies. Those strategies ensured localised Catholic persistence, allied as they often were to minority landed power in particular and sometimes isolated places. But until the overwhelming and forceful migratory repercussions of the Great Irish Famine, this higher proclivity to geographical survival came with a certain geographical inflexibility that set Catholicism apart from Protestant nonconformity, and we have seen that this was in some ways a disadvantage for the Catholic faith.

We should end with questions of methodology in religious history and cultural geography. To some extent historical surprise at weak denominational continuities is related to the shifting direction in historiographical method for religious history, a subject that has not been precipitate in taking up quantitative approaches.[76] When using more *qualitative* documentation than we have done, looking for example at Catholic estate papers and Quarter Session registration, or studying continuities in the architectural presence of churches and chapels, historians are predisposed to be more struck by continuity than by its absence. They see the visible and the seemingly enduring, and they try to account for it. Furthermore, denominational historians, who have played such a distinguished role in the writing of reli-

[76] See K. D. M. Snell, *Church and Chapel in the North Midlands: Religious Observance in the Nineteenth Century* (Leicester, 1991), ch. 1.

gious history, have often written for present-centred reasons and loyalties. Historians, unlike Welsh poets, do not always notice the things that have tumbled by the wayside: the failures, the collapsed or sold chapels with their decayed rendering, the prematurely dead preachers, the dissipated, depleted and disillusioned congregations, the hapless or thwarted missions. Rather than only the past brittle with relics, it is the stories of steadfast success that usually strike them: for these are the narratives to be told, as of Robert Hall's chapel at Arnesby, of the Unitarian Great Meeting in Leicester, of the Catholic traditions of Llanarth, Hathersage, Sawston or Everingham, or of many other long-lasting outcomes. There are merits and convincing purposes in such history, not least because it helps the present to be interpreted. However, one advantage of a more quantitative approach, like that taken here, is that it tends to eschew linear and survivalist kinds of thinking, and thus may throw up alternative perspectives missed by other lines of study.

9

The Sunday school movement: child labour, denominational control and working-class culture

'Train up a child in the way he should go:
and when he is old, he will not depart from it.' (Proverbs, xxii.6)

Introduction

Sunday schools were perhaps the most important, but are now among the most neglected, of nineteenth-century religious and educational subjects. Often humble institutions, neither charismatic nor stirring to modern minds as a field of study, they are easily brushed aside by historians.[1] Nor did they usually leave impressive architectural reminders of what they once were.[2] Yet contemporaries like John

[1] T. W. Laqueur, *Religion and Respectability: Sunday Schools and Working Class Culture, 1780–1850* (1976), and P. B. Cliff, *The Rise and Development of the Sunday School Movement in England, 1780–1980* (Redhill, 1986), have been the two main publications in recent decades on them. Trends in the numbers of Sunday school pupils are well documented for many denominations in the appendices of R. Currie, A. D. Gilbert and L. Horsley, *Churches and Churchgoers: Patterns of Church Growth in the British Isles since 1700* (Oxford, 1977), although the series are strongest on periods after 1851.

[2] Sunday schools were usually held in houses, barns, rented buildings, chapels, the aisles of churches and even their porches – as in Malmesbury (Wilts.,) or Berkeley (Glos.,) – or charity and day-school premises. In rural Wales, many Sunday schools were held in scattered farmhouses, a practice that continued into the twentieth century. In both Wales and England, chapel and church building from around the 1840s often made special internal provision for them (as with the Congregational chapel of Newcastle-under-Lyme, the Methodists at Hanley, and so on), and from about this time separate buildings were sometimes specially built, although these were rarely notable for their enduring architectural value. Examples of purpose-built buildings can be found in places like Dunkerton (Som., Baptist), Dulverton (Som., Congregational), East Tytherton (Wilts., Moravian) or Wokingham (Berks., Baptist). Sometimes older chapels were converted into Sunday schools, as new chapels were built to replace them (e.g., the Congregational Chapel in Halifax in 1857). Among the denominations, the Anglican Church was probably the most prone to use separate buildings: *1851 Census Great Britain: Reports and Tables on Education, England and Wales*, xc (1852–3; I.U.P. edn, Population 11, Shannon 1970); hereafter *Education Census, 1851*), p. 91.

Wesley, Adam Smith or Thomas Malthus, and many earlier generations of historians, were in little doubt about their outstanding significance. 'One of the noblest institutions which has been seen in Europe for some centuries', wrote Wesley.[3] Their functions seem all the greater when we remember that they served a society in which almost half the population were children.[4] 'The Sunday Schools of the industrial North form not only a vast moral and educational engine, but a curious and characteristic social fact', reported Angus Bethune Reach, writing as the investigator for the *Morning Chronicle* in 1849–50. And he summarised a view he had frequently heard expressed: 'Were it not for the Sunday Schools . . . Lancashire would have been a hell upon earth.'[5]

Strongly worded judgements like this were shared by many educational historians. For Frank Smith, the 'success of the Sunday Schools is an event of enormous significance . . . They were the chief instrument for humanising the poor, and for two generations they were the chief means of giving secular instruction to the new working class in the factories.'[6] State education grew from the example and lessons established by these schools: 'It was through the Sunday School that

[3] See *Wesleyan Methodist Magazine* (1843), 118, in a letter to Charles Amore.

[4] P. Laslett, *The World We Have Lost* (1968, 1971 edn), pp. 108–9. About 49 per cent of the population was under 20 years old. Sunday scholars commonly went to such schools for about 8–10 years. See E. G. West, *Education and the Industrial Revolution* (1975), p. 18. W. B. Stephens, *Education, Literacy and Society, 1830–1870: the Geography of Diversity in Provincial England* (Manchester, 1987), p. 38, gives the normal ages at between 5 and 16, which seems to match Sunday school membership rolls in Leicestershire – for example, Leics. C.R.O., N/B/207 A/71 (Baptists, Loughborough, 1815–25).

[5] J. Ginswick (ed.), *Labour and the Poor in England and Wales, 1849–1851, vol. 1: Lancashire, Cheshire, Yorkshire* (1983), p. 67, also in A. B. Reach, *Manchester and the Textile Districts in 1849*, ed. by C. Aspin (Helmshore, 1972), pp. 43–52. The 'vast . . . influence' of Sunday schools was repeatedly commented upon in the *Education Census, 1851*, e.g., pp. 83, 85. Similar views were expressed in 1845 by Thomas Alsopp of Hinckley, Leicestershire: 'Hundreds of children . . . never knew what it is to go to any other school . . . If it was not for the Sunday schools . . . I think we should be at the lowest pitch of depravity that human mind is capable of conceiving'. Cited by Stephens, *Education, Literacy and Society*, p. 156. As Owen Chadwick pointed out, many contemporaries considered Sunday schools 'the most important and effective of the religious influences upon the English population'. *The Victorian Church*, pt. 2 (1970, 1980 edn), p. 257. Among these was John Bright: 'I don't believe that all the statesmen in existence – I don't believe all the efforts they have ever made – have tended so much to the greatness and true happiness, the security and glory of this country, as have the efforts of Sunday school teachers.' *Ibid.*, p. 257.

[6] F. Smith, *A History of English Elementary Education, 1760–1902* (1931), p. 63.

the idea of universal education was first conceived possible. While discussion was still raging whether the labouring poor should be taught to write, a knowledge of reading was spreading throughout the country . . . the Sunday School was all-embracing and free . . . The faith of those early promoters was heroic.'[7] According to Wadsworth, no other reform movement ever spread so rapidly in England.[8] George Unwin wrote of how these schools 'were the sole organs of a community that transcended the fierce antagonism of misconceived class interests. In them the masters, foremen and workers of the factory met on the common ground of mutual service.'[9] Assessments of this sort were made of Sunday schools in America too. They produced, wrote Sydney Ahlstrom in his erudite work, 'a pious and knowledgeable laity on a scale unequaled anywhere in Christendom'.[10] The growth of Sunday schools, it has been said, 'is one of the most important themes not just of English educational history but of working-class culture in its widest sense'.[11] In short, as Smith concluded, 'The growth of Sunday Schools . . . is a phenomenon in the history of education which is without a parallel . . . they performed the gigantic task of assembling together, under some sort of discipline, the majority of the

[7] *Ibid.*, p. 60. Or see J. Foster, *Class Struggle and the Industrial Revolution: Early Industrial Capitalism in Three English Towns* (1974, 1979 edn), p. 216, on the great social influence of the Sunday schools, given 'the almost complete lack of any other form of mass education for working children' till the 1870s.

[8] A. P. Wadsworth, 'The first Manchester Sunday schools', in M. W. Flinn and T. C. Smout (eds.), *Essays in Social History* (Oxford, 1974), p. 102. Despite Wadsworth's verdicts, Flinn and Smout observed in their 'Bibliographical note' that 'there has been little further exploration of the social history of the Sunday School movement since Wadsworth wrote this essay'. *Ibid.*, p. 120.

[9] G. Unwin, *Samuel Oldknow and the Arkwrights: the Industrial Revolution at Stockport and Marple* (1924), p. 41. This theme of Sunday schools having defused social unrest featured also in *Education Census, 1851*, pp. 85–7: they have 'increased attachment to the cause of order and sobriety' helping to heal 'the sad estrangement . . . between the different sections of society . . . a most invaluable agent for promoting the religious education of the people and securing social peace'. For a stress on their popularity in the manufacturing districts, see also S. C. Parker, *The History of Modern Elementary Education* (1912), p. 229; or Cliff, *Rise and Development of the Sunday School Movement*, p. 5.

[10] S. Ahlstrom, *A Religious History of the American People* (1972, New Haven, 1974 edn), p. 742.

[11] D. Hempton, *Methodism and Politics in British Society, 1750–1850* (1984, 1987 edn), p. 86. For a slightly more sceptical view, see J. K. Walton, 'The north-west', in F. M. L. Thompson (ed.), *The Cambridge Social History of Britain, 1750–1950, vol. 1, Regions and Communities* (Cambridge, 1990), pp. 376–7.

children of the poor, and of giving to them some notions of behaviour and some ideas of religion.'[12]

We should remind ourselves of the huge numbers of children and adults involved as pupils and teachers in Sunday school education.[13] In many areas, and nationally by 1833, these completely outnumbered those in day schools.[14] Between a quarter and three-quarters of children who attended Sunday school were not receiving any other education.[15] The number of Sunday school pupils in Britain in 1818 was 425,000;[16] in 1830, this figure had risen to between 800,000

[12] Smith, *English Elementary Education*, p. 65; P. Joyce, *Work, Society and Politics: the Culture of the Factory in Later Victorian England* (1980), p. 246: 'The Sunday school was the one great institution that reached into the lives of the mass . . . the number of teachers was vast.' Raymond Williams pointed out in *The Long Revolution* (1961, Harmondsworth, 1971 edn), p. 157, that Sunday schools were 'much more important' than the industrial schools of the early nineteenth century.

[13] Many adults also attended Sunday schools, and indeed some of the schools were for adults, like the three Welsh-speaking ones in Dowlais mentioned by the *Morning Chronicle* correspondent. See Ginswick, *Labour and the Poor, vol. 3: the Mining and Manufacturing Districts of South Wales and North Wales* (1983), p. 79; or A. D. Rees, *Life in a Welsh Countryside: a Social Study of Llanfihangel yng Ngwynfa* (1950, Cardiff, 1996 edn), p. 125. These schools could be attached to agencies like savings funds, social clubs, benefit and coal societies, technical classes and so on. See e.g., W. C. Braithwaite, 'The adult-school movement', in R. Mudie-Smith (ed.), *The Religious Life of London* (1904), pp. 331–3. As was advocated by Thomas Pole in 1814, adult Sunday schools came to have a wider-ranging educational agenda than had been envisaged by Hannah and Martha More in the 1790s. See W. A. Devereux, *Adult Education in Inner London, 1870–1980* (1982), pp. 2–3. Adult schools often shared the motives behind Sunday schools, like concerns over morals and crime, and they were frequently denominational. A desire to educate female lace workers underpinned what was probably the first adult school, in 1798 in Nottingham.

[14] See, for example, Wadsworth, 'First Manchester Sunday schools', pp. 116–17, on Salford and Manchester; West, *Education and the Industrial Revolution*, p. 80; Stephens, *Education, Literacy and Society*, pp. 26, 38–9, 155, commenting particularly on the midland and northern towns, and see his appendix J; Smith, *English Elementary Education*, p. 220; N. J. Smelser, *Social Paralysis and Social Change: British Working-class Education in the Nineteenth Century* (Berkeley, 1991), pp. 165–9. Percentages of the children in major cities who *only* attended Sunday schools can be seen in T. Kelly, *George Birkbeck: Pioneer of Adult Education* (Liverpool, 1957), p. 337, as taken from *Select Committee on the Education of the Poorer Classes* (1838): for example, in Manchester and Salford, 52.6 per cent; in Birmingham, 45.6 per cent; Bury, 54.2 per cent.

[15] Laqueur, *Religion and Respectability*, p. 100; or see P. Horn (ed.), *Village Education in Nineteenth-century Oxfordshire: the Whitchurch School Log Book (1868–93) and Other Documents* (Oxfordshire Record Society, vol. 51, 1979), p. xvii.

[16] G. R. Porter, *The Progress of the Nation* (1836, 1851 edn), p. 695, taking data from a return to the House of Commons in 1833.

and 1,500,000; by 1833, it had certainly climbed to over 1,500,000;[17] by 1851, it reached about 2,600,000; and it stood at over 6,000,000 in 1911.[18] About 13 per cent of the English and Welsh population was enrolled in Sunday schools in 1851 (or about three-quarters of working-class children aged between 5 and 15), and this rose further in subsequent decades.[19] Most people would have experienced them at some point in their childhood.[20] The numbers of pupils were especially impressive in some of the major cities. When the Queen visited Leeds in September 1858, over 32,000 Sunday school children turned out at Woodhouse Moor to see her.[21] According to the *Morning Chronicle*, Manchester had about 25,000 Sunday school children in 1849–50; and the Bennet Street Sunday School in that city had 2,611 pupils on its books.[22] The 1851 Religious Census indicates that over 25,000 people attended Manchester Sunday schools on 30 March 1851, nearly 9,000 of them being Anglican morning scholars. Extremely high numbers can also be found in many other places, often in Lancashire, including Liverpool, Bury, Bolton, Blackburn, Wigan, Prestwich, Rochdale, Glossop in Derbyshire, or St Margaret's in Leicester. Impressive numbers were to be found in parts of London

[17] L. James, *Fiction for the Working Man, 1830–1850* (1963, Harmondsworth, 1974 edn), p. 3. In its entry for Robert Raikes (1735–1811), the *Dictionary of National Biography* (1896), vol. 47, pp. 168–70, gave figures of 1,250,000 Sunday school scholars and 100,000 teachers in Great Britain by 1831. Raikes had opened the first of his Sunday schools in July 1780. See also R. Gill, *The Myth of the Empty Church* (1993), p. 113.

[18] Laqueur, *Religion and Respectability*, p. 246 (cf. Chadwick, *The Victorian Church*, pt. 2, p. 192). In the later 1890s, there were about 7,500,000 pupils in English Sunday schools, according to Smith, *English Elementary Education*, p. 220, giving a figure for 1897, which to judge from Laqueur's data (*Religion and Respectability*, p. 246) is perhaps too high. The figures for the Baptists, Congregationalists, Primitives and Wesleyans all appear to have peaked around 1906. See G. I. T. Machin, *Politics and the Churches in Great Britain, 1832–1868* (Oxford, 1977), p. 12. Even as late as 1961, there were over 2.5 million children enrolled at Sunday schools. See Laqueur, *Religion and Respectability*, p. 246.

[19] Laquer, *Religion and Respectability*, pp. 44, 246. See also the figures in Gill, *Myth of the Empty Church*, pp. 23–4, 113, 301, and his references. Wesleyan, Baptist and Congregational Sunday school enrolment finally began to decline after c. 1906, in which year there were over a million Wesleyan enrolments. A. D. Gilbert, *Religion and Society in Industrial England: Church, Chapel and Social Change, 1740–1914* (1976, Harlow, 1984 edn), p. 202.

[20] S. J. D. Green, *Religion in the Age of Decline: Organisation and Experience in Industrial Yorkshire, 1870–1920* (Cambridge, 1996), p. 22: 'Virtually everyone went to Sunday school.'

[21] A. Briggs, *Victorian Cities* (1963, Harmondsworth, 1982 edn), p. 175.

[22] Ginswick, *Labour and the Poor*, vol. 1, pp. 69–70.

too.[23] There were even a few parishes, like Dalton in Furness, that had over half their entire populations attending Sunday schools.[24] Across the country, about 318,000 amateur teachers were working in Sunday schools in 1851.[25] Asa Briggs' comments on Middlesborough can also be applied to many other urban areas: 'Sunday schools were the most powerful educational influence from the start, and the Sunday School Union one of the most carefully organized local voluntary bodies.'[26]

In Wales, the influence of *Ysgolion Sabothol* was arguably even greater than in England. The Sabbath schools were generally introduced rather later, and more gradually. This was because of the earlier traditions of Welsh peripatetic charity schools, as established by the Revd Griffith Jones after about 1730, and revived later by the Revd Thomas Charles of Bala (who felt even until the late 1790s that they had more promise than Sunday schools). There was, from the start, but most notably in the form they were adopted by Thomas Charles, more stress on personal religious improvement through Sunday schools in Wales than was true in the early years of the movement in England. For the Welsh these schools 'represented a folk movement. Catering for popular needs, they were organized by ordinary people

[23] P. S. Bagwell, *Outcast London, a Christian Response: the West London Mission of the Methodist Church, 1887–1987* (1987), p. 89, citing the case of Hinde Street and its branch schools nearby.

[24] These figures are calculated from the original enumerators' returns, 1851 *Census of Religious Worship*. For each place of worship, the census enumerators could provide three possible Sunday school figures: morning, afternoon and evening attendances, and there were also time-unspecified attendances in some cases. The parish figures reported in the text here are totals of the maximum denomination-specific attendance during the day. In other words, they do not count less well attended gatherings during the day for each denomination, and in that regard should be seen as minimum total figures for each parish.

[25] Smith, *English Elementary Education*, p. 223; D. Wardle, *English Popular Education, 1780–1970* (Cambridge, 1970), p. 62. Such numbers, he added, helped 'to keep the teaching profession in its chronically depressed state throughout the nineteenth century'! Laqueur, *Religion and Respectability*, p. 158, gives a seemingly lower figure of above 200,000 in 1850. Such teachers contributed to the exceptionally low cost of teaching each pupil: about two shillings a year. James, *Fiction for the Working Man*, p. 3.

[26] Briggs, *Victorian Cities*, p. 255. As Foster commented, 'going to Sunday school was definitely a mass experience', *Class Struggle and the Industrial Revolution*, p. 215. To similar effect, see P. and H. Silver, *The Education of the Poor: the History of a National School, 1824–1974* (1974), p. 7; J. Simon, 'Was there a Charity School Movement? The Leicestershire Evidence', in B. Simon (ed.), *Education in Leicestershire, 1540–1914* (Leicester, 1968), p. 94: 'it was the Sunday Schools that paved the way for the mass daily school'.

themselves, largely unsupervised from the outside.'[27] Philip Jenkins referred to Sunday schools as 'one of the distinctive national institutions', central to Welsh social life.[28] They were certainly more independent of middle- and upper-class patronage than in England, and much more dominated by the dissenting congregations.[29] Following a different path from their English equivalents, usually teaching in Welsh, and developing largely independent of English influence after about 1814, they were 'a chief centre in the religious life of the people and a custodian of the national language and ideals'.[30] It has been said that most farmers' households, including many adults, attended Sunday schools.[31] As an example of the staggering numbers involved, nearly a quarter of the entire population of north-east Wales was registered in Sunday schools in 1846.[32] This was despite the mountainous nature of much of the land, which had earlier led Thomas Charles to doubt whether Sunday schools could ever be established in such regions. Welsh parishes like Llanbadarn Fawr (Cards.), Bedwelty (Mon.) or Trevethin (Mon.) each had 1851 census-day Sunday school attendance of between 2,000 and 3,500, ranking alongside some of the highest in Lancashire.[33]

Sunday schools provided a basic religious education, one that was often informed by the late eighteenth-century emphasis on salvation through faith, which owed so much to Methodist influence. They also taught some secular subjects, reading and sometimes writing.

27 W. T. R. Pryce, 'Industrialism, urbanization and the maintenance of culture areas: north-east Wales in the mid-nineteenth century', *Welsh History Review*, 7 (1974–5), 318.

28 P. Jenkins, *A History of Modern Wales, 1536–1990* (1992), p. 312.

29 In Anglesey, Cardiganshire, Caernarvonshire and Monmouthshire, dissenting Sunday school scholars were, respectively, 88.4, 85.0, 90.8 and 81.8 per cent of total Sunday school scholars in 1847: Smelser, *Social Paralysis*, p. 167 (giving figures from the 1847 Commission on Education in Wales), pp. 168–9 (for the 1858–61 data, showing that the Welsh percentages of dissenters among Sunday scholars were much higher than for England).

30 Smith, *English Elementary Education*, p. 61; Smelser, *Social Paralysis*, pp. 146–58.

31 J. Rhys and D. Brynmor-Jones, *The Welsh People* (1923, New York, 1969 edn), p. 588. They also stressed these schools' influence upon the Welsh language after about 1785, especially via the Welsh Bible (pp. 506, 508).

32 Pryce, 'Industrialism', 320. H. V. Johnson commented in 1847 on north Wales that 'The humble position and attainments of the individuals engaged in the establishment and support of Welsh Sunday-schools enhance the value of this spontaneous effort for education . . . it is impossible not to admire the vast number of schools which they have established.' Cited in Smelser, *Social Paralysis*, p. 170.

33 Figures calculated from the enumerators' returns.

Whether writing should be taught on the Sabbath was open to argument and denominational judgement; the controversy much preoccupied Evangelicals and others, notably men such as Jabez Bunting.[34] Like contemporaries, historians have placed varying emphases on the importance of these schools in teaching writing, but most have agreed that prior to the 1870 Education Act they were crucial in creating mass literacy.[35] An enormous number of bibles, magazines, periodicals, sermons, catechisms, handbooks, hymnbooks, primers of reading and spelling, and so on, were published for the use of Sunday scholars, notably by the Sunday School Union and the Sunday School Society. In addition, the schools were key agencies in the inculcation of orderliness, punctuality, sobriety, cleanliness, and related virtues governing personal behaviour and social discipline.[36] Robert Raikes, seen as their founder in the early 1780s,[37] had been especially concerned with gaol reform, the control of crime around Gloucester, and the unruly behaviour and disrespect for property among children employed in local pin factories during the

[34] See E. P. Thompson, *The Making of the English Working Class* (1963, Harmondsworth, 1975 edn), pp. 389–90; Laqueur, *Religion and Respectability*, pp. 124–5; Cliff, *Rise and Development of the Sunday School Movement*, pp. 80–3; R. A. Soloway, *Prelates and People: Ecclesiastical Social Thought in England, 1783–1852* (1969), p. 352.

[35] See for example, Laqueur, *Religion and Respectability*, p. 123; Stephens, *Education, Literacy and Society*, p. 158; cf., Smelser, *Social Paralysis*, p. 24. Anglican and Wesleyan Sunday schools were often to the fore in resisting Sabbatarian teaching of writing, although some of them made provision for it to be taught on other days. The Wesleyan Conference decided against it in 1814 and again in 1827, although there was difficulty enforcing a prohibition. Other denominations, like the Quakers, supposedly had little or no such objection, but compare F. Engels, *The Condition of the Working Class in England* (1845, Glasgow, 1984 edn), p. 142: 'The Sunday schools of the State Church, of the Quakers, and, I think, of several other sects, do not teach writing, "because it is too worldly an employment for Sunday!"'

[36] This stress on *order* (as among children in Newcastle and the north-eastern mining villages) is well made in R. Colls, *The Pitmen of the Northern Coalfield: Work, Culture and Protest, 1790–1851* (Manchester, 1987), pp. 128–30, 184–6. See also R. Colls, *The Collier's Rant: Song and Culture in the Industrial Village* (1977), pp. 84–5, 89–90. As with charity schools, there was also the hope that in inculcating such values Sunday schools would help to reduce poor rates. Soloway, *Prelates and People*, p. 352.

[37] His first Sunday school opened in July 1780. There is debate over the origins of Sunday schools. See, for example, A. Temple Patterson, *Radical Leicester: a History of Leicester, 1780–1850* (Leicester, 1975), p. 20; A. Gregory, *Robert Raikes: Journalist and Philanthropist: a History of the Origin of Sunday Schools* (1877); J. Stratford, *Robert Raikes and Others: the Founders of Sunday Schools* (1880); F. Booth, *Robert Raikes of Gloucester* (Redhill, 1980); Cliff, *Rise and Development of the Sunday School Movement*, ch. 3 and p. 39.

week.[38] In this, he was supported by many magistrates and by the Proclamation Society of 1787, which advocated a 'reformation of manners'. The English schools were frequently dedicated to this end. William Fox, Hannah More and her sisters in the Mendips, and other early promoters of the schools were all motivated by moral concerns of this sort, and by worries over irreligion among the young.

In addition to the functions they may have had in these regards, the schools were major social and recreational centres. Their libraries, teachers' meetings and conferences, 'charity sermons', Whitsun outings, 'treats' and prizes, processions (like those described by Arnold Bennett), galas, music, singing classes, Bands of Hope, anniversary festivities, football clubs, mutual improvement societies, needlework classes, sick, clothing, benefit and burial clubs, funerals and other activities played an exceptionally important role in many districts.[39] Their jubilees and activities were even celebrated in popular lithographs.[40] Through the Sunday schools children became closely involved in charitable activity and missions.[41] The schools

[38] Smith, *English Elementary Education*, p. 48. Or see A. Briggs, 'Innovation and adaptation: the eighteenth-century setting', in J. Ferguson (ed.), *Christianity, Society and Education: Robert Raikes, Past, Present and Future* (1981), p. 18; F. Booth, 'Robert Raikes: founder of the Sunday-school movement', in *ibid.*, pp. 25–34; D. M. Griffith, *Nationality in the Sunday School Movement: a Comparative Study of the Sunday School Movement in England and in Wales* (Bangor, 1925), p. 11. R. Raikes, 'On Sunday schools', *Gentleman's Magazine* (June, 1784), 410–12, and 'Eusebius', 'A little learning is a dangerous thing', *Gentleman's Magazine* (Oct., 1797), 819–20, reprinted in J. M. Goldstrom (ed.), *Education: Elementary Education, 1780–1900* (Newton Abbot, 1972), pp. 15–23, provides Raikes' views, and those of an early detractor.

[39] *Education Census, 1851*, p. 86. The Harborough Congregational Sunday School in Leicestershire, dating from before 1794, had frequent outings, a Young Men's Institute, a Young Men's Bible Class, a gymnasium, a debating society, a Band of Hope, a Christian Endeavour Society, and football and cricket clubs. There was a sick fund associated with the school, which also had many ties with foreign missions, a Missionary Clothing Society, and a Juvenile Missionary Society. See Leics. C.R.O., N/C/215/23–24; N/C/215/245; N/C/215/22; *The Sunday School Chronicle*, 4 Jan. 1906, p. 10; *ibid.*, 9 Jan. 1891; W. H. Pool, *A Brief History of the Congregational Sunday School, Market Harborough* (Market Harborough, 1886). In Leicester, Thomas Cook was involved in organising Sunday school trips. See Temple Patterson, *Radical Leicester*, p. 269.

[40] Like that produced as a souvenir of the jubilee of the Orange Street Sunday Schools, 21 Sept. 1862. Westminster City Archives, Box 42, no. 15.

[41] This is very well documented in F. K. Prochaska, *Women and Philanthropy in Nineteenth-century England* (Oxford, 1980), ch. 3. Some Sunday schools were themselves founded or financed as charities, usually controlled by the Anglican Church, as for example at North Luffenham in Rutland, where in the early nineteenth century a master was paid from the Town Land's Charity to teach. D. Thomson, 'Charities in Rutland' (unpub. MA dissertation, Dept. of English Local History, University of Leicester, 1999), p. 24.

were also in many cases linked to other educational establishments and societies, like mechanics' institutes. Indeed, some mechanics' institutes developed out of Sunday schools, like the Brotherly Society of Birmingham after 1796, in which the local manufacturer James Luckcock played a key role.[42] These schools were also crucial venues for the public activities of lower- and middle-class women. Although this country had no direct counterpart to the American 'Female Union Society for the Promotion of Sabbath-Schools' (1816), many women were Sunday school founders, or textbook writers. They were often organised in local female associations, holding offices and managing finances. Probably a majority of Sunday school teachers were women. And as further confirmation of the schools' importance, it is worth remembering that among those taught or teaching in them were Samuel Bamford, William Lovett, George Holyoake, Francis Soutter, Joseph Barker, Marianne Farningham,[43] John Wilson, Thomas Cooper, George Edwards,[44] Ben Tillett, Benjamin Brierley, Edmund Gosse[45] and many other outstanding figures in the annals of working-class or religious history.

The early Evangelical enthusiasm for Sunday schools as a way of inculcating values normally more associated with the middle orders of society, coupled with the nineteenth-century debates about who controlled schooling, led many historians, from E. P. Thompson to Asa Briggs, to see Sunday schools as agencies of middle-class moral and political influence, or even indoctrination. The resulting arguments have taken various forms, which need not be elaborated in detail.[46] Standing against such views, Laqueur's *Religion and*

[42] Kelly, *George Birkbeck*, p. 67.

[43] M. Farningham, *A Working Woman's Life* (1907).

[44] The agricultural trade unionist George Edwards wrote of his Sunday school that 'This was the only schooling I ever had.' *From Crow-scaring to Westminster* (1922), p. 21. Many of his fellow rural union leaders had been Sunday school superintendents, commonly with the Primitive Methodists. See N. Scotland, *Methodism and the Revolt of the Field* (Gloucester, 1981), pp. 48, 62–4, 72–3.

[45] A. Thwaite, *Edmund Gosse: a Literary Landscape, 1849–1928* (Oxford, 1985), pp. 112–13, 151.

[46] J. F. C. Harrison, *Learning and Living, 1790–1860: a Study in the History of the English Adult Education Movement* (1961), p. 40; Thompson, *Making of the English Working Class*, pp. 389–90, 397, 414–15, refers to the 'emotional bullying' and even 'religious terrorism' of the Sunday schools, seeing them as 'a dreadful exchange even for the village dame's schools' of the eighteenth century. The schools were 'poisoned by the dominant attitude of the Evangelicals' in the counter-revolutionary years; E. P. Thompson, 'Time, work-discipline and industrial capitalism', in M. W. Flinn and T. C. Smout (eds.), *Essays in Social History* (Oxford, 1974), pp. 59–60; Foster, *Class Struggle and the Industrial Revolution*, p. 28: 'there seems to have been active use of Sunday schools to discipline the new child labour

Respectability was an exceptional advance in detailed inquiry and proposed at length a rather different thesis. His stress throughout was on 'the integration of the Sunday schools with the working-class community'.[47] Sunday schools were 'one strand of a uniquely working-class cultural constellation'.[48] They were 'indigenous institutions of the working-class community rather than an imposition on it from the outside'.[49] While he carefully qualified this view in various ways, stressing that no one group monopolised the institution, his emphasis was nevertheless on their role as 'an institution of the working class'.[50] 'The Sunday school was largely the creation of the working-class community', and 'grew out of the working class'; it was 'a part of, and not an imposition on to, popular culture'.[51] Supplied very largely with working-class teachers, and pupils, almost all of whom were from the lowest orders, it was, Laqueur argued, 'a relatively autonomous, largely working-class institution'.[52]

Some scholars have had misgivings about these emphases. On the one hand, the evident patronage of many of the southern Lancashire schools by mill-owners and local employers led Patrick Joyce to raise doubts about just how integral they were to an independently generated working-class culture, especially before the mid nineteenth century.[53] Middle-class funding and ideas were, he pointed out, fundamental to many of these institutions, and in towns like Bolton, Bury, Blackburn or Keighley, they often had very close connections with masters and factories.[54] Employers often set up Sunday schools and

Footnote 46 (*cont.*)
force in the factories'; H. Silver, *The Concept of Popular Education: a Study of Ideas and Social Movements in the Early Nineteenth Century* (1965), pp. 36–40; S. Pollard, *The Genesis of Modern Management* (1965, Harmondsworth, 1968 edn), pp. 228–31, 243; Hempton, *Methodism and Politics*, pp. 86–92. Argument about the class origination and control of Sunday schools parallels similar debate about mechanics' institutes. See for example M. Tylecote, *The Mechanics Institutes of Lancashire and Yorkshire before 1851* (1957); Harrison, *Learning and Living*, pp. 57–74; B. Simon, *Studies in the History of Education, 1780–1870* (1960), pp. 215–22; I. Inkster (ed.), *The Steam Intellect Societies: Essays on Culture, Education and Industry, c.1820–1914* (1985).

47 Laqueur, *Religion and Respectability*, p. 74.

48 *Ibid.*, p. 239.

49 *Ibid.*, p. 61.

50 *Ibid.*, p. 62.

51 *Ibid.*, pp. xi–xii, 189, 241. See also pp. 3, 28–30, where the stress is on the humble people starting them.

52 *Ibid.*, p. 63, and see p. 42 on their independent localism. Other historians have come close to such views on the Sunday school. See for example Chadwick, *Victorian Church*, pt. 2, p. 261: 'working men felt that it belonged to them and they to it'.

53 Joyce, *Work, Society and Politics*, pp. 246–8; and see Foster, *Class Struggle and the Industrial Revolution*, pp. 28, 171, 191, 215.

54 Joyce, *Work, Society and Politics*, pp. 178–9, 247–8. On Keighley and the attitude of

even personally ran the 'treats' and outings.[55] Further reservations have come from historians who have underscored the conservative and evangelical nature of Sunday schools, stressing their control by higher-class individuals who wanted to curb the activities of the labouring poor and improve their supposedly degraded morals. It has been suggested in particular that Sunday schools (especially before the 1830s) were rarely set up by working-class people, that most teachers had not been pupils, and that teachers and school authorities rarely espoused values held by the working classes.[56] One thinks, for example, of Patrick Branwell Brontë teaching at the 'National Church Sunday School' built adjacent to the Haworth parsonage, impatient and disdainful of his rough pupils, whom he would lift up by their hair and rap with his knuckles.[57]

These rival interpretations need to be kept in mind while considering the more empirical analysis that follows, which is rather different in style and method from most of the earlier historical writing on Sunday schools. While historians have commented on the wide variations that existed in Sunday schools in different parts of the country, and their varying modes of development, as yet almost no systematic work has been conducted on these features and the contexts within which the schools flourished.[58] Laqueur probed in this direction only

the Methodist manufacturer James Sugden, see Green, *Religion in the Age of Decline*, p. 67. However, there seems to have been very little involvement in Sunday schools by coalowners in the north-east, and here company schools were rare until the 1840s and 1850s – see Colls, *Pitmen of the Northern Coalfield*, pp. 130–1.

55 Joyce, *Work, Society and Politics*, pp. 164, 173; Smith, *English Elementary Education*, p. 64, noting for example the Strutts, who required all workers under the age of twenty to attend Sunday schools.

56 The most sustained argument along these lines is M. Dick, 'The myth of the working-class Sunday school', *History of Education*, 9 (1980). The Education Census stated that their teachers were 'members of the middle class': *Education Census, 1851*, p. 85. See also Cliff, *Rise and Development of the Sunday School Movement*, pp. 43–6, 150–2; and H. McLeod, 'Recent studies in Victorian religious history', *Victorian Studies*, 21 (1978), 247–8, for observant comments on Laqueur's thesis. Among other points, McLeod stresses the wide differences between Sunday schools, the high proportion of pupils enrolled in Anglican Sunday schools, and the need for caution in generalising from the industrial north-west, which may be atypical.

57 J. R. V. Barker, *The Brontës* (1994, 1995 edn), pp. 183–4. All the Brontë sisters taught at this Sunday school, which was purpose built in 1832.

58 See Stephens, *Education, Literacy and Society*, p. 29; Smith, *Elementary Education*, p. 59. Hempton, *Methodism and Politics*, p. 88, refers to 'the incompleteness of the research' done on 'genuine regional differences' and 'the colourful diversity of the Sunday schools'. Certainly there has been considerable emphasis on Stockport and certain other major Lancashire schools, to the exclusion of extensive regions of England and Wales.

to conclude that the distribution of Sunday school enrolment 'bears no clear relationship to any obvious social or economic determinants'.[59] He argued that the schools were not related to industrialisation, as many traditional towns like Chippenham or Shaftesbury had high levels of enrolment. Nor were they seemingly connected to degrees of population increase.[60] The prevalence of Sunday schools was, he believed, highly related to the overall strength of dissent;[61] and, he continued, 'the Sunday school was generally more a part of Non-conformist than Anglican religious culture, but the question still remains why the Church was strong or weak in a particular area. And here the historical sociology of religion, still in its infancy, fails to provide an answer.'[62]

It is well known that the *Census of Religious Worship* gave impressively detailed figures for Sunday school attendances on Census Sunday, 30 March 1851, alongside the other figures provided by the enumerators. As Cliff and others have commented, it was the first time that complete and reasonably accurate figures became available, and these were carefully scrutinised at the time.[63] These enumerators' returns are my main source of Sunday school data here. Like the data for religious attendances, the Sunday school figures were supplied for morning, afternoon and evening, by places of worship returning to the census.

For the general religious attendances, the problems of multiple attendance – across the three possible service times on Census Sunday – are such that historians normally calculate an 'index of total attendances', over all three possible service times.[64] The 1851 Sunday school data are rather different. One of their common features is that the attendance numbers given for each school at different times on Census Sunday are very similar. More or less the same people were attending the school at different times of the day. I therefore took the maximum attendance figure for each denomination in each parish (figures having been added together if a denomination operated more than one school), and from the figures for maximum attendants during the day a denomination-specific index of maximum Sunday

59 Laqueur, *Religion and Respectability*, p. 59.
60 *Ibid.*, pp. 58–9.
61 *Ibid.*, p. 60.
62 *Ibid.*, p. 60.
63 Cliff, *Rise and Development of the Sunday School Movement*, pp. 102, 131–2. On the problems of other Sunday school data, see Smelser, *Social Paralysis*, pp. 165, 411–12.
64 The 'index of total attendances' is calculated by summing the morning, afternoon and evening attendances for each denomination in each parish, dividing by parish population size, and multiplying by 100. See appendix C.

school attendance was calculated, which in each case relates the maximum attendance to the parish population.[65] Unless otherwise indicated, the parish Sunday school index of maximum attendance used here therefore refers to attendants, not to the total attendances (over all times of the day) which are often used in creating measures from the Religious Census.[66]

In the later eighteenth century, Sunday schools had often served a religiously varied group of local people and, in some cases, they were only weakly linked to particular denominations. This situation rapidly broke down, however, notably during the Napoleonic Wars, when many Anglicans expressed strong anti-Methodist opinions and Sunday schools were attacked as promoting revolutionary ideas among the poor.[67] By the 1851 census there was virtually no ambiguity in any of the enumerators' returns about which denomination each Sunday school 'belonged' to.[68] Any earlier faith in inter-denominationalism

65 The index is calculated by taking the maximum Sunday school attendance figure during the day, for each denomination in each parish, dividing by the 1851 parish population size, and multiplying by 100. Where necessary – as often in counties like Lancashire or Derbyshire – township or hamlet data were amalgamated into parish units. Indexes of this sort are of course essential to relate attendance data to local population size.

66 The index of maximum attendance is likely to underestimate slightly the total numbers attending Sunday schools at some time on Census Sunday, 30 March 1851. Close examination of the denominational figures and ratios between alternative measures does not indicate that this is a problem. A further possible difficulty lies in adult attendance at Sunday schools. Other than the very occasional comment, the 1851 enumerators' returns gave no information on this issue, and one is unable to take it into account. It *may* have the effect of marginally raising the Sunday school numbers for parts of Wales relative to England, but this has not been established. This would have only a very minor effect on the calculations. It is more probable that adult attendance was at separate schools, not documented in 1851, and most of these developed later.

67 E. Halévy, *A History of the English People in the Nineteenth Century: vol. 1, England in 1815* (1913, 1970 edn), p. 529; Smelser, *Social Paralysis*, pp. 51, 66, 197; Laqueur, *Religion and Respectability*, p. 32; Cliff, *Rise and Development of the Sunday School Movement*, pp. 11, 49, 72–3; J. M. Goldstrom, *Education: Elementary Education, 1780–1900* (Newton Abbot, 1972), pp. 22–3; E. R. Norman, *Church and Society in England, 1770–1970: a Historical Study* (Oxford, 1976), pp. 35–6; Silver, *Education of the Poor*, p. 7; Wadsworth, 'First Manchester Sunday schools', pp. 113–15. At the same time, William Godwin and other radicals were attacking Sunday schools for instilling habits of deference, obedience to one's station and respect for the Church of England.

68 See for example *Education Census, 1851*, p. 83: 'In general, every local Sunday school is the offshoot of an individual congregation.' Very exceptionally indeed, Sunday schools were said to be non-denominational. The Sunday school room in Little Hucklow (Derbyshire) came close to this: 'Open to Prodestants [sic] if they please to give us a sermon. Under no religious denomination. It belongs to Freeholders within the Township.' (The return was signed by one of the Chapmans, local Wesleyan Methodists, and was probably controlled by the denomination.) M. Tranter (ed.), *The Derbyshire Returns to the 1851 Religious Census*, Derbyshire Record Society, vol. 23 (Chesterfield, 1995), pp. 197–8.

had long since died away. This development was compounded by the prevalence of anti-Anglican sentiments, the antagonism to Henry Brougham's initiatives over state education in 1820 and the religious provisions of Sir James Graham's Factory Bill of 1843. It was intensified by Nonconformist distrust of the Tractarians. The principle of voluntary teaching had also asserted itself, further ensuring that schools became firmly sectarian. The census returns and accompanying comments indicate very tight relationships between church or chapel and the Sunday school. That school was often held in a distinct building, separate from the place of worship, but it was almost always organised under denominational authority.[69]

As we proceed, we need to recall a portentous reality of religious education, one which has been lost sight of in some historical writing on Sunday schools. The question of who controlled schooling was gravely important. This was central to the rival purposes of the British and National Societies, founded in 1811–12, as it had been to the Anglican charity schools of the eighteenth century. For the future success of any denomination it was absolutely vital that it teach its children the principles and tenets of its faith, and that it incline them strongly towards denominational obedience. This was not so much a matter of 'social control', but rather of denominational control at a time of openly competing religious rivalries and intolerances.[70] Sunday schools, like other denominational schools,[71] were the major means by which this was undertaken.[72] In due course the religiously disciplined children, often marrying within their Sunday school peer group, would form the adult church society. In some cases, especially

69 Such points have also been made by other historians. See for example I. Sellers, *Nineteenth-Century Nonconformity* (1977), p. 36; Foster, *Class Struggle and the Industrial Revolution*, p. 216, on the schools being directly linked to religious denominations by 1851. On schooling more generally 'becoming rapidly a matter of *denominational* activity', particularly after the controversies of the 1840s, 'intended as a sort of bulwark' for the denominations, see *Education Census, 1851*, pp. liii–liv.

70 There were many indications of such denominational competition, between rival Sunday schools. See Public Record Office, HO 129/225/48, remarks by the Revd R. Kemp, minister for Walpole, Suffolk: 'At present we have but few Sunday school children at the church, owing to the Chapel Sunday school, but means will be used to increase the numbers.' Whit-Monday processions and public events staged by Sunday schools were often informed by such rivalry.

71 Engels, *Condition of the Working Class*, p. 141.

72 As Green says, through Sunday schools religious organisations aimed 'to provide themselves with a regular and disciplined supply of religious conscripts for their congregations and societies'. Green, *Religion in the Age of Decline*, pp. 29–30.

in Wales, Sunday scholars even became the nucleus of new congregations. If a denomination failed to educate in this way, and was unable to make any significant compensation for such neglect through other activities, it would in all probability suffer the consequences in future years, as its culture and doctrine lost the attachment of younger generations, and its pews emptied. This recruiting role was especially important prior to the 1870 Education Act. Sunday schools were crucial not only for the inculcation of literacy and basic education, but also for the relative success of different denominations,[73] and, indeed, for the future of religious adherence as a whole. Neglecting to teach its theological and moral tenets would presage not only the progressive decline of a denomination over future decades, but more broadly would imply the failure of religious faith itself as something real to the population. These issues, which centred on Sunday schools, relating as they do to questions of 'secularisation', are therefore of huge social, ideological and institutional significance in the history of this country. They also remind us how pivotal education is in the broader transmission of culture, morality and belief, and what the consequences of overlooking it can be.

County- and registration-district level analyses

I have mentioned the virtual absence of quantitative studies of Sunday schools, despite the availability of data. This can now be remedied. My method involves cross-sectional analyses for three spatial units: the county, the registration district and, particularly, the parish. This allows the examination of these issues via different datasets and the validation of results across separate units of analysis. Before looking at detailed parish-level results from the 1851 enumerators' returns, some broader findings can be outlined. By the mid nineteenth century, Sunday schools were strongest in terms of attendance throughout Wales, and in a swathe of English counties running from Buckinghamshire to Lancashire, most notably Bedfordshire, Buckinghamshire, Derbyshire, Nottinghamshire, the West Riding and Lancashire. Counties like Dorset, Wiltshire, Gloucestershire and Staffordshire also showed quite high attendance. At the other

[73] This may have been especially true for dissenting and evangelical traditions; for the Roman Catholics and Tractarians a reliance upon the Mass may have been more important than Sunday schools.

extreme, counties like Kent, Sussex, Surrey, Middlesex or Herefordshire had much lower Sunday school attendance. In figure 9.1 this distribution is mapped for England and Wales at registration-district level. I have expressed these figures as percentages of registration-district populations.[74] It is clear from this map that we are dealing with an irregular geography, and with an educational phenomenon that had a distinctive and as yet unexplained pattern. It also demonstrates how separate Wales was as a whole, and when compared to neighbouring English counties.

Taking English Sunday school data at *county* level, and relating them in a cross-sectional analysis to county social, demographic and economic data, indicates some broad conclusions. My most striking finding at county level is the very clear-cut relationship between Sunday school enrolment and the prevalence of child labour. Sunday schools provided an education that did not interfere with the working lives of children during the week. Figure 9.2 shows this relationship for all English counties ($r=0.733$, $p=.000$).[75] If this issue is investigated for boys and girls separately, there is little difference. Some historians have been puzzled by the seeming absence of any exclusive ties between factory industrialisation and Sunday schools. While pointing to Sunday school successes in counties like Lancashire and the West Riding, they have also been aware how strong they were in counties like Bedfordshire or Buckinghamshire.[76] It requires knowledge of some neglected Victorian industries to appreciate the prevalence of child labour in the latter two counties. Bedfordshire had very considerable child labour in straw-plaiting and in lace-working. It was also the county ranked highest for Sunday school enrolments in

[74] The Sunday school data mapped here are from *Education Census, 1851*, pp. 234–75: the column headed 'Sunday schools. Scholars. Attending at the Schools on Sunday March 30, 1851. Both sexes'.

[75] Data on Sunday school pupils as a percentage of total population, Census Sunday 1851, were used, alongside data for all children returned as occupied in 1851 as a percentage of the age group 10–14. The data were from Stephens, *Education, Literacy and Society*, pp. 319, 352, with some of the other data used here. Forty variables were taken from a variety of different sources, and there is no need to list in detail variables found to be less important. The 1851 measure of Sunday school strength is very highly correlated with the similarly defined 1833 Sunday school data, and is clearly a very reliable measure. Welsh counties were not used for this analysis, because of the rather different cultural qualities of Sunday schools in Wales compared to England, and because of the inaccessibility of comparable Welsh data for some variables.

[76] Laqueur, *Religion and Respectability*, p. 216.

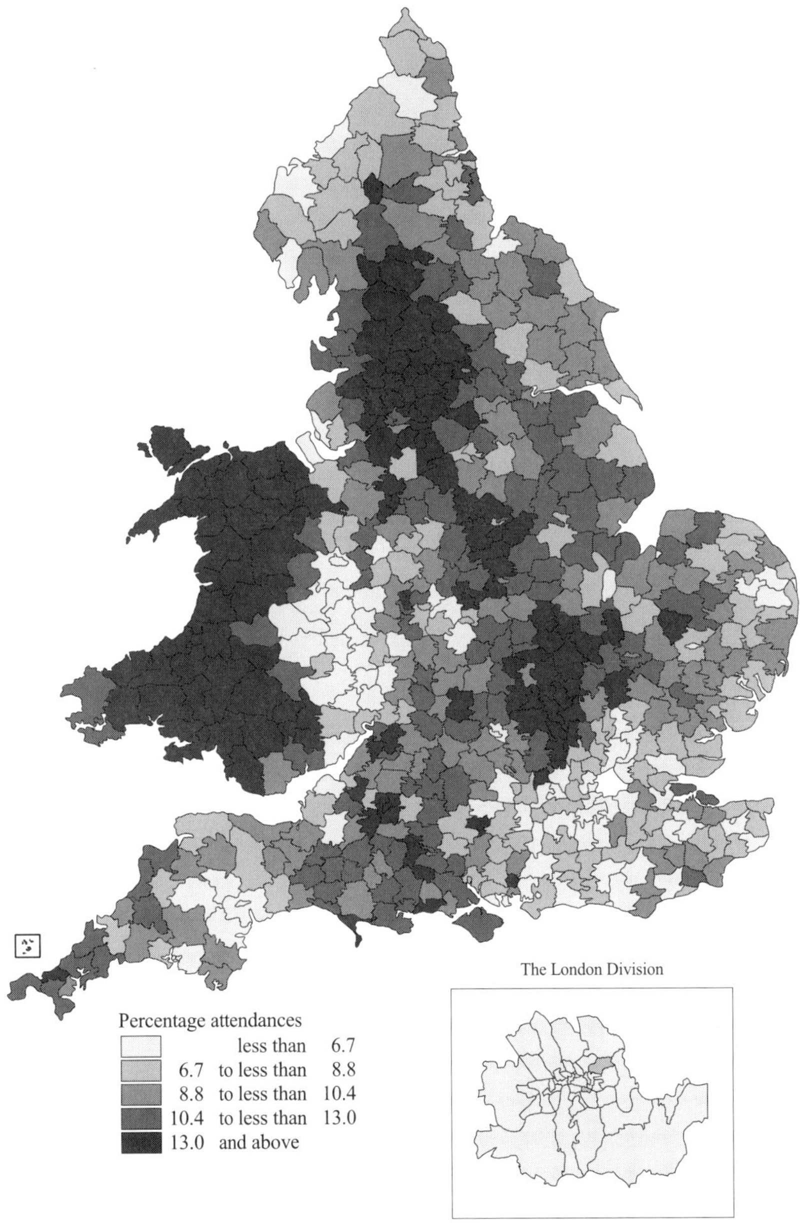

Figure 9.1. Sunday school attendances in 1851 as a percentage of registration-district population

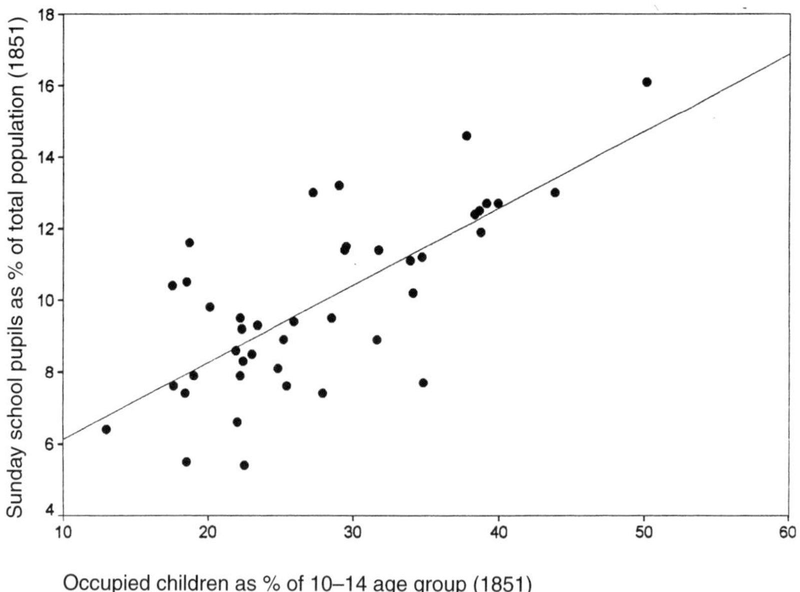

Figure 9.2. Sunday school enrolment and child labour in 1851

1851.[77] Buckinghamshire shared similar characteristics. The three framework-knitting east Midland counties (Leicestershire, Derbyshire and Nottinghamshire) also all had high Sunday school enrolment, which appears to have gone hand-in-glove with their high dependence upon child labour in certain work processes of this trade.

In very many areas and industries, child workers resorted widely to Sunday school education. This was true, for example, in the weaving, framework-knitting, and dyeing trades, where children worked and had neither time nor money for any other schooling.[78] It was especially so in some manufacturing towns.[79] A *Morning Chronicle*

[77] *Ibid.*, p. 49. On child labour in the straw-plait and lace industries, see A. J. Tansley, 'On the straw plait trade', *Journal of the Society of Arts*, 9 (21 December 1860); P. Horn, *The Victorian Country Child* (1974, Stroud, 1990 edn), pp. 126–7; P. Horn, 'Child workers in the pillow lace and straw plait trades of Victorian Buckinghamshire and Bedfordshire', *Historical Journal*, 17 (1974); D. H. Kennett, 'Lacemaking by Bedfordshire paupers in the late eighteenth century', *Textile History*, 5 (1974); Smelser, *Social Paralysis*, p. 258.

[78] Laqueur, *Religion and Respectability*, p. 152; Stephens, *Education, Literacy and Society*, p. 156; Smelser, *Social Paralysis*, p. 258.

[79] Griffith, *Nationality in the Sunday School Movement*, pp. 47–8; *Education Census, 1851*, pp. 49–50.

reporter interviewed Sunday school children in Manchester in 1849–50, and found that they worked during the week in weaving or painting, in shops, warehouses, foundries, engine shops, brickyards or stoneyards, in factories or in the fields.[80] Parents in places like Oldham talked of Sunday schools as '*the* schools', so reliant were their children upon them.[81] Child labour in the cotton manufacturing town of Stockport produced the largest Sunday school in the world.[82] In the potteries, and the Macclesfield silk mills, such education accompanied child employment.[83] In some areas, children employed in 'manufactories' were given preference as to Sunday school admission.[84] Similarly, the lack of weekly education in Merthyr Tydfil was said by the *Morning Chronicle* correspondent to engender Sunday schools.[85] Miners were blamed for neglecting child education, but they had no objection to Sunday schools because these did not interfere with children working.[86] Where there was relatively little child labour, as in Liverpool, Sunday schools were less conspicuous.[87] Examples of this relationship between Sunday schooling and child weekly labour can be extended considerably, adding regional and occupational detail to the quantitative relationship shown in figure 9.2.

As well as being associated with child labour, Sunday school pupils as a percentage of the population (1851) were correlated with a number of other variables at county level. Among these variables, the presence of dissent,[88] the total Methodist index of attendances in 1851 ($r=0.572$), the county total index of attendances for all denominations in 1851, and a high incidence of marriages under 21 years of age

80 Ginswick, *Labour and the Poor, vol. 1: Lancashire, Cheshire, Yorkshire*, pp. 70–4; or see Wadsworth, 'First Manchester Sunday schools', pp. 106–9. Some Sunday schools were even held in factories.

81 Stephens, *Education, Literacy and Society*, p. 93.

82 M. Dick, 'Urban growth and the social role of the Stockport Sunday school, c. 1784–1833', in J. Ferguson (ed.), *Christianity, Society and Education: Robert Raikes, Past, Present and Future* (1981), p. 54. Sunday schools were also advocated in Glasgow (in 1787) to educate cotton 'apprentices' on their only day of rest. C. G. Brown, *The Social History of Religion in Scotland since 1730* (1987), p. 131.

83 Smith, *English Elementary Education*, p. 64.

84 Cliff, *Rise and Development of the Sunday School Movement*, p. 35, citing 'Rules and Orders' for Sunday schools in Birmingham, 1784.

85 Ginswick, *Labour and the Poor*, vol. 3, p. 74.

86 Stephens, *Education, Literacy and Society*, pp. 56, 156.

87 *Ibid.*, p. 93.

88 A ranked variable was used of the percentage of total sittings which were dissenting in 1851, and another of Protestant dissenters as a percentage of the population present at the most numerously attended service on Census Sunday.

(r=0.612) are conspicuous.[89] The Sunday school measure was negatively correlated with domestic servants per 1,000 of the 1841 population (r=−0.637), a variable sometimes taken as a measure of the presence of middle-class households. (In all of these paired correlations, p=.000.) The measure for Sunday school pupils was also positively associated with illiteracy (r=0.465, p=.002). This was an indication, not so much of the ineffectiveness of the schooling they provided, but rather of the fact that weekly education was lacking.[90] A slight association existed between the percentage of males aged over twenty in manufacturing employment and Sunday school pupils (r =0.281, p=.071). A weak negative relationship also existed between Sunday school pupils and day school pupils as a percentage of the population (r=−0.199, p=.206).[91]

These and other county variables were also studied with multiple regression, a method that takes account of every variable in the equation. The conclusions highlighted child employment, the total index

[89] Using 1844 data, of percentages of such marriages above or below the national average. (See note 92 below.)

[90] This is a striking result which was also checked with registration-district data from the *Annual Report of the Registrar General of Births, Deaths, and Marriages in England* (London, 1855), pp. 6–25, for 1851: 'Total marriages and signed the marriage register with marks', men and women. At that registration-district level, the percentage illiterate in 1851 was again positively correlated with the variable 'all pupils attending Sunday schools on 30 March 1851 (as a percentage of registration-district population)'. The results were almost identical to those at county level. In England the Pearson coefficient was 0.455 (sig. at .001). In Wales it was 0.345 (sig. at .05). Across both countries combined, the coefficient was 0.487 (sig. at .001). By comparison, the variable 'all pupils attending at day schools on 31 March 1851 (as a percentage of registration-district population)' was negatively correlated with illiteracy (measured as above), the respective coefficients being −0.285, −0.274, and −0.374.

Many regional examples could be given of this relationship between child labour, illiteracy and Sunday schools. For example, east midland framework-knitters were often illiterate, their reliance on child and family labour hindering child education during the week. M. Palmer, *Framework Knitting* (1984, 1990 edn), p. 20; Stephens, *Education, Literacy and Society*, p. 40. It is clear from the Religious Census returns for the framework-knitting parishes that this induced a dependency upon (often dissenting) Sunday schools.

[91] The 1851 Education Census thought that Sunday scholars were most common where day school education was lacking, e.g., in Wales, Lancashire and Yorkshire. *Education Census, 1851*, p. 88. The Spearman correlation coefficient between the indexes of Sunday school attendances and day school attendances at registration-district level (England and Wales) is negative, at −0.218 (p = .000). (Day school data are from *Education Census, 1851*, pp. 234–74, column headed 'Day schools. In all the schools. Attending at the schools on March 31, 1851. Both sexes'. Sunday school data are from *ibid.*, and see my note 74. On day schools, see also my note 90.)

Table 9.1. *English county-level analysis of the determinants of Sunday school pupils as a percentage of total population on census day, 1851 (stepwise multiple regression)*

Multiple R	0.896
R square	0.802
Adjusted R square	0.779
Standard error	1.177

Analysis of variance

	DF	Sum of squares	Mean square
Regression	4	191.271	47.818
Residual	34	47.098	1.385

F = 34.519 Signif. F = .0000

Variable	B	SE B	Beta	T	Sig. T
totalia	0.084	0.019	0.544	4.418	.0001
wages50	0.293	0.091	0.285	3.201	.0030
childocc	0.163	0.028	0.553	5.828	.0000
reliefpc	−0.141	0.065	−0.252	−2.159	.0380
(constant)	−1.317	1.493	–	−0.882	.3838

of religious attendances across all denominations, wage levels in 1850, and *per capita* poor relief as explanatory variables. Table 9.1 gives the results for these variables, selected out of a much wider range of variables by stepwise regression. The R square value indicates that 80 per cent of the Sunday school measure is explained by these four factors alone. It is worth noting that child employment ('childocc') had even higher explanatory significance than the overall index of religious attendances ('totalia'). (In parish-level analyses of this and related subjects, one rarely finds that an economic variable like this has greater explanatory power than the cultural variables.) There was also a clear association of the Sunday school measure with high wages and low levels of *per capita* poor relief.[92]

92 Fifteen different socio-economic variables were used in these correlation and multiple regression analyses. Only those accepted into the equation by the SPSS default criteria are shown here. The Sunday school variable used data from Stephens, *Education, Literacy and Society*, p. 352. The variable 'childocc' was of children aged between 10 and 14, returned as occupied in 1851. (*Ibid.*, p. 319.) *Per-capita* relief ('reliefpc') is for 1831, and was taken from M. Blaug, 'The myth of the old poor law', reprinted in M. W. Flinn and T. C. Smout (eds.), *Essays in Social History* (Oxford, 1974), p. 145. 'Wages50'

By taking the excess of Sunday school pupils over day school pupils as a variable to be explained,[93] a comparable picture emerges. This measure, in particular, was even more strongly correlated with child employment ($r=0.792$, $p=.000$). It was also correlated with a relatively high incidence of early marriage ($r=0.551$, $p=.000$), with illiteracy ($r=0.631$, $p=.000$), with the total Methodist index of attendances ($r=0.548$, $p=.000$), with the total index of religious attendances for all denominations ($r=0.477$, $p=.001$), and slightly less strongly with mining and manufacturing employment. It seems to have been largely unrelated to the strength of the Church of England, illegitimacy, and most of my other county variables.

The broad conclusions therefore are clear. Sunday school pupils at the county level were very strongly related to the incidence of child employment, for the most part seemingly in manufacturing, broadly defined. They were also associated to a significant extent with a general high level of religious attendance, relatively high wages and the low *per capita* relief costs of the midlands and northern counties.[94] Regional dissenting strength, above average illiteracy and early marriage were also features of counties in which Sunday schools were strongly established.

Denominations and Sunday schools in the parishes

Such firm generalisations can be made by using county-level data, but the analytical potential of those data is inevitably limited. Other

Footnote 92 (*cont.*)
was of weekly money wages for agricultural workers in 1850, from Blaug, 'Myth of the old poor law', pp. 147–50, i.e. from James Caird, as used by A. L. Bowley in his 'The statistics of wages in the United Kingdom during the last hundred years', pt. 1, 'Agricultural wages', *Journal of the Royal Statistical Society*, 61 (December, 1898). Other county-level variables mentioned here and in the preceding paragraphs were from Stephens, *Education, Literacy and Society*, pp. 317, 350, 359–61.

93 That is, Sunday school pupils as a percentage of the total population in 1851 *minus* day school pupils as a percentage of the total population in 1851.

94 High poor-relief costs were a feature of the southern agricultural counties in the early–mid nineteenth century, associated with a decline of farm service and consequent juvenile unemployment, surplus labour problems in agriculture, a frequent lack of alternative work, and in some regions with de-industrialisation. In other words, these were all circumstances not favourable to high reliance on child labour, and thus not conducive to the success of Sunday schools. See K. D. M. Snell, *Annals of the Labouring Poor: Social Change and Agrarian England, 1660–1900* (Cambridge, 1985), chs. 1–4.

limitations have existed until now for the parish data on Sunday schools. Laqueur commented that 'while data on enrolment are available for individual parishes, commensurate material for other variables is not readily accessible at the local level'.[95] This situation can now be redressed with the socio-economic, religious and Sunday school data created as part of the huge datasets for the 2,443 parishes. These support the county analyses and can provide more detailed insight into the contexts in which these schools flourished. They also make it possible to pursue and refine questions about how integrated within working-class communities Sunday schools really were.

The parish data were computed to provide Sunday school indexes of maximum attendance, based on the highest school attendance figure for each denomination on Census Sunday. Table 9.2 reveals how the different denominations performed in each county in respect of their Sunday schools. It gives the total maximum-figure Sunday school attendance for each denomination, expressed as a percentage of the total maximum-figure Sunday school attendance for all denominations. Only the most prominent denominations have been shown.

As table 9.2 demonstrates, the Welsh Calvinistic Methodists commanded nearly 60 per cent of the total Sunday school attendance for Anglesey and Caernarvonshire. They also did well in Cardiganshire. At the other extreme of the cultural–religious divide, the Anglican Church had nearly 70 per cent of school attendance in Dorset, and over 50 per cent in Sussex, Suffolk, Rutland, Cambridgeshire, Leicestershire and the East Riding. It was almost insignificant in the northern Welsh counties and very weak in Cardiganshire and Monmouthshire, but it amassed high figures nevertheless in all the English counties, even the industrialising ones.

The Welsh phenomenon aside, none of the other major denominations came anywhere near the Anglican Church, even when all of the Baptists are grouped together.[96] The overall figure for the Anglican Church, 43.6 per cent, lowered by the Welsh experience, was still exceptionally high. The other denominations were very minor by comparison. It is worth observing just how dominant the 'establishment' Sunday schools were in England. For the most part these schools were organised by the Anglican clergy, their families and

[95] Laqueur, *Religion and Respectability*, p. 54.

[96] There were high numbers of unspecified Baptists in the enumerators' returns, and so the Baptists have been grouped together for this analysis.

Table 9.2. *Total maximum-figure Sunday school attendance for selected denominations, as a percentage of total maximum-figure Sunday school attendance for all denominations, in each county*

	Church of England	Independents	Total Baptists	Wesleyan Methodists	Primitive Methodists	Welsh Calvinistic Methodists
Ang.	5.5	17.0	7.1	9.5	0.0	58.8
Beds.	49.2	9.1	14.1	24.4	2.3	0.0
Caerns.	5.4	14.8	8.0	11.1	0.0	59.5
Cambs.	56.8	6.7	15.0	14.1	4.8	0.0
Cards.	18.1	22.0	16.7	1.0	0.0	36.5
Derbs.	40.4	8.7	7.5	21.8	11.6	0.0
Dors.	69.7	13.8	2.1	11.6	1.1	0.0
Lancs.	41.2	9.5	4.8	15.5	4.4	1.2
Leics.	53.1	8.6	17.9	11.6	4.7	0.0
Mon.	22.9	24.4	23.8	13.0	5.3	8.7
N'umb.	42.2	5.3	3.0	1.2	9.4	0.0
Rut.	64.2	10.9	9.5	9.6	1.8	0.0
Suff.	64.5	13.8	14.1	4.7	2.1	0.0
Suss.	67.8	11.3	4.8	10.0	1.1	0.0
York, E. Rid.	50.2	8.1	2.2	26.3	7.5	0.0
Total	43.6	11.2	8.6	13.5	4.2	6.5

others closely connected with them (such as local landed proprietors). Primitive Methodism, perhaps the most 'proletarian' denomination, while clearly making a small impression in Derbyshire or Northumberland, was by comparison negligible as a provider of Sunday school education. A somewhat stronger case could be made for the Independents and the Wesleyan Methodists but, again, their efforts in England were fairly limited compared with those of the Anglican Church. At first glance, therefore, aggregate results like these might raise questions about just how 'working-class' the organisation of Sunday schools really was.

This is clearly a matter worth pursuing further. Table 9.3 gives the percentage of parishes with churches or chapels for each denomination which were providing *any* Sunday school education on Census Sunday in 1851. The calculations have been performed on a parish basis, for every parish indicating such data, across all fifteen counties. The table supplies, for each denomination, the number of parishes where the denomination had Sunday schools, the number of parishes with the denomination, and the percentage of parishes where the respective places of worship had Sunday school education.[97]

The results of table 9.3 confirm those of table 9.2. Of the 2,323 parishes in which the Anglican Church had a place of worship, 1,679 (72.3 per cent) had Anglican Sunday schools. This is a high figure and contrary to many suppositions in the secondary literature. Only the Welsh Calvinistic Methodists (89.0 per cent), the Wesleyan Methodist New Connexion (77.1 per cent), the Baptist New Connexion (83.3 per cent), the Moravians (100 per cent),[98] the Countess of Huntingdon's Connexion (100 per cent) and the New Church (86.7 per cent) exceeded this percentage, and, of these, the last four were numerically very small indeed. The Wesleyan Methodists (i.e. the Original Connexion) fell well below the Anglican Church, as did the large number of unspecified Baptists, the Particular Baptists and the Roman Catholics. The most proletarian denominations – notably the Roman Catholics (by 1851), the Bible Christians, and the Primitive Methodists – were the least likely to supply Sunday school education alongside their other religious provision. The Quakers had a long tradition of attaching little importance to Sunday schools and, indeed, to religious education generally. Their low percentage is therefore not surprising. Quaker Sunday schools were only started from the 1840s.

A further way in which these questions may be raised is to ask how important Sunday schools were for each denomination relative to its maximum religious attendance – in other words, by summing here the denomination's maximum Sunday school attendance, and expressing that figure as a ratio of the denomination's maximum religious attendance in each county. This has been done in table 9.4 for the most important denominations. The higher the ratio, the greater the weight attached by the denomination to education via its Sunday schools.[99]

97 Where a parish had more than one place of worship for any particular denomination, this has been counted as one for these calculations. The same has been done for Sunday schools for each denomination. Some Welsh parishes, for example, had more than one Welsh Calvinistic Methodist chapel. On both counts, the interest here is in the numbers of parishes, not the total number of Sunday schools.

98 The Moravians lived in settlements with schools (for example, Ockbrook, Fullneck), and they placed heavy emphasis on education.

99 This use of maximum religious attendance from the Religious Census differs from the usual practice of taking total attendances, but is clearly best suited for comparison with a similar measure for Sunday schools. The ratios should not be translated into percentages however, because of the problem of multiple religious attendance across morning, afternoon and evening services in 1851.

Table 9.3. *The percentage of denominational churches or chapels (by parish) which had any Sunday schools*

Denomination	Parishes with Sunday schools	Parishes with the denomination	% with Sunday schools
Church of England	1,679	2,323	72.3
Church of Scotland	5	11	45.5
United Presbyterian Synod	10	20	50.0
Presbyterian Church in England	25	44	56.8
Independents	353	522	67.6
General Baptists	59	82	72.0
Particular Baptists	95	177	53.7
New Connexion General Baptists	10	12	83.3
Baptists (unspecified)	178	303	58.7
Society of Friends	3	60	5.0
Unitarians	31	50	62.0
Moravians	4	4	100.0
Wesleyan Methodist	438	786	55.7
Methodist New Connexion	27	35	77.1
Primitive Methodist	157	403	39.0
Bible Christian	4	22	18.2
Wesleyan Methodist Association	54	75	72.0
Independent Methodist	20	30	66.7
Wesleyan Reformers	32	59	54.2
Welsh Calvinistic Methodists	145	163	89.0
Countess of Huntingdon's Connexion	11	11	100.0
New Church	13	15	86.7
Brethren	5	9	55.6
Other Isolated Congregations	28	108	25.9
Roman Catholics	53	106	50.0
Catholic & Apostolic Church	18	31	58.1
Mormons	10	47	21.3

This does not take account of the varying levels of apparent religious indifference in each county, but rather indicates the importance of Sunday school education compared to each denomination's religious strength.

Once again, the Church of England did remarkably well on this measure, despite its very large number of parishes. Its ratio for 2,101 parishes was virtually the same as that of the Independents and

Table 9.4. *Ratios of the total of each denomination's maximum Sunday school attendance to the denomination's maximum religious attendance*

	Church of England		Independents		Total Baptists		Wesleyan Methodists		Primitive Methodists		Welsh Calvinistic Methodists	
		n.		n.		n.		n.		n.		n.
Ang.	0.22	47	0.48	29	0.37	19	0.49	18			0.48	48
Beds.	0.46	112	0.37	18	0.19	42	0.31	68	0.14	17		
Caerns.	0.23	39	0.39	29	0.46	22	0.39	26			0.49	48
Cambs.	0.32	135	0.24	28	0.22	50	0.30	45	0.18	33		
Cards.	0.37	80	0.31	46	0.33	33	0.45	5			0.43	45
Derbs.	0.58	101	0.58	22	0.47	24	0.54	73	0.35	49	0.00	1
Dors.	0.31	248	0.28	49	0.27	13	0.21	80	0.08	34		
Lancs.	0.46	72	0.51	43	0.55	28	0.59	55	0.66	31	0.45	5
Leics.	0.45	210	0.38	38	0.36	65	0.29	100	0.23	46		
Mon.	0.28	95	0.41	26	0.23	36	0.24	30	0.38	13	0.36	16
N'umb.	0.27	82	0.30	13	0.28	11	0.16	9	0.32	25		
Rut.	0.37	52	0.76	5	0.24	10	0.21	18	0.32	1		
Suff.	0.29	423	0.24	76	0.25	74	0.21	64	0.13	55		
Suss.	0.22	253	0.24	54	0.14	41	0.32	51	0.69	3		
York, E. Rid.	0.35	152	0.26	22	0.31	10	0.20	129	0.10	86		
Total	0.37	2,101	0.37	498	0.30	478	0.38	771	0.30	393	0.46	163

Notes: n. = number of parishes in which the denomination was present and had attendances greater than zero.[100]

100 These figures usually differ from those of table 9.3 because of parishes where churches were present, but did not have any attendance registered.

Wesleyans, and exceeded that of the other major denominations, except the Welsh Calvinistic Methodists. In Bedfordshire, Derbyshire, Lancashire and Leicestershire – all counties with high child labour and associated industries – it was notably impressive. Given the frequency of accounts which stress the Anglican Church's inertia or its earlier ideological suspicion of Sunday schools and their educational effects, results like these come as a surprise.[101] The Welsh Calvinistic Methodists, in table 9.4, were also exceptionally strong when considered in this way, particularly in the Welsh-language counties.[102] Among the other findings, those for the Independents and Wesleyans in Derbyshire and Lancashire, and the Primitive Methodists in Lancashire, are striking. That very high Primitive Methodist ratio for Lancashire (0.66) is revealing – for a county whose Sunday schools have attracted considerable attention – but it was very atypical for the denomination more generally. In the agricultural working-class communities which were often associated with this denomination, in Suffolk, Cambridgeshire, Bedfordshire, Dorset and the East Riding, or in the agrarian and industrial outworking villages of Leicestershire, the ratio was very much lower,[103] usually well below even the level of the Anglican Church in Anglesey. Such a distinctive Lancashire experience cannot therefore be generalised.

The local geography of Sunday schools was, of course, overwhelmingly influenced by the location of host denominations, discussed earlier in this book. One way of extending the analysis is through

[101] The early ambivalence of the Church of England to Sunday schools is well covered in Soloway, *Prelates and People*, e.g., pp. 350–3, 355–9, 363–6, 393. Even so, as many as 45 per cent of all Sunday schools in England were Anglican in 1851, and 56 per cent had been Anglican in 1801. See Cliff, *Rise and Development of the Sunday School Movement*, p. 102, and see p. 36: 'Sunday Schools were seen in their early days in many places . . . as almost exclusively Anglican in personnel and control.' See *ibid*., p. 45, on the Anglican desire to control the schools.

[102] The concern of Welsh Calvinistic Methodists to defend their own Sunday schools is frequently documented in Welsh visitation returns. See for example the extended statement by the incumbent of Rhiw: National Library of Wales (Aberystwyth), Diocese of Bangor, B/QA/22, vol. 1 (1814), who complained of their Sunday school, the way in which its timing deliberately affected his services ('very painful to me'), their neglect of his own prayers, creed and commandments, and the way they prevented his own efforts to start a Sunday school. He found that opposing them was 'an arduous task and next to impossibility at the present factious time'. His attitude towards 'sectaries . . . swinish Anabaptists . . . their natural filthiness . . . hoarse in bawling & stiff in jumping', etc., cannot have helped his position.

[103] Sussex is a seeming exception, but as the number indicates, the Primitives were very weak there.

denominational correlations between Sunday school indexes of maximum attendance, and the 1851 religious indexes of total attendances. Denominational attendances usually correlated with the respective Sunday school data, but this was much truer for some denominations than others. The Countess of Huntingdon's Connexion, Welsh Calvinistic Methodists, General Baptists, Independents, the Church of England and Unitarians had relatively high correlations,[104] suggesting that their congregations and the education of their young in Sunday schools were fairly closely interlocked. Many others produced lower coefficients, including the Particular Baptists, United Presbyterian Synod, Wesleyan Methodists, Methodist New Connexion, Independent Methodists, Wesleyan Methodist Association and Wesleyan Reformers. For some denominations, however, there were remarkably weak or even negative associations between their general religious attendances and Sunday school attendance: notably the Roman Catholics, Mormons, Primitive Methodists, Quakers and Bible Christians.[105] There is no simple class explanation for such results, yet, in connection with arguments about the 'working-class' character of Sunday schools, it is worth pointing out that denominations which probably had among the most proletarian adherence showed particularly weak associations between their general religious attendance and their education of Sunday school pupils. This contrasted strongly with certain denominations which probably had more elitist backing and membership.

Landownership and the Sunday schools

These results indicate that the role of middle- or upper-class managed denominations in the Sunday school movement has been significantly underestimated in some of the literature. The importance of the Church of England emerges very clearly, while the denominations usually most associated with working-class cultures by 1851 – for example, post-Famine Roman Catholicism, Primitive Methodism or Bible Christianity – seem to have been less effective in providing

104 Spearman coefficients between 0.390 and 0.809. Correlations were conducted only for parishes where the denominational index of total religious attendances was greater than zero.

105 Spearman coefficients between 0.183 and −0.286, the last three denominations being negative.

Sunday school education. Given these emphases, it is possible that Sunday schools, of whatever denomination, may even have been most effective in parishes of concentrated landownership, rather than in the more 'open' parishes that were often associated with dissent among the working classes, and with more overt occupational and plebeian cultures.[106] If the schools were most successful in so-called 'closed' or estate parishes,[107] where property ownership was narrowly concentrated and where the Anglican Church often had no rivals, it would be necessary to adopt a more paternalistic, elite-coordinated, conception of them.

Such possibilities can be examined by using the index of maximum Sunday school attendance in conjunction with the landownership categories provided for each parish by the *Imperial Gazetteer*.[108] The following tables show mean and median Sunday school indexes of maximum attendance for the major denominational groupings, by landownership category, and the results of statistical tests of significance.[109]

It is clear from tables 9.5–9.8 that the success of Sunday schools when measured in this way, for some of the major denominations, was heavily dependent upon the nature of landownership. The parishes with the most concentrated property ownership, with land owned by one family or in a few hands – that is the 'estate' or 'closed' parishes – usually had the highest Sunday school indexes of attendance. This set them apart from the parishes with more scattered

[106] On the implications of 'open' or 'closed' parishes for the situation of dissent, see in particular A. Everitt, *The Pattern of Rural Dissent: the Nineteenth Century* (Leicester, 1972), and ch. 11 of this book.

[107] This is not the place to rehearse points about parish classifications, but on the issue of 'open' and 'closed' (or estate) parishes, see ch. 11 below; M. A. Havinden, *Estate Villages* (1966); B. A. Holderness, '"Open" and "close" parishes in England in the eighteenth and nineteenth centuries', *Agricultural History Review*, 20 (1972); G. Darley, *Villages of Vision* (1978); D. R. Mills, *Lord and Peasant in Nineteenth-century Britain* (1980); S. Banks, 'Nineteenth-century scandal or twentieth-century model? A new look at "open" and "close" parishes', *Economic History Review*, 2nd ser., 41 (1988).

[108] J. M. Wilson, *The Imperial Gazetteer of England and Wales*, 6 vols. (Edinburgh, n.d., c.1870–2). This source, and its later editions, classified parishes into four groups: with landownership being 'in one hand [or family]', 'in a few hands', 'sub-divided', or 'much sub-divided'. In the absence of other readily accessible national data on parochial landowning at this time, these classifications have been used here. Their reliability is tested and affirmed in appendix E.

[109] Only parishes where the Sunday school indices are greater than zero have been used for these tables; n. = number of parishes.

Table 9.5. *Church of England Sunday school index of maximum attendance, by categories of landownership*

Landownership	mean	median	n.
In one family	20. 3	13.3	53
In a few hands	10.3	8.9	547
Sub-divided	8.3	7.3	202
Much sub-divided	7.4	6.3	269

Notes:
ANOVA: F ratio = 37.8013
F prob. = .0000

ownership, and the differences can be statistically very significant. Table 9.5 shows this for the Church of England's Sunday schools.

If this calculation is performed for only the English counties, the result is even stronger. It is fascinating to note, however, that the equivalent result was not significant for the four Welsh counties when they were analysed alone. In other words, the influence of landownership was exceptionally marked in the English counties, and this points to one of the reasons for the success of Anglican Sunday schools. Local propertied structures which were often characterised by patronage and social controls fostered the greatest success of Sunday schools. Yet in Wales this factor was irrelevant – other cultural or economic considerations underlay the fortunes of the Church of England Sunday schools there.

These results were much less extreme for old dissent taken as a whole, as shown in table 9.6.[110] Separate analyses for the Baptists and Independents show a slight effect, particularly for England. Once again, this influence of landownership on old dissenting Sunday schools was weaker and not significant when one takes Wales separately.

Table 9.7 gives the results for all Methodists, including the Welsh Calvinistic Methodists. Landownership once more had a marked effect on Sunday school attendance. In the parishes of most concentrated ownership the index of attendance was twice as high as in the 'much

[110] 'Old dissent' is taken here as the General Baptists, Particular Baptists, unspecified Baptists, Quakers, Presbyterian Church in England, Unitarians and Independents. The comparable Kruskal–Wallis test gives significant results for this group: chi-square = 16.8; signif. = .0008.

Table 9.6. *Total old dissent Sunday school index of maximum attendance, by categories of landownership*

Landownership	mean	median	n.
In one family	6.2	4.1	3
In a few hands	9.2	7.0	105
Sub-divided	6.8	4.6	44
Much sub-divided	6.6	4.0	102

Notes:
ANOVA: F ratio = 1.1283
F prob. = .3382

Table 9.7. *Total Methodist Sunday school index of maximum attendance, by categories of landownership*

Landownership	mean	median	n.
In one family	13.5	9.0	5
In a few hands	12.2	8.0	162
Sub-divided	8.7	5.8	82
Much sub-divided	6.7	4.3	134

Notes:
ANOVA: F ratio = 7.8594
F prob. = .0000

sub-divided' ones. That effect was much less marked for Wales alone. Similar results to these were obtained for the Wesleyan Methodists separately. However, it is worth observing that the Primitive Methodist Sunday school attendance was largely independent of landownership. For a denomination which appealed to 'the ruder of the lower class', as Kendall put it, this result is what one might anticipate.[111]

The other leading denomination which did not share these features was Welsh Calvinistic Methodism. Situated almost entirely in Wales, its Sunday school record was largely independent of landownership,

[111] H. B. Kendall, *The Origin and History of the Primitive Methodist Church*, 2 vols. (London, n.d., c.1905), vol. 1, pp. 160–2; J. Obelkevich, *Religion and Rural Society: South Lindsey, 1825–1875* (Oxford, 1976), pp. 220–58. There are insufficient cases to test this hypothesis for the Bible Christians.

Table 9.8. *Welsh Calvinistic Methodist Sunday school index of maximum attendance, by categories of landownership*

Landownership	mean	median	n.
In one family	18.7	18.7	2
In a few hands	19.4	15.5	65
Sub-divided	16.9	16.6	17
Much sub-divided	13.7	7.7	23

Notes:
ANOVA: F ratio = 0.9509
F prob. = .4190

as seen in table 9.8. In this, it was similar to the other denominations when they are analysed only in their Welsh contexts.

These findings are striking. Wales was distinctive and separate from England insofar as the influence of landownership was inconsequential for Sunday schools. Large parishes, frequently scattered settlements and absentee landlords, a tradition of self-government in the Welsh schools as compared with the oligarchic nature of so many English Sunday schools, and the dominance of folk religious traditions not much controlled from above, seem to underlie the Welsh results. They also recall the almost uniform Welsh pattern of figure 9.1. By comparison, English Sunday schools with the highest indexes of attendance tended to be found in local environments of a 'closed' nature, where property ownership was concentrated. Such parishes were very commonly marked by paternalism and social controls, however the latter might be defined. It seems as if the local structures of property-holding and related features of the parish economy had a primary effect on the comprehensiveness of Sunday schooling, almost regardless of the denomination responsible. The relationship was strongest for the Church of England, as might be anticipated, but it was also true of other denominations in England. These findings highlight the social controls, paternalism, and related constraints which operated in the more 'closed' parishes and had themselves influenced the siting of denominations.[112] The authorities of those parishes accepted, and took advantage of, the possibilities offered by Sunday

[112] See chapter 11, and Everitt, *Pattern of Rural Dissent*.

Table 9.9. *Total denominational Sunday school maximum attendance, by categories of landownership*

Landownership	mean	median	n.
In one family	52.7	30.0	55
In a few hands	95.1	50.0	650
Sub-divided	119.7	68.0	231
Much sub-divided	267.8	108.5	306

Notes
ANOVA: F ratio = 15.4581
F prob. = .0000

schools in such a way as to achieve higher attendances relative to population than was the case in other, more 'open', parishes. Where Sunday school recruitment was highest relative to population, therefore, it seems unlikely that these schools were autonomous cultural agencies of an emerging 'working class'. Nor were they most effective (when judged in this way) in the less controlled, more socially variegated, populous and 'open' parishes, where less deferential working-class cultures were most evident. In Wales they were clearly more independent of upper- or middle-class influence (and the same was true generally of the Primitive Methodists); however, as a rule, such social influences from above had a strong effect on indexes of Sunday school attendance in England.

Much depends upon the measures that are used. These calculations all use indexes of attendance to measure the success of Sunday schools, extending the conventional measures that historians derive from the 1851 Religious Census. These indexes take account of the size of populations, relating Sunday school pupils to parish populations. It would normally be thought most appropriate to assess the schools in such a way. However, the parishes of concentrated landownership were, of course, also the least populous and, perhaps by this token, the easiest in which to achieve high levels of Sunday school attendance. If one looks at the total attendances *alone*, without calculating any index of attendance, then the patterns shown here change. The *total numbers* of Sunday school pupils tended to be highest in parishes of much sub-divided property and lowest in those of concentrated property. Table 9.9 gives an overall analysis of this, using simply the total maximum Sunday school attendance for all denominations.

Historians would probably prefer to use indexes of attendance in making their arguments, for these relate school attendance to the size of population. They need, however, to be aware that an argument could still be made which stressed that the largest numbers of Sunday scholars were in the most sub-divided parishes, and those included most towns. Much of the discussion about Sunday schools derives, often in an unappreciated way, from various historians adopting dissimilar notions of how and why they were 'successful'. Rather different points about social context (to those made here) would follow if one concentrated on absolute numbers *per se*, for, although indexes of attendance were lowest in the more sub-divided parishes, the total numbers educated in them were nevertheless very substantial. And the vast majority of these pupils were certainly working class.

Clerical livings and Sunday schools

Critics of the Church in the early nineteenth century often attacked the consequences of a shortage of clerical housing and associated non-residency. The different status of livings (whether perpetual curacies, vicarages or rectories) was also sometimes blamed for clerical inadequacies. The provision of a well-attended Sunday school by the Anglican Church was a very good indication of the effectiveness of a clergyman, and of his preparedness to go beyond the 59th canon. I therefore examined the implications for Sunday school attendance of the type of living and whether it included habitable accommodation.[113] The latter made no impression at all on Anglican Sunday school attendance; however, there was a tendency for Anglican indexes of maximum Sunday school attendance to be highest in the rectories (the most valuable livings), and rather lower in the vicarages and perpetual curacies.[114] The Anglican types of livings had little significant implication for any other denomination's Sunday school attendance, with the exception of the Welsh Calvinistic Methodists, whose Sunday schools were most successful where there were perpetual curacies – where the Church of England livings were lowest in value, and where it was likely to have been weakest. Here, as in other

[113] Types and values of livings, and whether they contained habitable accommodation, were obtained for parishes from Wilson, *Imperial Gazetteer*.

[114] Using the Kruskal–Wallis test, mean ranks were as follows: perpetual curacies (708), vicarages (675), rectories (880); chi-sq. = 74.2, signif. = .0000.

regards, this most Welsh denomination presented an opposing aspect to the Anglican Church, challenging or reciprocating it culturally, and taking advantage of its regional deficiencies and its failure to gain popularity in many Welsh regions.

Sunday schools and local socio-economic contexts

To examine the effect of other local conditions on Sunday schools, I conducted multiple regression tests with cultural and socio-economic variables most likely to have influenced the schools. For every denomination, taken separately, regressions were run on those parishes where the denomination had a Sunday school, to see which variables were associated with the strongest Sunday school attendance. In each case the Sunday school index of maximum attendance was used as the variable to be explained. The possible explanatory variables were wide-ranging. They included all the 1831 census occupational data, 1851 parish acreages, and derived variables such as mean household size in 1851, population growth rates (1811–51), and density of population.[115] For each denomination, regressions were run first with the socio-economic data alone and, secondly, with the addition of the relevant denomination's index of total religious attendances. The addition of this cultural variable has the effect of raising the R square value, for in almost every case it was the single most important explanatory factor. It did not usually seriously distort the contribution of the other socio-economic variables in the equations.

The broadest analysis is that of table 9.10, where all the Sunday schools' maximum attendances are combined into one index, for all parishes with such schools in the fifteen counties. Every denomina-

[115] Larger regressions were also conducted with parochial variables such as the value of the clerical living, property values, poor relief, and derived measures like the value of property *per capita*, the ratio of the value of the living to total property values, the ratio of the value of the living to the population size, and so on. The parishes with such data are a fairly large subset of the whole. While some very interesting results were obtained, the effect was to reduce the size of the Sunday school denominational data being used for each denomination, as multiple regression deselects cases on a 'listwise' basis (i.e., if one variable is missing for a parish, the entire parish is dropped from the equation). When one selects for analysis only those parishes where a particular denomination had a Sunday school, the dataset is cut further, and this can produce somewhat illusory results based on small numbers. Therefore, the concentration here is on the results for the fullest possible number of parishes, using data only from the religious, demographic and occupational censuses. Landownership was not used because of the nature of the *Imperial Gazetteer* evidence, and, at parish level, there is no usable data on child employment, although proxies exist.

Table 9.10. *Parish-level analysis of the total maximum Sunday school index of attendance, for all denominations combined (stepwise multiple regression)*

Multiple R	0.562
R square	0.316
Adjusted R square	0.312
Standard error	7.093

Analysis of variance

	DF	Sum of squares	Mean square
Regression	7	29272.6	4181.8
Residual	1258	63286.7	50.3

F = 83.125 Signif. F = .0000

Variable	B	SE B	Beta	T	Sig. T
mhs51	−0.775	0.302	−0.062	−2.562	.0105
retpop	−0.380	0 .072	−0.125	−5.253	.0000
manpop	0.378	0.076	0.119	4.972	.0000
msepop	0.827	0.166	0.120	4.968	.0000
acre51	−8.136 −05	2.817 −05	−0.071	−2.888	.0039
ocnpop	0.617	0.128	0.115	4.809	.0000
ita	0.129	0.007	0.475	19.524	.0000
(constant)	8.981	1.708		5.258	.0000

tion is used and the results allow generalisations about the overall characteristics of the Sunday school movement.[116] The R square value indicates that the variables explain 32 per cent of the parochial variance in Sunday schools. This is fairly low, but then this regression combines a huge localised variety of denominational experience.

As would be expected, Sunday schools were strongest in the parishes with the highest indexes of total religious attendance (the variable named 'ita' in table 9.10). But beyond this variable, which was by far the most prominent, those parishes with concentrations of agricultural 'occupiers not employing labourers' ('ocnpop') tended to make use of these schools,[117] as did parishes with relatively high

[116] Variables rejected by stepwise regression are not shown here.

[117] The agricultural classification is from the 1831 census, contrasted there with 'occupiers employing labourers'. That contrast is an important regional indicator of farming structures. The smaller family farms (as in many western or northern pastoral regions) were least likely to employ labourers. The variable I have used is defined as occupiers not employing labour in 1831, expressed as a percentage of parish population.

dependence upon male servants ('msepop').[118] Both of these point to child labour. In the former, the farming occupiers were clearly dependent upon their own families for workers and released their children for education on Sundays rather than during the week. In the latter, the servants were usually below marriageable age and under 'paternalistic' control in their households of employment. Their limited education took place on Sunday, usually in the local Sunday school of the employer's religious denomination. The role of manufacturing employment ('manpop'), while a little vague (for the 1831 census category covered a diversity of 'manufacturing'), also points to child employment as the underpinning factor.[119] It is clear that parishes of large acreage ('acre51') tended to restrict the likelihood of children attending Sunday schools. This was found in all denominational regressions except those for the Unitarians and the Presbyterian Church in England. Employment in retail trade and handicraft ('retpop') appears not to have been a pointer to Sunday schools; perhaps it required less child labour than more directly productive occupations. The small negative influence of mean household size ('mhs51') is hard to explain, for this measure was surprisingly independent of almost all other variables.[120]

Each denomination's Sunday school figures were also analysed separately, from which a number of points can be summarised. For many denominations, an additional explanatory variable was the incidence of agricultural 'occupiers employing labour' in the parish population. This was so for the Baptists, Independents, for all of old dissent combined, for the Wesleyan Methodists, Primitives, Wesleyan Methodist Association, total Methodists in England (but not in Wales), and the effect was very strong indeed for the Methodist New Connexion and the Countess of Huntingdon's followers. Given the influence of occupiers *not* employing labourers on overall Sunday school attendance, as seen above, it would appear that the prevalence of occupiers of either sort was influential, as both required children to work their land. Among the other variables of interest, manufacturing employment had a strong effect on the combined Methodists in

[118] This variable is of male servants in 1831 as a percentage of the 1831 parish population.

[119] The variable is defined as the percentage of the parish population employed in manufacture or in making manufacturing machinery.

[120] 'Mean household size' is defined here as the 1851 parish population divided by the number of habitable houses.

England, as did female servants as a percentage of population. The picture for the Church of England was one in which population growth rates, size of parish, and retail or handicraft employment, had a negative influence on Sunday school attendance, while manufacturing employment, the proportion of labourers in the population and, particularly, the incidence of male servants all had a positive influence. Once more, child labour and dependency employment relationships are indicated as underpinning Sunday schools.

When Wales is analysed in its own right, some important conclusions emerge. Not only were Welsh Sunday schools almost unique in being independent of landowning structures but, beyond that, Welsh Sunday school attendance, taking all denominations into account, was also more independent of the other socio-economic variables than was the case for denominations in England. There was clearly some association between old dissenting Sunday schools and occupiers employing labour in Wales. And the parochial sex ratio had a negative effect on Sunday school attendance in Wales – that is, Welsh Sunday school measures tended to be higher where females outnumbered males.[121] But, whatever the denominational grouping analysed in the Welsh counties – whether all denominations combined, or total Welsh dissent, or all Methodists in Wales, or the Welsh Calvinistic Methodists alone – usually the only significant variables explaining Sunday school attendance were the respective religious attendances. The stepwise regression procedures, when applied to the Welsh parish Sunday school data, rejected almost all possible explanatory variables, many of which had been readily accepted into equivalent regression equations for the English parishes.[122] Welsh religious cultures would seem to have been more autonomous of socio-economic conditions

[121] This finding may be indicative of religious and educational proclivities among many Welsh women; but one needs to note that women outnumbered men in many Welsh small-farm pastoral parishes. Women also comprised 18% of farm occupiers in Wales, compared to only 7% in England. (J. Rhys and D. Brynmor-Jones, *The Welsh People* (1923, New York, 1969 edn), p. 434, using 1861 data for farmers and graziers.) The importance of female work on such farms was probably also associated with considerable child labour, with its implications for Sunday schools. (High female participation rates often coincided with similar rates for children.) Men were more prone than women to migrate to the Welsh areas of heavy industry, where there was less work for women and children, but they took their religious culture and faith in Sunday schools with them.

[122] A number of further tests, involving much smaller samples of the English data, suggested that this was not an effect of differential data sizes between the two countries.

than their equivalents in England, where a greater variety of contributory local factors is striking, varying by denomination and region. (This was borne out in the border contrasts and homogeneity of Welsh districts shown in figure 9.1.) In Wales the strength of the culture, nuanced by its denominational forms, stood independently of almost all local socio-economic determinism. This is a most suggestive contrast between the two countries, albeit one that may not surprise Welsh readers.[123]

Conclusion

My discussion here has concentrated upon explaining Sunday school successes relative to population sizes, but there are precautions to bear in mind. First, there must have been cases where children were sent across parish boundaries for their Sunday school education, and this would have been most conspicuous for some of the dissenting congregations, rather than the Anglican Church. While such mobility of children should not be exaggerated, for they usually returned home intermittently during the day from such schooling – and child mobility was a harassing proposition even in the nineteenth century – it slightly weakens the explanatory effect of the parish variables used here.

Secondly, in my discussion of landownership, mention was made of rival measures that can be used to describe Sunday school success or failure. The larger parishes, usually with sub-divided property ownership, were inevitably the ones where the largest Sunday school numbers were found. These are the places that have received the most attention in Sunday school historiography. I gave many examples of them at the start of this chapter, and such cases could be multiplied considerably, particularly for the Lancashire towns. These centres also had high concentrations of the population in the 'working class'. In this sense, much of the argument made by Laqueur is acceptable in its general emphases.[124] Examples of humble people helping to organise Sunday schools can certainly be found, and not only in the large

123 For a fascinating early discussion of the contrasts between English and Welsh Sunday schools, which much of my analysis bears out, see Griffith, *Nationality in the Sunday School Movement*.

124 One could add that many Chartists supported Sunday schools. D. Thompson, *The Chartists: Popular Politics in the Industrial Revolution* (Aldershot, 1984), p. 260.

towns. There was, for instance, the case of the gardener, George Roberts of Erddig (Denbighshire), who also served on the Parish Council in the 1890s.[125] Laqueur lists many more, although the working-class upbringing of some is open to question.[126] Nor is there any doubt that the large majority of people attending Sunday schools were working class. A concentration on poorer pupils was inevitable, and was sometimes insisted upon in school regulations. Raikes commented on the schools as 'calculated to receive the poorest and most neglected'.[127] It is also probable that many teachers were drawn from the working class, especially after the 1830s;[128] but this cannot be calculated, and many voluntary teachers after the turn of the century came from 'respectable' families. Working-class involvement may have been particularly high in Lancashire, although it is a county that should not be relied upon too heavily.[129] Stockport, Manchester, Whaley Bridge, as with Hanley, Newcastle-under-Lyme and other famous examples elsewhere, were indeed remarkable in fact and documentation; their Congregationalists and Methodists in particular often educating huge numbers of children. However, there were very much wider regional dimensions beyond such towns. Quantitative studies allow us to appreciate this point, and the role of the Church of England, and suggest rather different emphases than those found in much of the literature.

Historians need to define their thoughts and measures precisely if these debates are to progress. Much of my discussion has concentrated on indexes of Sunday school attendance, for it seems best to relate the schools to the size of the local population they might educate. There is little doubt on this score that the most paternalistic or 'closed' parishes – by which is meant here those of consolidated landownership – enlisted the largest proportions of Sunday scholars from their populations. This held true across almost all denominations in England. Accounts of 'social control' (or denominational

125 M. Waterson, *The Servants' Hall: a Domestic History of Erddig* (1980), p. 161.

126 Laqueur, *Religion and Respectability*, pp. 252–4; cf. Dick, 'Myth of the working-class Sunday school', pp. 37–40.

127 Cliff, *Rise and Development of the Sunday School Movement*, p. 38, and see pp. 44–5.

128 Rather later, large numbers of Sunday school teachers in Cardiganshire were said to be farm servants. See D. W. Howell and C. Baber, 'Wales', in F. M. L. Thompson (ed.), *The Cambridge Social History of Britain, 1750–1950, vol. 1, Regions and Communities* (Cambridge, 1990), p. 330.

129 A similar caveat with regard to Laqueur's evidence is made in McLeod, 'Recent studies in Victorian religious history', 247.

control) in these contexts should certainly incorporate many denominational Sunday schools as important agencies in the exercise of such control. And 'social control' itself, as a commonly used term, should perhaps more often give way to the term 'denominational control', for that is often what I am documenting: a form of religious control that operated with varying degrees of effectiveness, harmonising with local economic interests, strongly influenced by matters like landownership and local employment structure.

Perhaps we should not be surprised by such findings. The 'closed' parishes were after all the ones where an insistence on deferential behaviour was most conspicuous, and the Sunday school was a key instrument in promulgating this. In so many parishes the founders of Sunday schools were the local clergy and gentry, who formed committees to collect subscriptions, adopt rules, appoint masters or mistresses, visit the schools to inspect them, audit the accounts, and so on.[130] This kind of initiation and management was easily coordinated in the more 'closed' parishes. In parishes such as these, particularly in England, patrons could easily control teachers and penalise those parents or children who held out against such education, by withdrawing charitable alms, poor relief, employment and other preferential treatment. Child labour could of course be as important in these parishes as in much larger urban ones. Indeed, labour shortages were incidental to parishes that restricted entry, and those shortages could induce more reliance upon child labour, as the reports in the late 1860s on the employment of women and children in agriculture documented for the 'ganging' areas.[131] To make such points is not to undermine the enormous role of the Sunday schools in many larger parishes or towns of a more manufacturing character, where recruitment could be much smaller as a percentage of the eligible population. Certainly there were factory masters and others exercising forms of patronage that were as strong as those found in many rural areas, and those masters could play a major role, as Patrick Joyce and others have pointed out. Clearly there were also many varieties of Sunday school,

[130] In many parts of Dorset, for example Purbeck, the gentry set them up, or encouraged religious societies to do so, one motive being to reduce lawlessness among children and to 'pacify' the poor. M. J. Flame, '"All the common rules of social life": the reconstruction of social and political identities by the Dorset gentry, c.1790–c.1834' (Univ. of Warwick Ph.D. thesis, 1998), pp. 260–1.

[131] *Report on the Employment of Women and Children in Agriculture*, xvii (1867–8); *Report on the Employment of Children, Young Persons, and Women in Agriculture*, xiii (1868–9).

and, even within denominations, these might vary considerably by location. There is still scope, in many places, to see these schools as cultural expressions of the 'working class', serving key roles in its formation, and coming to articulate many of its values, especially if we accept a more gradual and later chronology for the emergence of that class than some arguments have posited.[132]

The prospect for denominations lay partly in the effectiveness of their Sunday schools. In the narrow monetary language of the late twentieth century, this was one way in which they could 'invest' in their young, socialising them in denominational doctrine. The Wesleyan Methodists referred to their Sunday schools as 'the nursery of the church'.[133] Indeed, Sunday schools have been recommended in more recent years as a way of reversing numerical religious decline.[134] There were very many factors influencing a denomination's fortunes, as Currie, Gilbert and Horsley have so admirably shown, but, as they indicated, Sunday school education was a significant consideration in this regard. I have drawn particular attention to the role of the Anglican Church in the Sunday school movement. It is necessary only to remember the arguments of Gilbert and others on the successes of the established church after the mid nineteenth century to appreciate that there was probably a very strong link between its Sunday school efforts and its later fortunes.[135] After all, the Anglicans had captured 42 per cent of all English Sunday school enrolments at this time.[136] Welsh Calvinistic Methodism, certainly among the most impressive of denominations, was also to gain considerable ground. It was intimately involved in the expansion after 1851 of the total numbers speaking Welsh,[137] and

[132] My sympathies here are closer to E. J. Hobsbawm, 'The making of the working class, 1870–1914', in his *Worlds of Labour* (1984), than to Thompson, *Making of the English Working Class*.

[133] B. Crofts (ed.), *At Satan's Throne: the Story of Methodism in Bath over 250 Years* (Bristol, 1990), p. 123.

[134] Gill, *Myth of the Empty Church*, p. 291, suggesting rural subsidies to support mobile Sunday schools in rural areas.

[135] Gilbert, *Religion and Society*, pp. 27–9; Currie, Gilbert and Horsley, *Churches and Churchgoers*, pp. 128–9, 167–8. On falling Sunday school enrolment and church membership in Scotland after 1890, see Brown, *The Social History of Religion*, pp. 85–6.

[136] Cliff, *Rise and Development of the Sunday School Movement*, p. 102. My table 9.2, including four Welsh counties, gives a very similar percentage of 43.6.

[137] The absolute numbers speaking Welsh rose until 1911, although as a *written* language Welsh was probably on the decline by the 1880s. See for example Howell and Baber, 'Wales', pp. 340–1.

in Welsh nationalism and its associated developments. Its subsequent attainments should be seen in the light of its educational efforts demonstrated here. With the benefit of hindsight, it is possible to see that some of the other denominations which were to enjoy further growth were also ones with creditable Sunday school records, like the Methodist New Connexion, the New Church or the Independents. Others, like the Primitive Methodists, seemingly rather unimpressive in Sunday school provision in 1851, were nevertheless to achieve expansion of Sunday scholars after 1851 and large denominational growth as well.[138] Denominations like the Society of Friends or the Latter Day Saints were weak providers of Sunday schooling in 1851, and their indifferent records in the second half of the nineteenth century may be partly a consequence of this.[139]

The main exception to this was Roman Catholicism, which put relatively little effort into its Sunday schools, perhaps because it did not need them. Nor did it need to compete in the Protestant denominational 'market'. It lacked schisms and their competitive effects; for the wayward, there was easy return to the faith; and it differed from many other denominations in its emphasis upon worship. Roman Catholicism in 1851 was clearly distinctive with regard to Sunday school education, given its different traditions, its stress on catechism and the huge accessions it was to gain in England and south Wales from the Irish Famine.

Finally, I return to the issue that has emerged many times in this chapter. From the earliest days, with Raikes' worries in the 1780s about the education of children employed in the Gloucestershire pin factories, child labour seems to have been a very common factor influencing Sunday schools. This was true for diverse regions, whether of handloom or powerloom weaving, other factory work, or framework knitting, the dyeing trades, lace-making, straw-plaiting, much agricultural labour and the family economies of numerous artisan trades. It is worth remembering that Raikes had wanted Sunday schools to be

[138] Currie, Gilbert and Horsley, *Churches and Churchgoers*, p. 189; J. Ritson, *The Romance of Primitive Methodism* (1909), p. 300. There is little doubt that Hugh Bourne had a deep conviction of the need for elementary education among the people he wished to attract to the Primitive Methodist schools.

[139] The decline in the numbers of the Latter Day Saints also owed much to emigration to America. See Currie, Gilbert and Horsley, *Churches and Churchgoers*, for detailed examination of the fluctuations of denominations. This work is invaluable, and its appendices inform the textual comments above.

closely tied to Schools of Industry.[140] It is perhaps a paradox, at least for us today, to think that those areas most exploiting child labour were the ones that leaned most heavily on primarily religious education for their youth. This was clear to many contemporaries, even if they were less critical than Robert Southey. He complained to Lord Ashley that the manufacturers knew 'that a cry would be raised against them if their little white slaves received no instruction; and so they have converted Sunday into a school-day!' Used in such a way, he felt that Sunday schools became 'a compromise between covetousness and hypocrisy'.[141] Such religious education may have had the blessing of those who benefited from child labour, but it was also based on denominational assertiveness: employer and religious sources of power which were by no means always synonymous. It certainly had particular relevance in those areas most associated with the first phases of industrialisation, areas where child employment was often most capitalised upon. The emergence of the Sunday school movement, from around 1780, therefore cannot be divorced from the changing patterns of child employment over this crucial period for the British economy. It was in many ways a facilitating response to the problems created by those patterns of child labour, and to what was probably an intensified work discipline affecting children and teenagers during the working week.[142]

Without entering into the more cynical interpretations, it is possible to draw lessons from this on the role of religion in inculcating values of work discipline in working-class youngsters. This most religious form of education, provided by *both* the Anglican and dissenting Sunday schools, coloured many of the agrarian, cottage-industrial and industrial settlements that relied on child labour in the first half century of the Industrial Revolution. Furthermore, the Anglican Church played a much more dominant role in this provision than is usually acknowledged and, in its schools, 'clerical control was often

140 Cliff, *Rise and Development of the Sunday School Movement*, p. 19.

141 Cited in B. Inglis, *Poverty and the Industrial Revolution* (1971, 1972 edn), p. 448. See also the dismissive views of Frederick Engels on Sunday schools, which he clearly felt were associated with manufacturing environments reliant on child labour: *Condition of the Working Class*, pp. 140–1.

142 On work discipline, to which my argument clearly relates, the key discussion remains E. P. Thompson, 'Time, work-discipline, and industrial capitalism', in Flinn and Smout, *Essays in Social History*. It was originally published in *Past and Present*, 38 (1967).

strict and the syllabus narrow'.[143] These points raise questions for many historical interpretations. When readers reconsider questions of moral and work discipline in agriculture, cottage industry and the factory, when they think of how new technologies and working experiences co-existed with more traditional and establishment religious mentalities, and when they write the larger historical syntheses, they will surely need to pay much more attention to the instruction of the Sunday schools.

[143] McLeod, 'Recent studies in Victorian religious history', 247.

10

Free or appropriated sittings: the Anglican Church in perspective

Looking back over the seventeenth century, Richard Gough organised his *History of Myddle* around the seating plan of its parish church.[1] As he was so well aware, the spatial apportionment of religious seating was of great significance for the local social order, for parochial belonging and for denominational allegiance. It was an issue of considerable symbolic importance, a hinge that seemed to connect the social order with religious belief. The realities of the local social structure were proclaimed through church seating arrangements, preserved as unquestioned within the House of God, plied into hierarchic forms by master carpenters, and sometimes annointed with a varnished finish. Long after Gough had rung down his curtain, the Victorians remained as fascinated as he had been with the internal seating arrangements of churches and chapels. This concern almost rivalled their interest in external architecture, and it focused upon issues like the availability of sittings, pew appropriation, seat rents and incomes, the relation of sittings to liturgy, the symbolic and social connotations of church seating, or historical precedents for such arrangements.

It is hardly surprising therefore that questions about seating were asked in the *Census of Religious Worship*. Those questions are of interest to us today not only because they bear on more general issues of religious provision and accessibility, but also because they bring us into touch with certain aspects of local custom and community rather different from the customs researched by social historians. Because this subject involves religion – rather than the popular rights addressed by the term 'customs in common' – it has not received much attention. And if one looks further, into other areas of study, one would find that architectural histories of ecclesiastical buildings

[1] R. Gough, *History of Myddle* (written in 1701, Harmondsworth, 1981 edn); D. Hey, *An English Rural Community: Myddle under the Tudors and Stuarts* (Leicester, 1974).

– as well as denominational histories – have usually paid little attention to internal questions of seating. Nevertheless, the ways that internal church space was used, especially the contemporary division between 'free' and 'appropriated' sittings, is of much inter-disciplinary interest and warrants consideration here.[2]

Church seating and precedence at communion made a forceful impression on many in the nineteenth century. One of the most vehement testaments to this is the *Autobiography* of Joseph Arch, the agricultural labourers' leader and Methodist lay preacher, who was born in Barford, Warwickshire, in 1826. 'I can remember', he wrote, 'when the squire and the other local magnates used to sit in state in the centre of the aisle. They did not, if you please, like the look of the agricultural labourers. Hodge sat too near them, and even in his Sunday best he was an offence to their eyes. They also objected to Hodge looking at them, so they had curtains put up to hide them from the vulgar gaze. And yet, while all this was going on, while the poor had to bear with such high-handed dealings, people wondered why the Church had lost its hold, and continued to lose its hold, on the labourers in the country districts!' As a small boy Joseph looked through the church keyhole, and saw in succession the squire, then the farmers, then the tradesmen, then the shopkeepers, then the wheelwright, then the blacksmith, and finally the smock-frocked agricultural

[2] Discussions of this subject may be found in R. Burn, *Ecclesiastical Law* (1781 edn); J. M. Neale, *The History of Pews* (Cambridge, 1841); G. H. H. Oliphant, *The Law of Pews in Churches and Chapels* (1853); A. Heales, *The History and Law of Church Seats, or Pews*, 2 vols. (1872); W. J. Hardy, 'Remarks on the history of seat-reservation in churches', *Archaeologia*, 53 (1892), 95–106; H. J. Hodgson, *Steer's Parish Law* (1857 edn), pp. 29–39, 289; H. Miller, *A Guide to Ecclesiastical Law for Churchwardens and Parishioners* (1899 edn), pp. 9–11; K. M. Macmorran, *A Handbook for Churchwardens and Church Councillors* (1921, 1945 edn); W. L. Dale, *The Law of the Parish Church* (1946), pp. 82–6; Viscount Simonds (ed.), *Ecclesiastical Law, Being a Reprint of the Title Ecclesiastical Law from Halsbury's Laws of England: Church Assembly Edition* (3rd edn, 1957), pp. 171–2, 406–9; W. E. Tate, *The Parish Chest* (1946, Cambridge, 1960 edn), pp. 89–92. More recently, see C. G. Brown, 'The costs of pew-renting: church management, church-going and social class in nineteenth-century Glasgow', *Journal of Ecclesiastical History*, 38 (1987), 347–61; M. Aston, 'Segregation in church', in W. J. Sheils and D. Wood (eds.), *Women in the Church* (Oxford, 1990); S. J. D. Green, 'The death of pew-rents, the rise of bazaars, and the end of the traditional political economy of voluntary organizations: the case of the West Riding of Yorkshire, c.1870–1914', *Northern History*, 27 (1991), 198–235; R. Tittler, 'Seats of honor, seats of power: the symbolism of public seating in the English urban community, c.1560–1620', *Albion*, 24 (1992), 205–23; D. Dymond, 'Sitting apart in church', in C. Rawcliffe, R. Virgoe and R. Wilson (eds.), *Counties and Communities: Essays on East Anglian History* (Norwich, 1996), pp. 213–24.

labourers, walk up to the communion rails. Nobody knelt with the latter: 'it was as if they were unclean'. He wrote of how these things 'will be engraved on my mind until the last day of my life . . . a wound which has never been healed . . . I wanted to know why my father was not as good in the eyes of God as the squire'.[3]

A few decades after Arch witnessed this, and shortly before the rise of his National Agricultural Labourers' Union, Thomas Wright – 'a journeyman engineer' – complained that 'if a working man . . . does go into a church, he is put into a free sitting, where he probably finds himself in company with a lot of sniggering children, while any well-dressed individual who enters the church, and who has no greater claim upon it than the working man, is obsequiously shown into a pew. This . . . touches the working man on a tender chord.'[4] Horace Mann summarised a very similar view in his Census 'Report'. 'One chief cause', he wrote, 'of the dislike which the labouring population entertains for religious services is thought to be the maintenance of those distinctions by which they are separated as a class from the class above them. Working men, it is contended, cannot enter our religious structures without having pressed upon their notice some memento of inferiority. The existence of pews and the position of free seats are, it is said, alone sufficient to deter them from our churches;

[3] J. Arch, *The Autobiography of Joseph Arch* (1898, 1966 edn), pp. 25–6. Concern over hygiene was in fact an argument advanced in favour of pew-renting. See Brown, 'Costs of pew-renting', 353–4. In the same year as the Religious Census, John Noake satirised appropriated seating in the following terms:

'O my own darling pue, which might serve for a bed,
With its cushions so soft and its curtains of red;
Of my half waking visions that pue is the theme,
And when sleep seals my eyes, of my pue still I dream.
Foul fall the despoiler, whose ruthless award
Has condemned me to squat, like the poor, on a board,
To be crowded and shov'd, as I sit at my prayers,
As though my devotions could mingle with theirs.'

J. Noake, *The Rambler in Worcestershire* (1851), cited in J. Betjeman (ed.), *English Parish Churches* (1958), p. 38. See also Disraeli's description of the 'vast pew, that occupied half the gallery . . . lined with crimson damask, and furnished with easy chairs' belonging to Lord and Lady Marney, in *Sybil* (1845, Harmondsworth, 1984 edn), pp. 82–3. He juxtaposed their pew against the 'conventicles, which abounded; little plain buildings of pale brick' in which 'the people of Marney took refuge'. *Ibid.*, p. 83.

[4] T. Wright, *Some Habits and Customs of the Working Classes by a Journeyman Engineer* (1867, New York, 1967 edn), p. 245. Apparently 'the Chartists made it a practice to march in procession to churches and occupy their seats before their tenants arrived'. See C. Garbett, *The Claims of the Church of England* (1947, 1948 edn), p. 207.

and religion has thus come to be regarded as a purely middle-class propriety or luxury. It is therefore, by some, proposed to abandon altogether the pew system, and to raise by voluntary contributions the amount now paid as seat rents.'[5]

This socially demarcated seating imprinted itself on some people from a very different class from Arch or Wright, or those Mann was describing. The seventh Earl of Shaftesbury is best known for his political initiatives in other realms of social and economic life, but he also complained about the way working people were treated in Anglican churches. In his impressive speech on the Religious Worship Act Amendment Bill (1857), during the Exeter Hall controversy and debates about the adequacy of the parochial system, he claimed that 'the working-classes, when they attend the services of the Establishment, generally find the churches pewed up in the very aisles . . . they are shut out from places where they can hear and be well accommodated, and not placed on a footing of equality with the rest of the congregation. They see many nooks and corners reserved for the working-classes; they find free seats set apart for them; but they will not occupy these places; they think they are looked upon as a distinct order of beings, and that they are looked down upon and despised. Unless, therefore, you show them proper respect . . . the vast proportion of the labouring population in London, will never be brought to attend the worship of the Establishment'.[6] It is also worth noting here that the provision of free seats did not necessarily safeguard a church from imputations of condescension or patronising attitudes. Rather later Cyril Garbett, the Archbishop of York, reminisced about the hierarchical seating in the Surrey agricultural village of Tongham near Aldershot (Hampshire), where he grew up during the 1870s and 1880s. 'In the morning the "quality" came to church, occupying the front pews; the farmers and small tradespeople sat just behind them; and the Sunday School away at the back. In the evening

5 *Census of Religious Worship*, p. clix. This introduction to the Religious Census was also published as H. Mann, *Sketches of the Religious Denominations of the Present Day* (1854), where the passage cited is on p. 94. Such concern over pew-rents, especially in private chapels, was apparently being voiced by some in the Anglican Church as early as the late seventeenth century. See G. F. A. Best, *Temporal Pillars: Queen Anne's Bounty, the Ecclesiastical Commissioners, and the Church of England* (Cambridge, 1964), p. 15.

6 *Hansard's Parliamentary Debates*, CXLVIII (8 December, 1857), 329; J. Wesley Bready, *Lord Shaftesbury and Social-Industrial Progress* (1926), p. 30; G. Battiscombe, *Shaftesbury: a Biography of the Seventh Earl, 1801–1885* (1974), p. 252.

these places, with the exception of the front pews, were taken by the servants and the villagers; at the last stroke of the bell a crowd of lads clattered in and rather noisily filled the back seats.'[7]

Such contemporary remarks are encompassing in their social derivation. The 1851 *Census of Religious Worship* figures on the extent of seat appropriation are staggering, and confirm the reality of this phenomenon. There were 5,407,968 appropriated sittings across all denominations recorded on Census Sunday: 53 per cent of all sittings.[8] Horace Mann estimated that there were 10,427,609 people in England and Wales who were able to attend divine service, that is, who were not absent 'of necessity'.[9] If one assumes that those who could not attend services did not appropriate sittings, it would therefore appear that of those who were able to attend services, 52 per cent must have had access to a seat that was appropriated to them in some way. This must be a low estimate, for many who were able to attend services in fact never did so, although perhaps their decision was influenced by seating arrangements.[10] Another way to think about this would be to take Mann's (very improvised) estimate of the numbers of separate attendants at some service on Census Sunday (7,261,032),[11] and make the forced assumption that all those who had appropriated a seat actually sat in it on that important day. (Seat appropriation was, to a denominationally varied extent, a measure of numbers committed to the support of a church.) This would imply that 74 per cent of all separate attendants had access to an appropriated seat. These are very rough calculations, to which exceptions can readily be made. Yet they do demonstrate a contrast with late twentieth-century religious practice that is quite phenomenal. The mid nineteenth-century figures suggest a sweeping extension of the principles of private or rented property

7 Garbett, *Claims of the Church of England*, p. 211.

8 *Census of Religious Worship*, p. cxxxv. There were a total of 10,212,563 free and appropriated sittings recorded in 1851. *Ibid.*, p. cxlviii, cf. p. clxxi.

9 This was 58 per cent of the 1851 population. Mann discounted young children, the sick or debilitated, the very aged, those engaged in household duties, transport workers and the like in making this rough estimate. It is fair to assume that such persons would rarely have appropriated seats. The 1851 total population was 17,927,609. Mann discounted 7,500,000 persons as absent from worship 'of necessity'. *Census of Religious Worship*, pp. cxx–cxxi.

10 Mann estimated that 5,288,294 people able to attend religious services neglected to do so on Census Sunday. *Census of Religious Worship*, p. cliii. Habitual non-attenders were an unknown but probably quite high proportion of these.

11 *Census of Religious Worship*, p. clii.

into these material aspects of religious conduct.[12] They show just how important appropriated seating was.

The contemporary remarks I have cited, and these gross figures from the Religious Census, invite us first to delve into the history and conditions regulating sittings. The evidence suggests that pews and seats in church naves were frequent in the fifteenth century, and probably much earlier too. One view is that fixed seats were uncommon in churches and cathedrals until the Reformation, except in chancels, with people standing to worship.[13] Even so, many examples of pre-Reformation benches can be found – like those of Croxton Kerrial or Gaddesby (both in Leicestershire) – and it seems likely that some movable and other forms of seating date back to at least the thirteenth century.[14] Pews for wives and widows were mentioned in *Piers Plowman*, written in the late fourteenth century, and it seems likely that the earliest seats were for women.[15] Earlier practice had frequently been for women to sit in the north sides of churches, and men in the south, and in the medieval and early modern periods one can find much evidence of gendered separation.[16] From the late sixteenth century gendered segregation had been giving way to family seating, although servants and the young were often still segregated as groups.[17] From an early date some churches had masonry benches along outer walls or aisles, by internal partition walls,[18] or around columns, and examples may be seen at Moulton or Skirbeck (both in Lincolnshire), Campsall in Yorkshire, Rickinghall Superior in

[12] Appropriation may have been even more pronounced half a century or more before 1851, given the enactments governing availability of sittings in the Church Building Acts, and the campaign against reservation associated with the ecclesiological movement. Of course, in the late twentieth century the often very low levels of church attendance make seat reservation unnecessary. In rural parishes after the mid nineteenth century, it was hard to see high levels of appropriation continuing when out-migration made over-provision of sittings a problem for all denominations. If one views the phenomenon in a long-term perspective, the decline of seat appropriation might seem as much a consequence of declining attendances as a conscious effort to maintain attendances. Low attendance caused by out-migration is covered by R. Gill, *The Myth of the Empty Church* (1993), pp. 47–9, 68–9.

[13] Tittler, 'Seats of honor', 217–18.

[14] Hardy, 'Remarks on the history of seat-reservation', 104. Seating often had to be movable to facilitate burials, and to allow other communal uses of the church which subsequently declined.

[15] Aston, 'Segregation in church', pp. 259, 264.

[16] *Ibid., passim*. This was found for example at Staunton Harold (Leicestershire): G. Jackson-Stops and R. Fedden, *Staunton Harold Church* (1975), p. 9.

[17] Aston,'Segregation in church', pp. 283–91.

[18] D. Parsons, *Churches and Chapels: Investigating Places of Worship* (1989), pp. 41–2.

Suffolk, or Weston on Trent in Derbyshire. Such seating was said to be the origin of the phrase 'the weakest go to the wall'. As this suggests, it seems likely that these and early benches were intended for elderly or infirm people.[19] Thirteenth-century wooden benches, like those at Dunsfold in Surrey, can certainly be found; but it is not known how common they were, or the extent of their appropriation.[20] Distinct parts of churches were probably not usually allocated to particular inhabitants, with the exception of those of considerable eminence. It is worth remembering that the word 'pew' in Middle English usually referred to a (frequently enclosed) place raised on a footpace, appropriated for certain great personages or families. It could also refer to a raised seat or bench for judges or public speakers. The word "pew" derives from the Latin *podium*: an elevated place, parapet or balcony, and it appears to have had an elite connotation. Family pews often had such an elevated aspect, in due course taken to their fullest extent in cases like the famous Milbanke Pew of c.1670–80, at Croft in the North Riding,[21] or the Vaughan family pew, emblazoned with their ancestral coats of arms, which dominated the chancel of Llanfihangel yng Ngwynfa (Montgomeryshire) church until 1862.[22] Family seats may often have been related to the proprietorial origin of many, if not the majority, of parish churches, and although this was ignored by many later critics it is worth bearing in mind. There were countless families who, like the Shirleys of Breedon-on-the-Hill (Leicestershire), turned over most of their own property to the parish for public attendance at worship, retaining a small portion for themselves which later came to be attacked as appropriation. Whatever their origins, from the early fifteenth century 'we frequently meet with

[19] D. Smith, *Old Furniture and Woodwork: an Introductory Historical Study* (1937, 1949 edn), pp. 28, 60; B. Kümin, *The Shaping of a Community: the Rise and Reformation of the English Parish, c. 1400–1560* (Aldershot, 1996), p. 233. Rather later, some elderly people could be placed near the pulpit to help them hear. Aston, 'Segregation in church', p. 288.

[20] Bishop Quivil's Exeter synod passed an injunction against seat reservation in 1287. J. C. Cox and A. Harvey, *English Church Furniture* (1907), p. 283; Aston, 'Segregation in church', p. 251. N. Pevsner, *The Buildings of England: North-West and South Norfolk* (1962, Harmondsworth, 1990 edn), p. 47, wrote that 'Benches were apparently not provided in churches before the C15', but on this matter his source of information may not have been strictly correct.

[21] An illustration of this is in G. Randall, *Church Furnishing and Decoration in England and Wales* (1980), p. 63.

[22] A. D. Rees, *Life in a Welsh Countryside: a Social Study of Llanfihangel yng Ngwynfa* (1950, Cardiff, 1996 edn), p. 17.

references to seats in churches belonging to and reserved for particular individuals', and some churches were charging rents at that time, which varied according to the place in the church.[23]

After the Reformation pews and benches became more prevalent and elaborate, with their characteristic carved oak ends and arm rests, poppy-head finials and the like. They were also more commonly enclosed by doors, often with locks on them.[24] Seats and pews for general use developed much further during the seventeenth century,[25] partly because of an emphasis on the sermon, and box pews became most fully established in this and the following century.

Under common law, every parishioner was entitled to a seat in the church, provided there was room, but was not enabled to sit wherever s/he chose. Even if there was no seat available, a parishioner still had the right to enter the church to attend divine service, as instructed under the Act of Uniformity. Indeed, a parishioner had priority over occupiers of pews who were not parishioners.[26] The term *pew-fellow* – one who sits in the same pew – meant a local associate. Those who were not parishioners could not claim a seat as a matter of right, but they were not to be excluded from church services. Any person might be permitted to sit in a vacant allotted seat once the service had begun. The apportionment of seats throughout the church was in the hands of the churchwardens, as deputies taking their authority from the Ordinary, rather than the minister.[27]

23 Hardy, 'Remarks on the history of seat-reservation', 98–9; Kümin, *Shaping of a Community*, p. 233.

24 Hardy, 'Remarks on the history of seat-reservation', 104. Like many other nineteenth-century reformers, Hardy was strongly opposed to seat appropriation. But he argued that the Reformation had little effect on church seating, and that seat reservation was prevalent long before.

25 And were extended also to youths: Aston, 'Segregation in church', p. 289. A. W. N. Pugin, *Contrasts* (1836, Leicester, 1969 edn), pp. 31–3, believed that 'dozing-pens, termed pews' in naves and aisles – those 'wretched mutilations', 'enormities' and 'abominations' – attained their full growth under Charles II, having initially emerged from the reign of Edward VI. To him they epitomised Protestant principles and the decline of ecclesiastical architecture. Capping it all, stalls for church dignitaries had come to be occupied by lay people, 'and not unfrequently the bishop's throne . . . by some consequential dame'. *Ibid.*, p. 39.

26 W. A. Holdsworth, *The Handy Book of Parish Law* (1859, 1872 edn), p. 7.

27 'The Ordinary hath a proper Jurisdiction over them [seats in churches], and may place and displace whom he thinks fit: But where Custom or Prescription interposeth, there his Jurisdiction ceaseth'. W. Nelson, *The Office and Authority of a Justice of Peace* (1729), p. 152; J. Shaw, *The Parochial Lawyer; or, Churchwarden and Overseer's Guide and Assistant* (1833), p. 29.

Churchwardens also collected seat rents. Where an aisle, chapel or a particular pew was the property of a private person, or where he had a perpetual right to occupy it through a faculty, the churchwardens had no authority over the sittings it contained during his resident lifetime. Occupation of a seat for a considerable time (usually twenty years at least) conferred a claim to it, one that churchwardens were obliged to respect and to treat reasonably when arbitrating on these matters.

A great deal of parliamentary, ecclesiastical and localised debate occurred over prescriptive and other rights to Anglican pews, and whether people could be displaced from them. Archbishop Laud involved himself in controversy by criticising reserved and high pews facing in indiscriminate directions, and in the seventeenth century there is growing evidence of disputes over the appropriation of sittings, and over who was eligible to be seated. Such debate concerned for example the length of long-term occupancy; the implications for occupancy of repairs to a pew having been conducted by someone 'time out of mind' (and what the latter meant); whether the inhabitants of the same house had conducted such repairs; what the consequences were for pew entitlement when a house had been sub-divided, or when a family found itself reduced in size; whether a seat was part of the parson's freehold; and whether an action for trespass could be brought in cases of intrusion into a pew. There could also be difficulties if a new church was built in a parish, replacing the old parish church. In such circumstances the bishop could institute enquiries as to which people had rights to hold pews, and they could then be assigned seats in the new church.[28]

If a church was re-pewed, rebuilt or enlarged, those who had had seats, by faculty or prescription, were usually allotted others as near as possible to the sites of their previous seats. This occurred for example with the Moores' family pews at Appleby Magna (Leicestershire) upon restoration in 1829–32.[29] Those who had contributed to the expenses of church building or repairs were allotted sittings according to their social rank, the sums they had expended, and the size of their families, assuming that they still lived in the

[28] 8 & 9 Vic. c. 70, s. 1.

[29] R. J. Eyre, 'The nineteenth century restorations at St Michael and All Angels, Appleby Magna', *Leicestershire Archaeological and Historical Society Transactions*, 61 (1987), 45; Leics. C.R.O., 15 D 55/12.

parish.[30] Remaining inhabitants were then granted seats according to their social status and needs.[31] Changes in property demarcation in the parish, or the resiting of farm buildings, as upon enclosure, often raised major problems for customs aligning particular seats with parcels of land.

It seems likely that most urban sittings, and very many in rural areas, were appropriated in various ways, especially before 1818. Often pews were felt to be 'owned' by particular families, and in many parishes they had come to be closely tied to properties, in some cases leaving little room for outsiders or for poorer parishioners. As Humphreys commented on Montgomeryshire, churches often did not possess adequate seating, 'for pews were a form of property, carefully earmarked and jealously guarded by the parish freeholders'.[32] The 'owners' of pews were normally liable for their upkeep. In many parishes such appropriation had become more problematic with growing demand for church sittings during the eighteenth century, and it was linked closely to church enlargement or rebuilding. The 'principal inhabitants' would often possess box pews, even with their initials or the names of their property inscribed on them.[33] Thus one finds the names of farms painted on the backs of benches in West Grinstead church (West Sussex),[34] or on the box pews dating from 1742 in Thurning church (Norfolk), which were still being used by the allocated households in the 1920s.[35] The main point is that such pews were held as a right appurtenant to the occupation of a dwelling-house within the parish.[36] In some leases one also finds church pews or seats

[30] In some cases allocation of pews books (half-page duplicates of which could be given to the seat occupiers) specified the sums donated to the church or its repair, that had warranted seat appropriation. See e.g. Leics. C.R.O., 15 D 55/17, for the allocation book of Appleby, whose church underwent major and exceptionally well-documented restoration from 1827.

[31] Holdsworth, *Handy Book of Parish Law*, p. 8.

[32] M. Humphreys, *The Crisis of Community: Montgomeryshire, 1680–1815* (Cardiff, 1996), p. 180.

[33] At Astbury (Cheshire) the top rails of many of the enclosed benches with doors are carved with incised lettering indicating personal ownership: 'Half of this Pew belongs to Ms Margret Leigh', or 'Green 1761 Since Sould [*sic*] to Sam'l . . . ' etc. I am grateful to David Parsons for this information.

[34] Parsons, *Churches and Chapels*, p. 42.

[35] Names like Lime Tree Farm, Roundabout Farm, Rookery Farm, Burnt House Farm, Hall Farm are on the box pews of Thurning. Curtained pews for Rectory and Hall servants, and the rector's coachmen, were at the back of the church.

[36] The seating arrangements described in 1717–18 for West Woodhay (Berkshire) allocated seats to individuals 'for their Lease & Copy-holds', 'for the Parsonage, Hatch House Farm & Knights Copyhold', 'for Blandys & the Malthouse farms', 'for their Copy Holds', and 'for their Copy & Lease Holds'. See the allotment of seating printed

described as 'belonging' to occupiers 'in right of or as appurtenant to' property held by them.[37] This practice appears to have developed particularly during the seventeenth and eighteenth centuries. Such a pew was held in respect of a house, and came with that house's habitation, as a privilege confined to occupation of the house.[38] It was thought unreasonable for any person to retain their seat if s/he moved elsewhere, for seats were for the inhabitants of a parish, not for others.[39] As James Shaw put it: 'Resiants [*sic*] only are capable of acquiring a Right in Pews'.[40] As Shaw wrote in another book, 'there can be no permanent property in pews'.[41] That was the situation under common law. Yet in practice it seems that pews were often regarded as freehold

as appendix 1 in B. F. L. Clarke, *The Building of the Eighteenth-century Church* (1963), pp. 214–15, from the Oxford archdeaconry papers. J. Shaw, *Parish Law* (1753), p. 91, argued (like other commentators) that seats were appendant only to houses, not to land.

37 See for example the 1824 indentures of lease and release of property and pew in the parish church of North Kilworth (Leicestershire), from a father to his son: Leics. C.R.O., DE 3853/5,6.

38 Nelson, *Office and Authority of a Justice of Peace*, p. 153; Shaw, *Parish Law*, p. 90; Clarke, *Building of the Eighteenth-century Church*, p. 23, on an early nineteenth-century case concerning St Werburgh's Church, Derby; G. W. O. Addleshaw and F. Etchells, *The Architectural Setting of Anglican Worship* (1948, 1956 edn), p. 95; Leics. C.R.O., DE 3178/4 (1807), Oakham (Rutland) pew allocations, 1652–1793, as recorded in the Old Parish Book, where allocations were clearly specified to houses and freeholds, often 'for ever'.

39 Shaw, *Parish Law*, pp. 90–1. For an unpunctuated example of this and the process of allocation, see Leics. C.R.O., 15 D 55/28/22: Faculty for new pewing the church of Appleby: The rector, churchwardens and clerk 'or the major part of them to allott and appropriate all the said Seats Stalls or Pews in the said church (except the free Seats) when erected and built or sitting places therein unto and amongst all and every the parishioners and Inhabitants of the said parish paying towards the repairs of the said Church and proprietors or occupiers of messuages or Tenements therein so long as such persons or their families shall continue Inhabitants of the said parish and continue possessors or occupiers of the messuages or tenements they now own or rent therein as they the several persons above named or the major part of them shall think proper fit and convenient and wherein for the said several parishioners and Inhabitants and their families respectively to whom the said several seats stalls and pews in the said Church shall be allotted and appropriated in manner as aforesaid to sit stand kneel and hear divine Service and Sermons read and preached in the said Church exclusive of all other persons whomsoever so long as they the said several persons or their families shall remain parishioners and Inhabitants of the said parish and continue possessors or occupiers of the messuages or Tenements they now own or rent therein and no longer and further . . . to act and do as law and justice shall require.'

40 Shaw, *Parish Law*, p. 90. In fact, if someone erected a pew, it became church property (even if not donated to the church), and might not afterwards be removed. Churchwardens could sue someone for removing such a pew. *Ibid*., pp. 89, 92.

41 Shaw, *Parochial Lawyer*, p. 31.

property, saleable by the owner, and seen as part of a person's physical assets. This appears to have been most common in towns.[42] In Sheffield for example, it was possible for such an 'owner' to rent them out, sums of between about 1s. 6d. and 2s. 6d. per annum being payable as rents in the early nineteenth century.[43] In 1766, a seat in Kilsby church (Northamptonshire) 'belonging to . . . Thomas Hall at his decease' was 'Bargined [*sic*] with and sold' for 10s. 6d. by Hall's executor to another man in the parish, as a surviving declaration of sale informs us.[44]

Like the social precedence manifest in communion-taking, seating symbolically represented the ranking of local society. As James Shaw put it: 'The parishioners have, indeed, a claim to be seated according to their rank and station, but the churchwardens are not, in providing for this claim, to overlook the claim of all the parishioners to be seated, if sittings can be afforded them. They must, therefore, not accommodate the higher classes beyond their real wants, (that is their rank, extent of property, number of family, and length of inhabitancy in the parish,) to the exclusion of their poorer neighbours, who are equally entitled to accommodation with the rest, though they are not entitled to the same accommodation, supposing the seats to be not all equally convenient.'[45] This vexatious balance between the various claims of status and general entitlement was hardly one that was smoothly arrived at. In developing local societies as socially con-

[42] Addleshaw and Etchells, *Architectural Setting*, p. 90.

[43] E. R. Wickham, *Church and People in an Industrial City* (1957, 1969 edn), pp. 42–3. He comments that 'The selling and private appropriation of seating in the parish churches was in fact contrary to common law, whereby all parishioners equally have rights within their parish churches; but this did not prevent the widespread development of the practice' (p. 42). See also Clarke, *Building of the Eighteenth-century Church*, pp. 23–4; Brown, 'Costs of pew-renting', 351: 'a complicated system of preferential rights to seats developed in the seventeenth and eighteenth centuries whereby families had "first call" on their traditional pews. The exact status of these rights is unclear, but they were certainly passed from one generation to the next as heritable property.' Seats in the Established Church of Scotland could also be sold by auction.

[44] Leics. C.R.O., DE 2615/50.

[45] Shaw, *Parochial Lawyer*, p. 31. And he added, 'With respect to pews held by householders dying or leaving the parish, such vacant pews may be allotted to those parishioners who have the best claim to them in point of standing in the parish and general respectability.' *Ibid.*, p. 32. For the early modern period, there is a discussion of the reasons for seating precedence in N. Alldridge, 'Loyalty and identity in Chester parishes, 1540–1640', in S. J. Wright (ed.), *Parish, Church and People: Local Studies in Lay Religion, 1350–1750* (1988), pp. 94–7. This assesses the rival claims of rate-paying, house occupancy, social rank, and so on: 'placement in church was an order consciously devised to project an artificially conceived social image corresponding to the local community's particular conception of status'.

scious as those of the nineteenth century, the results often led to muttering in the ranks.[46]

Farnborough church (Warwickshire) in the early nineteenth century was described by Thomas Hall as follows: 'In the chancel on the left-hand side sat the ladies and gentlemen from the Hall; on the right-hand side sat the servants and we school children occupied the steps leading to the communion table. We children always watched the arrival of occupants of these pews with great interest and when the gentlemen and ladies had taken their seats the butler and footman also took theirs.'[47] Flora Thompson described something very similar for the church in the mother village of her hamlet Juniper Hill in north-east Oxfordshire: 'The Squire's and clergyman's families had pews in the chancel, with backs to the wall on either side, and between them stood two long benches for the school children, well under the eyes of authority. Below the steps down into the nave . . . came the rank and file of the congregation, nicely graded, with the farmer's family in the front row, then the Squire's gardener and coachmen, the schoolmistress, the maidservants, and the cottagers, with the Parish Clerk at the back to keep order.' In his sermons, the rector's 'favourite subject was the supreme rightness of the social order as it then existed'.[48] School children were sometimes put apart in galleries (as in Appleby,[49] or St Nicholas's, Newcastle upon Tyne),[50] or in other parts of the church, as in St Peter's Netherseal (Derbyshire), where the post-restoration 'Ground Plan' of 1874 shows a large area of the north aisle designated as 'children's seats'.[51] Sunday school children were

[46] And when exclusion resulted, seat appropriation spilt over into the controversies about church rates, the point being made that those who had excluded others from church ought to be the only people rated.

[47] Cited in P. Horn, *The Victorian Country Child* (1974, 1985 edn), p. 162.

[48] F. Thompson, *Lark Rise to Candleford* (1939, Harmondsworth, 1976 edn), pp. 210–12. A similar description is found in L. Lee, *Cider with Rosie* (1959, Harmondsworth, 1962 edn), pp. 218–19, on the Cotswold village of Slad, just north of Stroud. A surviving example of rigidly stratified seating is Wilby (Norfolk), where labourers sat on open benches at the back: T. Williamson and L. Bellamy, *Property and Landscape: a Social History of Land Ownership and the English Countryside* (1987), pp. 186–7.

[49] Appleby church (Leicestershire) had a gallery belonging to a school. Leics. C.R.O., 15 D 55/28/35. Or see the attractive Hallaton church plan: Leics. C.R.O., DE 1556/60.

[50] Addleshaw and Etchells, *Architectural Setting*, p. 91.

[51] A copy of the Netherseal church plan was generously provided to me by the Revd William Bates. At Barwell (Leicestershire) there is 'Unusual raked children's seating at the W end of the N aisle: it dates from the 1854 restoration by H. Goddard'. See N. Pevsner, E. Williamson and G. K. Brandwood, *The Buildings of England: Leicestershire and Rutland* (1960, Harmondsworth, 1989 edn), p. 93, kindly drawn to my attention by David Parsons.

also often seated in particular and separate parts of churches, with occasional argument in both churches and chapels as to whether they should be so seated, or sit with their families.[52]

In Christ Church, Timperley (Cheshire), an attractive cruciform church built in 1849, the gentry worshipped in the main body of the church, whereas their attendant coachmen gained access to the inner balcony via a separate external entrance in the tower.[53] The churches of Tintinhull, Baltonsborough and Catcott (all in the Bridgwater–Glastonbury–Yeovil triangle of Somerset) had small auxiliary flap- or pull-out seats connected to bench-ends for the servants to sit on, thus allowing them to remain proximate but separate from their employing family seated in the pew. At Clovelly (Devon) these took a more durable form.[54] Many churches undergoing nineteenth-century restoration and re-pewing provide documentation of families asking for seating space alongside them for their servants.[55] There were further nuanced sub-divisions manifest in church seating. For example, ranks of servants were sometimes expected to sit in a sequential order at church that reflected their status within the occupation.[56] Male and female servants were often seated in different places. Servants of separate families sometimes sat in specially allocated seats, as at Buckerell in Devon, where this was clearly shown on the church plan of 1773, alongside other allocations like 'Poor Women Seats', 'Women Servants Seats', 'Vacant Seats for poor men', all of

[52] Leics. C.R.O., N/M/179/280, Millstone Lane Sunday School, Wesleyan Methodist Minutes, 4 January 1849. It was ordained 'That the children whose parents wish them to sit in their private pews during service be permitted to do so, if a special request to that effect be made by the parents to the Officers of the School'. Or see P. B. Cliff, *The Rise and Development of the Sunday Schol Movement in England, 1780–1980* (1986), p. 46, citing East Dereham (Norfolk). This was sometimes objected to on the grounds that the place of worship could not then charge rents for the seats Sunday school children occupied. *Ibid.*, pp. 83–4. S. C. Carpenter, *Church and People, 1789–1889: a History of the Church of England from William Wilberforce to 'Lux Mundi'* (1933), pp. 19–20: letter of Vicar of Stretton to Joshua Watson (founder of the National Society) about his seating plans, separating Sunday school boys, men, women, farmers' servant-lads, deaf and infirm: 'thus promoting the progress of our holy faith'.

[53] Information kindly supplied by Mr and Mrs Redpath.

[54] J. C. D. Smith, *Church Woodcarvings: a West Country Study* (Newton Abbot, 1969), pp. 14–15. Clovelly also had 'small, bracket-seats, known as pauper-pews . . . Pauper children sat on these tiny uncomfortable seats.' See S. Ellis, *Down a Cobbled Street: the Story of Clovelly* (Bideford, 1987), p. 49. Tablets or plaques commemorating people could be placed over or near 'their' seats. *Ibid.*, p. 47.

[55] For example, Leics. C.R.O., 15 D 55/16 (Appleby): an allocation of pews book specifying who has what pews, and what they require for themselves, servants and tenants when the church is re-pewed.

[56] Horn, *Victorian Country Child*, p. 140.

these being in much less eligible positions than the gender-divided pews occupied by the named principal inhabitants.[57] At West Woodhay (Berkshire), in the early eighteenth century, male servants sat on the north side of the tower, and female servants on the south side; and they sat with the children of those who paid no scot or lot in the parish, the latter again separated by sex.[58] In Thurning (Norfolk), girls sat on the left of the central benches and boys and men on the right, a custom lasting into the 1920s. And as is well known, some churches (like Appleby) also had a pew for women immediately following childbirth, 'as a Churching Pew for the said Parish'.[59]

Church seating plans like those mentioned above were very largely a result of seating appropriation, and examples of such plans survive for almost all denominations.[60] Plans for the Church of England (usually made by churchwardens, or sometimes by builders upon church re-pewing or restoration) are available for Netherseal (Derbyshire), Overseal (Derbyshire), Appleby, Hallaton or Knossington in Leicestershire,[61] Burley on the Hill (Rutland),[62] Monks Kirby in

57 A. Warne, *Church and Society in Eighteenth-century Devon* (Newton Abbot, 1969), pp. 60–1: 'The squire's seat occupied a commanding position with a view of the whole church, from which he could take note of absentees . . . the parishioners were graded according to the importance of their holdings down to the smallholders in the rear, and finally behind them the poor . . . The arrangement of seats had a theological as well as a social significance, for the more "important" seats had the pulpit in view rather than the altar, suggesting that the ministry of the word had precedence over that of the sacraments' (p. 57).

58 Clarke, *Building of the Eighteenth-century Church*, pp. 214–15.

59 In Appleby this was Pew no. 15 in the middle aisle on the north side. Leics. C.R.O., 15 D 55/17. Sedgefield, in county Durham, had a pew marked 'the sick wife's stall', meaning a churching pew. Addleshaw and Etchells, *Architectural Setting*, p. 94.

60 Pew charts and gaps in seating were sometimes used to see who was absent from service. E. Carlson, 'The origins, function, and status of the office of churchwarden, with particular reference to the diocese of Ely', in M. Spufford (ed.), *The World of Rural Dissenters, 1520–1725* (Cambridge, 1995), p. 172; Aston, 'Segregation in church', p. 258. An early plan is discussed in J. Popplewell, 'A seating plan for North Nibley church in 1629', *Transactions of the Bristol and Gloucestershire Archaeological Society*, 103 (1985).

61 See the 1841 seating plan for St Matthews, Overseal, in Derbyshire C.R.O. (Gresley Papers), 77M Box 23, Folder 5. The Revd William Bates kindly drew my attention to this and related documentation. For the church seating plan of c. 1882 for Knossington, see Leics. C.R.O., DE 1318/23. This also lists 'houses to which sittings are allotted' and those to which no sittings are allotted: 'The 24 Pews are occupied by the families inhabiting *22* out of the *68* houses in the Parish.' For plans of Appleby church, see Leics. C.R.O., 15 D 55/28/54 and 15 D 55/30 (c. 1827), and for Hallaton, see Leics. C.R.O., DE 1556/60.

62 Leics. C.R.O., DG7/4/30–31, with seats for charity children, cottagers and different categories of servants.

Warwickshire, South Carlton in Lincolnshire,[63] Buckerell in Devon,[64] Sutton in Cambridgeshire,[65] St Paul's Covent Garden,[66] among many other places. In most plans, the pews were numbered. In some cases (as at Overseal) such numbers survive on the church pews, a fairly clear indication that seating plans were used before the modern era of comparatively free access to seating. A seating plan is a fascinating source of much potential, for the names of pew occupiers can be matched against census returns or directories to produce a spatial outline of parochial social structure, sketched out in its seating allocation. Indeed, something similar can be done for church burial grounds; although no one has compared the two as joint evidence on personal status, and considered whether they relate spatially to geographical residences of families within a parish. In addition, where various hamlets or gentry seats existed within a parish, one can find these having geographically corresponding allocations in the church plans, as was clearly the case for Quenby, Ingoldsby, Baggrave and Hungarton in Hungarton church, Leicestershire.[67]

Pew rents 'were a legacy from the later Middle Ages', according to one source.[68] Whatever their origin, they certainly accompanied the pewing-up of old parish churches from the sixteenth century, and became common in seventeenth-century churches and chapels.[69] A

[63] J. Obelkevich, *Religion and Rural Society: South Lindsey, 1825–1875* (Oxford, 1976), pp. 109–10. As he says, it is possible from such a plan 'to retrace the social map of the entire village'. He also suggests that gendered separation in seating, which he did not find in his region, 'would have been appropriate in a more communal society in which class differences were less salient than they were in the nineteenth century'. Compare the discussion of earlier separation of unmarried people by gender, and upon marriage by family, in Addleshaw and Etchells, *Architectural Setting*, p. 90.

[64] See Warne, *Church and Society*, pp. 56–7, 60–1. This very detailed plan even has 'Seats for Witch' and 'Vacant Seats for Servants of Witch' in its north aisle!

[65] Cambs. C.R.O., P148/06/04, a less detailed plan than some, but showing which pews were 'appropriated'.

[66] Westminster City Archives, Box 26, no. 13 (1798). This shows the children's gallery, churchwardens' pew, rector's pew, and that for 'His Grace the Duke of Bedford'. All other seats are numbered.

[67] Leics. C.R.O., 12 D 43/44/7–9. There were long-running disputes here (1765–1877) over seating arrangements and responsibility to repair parts of Hungarton church that were proximate to one's seating allocation. See *ibid.*, 12 D 43/44/1–4, 6, 20–64.

[68] Addleshaw and Etchells, *Architectural Setting*, p. 92.

[69] Tittler, 'Seats of honor', 218–19, usefully describes three phases of rented seat adoption, from the late fifteenth to the early seventeenth century. A shift from gender-based to family-based seating may also have facilitated rent payments. It seems likely that pew rents were one of the expedients adopted to replace earlier festive sources of parish income (church ales, May games, Hocktide gatherings, hoggling, plough

parishioner in fact had a right to a seat without such payment,[70] and the extent of payment in different periods has yet to be researched. Such rent was sometimes referred to as *pewage*, and it was evidently very prevalent. As Wickham commented, 'the custom had profound consequences for the relation of the churches to the common people'; and he observed about beliefs in private and transferable property in pews that 'It is of immense sociological value to know the exact practices that obtained.'[71] The rents were collected by churchwardens,[72] and might be put to almost any use connected with the church. The minister was normally entitled to a share of the proceeds, but these usually comprised only a small part of his income.[73]

It was partly in response to these proprietary and monetary customs that the Church Building Acts after 1818, the Incorporated Church Building Society, and the New Parishes Acts from 1843 aimed to extend the free accommodation available in churches.[74] The 1818 Act laid down that two pews close to the pulpit should be reserved for the use of the minister, his family and servants, while not less than one-fifth of the seats (known as 'free seats') were to be retained for the poor of the parish without payment.[75] Whatever the

Monday collections and the like) which had been in decline (as sources of parochial finance) since Elizabeth's reign. R. Hutton, *The Rise and Fall of Merry England: the Ritual Year, 1400–1700* (1994, Oxford, 1996 edn), pp. 119–20.

70 Shaw, *Parochial Lawyer*, pp. 30, 33; Holdsworth, *Handy Book of Parish Law*, p. 7.

71 Wickham, *Church and People*, pp. 42, 44.

72 See 58 Geo. III, c. 45, s. 73; 59 Geo. III, c. 134, ss. 26 & 32; 3 Geo. IV, c. 72; 1 & 2 Wm. IV, c. 48; Miller, *Guide to Ecclesiastical Law*, p. 10; Shaw, *Parochial Lawyer*, p. 33. And see *ibid.*, pp. 44–7, on the roles and procedures for churchwardens respecting seats in churches or chapels built or appropriated under the first three of these Acts, and under 5 Geo. IV, c. 103. It is of interest to note that provision was now made for vacant pews to be rented 'to any inhabitant of any adjoining parish or place'.

73 There were exceptions to this. See e.g. P.R.O., HO 129/227/42 (St Mary's Chapel, Gorleston, Suffolk), where the mid nineteenth-century pew rents from 800 non-free sittings came to £120.

74 The 1818 Church Building Act (58 Geo. III, c. 45, s. 73) nevertheless empowered churchwardens of places of worship to which the Act applied to sue for and recover unpaid rents of seats and pews, making the churchwardens a 'corporation' for this purpose. On free seats and the new churches, see M. H. Port, *Six Hundred New Churches: a Study of the Church Building Commission, 1818–1856, and its Church Building Activities* (1961), pp. 5–10, 24–5, 40; R. A. Soloway, *Prelates and People: Ecclesiastical Social Thought in England, 1783–1852* (1969), pp. 271, 278. The 1843 New Parishes Act did not allow pew rents, but they were subsequently permitted as a last resort in 1856. See Macmorran, *Handbook for Churchwardens*, p. 41; R. E. Rodes, *Law and Modernization in the Church of England: Charles II to the Welfare State* (Notre Dame, Indiana, 1991), pp. 168–9, and n. 48; 6–7 Vic. c. 37; 19–20 Vic. c. 104.

75 58 Geo. III, c. 45, s. 75.

origins of the church, some Victorian photographs show pews with 'FREE' inscribed on their doors, like St Mary's Parish Church, Whitby, as photographed by Frank Meadow Sutcliffe.[76] This detail survives in some churches today, as for example with the metal plates indicating that certain of the pews in Billesdon (Leicestershire) are 'free'.[77] The popular image of a miscellany of characters resorting to such pews was captured in J. Lobley's oil painting, 'The Free Seat'.[78] In Husbands Bosworth (Leicestershire), seats for the poor survive from 1812 in the north-west corner of All Saints Church.[79] In the 'Plan of the Isles and Pews in Seale CHURCH. 1830', an outlying northern area of the nave, lacking any possible view of the altar, was reserved 'For cottagers and all who have no Sittings allotted them'.[80] After 1818, in the appropriate churches, pews were nevertheless still to be available for letting to parishioners, at rates fixed by the commissioners, and part of the proceeds were intended to pay for the minister and clerk.[81] Grants for churches by the I.C.B.S. were made on the condition that a half or more (sometimes all) of the sittings would be free, and one can find plaques on some church walls reminding parishioners of this resolution.[82] As in Whitby and many older churches, such seats were often clearly marked as free sittings, and in the later 1850s it was held that they should be as well placed as those seats enjoyed by higher classes of local inhabitants, being near

[76] B. E. Shaw (compiler), *Frank Meadow Sutcliffe: a Second Edition* (Whitby, 1979, 1982 edn), p. 39, a detail still present in faded form.

[77] See also Leics. C.R.O., DE 4751/51 (c. 1870) on Billesdon church seating, including seats for 'farm servants', 'Coplow servants', 'Coplow cottages', 'servant girls', 'school benches' and 'Vicarage servants'. Most are reserved by name of person.

[78] J. Lobley (1829–88), 'The Free Seat', which can be seen in the Birmingham City Museum and Art Gallery.

[79] R. B. Pugh (ed.), *The Victoria County History of the Counties of England* (1964), vol. 5, p. 36.

[80] Plan of St Peter's, Netherseal (Derbyshire), 1830, an older arrangement dating from the seventeenth century, showing all the numbered pews. This was kindly supplied by the Revd William Bates. Some enumerators' returns in 1851 referred to 'cottagers' pews'. See e.g. the return for Exton in Hampshire: J. A. Vickers (ed.), *The Religious Census of Hampshire, 1851* (Hampshire Record Series, Winchester, 1993), p. 141. The restoration of Appleby Magna (Leicestershire), 1829–32, provided 17 oak benches placed in the centre of the aisle of the nave for 51 poor people, and this kind of placement was common at that time. See Eyre, 'The nineteenth century restorations', 45. For free pews in the church of St Helens, Ashby-de-la-Zouch (Leicestershire), see Leics. C.R.O., DE 4830/9 (1843–51). Some seats there were also rented for servants.

[81] See also 59 Geo. III, c. 134, s. 6; 5 Geo. IV, c. 103, s. 5; 1 & 2 Wm. IV, c. 78, s. 4.

[82] For example the porch of the Church of St Peter and St Paul, Exton, Rutland.

the reading desk and pulpit.[83] Clearly in many cases this had not hitherto been the case; and to judge from later church seating plans (like that of Knossington),[84] free seats frequently remained those least favoured by better off parishioners.[85]

There seems little doubt that the proportions of Anglican free seats increased from around 1818 onwards, although pew rents (or payments that were very close to this in their practical effects) lasted well into the twentieth century in some churches.[86] This reinforced efforts being made from the later eighteenth century to rearrange pulpits, reading desks and sittings, changes which were linked to liturgical reforms and the challenge of Nonconformity. In due course these moves were further expedited by the ecclesiological desire to banish large box pews and sittings which obscured the view of the chancel and communion table, to replace them with open 'medieval' benches, and so increase the numbers of sittings and terminate the custom of appropriating pews or seats. Church restorations often engendered larger numbers of free sittings, for many reformers intensely disliked exclusivity in seating.[87] In many cases however, the vested interests and pre-existing appropriations militated against such expanded

[83] 19 & 20 Vict. c. 104, s. 6; Holdsworth, *Handy Book of Parish Law*, p. 9.

[84] Leics. C.R.O., DE 1318/23 (c. 1882).

[85] Visitation returns increasingly discuss the availability of free or 'open seats' in the first half of the nineteenth century. It is clear that many of these seats were 'old and in parts decayed', 'rotten and bad', 'falling to pieces', 'not in a good state', and 'want repair', comments that were frequently made about Leicestershire churches. See e.g. the Parochial Visitation of Revd Thomas Bonney, Leics., C.R.O., 245' 50/9 (1842), pp. 1, 5, 29, 67, 79, 101, among many other examples of such comment, found also in Revd Bonney's other diligently conducted visitations. The need for more seats for the poor was often expressed, as e.g. Leics., C.R.O., 245' 50/1 (1832), p. 67. Provision of hassocks for the poor (or substitutes, like planks covered with sacking) was an equal concern (e.g. *ibid.*, p. 120). In some cases however, one finds comments like 'oak seats for the poor' (*ibid.*, p. 160, Swepstone, or p. 184, Whatton), and in many Anglican churches new free seats for the poor were being provided between c. 1820 and 1845. The problem of seating 'the poor' continued however. In 1890 the Rector of Oxhill (Warwickshire) wrote to the *Banbury Guardian* that 'the poor have no seats but under a low west gallery where it is dark and draughty'. Cited in B. Smith, *The Village of Oxhill and the Church of Saint Lawrence* (Oxhill, 1971), p. 42.

[86] The *Imperial Gazetteer*, 2 vols. (1875 edn), p. 1190, commented on the Anglican Church that 'All the pew-sittings in some of the recently-erected churches are free; many also in not a few other recently-erected churches are free; but the great majority of those in town-churches are charged each from 5s. to 10s. or upwards a-year.'

[87] Examples of complaints against such pews in the 1851 Religious Census may be found in R. W. Ambler (ed.), *Lincolnshire Returns of the Census of Religious Worship, 1851* (Lincolnshire Record Society, 72, 1979), p. xxxiv.

availability. In Appleby (Leicestershire) for example, the intention in 1827 was clearly to enlarge the number of free seats (to be constructed 'in a handsome workmanlike and uniform manner' and in the best Norway oak like the other sittings, rather than in deal): 'Our wish, is to accommodate the poor as much as we can.' However, highly confidential correspondence made it clear that they had precious little room in the church to achieve this, given previous stakes in the sittings, and legal advice was taken not to commit themselves openly to any such purpose.[88] To judge from the more general legal arguments surrounding pew appropriation and precedence, and the centrality of social position in people's local priorities, the ecclesiological reforming mission must often have brought local obstruction and ill-feeling from established interests. This problem was accentuated by the fact that ecclesiological clergy often arrived in parishes as complete outsiders.

Pew rents were an important means to support church fabric. Nonconformists in both England and Wales found them crucial to pay off costs incurred in chapel building. Many chapels competed in architectural terms against other denominations, and this added to their debts. Whatever the idealism of a belief in free accommodation, such indebtedness ensured that pew rents persisted as a source of funding for chapels.[89] In some (like the Independent chapels in Sheffield) there were very few free seats. This suggests 'on the one hand the sense of possession of their chapel by the group of families making up the membership of the church, and on the other the feeling of exclusion that would mark the attitude of outsiders even were they to consider the possibility of attendance'.[90] Much about the external appearance of chapels deliberately set them apart from most Anglican churches: until the mid nineteenth century their architecture was usually classical rather than gothic. There were often key internal differences too, like their common tendency to focus upon the pulpit. However, many chapels still operated seating prerogatives and allocations comparable to those found in seating plans for the Church of England. For example,

88 Leics. C.R.O., 15 D 55/26/4; 15 D 55/28/44; 15 D 55/16; 15 D 55/28/22; 15 D 55/28/27; 15 D 55/17. The eventual provision here was for 51 free seats for the poor.

89 R. Dixon and S. Muthesius, *Victorian Architecture* (1978, 1995 edn), p. 229.

90 Wickham, *Church and People*, p. 48. Some churches had seats for 'strangers'. See Addleshaw and Etchells, *Architectural Setting*, p. 93, on Little Barningham, Norfolk, a pew also used for brides and grooms.

the seating plan of 1851 for the Wymondham Independent Chapel (Norfolk) gives very detailed named specification of appropriated box pews.[91] Seating designation like this is found in many Nonconformist seating plans and pew rent books. Oral testimony for a later period demonstrates how important sitting position could be in chapels, even among children.[92] As well as the multiplicity of personally named allocations, there were many references to seats reserved for categories of the poor, just as one finds with the Anglican Church.[93] In the Unitarian Great Meeting Chapel, Leicester, there were seats variously designated in words such as 'Under the Gallery formerly for the Poor', and 'Poors Seat under the Gallery', and 'Now Charity Children', 'Servants', 'Under the Gallery for the Poor Gratis', 'The Singers', and seats 'for the children belonging to the Charity and Sunday Schools'.[94] In the same county, the Hinckley Congregational Church had pews 'used as free', and others 'Kept as Free for Stray Worshipers'.[95]

In other ways the organisational details of Nonconformist seat appropriation differed from the Anglican Church. There was greater emphasis on what people could pay, and on their service to the church, rather than on the position and property individuals held in a parish. As an example of one way of allocating seats and rents, there is the rare surviving set of 'Rules for Disposing of the Pews' drawn up around 1812 by the Deacons of the Baptist Chapel in Blaby, Leicestershire.[96] At that time the custom in this chapel was for members and others 'to subscribe what they please'. The largest subscriber was then given the opportunity to choose a seat first, with the subsequent order of choice descending down through the subscription list to those who had offered the smallest sums. Previously occupied pews had precedence.

91 The plan is helpfully reproduced in J. Ede, N. Virgoe and T. Williamson, *Halls of Zion: Chapels and Meeting-Houses in Norfolk* (Norwich, 1994), p. 19.

92 See Leicestershire and Rutland Federation of Women's Institutes (comp.), *Leicestershire and Rutland: Within Living Memory* (Newbury, Berks., 1994), p. 42. On Congregationalist, Primitive Methodist and Wesleyan Methodist practice in the Anstey district of Leicestershire: 'The churches erected special tiered galleries to accommodate scholars for the Sermons, the youngest sitting at the bottom. Great importance was attached to position on the gallery and how high up you were.'

93 And see M. R. Watts, *The Dissenters. Vol. 1: From the Reformation to the French Revolution* (Oxford, 1978), p. 358.

94 Leics. C.R.O., N/U/179/53; N/U/179/52. In the Presbyterian church at Ford (Northumberland), 'Members of the congregation in indigent circumstances are not called upon to pay pew rents'. P.R.O., HO 129, 552–563 (Ford).

95 Leics. C.R.O., N/C/142/18, Hinckley Congregational Pew Book.

96 Leics. C.R.O., N/B/38/18: Blaby Baptist Church, no date, but the watermark is 1812.

'If any one lowers his subscription, he shall lose his claim to the pew he chose first, and shall be entitled to chose according to his then subscription of the pews then disengaged. Lenity is recommended towards those that are reduced through misfortune & old age or sickness.' Families sat together in this Baptist chapel. The deacons were empowered to fill empty spaces with other people 'according to the subscription, and choice of the persons applying'.

This was not a uniform payment system, like that sometimes advocated.[97] As in most chapels, sums varied by position of the seat or pew. Nor was a price fixed for particular seats regardless of occupier. This system had the advantage of flexibility: taking account of what people could pay, and of vicissitudes in their personal situation. Most chapels required quarterly payment, but Nonconformist pew rent books contain many details of arrears, in some cases making clear that considerable indulgence could be granted according to circumstances.[98] This form of appropriation might thus maximise income, while also ensuring that those reduced in livelihood were not excluded from the chapel they had hitherto supported.[99] By these

[97] For example, the Unitarian Great Meeting, Leicester, in its desire to establish a regular source of income, complained in 1820 that 'much irregularity has existed in the respective rates of single sittings, and in several instances of the rates of whole Pews, so that considerable loss has been experienced by the Society so long back as from the year 1808'. Instead 'one uniform system of rate' was advocated throughout the chapel; but with differences below stairs and in the galleries. 'The same Seats both below Stairs, and in the Gallerys to be continued as usual for the use of Strangers.' Leics. C.R.O., N/U/179/57. To judge from the chapel's subsequent records, this was not long acted upon.

[98] Tolerance of arrears seems to have been common for example at the Unitarian Great Meeting Chapel, Leicester. See Leics. C.R.O., N/U/179/60. Sittings were charged quarterly at about 2s. 6d. upwards in the 1830s, and at about 5s. in the 1870s, a sum slightly greater than many other Leicestershire Nonconformist quarterly charges, which commonly seem to have been between 1s. to 4s. for individual sittings. In 1830 'New comers' at this famous chapel sat in the front rows of the galleries. See Leics. C.R.O., N/U.179/58. Entries in pew rent books indicating that certain entered names paid nothing can readily be found, as for the Hinckley Congregational Church: 'P [pew] 2, Roberts Mr. do not give anything'. Leics. C.R.O., N/C/142/18. See also Green, 'Death of pew-rents', p. 212. As he comments, such leniency and other considerations affecting the pew-rent system meant that it was 'an altogether more socially inclusive institution than it has hitherto been given credit for. It encouraged those who could give generously to do so. It enabled those who could give little to do so' (p. 214).

[99] This respect for a prior claim on sittings is often found in chapels. The Unitarian Great Meeting, Leicester, was careful in 1804 to qualify one resolution by adding 'That no removal of Familys or individuals is intended should take place. But by the Free will of themselves they may be accommodated in other situations if preferd by them as soon as an opportunity presents itself'. Leics. C.R.O., N/U/179/55.

means, a major part of the chapel's income was closely linked to the committed attendance of a core hierarchy of members. This was unlike some of the income generating expedients (bazaars, 'at homes', tea meetings, offertories and so on) that gained ground in the later nineteenth century, and that often separated monetary collection from the act of worship.[100] Those newer expedients generated income from a larger, more miscellaneous but probably less committed public, and tied people to the church in different and perhaps less effective ways.

Seating categories and the 1851 census

The 1851 Religious Census is a source that allows very detailed comparison between denominations with regard to the appropriation of sittings. The census forms asked for this information, and we have seen earlier that the enumerators' returns gave figures for 'free' and 'other' (i.e. appropriated) sittings for places of worship. This was a most important matter for those who designed the census. They asked 'how much of the accommodation proved to be existing is available for the use of that great part of the community most needing spiritual education, and least able, by pecuniary outlay, to procure it? What proportion of the present provision is at the service of the poorer classes, without price?'[101] The meaning of the word 'free' was taken to be 'free to any persons wishing, without payment, to occupy them'.

Having explained this, the Census Report continued by stating the following caveat: 'The answers to this question were, unfortunately, not in every instance framed in accordance with this interpretation. In the case of ancient parish churches, sometimes *all* the sittings were returned as free – the meaning evidently being that no money payment was received from the occupants; but, as many of them were, no doubt, *appropriated*, either by custom or the authority of church officers, to particular persons, it is clear they would not be available indiscriminately to the poor, so as to make them "free sittings" in the sense above referred to. And with reference to Dissenters' chapels, it seems not unlikely that the term "free sittings" has been taken as

[100] On this issue, see Green, 'Death of pew-rents', *passim*.
[101] *Census of Religious Worship*, p. cxxxiv.

including sittings merely *unlet*, and not confined to sittings especially and permanently set apart for the use of the poorer classes.'[102]

Accordingly, in the tables that Horace Mann produced relating to sittings, a rather poorly explained correction to the Anglican data was introduced.[103] It aimed to deal with this problem of some supposedly 'free' sittings being not only free of money payment, but also being free in the sense that they were not appropriated in any way: 'sittings, in fact, devoted especially to the poorer classes, and which they might in freedom occupy at their own option and selection. In all such cases . . . it was deemed advisable, in order to secure an uniformity of meaning throughout the returns, to mention merely the total number of sittings – making no apportionment of them into "free" and "appropriated".'[104] All sittings enumerated in the published census tables as 'free' were thought to be free in the sense explained above,

[102] *Ibid.*, pp. cxxxiv–cxxxv. This problem for the Anglican Church of some sittings being free, but also appropriated (in the sense of being allotted to houses), was raised by some clergy. See for example P.R.O., HO 129/220/22 (St Mary Akenham, Suffolk); or most explicitly in P.R.O., HO 129/220/53 (John Adeney, Rector of Flowton, Suffolk): 'A Return is made of "Total sittings 240". These may be considered as all "free", inasmuch as *no rents* are paid for pews or sittings in these old parish Churches. Yet, because a pew is allotted to every house subject to the payment of certain rates – such pew, with the sittings in it, is, of course, *not absolutely free* to *all persons*, whether of the parochial poor, or to strangers. A difficulty also occurs in *estimating* the number of *available sittings* in these Churches; since a pew capable of holding *six* persons is frequently allotted to a family consisting but of *two* or *three*. Probably, however, of the 240 Sittings *here reported for Flowton Church, 190* may be considered as free to the poor, or others; and the *remaining 50* to belong to the *pew* allotted to *ratepaying inhabitant householders*.' (His emphases.) Such comments were rare however, and much more commonly either no remarks were made, or remarks such as that by the Rector of Kirton, Suffolk, P.R.O., HO 129/223/34: 'All the Church is free, with the exception of six or eight pews appropriated to certain farms, and two pews appropriated to the Rector's family & servants.'

[103] The instructions for filling up the schedule for Anglican churches seemingly failed to provide any guidance on section VI of the census form, on sittings. (Mann did not mention this.) Instructions for other denominations, however, were more explicit, providing the following guidance: 'The term "Free Sittings" is used to denote sittings which are not appropriated for the use of particular individuals, and to which, therefore, *any* person is entitled to have free access. "Other Sittings" are those which are either let, or have become private property, or which for any other reasons do not answer strictly the description of *free* sittings.' If this instruction had been circulated to all places of worship, any later problems would have been largely obviated. See *ibid.*, pp. clxxii–clxxv, showing copies of the forms and instructions issued with them. A few Anglican clergymen commented on this problem in their returns, like the Revd P. Jacob, of Crawley (Hampshire): 'no distinction is drawn between free sittings, i.e. unpaid for & appropriated & unappropriated'. Vickers, *The Religious Census of Hampshire*, p. 126.

[104] *Census of Religious Worship*, pp. clxx–clxxi.

while 'appropriated' sittings were those which, 'either from a money payment or from customary occupancy, are not accessible to anybody indiscriminately; and that the residue . . . not adequately described, may belong to either of these classes, but most likely in greater proportion to the latter'.[105] In other words, it would appear that where an Anglican church returned *all* its sittings as 'free', Horace Mann had decided to allocate this figure to 'the residue', and not to count *any* of them as 'free'. Over all denominations he thereby arrived at figures of 3,947,371 'free' sittings, 4,443,093 'appropriated', and 1,077,274 in 'the residue' category, a relatively large figure.[106]

The problem affects the Anglican Church much more than the other churches. It may be that large proportions of Anglican free sittings were being subtracted from its total by this method, or that the discounted Anglican figures (for churches where all sittings were returned as 'free') were broadly typical of those Anglican churches where more precise divisions were obtained between the two categories. There is little way of ascertaining further information on this point. In addition, some leeway is required to allow for differing denominational understandings of what the census instructions meant. My analysis here will proceed on the principle of accepting at face value the census enumerators' initial statements on free and appropriated, as taken from their original unpublished returns, while entering in notes alternative summary percentages for the Church of England based on other possible ratios obtainable for its returned data, ratios which take into account the kinds of reservations that Mann expressed. In this way, the original and literal data can be inspected across denominations and regions without the benefit of Mann's interventions, while bounds of credibility can be supplied for the unpublished Anglican figures via alternative calculations of greater sophistication than those which Mann and his clerks were able to make.

All enumerators' figures on denominational sittings were computerised for the 2,443 parishes in the fifteen counties, allowing detailed analysis of them, of the effects of seat appropriation, and of the local socio-economic contexts which may have influenced such appropriation or freedom of access. One of the most important initial questions to raise is whether the criticism so often directed against

105 *Ibid.*, p. clxxi. 106 *Ibid.*, p. clxxi, cf. p. cxxxv.

the Church of England for its seat appropriation is justified when it is compared with other denominations.

Table 10.1 gives the percentages of free sittings by county for the six strongest denominations. For the Church of England, 45.6 per cent of its total sittings were 'free', over the 2,071 parishes where such a calculation is possible.[107] This is certainly lower than for the Primitive Methodists and marginally lower than for the Baptists (here combined together), but much higher than the Welsh Calvinistic Methodists, somewhat higher than the Independents, and slightly greater than the Wesleyan Methodists. Any idea that the Church of England was, in these terms, the most exclusive of denominations therefore seems doubtful. Indeed in some counties the Anglican Church had higher proportions of free sittings than all the other denominations in the table: Suffolk, Cambridgeshire, Bedfordshire, the East Riding, Cardiganshire, Caernarvonshire and Anglesey.[108]

Data for all denominations are given in Table 10.2, which shows the percentages of free and appropriated sittings for denominations, and the number of parishes in the fifteen counties for which this could be calculated. In addition, the final column gives the percentage

[107] Calculations here are performed for all parishes where the denomination in question had stated total sittings greater than zero, and the number (n.) in the table refers to the number of parishes supplying data for the denomination. Where there are no entries in the table, the denomination was not present. In some parishes, a denomination may be present but be stated to have no sittings, or the enumerator's form may have been left blank on this issue, or the question otherwise avoided, and cases like these are omitted in the calculations.

[108] To consider Mann's hesitations over the Anglican data, I calculated the fifteen-county data for the Church of England in different ways. The census data on seating divides into three groups: free sittings, other (i.e. appropriated) sittings, and unspecified sittings. Total sittings are the sum of these three.

If one selects only parishes where free sittings were less than 100 per cent of total sittings, free sittings were 42.4 per cent of total sittings.

If one selects only parishes where unspecified sittings were not equal to total sittings, free sittings were 47.2 per cent of the total.

If one selects only parishes where free sittings were greater than zero, free sittings were 47.7 per cent.

If one expresses free sittings as a percentage only of free plus appropriated sittings, the result for free sittings is 53.9 per cent.

If one selects only parishes where free sittings and appropriated sittings were greater than zero, free sittings were 44.5 per cent of the total.

Without any selection qualification, the result is 45.6 per cent, the figure in my table. All the above results are close to this, which is near to being an average of the different interpretative possibilities.

Table 10.1. *County percentages of free sittings by denomination*

	Church of England		Independents		Total Baptists		Wesleyan Methodists		Primitive Methodists		Welsh Calvinistic Methodists	
		n.		n.		n.		n.		n.		n.
Ang.	53.1	62	22.3	30	16.5	18	17.0	19			26.1	47
Beds.	54.6	105	38.3	17	38.2	45	49.4	68	54.2	17		
Caerns.	47.2	55	18.1	32	37.3	21	22.1	26			21.6	46
Cambs.	53.6	111	50.9	26	38.1	48	40.4	45	49.4	32		
Cards.	68.0	80	50.5	42	49.9	29	49.6	5			33.4	42
Derbs.	43.2	102	38.9	21	48.9	24	54.1	68	64.5	46	100.0	1
Dors.	53.1	236	46.4	46	44.0	11	50.6	73	62.2	31		
Lancs.	37.5	75	33.0	44	37.0	28	43.2	53	60.0	31	33.4	5
Leics.	46.0	205	32.7	36	55.4	64	53.3	100	65.7	46		
Mon.	49.4	108	58.8	25	65.1	36	56.5	27	64.8	13	58.9	16
N'umb.	36.2	83	31.5	14	69.7	9	70.3	7	64.2	23		
Rut.	33.6	53	46.8	5	73.6	10	59.1	18	80.0	1		
Suff.	54.6	425	46.8	73	47.2	73	46.2	65	48.4	55		
Suss.	51.4	222	59.7	49	60.4	36	51.1	49	53.8	4		
York, E. Rid.	48.9	149	31.7	26	19.9	9	34.5	120	32.3	82		
Total	45.6	2,071	40.1	486	47.9	461	45.4	743	56.0	381	30.4	157

Table 10.2. *Free and appropriated sittings, by denomination, for the fifteen counties and nationally*

Denomination	% free sittings, 15 counties	% appropriated sittings, 15 counties	N. parishes (from the 15 counties) with sittings for that denomination	% appropriated nationally
Church of England	45.6	48.4	2,071	43.1
Church of Scotland	13.4	83.5	8	73.5
United Presbyterian Synod	25.8	69.8	19	65.3
Presbyterian Church in England	13.6	77.7	43	81.3
Independents	40.1	57.2	486	57.7
General Baptists	56.3	43.5	79	37.2
Particular Baptists	46.8	49.9	164	51.1
New Connexion General Baptists	45.5	54.5	12	51.3
Baptists (unspecified)	46.6	51.1	273	36.7
Society of Friends	19.8	0.0	54	1.0
Unitarians	30.7	66.4	46	59.3
Moravians	65.9	0.0	4	5.2
Wesleyan Methodist	45.4	53.6	743	53.6
Methodist New Connexion	42.9	55.9	33	60.1
Primitive Methodist	56.0	43.5	381	44.7
Bible Christian	53.4	46.6	18	48.9
Wesleyan Methodist Association	52.6	46.9	71	50.6
Independent Methodist	61.9	35.6	26	21.0
Wesleyan Reformers	71.5	27.7	53	25.5
Welsh Calvinistic Methodists	30.4	69.6	157	60.9
Lady Huntingdon's Connexion	40.8	59.2	10	61.0
New Church	27.8	72.2	14	66.0
Brethren	100.0	0.0	7	10.2
Other Isolated Congregations	70.9	26.6	82	23.9
Roman Catholics	45.0	52.6	93	44.5
Catholic & Apostolic Church	40.4	49.9	28	5.3
Mormons	97.4	0.2	32	1.2

appropriated nationally, calculated from the published census.[109] Mann excluded a large number of Anglican churches which returned all their sittings as 'free' from his overall totals of 'free' sittings, as discussed above. His published data for appropriated sittings are more reliable, and so these data have been used here to calculate national percentages of appropriated sittings.[110]

The Church of England had relatively low levels of appropriated sittings nationally. If one refers to the final column showing national data, the lowest levels of appropriation were for the Quakers, Mormons, Moravians, the Catholic and Apostolic Church, and the Brethren. Other denominations like the Independent Methodists, the Wesleyan Reformers,[111] the General Baptists and Baptists (unspecified) were lower than the Church of England. The Primitive Methodists nationally came out much the same as the Church of England, as did the Roman Catholic Church.[112] Many other denominations – some of them (like the Bible Christians) with strong proletarian following – had higher levels of appropriation than the Anglican Church. This certainly seems to be true of Welsh Calvinistic Methodism. The Church of Scotland and the Presbyterian

[109] *Census of Religious Worship*, Table A, p. clxxviii. See also the discussion and caveats on pp. cxxxiv–cxxxvi, clxx–clxxi, clxxv.

Some very small denominations (not classed by Horace Mann as 'other isolated congregations'), were excluded from the analyses if they were almost entirely absent from the fifteen counties. However, it is of interest to note that the national percentages appropriated for them were as follows: French Protestants: 0.0. German Catholics: 66.7. German Protestant Reformers: 30.0. Greek Church: 0.0. Italian Reformers: 0.0. Jews: 67.2. Lutherans: 57.1. Reformed Church of the Netherlands: 0.0. Reformed Irish Presbyterians: 0.0. Sandemanians, or Glassites: 4.4. Scotch Baptists: 0.8. Seventh Day Baptists: 0.0. (See *ibid.*, p. clxxviii. Total sittings and other data for the 64 'other isolated congregations' may be found in *ibid.*, p. clxxx. This is not disaggregated by types of sittings.)

[110] The free and appropriated percentages for the fifteen counties will not usually add up to 100 because of the 'sittings unspecified' category, not analysed separately in this table.

[111] One needs to enter a *caveat* in the case of the recently formed Wesleyan Reformers, since in 1851 many of their congregations were meeting in private houses and similar venues, where there would only be free seats.

[112] On Roman Catholic practice after 1791, see S. Gilley, 'The Roman Catholic mission to the Irish in London, 1840–1860', *Recusant History*, 10 (1969), 131–3; J. C. H. Aveling, *The Handle and the Axe: the Catholic Recusants in England from Reformation to Emancipation* (1976), p. 302: 'Paying for missioners and buildings became a drain on Catholic resources, met by the introduction of proprietary pews, pew-rents and seat-rents. Inevitably the middle-class parishioners acquired fitted box-pews with lockable doors; the poor had to make do with hard, free sittings on benches by the door or standing outside it.'

Church in England had the highest appropriation, very far removed from many of the other denominations.

The fifteen-county parochial data provide a further way of considering such sittings, using explicit statements from the original returns on whether sittings were 'free' or 'other' (i.e. appropriated). The findings correspond very closely to the national data. For some denominations (e.g. the Wesleyan Methodists) they are exactly the same. This confirms the general representativeness of the fifteen counties. The Anglican data are also similar to those which Horace Mann produced nationally.

The figures here suggest much of comparative interest, and often display contrasts between denominations that become intelligible when one considers the differing social composition and hierarchical structures of the churches. In some cases there were enormous but easily anticipated differences, as between Quaker or Brethren practice and that of the Anglican Church, or at a further extreme the Church of Scotland or the Presbyterian Church in England. However, it should be stressed that denominational comparisons of this sort can be problematic, for reasons like those mentioned by Horace Mann. In particular, there must have been many effectively appropriated Anglican sittings which were free of charge to their occupants, and which were therefore entered as 'free' sittings. There were other Anglican seats which were appropriated *and* for which their occupants paid a pew rent. Despite the surviving church plans, we know relatively little about the form and extent of Anglican pew rent payments as compared with those documented in the rent books of the Nonconformists.

One could mention many further denomination-specific reasons for caution over these comparisons. The meaning of 'appropriation' varied considerably across denominations: there were differing theological and practical justifications for the practice; the sums paid could differ greatly, even in a particular church; 'appropriation' could occur for a variety of reasons without any rent being charged; the social nuances and repercussions were diverse. Yet when all such points and comparisons are made, and when the long-standing evolution of Anglican seating custom and social precedence is borne in mind, it is surprising that the Anglican Church produces such results. These show it in a more favourable light compared with its rivals than many of its historical critics might have anticipated. Those critics may have disliked the particular personalities and social differentials on display in an Anglican church; but to judge from what they substituted in dissenting chapels it should not have been the principle of appropriation *per se* that was being objected to.

The contexts of appropriation

An interesting question to raise here concerns the local contexts of free or appropriated pews. What sorts of parishes were most inclined to appropriate their Anglican church seats? Where might one find relatively large proportions of free seats? Such questions allow one to begin the task of relating church seating to the local social structure, an avenue in historical research as yet little explored, despite all the interest there has been in historical sociology during recent decades. There seems to be an implicit assumption in much historical writing that highly appropriated Anglican churches were likely to be found in the most 'traditional', 'closed', stable, agricultural parishes: those with the most hierarchical social order, in which everybody 'knew their place' outside the church as well as in it. Change to a more diversified parochial economy, introducing rival forms of wealth, faster population growth, and greater mobility of labour, might exert irresistible pressures upon an agrarian order, subverting many of the justifications and manifestations of its hierarchy. Prominent among those manifestations was traditional church seat appropriation. There are many reasons to suppose that these changes were well underway by 1851.

These historical questions require us first to see whether there was a relationship between landownership patterns and the extent of Anglican seat appropriation. The property classifications for each parish given in the *Imperial Gazetteer* will be used for this.[113] The importance of landownership is manifest elsewhere in this book, and this factor was also linked to the availability of free sittings. However, its effect was the opposite of that anticipated above. In parishes with property owned by only one family, the mean percentage of 'other' (or appropriated) Anglican sittings was 30 per cent. In parishes that were 'much sub-divided', the mean was 41 per cent, the intermediate

[113] For further discussion of landownership, parochial landed classifications and this source, see chapter 11 and appendix E.

parishes lying between these figures.[114] Combining all denominations, free sittings as a percentage of all sittings were highest (at 67 per cent) in parishes of most concentrated ownership. By comparison, the most 'open' parishes had significantly lower levels of free sittings (at 53 per cent), and higher percentages appropriated.[115]

Contrary to expectation, the most 'closed' parishes were *not* the ones with the most appropriated and demarcated church seating arrangements. Perhaps their social structure was such that parishioners felt less need to reinforce social hierarchy in this way. These parishes were also the least populous ones, and they had relatively little religious dissent. A high degree of concentrated wealth may have entailed select seating arrangements for the key families, but not for the rest of the parish. Benevolence towards the church from the leading family could make seat charges unnecessary. A more variegated parish, with diverse gradations of wealth, occupation and social position (and usually a higher population), may in fact have been more attracted by the demonstrative aspect of appropriated seating. Without paternalistic munificence, it may also have been the kind of parish that felt a practical need to charge pew rents.

To further examine parochial contexts we need to relate seat appropriation to other social and economic variables, like those in the occupational tables of the 1831 census.[116] Accordingly correlations were performed for the Church of England, Independents, all Baptists combined, Wesleyan Methodism, Primitive Methodism and Welsh Calvinistic Methodism, to test for parish-level associations between socio-economic variables and their proportions of sittings that were appropriated. After exploration with a wide range of variables, the results summarised below were found to be most significant.[117] Certain variables appeared consistently important across denominations, the most salient ones being measures of church or chapel size, retail and handicraft employment, population growth, and the proportions of servants and agricultural labourers among the occupied population.

[114] The calculations here are for parishes where Anglican total sittings exceeded zero.

[115] Calculations here were performed on parishes where total free sittings plus total other sittings exceeded zero.

[116] All parish occupational data used below were taken from the 1831 census.

[117] Almost all results reported below were significant at .001.

Church size was measured as the mean size in sittings of each denomination in 1851. This showed strongly significant results (except for Welsh Calvinistic Methodism), and it was clearly one of the most important influences upon the extent of appropriation. In every case the variables were positively associated. Where place of worship size was large, there also tended to be high percentages of seats appropriated. Small church sizes (as in many 'closed' parishes) tended to be associated with smaller percentages appropriated. A number of possible explanations might be offered for this. Larger places of worship may well have needed pew appropriation to raise revenues. They had usually been built in parishes where there was both demand and congregational funds for such appropriation. And perhaps their size, with their variety of possible seating, meant that there were fewer adverse social costs involved in allowing higher levels of appropriation.

Seat appropriation across denominations was also influenced by the level of retail and handicraft employment. The presence of a significant proportion of people in such work seems to have reinforced appropriation, and their incomes probably facilitated payment. Population growth (1811–51) was a further factor. Nonconformist seat appropriation in particular tended to be more pronounced in parishes of relatively rapid growth. Such growth may have raised demand for sittings, such that the renting of seats became one way of resolving or benefiting from such demand.

The presence of high proportions of servants was also linked to seat appropriation. The explanation for this is that servants were an indication of middle-class families, who could afford to pay seat rents. By contrast, poor relief *per capita* (1832–6) was inversely connected with appropriation, strongly so for the Independents.[118] High levels of relieved poverty were of course not conducive to payment of seat rents, among either ratepayers or relief recipients, whatever the denomination. The presence of high proportions of agricultural labourers generally had a similar consequence, very marked again for the Independents, and true for all denominations except the Primitive

[118] The poor-relief data are from the annual Returns to the Poor Law Commission covering these years. They have been amalgamated where necessary (mainly in northern counties) to parish units, and have been related to 1831 parish population sizes.

Methodists. It is of interest to note that the ratio of the value of the Anglican living to parish property value had no effect whatever for the Anglican Church;[119] but curiously it had a small negative influence for the other denominations. Where occupiers not employing labour were numerous relative to other occupiers, one tended to find higher appropriation within the two old dissenting denominations. Finally, total population size (1851) and population density in 1851 (a measure of urbanisation) both influenced the degree of appropriation. The larger, and more densely populated, parishes had higher percentages of appropriated sittings.[120] These were parishes where retail and handicraft employments were concentrated. They were also parishes of much sub-divided property ownership.

A separate exercise was conducted by dividing parishes into four groups according to their degree of urbanisation, and analysing free and appropriated sittings with different methods. The proportions appropriated were highest in urban environments, and declined as one moved to the more rural parishes. This was true for total sittings across all possible denominations combined; and among the six major denominations it was also true for the Anglican Church, the Independents, the Baptists, the Wesleyan Methodists, and the Primitive Methodists.[121] There was no significant difference in proportions of free or appropriated sittings for the Welsh Calvinistic Methodists according to the level of urbanisation.

The incidence of seat appropriation was therefore raised by population pressure, as in urban parishes, in conjunction with a varied parochial economy containing significant numbers of people who could pay seat rents. While one hesitates to apply simple economic ideas to explain appropriated religious seating – for many other unmeasurable customary and denominational factors had an influence too – there does appear to be compelling justification for 'market'

[119] Parochial data for both variables are from J. M. Wilson, *The Imperial Gazetteer of England and Wales*, 6 vols. (Edinburgh, n.d., c.1870–2).

[120] One might have expected topography to have played a part in seat appropriation, particularly in Wales – for who would wish to walk some miles to worship, perhaps over rough terrain, unless they were sure of a seat? But the results did not indicate much of an effect like this.

[121] Kruskal–Wallis and ANOVA tests were used. Of the major denominations, the Church of England, and then the Wesleyans, produced the strongest associations of appropriated sittings with urban parishes.

or demand-led explanations of the phenomenon of renting seats in places of worship.[122]

The Anglo–Welsh denominations' seating appropriation (particularly the Independents and Baptists) can be 'explained' more readily by these kinds of calculations than can the seating arrangements of Welsh Calvinistic Methodism. That most Welsh of denominations was more autonomous of socio-economic influences than were the others, almost always showing negligible and insignificant correlation coefficients. One recalls that such relative independence of socio-economic contexts was also found for its Sunday schools. Only one variable had a very significant bivariate association with Welsh Calvinistic Methodist seat appropriation, and that was the sex ratio in 1851. (This is defined as the number of men to 100 women.) Where that was low (i.e. where women outnumbered men), the proportions of seats appropriated in Welsh Calvinistic Methodism were high. We saw in chapter 9 that the same condition favoured this denomination's Sunday schools. It is sometimes suggested that women may have been steadier in their religious attachments than men. The numerical predominance of women over men in these western and northern Welsh parishes, coupled with female work and earnings in pastoral agriculture, or as small farmers, seem to have been circumstances favouring seat appropriation.[123]

[122] A similar argument on the free market's effects on church seating and rents has been made by Callum Brown for Glasgow between the 1780s and 1820. He pointed out that seat prices and church income from sittings rose alongside the population of the city, as the Church of Scotland and dissenting churches could not keep pace with the demand for seats. Middle-class people could afford to pay higher sums for sittings, and this process tended to exclude many of the poorer classes. It was compounded by middle-class concern over hygiene and other class ideas of refinement. Pew renting became a sign of 'respectability'. Many Glasgow churches abandoned free seats ('*gratis* seats') altogether in the first two decades of the nineteenth century. The higher income led to rising ministers' stipends and church improvements, but the consequent fall-off in working-class attendances became marked over the rest of the century, and increasingly the middle classes moved away from the city centre to suburban districts. Brown, 'Costs of pew-renting', 347–61. There is further discussion of Scottish pew renting and social status in C. G. Brown, *The Social History of Religion in Scotland since 1730* (1987), pp. 100–1, 114, 133, 142, 153–6, 161–2; A. A. MacLaren, *Religion and Social Class: the Disruption Years in Aberdeen* (1974), pp. 108–9, 111, 119, 134–5.

[123] Anglesey, Caernarvonshire and Cardiganshire (strongholds of Welsh Calvinistic Methodism) all had sex ratios below 100 (i.e. women outnumbered men). In Cardiganshire the mean parish sex ratio was as low as 86.5, showing the lowest number of men relative to women in all the fifteen counties.

The contexts of seat appropriation were also judged by using stepwise multiple regression, incorporating variables that correlation had indicated to be significant.[124] Similar results were obtained. Once again, church or chapel size proved to be the strongest explanatory variable in every case, with very strong statistical significance. Larger places of worship had higher proportions of seats appropriated. For the Church of England, the proportions of the occupied population which were agricultural labourers, population growth and *per capita* poor relief all had a negative influence, in that order. Much the same was true for the Independents and Baptists. Apart from chapel size, the measure of occupiers not employing labour as a percentage of all occupiers (1831) was the only variable accepted into the regression equation for the Welsh Calvinistic Methodists, having a positive influence upon appropriation.

The regression results indicated that the Independents' and the Baptists' seating appropriation were most amenable to explanation via these variables (which 'explained' 29 per cent and 20 per cent of the variance of their appropriation respectively). Equivalent values for the Methodists were 14 per cent (Wesleyans) and 20 per cent (Primitives). The breakdown of sittings for the Church of England and for Welsh Calvinistic Methodism were least susceptible to such statistical explanation, for such calculations explained respectively only 6 per cent and 11 per cent of appropriation. These two denominations most represented salient features of the English–Welsh religious, cultural and geographical polarity. These results suggest that the respective customary and cultural reasons for their seating patterns were largely independent of any such 'deterministic' factors which might be detected via multiple regression, and which more evidently affected old dissent and Arminian Methodism.

124 The parochial variables used were: retail trade and handicraft employment; total servants; occupiers not employing labour; labourers in agriculture; manufacturing employment; occupiers employing labourers; (all of the above 1831 occupational categories being expressed as percentages of occupied parish populations); mean church size (in sittings) for each denomination; parish population growth rates (1811–51); poor relief *per capita* (1832–6); parish property values *per capita* (from Wilson, *Imperial Gazetteer*, and related here to the 1851 parish population sizes); the 1851 sex ratio; population per square kilometre (1851); the ratio of the value of the clerical living to property values (from *ibid.*,); and the total population in 1851.

The consequences of appropriation

To judge from much of the literature, high levels of Anglican appropriation were associated with disenchantment, anti-clericalism, and a favourable inclination towards Nonconformity on the part of those, like Joseph Arch, who felt cold-shouldered by the church. Where free sittings were more available, it is possible that a contrary, more friendly, disposition towards the Church of England manifested itself. There is some slight statistical evidence to support such an interpretation. At parish level, Anglican free sittings as a percentage of the Anglican total were weakly correlated with Anglican churches as a percentage of total places of worship.[125] In other words, the greater the availability of Anglican free seats compared to appropriated ones, the smaller the number of rival churches. Similarly there was an extremely weak negative association between the proportions of Anglican free sittings, and dissenting attendances as a percentage of total attendances, a measure of religious 'pluralism'.[126] Anglican availability of free seats had thus seemingly helped to avoid the emergence of a pluralistic and religiously competitive situation, with the long-term adverse consequences that this could bring for overall religious practice, and the way in which it could contribute to 'secularisation'.[127] In this respect the Church Building Acts and the ecclesiologists' seating reforms were probably appropriate to the condition of the established church, even if they came rather late. These and other similar tests suggest that the Joseph Arch aversion effect is weakly supported in the data, but it is hardly as dramatic as the literary evidence for it.

If relatively high proportions of free sittings were a congenial and hospitable enticement to potential congregations, one might expect this to be manifest in attendance figures. It is therefore interesting to consider the relationship between the proportion of free sittings and

125 $r = 0.128$, $p = .000$, n. = 2,443 parishes.

126 $r = -0.059$, $p = .005$, n. = 2,273 parishes.

127 I refer here to findings due to be published by Alasdair Crockett. The greater the religious pluralism shown in the Compton Census of 1676, the lower the levels of religious practice in 1851. However, in parishes where the Anglican Church had no dissenters in 1676, overall indexes of religious attendance (i.e. across all denominations) tended to be relatively high in 1851. Religious pluralism in England and Wales appears to have had a long-term localised tendency to 'secularise', partly because of disillusionment with the adversarial options available.

the index of total attendances for every denomination. The results can be summarised here. Over twenty-five denominations, there was no clear general relationship between the two measures. For some denominations they were positively associated in a significant manner. This was true for the Church of England, the General Baptists, Unitarians, and Lady Huntingdon's Connexion. In these, high proportions of free sittings and high attendance indexes went hand in hand. For others the reverse was the case. The Wesleyan Methodists, Primitive Methodists, Welsh Calvinistic Methodists, Wesleyan Reformers, Wesleyan Methodist Association and the Mormons were the main groups whose attendances seem to have suffered by having high levels of free sittings. These were also the ones whose indexes of attendance seem to have been enhanced by having higher levels of appropriated sittings.

One might bear in mind another causal possibility: that the very popularity of a chapel allowed it to charge seat rents, rather than seat rents being a factor that tied a congregation to its chapel. This possibility, and the diverse denominational results, make it hard to generalise overall about the *effects* of free or appropriated sittings. One is struck by denominational variety. It would certainly appear that in some denominations – where followers felt that they had a stake, via quarterly money payment, in 'their' sittings – such appropriative practice could be beneficial to the church's index of attendances as well as to its finances. Most of the Methodist denominations loom large in this style of thinking, and for them the payment of seat rents would seem to have been a compelling sign of belonging and allegiance, one that augmented their attendances. In other churches, free sittings were an attraction that helped to boost attendances. As much of the literature suggests, this was so for the Anglican Church.[128]

It is possible that the relative availability of free or appropriated sittings for each denomination also had an effect on the 'index of occupancy' (which relates total attendances, including Sunday scholars, to

[128] The Anglican Church's data here were calculated in a variety of ways, using different selection criteria in computations to take account of Mann's hesitations. All results of such correlations between the proportions of free sittings and the Anglican index of attendance were positive, usually at an acceptable significance level.

In the analysis of all denominations, data for these correlations were selected only for those parishes where the denomination in question had total sittings greater than zero.

total sittings in each place of worship).[129] Once more, there were contrasts between the major denominations. The Wesleyan Methodists, Roman Catholics, Independents and Baptists (undefined) had strong associations between appropriated sittings and their indexes of occupancy. In these cases, high levels of seat appropriation were very clearly linked to high levels of occupancy (i.e. to high attendances relative to seating capacity).[130] Yet this was not a consistent result for all denominations. For many others this relationship was negative rather than positive, often significantly so. This was true for example of the Anglican Church, the Church of Scotland, the United Presbyterian Synod, the Presbyterian Church in England and the Welsh Calvinistic Methodists. Seat appropriation in these latter denominations seems to have been connected with a tendency for seats to be relatively empty. As one would expect, in parishes where these denominations had relatively high proportions of *free* sittings, the index of occupancy tended to be high. This was most noticeable (in terms of significant results) for the Church of England.

Conclusion

Generalisations about the meaning of pew rent as a system, and its implications for denominations and for local societies, have been common in documentation and religious history. On the one hand, there were attacks on the Church of England of the sort made by Joseph Arch and many others, taking pew appropriation as a focus and justification for anti-Anglican sentiment and Nonconformist activity. On the other hand, there have been rather different accounts stressing the way in which seat reservation could attach congregations dutifully to their place of worship, while also providing a major source of beneficial income for churches. These perspectives offer differing interpretations of the effects of seating arrangements upon church attendance and the preservation of belief. Both emphases have much justification and make very telling points – but neither seems wholly correct as a generalisation.

[129] The denominational index of occupancy is defined as total attendances across all three services, including Sunday scholars, divided by total sittings for the denomination, multiplied by 100. See appendix C for further explanation.

[130] Calculations were made for parishes in which total attendance for the denomination in question was greater than zero.

One is struck instead by denominational diversity. This is striking when one compares levels of appropriation across all denominations. Many denominations had much higher appropriation than the Anglican Church. It is perhaps surprising that some dissenters criticised the established church on this score. The socio-economic contexts of appropriation had much in common across churches; but diversity becomes apparent again when one explores what the consequences of free or appropriated sittings were for denominations. Where the Church of England had high levels of appropriation, it would indeed seem to have forfeited some adherence as a result. Reservation in Anglican churches frequently indicated at best the desire of the upper classes for personal comfort and convenience, and at worst exclusivity and the social divisions in the community. Something similar applied to certain other denominations. However, and leaving aside the important issue of funding, there were churches for which appropriation rather than free access was probably a sensible policy. The Wesleyan Methodists were a good example of this, as were the Independents and the Welsh Calvinistic Methodists. For groups like these, appropriation could be read positively as a statement of commitment to an originally unfashionable or illegal cause.

In retrospect, it would be easy to make a rational case for pew rents in such cases. For denominations like these, rents appear to have had little detrimental effect on attendances. They conferred many advantages in terms of funding, personal commitment, and a financially incorporated sense of religious community. This could be so for churches of very different social complexions: the same beneficial effect for the church could accrue through this mechanism of appropriation, regardless of the social level and the different sums being charged by denominations. As Horace Mann suggested, where 'the labouring myriads' formed themselves into 'a world apart', in religious services 'exclusively their own . . . as amongst the Methodists', 'multitudes will readily frequent such places, where of course there is a total absence of all class distinctions'.[131] The Primitive Methodists, and other such denominations, could in such situations rely on levied appropriation without detriment to their attendances, making a safe and clever use of small nuanced differences of rank and income within the working and lower-middle classes.

[131] *Census of Religious Worship*, p. clix.

However, the damage for English working-class faith was done when sittings and their rents excluded people from their rights as parishioners, and established further differentials which were perceived as an obvious extension of the grosser external class inequalities: when such seating reinforced those larger inequalities and seemed to embellish them, rather than appearing as a small matter of occupational intermixture, put to good use to support a community of shared religious and other concerns. Among the denominations such an effect was most pronounced in the Church of England, because of expectations of widespread attendance, ideas of parishioner's rights, and the social breadth of its congregations. This effect was probably most regionally pronounced in those areas where class division and social conflict outside the church were most explicit, like the cereal-producing regions of lowland England, long-established towns, and manufacturing areas. In other regions – for example in many small-farm pastoral areas – seat appropriation could co-exist with a more harmonious acceptance of social inequality. This was particularly the case where personal and group identities were conceived mainly in kinship, cultural and linguistic (rather than class) terms, as in many parts of rural Wales.[132]

This discussion has covered in general quantitative terms the phenomenon of free and appropriated sittings, placing stress on comparisons between denominations. Enough has been written to demonstrate how primed the subject is for further exploration. In the rules and seating regulations drawn up by different religious groups, there were expressed assumptions about government and attitudes towards authority. This issue opens up many matters of an internal denominational nature not addressed here. It has a crucial bearing upon issues like church regulation, hierarchy, custom and the sense of order within religious communities. The economic history of the Church of England – the most neglected subject in British social and economic history – would be significantly advanced by study of the customs and finances of pew renting. Seat appropriation also raises many comparative questions about the influence of theology on the practical administration of worship, as

[132] On regional variations in class experience within agriculture, see K. D. M. Snell, 'Deferential bitterness: the social outlook of the rural proletariat in eighteenth- and nineteenth-century England and Wales', in M. L. Bush (ed.), *Social Orders and Social Classes in Europe since 1500: Studies in Social Stratification* (1992), pp. 158–84.

well as anthropological questions relating religious cosmology to an exhibited denominational hierarchy, or lack of it. It would be instructive to know much more about comparisons across parishes, regions and denominations. More needs to be ascertained about the types of parishes supplying 'free' seats, and where in the place of worship these were situated. Precisely *who* appropriated seats, through what mechanisms, and why? How far were the criteria and allocations involved common across different parishes and regions? Were they affected by regional expectations that ran across denominations? If so, what does that tell us about regional cultures? How did the sums paid as pew rents (and their variances) compare across denominations, and what can one infer from this about the congregations? How were the important issues of belonging, outsiders, kinship, gender, life-cycle and possible seniority by age dealt with in seating arrangements? Beyond the obvious cases of the minister and his family, one needs to ask whether there were certain occupations, interests or groups that tended to be situated in certain parts of churches, and if so why such standardisation occurred, how regional it was, and how it changed. Did seating patterns embody notions taken for granted across denominations, or were they more distinctive than that? The majestic private family pews or closed seats of the gentry, with their heraldry and memorials, have been studied by genealogists and art historians – but who has studied where and how 'the poor' were seated, lurking with their thoughts in the dark side of the church?

The archival and other documentation covering this subject extends far beyond that contained in the *Census of Religious Worship*, being diverse and of fascinating potential. Seating plans, church restoration records, documents on re-pewing and rent books survive for many denominations. These often list members of the paying congregation at precise moments in time, allowing comparative turnover study of individuals who were long-term attenders, and others who had 'Left the district'.[133] They suggest how such people's circumstances and religious motivations may have changed over time, and during their life-cycles. With their details of sums paid for seats, they are indicative of social status and wealth – especially

[133] A commonly found report in ledgers of rents. See for example Leics. C.R.O., N/M/73/30.

when combined with local directories, baptism registers and other sources – symbolically representing aspects of the local social structure through church seating, and perhaps the status that individuals hoped to command within the church. In an understanding of local social and religious order, comparative denominational financial history, and the reasons for attachment to or alienation from religious worship, the study of church seating practice may yet prove historically instructive in many further ways.

11

Conformity, dissent and the influence of landownership

Introduction

Historians have had a long-standing interest in the consequences of landownership for local religious geography. The discussion has involved pioneering scholars like Alan Everitt, in his *The Pattern of Rural Dissent*, Dennis Mills in his *Lord and Peasant in Nineteenth-century Britain*, Margaret Spufford, James Obelkevich, Brian Short and many others.[1] Most have discussed the issues with reference to

[1] For discussion of 'open' and 'close' issues and religious questions, see A. Everitt, *The Pattern of Rural Dissent: the Nineteenth Century* (Leicester, 1972), and his 'Nonconformity in country parishes', in J. Thirsk (ed.), *Land, Church and People: Essays Presented to Professor H. P. R. Finberg* (Reading, 1970); M. Spufford, *Contrasting Communities: English Villagers in the Sixteenth and Seventeenth Centuries* (Cambridge, 1974), ch. 12; J. Obelkevich, *Religion and Rural Society: South Lindsey, 1825–1875* (Oxford, 1976); D. R. Mills, *Lord and Peasant in the Nineteenth-century Britain* (1980); D. R. Mills, 'English villages in the eighteenth and nineteenth centuries: a sociological approach', *Amateur Historian*, 6 (1963–5); M. Tranter (ed.), *The Derbyshire Returns to the 1851 Religious Census*, Derbyshire Record Society, 23 (Chesterfield, 1995), pp. xxxiii–xxxv; T. Williamson and L. Bellamy, *Property and Landscape: a Social History of Land Ownership and the English Countryside* (1987), pp. 162–4. More general discussion of nineteenth-century 'open–close' questions can be found in B. A. Holderness, '"Open" and "close" parishes in England in the eighteenth and nineteenth centuries', *Agricultural History Review*, 20 (1972), 126–39; D. R. Mills and B. M. Short, 'Social change and social conflict in nineteenth-century England: the use of the open-closed village model', *Journal of Peasant Studies*, 10 (1983), also in M. Reed and R. Wells (eds.), *Class, Conflict and Protest in the English Countryside, 1700–1880* (1990), pp. 93–4; S. Banks, 'Nineteenth-century scandal or twentieth-century model? A new look at "open" and "close" parishes', *Economic History Review*, 2nd series, 41 (1988), 51–73; D. R. Mills, 'The geographical effects of the laws of settlement in Nottinghamshire: an analysis of Francis Howell's report, 1848', in his (ed.), *English Rural Communities* (1978); M. E. Rose, 'Settlement, removal and the New Poor Law', in D. Fraser (ed.), *The New Poor Law in the Nineteenth Century* (1976); D. Ashforth, 'Settlement and removal in urban areas: Bradford, 1834–71', in M. E. Rose (ed.), *The Poor and the City: the English Poor Law in its Urban Context, 1834–1914* (Leicester, 1985); K. D. M. Snell, 'Settlement, poor law and the rural historian: new approaches and opportunities', *Rural History*, 3:2 (1992), 145–72. Among contemporary reports, see *S.C. on Settlement and Poor Removal*, VIII, XI (1847); *Report of George Coode to the Poor Law Board on the Law of Settlement*

smaller areas or groups of parishes than are covered in this book, and it is now worth developing the analysis further with larger-scale data which might further resolve some of the questions.

There are many important historical issues that need to be addressed. It is often said that 'open' parishes, of varied and wide landownership, were most prone to accommodate dissent, while 'close' parishes were much more conformist. Some historians even suggest that religion is a defining element in the historical considerations that set the more extreme so-called 'open' and 'close' villages apart from each other: that religion expressed the different ways in which landed power was exercised, and the parochially varied leeway for independence of mind. In the 'close' settlements, it has been argued, land could be made inaccessible for chapel building, much as there was often control over housing in the interests of keeping the population low and manageable. In places like Ashburnham (Sussex), Penhurst (Sussex), Ardington (Berkshire) or Lockinge (Berkshire), tenants were often checked for their religious and political sentiments, and superintended through restrictive clauses in leases;[2] almshouses, charities, schools, reading rooms and the like were frequently provided, but carefully controlled; vestries were often 'closed' rather than 'open'. Here the church commonly asserted the position and taste of the local gentry family, its own construction sometimes even complementing the architecture and fittings of the dominant residence, as at Belsay in Northumberland. The church was often an appendage of the emparked land that contained the landed house, as one finds for example in Sudbury (Derbyshire), Brocklesby (Lincolnshire) and many other such places. Within such a church, the position of the landed family was further embellished and celebrated by memorials, elite seating prerogatives, family crests and other related iconography like hatchments, the latter at their most widespread during the mid nineteenth century. Church restoration or rebuilding at that time further asserted the authority and prestige of such a family. Unlike the usually much more crowded and miscellaneously owned 'open' parishes, it is commonly suggested that closed villages were not likely

and Removal of the Poor, XXVI (1851); *S.C. on Irremovable Poor*, VII (1859); *Report on the Employment of Women and Children in Agriculture*, XVII (1867–8); *Report on the Employment of Children, Young Persons, and Women in Agriculture*, XIII (1868–9).

2 Although there were certainly some major Anglican landlords who tolerated Nonconformists, like Lord Yarborough in north Lincolnshire. See R. J. Olney, *Lincolnshire Politics, 1832–1885* (Oxford, 1973), p. 40.

to be environments in which religious dissent thrived, except of course in those well-known but few cases where the dominant landowners or employers were themselves dissenters.

Whatever one's views on parochial classifications, these are important arguments, and they have promoted much historical understanding. They require the comparative study of religion at the local level, in relation to local societies and the many varied forms that these have taken. The approach here is along such lines, using the parish-level data, informed also by fieldwork, literary evidence, accounts of authority and deference, examining broader contrasts between regions and between Wales and England, and benefiting from more rigorous quantitative testing of the possible links between local contexts and religious adherence.

'Open–close' parishes: historiography and precautions

Almost inevitably, the words 'open' and 'close' parishes occur frequently here, as elsewhere in this book. These have a troubled and sometimes contradictory historical record, firing controversy in the nineteenth century (and probably earlier), as well as between scholars from geography and history who have often used separate disciplinary terminology and concepts. The terms are used in this book in a conservative and restricted manner, with the following caveats. The argument is not that 'open–close' or other such parish classifications comprise causal models of a strongly predictive value. Rather, the intention is to explore and define more precisely the relevance of landed parochial character for religious features, and discuss them as predisposing considerations, among many others, which facilitated the parochial location of certain denominations. Quite precise *descriptive* pictures will be developed of the role of landownership in conjunction with other variables, as associated with the geography of religion; but this exercise does not extend to proposing predictive models which can be applied generally in Wales and England. There is no objection in principle to such models, so long as their internal linkages and supposed causalities are established warily and with appropriate statistical weights, and so long as the great variety of regional experience is taken account of by separate models. To satisfy these caveats, however, is a demanding and space-consuming exercise, and so my aim is the less ambitious task of more general description and explanation.

Insofar as 'open–close' classifications are used here, they serve as basic descriptions of property ownership, without any particular respect for historiographical precedent, or for any prior definitions that may have been offered by other historians. No historian ought to be fastened by historiographical precedent, nor is there much reason to expect historians to agree with each other when contemporaries, from so many regions, came up with such differing accounts. The usage in this chapter reflects the more inexact and theoretically unattached meaning that these terms had in the nineteenth century. As Holderness pointed out, for contemporaries who analysed the distinction, 'the "close" parish was simply one in which ownership of land and house accommodation was in the hands of one, or at the most three, proprietors who shared similar interests'.[3] He went on to define 'open' and 'close' rather differently for his purposes – stressing the effects sometimes associated with these parish divisions on the labour market and inter-parish mobility to work. But the terms will be used here as narrower descriptions of constrained, extending to more varied, property ownership.

In this way, confusion between the root causes or frequent enabling factors underpinning 'open' and 'close' parishes (landownership characteristics) may be more clearly distinguished from the *effects* of such differences (whether on poor-law settlement, relief expenditure, local labour mobility, cottage destruction, density of population and so on). In other words, I use the terms in the manner of many contemporaries, as applying rather loosely to the nature of ownership. This is partly because parochial and regional variety make it impossible to squeeze parishes into tight definitions. Nor do these terms *necessarily* describe a socio-economic condition that was associated in any invariable or linear manner with other variables. Many other features were woven across them, linking parishes together into different groupings or potential configurations, and these often operated with greater divisive strength than any 'open–close' dichotomy or continuum. Furthermore, in different regions, whether on the large scale between Wales and England, or smaller areas within the two countries, the importance of landownership in socio-economic terms varied very considerably indeed.

In many ways, the term 'estate' parish is preferable to the term

[3] Holderness, '"Open" and "close" parishes', 131.

'closed' parish, although estate parishes (leaving aside the later suburban 'estates') were probably a smaller sub-set of closed parishes. 'Estate' parishes may have had fuller gentry residency compared with 'close' parishes as a whole, and may have experienced a more concentrated exercise of power and paternalism as a consequence. After all, many estate parishes – like the Vernon family's south Derbyshire village of Sudbury – were very much tailored to gentry residence and living convenience. However, one can also find 'estate' parishes in which property was held by a larger group of people than the local gentry or other leading family. Or one can find 'estate *townships*' within northern and other 'open' parishes. For these and other reasons, the terms 'estate' and 'close' in this connection cannot be taken to mean exactly the same thing, although there is no need to define precise differences. Another label sometimes used is 'model village', which normally describes types of carefully 'planned' and built 'estate' villages. These take a variety of forms, and readers will probably think here of places like Milton Abbas (Dorset), Canford Magna (Dorset),[4] Nuneham Courtenay (Oxfordshire), New Houghton (Norfolk), Edensor (Derbyshire), Chippenham (Cambridgeshire), Blaise Hamlet (Gloucestershire), Somerleyton (Norfolk), Old Warden (Bedfordshire), Ilam (Staffordshire), Harewood (Yorkshire), Blanchland (Northumberland), Tremadoc (Caernarvonshire) and the like. These may be roadside villages, or they may be variants on squarer plans; they may be classical in architecture, or 'picturesque' in the 'vernacular' styles of Gilpin, Price or Loudon; in some cases they were painstakingly 'romantic', in a supposedly rustic sense; in others they were built to house industrial workers (e.g. the lead miners of Blanchland). They tend to have a stronger contrived and architecturally styled appearance than the broader notion of 'estate parishes' (of which they are perhaps the paragon example), often also having more pronounced emblems of ownership (landowners' initials or heraldry on houses, standardised colour schemes for parts of property, and so on).[5] There is

[4] For example, Pevsner and Newman wrote 'The village is a very complete example of the Victorian model estate, meticulously, if not stiflingly, philanthropic.' N. Pevsner and J. Newman, *The Buildings of England: Dorset* (1972, Harmondsworth, 1985 edn), p. 129.

[5] Among an extensive literature on the aesthetic issues, see C. Hussey, *The Picturesque: Studies in a Point of View* (1927); S. Copley and P. Garside (eds.), *The Politics of the Picturesque: Literature, Landscape and Aesthetics since 1770* (Cambridge, 1994); G. Darley, *Villages of Vision* (1978), chs. 1–7. Other classificatory

little need to use the term 'model' or 'planned' village here, for while such villages are of fascinating interest in architectural and rural planning history, they are comparatively small in number, and so their analytical usefulness for a project like this one is limited.

At the other classificatory extreme, an argument could certainly be made for the term 'open' parish having rather limited analytical utility in this context. Under many definitions it can refer to a great variety of cases, from Manchester to Castle Acre in Norfolk. Indeed, almost any urban parish was an 'open' parish, having sub-divided property ownership.[6] Many small rural parishes might also be labelled 'open'. There were plenty of southern parishes with tight nucleated settlement which were termed 'open' by contemporaries, but then (whatever the definition used) so too were some of the huge mountainous parishes of Caernarvonshire. One might argue that such diverse examples had little in common. For such reasons, the term 'open' parish probably has lesser relevance here than the term 'closed' or 'estate' parish, even though it is needed for comparative balance. It is clear also that the most 'closed' category of parishes has the strongest analytical viability, when one relates the *Imperial Gazetteer* evidence to other evidence on landholding, as in appendix E. For reasons such as these, there will be rather more emphasis in this chapter on the repercussions of 'closed' parishes than 'open' ones.

One further precautionary statement needs to be made, although it should be obvious to any sympathetic reader. It is not being claimed at any point in this discussion that local religious characteristics can be 'explained' in any full sense by landownership. For a proper interpretation it is axiomatic that one needs to consider a far wider range of matters, like preachers' personalities and charisma, the relation between preachers and local cultures, the cohesion and regionally varied attractiveness of theological tenets, the local political significance of religious views, the broader cultural regions within which denominations gained ground, the presence and rivalry of other denominations and the prior standing and disposition of the Church of England, and so on. My aim is narrower here, and focuses on one of

terms sometimes found are 'manorial village' and 'squire's village'. These are fairly uncommon in the nineteenth-century literature however, and have not been applied here.

6 The most heavily urban parishes have necessarily been omitted from this analysis, as explained in appendix E.

the most tangible, ascertainable lines of interpretation. The ensuing discussion will show that landownership is an aid to interpret only part (often a small part) of local religious geography. It should never be taken as a key explanation, one that allows historians or geographers crudely to lay aside the fuller historical picture. It is important to make such qualifications from the start, to indicate what one is *not* trying to achieve here.

The *Imperial Gazetteer* and landownership

One of the main sources in this analysis of the Religious Census is the *Imperial Gazetteer*, with its classifications of the type of landowning in each parish. This major Victorian source divided parishes into four groups: where land was held 'in one hand'; where it was 'not much divided' or 'in few hands'; where it was 'sub-divided'; and those where it was 'much sub-divided'. These were fairly simple classifications, cutting across a multi-layered continuum of parochial landownership patterns. Close testing of the *Gazetteer* against data from the 1832 Leicestershire land-tax returns, described in appendix E, shows that its classifications can be treated confidently by historians. The Leicestershire land-tax data can also be used to confirm some results below. The *Imperial Gazetteer* categories have been used by previous historians, particularly Alan Everitt and Brian Short, and my use of them therefore bears comparison with important earlier historiography.[7] They are also well suited to the types of quantitative analyses pursued here.

There is little doubt that the authors of the *Imperial Gazetteer*, and similar contemporary gazetteers and directories, had their eyes open to important differences between parishes when they used the divisions they did. They knew that such classifications often had important implications for other features of parish life. One of the purposes of the *Imperial Gazetteer* was to inform potential incumbents about the nature of the parish, as well as to advise visitors, tourists, com-

[7] Everitt, *Pattern of Rural Dissent*; B. Short, 'The changing rural society and economy of Sussex, 1750–1945', in The Geography Editorial Committee (University of Sussex) (ed.), *Sussex: Environment, Landscape and Society* (Gloucester, 1983). To similar telling effect, R. W. Ambler uses a fourfold landownership division from White's *Directory* (1856) in analysing his (ed.), *Lincolnshire Returns of the Census of Religious Worship, 1851* (Lincolnshire Record Society, 72, 1979), pp. lxiii–lxxii. For further discussion of the *Imperial Gazetteer*, see appendix E.

Table 11.1. *Landownership category and the size of parishes*

Landownership	mean 1851 population	mean 1851 acreage	N. of parishes
In one hand	280	1,697	88
In few hands	663	3,143	816
Sub-divided	924	3,775	271
Much sub-divided	2,913	5,332	349
All parishes	1,202	3,670	1,524

mercial travellers and others about its key features. Many readers must have been alert to the possible implications suggested by descriptions like 'the property is all with one family', or 'the property is much sub-divided'. Furthermore, the *Gazetteer* also mentioned dissenting chapels in its entries, taking that information from the *Religious Census*, and some contemporaries were surely conscious of probable links between the presence of such denominations and the nature of landownership.

However, one must bear in mind that parish classifications seem to have been subjectively made in the *Gazetteer*, albeit by people who were locally well informed. And the *Gazetteer* is weak by modern standards in referencing its sources of information. 'Open' and 'close' labels, therefore, especially when applied in a shorthand way to this source's categories, comprise fairly unrefined description, and should be handled with caution. In the absence of systematic and reliable data on landowning up to 1851 for parishes in all the fifteen counties, there is in fact little else readily available on this encompassing scale to discuss these issues.

Landownership, parish size and 'urbanisation'

The parishes classified in this way had different characteristics. One aspect of this was that close parishes were generally smaller (in population and acreage) than the open ones. There was a marked pattern to this, as seen in Table 11.1.[8]

This raises complications for arguments that close or open parishes had a predisposition respectively towards Anglican conformity or

8 The results are highly significant statistically. Using one-way analysis of variance (ANOVA), for population size the F ratio is 8.966, with a probability of .0000; and for acreage the F ratio is 20.561, probability again .0000.

dissent. It could well be the case, as Margaret Spufford suggested for the seventeenth century,[9] that religious dissent found a natural home in the larger parishes, and that by virtue of their size these happened also to be 'open' parishes. She pointed out that the causal links between the pattern of landownership and religion which historians have observed may be a feature of the open parishes being larger, and therefore (other influences perhaps being neutral) more likely to be religiously pluralistic. This is a point that needs to be borne in mind. There is some justification for this hypothesis, mainly with regard to parishes' acreages rather than population sizes, but it can be shown statistically that this point does not much interfere with the greater importance of landownership as an influence.

As one would expect from table 11.1, the parish population densities varied. These ranged from an average of 39 people per square kilometre for the most 'closed' parishes up to an average of 262 for the most 'open'. Indeed, some of the most open parishes would be classed as 'urban' settlements under many definitions of that term. I will concentrate on the theme of landownership rather than 'urbanisation' here, because of the rural dispositions of the majority of parishes that are classifiable in open–closed terms, and because of the strong historiographical orientation stressing landownership as affecting religion. Insofar as it is possible to disentangle effects, factors associated with 'urbanisation' will be controlled for. However, some points about the importance of landownership could also be made for 'urbanisation'. There is close overlap between their respective influences, for similar reasons. Fragmented landownership often facilitated both the building of a variety of places of worship and an independency of mind that could more readily choose between religious alternatives – but much in urban environments had a similar effect. It is difficult to uncover the various circumstances in closed or open villages predisposing to certain cultural and religious results, just as the great variety of towns makes it hard to generalise about the religious effects of 'urbanisation'. This will be considered in the final chapter, while confining discussion here to the implications for local religion of landownership.

9 Spufford, *Contrasting Communities*, p. 313, where she enters doubts on this issue as against Everitt's hypotheses.

Table 11.2. *Landownership and the Church of England's index of sittings*

Landownership	mean Anglican index of sittings	median Anglican index of sittings	valid n.
In one hand	86	62	88
In few hands	51	46	816
Sub-divided	41	40	271
Much sub-divided	37	34	349
All parishes	48	42	1,524

The Church of England and landownership

The Anglican Church is often said to have been strongest in the closed parishes, and much historical discussion has centred upon this and the implications that flow from it. There is no doubt that this is true. In whatever way the issue is tested, the results show the established church as most successful in parishes of highly concentrated ownership. Table 11.2 indicates this, taking the Church of England's index of sittings as the measure examined.[10] In this case, the Anglican Church was about twice as strong in the most closed parishes compared with those of much sub-divided ownership.[11] Much the same results were obtained by using the Anglican index of total attendances. At such a level of analysis, with 1,524 parishes over such diverse counties, this historical view can now be regarded as definitively proven.

The question of whether these findings were due to variations in the size of parishes was examined, a consideration (as explained above) that may lurk behind 'landownership'. Three approaches were adopted. First, the ordinal variable for landownership was transformed into four 'dummy' variables, and these were run in multiple regressions alongside variables for population size and acreage in 1851. Secondly, multiple analysis of variance procedures were used to

[10] This variable best represents the physical reality of the Church on the ground relative to the local population.

[11] These results are highly significant statistically. The Kruskal–Wallis 1-way ANOVA gives a chi-square of 61, with a probability of .0000. The parametric ANOVA gives an F ratio of 36, with the same probability. A median test gives equally strong results.

analyse the effects of landownership on the religious variable while controlling for the effects of population size and acreage. Thirdly, tests examined data selected only for parishes with 1851 populations under 1,000, and then under 500. All the tests demonstrated that landownership was the dominant factor affecting the religious variable. The explained sum of squares in the manova procedure due to landownership was nearly three times larger than for the covariates combined. Acreage had a larger role to play than population (as with landownership, being significant at .0000); but neither population nor acreage matched the statistical effect induced by landownership.[12] The results describing the influence of landownership are not largely due to the effects of different parish sizes.

[12] For the multiple regression, changing the landownership variable into four dummy variables, the results were:

	Beta	T	sig. T
tpop51	−0.0399	−1.599	.1101
acre51	−0.1362	−5.400	.0000
dum1/in one hand	0.1774	7.046	.0000
dum3/sub-divided	−0.0799	−3.103	.0020
dum4/much sub-divided	−0.1060	−4.025	.0001

(dum2/in few hands was not accepted into the equation under SPSS default entry requirements). R square was 0.0861.

Depending on what denomination or groups of denominations are being analysed, the R squares in such regressions usually vary between 0.03 and 0.16. In other words, one should not exaggerate the role of landownership and parish size generally in explaining religious phenomena, as they account for only about 3–16 per cent of variation in the latter at parish level.

The landownership data from the 1832 Land Tax for parishes in Leicestershire (discussed in appendix E) allowed the relationship between number of landowners and the Church of England index of sittings to be analysed through partial correlation. The simple bivariate correlation coefficient was −0.303 (p = .000). The partial correlation coefficient (controlling for population size) was −0.195 (p = .010). The results were almost identical when controlling for acreage.

The Kruskal–Wallis and ANOVA tests on the entire dataset for parishes of under 500 population (a total of 752 parishes), using the same Anglican variable, gave respectively chi-square results of 24.1 (signif.= .0000); and an F ratio of 11.7 (F prob. = .0000). These results can be compared with those in the note above, which refers to the entire dataset. It will be seen that there is some reduction of effect due to parish size, but this does little to minimise the effect of landownership on the Anglican Church.

Table 11.3. *Landownership and the total dissenting index of sittings*

Landownership	mean dissenting index of sittings	median dissenting index of sittings	valid n.
In one hand	5	0	88
In few hands	24	9	816
Sub-divided	27	22	271
Much sub-divided	30	25	349
All parishes	25	15	1,524

Landownership, dissent and religious pluralism

In conjunction with the view examined above, it is frequently claimed that 'open' parishes were much more accommodating of dissent, and more likely to be religiously pluralistic. This was so, it is suggested, because of considerations like diverse property ownership, lesser possibilities of social control, heterogeneity of inhabitants, experiences of migratory labour, or an independency of mind bred by the different kinds of marginal, upland, dispersed settlement, rural slum, or semi-industrial contexts often associated with such parishes. There have been quite complex explanations like these advanced, varying with the regions historians and geographers have examined. If one turns to table 11.3, it will be seen that an association of dissent with complex landownership is entirely convincing.

These four different types of parish contrasted markedly in their receptivity to dissent when, as here, all dissenting groups across the fifteen counties are combined. The total dissenting index of sittings rose very markedly as one moved from close to open parishes.[13] The analysis was pursued with Kruskal–Wallis and ANOVA tests, and the results were highly significant.[14] Further analysis demonstrated that these results were affected to some extent by population or acreage, but that landownership was a stronger influence than either of those

[13] The total dissenting index of sittings is here defined as ((ts-cofets)/tpop51) × 100, where ts = total sittings for all denominations, cofets = Church of England total sittings, and tpop51 = total parish population.

[14] Kruskal–Wallis chi-square = 101 (109 when corrected for ties), significance = .0000. The F ratio resulting from ANOVA was 12.3, and the probability was .0000. The chi-square on the median test was 120, with the same significance.

variables.[15] The index of sittings used here represents well the physical strength of dissent relative to population size. The same exercise was also conducted by using a different measure of dissenting strength: the total dissenting percentage share of all attendances.[16] The results confirmed those reported here.

There are other ways of looking at such relationships. In particular one can focus on the issue of religious 'pluralism', and ask whether the open parishes were more religiously pluralistic than the closed ones. This is rather different from analysing dissenting strength in the way just done, for it takes into account the range and number of denominations. It does so in a neutral way, without labelling almost all 'dissenting' and one 'established'. The reader will be aware that one can find high dissenting measures of the kind just described, but that these could be based on simply one denomination, as for example the Welsh Calvinistic Methodists in one of the parishes in which they were almost hegemonic. From a Welsh perspective, in such a parish, it was the Calvinistic Methodists that were culturally orthodox, while the minority Anglican Church in Wales was aberrant. In this regard, statistical variables as defined from an English 'establishment' point of view would appear irrelevant or an affront to practical cultural realities.

In this analysis one needs therefore to ask a further question: whether religious pluralism or diversity was most pronounced in the open parishes? For this purpose an index of religious diversity will be used. The measure itself is statistically complex, and was developed by Alasdair Crockett from quantitative indexes used in sociological and other studies of religious pluralism in America.[17] There are

[15] The data were examined with the same tests as for table 11.2. Multiple regression with dummy variables for landownership pointed to the key negative effect of parishes 'in one hand' (T = −4.372), the only variable for which the T value had significance of .0000. Acreage, and parishes that were much sub-divided, had secondary positive effects (T values respectively of 2.565 and 2.455, their significance being .0104 and .0142).

The data for Leicestershire were separately analysed, with the 1832 Land Tax returns. This produced a correlation between the dissenting index of total sittings and the numbers of owners of r = 0.248 (p = .001). A reduction to r = 0.176 occurred with partial correlation controlling for population size, and to 0.120 when controlling for acreage. Here (as in most of my analyses along these lines) acreage had a greater effect than population size, but in none of the tests can parish size *per se* be said to determine an association between landownership and religious activity.

[16] This is defined as ((ta-cofeta)/ta) × 100, where ta = total attendances for all denominations, and cofeta = Church of England total attendances.

[17] It is described in appendix C, pp. 436–7.

Table 11.4. *Landownership and religious diversity*

Landownership	mean index of 'religious diversity'	median index of 'religious diversity'	valid n.
In one hand	0.059	0.000	70
In few hands	0.249	0.213	766
Sub-divided	0.346	0.434	265
Much sub-divided	0.398	0.473	337
All parishes	0.292	0.341	1,438

various quantitative ways of thinking about and defining religious pluralism, and this measure may be said to measure 'pluralism' from the point of view of diversity. The measure can vary between zero and one: a score of '0' describes a situation of total monopoly by any one denomination (whether it be for example the Church of England, or the Welsh Calvinistic Methodists), while a score of '1' would mean 'total diversity' (which in historical practice is unobtainable).

Table 11.4 gives the results, again for all fifteen counties combined. It is immediately apparent that parishes became more religiously diversified as one moved from closed to open contexts. The most closed group of parishes exhibit very limited diversity indeed, with extremely low means and medians.[18] Then there is a jump to the figures for parishes 'in few hands', and progressive increase through the other two groups. The index of religious diversity rises markedly according to the greater division of landownership. The statistical significance of these results is exceptionally strong.[19]

The fourfold landownership coding is imperfect partly because it does not cover some of the more urbanised parishes. If it did, the

[18] The numbers of parishes can vary across these and other analyses because of the differing incidence of missing values for variables being used in the calculations.

[19] The Kruskal–Wallis chi-square is 127 (136 when corrected for ties), with .0000 significance. ANOVA gives an F ratio of 50 and the same significance. The chi-square on the median test is 104, again with the same significance.

Marginally weaker results of this sort were also obtained with sub-divisions of the data into groups based on parish size. However, multiple analysis of variance demonstrated that landownership had an effect on religious diversity that slightly exceeded the combined effect of population and acreage. Acreage was a very much stronger influence than population, although the t-values of both had significance of .000. Population per square kilometre (another measure of 'urbanisation') was irrelevant when adopted as a covariate with population and acreage, having a t-value of only 0.873. Landownership dummy variables explained 9.4 per cent of the variance in 'religious diversity'. Adding population and acreage increased this to 15.5 per cent.

results in all these tables would be even stronger. Analysis of the Leicestershire Land Tax data in connection with religious diversity revealed further differentiation of the kind described.[20] Taking other individual counties, it was clear that religious diversity, and the presence of dissent, were markedly affected by the nature of landownership in England. The social, economic and cultural ramifications of this factor in the English counties undoubtedly had a pronounced influence on whether parishes stayed with the Church of England alone, or moved towards religious pluralism. This is an effect that is much harder to document in the Welsh counties, as will be seen in considering Welsh–English contrasts.

Landownership and the denominations

This account has not yet paid any regard to individual denominations, but has combined dissent together. And the focus has largely been on the index of sittings – the actual physical presence – of denominations. The results can be expanded now by looking at some separate denominations, taking their index of total attendances, and analysing these by categories of landownership. This has been done in table 11.5 for the major denominations. In every case of dissent from the Anglican Church, the previous analysis is further reinforced. The strength of these denominations increases from 'closed' to 'open' parishes. The Church of England, as one would expect, shows the contrary pattern: of a high index of attendances in the 'closed' parishes, falling progressively as one moves into the more 'open' parishes. Its figure for the much sub-divided parishes is almost half that for the parishes held 'in one hand'. This is in marked contrast to all the other denominations. In some of these, like the Particular Baptists, the Wesleyan Methodists, or the Primitive Methodists, there is a striking upward progression of their figures as one looks from left to right in the table: from 'closed' to 'open' parishes – reversing the sequence of the Church of England.[21]

[20] The Pearson correlation coefficient for 168 Leicestershire parishes between numbers of owners and the index of religious diversity was 0.547, significant at .001. Controlling for population size with partial correlation reduced this to 0.387, significant at .001. The reduction was almost identical when controlling for parish acreage.

[21] These denominational differences balance themselves out when one considers the index of total attendances (all denominations, including the Anglican Church) by

Table 11.5. *Mean denominational index of total attendances by landownership category (ANOVA results)*[22]

	1	2	3	4	F ratio	F prob.
Church of England	46.12	33.26	27.28	25.23	12.80	.0000
Roman Catholics	0.00	0.52	0.22	0.44	0.47	.7040
Independents	0.41	4.97	4.17	8.06	4.27	.0052
General Baptists	0.11	0.28	0.35	0.79	2.11	.0975
Particular Baptists	0.67	0.73	3.44	2.67	5.73	.0007
Quakers	0.00	0.01	0.01	0.03	3.19	.0229
Wesleyan Methodists	2.15	5.79	8.76	7.45	7.39	.0001
Methodist New Connexion	0.00	0.06	0.07	0.23	1.15	.3275
Primitive Methodists	0.15	1.89	2.77	3.28	5.92	.0005
Wesleyan Reformers	0.00	0.09	0.15	0.28	2.41	.0651
Welsh Calvinistic Methodism (in Wales)	5.59	26.92	29.80	16.55	1.71	.1661

Notes:
Column landownership coding:
1 = in one hand
2 = in few hands
3 = sub-divided
4 = much sub-divided

The Welsh Calvinistic Methodists break away to some extent from this English pattern of socio-economic influence. Even their measure was lowest in the 'closed' parishes; but in the other types of parish landownership did not have the anticipated effect. For them, unlike almost all the others, the 'much sub-divided' parishes seem to have offered no special advantages, and their figure for these most 'open' parishes is appreciably lower than for parishes which were 'in a few hands' or 'sub-divided'. It may be that open–close divisions were less meaningful in many Welsh areas than in England, given contrasts in the size and topography of parishes, and the incidence of absentee

landownership. The mean figures by landed category were: 1 = 52.9; 2 = 59.3; 3 = 56.4; 4 = 56.7. Total = 57.8. Using ANOVA, the F ratio was only 0.546, its probability being .6512. In other words, the results are not significant.

22 Only the more important denominations have been presented. All parish cases with a value of zero are included, as this bears on the issue of whether a denomination was present in different landownership contexts. For the Welsh Calvinistic Methodists (almost wholly absent in England), the tests were conducted only for parishes in the four Welsh counties. If one takes England and Wales together, this Welsh denomination's results are of course much lower, but show a similar progression by landownership, with an F ratio of 2.58, and a probability of .0519.

landowners, although this is largely unresearched. The main point though, as when discussing other subjects like Sunday schools, is that here one observes a religious culture and *seiat*-based organisation sufficiently strong to withstand the pressures that landed power had over the situation of dissent in England. This was often coupled with historically high levels of pluralism in the established church in Wales, inadequate endowments, external lay impropriation of tithes, greater non-residency of both clergy and landowners, clergy who often could not speak Welsh, an unusually high reliance upon lowly paid and demoralised curates, and churches which were sometimes in a dismal state.[23] Furthermore, in many parishes Calvinistic Methodism and its integrated *seiadau* benefited from Welsh landowners who were themselves associated for cultural reasons with this Welsh-speaking denomination, and who were tolerant or supportive of it.

Wales, England and the counties compared

Most of the analysis so far has taken all available parishes in the fifteen English and Welsh counties together. It is worth considering these issues by county however, as there are distinct regional contrasts. Table 11.6 gives the results of such analysis, studying the issue via the index of religious diversity used earlier. The landownership columns show a fairly consistent change from very low average figures for the most 'closed' parishes through to the most 'open' ones. The final three columns of the table give the F ratios from the Scheffé tests, their probabilities, and the number of parishes used for each county.

[23] Clerical non-residency and absence from duty in Wales were as high as 60 per cent in 1810 (85 per cent in the Diocese of Llandaff). And poor livings were more common in Wales than in England. See C. Brooks and A. Saint (eds.), *The Victorian Church: Architecture and Society* (Manchester, 1995), p. 14. In the data from the *Imperial Gazetteer*, the mean and median values (£) of Welsh and English livings in the fifteen counties were as follows:

	mean	median	min.	max.	n.
Welsh counties	213	165	25	900	268
English counties	390	295	13	7,306	1,858
All counties	368	274			2,126

Table 11.6. *County mean 'religious diversity' measures, by landownership category (ANOVA results)*

County	1	2	3	4	F ratio	F prob.	N. parishes
Ang.	0.00	0.33	0.56	0.37	3.93	.014	53
Beds.	0.10	0.38	0.46	0.53	6.87	.000	81
Caerns.	0.38	0.38	0.60	0.48	0.91	.443	45
Cambs.	0.00	0.22	0.44	0.44	7.35	.000	78
Cards.	–	0.34	0.49	0.35	0.73	.488	63
Derbs.	0.00	0.31	0.55	0.65	12.34	.000	65
Dors.	0.01	0.24	0.16	0.33	8.00	.000	157
Lancs.	–	0.29	0.44	0.42	0.71	.498	40
Leics.	0.14	0.28	0.38	0.49	6.24	.000	130
Mon.	0.18	0.20	0.29	0.37	2.00	.120	96
N'umb.	–	0.31	0.31	0.33	0.02	.977	54
Rut.	0.00	0.20	0.17	0.27	0.60	.625	22
Suff.	0.03	0.16	0.24	0.24	4.39	.005	267
Suss.	0.00	0.10	0.24	0.32	13.41	.000	167
York, E. Rid.	0.33	0.38	0.44	0.55	3.56	.017	120
All counties	0.06	0.25	0.35	0.40	49.63	.000	1,438

Notes:
Column landownership coding:
1 = in one hand
2 = in few hands
3 = sub-divided
4 = much sub-divided

A number of points strike one from this table. The Welsh counties demonstrate among the weakest progression of religious diversity according to parish landownership, and indeed this pattern is largely absent for Caernarvonshire and Cardiganshire. Northumberland and Lancashire were similar to these Welsh counties, with religious diversity as measured in this way being largely independent of landownership. These two English counties were, like Monmouthshire, ones with relatively highly developed industries, and they also contained some very extensive parishes. Rutland (with its small number of parishes) was an exception to the general observation one would make about this table: that the Welsh and the industrial English counties stood apart from such an influence of landownership. For the Welsh this was largely because of topographical and long-standing cultural/linguistic reasons. For the industrial English counties it was seemingly because the traditional hold of landed power over cultural and religious life was disintegrating under the influence of non-agricultural sources of employment, which conferred greater independency from any domineering nucleus of agrarian control.

This is only a simple reason for the cardinal differences in the table, but it is surely the basic explanation to be elaborated upon. The other counties with very strong relationships between landowning and religion were usually more highly agricultural and 'traditional' in their economic structures: Anglesey, Bedfordshire, Cambridgeshire, Derbyshire, Dorset, Leicestershire, Suffolk, Sussex and the East Riding. Anglesey provides similar results to the East Riding, but with that exception these latter counties are English rather than Welsh. As so often in this book, the Welsh geographies of religion display a relative independence of social and economic influences that separates them from the patterns very clearly manifest in England.

Contemporary discussion about the repercussions of 'open' and 'close' parishes focused upon socio-economic and demographic effects, rather than having much to say about religious geographies. Such discussion was therefore differently orientated from this chapter. However, it is worth noting that the nineteenth-century investigations centred especially on southern and lowland English regions, often those with relatively high poor expenditure, de-industrialisation, narrow occupational choice, problems of surplus population and seasonally intermittent demand for agricultural labour. These had long been the poor-law reformers' main concern, and in connection with 'open–close' issues they were the ones highlighted by authors like James Caird.[24] The richest source for such description – the 1847 *Select Committee on Settlement and Poor Removal* – found its most forthright witnesses on these issues from counties like Dorset, Oxfordshire, Warwickshire, Leicestershire, Berkshire, Lincolnshire, Suffolk, albeit with more northern or western complaints coming from parts of Pembrokeshire, Worcestershire,

[24] J. Caird, *English Agriculture in 1850–1* (1852, Farnborough, 1968 edn), for example p. 516. For county and Welsh–English contrasts in wages and agricultural employment, see E. H. Hunt, *Regional Wage Variations in Britain, 1850–1914* (Oxford, 1973); K. D. M. Snell, *Annals of the Labouring Poor: Social Change and Agrarian England, 1660–1900* (Cambridge, 1985), pp. 96–7, 130; and for relief expenditure, M. Blaug, 'The myth of the old poor law and the making of the new', in M. W. Flinn and T. C. Smout (eds.), *Essays in Social History* (Oxford, 1974), pp. 145–50. For cartographically presented ratios of pauperism to population in 1872, see F. Driver, *Power and Pauperism: the Workhouse System, 1834–1884* (Cambridge, 1993), p. 55.

Shropshire and the Thirsk Union in Yorkshire. Norfolk, Cambridgeshire, Lincolnshire and Dorset were probably the counties most notorious for the 'gang' system, and for the parochial policies associated with it. There were no Welsh or northern English equivalents to rival the contemporary reputation of places like Castle Acre (Norfolk), or even lesser known centres like Binbrook (Lincolnshire), Middle Rasen (Lincolnshire), Tealby (Lincolnshire), Middle Barton (Oxfordshire) and their like. It was that kind of reputation, and the labour-market and supposed moral effects associated with it, which stimulated investigations in the later 1860s into child and women's labour in agriculture. The *Imperial Gazetteer* bears out this regional distribution to some extent. If one takes the counties with the highest percentage of parishes in the category 'property all in one hand', one finds Dorset (14.9 per cent), Rutland (13.0 per cent), Bedfordshire (11.9 per cent), and Sussex (9.3 per cent) as being the ones that are above the fifteen-county average (which was 5.8 per cent over 1,524 parishes).[25] The analysis here of the influence of landownership on religion thus extends in a regionally intelligible way contemporary concerns about other social and economic implications of 'open–close' parishes.

Explanatory socio-economic contexts

The explanations for these relationships between landownership and religion are to be found primarily in the nature of dependency and the exercise of power in the different types of parish. It is hard to generalise about this across so many parishes. The ways in which influence was exercised in closed parishes differed markedly. Some monopoly landowners were flexible and tolerant of dissent. Many others were not. Both cases could be extensively documented. This was not only a matter of insecurity and local subordination: closed parishes could

25 This point should not be exaggerated however. If one takes the two categories of most concentrated ownership, and defines these as 'closed' parishes, then the counties which emerge as having percentages of closed parishes above the fifteen-county average (which is 59.3% for 1,524 parishes) are Caernarvonshire (79.2%), Rutland (78.3%), Dorset (75.0%), Anglesey (66.7%), Northumberland (66.1%), Bedfordshire (64.3%) and Monmouthshire (64.2%). One sees the Welsh counties emerging much more prominently in any such ranking, although in these Welsh counties the proportions of non-resident landowners were high by English standards. And needless to say, there were many parishes in this definition of 'closed' parishes in which landowners did not act in concert, in any way that might fit into the classic notions of 'closed' parishes.

often manifest marked loyalty to the main landowner, conducing to a 'voluntary' disinclination to countenance dissent, and indeed outsiders generally. One thinks of the readiness with which some such parishes – for example in the Vale of Belvoir – acted collectively against the intrusions of Methodist itinerant preachers, a matter well documented in the annals of Wesleyan and Primitive Methodist history.[26] This book need add little to the considerable evidence of how local landed power operated, or was acquiesced in, but it bears witness to the effectiveness of territorial authority.

What can be further explored are certain socio-economic features of the different kinds of landed parish. Such examination indicates very clearly the ties and dependencies of the closed parishes, their constrained opportunities, and the limited nature of their economic base. It is worth outlining such contrasts, for they provide a useful structure for interpretation, one that makes clearer why the religious contrasts between parochial environments were so striking.

The average values of ecclesiastical livings in the more open parishes were certainly greater than in the closed, as one would expect given the larger sizes of the parishes with fragmented ownership. But one can also see from table 11.7 that the annual values of the Anglican living relative to population, and to the annual values of parish real property, were highest in the closed parishes.

It is worth noticing how strong economically the Anglican Church could be in the closed parishes, where the values of its livings aver-

[26] See for example H. B. Kendall, *The Origin and History of the Primitive Methodist Church* (n.d., c. 1905), pp. 229, 238–9, 252, 270–5, on the opposition to Primitive Methodism in the Vale of Belvoir, 'in the more purely agricultural parts' of Nottinghamshire, in the Trent valley, Rutland and certain parts of Lincolnshire. Some of the places most resistant to Primitive Methodism included Kinoulton, Cropwell Bishop, Shelford, Oakham, Bingham, Newark, Grantham, Cotgrave, the area around Belvoir Castle, and especially Bottesford. At Car Colston Green, 'gentry were numerous in the neighbourhood, and they watched the progress of the movement with a dislike they took no pains to conceal'. *Ibid.*, p. 252. Kendall commented that 'in a very real sense Persecution is "racy of the soil"; that, in proportion as men are tied to the soil which is not their own freehold, there are the conditions most likely to be found favourable to the propagation of the persecuting spirit'. *Ibid.*, pp. 308–9. For further discussion, see A. Rattenbury, 'Methodism and the Tatterdemalions', in E. Yeo and S. Yeo (eds.), *Popular Culture and Class Conflict, 1590–1914* (Brighton, 1981), pp. 34–5; J. Walsh, 'Methodism and the mob in the eighteenth century', in G. J. Cuming and D. Baker (eds.), *Studies in Church History: Popular Belief and Practice* (Cambridge, 1972), pp. 213–28.

Table 11.7. *Values of the Anglican living and landownership (ANOVA: 1,364 parishes, 15 counties)*[27]

	1	2	3	4	F ratio	F prob.
Mean value of the living (£)	223	305	379	452	16.80	.0000
Mean ratio of the value of the living to parish population size	1.47	0.81	0.64	0.44	42.68	.0000
Mean ratio of the value of the living to annual value of real property	0.121	0.115	0.087	0.071	1.92	.1252

Notes:
Column landownership coding:
1 = in one hand
2 = in few hands
3 = sub-divided
4 = much sub-divided

aged over 12 per cent of parish property values.[28] Such an economic position, based on beneficial landed standing and property ownership, post-enclosure status, tithes and so on, suggests a church well placed to exercise influence locally, however the incumbent and his supporters chose to do that.[29]

27 The count for each landownership category was as follows: 1 = 67; 2 = 727; 3 = 253; 4 = 317. This is based on the first row. Subsequent rows differ slightly because of the different numbers of cases that permit the ratios to be calculated.

28 The ratio is a preferable figure, for the value of the living cannot be seen as a subset of the annual value of real property in each parish: it included income from glebe, surplice-fees, pew rents, stipends, commuted tithe-rent, external augmentations and the like.

29 Many possible inter-relationships were examined between types of living (rectory, vicarage or perpetual curacy), their values, clerical residency, and 'open–close' differences. Space is lacking to develop these issues here. But in this context a matter of interest was the possibility that the type of living had implications for clerical income, residency and perhaps efficiency of religious control, and that if type of living was related to 'open–close' differences it could help explain some findings of this chapter. There was a predictably marked variation in the values of living by their type, the average value of perpetual curacies in the fifteen counties being £145, vicarages £268, and rectories £407. (2,029 parishes provided data on both the type of living and its value.) This is not surprising, as for rectors the tithes were entire, for vicars great tithes were in secular hands, and for perpetual curates tithes were all appropriated or impropriated. And *within* each of the three types of living, there was a distinctive and progressive increase in the value of living from closed to open parishes: the median

If one turns to property values and relief expenditure (table 11.8), one can see that the closed parishes also had higher *per capita* values and poor relief payments than the open parishes. The latter were of course richer in total terms, being larger, and having a more varied range of economic assets and employment. The first row of table 11.8 shows this clearly. But in *per capita* terms the picture was very different. Here the average values and acreages of property per inhabitant in a closed parish were well over twice the level found in the most open parishes. There were simply more assets available to individual inhabitants in the closed parishes than to their counterparts in the open ones, both in value and in acreage. As one might therefore expect, with the poor rate levied on fixed property, the *per capita* poor relief payments of the most closed parishes were considerably higher than those of the most open ones.[30] This came on top of the fact that

Footnote 29 (*cont.*)
values rising steadily from 'closed' to 'open' perpetual curacies, through 'closed' to 'open' vicarages, and then through 'closed' to 'open' rectories. This forms a very striking pattern in boxplot displays, with this sequence of types of living on the x axis. However, there was no relationship between the type of living and the parish landownership categories, a finding that requires considerable historical knowledge fully to explain.

On another issue, many visitation returns complained about poor clerical housing, particularly for an earlier period; but I could find no significant relation between landed category of parish and whether the clerical living included habitable accommodation for the incumbent. Data on these matters, and on the value of the living, were taken from the *Imperial Gazetteer* for every possible parish in the fifteen counties. As agenda for the economic history of the Anglican Church, these issues deserve much more research.

30 The 1832–6 parochial returns of poor relief expenditure were used, taking the published annual averages of those data for this purpose. The data for these counties is from appendices C and D to the *Annual Reports of the Poor Law Commissioners for England and Wales* (1836–7). Township data, or data for other sub-parish units, have been amalgamated to the 1851 parish areas for this book. A great deal of poor-law data is available in government reports, and parochial contrasts in relief expenditure tend to be quite long-standing. These dates were chosen because they document the situation prior to 1851, back in a period when the religious geography described by the census was being formed. It was also preferable here to take a period prior to the full application of the New Poor Law, which outside the incorporated hundreds started to function effectively in some regions from about 1836/7. This is partly because the 1851 local geographies of religion were very largely in place by 1834, and also because the differing parochial, union and regional policies of avoidance or compliance with the 1834 Act (the use of the Highway Rate for poor relief, the north–south contrasts in workhouse building, the local variations of out- and in-relief, etc) make parochial comparisons between parish relief data more problematical after the Act became functional. The relief expenditure data are here related to 1831 population sizes for *per capita* calculations.

Table 11.8. *Average property values, population growth rates, acres per person and poor relief by landownership (ANOVA: 1,364 parishes, 15 counties)*[31]

	1	2	3	4	F ratio	F prob.
Average value of parish property (£)	2,889	4,189	5,587	16,367	7.77	.0000
Average parish population growth rate, 1811–51	0.595	0.720	0.830	0.965	12.27	.0000
Average parish property value *per capita*	15.52	7.99	7.42	6.34	41.06	.0000
Average parish acreage *per capita*, 1851	11.00	6.36	5.03	4.61	30.55	.0000
Average annual value of parish poor relief *per capita* (1832–36)	0.972	0.703	0.741	0.637	7.10	.0001

Notes:
Column landownership coding:
1 = in one hand
2 = in few hands
3 = sub-divided
4 = much sub-divided

the closed parishes extended relatively full employment to their fewer inhabitants, and also usually dispensed a much more generous array of housing, almshouses, 'pensions', charities, allotments and other perks per inhabitant. Such parishioners were less in need of relief, and when they obtained it, they did so on much more generous terms. They obtained it also, in very many cases, through the instigation or influence of the Anglican clergyman, whether that was under the old or the new poor laws; and the clergy were also controllers of many parish charities.

In short, there was greatest dependency *and* advantage in dependency in the closed parishes compared to the open. Employment was relatively secure and well-paid. This was by virtue of the controls over population, the low growth rates, and the arrangements often made to ensure that only preferential inhabitants could legally settle or gain irremovability status. With their high levels of wealth per inhabitant,

[31] The count for each landownership category was as follows: 1 = 67; 2 = 727; 3 = 253; 4 = 317. This is based on the first row. Subsequent rows differ somewhat because of the different numbers of cases that permit ratios to be calculated.

these 'closed' parishes could afford to be generous to 'their own'. They were the more inclined to be so, given the long-standing employment records that many of these inhabitants would have had: knowing they were favourably situated, that 'their' parish was well worth being legally settled in, they would often have built up friendly and face-to-face relationships with employers who had facilitated their settlement, and who themselves took pride in the way they managed a village where they had proprietorial and residential interests. Much the same is often commented upon by inhabitants of estate villages in more recent times.[32] 'Coming of age' festivities in which the whole village celebrated with the dominant family, communal calendrical events patronised by that family, marriage within the estate, a clear and acquiesced-in sense of place and hierarchy, manifest in church seating and burial placement, tombstones erected by the landowner to commend dutiful and lengthy service of employees – these were so often part of the experience of close-parish inhabitants. Their housing, employment and 'social capital' were comparatively durable and long-lasting – and these were interests that needed to be carefully preserved, both internally and against interlopers. It is easy to see why Anglican authorities in such parishes could gain the support of inhabitants against religious and other 'outsiders'.

Such parishes and estates were widely criticised by liberals and radicals in the nineteenth century who disliked 'paternalism and interference' in everyday lives: doing for people what they might be doing for themselves.[33] Critics condemned the lack of religious and political freedom in such villages, and were aware of the risks and costs that

[32] This point could be documented with reference to many such villages. One thinks for example of Sudbury in south Derbyshire (where Sudbury Hall is situated), which I have studied for a number of years. The village was historically owned by the Vernons, a Whig or Liberal family. To judge from poll books, a large number of enfranchised inhabitants voted Whig. It is a village where the inhabitants display considerable loyalty to the Vernon family, and one that was remarkably well supplied with assets from an early date. These included an excellent school, a mechanics' institute, reading room, high quality 'grace and favour cottages', the 'Vernon Arms' public house, exceptionally early village gas works and supply, bowling green, sporting facilities, and so on. Needless to say, there is no chapel in the village, and in this case one doubts that the Derbyshire inhabitants felt the slightest penchant for Nonconformity.

[33] M. A. Havinden, *Estate Villages* (1966), pp. 114–18, on Ardington and Lockinge in Berkshire, as owned by Lord Wantage and Lord Overstone. The Liberal *Daily News* commented on these villages as being little self-contained worlds 'in which nobody is idle, nobody is in absolute want, in which there is no squalor or hunger'. (Cited in *ibid.*, p. 114.) No dissenting chapels were allowed in either village. *Ibid.*, p. 70.

could be incurred by straying objectionably from the established order. In these parishes, Nonconformity was one of the most overt options by which to deviate, almost akin to joining an agricultural union, and it is small wonder that few chose this when they had so much to lose. In addition to such deference and dependency, the hierarchical structures of a relatively simple agrarian order and economy seem to have raised few problems for shielded Anglican doctrine.

However, the costs of dissent were much less apparent to inhabitants of more open parishes, where rack-renting, squalid housing, pressure on employment and poor relief, exploitative relations of work, inadequate charity provision, anti-clericalism and the like were frequently the order of the day. Here, across a great variety of local societies, dissent from the established church came more naturally as a habit of mind. And in populous and heterogeneous parishes it came with few penalties attached. Itinerant preaching was but another form of the migration that inhabitants were so accustomed to. Dissent was facilitated also in the open parishes by the diversity of economic livelihoods, by larger populations, more extensive clients and markets, all of which might fortify independency of mind. Access to land for chapels was made easier by the fragmented nature of property ownership. Economic pluralism habituated inhabitants to handling conflicts of allegiance – for it was characterised by competing interests and factions, in-fighting over resources, haggling over price, disputed barter between interdependent but jostling trades, rivalry between workers with insecure employment, and conflicts between small employers and the labouring poor. This provided a context in which religious choice was coextensive with choices made in other areas of daily life. Here, religious faith was often a logical extension of one's affiliations outside the chapel or church, just as it was (in a different way) in the closed parishes.

The subjective experience of these contrasts can only be hinted at through quantitative data, which has evident limitations in conveying any sense of differing mentalities. Yet an aggregate description of the economic profiles of the open and closed parishes can be gained from the 1831 occupational census. Among the census data were parish figures for the numbers of families chiefly employed in agriculture, the number chiefly employed in trade, manufactures and handicraft, and the number of all other families not comprised in those two preceding classes. Having reworked those data as parish percentages of total families employed in each of the three classes, table 11.9

Table 11.9. *Landownership categories and average parish employment of families (1831 occupational census) (ANOVA: 1,518 parishes, 15 counties)*

	1	2	3	4	F ratio	F prob.
% of families chiefly in agriculture	74.4	66.5	63.0	56.6	27.75	.0000
% of families chiefly in trade, manufactures & handicraft	12.9	18.9	22.9	26.3	37.98	.0000
% of other families	12.7	14.7	14.1	17.1	3.97	.0079

Notes:
Column landownership coding:
1 = in one hand
2 = in few hands
3 = sub-divided
4 = much sub-divided

analyses the data by type of parish, giving averages of the parish percentages. Across the fifteen counties, the percentage of families in agriculture was highest for the closed parishes, at 74 per cent, falling noticeably into the open parishes. The reverse pattern was found for families in trade, manufactures and handicrafts, and to a lesser extent also for the 'other families', including people like miners, quarrymen, transport workers, fishermen and so on. The results are clear cut and securely based, as seen from the F ratios and their probabilities.

Fuller investigation of the more specific 1831 census occupational data, by landownership category, may be found in table 11.10. All occupational figures for every parish were expressed as a percentage of the 'total occupied population' for the parish.[34] ANOVA tests were then run on those data. The columns headed 1–4 give the average percentages for occupational groups within each landed category, followed by the statistical significance of results. Thus for example, in

[34] 'Total occupied population' means here the total population thus accounted for in the census. There are difficulties in the concept of 'total occupied population' as derived from the 1831 occupational census. It is most problematical in connection with women's work, and raises further issues about the inter-parochial age structures of the working population. These cannot be addressed in this context but, after much examination of the 1831 occupational data, it was clear that such issues do not materially affect the socio-economic and cultural relationships explored here. Similar calculations were undertaken using each occupational category expressed as a percentage of the total parish population, and these fully support the results presented.

Table 11.10. *Landownership categories and average parish percentages of the occupied population (1831) in different occupational categories (ANOVA: 1,515 parishes, 15 counties)*

	1	2	3	4	F ratio	F prob.
Labourers in agriculture	53.1	43.8	41.8	36.1	29.97	.0000
Labourers not agricultural	3.6	5.3	5.1	6.4	2.37	.0688
Female servants	16.0	14.1	12.8	13.6	5.22	.0014
Male servants (all ages)	2.5	1.9	1.9	1.7	1.62	.1827
Total servants (all ages)	18.4	15.9	14.6	15.3	5.57	.0009
Retail trade and handicraft	9.2	14.1	15.7	17.4	29.31	.0000
Manufacture	0.3	1.4	3.3	4.3	15.46	.0000
Capitalists, bankers, professional & other educated men	1.8	1.5	1.8	2.0	7.81	.0000
Occupiers employing labourers	8.3	9.1	8.5	8.0	3.89	.0088
Occupiers not employing labourers	2.3	4.9	4.9	6.0	8.59	.0000
Other males, aged 20 or more	3.0	4.0	4.3	4.4	2.15	.0922
Occupiers not employing labour as a % of total occupiers	16.0	27.5	29.9	38.0	27.59	.0000

Notes:
Column landownership coding:
1 = in one hand
2 = in few hands
3 = sub-divided
4 = much sub-divided

the most closed parishes (column '1'), an average of 53.1 per cent of the total occupied population were 'labourers in agriculture'.[35] The findings extend the previous table, with more discriminating occupational detail. They show clear contrasts across the four parish categories. Much higher proportions of the occupied population were agricultural labourers in the most closed parishes. The same applies for female and male servants. In fact, 72 per cent of the total occupied population in the most closed parishes were servants or agricultural labourers. These two classes of occupation were those most likely to have been in a dependent position *vis-à-vis* landed employers, and

[35] The columns add to more than 100 because of the addition of rows on 'total servants' and 'occupiers not employing labour as a percentage of total occupiers'.

most vulnerable to pressure as to where they worshipped. By contrast, in the parishes with most fragmented property ownership, 51 per cent of the occupied population were servants or agricultural labourers. These latter parishes were more sophisticated economically, experiencing greater division and complexity of labour. They had higher proportions of the occupied population in what are usually regarded as more self-reliant occupations, like retail trade and handicraft, manufacture, occupiers not employing labourers (making use of their own families), labourers not in agriculture, 'other males', capitalists, bankers, professional and other educated men. Some of these would have been susceptible and vulnerable in much the same way that most agricultural labourers and servants were – but the overall contrasts and their significance for religious freedom to set up places of worship, and attend them without hindrance, are striking.

Table 11.10 also gives figures for occupiers not employing labour as a percentage of total occupiers, which is an interesting measure of occupiers' family self-reliance (or even 'peasant'-like) status. This figure is much higher for the most 'open' parishes compared to the 'closed'. One should also note how almost all percentages in the table show clear progressions between the landed categories of parish, and how statistically reliable they are. One needs to be very careful indeed in drawing deductions about personal behaviour from such occupational data, especially on a subject like religion. It is certainly not the intention to suggest that there are straightforward linkages between occupational status and religious observance. The many ways and means by which people in different occupations could be religiously or politically constrained is not a subject that can be entered into here.[36] However, the implications for rather greater freedom of action, organisation and choice in the open parishes than the closed seem well demonstrated by this examination of the occupational and socio-economic structures of the different parishes.[37]

[36] Indeed, beyond the agricultural labourers considered in many works like F. E. Green, *The Tyranny of the Countryside* (1913), E. J. Hobsbawm and G. Rudé, *Captain Swing* (1969), or H. Newby, *The Deferential Worker* (1977), these pressures have been little studied for individual occupations, and there has been even less attention paid to regional differences. For a fascinating discussion of one occupation, see E. J. Hobsbawm and J. W. Scott, 'Political shoemakers', *Past and Present*, 89 (1980), also in E. J. Hobsbawm, *Worlds of Labour* (1984).

[37] Landownership variables stand alongside the strongest variables in multiple regressions aimed to 'explain' other religious measures. For example, in connection with the 'religious diversity' measure in England and Wales, the variables with the

Conclusion

As was observed earlier, there were many other influences operating alongside or ancillary to landownership, in what are issues both of parochial contrast and historical process affecting the local geography of religion. One should not minimise such other factors, even though they are much harder or impossible to measure. As the methods and quantitative variables indicate, in this chapter the argument has proceeded with considerable precision but within restricted terms of reference: supplying an encapsulated subset of analysis within what is ultimately a much larger and often indeterminate historical picture, spreading across many areas of enquiry. These areas are often hard to splice together because of their varied evidential nature, and because of the difficulties of marrying quantitative and qualitative types of evidence.

There is little doubt that landownership variations, with their implications for the exercise of power and independency of mind, had important local repercussions. The 'closed' parishes were commonly habituated to unitary authority, in what often seemed self-contained parochial worlds with clear-cut social and economic hierarchies, symbols and precedences, and strong senses of boundary. It is of broader relevance that these were the parishes that retained greatest apparent solidarity and consensus of religious belief. They were to dwindle in number and significance as a consequence of the later nineteenth-century agricultural depression, and of the First World War, with the widespread fragmentation of great estates and property sales.[38] In view of those later changes, it is of considerable interest

highest significance in multiple regression were retail trade and handicraft employment, parish acreage, manufacturing employment, occupiers not employing labour, the dummy variables for the two most subdivided categories of parish, and labourers not employed in agriculture. Out of seventeen independent variables used (including population size), these were the ones significant at 0.0001. Multiple regression to 'explain' the Church of England's index of sittings produced results in which the highest significance was for the dummy variable of landownership 'in one hand', followed by acreage and retail trade (the latter two having negative influence). Again, of seventeen variables these were the only ones significant at 0.0001. The same dummy variable had the highest positive influence in 'explaining' the Anglican Church's index of total attendances, as against the negative effects of variables like retail employment, acreage, non-agricultural labourers and occupiers not employing labour.

38 On those later rural changes, see F. M. L. Thompson, *English Landed Society in the Nineteenth Century* (1963), chs. 10–12; P. J. Perry, *British Farming in the Great Depression, 1870–1914: an Historical Geography* (Newton Abbot, 1974); A. Howkins, *Reshaping Rural England: a Social History, 1850–1925* (1991).

that fragmented landownership, and the local social and economic structures found with it, provided contexts for markedly greater religious pluralism and diversity. In a later book using these religious and socio-economic data, Alasdair Crockett will argue that religious pluralism was intrinsically bound up with a process of 'secularisation', being a major factor and phase in its development. Important aspects of the development towards religious pluralism have been seen here, in the comparison of the 1851 Religious Census with the 1676 Compton data.[39] In the light of this chapter, another piece of the larger historical picture comes into focus. An historical and cultural effect of the religiously heterogeneous 'open' parishes, whether rural *or* urban,[40] was an environment of relative freedom of choice, one less defensive of received doctrine, one in which more irreligious and secularised habits of thought and practice might be adopted than had been the case in agrarian parishes of unified authority. As an increasingly evident structural feature of rural societies, particularly with the changes from the late nineteenth century, this facilitated one of the most important shifts of mass belief in modern history: the drift towards secularisation, and towards the crises of belief and the search for belonging that supplied converts to the ideologies and nationalisms of the twentieth century.

[39] See chapter 8, esp. pp. 265–6.

[40] On the partial role of urbanisation in a process of 'secularisation', see chapter 12.

12

Urbanisation and regional secularisation

The growth of 'secularisation' is one of the most important subjects of modern history. It has been approached in a great variety of ways, across sociology, politics, anthropology, theology and biblical criticism, the history of ideas and of science, and many other historical sub-disciplines. There is no doubt that a spatial or geographical approach, using the data of this book, can deepen understanding of secularisation. It can do this most obviously by studying the effects of urbanisation upon religious attendance, and by looking at the cartography of low religious attendance to examine what scholars in some countries call areas of 'de-Christianisation'.

The view that 'urbanisation', or a growing proportion of the population living in towns and cities, adversely affected religious belief and attendance in the nineteenth century was for a long time considered almost axiomatic among historians. Indeed, a concern with possible shortcomings of religious provision in larger towns was prominent in the Religious Census itself, as revealed in the summary urban tables that Horace Mann supplied to evaluate 'spiritual provision and destitution'.[1] The arguments varied, but they included the views that urban parochial supervision was relatively ineffective, that a sense of religious community was destroyed by industrial cities, that urban churches and sittings were inadequate to demographic requirements, that non-agricultural employment was inimical to religious belief and fostered more secular forms of class organisation, and that the pluralistic environment and diverse ideas available to town inhabitants militated against steadfastly held older doctrines.[2] In many cases,

1 *Census of Religious Worship*, pp. cxix–clv, cclii–cclxxii. Those tables have led to some informative historical work, such as K. S. Inglis, 'Patterns of religious worship in 1851', *Journal of Ecclesiastical History*, 11 (1960).

2 Such arguments about urbanisation have also been made by many French and other European historians, like Vovelle, to whom this 'religious cleavage is one of the most expressive symptoms' of the urban–rural divide. M. Vovelle, *Ideologies and Mentalities* (Cambridge, 1990), p. 113.

observations about the most highly urbanised areas – whether Sheffield, the east end of London, the Black Country or elsewhere (such towns usually being English rather than Welsh) – were clearly based on accurate observation, and should be taken very seriously. In much literature however, local examples of the decline of urban religious belief were extended to more sweeping or theoretical statements, claiming that towns in general were more inhospitable to religious faith than the countryside.

This view of the historical effects of urbanisation upon religious attendance in Britain has been thrown into doubt over the past decade or so, most notably by Callum Brown,[3] although it is still compelling for many other countries. On the scale dealt with in this book, and using both the registration-district data for England and Wales and the fifteen-county parish data for 2,443 parishes, it is possible to resolve more fully the issue of the effects of town life. The data analysed here do not extend after 1851, so later urban influences remain a more open question. But the computerised Religious Census allows unprecedented analysis of the relationships between 'urbanisation' (measured by population per square kilometre and population size) and indexes of religious attendances in 1851. Some very significant conclusions emerge. Some of them will be outlined here, opening up the complex theoretical and empirical questions of 'secularisation' and its contexts, due to be explored elsewhere via these data.[4]

The urban or rural provenance of separate denominations has been touched upon earlier in this book, and is further addressed in table 12.1. Both registration-district and parish data have been used here.

[3] C. G. Brown, 'Did urbanization secularize Britain?', *Urban History Yearbook* (1988).

[4] For a preliminary statement, see pp. 16–17, 357, 394 above, and A. C. Crockett, 'A Secularising Geography? Patterns and Processes of Religious Change in England and Wales, 1676–1851' (unpub. Ph.D thesis, University of Leicester, 1998). This chapter aims to set the stage for the more intensive theoretical and empirical work due to be published by Alasdair Crockett.

[5] (*Opposite page*) Only districts, or parishes, in which the denomination being analysed recorded attendances have been used for this table, to avoid correlation with zero values. Thus for example the Church of England parochial sample is 2,095 parishes, while the Welsh Calvinistic Methodist parochial sample is 161. While this is the most meaningful way to proceed, the results need to be handled carefully, for one is not strictly comparing like with like. The correlations refer to the parishes or districts containing each denomination, but not to those where that denomination was absent.

One needs to bear in mind here, and for tables below, that the registration-district data include the 36 census districts of the London division, while the parish-level data from the fifteen counties are wholly extra-metropolitan. A more urban bias is thus imparted to the registration-district calculations.

Table 12.1. *Spearman (rank) correlation coefficients between denominational indexes of attendance and population per square kilometre, at registration-district level for all of England and Wales (column 2); at parish level for all parishes in the fifteen counties (column 3); and at parish level between indexes of attendance and population growth rates, 1811–51 (column 4)*[5]

Denomination	Registration-district level: index of attendances and population per square kilometre	Parish-level: index of attendances and population per square kilometre	Parish-level: index of attendances and population growth rates
Church of England	−0.166**	−0.185**	−0.156**
Church of Scotland	−0.211	−0.527	−0.709
United Presbyterian Synod	−0.330	−0.379	−0.591*
Presbyterian Church in England	−0.382*	−0.694**	−0.742**
Independents	0.005	−0.319**	−0.273**
Total Baptists	−0.043	−0.265**	−0.197**
Society of Friends	0.081	−0.074	−0.206
Unitarians	0.044	−0.535**	−0.619**
Wesleyan Methodist	−0.215**	−0.293**	−0.170**
Methodist New Connexion	−0.127	−0.718**	−0.546**
Primitive Methodist	−0.288**	−0.396**	−0.238**
Bible Christian	−0.442**	−0.562*	−0.278
Wesleyan Methodist Association	0.199	0.482**	0.608**
Independent Methodist	−0.405	−0.629**	−0.747**
Wesleyan Reformers	−0.128	−0.345	−0.324
Welsh Calvinistic Methodists	−0.703**	−0.247*	−0.284**
Lady Huntingdon's Connexion	−0.049	−0.842*	−0.582
New Church	0.016	−0.874**	−0.600
Brethren	−0.556**	−0.821	−0.524
Roman Catholics	0.234**	−0.414**	−0.229
Mormons	0.083	−0.567**	−0.430*
'Old dissent'	0.077	−0.140**	−0.126**
'New dissent'	−0.265**	−0.228**	−0.067

Notes:
** = significant at .001
* = significant at .01

Indexes of attendance were correlated with population density to see how far each denomination was associated with urban environments. In the final column correlation coefficients are shown between parish population growth rates (1811–51) and denominational indexes of attendance, thus touching upon a closely related subject.

These results show major contrasts between the denominations' ability to adapt to urbanisation. Some denominations (showing high negative coefficients) were clearly very rural-based indeed – for example, Welsh Calvinistic Methodism, the Brethren, Bible Christianity, Independent Methodism, the Presbyterian Church in England or Primitive Methodism, to take the most obvious in descending order. The parish-level data support this, although there are some dissimilarities: Lady Huntingdon's Connexion, the New Church, the Methodist New Connexion, the Church of Scotland, and rather surprisingly Unitarianism and the Mormons all showing a pronounced anti-urban bias in the parish data. Such conclusions are largely reinforced by the relationship between denominations and population growth rates, which show certain denominations being more caught out by high demographic increase than others. One can mention here the Presbyterian Church in England, the Church of Scotland, Unitarianism, Independent Methodism, the Methodist New Connexion, the New Church and the Brethren. A very large majority of coefficients in table 12.1 are negative. The table shows that denominations were usually slow to adapt to urbanisation and population growth. Some, however, like Welsh Calvinistic Methodism, were highly rural, and a lack of significant urban growth in their heartlands did not compromise their position. Indeed, as many stranded and song-less rural Welsh chapels now testify, they were to suffer more from rural out-migration.

One denomination in particular – the Wesleyan Methodist Association – seems to have been much more compatible with the towns, and with areas of rapid population growth. No other denomination could approach its urban compatibility when measured in this way, not even other recently formed ones like the Wesleyan Reformers, although the Society of Friends, the Catholics and Mormons show rather more adaptability to urbanisation than most. Only the Wesleyan Methodist Association was positively associated with population growth – indeed, it seems to have thrived on such growth in a remarkable manner.

Nothing has been said so far about the Church of England. It is a widely held view that the established church did not keep up with the growth of towns and demographic increase, and that it performed best in rural society. Urbanisation and the Industrial Revolution are usually thought to have put the established church into an increasingly anachronistic position, and other denominations gained as a result. It is true that the Church of England was well acclimatised to rural parishes, especially those with slight population growth. However, table 12.1 suggests that it did better in urban locations than most of its rivals, despite its longer rural traditions and inheritance. It seems to have been more adaptable to the towns than 'new dissent' as a whole, although it was slightly more rural-based than combined 'old dissent', which often had strongholds in market towns.[6] The differences in the table between the Anglican Church, and the general groupings of 'old' and 'new' dissent, are very minor. And the Church of England emerges in a remarkably favourable light from the contrasts between separate denominations. It would take further analysis to judge whether this was a longer-term situation, to be found also in the seventeenth and eighteenth centuries,[7] or whether the administrative and financial reforms before 1851, the Church Building and New Parishes Acts, the new or refurbished churches, and the initiatives associated with the Oxford Movement and Gothic Revival, had accomplished this. To take a more visible form of evidence than census returns, many of the most famous Gothic Revival churches – like Butterfield's All Saints Margaret Street, or R. C. Carpenter's St Mary Magdalene, Munster Square – were being built at the time of the 1851 census in slum or working-class neighbourhoods, served by ritualist priests like A. D. Wagner in St Paul's, Brighton (another R. C. Carpenter church commissioned in the late 1840s). Like Father Wagner, they sometimes had a mixed reception. Once more, however, as with Sunday school provision or denominational seating, the Anglican Church emerges in a more favourable and responsive light than some portrayals of lethargy or conservatism have allowed.

6 Old and new dissent are as defined in chapters 3 and 4.

7 Rank correlation between the percentages of the 1676 (adjusted) Compton population that were Papist, Nonconformist or conformist, and the total (adjusted) Compton population per square kilometre, produced random results for each of the three 1676 denominational groups. There are of course problems with this, including some change in parish acreages, and doubts over the Compton figures.

Table 12.2. *Categories of 'urbanisation', and their corresponding average index of total attendances for all denominations, at registration–district and parish levels*[8]

Category of 'urbanisation'*	Registration districts (mean index of total attendances)	Parishes (mean index of total attendances)
Group 1	69.2	53.9
Group 2	73.2	54.5
Group 3	72.6	58.6
Group 4	53.5	59.5
Total	67.1	56.6

Notes: * The categories of 'urbanisation' are based upon quartile divisions of the variable 'population per square kilometre', separately calculated for the registration-district data and for the parish data. Group 1 represents the least urban (or most rural) districts or parishes, while group 4 represents the most urban ones. For the registration-district column, there are 156 districts in each group (a total of 624 districts), while for the parish column there are 595 parishes in each group (a total of 2,380 parishes).

Urbanisation and total religious attendances

After considering these rural–urban comparisons on a denominational basis, the effect of urbanisation upon *total* religious attendance can be considered. The best way of assessing this is in table 12.2, which uses the index of total attendances for all denominations, taking both registration-district and parish data. This index of total attendances has been related to four categories of 'urbanisation'. In the column headed 'category of urbanisation', group 1 is of the *least* urban districts or parishes, and the rows progress down through groups 2 and 3 to the *most* 'urban' ones, in group 4. If urbanisation had had an adverse effect upon religious attendance by 1851, there should be clear-cut reductions in the index of total attendances as one moves down from the least urban areas to the most urban ones.

This table throws doubt on the pessimistic view of urbanisation's effects, expressed as an historical generalisation about the rural–urban continuum. There is little support for it in these data, and

8 Using one-way analysis of variance and the Scheffé test, for registration districts the F ratio is 42.6 with a probability of .000. (Groups 1, 2 and 3 are significantly different from group 4 with a significance level of .05.) For parishes, the F ratio is 1.84 with a probability of .137. (No groups are significantly different from each other at the .05 level.)

analyses on this large scale eclipse the scope of previous British work.[9] All that can be said for the conventional view is that group 4 of the registration-district data (the *most* 'urban' group) shows a reduction from the other three groups,[10] although within those three groups there is no downward trend as one moves into more urban districts. However, the parish-level data show an even more surprising picture. As the spectrum of parishes became more urban, so their overall index of religious attendances consistently *rose*. While this rise was not sufficiently large to make it statistically significant, it is wholly contrary to expectations and to much of the historiography.[11]

These are important findings with considerable implications, so they should be tested one step further via rank correlation. Table 12.3 shows registration-district and parish-level findings alongside each other. It gives the Spearman coefficients between 'urbanisation' (population per square kilometre) and the index of total attendances for all denominations. England and Wales are shown separately, and

[9] The Spearman correlation coefficient between parish population size and population per square kilometre (1851) was 0.635, significant at .001. Both variables are good indicators of 'urbanisation', although population per square kilometre is technically preferable for these rank correlations. The parish data were also analysed using population size to indicate 'urbanisation', and the results were similar to those reported above. Divisions of parishes into four groups based on the quartiles of their 1851 population, and analysis (ANOVA and Scheffé test) of the index of total attendances for all denominations by those groups, produced an F ratio of only 1.49 (prob. = .214). No two groups were significantly different at the .05 level. Further analysis showed that for 113 parishes with populations over 5,000, the median index of total attendances was 47.3. This compared with 50.0 for 2,328 parishes with under 5,000 people. The difference was statistically insignificant, and suggests again that urbanisation *per se* is not an adequate explanation for variations in the index of total attendances.

[10] This effect is largely due to the inclusion of the 36 London registration districts, which fall into this group 4. They do not feature in the parish-level data from the fifteen counties.

[11] In Wales this beneficial effect of urbanisation upon parish-level religious attendances was even more pronounced, with a significance of .0002 (ANOVA). The least urban Welsh parishes (group 1) had a mean index of total attendances for all denominations of 53.7, which rose progressively to 92.9 for the most urban parishes (group 4). Their overall mean index of total attendances for all denominations was 69.2 (across 354 parishes in the four researched Welsh counties). If one takes only the English counties, the same effect was still present, albeit much less acutely: rising from 54.0 (group 1) to 55.3 (group 4). The overall English mean was much lower than the Welsh at 54.4 (across 2,026 parishes in eleven counties). In both England and Wales therefore, urbanisation enhanced religious attendances at the parish level, and this was very noticeable for Wales. The contrast of the parish data with the registration-district data is (as noted above) largely because the latter include London. The capital and its hinterland were, we shall see, marked by relatively low attendances.

Table 12.3. *Spearman (rank) correlation coefficients between 'urbanisation' and indexes of attendances for all denominations, at registration-district and parish levels*

	Registration-district level	Significance	Parish-level	Significance
England	−0.290	.000	0.080	.000
Wales	−0.050	.734	0.289	.000
England and Wales	−0.301	.000	0.108	.000

then combined in the bottom row. If urbanisation induced low attendance at church, then all results should be clearly negative.

Once more the overall effect of urbanisation in reducing church or chapel attendance comes into some doubt. There is evidence for such a role in the registration-district data of table 12.3, partly because those data include London.[12] In the 48 Welsh districts urbanisation was irrelevant. At the parish level, however, the conclusions from the previous analysis are reinforced. There was a very small tendency for parochial indexes of attendance to rise with urbanisation, and this was most marked for Wales. The parish data are more tightly focused than those for the registration districts, they are not affected by the special case of London, and many 'urban' districts contained surrounding rural parishes, making them rather blunt analytically for my purpose. Nevertheless, close inspection of the district data reveals some further points. For the very largest 31 urban areas, with populations over 80,000, only one district (Dudley) had an index of total attendances for all denominations above the English average of 66.[13] In that sense, extreme urbanisation was inimical to above average attendances. Low indexes from the large English cities are readily found, and London districts were notable among them, as we shall see. Other highly urban districts with low indexes of total attendances (given in brackets) were Birmingham (38), Sheffield (38), Manchester (38), Liverpool (42), Bolton (45), Ashton under Lyme (46), and Wolverhampton (47).[14]

12 If one omits the 36 London districts, the English and Welsh rank correlation coefficient falls from −0.301 to −0.196.

13 The relation between population size and the index of total attendances in this group of 31 districts was completely random.

14 These districts were the ones with populations over 100,000 and indexes of total attendances of under 50. In London, the same criteria were met by Shoreditch (20), St

Yet one can find many districts with populations of between 20,000 and 80,000, some of them with quite high population densities, which had above average religious attendance. Moderate urbanisation did not inhibit high indexes of attendance in these.[15] Measured over the rural–urban continuum, and setting aside London and some other extreme cases for the moment, many urban environments were not detrimental to religious attendances in 1851.[16] It is also worth recalling that *per capita* church membership, and Anglican Easter Day

George (East) (23), Kensington (33), Stepney (34), Lambeth (34), Marylebone (39), and Pancras (46). Most of the smaller London districts had indexes under 50. Many urban districts in the north-east had indexes of total attendance below 50, including Durham (39), Gateshead (41), Tynemouth (43), Newcastle upon Tyne (44), Sunderland (47), and South Shields (49). In Lancashire and the West Riding, there were districts like Oldham (32), Salford (38), Barnsley (40), Preston (43), Bolton (45), Bury (48), and Stockport (48). West midland urban equivalents were Aston (33), Stoke-on-Trent (39), Stafford (41), Coventry (43), Walsall (46) and Solihull (46). (One needs to bear in mind that some of these districts still covered rural areas in 1851.)

Parishes with populations over 10,000 and low indexes of total attendance of between 15 and 40 included Newcastle (All Saints, or St John), Preston, Prestwich, Chorley, Manchester, Bury, Rochdale, Wigan, Lancaster, Leicester (St Margaret), Blackburn, Liverpool and Glossop. However, there were extremely large numbers of rural parishes with exceptionally low indexes, often much lower than these urban ones.

Among the registration districts, the very lowest indexes of total attendances (below 30) were found in the following *urban and rural* districts: Longtown (17), Shoreditch (20), St George (East) (23), Haltwhistle (23), Poplar (26), Radford (26), Wigton (27), Saddleworth (28), Ecclesall Bierlow (28), Bethnal Green (28), Brampton (28), Clerkenwell (29) and Strand (29). Population per square kilometre in these districts could hardly range more widely: from 21 (Haltwhistle) to 63,139 (Strand). This unpredictable but crucial mix particularly of border and/or rural districts, with those of London and a few other industrial districts, will be interpreted below.

15 High indexes of over 90 (given in brackets) were found in districts like Colchester (92), Marlborough (92), Carmarthen (92), Kettering (95), Newport Pagnell (99), Bradford (100), Llanelly (100), Bedford (102), Luton (103), Stroud (103), Bangor (108), Cardigan (110), Royston (112), Dursley (121), Salisbury (124), or Aberystwyth (131), although these were certainly not as densely urban as the urban districts with the lowest indexes of attendance, and they often included rural parishes. Aberystwyth had the highest index of total attendances for all denominations of any registration district in England and Wales, although it was exceeded by the Scilly Isles (133).

Many examples of high indexes of total attendances (between 80 and 172) can be documented for urban parishes, like Beverley (St Martin, or St Mary), Newcastle (St Nicholas), Lowestoft, Poole (St James), Woodbridge, Biggleswade, Luton, Bridport, Blandford Forum, Leicester (All Saints), Dunstable or Stowmarket.

16 Similar doubts are raised for Scotland in C. G. Brown, *The Social History of Religion in Scotland since 1730* (1987), pp. 81–3; and more generally his 'Did urbanization secularize Britain?'. The adequacy of an interpretative stress in religious history between the rural and urban is discussed in D. Thompson, 'The churches and society in nineteenth-century England: a rural perspective', in G. J. Cuming and D. Baker (eds.), *Studies in Church History: Popular Belief and Practice* (Cambridge, 1972), p. 270; I. Sellers, *Nineteenth-Century Nonconformity* (1977), pp. 54–5.

communicant density, seem not to have declined in the nineteenth century.[17] Furthermore, the classic period of industrialisation, with its rapid urbanisation, witnessed a growth of new denominations and of church building that is completely unrivalled in British history. The remarkable growth of religious pluralism was touched upon in chapter 8, when comparisons were made between 1676 and 1851.[18] If one includes the many 'other isolated congregations', there were about *seventy* sects and denominations named in the Religious Census which had not existed in 1700. Since then, over half of the thirty-five denominations separately tabulated by Horace Mann had come into being in Britain. 4,410 (out of 14,077) Anglican churches had been built after 1801 (figures are not available for the eighteenth century). It is difficult to be exact on this, but if one considers all sects and denominations, over half of their 34,467 total places of worship in England and Wales (1851) must have been built or designated between 1750 and 1851, and probably most of these were in urban areas.

Extreme urbanisation in London and some of the largest English industrial cities did therefore tend to reduce religious attendances – but one should be sceptical about whether this was true of urbanisation more generally. This need not surprise us. After all, most towns were integrated within their rural surroundings to a greater extent than is true today. They were supplied by large numbers of short-distance migrants from country areas, bringing their beliefs with them, many of whom periodically returned to the country, where they were often legally settled for poor-law purposes. Urban dwellers faced exceptionally high mortality, and this may have heightened religious susceptibilities. Their accommodation to town life was often facilitated by religious fellowship, which could help them overcome any sense of dislocation. In the short term, urban religious pluralism may have augmented overall attendances. There were many ways in which urban life could foster religious variety and rivalry, and allow the churches greater freedoms than they had in the country. In Welsh towns, religion had a cultural centrality that was augmented by its roles in national and class consciousness. The findings here add to historiographical doubts about some of the cultural implications of rural–urban difference. British (and particularly English) scholars

[17] A. D. Gilbert, *Religion and Society in Industrial England: Church, Chapel and Social Change, 1740–1914* (1976, Harlow, 1984 edn), pp. 27–32; Brown 'Did urbanization secularize Britain?', pp. 4, 6, 11–13.

[18] See pp. 265–6 above.

have often been inclined to idealise the countryside, and to disparage the towns, which attracted such a relatively large proportion of the population compared with Europe.[19] To argue that 'towns secularised people' comes easily to such an academic culture. However, one would stay closer to historical record by appraising towns more positively *vis-à-vis* religious behaviour.

The national cartography of 'religiosity'

Following these denominational comparisons and points about the effects of urbanisation, further questions arise concerning regional levels of 'religiosity': admittedly a crude word, but one that can serve within the terms of these data and analyses. The questions may be pitched in many different ways, opening up complex agenda in the theory and empirical evaluation of 'secularisation', which will be developed more fully elsewhere. To end this book with a hypothesis about the conditions for high and low 'religiosity', my emphasis will now be on the cartography of differing levels of religious performance over England and Wales when the denominations are combined.

Figure 12.1 takes all sittings across all denominations, and shows them relative to population as an index of total sittings. There was highest seating availability over most of Wales, north Cornwall, parts of Dorset, Leicestershire, Rutland, Northamptonshire, north Norfolk, Lincolnshire, and a large region of the East and North Ridings across to north Lancashire. Other scattered areas had high indexes, as, for example, along the south coast and in parts of the midlands, Suffolk and Essex. These districts contrasted with many others which had much lower figures, and most prominent among them were London and its surrounding area, the English borders with Wales and Scotland, and Lancashire and the West Riding. Almost all London was poorly supplied, and it is interesting to see how undifferentiated the capital was in this regard. There was almost no difference between its west and east ends, despite (or perhaps because of) the mission efforts at this time.

Where the Anglican Church had always been strong – in many parts of the south-east – a relative lack of denominational competition

[19] Among many discussions, see M. J. Wiener, *English Culture and the Decline of the Industrial Spirit, 1850–1980* (Cambridge, 1981); D. Lowenthal, 'British national identity and the English landscape', *Rural History*, 2 (1991).

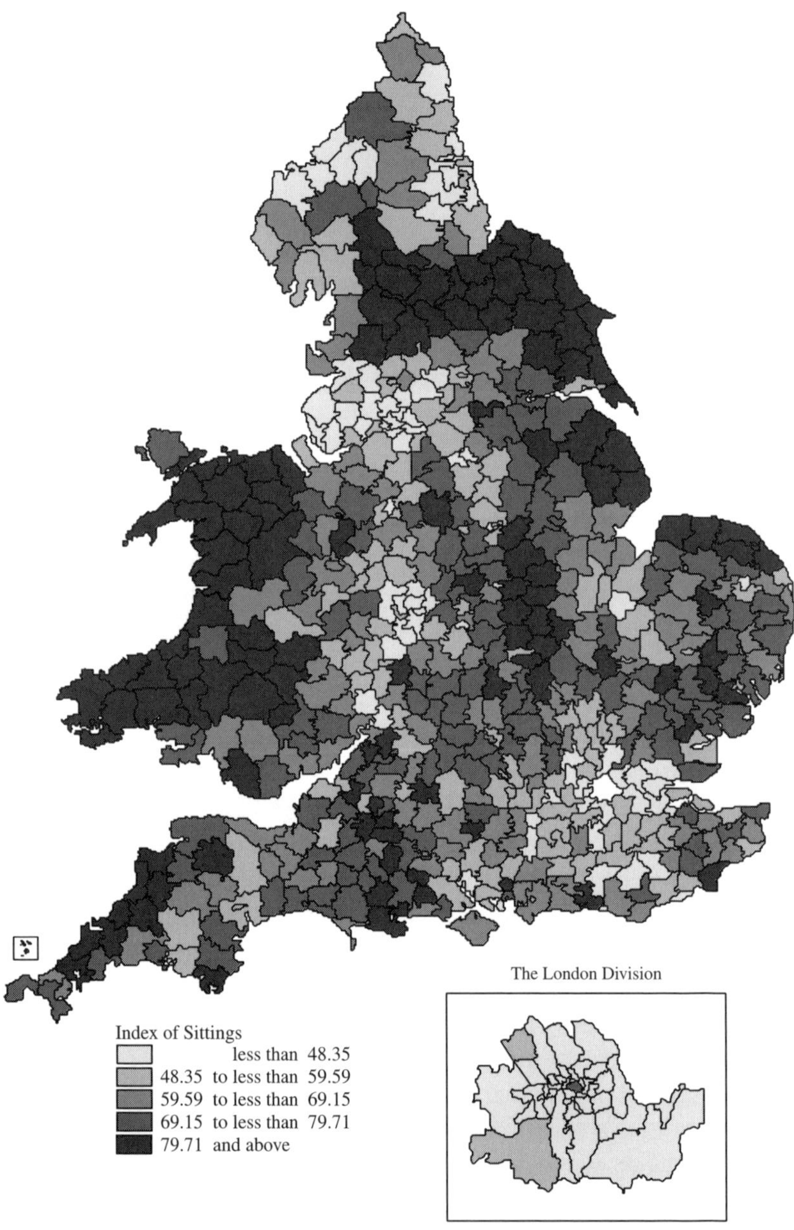

Figure 12.1. Index of total sittings (all denominations) in 1851

meant that provision of sittings could be quite low. By contrast, large medieval churches which were under-utilised and sited in areas of depopulation or circumscribed employment (in Norfolk, other parts of East Anglia, Rutland, Lincolnshire, Dorset), provided a ready availability of sittings. This was particularly notable where such Anglican provision was heavily supplemented by Nonconformist chapels: in the south midlands, Lincolnshire and Norfolk. The contribution made by Methodism was very evident in the latter two counties, in Wales, north Cornwall and Yorkshire, augmenting established churches that were sometimes poorly maintained and attended. With regard to 'secularisation', the main point to bear in mind from figure 12.1 is the low provision of sittings around London, in the industrial north-west, and the rural border regions.

Figure 12.2 complements figure 12.1 by providing the index of total attendances for all denominations. It is, in effect, a map of 'religiosity' measured by the tendency of regional populations to attend services. Alternatively, in the terms of these data it may be seen as the pattern of regional 'secularisation' across Wales and England – the lightest areas being the most 'secular', if one allows that problematical term to be used in this fairly narrow way. Most denominations showed close matches between their indexes of attendances and sittings, and the data for these two maps are closely associated.[20] As expected, much of Wales had very high attendances.[21] The English south midlands produced high attendance indexes, overlapping with much of figure 12.1, and this extended down to Dorset. There was also the area of strong old dissent, overlapping with some Anglican 'core' areas, from the south midlands through to the Essex coast. The large area of Yorkshire and nearby districts where Methodism had established so many chapels, showing so visibly in figure 12.1, is rather less obvious from the index of total attendances. This contrast between the maps recalls

[20] Their relation is very linear, and the Spearman correlation is 0.723, significant at .001.

[21] One recalls that the registration-district data include Sunday school attendances. The parish data were therefore analysed to see whether double or multiple attendance at such schools in Wales was more common than in England, perhaps thus contributing to the high Welsh attendance indexes. There was not much variation in this across English counties, but such multiple attendance at Sunday schools was rather *less* common in Cardiganshire, Anglesey and Caernarvonshire than in the English counties, probably for topographical reasons. Welsh indexes of total attendances reach extremely high levels despite this.

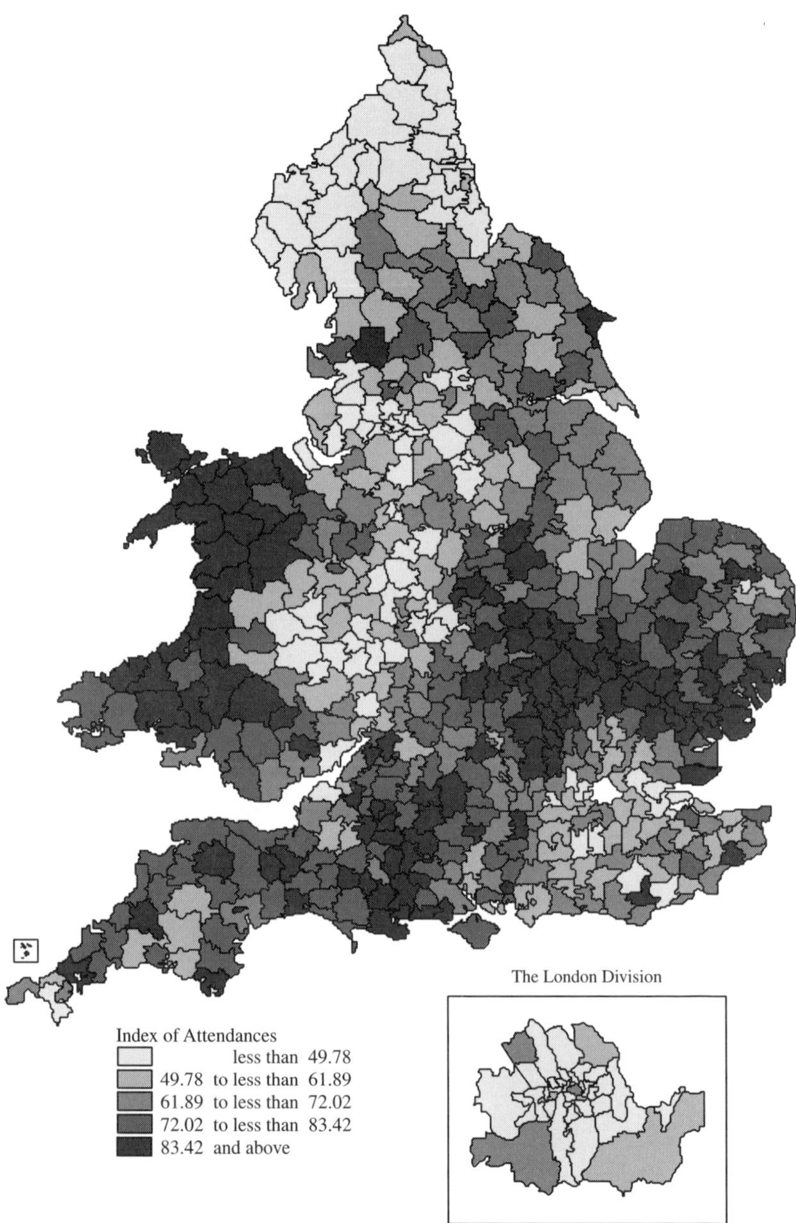

Figure 12.2. Index of total attendances (all denominations) in 1851

the earlier point that Methodism had over-provided in some of these northern areas.[22]

The most 'secular' regions did not correspond in any simple way with divisions between north and south, or west and east, or upland and lowland.[23] It is premature to relate them to political geography.[24] They were not strictly coterminous with urban areas as compared with the countryside, although there were certainly salient cases documenting that view. Figure 12.3 shows the 1851 population density of England and Wales, indicating the pattern of urbanisation. There were indeed regions where low attendances coincided with high urbanisation, like Lancashire and the West Riding, London and

22 The two figures (and a highly linear association between total sittings and total attendances, the Pearson correlation coefficient for those registration-district data being 0.956), seem not to demonstrate any overall relation in 1851 between excessive religious provision and falling attendances, although this may have occurred after the mid nineteenth century. See the interesting discussion in R. Gill, *The Myth of the Empty Church* (1993), *passim*, much of whose argument does indeed cover later decades. One would expect a non-linear relation between sittings and attendances if this thesis had become evident by 1851, with larger numbers of sittings depressing attendances. But one does not find such a relation with registration-district data, either nationally or in any of the published census divisions. Nor is it apparent in parish-level data (for which the Pearson coefficient between total sittings and total attendances is 0.969). The association between sittings and attendances is highly linear in all cases, and insofar as any non-linearity is apparent, the fitted line turns slightly in extreme cases towards the attendance axis. If excess sittings led to falling attendances, one would expect the opposite of that. Crockett, in 'A Secularising Geography?', pp. 298–343, examines this issue further.

23 Nor do the religious maps bear a resemblance to regional patterns of fertility and mortality, or to the surviving incidence of farm service (in the west and north). A study of registration-district illiteracy in 1851 was conducted, which showed high literacy in the extreme north, around London, and along the south coast, and high illiteracy in south Wales, the south midlands, East Anglia, Lancashire and the West Riding. These patterns seem to have little bearing on religious attendances. However, the more interesting relationship between indexes of total attendance and regional illegitimacy is discussed in note 35.

24 We saw in chapters 2, 3 and 4 how different denominations related to the geography of nineteenth-century politics. When considering the cartography of English 'secularisation', some of the most 'secular' areas coincide with patterns of political radicalism, as in London, or the West Riding and east Lancashire, which had large numbers of Chartist associations. See A. Charlesworth, 'Labour protest, 1780–1850', in J. Langton and R. J. Morris (eds.), *Atlas of Industrializing Britain, 1780–1914* (1986), p. 188; D. Thompson, *The Chartists: Popular Politics in the Industrial Revolution* (Aldershot, 1984), pp. 242, 341–68, on the location of the various Chartist organisations. However, the historiography on the half century before 1851 does not always facilitate a view of radicalism in regional terms, being stronger on issues of class than of region. Nor, as yet, can the data of this book be related statistically to regional voting patterns, although that will become possible in the future.

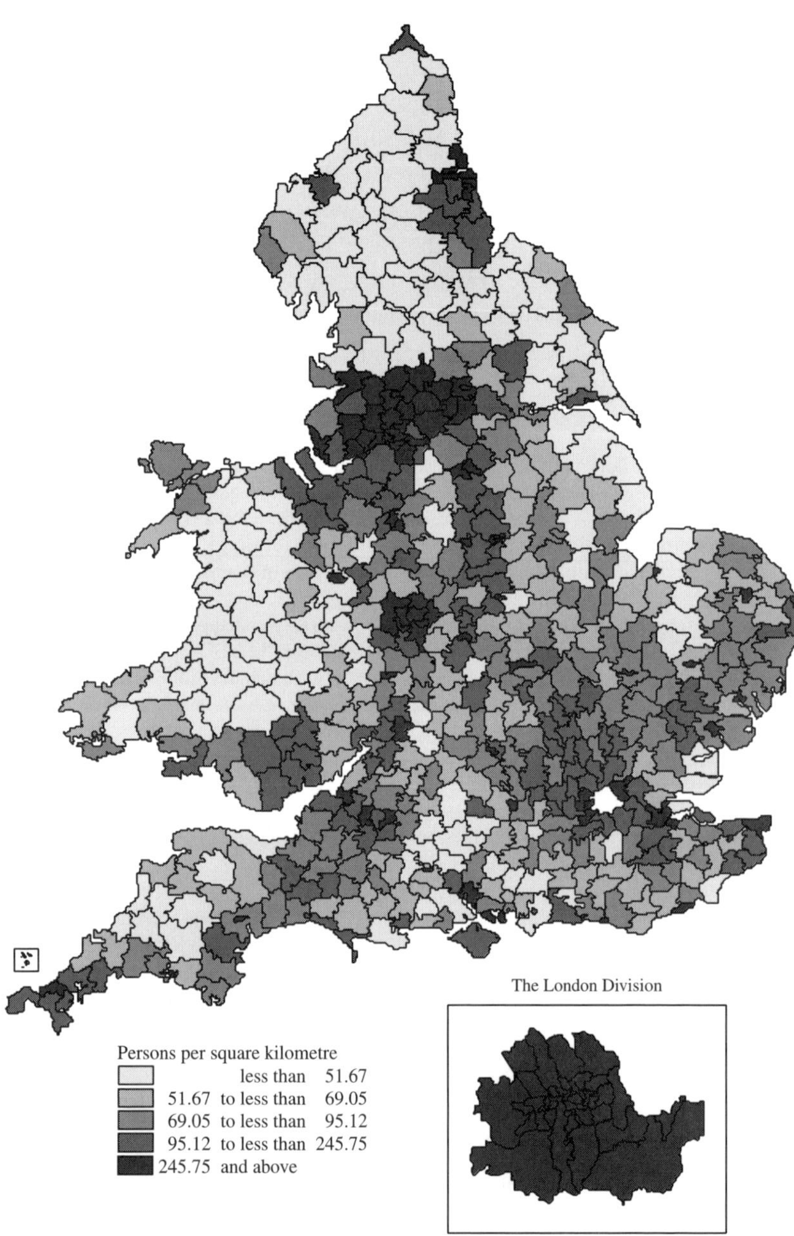

Figure 12.3. Population density in 1851

the surrounding districts, some districts in the Black Country like Aston, Birmingham, Walsall and Wolverhampton, and parts of the north-east like Gateshead, Newcastle, South Shields and Tynemouth. Horace Mann and other contemporaries were very alive to this, and argued that it was an important matter to remedy. Their view was that people did not attend worship because there were insufficient churches and accessible sittings in the towns and cities. Aspects of that argument are confirmed by figure 12.4, which shows persons per place of worship in 1851, clarifying the nature of urban provision.[25] The relation between these four maps is readily apparent, especially when one looks at London, the west midlands, Lancashire, the West Riding, and the industrial north-east. Those areas do suggest that English urbanisation was important where it was most pronounced.

However, a direct equation between secularisation and urbanisation was called into doubt by the earlier statistics, and one cannot carry it too far because there were very significant exceptions. The caveat is that very many *agricultural* areas had low indexes of sittings and attendances, and high numbers of people per place of worship (figure 12.4), and in these districts population density was usually very *low*. This was true in much of Surrey, Kent, the Sussex Weald,[26] Herefordshire, Worcestershire, Shropshire, Cheshire, and further north in Cumberland, Westmorland, Northumberland and Durham. It was these many *rural* and often border districts of low religious attendance that led to the statistical results shown above, undermining a clear-cut role for urbanisation *per se*.

A hypothesis about secularisation, therefore, has to be one that can *combine* the effects of intense urbanisation with the low religiosity of these rural areas. At first glance, one would be tempted to argue that these rural and urban areas shared a common problem in being poorly provided for – they both had high numbers of people per place of worship and low indexes of sittings – and that this was the key to the regional patterns. There is obviously a great deal of truth in such an emphasis, but it is not entirely adequate. One can see this by looking at figure 12.5, the index of occupancy for all denominations. This

[25] This measure of course correlates negatively with the index of total sittings. The Spearman coefficient between them is −0.831.

[26] R. Heath, *The English Peasant* (1893, Wakefield, 1978 edn), ch. 11, described very pervasive indifference towards religion in the Weald, and his comments on this are confirmed by figures 12.1 and 12.2.

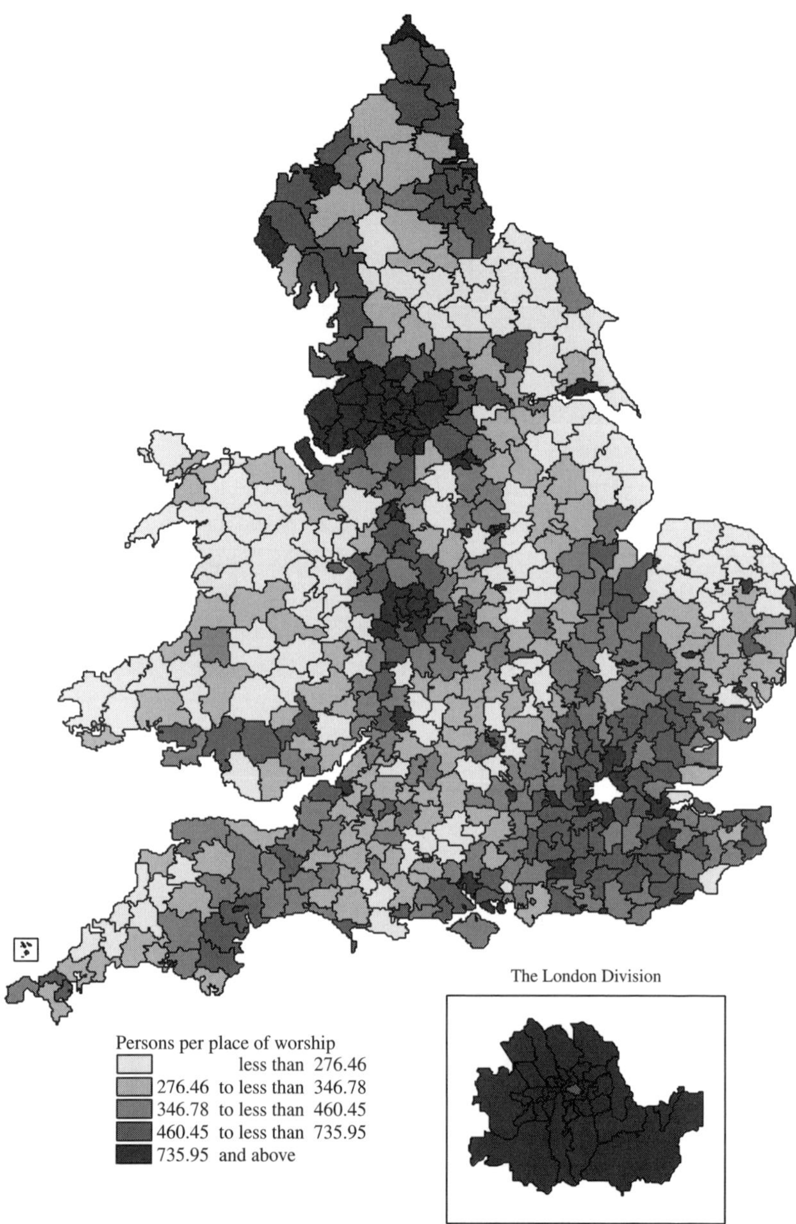

Figure 12.4. Persons per place of worship for all denominations in 1851

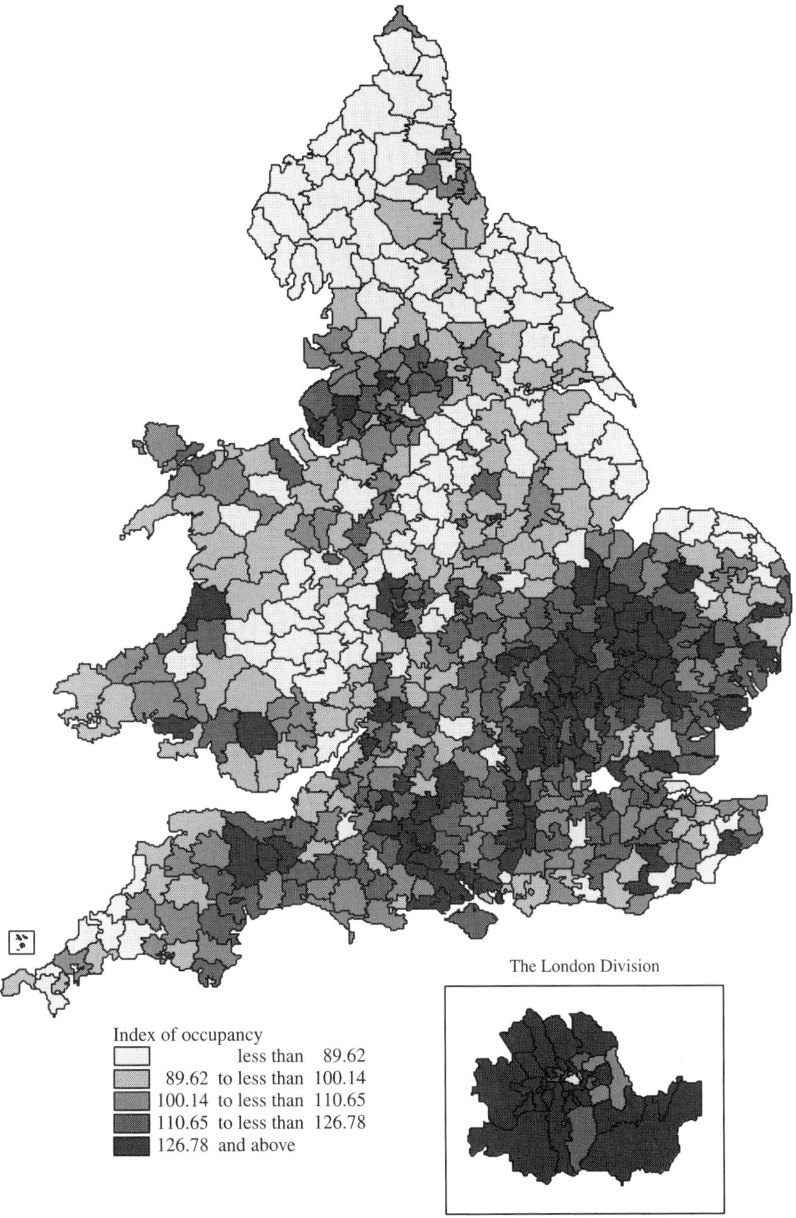

Figure 12.5. Index of occupancy for all denominations in 1851

measure (which relates attendances to sittings) shows predictably high pressure upon available seating in London, and in certain urban areas of the west midlands and the north-west. But it also shows very low pressure upon seating in the rural border areas, which does not suggest that inadequate provision in those areas was the key to low attendances. Although the index of occupancy is notoriously difficult to interpret – raising many chicken-and-egg questions about provision and demand[27] – there is little sign in figure 12.5 that there was thwarted demand for more sittings in the border regions, for that would have led to much higher indexes of occupancy there. Those border churches and sittings were few relative to population but, even so, there was very scant demand for them.

In presenting a fuller hypothesis that takes account of these findings, it is helpful to look particularly at regional differences within Wales, at the English border zones, London, and the three main areas of intense English urbanisation (the north-east, north-west and the west midlands). Wales had very high indexes of attendance throughout, but those indexes were somewhat lower across rural *and* industrial south Wales (figure 12.2). Pembrokeshire, south Gower,[28] and the industrial valleys had the highest proportions of English speakers, having in distant or recent history received the most Saxon, Norman and English immigrants. By comparison, the most religiously attending regions of Wales – in the west and north – were the regions of strongest Welsh language and associated culture. These were also areas of low in-migration, for (leaving aside local exceptions like the copper, lead and slate workings) they tended to lose population to the more heavily industrial regions of the south. In the north and west Welsh areas where a lack of cultural heterogeneity was most obvious – in *Cymru Gymraeg* – one found the highest religious attendances (figure 12.2). The strongest senses of Welsh linguistic and cultural identity were linked with exceptionally high religious attendances.

Now let us look down from the Welsh hills towards England. The rural borders adjoining Wales and Scotland were among the regions of lowest attendance, and they shared this with London and industrial

[27] See appendix C, pp. 434–5.

[28] North Gower, where part of my family is from, has long seen itself as more Welsh than south Gower, with a reluctance to marry southwards, and this north–south cultural division is still apparent in blood-group maps for the peninsula. Gower was in this regard a microcosm of many similar situations across south Wales.

Table 12.4. *Indexes of total religious attendance (all denominations) for the English border districts, the London districts, all Wales, all England, and English urban/industrial districts in the west midlands, the north-east and the north-west*[29]

	N. of districts	Mean index	Median index	Min. index	Max. index
English districts bordering Wales and Scotland[30]	16	47.8	49.0	16.9	73.2
London districts	36	40.1	38.1	19.9	67.5
West midlands urban districts[31]	7	48.8	47.2	32.9	68.7
North-east urban districts[32]	4	43.7	43.5	40.7	47.0
North-west urban districts[33]	26	49.9	48.0	32.0	78.3
Wales	48	84.3	85.3	37.0	130.7
All England	576	65.7	65.6	16.9	133.4

parts of the north and west midlands. Precise figures are given in table 12.4.

London had very low attendance indexes, and the most urban districts of the north-east, west midlands and the north-west were nearly as low. The English border districts were as low as these urban areas and, indeed, this held for Herefordshire, Shropshire, Cheshire, Cumberland and Northumberland as a whole.[34] If one refers back to

[29] The districts chosen for the three non-metropolitan urban/industrial regions are listed in notes below. These were selected because they were highly urbanised, each of them having in 1851 over 150 people per square kilometre and a total population of over 40,000.

[30] The border districts used are those which immediately adjoined the border. However, much the same point applies if one takes 'border' areas that lie somewhat deeper within England.

[31] Wolverhampton, Walsall, West Bromwich, Dudley, Stourbridge, Aston and Birmingham.

[32] Newcastle upon Tyne, Gateshead, Sunderland and Tynemouth.

[33] Preston, Wigan, Prescot, West Derby, Liverpool, Salford, Manchester, Chorlton, Ashton-under-Lyne, Oldham, Bury, Bolton, Blackburn, Burnley, Rochdale, Haslingden, Stockport, Halifax, Bradford, Huddersfield, Sheffield, Hunslet, Leeds, Wakefield, Dewsbury and Keighley.

[34] This was a border geography which contrasted markedly with the French situation, where border, fringe or non-central regions (Brittany, the Pyrenees, the Massif Central, and the Jura, away from cities and industrial areas) consistently indicated the highest religious attendances, while French central and urban areas demonstrated much lower religious vitality. J. D. Gay, *The Geography of Religion in England* (1971), pp. 5–6, 264. 'De-Christianisation' in France was related much more strongly than in England to urbanisation and the presence of industry.

chapter 9 on Sunday schools (p. 291), it will be seen from the map there that these border areas, with London and its hinterland, had the lowest percentages of population attending denominational Sunday schools. As regions of low religious attendance, these areas were breeding successive generations relatively indifferent to religious belief, a process which had a regional identity and momentum of its own.[35]

As noted above, there had often been poor institutional provision in the borders, much as there was in the largest industrial cities. The border parishes were sometimes upland, with scattered farms, and they were often very expansive – to the point of being almost meaningless as administrative and religious units. This did not favour high church attendance. They were usually fragmented in landownership and not subject to tight controls. They did not normally provide rich clerical livings, and their clergy did not gain much from parliamentary enclosure.[36] As we have seen, these border areas had high numbers of people per place of worship (figure 12.4) and low indexes of sittings (figure 12.1) – similar to London or industrial Lancashire – but (unlike such cities) they featured low attendances relative to sittings (figure 12.5).

Superimposed upon poor religious provision in the borders was another factor, which probably accentuated secular outlooks, and

[35] As a possibly related indicator, illegitimacy was highest in the English–Welsh borders, in the far north and along the border with Scotland. It coincided with the low index of total attendances in the borders. P. Laslett, *Family Life and Illicit Love in Earlier Generations* (Cambridge, 1977), pp. 136–48, 156–7. Laslett's results (for 1842) are well supported by detailed registration-district maps of illegitimacy, which Crockett and Snell will publish elsewhere. Laslett commented, 'regional variation has been a well-marked feature of English bastardy . . . the western and north-western counties were the counties of high illegitimacy'. *Ibid.*, pp. 144–7. He correctly showed lowest illegitimacy in the south and south midlands (*ibid.*, pp. 146–8, 156–7). One should add that illegitimacy was also low in south Wales, Anglesey and Caernarvonshire, and along the southern English coast: all areas of high religious attendances. Urbanisation was not associated with high illegitimacy, unlike in France. In the borders, low church provision, long distances to worship, and cultural pluralism may have induced tolerance of both extra-marital sexuality and indifferent religious attendance.

[36] These English regions of high attendance coincide well with the 'triangle' most affected by parliamentary enclosure between Dorset, the East Riding and Essex. M. E. Turner, *English Parliamentary Enclosure* (Folkestone, 1980), pp. 35, 59. The Anglican clergy were major beneficiaries of this agricultural reorganisation, which reinforced the established church (and in so doing fortified its opposition). Any long-term perspective on English secularisation would do well to relate that subject to the changing regional economic history and status of the Church of England.

which these very rural districts shared with areas of considerable urbanisation. In the border regions cultural pluralism was a matter of everyday experience. There were ambiguous, weak, or two-sided senses of national identity. People had a cross-cultural familiarity with different languages, accents, place-names, personal names, kin and farm organisation. Much local migration and inter-marriage across borders had ensured this. Many other cultural and national markers of identity were vague and equivocal. It seems significant therefore that such border conditions were associated with relatively high indifference towards religious attendance. This was one of the few things the borders shared with the metropolis – the extreme case of urbanisation – where cultural pluralism took very different forms, but was again a common experience. For London was also a 'border' area, and had been so long before this period: a border area with Europe, and by 1851 with the rest of the world, having become the mercantile centre of international communication. Certainly, it had its 'tribes' – described by Mayhew and others – but there were many of them, living in close quarters with each other. In such culturally pluralistic (or 'socially differentiated') areas – regardless of their very rural or very urban character – personal religious beliefs (in whatever denominational form) were constantly confronted to the point of scepticism by options and alternatives. In them, it may not be surprising that religious commitment expressed in church attendance seems to have become dubiously regarded by comparatively large numbers of inter-mixed people. For these were areas, if one returns to George Eliot's *Silas Marner* – to the quotation that started this book – *where people's lives 'have been made various'*: territories no longer inhabited and ruled by their 'own divinities' or 'native gods'. In them one found that inter-weaving of views which Eliot diagnosed as underlying Silas Marner's religious disillusionment: 'frustrated belief . . . a curtain broad enough to create for him the blackness of night'.[37]

The highest total attendances were found where national and cultural identities were *least* ambivalent, furthest away from border zones and apart from the largest cities – in west and north Wales, or in the southern and south midland English counties beyond the metropolis

[37] George Eliot, *Silas Marner* (1861, Harmondsworth, 1969 edn), ch. 2, pp. 62–4. Compare T. S. Eliot, 'Journey of the Magi', *Collected Poems, 1909–1962* (1936, 1963 edn), pp. 109–10: for another journey 'down to a temperate valley', leaving them 'no longer at ease . . . in the old dispensation'.

and its immediate influence. It has been shown how Welsh Calvinistic Methodism, and the Church of England, epitomised salient contrasts of a national kind between the two countries of this book. The English areas of highest attendance (figure 12.2) owed most to the geography of the Anglican Church. As in Wales, such highest attending regions were situated where national commitment and cultures took their most adamant and unquestioning forms, where they were not confronted with the more far-reaching cultural and national options raised by the Welsh (or English), the Scottish, the Irish and perhaps (locally) by the Cornish – and where, in the more outlying districts of the aptly named 'home counties', they were not (as yet) subjected to daily contact with the cultural heterogeneity and low religiosity of London. By contrast, in the rural-border *and* urban-industrial areas of most marked cultural pluralism, 'secularisation' (as measured here) was most advanced by 1851. Cultural diversity – whether very urban, or in the form of the ambivalent loyalties and poor provision of the very rural Welsh and Scottish borderlands – proved uncongenial to religious attendance. The effects of these linkages between cultural and religious pluralism, extreme urban growth, poor provision and 'secularisation' would intensify in the century ahead, penetrating further from the borders into the key English and Welsh strongholds of faith, just as they would spread outwards from the metropolis and, to a lesser extent, from a few other areas of marked urbanisation.

The hypothesis sketched above is tentative, broad-brushed and can be further refined. A stress upon borders and pluralism – whether rural *or* urban – fits the religious patterns better than arguments for urbanisation *per se*. One allows the secularising effects of extreme urbanisation in a few regions – where poor religious provision and a metropolitan pluralistic effect were produced by very high in-migration. Such a stress is congruent with the long-term relationship (in England and Wales) between religious pluralism and secularisation, which Alasdair Crockett will describe in due course.

Maps like those I have discussed raise many further questions about the relation between religion and cultural identities, some of which can be pursued elsewhere. Religious cartography does not by itself 'explain' the phenomena delineated, although it opens up explanatory possibilities, shows associations, and helps to focus questions. Allied to such cartography in this book have been methods and approaches which are relatively new in the historical study of British religion.

The book began with such an agenda, now partly realised, although there is still much to do in studying British religious and cultural regions. So for the ending here, it seems instructive to bring this discussion back to questions of method.

As is clear from analysis of 'urbanisation' and its correlates in this chapter, and as has been clear from many of the book's other findings, there are limitations to how far one can use economic or social factors in an explanation of religious attendance. Local conditions – of 'open' or 'closed'/estate parishes, of multiple- or mono-employment, of rural or urban – with their associated varieties of social structure, undoubtedly influenced the siting of denominations. There have been many examples of such partially contextual explanation in this book. Modern methods make these increasingly visible to researchers, and allow co-associations to be precisely judged. Even readers studying religion from viewpoints strictly within the history of ideas would probably agree that it is impossible to explain local religious patterns without reference to such economic, topographical and societal features.

However, detailed national maps often suggest that such features were influential in contrasted localities *within* larger regions, and that they may not have determined which broader regions became crucial in the history of separate denominations. At the broader level one looks for larger historical courses: for national, political and cultural affinities, for denominational policy-making and biographical choices. It was often those choices that influenced where and when the local factors came into effect. At the national scale, such local determinations are less persuasive to the historian – their preponderance in some regions rather than others was not necessarily a crucial matter. National patterns of religious attendance perhaps bear witness above all to the regional initiatives, choices and remarkable staying-power of people like John Wesley, George Whitefield, Lady Huntingdon, Howel Harris, Daniel Rowland and their old dissenting counterparts, let alone the cumulative effect of diocesan decisions by the Anglican authorities. No doubt such people were swayed by personal interpretations of cultural differences in England and Wales. Certainly they were carried to some extent on the shoulders of indigenous revivals. Yet their experiences and differences had far-reaching implications, affecting for example many of the contrasts between English and Welsh religion. The regional background of John Wesley, in north Lincolnshire, may well have had a geographical influence on Methodism that overshadowed any reductionist factors. Religious denominations were the cultural products of experienced, exceptionally forceful human personalities and their followers, variously aware of the contexts in which they acted. It was the pluralistic overlay of those human concerns that created the cartographic contours of mid-century Victorian religion. When one examines the geography of religion, the efforts of charismatic evangelists often over-ride the panoply of local deterministic factors that technical scholarship now elucidates. This may seem an old-fashioned historical point, made in the face of many of the 'social-scientific' methods and approaches of this book, but it is one that studies of religion will always do well to remember and respect.

Technical appendices

Appendix A

Table A.1. *Summary statistics for the major denominations, England and Wales*

Denomination	N. places of worship	N. sittings	Total attendances
Church of England	14,077	5,317,915	5,292,551
Church of Scotland	18	13,789	11,758
United Presbyterian Synod	66	31,351	31,628
Presbyterian Church in England	76	41,552	37,124
Independents	3,244	1,067,760	1,214,059
General Baptists	93	20,539	22.096
Particular Baptists	1,947	582,953	740,752
New Connexion General Baptists	182	52,604	64,321
Baptists (unspecified)	550	93,310	100,991
Society of Friends	371	91,599	22,478
Unitarians	229	68,554	50,061
Moravians	32	9,305	10,874
Wesleyan Methodist	6,579	1,447,580	1,544,528
Methodist New Connexion	297	96,964	99,045
Primitive Methodist	2,871	414,030	511,195
Bible Christian	482	66,834	73,859
Wesleyan Methodist Association	419	98,813	94,103
Independent Methodist	20	2,263	3,120
Wesleyan Reformers	339	67,814	91,503
Welsh Calvinistic Methodists	828	211,951	264,112
Lady Huntingdon's Connexion	109	38,727	44,642
New Church	50	12,107	10,352
Brethren	132	18,529	17,592
Other Isolated Congregations	539	104,481	104,675
Roman Catholics	570	186,111	383,630
Catholic & Apostolic Church	32	7,437	7,542
Mormons	222	30,783	35,626
Jews	53	8,438	6,030
Total for all denominations	34,467	10,212,563	10,896,066

Source: *Census of Religious Worship*, pp. clxxxi–clxxxii. Supplements 1 and 2 to Table A, including the estimates made by Horace Mann for defective returns.

Separate figures for the following minor denominations are not given in the above appendix, but they are included in the final 'total for all denominations':

Reformed Irish Presbyterians, Seventh-Day Baptists, Scotch Baptists, Sandemanians, Lutherans, French Protestants, Reformed Church of the Netherlands, German Protestant Reformers, Greek Church, German Catholics, and Italian Reformers.

For the 64 sects comprising 'other isolated denominations', see *ibid.*, p. clxxx.

Appendix B

The correction of census data

This appendix discusses the method of correction used in the first part of the book, to adjust 1851 published registration-district data for missing values. For a variety of reasons, a small percentage of omissions occurred on the enumerators' forms. Such omissions were footnoted by Horace Mann in the published district tables of the census, although he did not make any changes to those tables. Mann did, however, provide overall tables in which he included estimates for 'defective returns'.[1] The problem is one that has commonly been ignored by historians.[2] They have been aware of the difficulties in supplying such missing data, and of the relatively small numbers of census figures affected. The view has usually been taken that these missing figures have little effect on calculations. For England and Wales, omissions of sittings affect 7.3 per cent of places of worship,

[1] *Census of Religious Worship*, pp. clxxxi–clxxxiii. His subsequent tables for the census divisions (pp. clxxxiv–cxciv), and for the individual counties (pp. cxcv–ccxxxiv), notified in footnotes the numbers of places of worship not returning sittings, and the same for attendances. These notes also provided a breakdown of defective returns for each denomination. Further details for sittings were supplied in *ibid.*, pp. ccxxxv–ccxxxviii, covering the numbers of places open for worship at the three main times of the day, but from which no information as to sittings was received. Mann interpolated figures for his main tables, to deal with defective returns, and he usually did this by basing such interpolations upon the average numbers of sittings and attendances for each denomination across the whole of England and Wales. (See *ibid.*, notes to pp. clxxxi–clxxxii, and the final column of Supplement I to Table A, on p. clxxxi, which gives those average numbers of sittings.) The exceptions to this were 'where the average number of sittings in any case is less than the number of persons actually attending at one service, [and here] the plan has been to put down the number of sittings in that case at one fourth more than the number of attendants'. (*Ibid.*, note to p. clxxxi, and see the first note to p. cxxiii.) There are small problems involved in such assumptions – for example the issue of standing rather than sitting at services – but these need not detain us. One is generally struck by the good sense of his methods.

[2] For example, B. I. Coleman, 'Southern England in the Census of Religious Worship, 1851', *Southern History*, 5 (1983), 155.

and of attendances 4.0 per cent.[3] There is no alternative source generally available to assess the 'real' historical values of missing figures. Even chronologically very proximate sources of local information – in the rare cases where they exist – may still be misleading in that they do not give precise information as to what happened on Census Sunday.[4]

Nevertheless it is possible to adjust the data to give rather more accurate values, taking some account of the missing figures which Mann alerted the reader to. In the registration-district analysis, on the scale covered here, it was felt that this matter needed to be addressed, to make the figures more accurate. The approach used was to correct the data where necessary by interpolating estimates that were based upon the calculation of mean values (i.e. for sittings or attendances) for the denomination in the affected registration district.[5] This was done where such omission was notified by Horace Mann in the footnotes to the published census, and where the other figures for that denomination in that district allowed the calculation of such an average.[6]

[3] *Census of Religious Worship*, calculated from the notes to Table A, on pp. clxxviii–clxxix. See also p. clxx.

[4] The census forms also invited the person making the return to comment (if he wished) on 'the estimated average number of attendants' on Sundays during the previous twelve months. See *Census of Religious Worship*, pp. clxxiv–clxxv. Such entries seem to be insufficiently reliable and regular to warrant much attention, and they were not published at national level.

Neither in registration-district nor parish analysis did we ever enter data from another source close to 1851 to fill any seeming gap in the 1851 returns. In a couple of cases alternative evidence inclines one to do so, but we opted instead to represent and analyse the Religious Census in and for itself.

[5] This approach is similar to Mann's, and differs from his mainly through our use of registration-district averages for each denomination when making corrections, rather than the use of national averages. This has the advantage of a more local siting for the interpolations, one that takes account of the local strengths and sizes of each denomination's churches and attendances, rather than using national averages much swayed by distant churches.

[6] The drawback to this method is as follows. In a small number of cases, usually affecting sittings data for some of the smaller denominations, it was impossible to calculate such an average figure, and so no data was interpolated, making such a missing figure zero. This has occurred for about 0.1 per cent of the 33,818 places of worship. For almost all denominations the problem is minute, less than a handful of churches normally being affected. Such non-interpolation is not a problem at all for some denominations, like the Church of England. It mainly affects sittings rather than attendance data, and is most noticeable for sittings for the Roman Catholics, Wesleyan Reformers and the Mormons. There is no problem of note for their attendance data, which is either complete in its interpolation or very nearly so.

Here is an example to illustrate this. The footnotes for the Cardiff district report that 'The returns omit to state the number of *sittings* in . . . two [places of worship] belonging to the CALVINISTIC METHODISTS.'[7] The recorded total number of sittings in Cardiff for the Calvinistic Methodists was 5,731. In this district they had 25 places of worship but, the footnote indicates, the sittings data relates to only 23 of them. One may easily calculate, therefore, that within the district the mean sittings for each of their places of worship was 249. The mean number of sittings is then multiplied by the number of missing returns, and this figure is added to the total given in the census. In this example, after correction the Cardiff sittings figure is increased by 498 to 6,229.

This method assumes that places of worship not providing data were neither typically above nor below the denominational registration-district mean in terms of sittings or attendances. This is an assumption that cannot always be defended. It might be argued that omissions were more likely to come from small places of worship, or places of worship with low attendance figures. As such it is conceivable that the corrected figures slightly overestimate the true values.

A figure based on national averages for these particular churches' sittings could be interpolated, following Mann, but we have not done so. These were denominations that usually had very few churches in each district – hence this problem – and they tended to comprise either very poor congregations, or newly recruited ones. Thus there are reasons to believe that their followers were as yet inadequately accommodated in any case. They may well have had no sittings (or very few) in their 'places of worship', and the occasional lack of sittings figures for them may simply document this, and render any interpolation superfluous. They usually have good data for attendances. We therefore opted to leave such figures without any interpolation by other methods.

The effect has probably been a tendency very slightly to underestimate the sittings data for a few of the smaller denominations. This will have little significant influence on most later variable creation and calculations, because missing values (resulting through use of a zero in their generation) will remove such questionable cases from overall measures. Nor does it have any real effect upon the published denominational maps, as we normally used attendance data for those, and any such affected figures (about one in a thousand) will almost always be imperceptible on national maps.

One could debate rival methods of interpolation. The best alternative option was that used by Horace Mann, interpolating a national average figure for the denomination where necessary, and so avoiding any inconsistency of treatment across cases. This would have broken with our principle of only using data for the district in question, and would have brought attendant difficulties in other regards. However, it seems to us that a reasonable case can be made for either approach, and both are certainly preferable to omitting interpolations altogether.

[7] *Census of Religious Worship*, p. 121, district number 581.

On the other hand, it might be argued that omissions tended to occur where the place of worship was large, making counting more difficult. Another way of thinking about this issue is to suggest that omissions of detail stemmed more from individual clerical oversights on the part of the person filling in the form, and that this could occur regardless of the size of the church or chapel he was returning for. One sometimes has this impression when reading the enumerators' forms. Whatever one's view on this matter, there is no doubt that the numbers of omissions are sufficiently small as a percentage of the total, and the leeway of interpolative error sufficiently slight, as to render the problem very minor for our calculations and cartography.

Other methods of correction are possible, some of them being cruder, or being based upon denomination-specific ratios between sittings and attendance figures.[8] The latter approach may have the potential to be more accurate, but it becomes complex where information for a number of places of worship is missing, and it is impossible to apply where neither sittings nor attendance data were provided, thus forcing one back to the interpolation of mean district or national values.

It was felt best to use one procedure throughout for the registration-district data, and we opted to interpolate mean values. Because of the relatively small proportions of omissions in the published census, and the fact that different correction methods usually produce results differing by only a couple of percentage points, it can be shown that the cartography and calculations are affected to only a minute degree by the different correction methods possible, or by inconsistencies within any one such method.

The above account describes the registration-district procedures for part 1 of the book, where the footnotes to the district data provided by Horace Mann were used to adjust the data. Any errors due to interpolative method were not likely to have much impact on the overall calculations and cartography at this level. For part 2 of the book however, no interpolations of any sort were conducted on the parish-level data. This was partly because of the considerable difficulty of doing so at such a local level. In addition, it seemed that Mann may have been making rather optimistic assumptions about religious prac-

[8] See e.g. J. D. Gay, *The Geography of Religion in England* (1971), pp. 50–1; cf. K. D. M. Snell, *Church and Chapel in the North Midlands: Religious Observance in the Nineteenth Century* (Leicester, 1991), p. 66, n. 7.

tice and provision, or indeed about churches 'open for worship' on Census Sunday, when he supposed that missing entries might be taken as missing evidence of a service actually having taken place, or of a church building that was a functioning reality, or one that was well supplied with seating (rather than relying on standing room).[9] To interpolate figures for the registration districts is more advantageous than misleading. But at parish level, where interpolated data can make such a difference to localised results, where the basis for interpolation is less clear (no methods exist to do this), and where no precedents have been established, it becomes more questionable whether one should proceed in that way. We decided to take the enumerators' returns as read for the parish returns, and to analyse them in their literal documented form only. If no attendance or sittings figures were given for a place of worship supposedly 'open for worship', we accepted the possibility that no service in fact took place – whether for reasons of clerical absenteeism, negligence, dereliction of the building, or whatever – or that the 'place of worship' simply had no seats. In such cases we entered a zero rather than guess or interpolate a figure.

As noted above, one deals here with a small proportion of cases, and the effects upon calculations of proceeding in this way are slight. This is partly because calculations with such a zero value result in the generation of missing values for many of the subsequent computed measures, and thus produces the targeted omission of such a questionable case from ensuing calculations. Where for various reasons this would not occur, care was taken in the SPSS syntax to cover this, for example by selecting cases in excess of zero. None of the work for this book involved summing our parish figures and cross-relating them to the census' published (and corrected) overall tables, where the different approaches at each spatial level would produce mismatches of

[9] In many such cases, the incumbent failed to give any figures for attendances on 30 March, did not write 'No service' (thus implying that the building was open for worship that Sunday), and gave average figures for a preceding period. We did not use such average figures, for to us (unlike the politically wary Horace Mann) it seemed dubious to suppose that such averages could be held to represent the true attendances on Census Sunday. If the incumbent was able to calculate averages and enter them on his form, why did he not also insert figures for his service(s) on Census Sunday? Our response is because there was in fact probably no service held on that day (or almost nobody attended), and that such incumbents adopted this strategy to circumvent disapproving comment. As is known, there were objections among some Anglican clergy to provide such data. See e.g. *Census of Religious Worship*, p. xxxix, note 3.

results. And all our registration-district data was taken from the published census alone.

We do not wish to lay down these procedures as rigid guidelines for future practice, for the data are amenable to different approaches. However, the results of such approaches are very close to each other, and these methods are among the best that can be devised to deal with the real or supposed problems of missing data.

Appendix C

The religious measures

In this appendix, we outline the different measures used in this book. If in doubt, the reader should use this section as a reference point for the chapters and maps, and for subsequent research. It should contribute a better understanding of the various measures that are made possible by the *Census of Religious Worship*, and that can be applied or adapted to some other religious sources.

The *'index of attendances'*. This is defined as total attendances (morning + afternoon + evening), expressed as a percentage of registration-district (or in part 2 of the book, parish) population. This is the measure we have used most commonly. It is well established in the historiography. We used the index of attendances partly because it allows our findings to be compared most readily with earlier arguments by other authors. It is one of the most direct measures available, and (unlike a sittings measure) has the main advantage of allowing one to discern the actual strength of worship on Census Sunday. As discussed in chapter 1, for the registration-district data the index of attendances (like other registration-district attendance measures) includes Sunday scholars, as Horace Mann added Sunday school attendances to general-congregation attendances in his published registration-district tables. For the parish data we kept Sunday scholars separate to allow greater precision in data handling.[1]

[1] See chapter 1, pp. 41–2. The parish-level index of attendances in this book uses general-congregation attendances alone. Many calculations and tests were conducted to consider how justifiable this was, and whether it was worth following Mann in adding Sunday school attendances to general religious attendances. The conclusion was that such addition made little difference, having very little effect on this book's calculations and arguments, and it was not worth noting such similar results. In addition, Mann's registration-district data were experimentally reconsidered, working up to district level from the enumerators' original data without using Sunday school attendances, but the results do not impair conclusions from his published data. Indeed, they showed how dependable Mann's calculations were. The index of

Care must be taken in the interpretation of the index of attendances. We referred in chapter 1 and elsewhere to the 'problem' of multiple attendances on Census Sunday: the fact that some worshippers attended church or chapel more than once, either at the same place of worship or at different denominational services. It is a measure of *attendances*, not of *attendants* or *attenders*. This is a general problem with all 1851 attendance-based measures but, in this instance, it certainly inflates index of attendance values. However, we found very close and consistent relationships between measures of total attendances, maximum attendance, those for sittings, and the wider range of measures, and we believe that the associations between attenders and attendances were fairly consistent. After very extensive examination of the inter-relationships between variables, for each denomination, we could find very little evidence that the index of attendances is an unreliable or distorting measure.

The *'index of maximum attendance'*. This is similar to the index of attendances, except that the *maximum* attendance during Census Sunday is used. (This can usually only be adopted with parish-level attendance data for the major denominations, as the registration districts amalgamate data for different services in a way that makes it inadmissible.) The same principle applies for the *'index of maximum Sunday school attendance'*, as justified and used in chapter 10. Some historians have preferred to use the index of maximum attendances for their main calculations, and so long as the measure is properly computed this is quite acceptable. The denominational index of maximum attendance is very highly correlated indeed with the index of total attendances. There are subtle issues following from this comparison, involving denominational ratios between morning, afternoon and evening figures, but these do not warrant exposition here.

The *'index of total attendances for all denominations'* takes the total of all denominational attendances at all times of the day (whether at parish or registration-district level), and expresses this

Footnote 1 (*cont.*)
attendances for registration districts tends to be higher than that for parishes (see for example p. 400), but such comparisons between district and parish data remain viable. These points largely derive, of course, from the fact that religious and Sunday school indexes of attendance were strongly correlated, Sunday school attendances being very dependent upon the size of general religious attendances.

total as a percentage of each registration-district or parish population in 1851. It indicates the overall proclivity of local populations to attend any form of worship on Census Sunday. Crudely expressed, it is a measure of the 'religiosity' of different areas; or, seen another way, it reflects one possible definition of the 'secularisation' of different areas. (We would make no claim that any such empirical definition of 'secularisation' should have priority over other ways of thinking about this term.) It is mapped for England and Wales in the last chapter.

The *'index of sittings'* takes total sittings for a denomination (both 'free' and 'other', or appropriated), and expresses them as a percentage of each registration-district (or parish) population in 1851. For example, a denominational index of sittings of 37 would indicate that 37 per cent of registration-district (or parish) population could be seated by that denomination. This is a measure of the physical capacity of denominations in their places of worship. It tends to be very accurate as such, for the numbers of sittings could be easily checked by others. Its drawback of course is that many places of worship, like those for the Anglican Church in some areas (such as parts of east Leicestershire), or sometimes for the Quakers, had sittings sizes which may have been appropriate to population requirements in the past, but which were out of line with local demand in 1851. Nevertheless, there are high correlations between sittings and attendances, and the measure is generally a reliable one. We have not gone further to use indexes of 'free', or of 'appropriated', sittings – feasible though these are – mainly because these extra refinements were superfluous for the purposes of this book.

The *'index of total sittings for all denominations'* takes the sum of all denominational sittings (whether at parish or registration-district level), and expresses this total as a percentage of each registration-district (or parish) population in 1851. It shows how well the populations of different areas were provided for in terms of sittings. For example, an index of total sittings of 100 would indicate that exactly all the population could be seated by the combined local body of churches and chapels. It is mapped for England and Wales in the concluding chapter.

The *'percentage share of sittings'* is a denomination's total sittings expressed as a percentage of all sittings for all denominations within the registration district, or parish. This is one of the three percentage share measures, which have not been used much in religious historiography. Like the other two such measures, it shows the relative strength of the denomination under consideration. It is highly reliable, but (like the index of sittings) refers to physical features of provision rather than actual attendances.

The *'percentage share of churches'* takes the number of churches for a denomination, and expresses that as a percentage of the total number of churches for all denominations. It is a crude but very reliable indicator, best applied at registration-district level, where church numbers make it worthwhile. Again, it is a measure of physical provision.

The *'percentage share of attendances'* is derived in a similar way as the other percentage-share measures, being calculated by taking the denomination's total attendances, expressed as a percentage of the total attendances for all denominations, at registration-district or parish level. One may also use a *'percentage share of maximum attendances'*, using each denomination's maximum attendance at parish level.

All three percentage-share measures have two main disadvantages. First, they take no account of regional levels of what we will here loosely term 'religiosity' or 'secularisation'. They measure a particular denomination's share of sittings, attendances or places of worship from the registration-district (or parish) total. Total levels of 'religiosity' (by which is meant total religious attendances as a percentage of the population) varied markedly throughout England and Wales. The same percentage share of sittings value for a denomination could occur in a district with high levels of 'secularisation', or a district with high levels of apparent 'religiosity' as judged by the general proclivity to attend worship. Secondly, any correlation or regression procedures between different denominations using the same percentage-share variable have to be treated with great caution. These measures are percentages, and due to the statistical closed number system, where one denomination performed well another by definition would tend to perform badly, resulting in negative correlations between them. Unfortunately a number of historians have failed to appreciate this, and have argued for strange conclusions on the basis of such (inevitable) negative correlations.

The *'index of occupancy'* measure is calculated by dividing each denomination's registration-district (or parish) total attendances by its total sittings, and multiplying the result by 100. This variable has not hitherto been used in the historiography. It provides an interesting insight into the demand for, or pressure upon, the accommodation provided by each denomination. A value in excess of 100 indicates that total attendances exceeded sittings. Of course, due to multiple services on Census Sunday, this does not necessarily mean that churches were full to overcrowding, but it does indicate that provision (in terms of seating) was being highly utilised. Values under 100, particularly values well under 100, clearly suggest a mismatch between accommodation and worshippers, with over-provision perhaps reflecting changes in the geography of religion, or declines in attendances at some time after the construction of the church or chapel, or a place of worship that never fulfilled its initial expectation. One needs to be aware of causal problems in interpreting this measure: an index of occupancy could be high because of high demand for a denomination's sittings in a region; *or* it might be high because a historically low level of demand had led to inadequate provision; *or* historically high demand may have led to over-provision, resulting in low indexes of occupancy. In other words, this is a complex measure that has to be interpreted tentatively, in the light of other religious measures, or with access to other forms of local historical knowledge.

'Persons per place of worship' is calculated by the registration-district (or parish) population being divided by the number of places of worship in the district (or parish) belonging to each denomination. This variable is limited in that it takes no account of accommodation in terms of seating or standing room provided by each place of worship. Hence if a denomination had a large number of places of worship in a district, but each place of worship was small, this measure would overestimate the denomination's strength. It may also underestimate religious provision in urban areas where places of worship tended to be large.

'Place of worship density' is another measure that allows one to examine religious provision. One generates this measure by expressing the number of places of worship for each denomination in terms of ten square kilometre units within each district or parish. This variable takes no account of registration-district (or parish) population density (and hence likely demand for religious provision); and so, particularly in urban areas, it needs to be interpreted with caution. For instance, 'place of worship density' in towns may be very high compared to rural

regions but, as a product of greater urban population densities, actual religious provision may, in fact, be less adequate.

'Place of worship mean size' is calculated by dividing a denomination's total sittings by its number of places of worship. The measure provides a further insight into the provision by each denomination and its response to factors such as population growth and urbanisation. As one would expect, it tends to be greatest in towns and cities, where large places of worship were most needed to accommodate the resident population. Comparative historical work on denominational mean sizes of churches or chapels, their relative effectiveness, and the chronological, architectural, administrative, economic and regional features of this, has as yet barely started,[2] and limitations of space have prevented us from exploring this issue in depth here.

The *'index of religious diversity'*. This 'diversity measure' is a type of *gini* index originally used to study linguistic diversity, which Alasdair Crockett developed as a measure of religious diversity.[3] (It was used as such in chapter 11). Using the 1851 religious census data, the most obvious translation of the index is to the formula

$$1-\sum_{x=1}^{x=n}(xa/ta)^2$$

where ta is the total attendance figure, xa is the attendance figure for denomination x, and n is the number of denominations in a parish or registration district. (Expressed differently, this is 1 minus the sum of the squared ratios of the attendances for each denomination to total religious attendances.) The measure ranges from zero where only one denomination is present, and tends towards unity under conditions of 'complete diversity'. In mathematical terms complete diversity is an infinite variety of equally strong denominations. This limit is of course never reached in the historical or present world, but, in mathematical language, is *tended towards*. This means that the diversity measure increases by ever decreasing amounts as the number of denominations increases. For example, two equally strong denominations would yield a diversity score of one half (0.5), three a

[2] The major exception to this statement being the fascinating work of R. Gill, *The Myth of the Empty Church* (1993).

[3] A. C. Crockett, 'A secularising geography? Patterns and processes of religious change in England and Wales, 1676–1851' (unpub. Ph.D thesis, University of Leicester, 1998).

score of two-thirds (0.66), four a score of three-quarters (0.75), and five a score of four-fifths (0.8), and so on.

A dissenting 'share of attendances' value of a certain magnitude, for example 50 per cent, can only arise from one set of circumstances, that is, half of the attendances in a given district or parish being of a dissenting nature. The value of the 'index of diversity' measure, however, results from the interaction of two factors, the number of denominations and their relative sizes (in terms of attendances). For example, the same value of diversity score can be recorded for a parish with few, but equally sized denominations, as a parish with many denominations one of which is predominant. The measure is neutral to all denominations when assessing religious diversity. For example, if only the Church of England is present a value of zero is recorded. The same value would be recorded if only the Welsh Calvinistic Methodists were present. Both situations represent an absence of religious diversity, and complete denominational hegemony.

These variables comprise the main possibilities offered by the Religious Census, although some further ones can be constructed for closely defined purposes. As has been pointed out, there are often very tight matches across variables, like the indexes of attendances and sittings. Most historians would wish to concentrate on the index of attendances for their work, and such an emphasis has been followed in this book. Limitations of space restrict the variables that can be used to analyse denominations on this scale, although fuller length treatment of specific denominations would warrant more detailed consideration of a range of measures, as shown for the Church of England in chapter 2.

Appendix D

Computer cartographic methods

One limitation in the historiography on the 1851 *Census of Religious Worship*, and indeed for the geography of religion more generally, is that very few detailed maps showing religious patterns have been produced. Hitherto, the best national maps were based on county units only. We have therefore taken this further – within constraints of publication space – by publishing maps here for most denominations as based upon registration-district units, for the whole of England and Wales, and at parish level for certain counties. We have provided national maps for almost all the main denominations, and for the Church of England this has been done with a diversity of possible measures.

Traditional methods of cartographic production are time-consuming and require skills that many historians, and some geographers, do not possess. At registration-district level, maps for the whole of England and Wales would be extremely difficult and time-consuming to draw with traditional methods. We made use of two computer cartographic packages – GIMMS and ARC/VIEW – that allowed us to map registration-district or parish data, and that offered new possibilities in terms of flexibility of data display.

The registration-district boundaries for these maps were derived from the original maps in the published 1851 census. Those census maps were put together for England and Wales, and all boundaries were digitised. County maps showing parishes were based upon those in *The Phillimore Atlas and Index of Parish Registers*,[1] with adaptations where necessary using other sources and the Ordnance Survey County series dating from the 1930s. These base maps are suitable for depicting the geography of religion here, although their accuracy

[1] C. R. Humphrey-Smith (ed.), *The Phillimore Atlas and Index of Parish Registers* (Canterbury, 1984).

would need to be further refined for selective enlargement with some modern geographical information systems. The computerised mapping of accurate historical parish and registration-district boundaries is a research project in itself, being worked on by others. The boundaries used here serve our purposes, given the scale of national cartography, and the need to communicate spatial patterns of religious denominations.

For all maps the issue of quantitative class divisions was considered carefully, and a consistent approach was followed throughout the book. In order to make the descriptions and interpretation as straightforward as possible, we adopted a legend grounded upon five classes. Class divisions were based on what is termed a 'quantile system'. That is, the same number of registration-district or parish observations fall into each class for each map.[2] A sixth class outside the quantile system was created to distinguish registration districts or parishes where a denomination was not recorded. For the registration-district maps this category also includes districts in which the denomination was present, but for which data were missing and could not be calculated using our data correction methods. One option considered was simply to devise a single set of class breaks and apply that to all denominations. This would have produced generally dark maps for the Church of England and the strongest dissenting denominations, very many registration-district values for them falling into the higher class categories. Much lighter maps would have resulted for the weaker and less common denominations. Many gradations of strength and weakness within particular denominations would have been lost with such standardisation. We therefore rejected this alternative, and the approach taken was to work with distinct quantiles calculated for each denominational measure in turn, where mapping took place. Hence the maps show the strengths and weaknesses of each denomination within the terms of its own data distribution, rather than relative to other denominations. Every map shows a full gradation of shading. But as the text and the class breaks indicated on each map make clear, some denominations were much stronger than others. The reader should bear this in mind when referring to the maps.

[2] An example may illustrate this point. Using the quantile system, if a denomination was recorded in 100 registration districts, then class breaks would be calculated in such a way as to ensure that 20 observations fell into each class.

Appendix E

Landownership and the *Imperial Gazetteer*

There has been use at various points in this book of the parish landownership classifications taken from the *Imperial Gazetteer*.[1] This impressive source provided data for this book on divisions of landed property, types of ecclesiastical living, value of ecclesiastical livings, whether those livings included accommodation for the incumbent, and real property values. It categorised parishes into four groups

[1] J. M. Wilson, *The Imperial Gazetteer of England and Wales*, 6 volumes (A. Fullarton and Co., Edinburgh, Glasgow, London, Dublin and New York, n.d., c. 1870–2). The six-volume work appeared in c. 1870–2, its information mainly relating to the 1860s. (Some libraries give the publication dates of the first two volumes as 1866 and 1867, while one dates the six-volume work as 1866–9, but it is not clear on what basis this is done.) There were very similar subsequent editions, for example a two-volume work in 1875, the entries of which appear to be identical to those for c.1870–2. The work superseded a previous *Gazetteer*, issued by the same publishers, called the *Parliamentary Gazetteer of England and Wales*, which had been published in 1838 and following years. The same company also produced J. M. Wilson, *The Imperial Gazetteer of Scotland; or, Dictionary of Scottish Topography, Compiled from the Most Recent Authorities, and Forming a Complete Body of Scottish Geography, Physical, Statistical, and Historical* (London, 1868), 2 volumes. *The Imperial Gazetteer of England and Wales* 'aims to be the best work of its class which has ever been produced'. (*Imperial Gazetteer*, 1875 edn, vol. 1, p. iii.) (The equivalent summary for the c. 1870–2 volumes is on pp. 1155–99). It used the 1851 registration districts for much of its data (*ibid.*, 1875 edn, vol. 1, p. iv). Its own statistics on churches and chapels (which we have not used) were accurately obtained from the 1851 Religious Census. It stressed the pains that had been taken to publish up-to-date and accurate data. Thousands of points 'have undergone revision by intelligent residents in the places which they describe' (*ibid.*, 1875 edn, vol. 1, p. iv). Some sources survive which illustrate this: see for example T. Bunn, *Answers to Inquiries Respecting Frome Selwood, in Somersetshire, Transmitted by the Editors of the Imperial Cyclopedia, in London, and of the Imperial Gazetteer, in Glasgow* (Frome, 1851, located in the National Library of Wales). Statements of real property values and of rated property in the *Imperial Gazetteer* were from returns of 1859 and 1860 (*ibid.*, 1875 edn, vol. 1, p. v). Its population figures were from the 1861 census. 'The values of very many of the benefices are given as admitted or corrected by the incumbents themselves' (*ibid.*, 1875 edn, vol. 1, p. v). It did not say how its parish and township property classifications had been arrived at.

according to their landownership: held in one hand; not much divided or in few hands; sub-divided; and much sub-divided. This was evidently a simple classification, a guide to one salient feature of the parish or township being described, and it has been used by earlier historians as well as ourselves.[2] It is well suited to the kinds of quantitative analyses pursued here. Almost no information was given in different editions of the *Imperial Gazetteer* about how its landownership divisions were arrived at, and contemporary readers seem to have taken those classifications as being relatively straightforward. By that time (with all the debate there had been on settlement and 'open' and 'close' parishes, and in 1867–9 on the gang system and female and child agricultural labour), they were well accustomed to thinking about parishes in such terms.

Despite some historians' prior use of the *Gazetteer*, and some preliminary tests with very limited numbers of parishes, there has been no rigorous examination of how reliable its coverage and classifications were. This appendix will therefore explore this further, taking the registration county of Leicestershire as a test case and comparing these four classifications with data on the number of owners from the land-tax returns. It will be argued that the *Imperial Gazetteer*'s data are remarkably dependable when tested in this way, and that as a general indicator it comprises a trustworthy basis for historical research of the sort conducted.

The *Imperial Gazetteer* certainly did not provide complete parish coverage when it gave information on landownership. Out of a total of 2,443 parishes in the fifteen counties, the source allowed us to take a landownership category for 1,524 parishes. This is a coverage of 62 per cent. In some cases, classifications were given for townships rather than for parishes, and this information had to be abandoned because of the use of the parish as our unit for statistical analysis. (It is usually impossible or unreasonable to combine classifications of this sort when given for various townships within a larger parish.) In other cases, where no classification was given, the parishes were often urbanised, and the source seems to have assumed that readers

[2] A. Everitt, *The Pattern of Rural Dissent: the Nineteenth Century* (Leicester, 1972); D. R. Mills, *Lord and Peasant in Nineteenth-century Britain* (1980); D. R. Mills and B. M. Short, 'Social change and social conflict in nineteenth-century England: the use of the open-closed village model', in M. Reed and R. Wells (eds.), *Class, Conflict and Protest in the English Countryside, 1700–1880* (1990), pp. 93–4.

Table E.1. *Landownership categories and source coverage by county*

County	Land in one family	Land in a few families	Land sub-divided	Land much sub-divided	% of parishes with data
Ang.	2	40	10	11	81.8
Beds.	10	44	21	9	67.7
Caerns.	2	36	4	6	76.2
Cambs.	2	43	9	25	53.0
Cards.	0	35	5	25	68.4
Derbs.	1	27	13	24	61.9
Dors.	25	101	13	29	59.2
Lancs.	0	7	11	24	53.8
Leics.	5	65	30	35	58.7
Mon.	6	62	17	21	88.3
N'umb.	1	36	10	9	61.5
Rut.	3	15	3	2	41.1
Suff.	12	155	58	60	58.9
Suss.	17	86	40	40	57.7
York, E. Rid.	2	64	27	29	71.3
Total	88	816	271	349	62.4

would be in no doubt about the sub-divided nature of ownership. Many urban parishes were omitted as a consequence of this, and one comes down to parishes of 5,000–14,000 people in 1851 (like Abergavenny, Ashbourne, Chesterfield or Bridlington) before classifications were usually registered. Coded data were only computed when explicitly given for parishes in the *Gazetteer*, and it was decided not to classify independently the more urbanised parishes. Information was also sometimes given in the source on manors rather than the parish, and this has been ignored. Table E.1 gives the resulting number of parishes in each landownership category for every county, and the overall county percentages of parishes for which information was available.

As can be seen from the final column, some counties had rather higher coverage than others: Monmouthshire, Anglesey, Caernarvonshire, the East Riding or Cardiganshire were prominent among them. Others, like Rutland, were much lower. The distributions by landownership category also varied between counties, which is an interesting subject in its own right. If one classed as 'closed' parishes those in the two most restricted *Gazetteer* categories, and used 'valid percentages' rather than the numbers above, it is clear that some counties had higher percentages of such parishes than others. The percentages of parishes that would be deemed 'closed' by this elementary approach were: Anglesey 66.7, Bedfordshire 64.3, Caernarvonshire 79.2, Cambridgeshire 57.0, Cardigan 53.8, Derbyshire 43.1, Dorset 75.0, Lancashire 16.7, Leicestershire 51.9, Monmouthshire 64.2, Northumberland 66.1, Rutland 78.3, Suffolk 58.6, Sussex 56.3, and the East Riding 54.1. The overall percentage for all counties was 59.3. Such variations accord (for some of the more extreme counties) with what is known impressionistically or in other documented ways: Caernarvonshire, Rutland and Dorset for example having high percentages of parishes in concentrated ownership,[3] contrasting with counties like Lancashire or Derbyshire.

There is no way at present of knowing how accurate these county distributions by landownership type were, and directly comparable measures that one could relate these distributions to are unavailable. This would require very considerable further work with other sources for validation. While such an exercise would clearly be valuable, it has seemed superfluous for the rather different priorities of this book. There are some counties with readily available land-tax data, like Leicestershire or Lincolnshire, but for most counties accessible parish-level historical data on landownership are surprisingly absent. The 1873 'New Domesday' survey of landownership does not supply detailed data in a form that can readily be used here. The enormous body of data from Lloyd George's 'Domesday' of landownership, consequent upon the 1909–10 Finance Act, is too late for this book, and that source's field and valuation books remain unresearched and poorly accessible because of the way they were separated between

[3] Among our English counties, Rutland and Dorset were also prominent in measures of the density of country aristocratic seats, and the percentage of their productive land taken up by estates of over 10,000 acres. See e.g. J. L. Sanford and M. Townsend, *The Great Governing Families of England* (1865), vol. 1, endplate map; J. Bateman, *The Great Landowners of Great Britain and Ireland* (1878, 1883 edn); H. A. Clemenson, *English Country Houses and Landed Estates* (1982), pp. 22, 25, 229–230: Rutland had nearly 70 per cent of its land held by 'great landowners' in 1880. However, Northumberland was also high in any such county list of estate prominence, and in making these comparisons (between the percentage of parishes that were 'closed' and the extent that land lay in great estates) one needs to stress that such measures are really quite different in some ways, and that a very diverse range of regional, topographical and north–south contrasts also had strong influences upon the extent of landed concentrations.

major archives.[4] The deficiency of *Gazetteer* information on landownership for some parishes is perhaps the main problem here, but it should not adversely affect calculations in a way that detracts from the argument. The most urban parishes were the ones most liable to be omitted;[5] but then they were at the farthest 'open' end of an 'open–close' ownership continuum, and their omission therefore serves to weaken the empirical contrasts and effects which have been displayed and argued from here. In other words, the arguments made in this book would be stronger if one chose to take account of this matter. Within a more rural environment, problems might arise only if certain kinds of estate (or other category) parishes were being systematically omitted, so as to render the categorised parishes unrepresentative. There is no reason to believe that this was the case.

What is more important is to verify that the *Imperial Gazetteer*'s classifications of parish type stand up when tested against other sources documenting landownership. The criteria used for the *Imperial Gazetteer* classifications were not made clear in that source, although it states that there had been much local consultation with incumbents. One suspects that subjective judgements were sometimes made, albeit by local people who presumably would have had good knowledge of the parish and familiarity with tithe surveys, rating valuations, and the land tax. The *Gazetteer* prided itself on the accuracy of its information, through a number of editions, but one would like more reassurance about its entries. To examine this, Leicestershire was used to test the *Gazetteer*'s data against the number of owners in the 1832 Land Tax returns.[6] This is the latest date for which land-tax data are usually available. There are a number of caveats to bear in mind. First, some time elapsed between 1832 and the publication of the *Imperial Gazetteer*, and this will weaken the comparisons made. However, landownership was a long-standing

4 For discussion, see B. Short, *The Geography of England and Wales in 1910: an Evaluation of Lloyd George's 'Domesday' of Landownership* (Historical Geography Research Series, no. 22, 1989); B. Short, *Land and Society in Edwardian Britain* (Cambridge, 1997).

5 The mean 1851 population size of the missing entries was 3,105, while the equivalent mean for 'much sub-divided' parishes was 2,913. The missing ones also had high population densities.

6 The data were taken from D. R. Mills, 'Landownership and rural population, with special reference to Leicestershire in the mid nineteenth century' (University of Leicester, Ph.D, 1963), Appendix 4. We have combined Mills' township data to parish level where necessary.

Table E.2. *Number of owners in Leicestershire in 1832, by categories of landownership*

Landownership	mean	median	n.
In one family	2.0	2	4
In a few hands	27.8	19	49
Sub-divided	54.8	46	24
Much sub-divided	80.1	64	30

Kruskal–Wallis 1-Way ANOVA

Landownership	mean rank	n.
In one family	5.5	4
In a few hands	38.5	49
Sub-divided	63.4	24
Much sub-divided	78.2	30
Total		107

Notes:

Chi-square	D.F.	Signif.
42.4	3	.0000

phenomenon: parish structures in this regard were not prone to change much over the short term, and certainly not during these few decades which came after the bulk of parliamentary enclosure and before the late nineteenth-century agricultural depression. Further, the land tax itself has been the subject of very detailed historical research, and plenty of doubts have accrued over the data it provides.[7] This is not the place to enter into an outline of the main difficulties with the source. But any inaccuracies, like the possible under-reporting of smallowners, work against the comparisons here – as does the chronological difference between the two sources – and so these (like the treatment of urban parishes) can be tolerated.

Accordingly the 1832 returns on the number of owners were collated into parish units, computerised, and compared with the *Gazetteer* data. The results, given in table E.2, are very reassuring. In

[7] For further discussion (out of a large literature) see especially G. E. Mingay, 'The Land Tax Assessments and the small landowner', *Economic History Review*, 17 (1964); D. R. Mills and M. E. Turner (eds.), *Land and Property: the English Land Tax, 1692–1832* (Gloucester, 1986); D. E. Ginter, *A Measure of Wealth: the English Land Tax in Historical Analysis* (1992).

Table E.3. *Median test on Leicestershire landownership*

Owners in 1832	In one hand	In a few hands	Sub-divided	Much sub-divided
GT median	0	13	14	26
LE median	4	36	10	4

Notes:

Cases	Median	Chi-square	D.F.	Signif.
107	38.0	31.6	3	.0000

both parts of the table, there were striking and predictable differences in the number of land-tax owners according to the *Imperial Gazetteer* classification. The mean and median number of owners for parishes where property was said to be 'in one hand' was 2. Where property was said to be 'much sub-divided', the mean was 80 and the median 64. There is consistent progression between these extremes in the two intervening categories of landownership. The results of the non-parametric Kruskal–Wallis test are highly significant statistically.

Table E.3 gives further analysis of the Leicestershire data, employing a median test. This shows in the top row the number of cases of *Imperial Gazetteer* categorisation that are greater than the overall median for land-tax owners, and in the bottom row the number of cases that are less than that median. As one would anticipate, the results strongly demonstrate consistency across the two historical sources. Other tests strongly support these findings.[8]

These results are highly confirmatory of the information in the *Imperial Gazetteer*. They become all the more so when one recalls the time gap between the two sources being used, and the questions that have dogged the land tax as an historical source. Any incongruities between land-tax data and that of the *Gazetteer* may of course have been due to errors emanating from the land-tax returns rather than from the *Gazetteer*. In fact, the tests show the two sources confirming each other very strongly indeed. This is remarkably the case for the most 'closed' parishes.[9] And if more urban parishes were included, the

[8] ANOVA produced an F ratio of 10.1, with an F probability of .0000.

[9] The findings of these tests are much more reassuring than Mills' earlier ones, which were based on smaller numbers, as reported in his *Lord and Peasant*, p. 88, and summarised again in his 'Peasants and conflict in nineteenth-century rural England: a comment on two recent articles', in M. Reed and R. Wells, *Class, Conflict and Protest in the English Countryside, 1700–1880* (1990), p. 118.

results would produce even starker contrasts, by raising the median number of owners for parishes that were 'much sub-divided'. There seems little doubt that similar results would emerge for other counties if the matter was to be pursued elsewhere in this manner.

Against this general picture, some occasional discrepancies do exist when the data are closely inspected by parish, and it is worth discussing these. There are a few cases where a Leicestershire parish described as 'not much divided', or with property 'among a few', had a considerable number of owners in 1832. In Nether Broughton, for example, there were 65 owners. Thornton had 54, Glenn Magna 57, Appleby 40, and Enderby 68. Breedon on the Hill had as many as 145. Examples like these were exceptional in showing such a mismatch between the sources. The sources were usually much more mutually supportive, and this was always so for the most 'closed' and 'open' parishes. In some cases it may be that there was a subsequent decline in owners, but even so the examples mentioned above are noticeable aberrations. There appear to be a number of reasons for them. The two sources document landownership in rather different ways, and the *Imperial Gazetteer* is the more subjective of the two. In some such examples, one has parishes containing separate townships and hamlets (e.g. Appleby, Breedon, Glenn Magna), and generalisations ostensibly about the parish may have been made without due regard to its full area. Breedon on the Hill, for example, contained the hamlets of Wilson and Tonge, and the townships of Staunton Harrold and Worthington. In others, conspicuous halls or manor houses in the parish (e.g. Enderby Hall, Appleby Hall, Broughton Lodge, all noticed by the source) might have inclined the *Gazetteer* to a conclusion about landownership not warranted by the real numbers of owners. One can for example envisage a parish in which over three-quarters of the land was owned by one family, but which also had a large number of much smaller owners. In Thornton, for example, 'most of the land belongs to Viscount Maynard and the Duke of Rutland'; but this was also a mining parish of rather more varied character than such a description might imply. Indeed, in such cases it may be that the subjective judgements of the *Gazetteer* are more helpful for the purposes of this book than data from a source like the land tax, for they may tell one more about the general character of a place. The *Gazetteer* coding was not altered for any parishes in the computerised dataset. It seems inevitable nevertheless that discrepancies of this sort render weaker some of the relationships demonstrated in this book, and that the quantitative results involving landownership would be stronger if they were eliminated. As the relatively few such anomalies work against this book's results and arguments, they can be tolerated here.

The overall conclusions derived from the quantitative tests are clear. In general terms, and allowing for the different style in which the phenomenon was described, the *Imperial Gazetteer* is a dependable source for landownership. Its categorisations are strongly supported by independent evidence. This conclusion suggests also that one may be optimistic about the other, more objective, quantitative information taken from the *Gazetteer*: on types and values of ecclesiastical living, whether the living included habitable accommodation for the incumbent, and parochial property values.

Appendix F

An 1861 Census of Religious Worship?

The 1851 Religious Census was not repeated for a variety of reasons, which are worth outlining here. They shed light both on the political importance of the subject at the time, and the ways in which the 1851 Religious Census was viewed in retrospect by many contemporaries.

There was extensive debate in 1860 as to whether there should be another such census in 1861. Some (particularly Nonconformists) wanted an exact repeat of the 1851 census. Others wished to see a simple statement of 'religious persuasion', while others balked at the idea in any form. The importance of the 1851 census was obvious to all: 'it was always used, and it has been over and over again quoted as exhibiting the numerical proportions of the different religious sects'.[1] As Lord Robert Cecil (MP for Stamford) stated, the Religious Census 'had been made the basis of reproaches against the Church of England, and attempts to undermine her position as an Establishment'. It 'had been appealed to in continual debates with very telling effect'.[2] This was despite his recollection that back in 1850 it had been intended 'to frame the census upon a plan which it was thought might be favourable to the religious body which had the greatest political organization, and could apply the sharpest whip to its members'.[3] It was clear that many Anglican parliamentarians felt that they had been adversely affected by the form of the census in 1851, and that its results had been used by dissenters to Anglican detriment. Rather than have a re-run of the 1851 census, the government proposed instead to have a question on 'religious profession' in 1861, which would be part of the normal census form.[4]

1 Sir George Lewis, *Hansard's Parliamentary Debates*, CLIX (11 July 1860), 1709.

2 *Hansard's Parliamentary Debates*, CLIX (11 July 1860), 1722.

3 *Hansard's Parliamentary Debates*, CLIX (11 July 1860), 1722.

4 J. Ridley, *Lord Palmerston* (1970, 1972 edn), p. 677.

However, this was opposed by Nonconformist interests, including even the Wesleyan Methodists.[5] The Nonconformists led by Edward Baines (MP for Leeds)[6] praised the 1851 Religious Census, and welcomed a re-run of it in 1861. They rejected any suggestion that the 1851 returns were unfair to the Church of England – Baines claimed that this suggestion 'was destitute of all real substance . . . there was no unfairness whatever'.[7] But they levelled a variety of criticisms against any simple statement of 'religious profession' in the forthcoming 1861 census. They felt that such a question was objectionable 'on the grounds of feeling and of principle'.[8] It was an 'authoritative demand' from government, that intruded into the 'domain of conscience',[9] and many petitions were received from local Nonconformist churches objecting to it. Bernal Osborne, the MP for Liskeard, argued that 'the Government has no right to inquire as to the religious persuasion of any member of the community'.[10] This objection to a clause on religion was shared by Scottish dissenters.[11] Such a question of profession also placed servants in a difficult position if they differed from their employers.[12] Probably the most crucial matter however, especially for the Nonconformists, was that many people were of no religion at all (clearly suggested in 1851).[13] As W. Monsell (MP for County Limerick) pointed out, these 'floating masses of the people, of no particular religious persuasion', would all be put down as belonging to the established church. Dissenting interests clearly feared that the result would be grossly unfair to themselves.[14]

Palmerston's second government of course had a very small majority.[15] With the Nonconformists led by Baines exercising their weighty

[5] E. D. Steele, *Palmerston and Liberalism, 1855–1865* (Cambridge, 1991), p. 178.
[6] Sir Edward Baines (1800–90), son of Edward Baines (1774–1848), both of whom were Liberal MPs for Leeds.
[7] *Hansard's Parliamentary Debates*, CLIX (11 July 1860), 1699, and see the entirety of Baines' speech, praising the 1851 Religious Census as a 'perfect success' (*ibid.*, 1700). He wanted another such census to teach the Establishment and the Nonconformists to respect each other (*ibid.*, 1702). See also Steele, *Palmerston and Liberalism*, p. 179.
[8] Edward Baines, in *Hansard's Parliamentary Debates*, CLIX (11 July 1860), 1696.
[9] *Hansard's Parliamentary Debates*, CLIX (11 July 1860), 1696–7.
[10] *Hansard's Parliamentary Debates*, CLIX (11 July 1860), 1717.
[11] *Hansard's Parliamentary Debates*, CLIX (11 July 1860), 1741.
[12] *Hansard's Parliamentary Debates*, CLIX (11 July 1860), 1697.
[13] *Hansard's Parliamentary Debates*, CLIX (11 July 1860), 1697–9. Baines used Mann's data to show that about 5,200,000 people who could have attended did not do so in 1851.
[14] *Hansard's Parliamentary Debates*, CLIX (11 July 1860), 1729, 1731–4.
[15] Steele, *Palmerston and Liberalism*, p. 178.

influence to block any such question of profession and its probable outcome, with the Anglican Church resolutely set against any direct repeat of the 1851 Religious Census, and with other MPs suggesting that 'Churchmen and Dissenters had a higher duty than quarrelling as to their respective numbers',[16] the prospects for any kind of religious census in 1861 looked unlikely.

Palmerston regretted the opposition of the Nonconformists.[17] It was his view that their claim to equality with the Church of England was doubtful. He thought that the Anglican Church had the adherence of two-thirds of the people of England and Wales, and the dissenters had a following of about a third of the population.[18] Gladstone came close to Palmerston's views on the utility of a religious census, despite their marked differences in ecclesiastical outlook. He appears to have regretted that a religious census had been proposed by the government for 1861 (his diary entry seeming a little ambiguous on that matter). But he felt that 'a religious census is not in itself mischievous', and that 'combined with a return of attendance it would be as nearly as possible fair . . . the Govt. may suffer from offending the Dissenters but cannot by merely conciliating them retain the character & strength necessary for its credit . . . My constituents call for the Census as a claim of justice.'[19]

They did not get it. Palmerston swallowed his vexation over the issue and 'settled to give up religious Enumeration in [1861] Census'.[20] J. Whiteside pointed out that the dissenting views were too strong for the government to withstand.[21] As Sir George Lewis stated, because of Nonconformist pressure, 'it is now impossible to carry a religious census into effect with a reasonable prospect of success'.[22]

16 *Hansard's Parliamentary Debates*, CLIX (11 July 1860), 1726, 1721.

17 *Hansard's Parliamentary Debates*, CLIX (11 July 1860), 1732–4.

18 See Palmerston's letter to Charles Wood, his Secretary of State for India, dated 20 November 1856, cited in Ridley, *Lord Palmerston*, p. 671. See also Steele, *Palmerston and Liberalism*, p. 169. Palmerston held this view despite the fact that 14,077 places of worship belonged to the Church of England in 1851, and 20,390 belonged to all other religious bodies (59.2 per cent of the total). The Church of England provided 5,317,915 sittings. The other churches provided 4,894,648 sittings (47.9 per cent of the total). See *Census of Religious Worship*, pp. viii, cxlviii.

19 Matthew (ed.), *The Gladstone Diaries, vol. V: 1855–1860* (Oxford, 1978), pp. 503–4.

20 Matthews, *The Gladstone Diaries, vol. V*, p. 503.

21 *Hansard's Parliamentary Debates*, CLIX (11 July 1860), 1735.

22 *Hansard's Parliamentary Debates*, CLIX (11 July 1860), 1715. See also the speech of Sir John Pakington (MP for Droitwich), blaming the dissenters for blocking the proposed 1861 Religious Census. *Ibid.*, 1731.

The government's plan had been brought down by MPs from such heartlands of dissent and Catholicism as Liskeard, Leeds and County Limerick. The reputation of Edward Baines soared even higher within dissenting and Liberal circles.[23] It was also held to be unnecessary to have another educational census, as such data was already available to the Education Commissioners.[24] A decade later the Free Church of Scotland requested a Religious Census for 1871, which Gladstone felt would 'go far to make the ground taken by the English non-conformists in /60 untenable'.[25] But religious enumeration for England and Wales was not included in the census bill of 1870 either.[26] Thus it was that the 1851 *Census of Religious Worship* continued as the main touchstone of contemporary debate for many decades to come, and became such an unrivalled source for historians of religion.

[23] Indeed, with regard to religious provision in towns, Horace Mann in his Census Report had already written that Baines was 'an excellent authority on subjects of this nature'. *Census of Religious Worship*, p. cxix, citing one of his publications.

[24] *Hansard's Parliamentary Debates*, CLIX (11 July 1860), 1739.

[25] H. C. G. Matthews (ed.), *The Gladstone Diaries, vol. VII: 1855–1860* (Oxford, 1982), p. 304: entry for 8 June 1870.

[26] Matthews, *The Gladstone Diaries, vol. VII*, p. 319: entry for 2 July 1870.

Bibliography

Sources of data

The 1851 Census of Religious Worship

Unpublished Public Record Office enumerators' returns:
Cambridgeshire, HO 129, 185–193.
Dorset, HO 129, 268–278.
Lancashire, HO 129, 461–486.
Leicestershire, HO 129, 408–418.
Northumberland, HO 129, 552–563.
Rutland, HO 129, 419–420.
Suffolk, HO 129, 211–227.
Yorkshire, East Riding, HO 129, 515–524.

Published enumerators' returns analysed in this book

D. W. Bushby (ed.), *Bedfordshire Ecclesiastical Census, 1851* (Bedfordshire Historical Record Society, vol. 54, Luton, 1975).

The Derbyshire data were made available, and later published, by M. Tranter (ed.), *The Derbyshire Returns to the 1851 Religious Census* (Derbyshire Record Society, 23, Chesterfield, 1995).

I. G. Jones and D. Williams (eds.), *The Religious Census of 1851: a Calendar of the Returns Relating to Wales, vol. 1: South Wales* (Cardiff, 1976).

I. G. Jones (ed.), *The Religious Census of 1851: a Calendar of the Returns Relating to Wales, vol. 2: North Wales* (Cardiff, 1981).

J. A. Vickers (ed.), *The Religious Returns of Sussex, 1851* (Sussex Record Society, 75, 1986–7).

1851 Census of Religious Worship (I.U.P. Shannon, 1970 edn), Population, vol. 11. (The source for Horace Mann's Report and the registration-district data.)

Other data sources

A. Whiteman (ed.), *The Compton Census of 1676: a Critical Edition* (Oxford, 1986).

J. M. Wilson, *The Imperial Gazetteer of England and Wales*, 6 volumes (A. Fullarton and Co., Edinburgh, Glasgow, London, Dublin and New York, n.d., c. 1870–2). The six-volume work appeared in c. 1870–2, its information mainly relating to the 1860s. (There were very similar subsequent editions, and we also sometimes cite the 1875 two-volume edition.) The c. 1870–2 six volumes provided data on division of landed property, types of ecclesiastical living, value of the living, whether the living included accommodation, and real property values.

The parochial occupational data were from the 1831 Population Census.

Parochial acreage data were from the 1831 and 1851 Population Censuses.

Parochial population figures were from the 1811, 1831 and 1851 Population Censuses.

Parochial poor-relief expenditure for each county (1832–6) was from Appendices C and D of the *Annual Reports of the Poor Law Commissioners for England and Wales* (1836–7).

Details of archival material (e.g. visitation returns, pew rent books, church seating plans, land tax returns or the 1829 religious returns), and of parliamentary debates, may be found in the notes for each chapter.

Other government reports

Select Committee on First Fruits and Tenths, and Administration of Queen Anne's Bounty, XIV (1837).

Select Committee on Settlement and Poor Removal, VIII, XI (1847).

Report of George Coode to the Poor Law Board on the Law of Settlement and Removal of the Poor, XXVI (1851).

1851 Census Great Britain: Reports and Tables on Education, England and Wales, XC (1852–3).

Census of Great Britain, 1851: Religious Worship, Scotland, Reports and Tables (1854).

Select Committee on the Irremovable Poor, VII (1859).

Report on the Employment of Women and Children in Agriculture, XVII (1867–8).

Report on the Employment of Children, Young Persons, and Women in Agriculture, XIII (1868–9).

Secondary bibliography

Only secondary items noted in the text are included here. Place of publication is London unless otherwise stated.

G. W. O. Addleshaw and F. Etchells, *The Architectural Setting of Anglican Worship* (1948, 1956 edn).

S. Ahlstrom, *A Religious History of the American People* (1972, New Haven, 1974 edn).

J. W. Aitchison and H. Carter, *The Welsh Language 1961–81: an Interpretative Atlas* (Cardiff, 1985).

'Rural Wales and the Welsh language', *Rural History*, 2 (1991).

N. Alldridge, 'Loyalty and identity in Chester parishes, 1540–1640', in S. J. Wright (ed.), *Parish, Church and People: Local Studies in Lay Religion, 1350–1750* (1988).

N. Alldridge (ed.), *The Hearth Tax: Problems and Possibilities* (Hull, 1983).

J. B. Allen and M. R. Thorp, 'The mission of the Twelve to England, 1840–41: Mormon Apostles and the working classes', *Brigham Young University Studies*, 15 (1975).

K. J. Allison, *The East Riding of Yorkshire Landscape* (1976).

R. W. Ambler, 'The 1851 Census of Religious Worship', *Local Historian*, 11 (1975).

'Social change and religious experience: aspects of rural society in south Lincolnshire, with specific reference to Primitive Methodism, 1815–1875' (unpublished Ph.D thesis, University of Hull, 1984).

'Religious life in Kesteven – a return of the number of places of worship not of the Church of England, 1829', *Lincolnshire History and Archaeology*, 220 (1985).

'A lost source? The 1829 returns of non-Anglican places of worship', *Local Historian*, 17 (1987).

Ranters, Revivalists and Reformers: Primitive Methodism and Rural Society, South Lincolnshire, 1817–1875 (Hull, 1989).

R. W. Ambler (ed.), *Lincolnshire Returns of the Census of Religious Worship, 1851*, Lincolnshire Record Society, 72 (1979).

O. Anderson, 'Gladstone's abolition of compulsory church rates: a minor political myth and its historiographical career', *Journal of Ecclesiastical History*, 25 (1974).

R. Anstey, 'Religion and British slave emancipation', in D. Eltis and J. Walvin (eds.), *The Abolition of the Atlantic Slave Trade* (Madison, Wisconsin, 1981).

J. Arch, *The Autobiography of Joseph Arch* (1898, 1966 edn).

T. Arkell, 'A method for estimating population totals from the Compton census returns', in K. Schurer and T. Arkell (eds.), *Surveying the People* (Oxford, 1992).

D. Ashforth, 'Settlement and removal in urban areas: Bradford, 1834–71', in M. E. Rose (ed.), *The Poor and the City: the English Poor Law in its Urban Context, 1834–1914* (Leicester, 1985).

T. S. Ashton, *The Industrial Revolution, 1760–1830* (Oxford, 1948).

M. Aston, 'Segregation in church', in W. J. Sheils and D. Wood (eds.), *Women in the Church* (Oxford, 1990).

D. Attwater, *The Catholic Church in Modern Wales* (1935).

M. R. Austin, 'Queen Anne's Bounty and the poor livings of Derbyshire', *Derbyshire Archaeological Journal*, 92 (1973).

'Religion and society in Derbyshire in the Industrial Revolution', *Derbyshire Archaeological Journal*, 93 (1974).

H. Aveling, *Post Reformation Catholicism in East Yorkshire, 1558–1790* (York, 1960).

J. C. H. Aveling, *The Handle and the Axe: the Catholic Recusants in England from the Reformation to Emancipation* (1976).

P. S. Bagwell, *Outcast London, a Christian Response: the West London Mission of the Methodist Church, 1887–1987* (1987).

S. Banks, 'Nineteenth-century scandal or twentieth-century model? A new look at "open" and "close" parishes', *Economic History Review*, 2nd series, 41 (1988).

J. R. V. Barker, *The Brontës* (1994, 1995 edn).

M. Barker, *Gladstone and Radicalism: the Reconstruction of Liberal Policy in Britain, 1885–94* (Hassocks, 1975).

F. A. Barnes, 'Settlement and landscape changes in a Caernarvonshire slate quarrying parish', in R. H. Osborne, F. A. Barnes and J. Doornkamp (eds.), *Geographical Essays in Honour of K. C. Edwards* (Nottingham, 1970).

D. A. Barton, 'William Griffith (1806–83): the Hercules of the Reform movement', *Proceedings of the Wesley Historical Society*, 43 (1982).

J. Bateman, *The Great Landowners of Great Britain and Ireland* (1878, 1883 edn).

G. Battiscombe, *Shaftesbury: a Biography of the Seventh Earl, 1801–1885* (1974).

D. E. D. Beales, *The Political Parties of Nineteenth-century England* (1971).

'The electorate before and after 1832: the right to vote, and the opportunity', *Parliamentary History*, 11 (1992).

E. D. Bebb, *Nonconformity and Social and Economic Life* (1935).

D. W. Bebbington, *The Nonconformist Conscience: Chapel and Politics, 1870–1914* (1982).

'Nonconformity and electoral sociology, 1867–1918', *Historical Journal*, 27 (1984).

O. A. Beckerlegge, *The United Methodist Free Churches* (1957).

D. Bellenger, 'The English Catholics and the French exiled clergy', *Recusant History*, 15 (1979–81).

The Exiled French Clergy in the British Isles after 1789 (Bath, 1986).

A. S. Bendall, *Maps, Land and Society: a History, with a Carto-bibliography of Cambridgeshire Estate Maps, c. 1600–1836* (Cambridge, 1992).

G. F. A. Best, *Temporal Pillars: Queen Anne's Bounty, the Ecclesiastical Commissioners, and the Church of England* (Cambridge, 1964).

'Popular Protestantism in Victorian Britain', in R. Robson (ed.), *Ideas and Institutions of Victorian Britain* (1967).

J. Betjeman (ed.), *English Parish Churches* (1958).

E. F. Biagini, *Liberty, Retrenchment and Reform: Popular Liberalism in the Age of Gladstone, 1860–1880* (Cambridge, 1992).

D. Bick and P. W. Davies, *Lewis Morris and the Cardiganshire Mines* (1994).

B. J. Biggs, *The Wesleys and the Early Dorset Methodists* (Gillingham, Dorset, 1987).

P. Bigmore, *The Bedfordshire and Huntingdonshire Landscape* (1979).

A. H. Birch, *Small-Town Politics: a Study of Political Life in Glossop* (Oxford, 1959).

B. G. Blackwood, 'Agrarian unrest and the early Lancashire Quakers', *Journal of the Friends' Historical Society*, 51 (1966).

R. Blake, *The Conservative Party from Peel to Churchill* (1972).

M. Blaug, 'The myth of the old poor law', in M. W. Flinn and T. C. Smout (eds.), *Essays in Social History* (Oxford, 1974).

N. Blewett, *The Peers, the Parties and the People: the General Elections of 1910* (1972).

F. O. Blundell, *Old Catholic Lancashire* (1925).

C. G. Bolam, J. Goring, H. L. Short and R. Thomas, *The English Presbyterians: from Elizabethan Puritanism to Modern Unitarianism* (1968).

F. Booth, *Robert Raikes of Gloucester* (Redhill, 1980).

'Robert Raikes: founder of the Sunday-school movement', in J. Ferguson (ed.), *Christianity, Society and Education: Robert Raikes, Past, Present and Future* (1981).

J. Bossy, 'Four Catholic congregations in rural Northumberland, 1750–1850', *Recusant History*, 9 (1967), 88–119.

'More Northumbrian congregations', *Recusant History*, 10 (1969).

The English Catholic Community, 1570–1850 (1975).

F. Boulard, *An Introduction to Religious Sociology* (1960).

F. Boulard and G. le Bras, *Carte Religieuse de la France Rurale* (Paris, 1952).

J. Bourke, '"I was always fond of my pillow": the handmade lace industry in the United Kingdom, 1870–1914', *Rural History*, 5 (1994).

F. W. Bourne, *The Bible Christians: their Origin and History, 1815–1900* (1905).

A. L. Bowley, 'The statistics of wages in the United Kingdom during the last hundred years. Agricultural wages', *Journal of the Royal Statistical Society*, 61 (December, 1898).

A. W. Braithwaite, 'Early tithe prosecutions: Friends as outlaws', *Journal of the Friends' Historical Society*, 49 (1960).

W. C. Braithwaite, 'The adult-school movement', in R. Mudie-Smith (ed.), *The Religious Life of London* (1904).

The Beginnings of Quakerism (1912, Cambridge, 1955 edn).

P. Brandon, *The Sussex Landscape* (1974).

P. Brandon and B. Short, *The South-East from A.D. 1000* (1990).

G. le Bras, *Etudes de Sociologie Religieuse* (Paris, 1956), 2 vols.

R. Brent, 'The Whigs and Protestant Dissent in the decade of reform: the case of the Church Rates, 1833–1841', *English Historical Review*, 102 (1987).

Liberal Anglican Politics: Whiggery, Religion and Reform, 1830–1841 (Oxford, 1987).

P. Brierley (M.A.R.C. Europe), *Christian England: What the 1989 English Church Census Reveals* (1991).

A. Briggs, *Victorian Cities* (1963, Harmondsworth, 1982 edn).

'Innovation and adaptation: the eighteenth-century setting', in J. Ferguson (ed.), *Christianity, Society and Education: Robert Raikes, Past, Present and Future* (1981).

C. Brooks and A. Saint (eds.), *The Victorian Church: Architecture and Society* (Manchester, 1995).

H. E. Broughton (ed.), *Nevill Holt: Studies of a Leicestershire Estate* (Leicester, 1985).

C. G. Brown, 'The costs of pew-renting: church management, church-going and social class in nineteenth-century Glasgow', *Journal of Ecclesiastical History*, 38 (1987).

The Social History of Religion in Scotland since 1730 (1987).

'Did urbanization secularize Britain?', *Urban History Yearbook* (1988).

R. Brown, *Church and State in Modern Britain, 1700–1850* (1991).

T. F. Bulmer, *History, Topography, and Directory of Northumberland* (Manchester, 1886).

R. Burn, *Ecclesiastical Law* (1781 edn).

D. W. Bushby (ed.), *Bedfordshire Ecclesiastical Census, 1851*, Bedfordshire Historical Record Society, vol. 54 (1975).

D. Butler and D. Stokes, *Political Change in Britain* (1969, 1974 edn).

J. Caird, *English Agriculture in 1850–51* (1852, Farnborough, 1968 edn).

N. Caplan, 'Sussex religious dissent, c. 1830', *Sussex Archaeological Collections*, 120 (1982).

E. Carlson, 'The origins, function, and status of the office of churchwarden, with particular reference to the diocese of Ely', in M. Spufford (ed.), *The World of Rural Dissenters, 1520–1725* (Cambridge, 1995).

S. C. Carpenter, *Church and People, 1789–1889: a History of the Church of England from William Wilberforce to 'Lux Mundi'* (1933).

S. Caunce, *Amongst Farm Horses: the Horselads of East Yorkshire* (Stroud, 1991).

O. Chadwick, *The Victorian Church*, pt. 2 (1970, 1980 edn).

C. W. Chalkin (ed.), *The Compton Census of 1676: the Dioceses of Canterbury and Rochester*, Kent Archaeological Society Records, 17 (1960).

A. Charlesworth, 'Labour protest, 1780–1850', in J. Langton and R. J. Morris (eds.), *Atlas of Industrializing Britain, 1780–1914* (1986).

R. Chew, *James Everett: a Biography* (1875).

M. Clark, 'Northern light? Parochial life in a "dark corner" of Tudor England', in K. L. French, G. G. Gibbs and B. A. Kümin (eds.), *The Parish in English Life, 1400–1600* (Manchester, 1997).

B. F. L. Clarke, *The Building of the Eighteenth-century Church* (1963).

P. F. Clarke, *Lancashire and the New Liberalism* (Cambridge, 1971).

'Electoral sociology of modern England', *History*, 57 (1972).

H. A. Clemenson, *English Country Houses and Landed Estates* (1982).

P. B. Cliff, *The Rise and Development of the Sunday School Movement in England, 1780–1980* (Redhill, 1986).

W. Clowes, *The Journals of William Clowes, a Primitive Methodist Preacher* (1844).

W. Cobbett, *Rural Rides* (1830, Harmondsworth, 1967 edn).

W. A. Cole, 'The social origins of the early Friends', *Journal of the Friends' Historical Society*, 48 (1957).

B. I. Coleman, *The Church of England in the Mid-Nineteenth Century: a Social Geography* (1980).

'Southern England in the Census of Religious Worship, 1851', *Southern History*, 5 (1983).

D. C. Coleman, 'Growth and decay during the Industrial Revolution: the case of East Anglia', *Scandinavian Economic History Review*, 10 (1962).

Courtaulds: an Economic and Social History, vol. 1 (Oxford, 1969).

R. Colls, *The Collier's Rant: Song and Culture in the Industrial Village* (1977).

The Pitmen of the Northern Coalfield: Work, Culture and Protest, 1790–1850 (Manchester, 1987).

R. J. Colyer, 'The gentry and the county in nineteenth-century Cardiganshire', *Welsh History Review*, 10 (1980–1).

J. H. Cooper, 'A religious census of Sussex in 1676', *Sussex Archaeological Collections*, 45 (1902).

S. Copley and P. Garside (eds.), *The Politics of the Picturesque: Literature, Landscape and Aesthetics since 1770* (Cambridge, 1994).

J. E. Coulson, *The Peasant Preacher: Memorials of Mr. Charles Richardson* (n.d., 2nd edn, 1866).

R. Cowherd, *The Politics of English Dissent, 1815–1848* (1956).

J. C. Cox, 'A religious census of Derbyshire, 1676', *Journal of the Derbyshire Archaeological and Natural History Society*, 7 (1885).

J. C. Cox and A. Harvey, *English Church Furniture* (1907).

A. C. Crockett, 'A secularising geography? Patterns and processes of religious change in England and Wales, 1676–1851' (unpublished Ph.D thesis, University of Leicester, 1998).

A. Crockett and K. D. M. Snell, 'From the 1676 Compton Census to the 1851 Census of Religious Worship: religious continuity or discontinuity?', *Rural History*, 8 (1997).

B. Crofts (ed.), *At Satan's Throne: the Story of Methodism in Bath over 250 Years* (Bristol, 1990).

F. L. Cross, *The Oxford Dictionary of the Christian Church* (1957).

H. Cunningham, 'The employment and unemployment of children in England, c. 1680–1851', *Past and Present*, 126 (1990).

R. Currie, 'A micro-theory of Methodist growth', *Proceedings of the Wesley Historical Society*, 36 (1967).

Methodism Divided: a Study in the Sociology of Ecumenicalism (1968).

R. Currie, A. D. Gilbert and L. Horsley, *Churches and Churchgoers: Patterns of Church Growth in the British Isles since 1700* (Oxford, 1977).

R. W. Dale, *History of English Congregationalism* (1907).

W. L. Dale, *The Law of the Parish Church* (1946).

G. Darley, *Villages of Vision* (1978).

E. T. Davies, *Religion in the Industrial Revolution in South Wales* (Cardiff, 1965).

H. Davies, *The English Free Churches* (1952, Oxford, 1963 edn).

J. Davies, *A History of Wales* (1990, Harmondsworth, 1993 edn).

S. Davies, *Quakerism in Lincolnshire: an Informal Study* (1989).

A. W. Davison, *Derby: its Rise and Progress* (Wakefield, 1970).

P. Deane and W. A. Cole, *British Economic Growth, 1688–1959* (Cambridge, 1962, 1969 edn).

P. Deffontaines, *Géographie et Religions* (Paris, 1948).

W. Densham and J. Ogle, *The Story of the Congregational Churches of Dorset, from their Foundation* (1899).

W. A. Devereux, *Adult Education in Inner London, 1870–1980* (1982).

M. Dick, 'The myth of the working-class Sunday school', *History of Education*, 9 (1980).

'Urban growth and the social role of the Stockport Sunday school, c. 1784–1833', in J. Ferguson (ed.), *Christianity, Society and Education: Robert Raikes, Past, Present and Future* (1981).

B. Disraeli, *Sybil* (1845, Harmondsworth, 1984 edn).

R. Dixon and S. Muthesius, *Victorian Architecture* (1978, 1995 edn).

A. H. Dodd, *A History of Caernarvonshire, 1284–1900* (1990).

A. P. Donajgrodzki, 'Twentieth-century rural England: a case for "peasant studies"?', *Journal of Peasant Studies*, 16 (1989).

F. Driver, *Power and Pauperism: the Workhouse System, 1834–1884* (Cambridge, 1993).

J. P. D. Dunbabin, *Rural Discontent in Nineteenth-century Britain* (1974).

'British elections in the nineteenth and twentieth centuries: a regional approach', *English Historical Review*, 95 (1980).

I. Dyck, *William Cobbett and Rural Popular Culture* (Cambridge, 1992).

D. Dymond, 'Sitting apart in church', in C. Rawcliffe, R. Virgoe and R. Wilson (eds.), *Counties and Communities: Essays on East Anglian History* (Norwich, 1996), pp. 213–24.

J. Eades, I. Duffy and B. Crofts, 'Methodism in the 19th century', in B. Crofts (ed.), *At Satan's Throne: the Story of Methodism in Bath over 250 Years* (Bristol, 1990).

J. Ede, N. Virgoe and T. Williamson, *Halls of Zion: Chapels and Meeting-Houses in Norfolk* (Norwich, 1994).

G. Edwards, *From Crow-scaring to Westminster* (1922).

George Eliot, *Silas Marner* (1861, Harmondsworth, 1969 edn).

T. S. Eliot, *Collected Poems, 1909–1962* (1936, 1963 edn).

P. S. Ell, 'An atlas of religious worship in England and Wales: an analysis of the 1851 Census of Religious Worship' (unpublished Ph.D thesis, University of Birmingham, 1992).

B. Elliott, 'Mount St Bernard's Reformatory, Leicestershire, 1856–81', *Recusant History*, 15 (1979).

'Mount St Bernard's Reformatory: a reply', *Recusant History*, 15 (1979–81).

'The return of the Cistercians to the Midlands', *Recusant History*, 16 (1982–3).

'A Leicestershire recusant family: the Nevills of Nevill Holt', *Recusant History*, 1st part, 17 (1984), pp. 173–80; 2nd part, *Recusant History*, 17 (1985), pp. 374–85; 3rd part, *Recusant History*, 18 (1986), pp. 220–24.

'The history of Catholicism in Market Harborough', *Harborough Historian*, 2 (1985).

'An eighteenth century Leicestershire business woman: the Countess Mary Migliorucci of Nevill Holt', *Leicestershire Archaeological and Historical Society*, 61 (1987).

S. Ellis, *Down a Cobbled Street: the Story of Clovelly* (Bideford, 1987).

T. M. Endelman, *The Jews of Georgian England, 1714–1830* (Philadelphia, 1979).

F. Engels, *The Condition of the Working Class in England* (1st German edn, 1845; Glasgow, 1984 edn).

'Eusebius', 'A little learning is a dangerous thing', *Gentleman's Magazine* (Oct., 1797), 819–20. (Reprinted in J. M. Goldstrom (ed.), *Education: Elementary Education, 1780–1900* (Newton Abbot, 1972), pp. 19–23.)

E. J. Evans, '"Our faithful testimony": the Society of Friends and tithe payments, 1690–1730', *Journal of the Friends' Historical Society*, 52 (1969).

'Some reasons for the growth of English rural anti-clericalism, c.1750–c.1830', *Past and Present*, 66 (1975).

The Contentious Tithe: the Tithe Problem and English Agriculture, 1750–1850 (1976).

H. A. Evans, *Monmouthshire* (1911).

A. Everitt, 'Nonconformity in country parishes', in J. Thirsk (ed.), *Land, Church and People: Essays Presented to Professor H. P. R. Finberg* (Reading, 1970), supplement to *Agricultural History Review*, 18 (1970).

The Pattern of Rural Dissent: the Nineteenth Century (Leicester, 1972).

R. J. Eyre, 'The nineteenth century restorations at St Michael and All Angels, Appleby Magna', *Leicestershire Archaeological and Historical Society Transactions*, 61 (1987).

M. Farningham, *A Working Woman's Life* (1907).

H. Faulkner, *Chartism and the Churches: a Study in Democracy* (1916, 1970 edn).

C. D. Field, 'The 1851 Religious Census: a select bibliography', *Proceedings of the Wesley Historical Society*, 41 (1978).

'The 1851 Religious Census of Great Britain: a bibliographical guide for local and regional historians', *The Local Historian*, 27 (1997).

M. J. Flame, '"All the common rules of social life": the reconstruction of social and political identities by the Dorset gentry, c.1790–c.1834' (unpublished Ph.D thesis, University of Warwick, 1998).

W. G. D. Fletcher, 'Religious census in Leicestershire in 1676', *Transactions of the Leicestershire Architectural and Archaeological Society*, 6 (1887).

'Religious census of Shropshire in 1676', *Transactions of the Shropshire Archaeological and Natural History Society*, 1 (1889).

M. W. Flinn, *The Origins of the Industrial Revolution* (1966, 1976 edn).

M. W. Flinn and T. C. Smout (eds.), *Essays in Social History* (Oxford, 1974).

J. Foster, *Class Struggle and the Industrial Revolution: Early Industrial Capitalism in Three English Towns* (1974, 1979 edn).

D. E. Fox, 'Families, farming and faith' (unpublished M.Phil thesis, University of Leicester, 1998).

C. Garbett, *The Claims of the Church of England* (1947, 1948 edn).

E. Gaskell, *The Life of Charlotte Brontë* (1857, Harmondsworth, 1983 edn).

R. D. Gastil, *Cultural Regions of the United States* (Washington, 1975).

E. S. Gaustad, *Historical Atlas of Religion in America* (New York, 1976).

J. D. Gay, *The Geography of Religion in England* (1971).

W. Gibson, 'The Tories and church patronage, 1812–30', *Journal of Ecclesiastical History*, 41 (1990).

A. Gilam, *The Emancipation of the Jews in England, 1830–1860* (New York, 1982).

A. D. Gilbert, *Religion and Society in Industrial England: Church, Chapel and Social Change, 1740–1914* (1976, Harlow, 1984 edn).

'Religion and political stability in early industrial England', in P. K. O'Brien and R. Quinault (eds.), *The Industrial Revolution and British Society* (Cambridge, 1993).

R. Gill, *Competing Convictions* (1989).

The Myth of the Empty Church (1993).

S. Gilley, 'The Roman Catholic mission to the Irish in London, 1840–1860', *Recusant History*, 10 (1969).

'Protestant London, No-Popery and the Irish poor, 1830–60', *Recusant History*, 10 (1970).

'Papists, Protestants and the Irish in London', in G. J. Cuming and D. Baker (eds.), *Studies in Church History: Popular Belief and Practice* (Cambridge, 1972).

J. Ginswick (ed.), *Labour and the Poor in England and Wales, 1849–1851* (1983), 4 volumes.

D. E. Ginter, *A Measure of Wealth: the English Land Tax in Historical Analysis* (1992).

J. M. Goldstrom, *Education: Elementary Education, 1780–1900* (Newton Abbot, 1972).

'Education in England and Wales in 1851: the Education Census of Great Britain, 1851', in R. Lawton (ed.), *The Census and Social Structure: an Interpretative Guide to Nineteenth Century Censuses for England and Wales* (1978).

R. M. Goodridge, 'The religious condition of the West Country in 1851', *Social Compass*, 14 (1967).

R. Gough, *History of Myddle* (written in 1701, Harmondsworth, 1981 edn).

F. E. Green, *The Tyranny of the Countryside* (1913).

I. Green, 'The first five years of Queen Anne's Bounty', in R. O'Day and F. Heal (eds.), *Princes and Paupers in the English Church, 1500–1800* (Leicester, 1981).

S. J. D. Green, 'The death of pew-rents, the rise of bazaars, and the end of the traditional political economy of voluntary organizations: the case of the West Riding of Yorkshire, c. 1870–1914', *Northern History*, 27 (1991).

Religion in the Age of Decline: Organisation and Experience in Industrial Yorkshire, 1870–1920 (Cambridge, 1996).

A. Gregory, *Robert Raikes: Journalist and Philanthropist: a History of the Origin of Sunday Schools* (1877).

C. Griffin, *The Leicestershire and South Derbyshire Miners, vol. 1, 1840–1914* (Coalville, 1981).

D. M. Griffith, *Nationality in the Sunday School Movement: a Comparative Study of the Sunday School Movement in England and in Wales* (Bangor, 1925).

G. Grigson, *Wessex* (1951).

E. L. Guilford, 'Nottinghamshire in 1676', *Transactions of the Thoroton Society*, 28 (1924).

H. Gurden, 'Primitive Methodism and agricultural trade unionism in Warwickshire, 1872–5', *Bulletin of the Society for the Study of Labour History*, 33 (1976).

J. R. Guy, 'The Anglican patronage of Monmouthshire recusants in the seventeenth and eighteenth centuries', *Recusant History*, 15 (1979–81).

'Eighteenth-century Gwent Catholics', *Recusant History*, 16 (1982–3).

E. E. Hagen, *On the Theory of Social Change: How Economic Growth Begins* (Cambridge, Mass., 1962).

E. Halévy, *A History of the English People in the Nineteenth Century: vol. 1: England in 1815* (1913, 1970 edn).

R. Halley, *Lancashire: its Puritanism and Nonconformity* (Manchester, 1869).

T. Hardy, *The Return of the Native* (1878, 1971 edn).

W. J. Hardy, 'Remarks on the history of seat-reservation in churches', *Archaeologia*, 53 (1892).

J. B. Harley, 'Place-names on the early Ordnance Survey maps of England and Wales', *Journal of the British Cartographic Society* (1971).

S. Harratt, 'Queen Anne's Bounty and the augmentation of Leicestershire livings in the age of reform', *Leicestershire Archaeological and Historical Society*, 61 (1987).

A. Harris, *The Rural Landscape of the East Riding of Yorkshire, 1700–1850* (Oxford, 1961).

J. F. C. Harrison, *Learning and Living, 1790–1860: a Study in the History of the English Adult Education Movement* (1961).

The Early Victorians, 1832–51 (1971).

The Second Coming: Popular Millenarianism, 1780–1850 (1979).

M. A. Havinden, *Estate Villages* (1966).

F. Heal and R. O'Day (eds.), *Princes and Paupers in the English Church, 1500–1800* (Leicester, 1981).

A. Heales, *The History and Law of Church Seats, or Pews*, 2 vols. (1872).

R. Heath, *The English Peasant* (1893, Wakefield, 1978 edn).

M. Hechter, *Internal Colonialism: the Celtic Fringe in British National Development, 1536–1966* (1975).

Dom B. Hemphill, *The Early Vicars Apostolic of England, 1685–1750* (1954).

D. Hempton, *Methodism and Politics in British Society, 1750–1850* (1984, 1987 edn).

D. Hey, 'The pattern of Nonconformity in south Yorkshire', *Northern History*, 8 (1973).

An English Rural Community: Myddle under the Tudors and Stuarts (Leicester, 1974).

Yorkshire from AD 1000 (1986).

J. Hickey, *Urban Catholics: Urban Catholicism in England and Wales from 1829 to the Present Day* (1967).

C. Hill, *Economic Problems of the Church* (Oxford, 1956).

G. Hill, *English Dioceses: a History of their Limits from the Earliest Times to the Present Day* (1900).

J. A. Hilton, *Catholic Lancashire* (1981).

The Lancastrian Catholic Heritage: a Historical Guide (Wigan, 1984).

M. Hirst, 'The electoral system', in J. Langton and R. J. Morris (eds.), *Atlas of Industrializing Britain, 1780–1914* (1986).

History, Gazetteer, and Directory of Cambridgeshire (no author, Peterborough, 1851).

E. J. Hobsbawm, 'Methodism and the threat of revolution', *History Today*, 7 (1957).

Primitive Rebels: Studies in Archaic Forms of Social Movement in the Nineteenth and Twentieth Centuries (Manchester, 1959, 1963 edn).

Labouring Men (1964).

Worlds of Labour (1984).

E. J. Hobsbawm and G. Rudé, *Captain Swing* (1969, Harmondsworth, 1973 edn).

E. J. Hobsbawm and J. W. Scott, 'Political shoemakers', *Past and Present*, 89 (1980).

C. H. Hodgson, *An Account of the Augmentation of Small Livings by the Governors of the Bounty of Queen Anne* (1826, 2nd edn, 1845).

H. J. Hodgson, *Steer's Parish Law* (1857 edn).

B. A. Holderness, '"Open" and "close" parishes in England in the eighteenth and nineteenth centuries', *Agricultural History Review*, 20 (1972).

W. A. Holdsworth, *The Handy Book of Parish Law* (1859, 1872 edn).

G. Holt, *The English Jesuits, 1650–1829* (1984).

R. V. Holt, *The Unitarian Contribution to Social Progress in England* (1938, 1952 edn).

T. G. Holt, 'A note on some eighteenth century statistics', *Recusant History*, 10 (1969).

'An eighteenth century chaplain: John Champion at Sawston Hall', *Recusant History*, 17 (1984).

K. T. Hoppen, 'Tories, Catholics and the General Election of 1859', *Historical Journal*, 13 (1970).

P. Horn, 'Methodism and agricultural trade unionism in Oxfordshire: the 1870s', *Proceedings of the Wesley Historical Society*, 37 (1969).

Joseph Arch (1971).

'Child workers in the pillow lace and straw plait trades of Victorian Buckinghamshire and Bedfordshire', *Historical Journal*, 17 (1974).

The Victorian Country Child (1974, 1985 edn).

P. Horn (ed.), *Village Education in Nineteenth-century Oxfordshire: the Whitchurch School Log Book (1868–93) and Other Documents* (Oxfordshire Record Society, vol. 51, 1979).

M. P. Hornsby-Smith, 'An unsecular America', in S. Bruce (ed.), *Religion and Modernization: Sociologists and Historians Debate the Secularization Thesis* (Oxford, 1992).

W. G. Hoskins, *Rutland* (Leicester, 1949).

'Landscapes of England: Marsh and Sea' (BBC programme, 1975).

R. Houston and K. D. M. Snell, 'Proto-industrialisation? Cottage industry, social change and the Industrial Revolution', *Historical Journal*, 27 (1984).

C. Howard, *A General View of the Agriculture of the East Riding of Yorkshire* (1835).

D. W. Howell, *Land and People in Nineteenth-century Wales* (1977).

D. W. Howell and C. Baber, 'Wales', in F. M. L. Thompson (ed.), *The Cambridge Social History of Britain, 1750–1950, vol. 1, Regions and Communities* (Cambridge, 1990).

P. Howell, 'Church and chapel in Wales', in C. Brooks and A. Saint (eds.), *The Victorian Church: Architecture and Society* (Manchester, 1995).

R. Howell, *A History of Gwent* (1988, Llandysul, Dyfed, 1989 edn).

A. Howkins, *Poor Labouring Men: Rural Radicalism in Norfolk, 1870–1923* (1985).

Reshaping Rural England: a Social History, 1850–1925 (1991).

'Peasants, servants and labourers: the marginal workforce in British agriculture, c. 1870–1914', *Agricultural History Review*, 42 (1994).

P. Hudson, *The Industrial Revolution* (1992, 1996 edn).

P. Hudson (ed.), *Regions and Industries: a Perspective on the Industrial Revolution in Britain* (Cambridge, 1989).

P. Hughes, 'The English Catholics in 1850', in G. A. Beck (ed.), *The English Catholics, 1850–1950* (1950).

A. Hume, *Remarks on the Census of Religious Worship for England and Wales, with Suggestions for an Improved Census in 1861, and a Map, Illustrating the Religious Condition of the Country* (1860).

C. R. Humphrey-Smith (ed.), *The Phillimore Atlas and Index of Parish Registers* (Canterbury, 1984).

M. Humphreys, *The Crisis of Community: Montgomeryshire, 1680–1815* (Cardiff, 1996).

E. H. Hunt, *Regional Wage Variations in Britain, 1850–1914* (Oxford, 1973).

C. Hussey, *The Picturesque: Studies in a Point of View* (1927).

R. Hutton, *The Rise and Fall of Merry England: the Ritual Year, 1400–1700* (1994, Oxford, 1996 edn).

B. Inglis, *Poverty and the Industrial Revolution* (1971, 1972 edn).

K. S. Inglis, 'Patterns of religious worship in 1851', *Journal of Ecclesiastical History*, 11 (1960).

I. Inkster (ed.), *The Steam Intellect Societies: Essays on Culture, Education and Industry, c. 1820–1914* (1985).

F. P. Isherwood, *Banished by the Revolution* (Jersey, 1972).

E. Isichei, 'From sect to denomination in English Quakerism', *British Journal of Sociology*, 15 (1964).

Victorian Quakers (Oxford, 1970).

J. A. Jackson, *The Irish in Britain* (1963).

P. Jackson, 'Nonconformity and the Compton census in late seventeenth-century Devon', in K. Schurer and T. Arkell (eds.), *Surveying the People* (Oxford, 1992).

R. H. Jackson, 'The Mormon experience: the plains as Sinai, the Great Salt Lake as the Dead Sea, and the Great Basin as desert-cum-promised land', *Journal of Historical Geography*, 18 (1992).

G. Jackson-Stops and R. Fedden, *Staunton Harold Church* (1975).

W. M. Jacob, 'Evidence for dissent in Norfolk, 1711–1800, from the records of the diocese of Norwich', in N. Virgoe and T. Williamson (eds.), *Religious Dissent in East Anglia: Historical Perspectives* (Norwich, 1993).

Lay People and Religion in the Early Eighteenth Century (Cambridge, 1996).

F. G. James, 'The population of the diocese of Carlisle in 1676', *Transactions of the Cumberland and Westmorland Antiquarian and Archaeological Society*, 51 (1952).

L. James, *Fiction for the Working Man, 1830–1850* (1963, Harmondsworth, 1974 edn).

P. Jenkins, '"A Welsh Lancashire"? Monmouthshire Catholics in the eighteenth century', *Recusant History*, 15 (1979–81).

A History of Modern Wales, 1536–1990 (1992).

L. Jewitt, *Guide to the Abbey of Mount St Bernard* (4th edn, 1897).

C. E. M. Joad, *The Untutored Townsman's Invasion of the Country* (1946).

J. H. Johnson, 'Harvest migration from nineteenth-century Ireland', *Transactions of the Institute of British Geographers*, 41 (1967).

A. M. Jones, *The Rural Industries of England and Wales, vol. 4: Wales* (1978).

D. J. V. Jones, *Before Rebecca: Popular Protests in Wales, 1793–1835* (1973).

The Last Rising: the Newport Insurrection of 1839 (1985).

Rebecca's Children: a Study of Rural Society, Crime, and Protest (Oxford, 1989).

I. G. Jones, 'Ecclesiastical economy: aspects of church building in Victorian Wales', in R. R. Davies *et al.* (eds.), *Welsh Society and Nationhood: Historical Essays Presented to Glanmor Williams* (Cardiff, 1984).

Communities: Essays in the Social History of Victorian Wales (Llandysul, 1987).

M. Jones, 'Y chwarelwyr: the slate quarrymen of North Wales', in R. Samuel (ed.), *Miners, Quarrymen and Saltworkers* (1977).

P. N. Jones, 'Baptist chapels as an index of cultural transition in the South Wales coalfield before 1914', *Journal of Historical Geography*, 2 (1976).

R. M. Jones, *The North Wales Quarrymen, 1874–1922* (Cardiff, 1981).

W. H. Jones, *History of the Wesleyan Reform Union* (1952).

P. Joyce, *Work, Society and Politics: the Culture of the Factory in Later Victorian England* (1980).

Visions of the People: Industrial England and the Question of Class, 1848–1914 (Cambridge, 1991).

R. J. P. Kain, *An Atlas and Index of the Tithe Files of Mid-nineteenth-century England and Wales* (Cambridge, 1986).

R. J. P. Kain and H. C. Prince, *The Tithe Surveys of England and Wales* (Cambridge, 1985).

S. Kaye-Smith, *The Tramping Methodist* (1908, 1924 edn).

Kelly's Directory of Leicester and Rutland (1922 edn).

T. Kelly, *George Birkbeck: Pioneer of Adult Education* (Liverpool, 1957).

Revd H. B. Kendall, *The Origin and History of the Primitive Methodist Church*, 2 vols. (London, n.d., c. 1905).

Handbook of Primitive Methodist Church Principles and Polity (1913).

J. Kennedy, 'On the Census returns respecting Congregational worship', *The Congregational Yearbook* (1855).

D. H. Kennett, 'Lacemaking by Bedfordshire paupers in the late eighteenth century', *Textile History*, 5 (1974).

B. M. Kerr, 'Irish seasonal migration to Great Britain, 1800–1838', *Irish Historical Studies*, 3 (1942–3).

Revd A. Kilham, *The Life of the Rev. Alexander Kilham . . . One of the Founders of the Methodist New Connexion in the Year 1797. Including a Full Account of the Disputes which Occasioned the Separation* (1838).

Charles Kingsley, *Alton Locke* (1850).

Yeast (1851, 1902 edn).

M. Kinnear, *The British Voter: an Atlas and Survey since 1885* (1968, 1981 edn).

P. Kriedte, H. Medick and J. Schlumbohm, *Industrialisation Before Industrialisation: Rural Industry in the Genesis of Capitalism* (Cambridge, 1981).

B. Kümin, *The Shaping of a Community: the Rise and Reformation of the English Parish, c. 1400–1560* (Aldershot, 1996).

A. Kussmaul, *Servants in Husbandry in Early Modern England* (Cambridge, 1981).

A. C. Lacey, *The Second Spring in Charnwood Forest* (Loughborough, 1985).

A. S. Langley, 'A religious census of 1676, A.D.', *Lincolnshire Notes and Queries*, 16 (April, 1920).

J. Langton, 'The Industrial Revolution and the regional geography of England', *Transactions of the Institute of British Geographers*, 9 (1984).

T. W. Laqueur, *Religion and Respectability: Sunday Schools and Working Class Culture, 1780–1850* (1976).

P. Laslett, *The World We Have Lost* (1968, 1971 edn).

'Clayworth and Cogenhoe', in his *Family Life and Illicit Love in Earlier Generations* (Cambridge, 1977).

Family Life and Illicit Love in Earlier Generations (Cambridge, 1977).

R. Lawton, 'Irish immigration to England and Wales in the mid-nineteenth century', *Irish Geography*, 4 (1959).

R. Lawton (ed.), *The Census and Social Structure: an Interpretative Guide to Nineteenth Century Censuses for England and Wales* (1978).

L. Lee, *Cider with Rosie* (1959, Harmondsworth, 1962 edn).

L. H. Lees, 'Patterns of lower-class life: Irish slum communities in nineteenth-century London', in S. Thernstrom and R. Sennett (eds.), *Nineteenth-century Cities* (New Haven, 1969).

Exiles of Erin: Irish Migrants in Victorian London (Manchester, 1979).

G. Legard, 'Farming of the East Riding of Yorkshire', *Journal of the Royal Agricultural Society*, 9 (1848).

E. Legg (ed.), *Buckinghamshire Returns of the Census of Religious Worship, 1851* (1991).

Leicestershire and Rutland Federation of Women's Institutes (comp.), *Leicestershire and Rutland: Within Living Memory* (Newbury, Berkshire, 1994).

G. J. Levine, 'On the geography of religion', *Transactions of the Institute of British Geographers*, 11 (1986).

G. J. Lewis, 'The geography of religion in the middle borderlands of Wales in 1851', *Transactions of the Honourable Society of Cymmrodorion* (1980).

J. G. Lewis, 'The middle borderland', in E. G. Bowen (ed.), *Wales: a Physical, Historical and Regional Geography* (1957).

J. O. Lindsay, *A History of the North Wales Slate Industry* (Newton Abbot, 1974).

R. W. Linker, 'English Catholics in the eighteenth century', *Church History*, 35 (1966).

V. D. Lipman, 'A survey of Anglo-Jewry in 1851', *Transactions of the Jewish Historical Society of England*, 17 (1951–2).

Social History of the Jews in England, 1850–1950 (1954).

K. M. Longley, *Heir of Two Traditions: the Catholic Church of St John the Baptist, Holme-on-Spalding-Moor, 1766–1966* (1966).

E. Lord, 'Communities of common interest: the social landscape of south-east Surrey, 1750–1850', in C. Phythian-Adams (ed.), *Societies, Cultures and Kinship, 1580–1850: Cultural Provinces and English Local History* (Leicester, 1993).

D. W. Lovegrove, *Established Church, Sectarian People: Itinerancy and the Transformation of Dissent, 1780–1830* (Cambridge, 1988).

D. Lowenthal, 'British national identity and the English landscape', *Rural History*, 2 (1991).

W. G. Lumley, 'The statistics of the Roman Catholic Church in England and Wales', *Journal of the Statistical Society of London*, 27 (1964).

G. I. T. Machin, *Politics and the Churches in Great Britain, 1832–1868* (Oxford, 1977).

Politics and the Churches in Great Britain, 1869–1921 (Oxford, 1987).

A. A. MacLaren, *Religion and Social Class: the Disruption Years in Aberdeen* (1974).

K. M. Macmorran, *A Handbook for Churchwardens and Church Councillors* (1921, 1945 edn).

H. Mann, *Sketches of the Religious Denominations of the Present Day* (1854).

'On the statistical position of religious bodies in England and Wales', *Journal of the Statistical Society*, 18 (1855).

H. C. G. Matthew (ed.), *The Gladstone Diaries, vol. V: 1855–1860* (Oxford, 1978).

J. H. Matthews, *The Vaughans of Courtfield* (1912).

H. McLeod, *Class and Religion in the Late Victorian City* (1974).

'Recent studies in Victorian religious history', *Victorian Studies*, 21 (1978).

Religion and the Working Class in Nineteenth-century Britain (1984).

'Religion', in J. Langton and R. J. Morris (eds.), *Atlas of Industrializing Britain, 1780–1914* (1986).

Religion and Society in England, 1850–1914 (1996).

G. E. Milburn, 'The Census of Worship of 1851', *Durham County Local History Society*, 17 (1974).

H. Miller, *A Guide to Ecclesiastical Law for Churchwardens and Parishioners* (1899).

W. Miller and G. Raab, 'The religious alignment at English elections between 1918 and 1970', *Political Studies*, 25 (1977).

D. R. Mills, 'Landownership and rural population, with special reference to Leicestershire in the mid nineteenth century' (unpublished Ph.D thesis, University of Leicester, 1963).

'English villages in the eighteenth and nineteenth centuries: a sociological approach', *Amateur Historian*, 6 (1963–5).

'The peasant tradition', *The Local Historian*, 11 (1974).

'The geographical effects of the laws of settlement in Nottinghamshire: an analysis of Francis Howell's report, 1848', in his (ed.), *English Rural Communities* (1978).

Lord and Peasant in Nineteenth-century Britain (1980).

D. R. Mills and B. M. Short, 'Social change and social conflict in nineteenth-century England: the use of the open-closed village model', *Journal of Peasant Studies*, 10 (1983). Reprinted in M. Reed and R. Wells (eds.), *Class, Conflict and Protest in the English Countryside, 1700–1880* (1990).

D. R. Mills and M. E. Turner (eds.), *Land and Property: the English Land Tax, 1692–1832* (Gloucester, 1986).

R. Millward and A. Robinson, *Landscapes of North Wales* (Newton Abbot, 1978).

W. E. Minchinton, 'Agricultural returns and the government during the Napoleonic Wars', *Agricultural History Review*, 1 (1953).

G. E. Mingay, 'The Land Tax Assessments and the small landowner', *Economic History Review*, 17 (1964).

W. Mooney, 'A religious census of Berkshire in 1676', *Berkshire, Buckinghamshire and Oxfordshire Archaeological Journal*, 4 (1889), pp. 112–15, and 5 (1900), pp. 55–9.

M. Moore, 'Stone quarrying in the Isle of Purbeck: an oral history' (unpub. MA dissertation, Dept. of English Local History, University of Leicester, 1992).

J. R. H. Moorman, *A History of the Church of England* (1973).

K. O. Morgan, *Rebirth of a Nation: Wales, 1880–1980* (Oxford, 1981, 1988 edn).

J. M. Neale, *The History of Pews* (Cambridge, 1841).

J. M. Neeson, *Commoners: Common Right, Enclosure and Social Change in England, 1700–1820* (Cambridge, 1993).

W. Nelson, *The Office and Authority of a Justice of Peace* (1729).

H. Newby, *The Deferential Worker* (1977, Harmondsworth, 1979 edn).

A. N. Newman, *The Board of Deputies of British Jews, 1760–1985: a Brief Survey* (1987).

A. N. Newman (ed.), *Provincial Jewry in Victorian Britain* (Jewish Historical Society of England, 1975).

J. Noake, *The Rambler in Worcestershire* (1851).

E. R. Norman, *Church and Society in England, 1770–1970: a Historical Study* (Oxford, 1976).

The English Catholic Church in the Nineteenth Century (Oxford, 1984).

E. R. Norman (ed.), *Anti-Catholicism in Victorian England* (1968).

T. J. Nossiter, 'Aspects of electoral behaviour in English constituencies, 1832–1868', in E. Allardt and S. Rokkan (eds.), *Mass Politics: Studies in Political Sociology* (New York, 1970).

'Voting behaviour, 1832–1872', *Political Studies*, 18 (1970).

Influence, Opinion and Political Idioms in Reformed England: Case Studies from the North-east, 1832–74 (Brighton, 1975).

J. Obelkevich, *Religion and Rural Society: South Lindsey, 1825–1875* (Oxford, 1976).

P. K. O'Brien and R. Quinault (eds.), *The Industrial Revolution and British Society* (Cambridge, 1993).

A. O'Dowd, *Spalpeens and Tattie Hokers: History and Folklore of the Irish Migratory Agricultural Worker in Ireland and Britain* (Dublin, 1991).

C. O'Grada, *The Great Irish Famine* (1989).

G. H. H. Oliphant, *The Law of Pews in Churches and Chapels* (1853).

R. J. Olney, *Lincolnshire Politics, 1832–1885* (Oxford, 1973).

M. A. G. Ò Tuathaigh, 'The Irish in nineteenth-century Britain: problems of integration', *Transactions of the Royal Historical Society*, 5th series, 3 (1981).

M. Overton, 'Agriculture', in J. Langton and R. J. Morris (eds.), *Atlas of Industrializing Britain, 1780–1914* (1986).

M. Palmer, *Framework Knitting* (1984, 1990 edn).

C. R. Park, *Sacred Worlds: an Introduction to Geography and Religion* (1994).

S. C. Parker, *The History of Modern Elementary Education* (1912).

D. Parry-Jones, *My Own Folk* (Llandysul, 1972).

D. Parsons, *Churches and Chapels: Investigating Places of Worship* (1989).

J. Patten, 'The Hearth Taxes, 1662–89', *Local Population Studies*, 7 (1971).

A. H. Patterson, *From Hayloft to Temple: Primitive Methodism in Yarmouth* (Norwich, 1903).

W. M. Patterson, *Northern Primitive Methodism* (1909).

I. C. Peate, *Tradition and Folk Life: a Welsh View* (1972).

H. Pelling, *Social Geography of British Elections, 1885–1910* (1967).

H. Perkin, *The Origins of Modern English Society, 1780–1880* (1969, 1976 edn).

P. J. Perry,'Working-class isolation and mobility in rural Dorset, 1837–1936', *Transactions of the Institute of British Geographers*, 46 (1969).

British Farming in the Great Depression, 1870–1914: an Historical Geography (Newton Abbot, 1974).

L. Petty, *The History of the Primitive Methodist Connexion* (1864, 1880 edn).

N. Pevsner, *The Buildings of England: Cambridgeshire* (Harmondsworth, 1954).

The Buildings of England: Yorkshire: York and the East Riding (Harmondsworth, 1972).

The Buildings of England: North-West and South Norfolk (1962, Harmondsworth, 1990 edn).

N. Pevsner, J. Harris and N. Antram, *The Buildings of England: Lincolnshire* (1964, Harmondsworth, 1990 edn).

N. Pevsner and J. Newman, *The Buildings of England: Dorset* (1972, Harmondsworth, 1985 edn).

N. Pevsner, E. Williamson and G. K. Brandwood, *The Buildings of England: Leicestershire and Rutland* (1960, Harmondsworth, 1989 edn).

S. A. Peyton, 'The religious census of 1676', *English Historical Review*, 48 (1933).

J. A. Phillips, *The Great Reform Bill in the Boroughs: English Electoral Behaviour, 1818–1841* (Oxford, 1992).

C. Phythian-Adams (ed.), *Societies, Cultures and Kinship, 1580–1850: Cultural Provinces and English Local History* (Leicester, 1993).

W. S. F. Pickering, 'The 1851 Religious Census – a useless experiment?', *British Journal of Sociology*, 18 (1967).

C. A. Piggott, 'A geography of religion in Scotland', *Scottish Geographical Magazine*, 96 (1980).

X. de Planhol and P. Claval, *An Historical Geography of France* (Cambridge, 1994).

S. Pollard, *The Genesis of Modern Management* (1965, Harmondsworth, 1968 edn).

W. H. Pool, *A Brief History of the Congregational Sunday School, Market Harborough* (Market Harborough, 1886).

J. Popplewell, 'A seating plan for North Nibley Church in 1629', *Transactions of the Bristol and Gloucestershire Archaeological Society*, 103 (1985).

M. H. Port, *Six Hundred New Churches: a Study of the Church Building Commission, 1818–1856, and its Church Building Activities* (1961).

G. R. Porter, *The Progress of the Nation* (1836, 1851 edn).

D. H. Pratt, *English Quakers and the First Industrial Revolution: a Study of the Quaker Community in Four Industrial Counties, Lancashire, York, Warwick and Gloucester, 1750–1830* (New York, 1985).

J. C. C. Probert, *The Sociology of Cornish Methodism to the Present Day* (Redruth, 1971).

F. K. Prochaska, *Women and Philanthropy in Nineteenth-century England* (Oxford, 1980).

L. J. Proudfoot, 'The extension of parish churches in medieval Warwickshire', *Journal of Historical Geography*, 9 (1983).

W. T. R. Pryce, 'Approaches to the linguistic geography of northeast Wales, 1750–1846', *National Library of Wales Journal*, 17 (1972).

'The 1851 Census of Religious Worship: Denbighshire', *Transactions of the Denbighshire Historical Society*, 23 (1974).

'Industrialism, urbanization and the maintenance of culture areas: northeast Wales in the mid-nineteenth century', *Welsh History Review*, 7 (1974–5).

'Migration and the evolution of culture areas: cultural and linguistic frontiers in north-east Wales, 1750 and 1851', *Transactions of the Institute of British Geographers*, 65 (1975).

'Wales as a culture region: patterns of change, 1750–1971', *Transactions of the Honourable Society of Cymmrodorion* (1978).

'Welsh and English in Wales, 1750–1971: a spatial analysis based on the linguistic affiliation of parochial communities', *Bulletin of the Board of Celtic Studies*, 28 (1978).

'The Welsh language, 1751–1961', in H. Carter and H. Griffiths (eds.), *The National Atlas of Wales* (Cardiff, 1981).

R. B. Pugh (ed.), *The Victoria County History of the Counties of England* (1964), vol. 5.

A. W. N. Pugin, *Contrasts* (1836, Leicester, 1969 edn).

H. D. Rack, *Reasonable Enthusiast: John Wesley and the Rise of Methodism* (1989, 1992 edn).

R. Raikes 'On Sunday schools', *Gentleman's Magazine* (June, 1784), 410–12.

(Reprinted in J. M. Goldstrom (ed.), *Education: Elementary Education, 1780–1900* (Newton Abbot, 1972), pp. 15–19.)

G. Randall, *Church Furnishing and Decoration in England and Wales* (1980).

N. Ratcliff (ed.), *The Journal of John Wesley, 1735–1790* (1940).

A. Rattenbury, 'Methodism and the Tatterdemalions', in E. Yeo and S. Yeo (eds.), *Popular Culture and Class Conflict, 1590–1914* (Brighton, 1981).

C. Rawding, 'The iconography of churches: a case study of landownership and power in nineteenth-century Lincolnshire', *Journal of Historical Geography*, 16 (1990).

A. B. Reach, *Manchester and the Textile Districts in 1849* (Helmshore, 1972, ed. C. Aspin).

B. Reay, 'Quaker opposition to tithes, 1652–1660', *Past and Present*, 86 (1980).

'The social origins of early Quakerism', *Journal of Interdisciplinary History*, 11 (1980).

The Quakers and the English Revolution (1985).

A. Redford, *Labour Migration in England, 1800–1850* (1926, Manchester, 1976 edn).

Redundant Churches Fund, *Churches in Retirement: a Gazetteer* (HMSO, 1990).

M. Reed, 'The peasantry of nineteenth-century England: a neglected class?', *History Workshop*, 18 (1984).

'Nineteenth-century rural England: a case for "peasant studies"', *Journal of Peasant Studies*, 14 (1986).

'"Gnawing it out": a new look at economic relations in nineteenth-century rural England', *Rural History*, 1 (1990).

M. Reed and R. Wells (eds.), *Class, Conflict and Protest in the English Countryside, 1700–1880* (1990).

D. Reeder, *Landowners and Landholding in Leicestershire and Rutland, 1873–1941* (Centre for Urban History, Leicester, 1994).

A. D. Rees, *Life in a Welsh Countryside: a Social Study of Llanfihangel yng Ngwynfa* (1950, Cardiff, 1996 edn).

J. Rhys and D. Brynmor-Jones, *The Welsh People* (1923, New York, 1969 edn).

T. Richards, 'The religious census of 1676: an inquiry into its historical value, mainly in reference to Wales', Supplement to the *Transactions of the Hon. Society of Cymmrodorion* (1925–7).

J. Ridley, *Lord Palmerston* (1970, 1972 edn).

J. Ritson, *The Romance of Primitive Methodism* (1909).

M. J. D. Roberts, 'Private patronage and the Church of England, 1800–1900', *Journal of Ecclesiastical History*, 32 (1981).

R. E. Rodes, *Law and Modernization in the Church of England: Charles II to the Welfare State* (Notre Dame, Indiana, 1991).

W. Rodwell, 'Archaeology and the Church', *Antiquity*, 49, no. 193 (1975).

J. Rogan, 'The Religious Census of 1851', *Theology* (1963).

A. Rogers, 'The 1851 Religious Census returns for the City of Nottingham', *Transactions of the Thoroton Society of Nottingham*, 76 (1972).

M. E. Rose, 'Settlement, removal and the New Poor Law', in D. Fraser (ed.), *The New Poor Law in the Nineteenth Century* (1976).

E. Routley, *English Religious Dissent* (Cambridge, 1960).

J. Rowlands, *Copper Mountain* (1966, Llangefni, 1981 edn).

M. Rowlands, 'The iron age of double taxes', *Staffordshire Catholic History*, 3 (1963).

Catholics of Parish and Town, 1558–1778 (Catholic Record Society, 1999).

J. G. Rule, 'The labouring miner in Cornwall, c.1740–1870' (unpublished Ph.D thesis, University of Warwick, 1971).

J. L. Sanford and M. Townsend, *The Great Governing Families of England* (1865).

N. Scotland, *Methodism and the Revolt of the Field* (Gloucester, 1981).

M. Seaborne, 'The Religious Census of 1851 and early chapel building in North Wales', *National Library of Wales Journal*, 26 (1990).

I. Sellers, *Nineteenth-Century Nonconformity* (1977).

P. Sharpe, 'The women's harvest: straw-plaiting and the representation of labouring women's employment, c. 1793–1885', *Rural History*, 5 (1994).

B. E. Shaw (compiler), *Frank Meadow Sutcliffe: a Second Edition* (Whitby, 1979, 1982 edn).

J. Shaw, *Parish Law* (1753).

The Parochial Lawyer; or, Churchwarden and Overseer's Guide and Assistant (1833).

T. Shaw, *The Bible Christians, 1815–1907* (1965).

W. J. Sheils, 'Catholics and their neighbours in a rural community: Egton Chapelry, 1590–1780', *Northern History*, 34 (1998).

B. Short, 'The changing rural society and economy of Sussex, 1750–1945', in The Geography Editorial Committee (University of Sussex) (ed.), *Sussex: Environment, Landscape and Society* (Gloucester, 1983).

The Geography of England and Wales in 1910: an Evaluation of Lloyd George's 'Domesday' of Landownership (Historical Geography Research Series, no. 22, 1989).

Land and Society in Edwardian Britain (Cambridge, 1997).

J. R. Shortridge, 'Religion', in J. F. Rooney, W. Zelinsky and D. R. Louder (eds.), *This Remarkable Continent: an Atlas of United States and Canadian Society and Cultures* (Texas, 1982).

H. Silver, *The Concept of Popular Education: a Study of Ideas and Social Movements in the Early Nineteenth Century* (1965).

P. and H. Silver, *The Education of the Poor: the History of a National School, 1824–1974* (1974).

B. Simon, *Studies in the History of Education, 1780–1870* (1960).

J. Simon, 'Was there a Charity School Movement? The Leicestershire evidence', in B. Simon (ed.), *Education in Leicestershire, 1540–1914* (Leicester, 1968).

Viscount Simonds (ed.), *Ecclesiastical Law, Being a Reprint of the Title Ecclesiastical Law from Halsbury's Laws of England: Church Assembly Edition* (3rd edn, 1957).

N. J. Smelser, *Social Paralysis and Social Change: British Working-class Education in the Nineteenth Century* (Berkeley, 1991).

B. Smith, *The Village of Oxhill and the Church of Saint Lawrence* (Oxhill, 1971).

D. Smith, *Old Furniture and Woodwork: an Introductory Historical Study* (1937, 1949 edn).

F. Smith, *A History of English Elementary Education, 1760–1902* (1931).

J. C. D. Smith, *Church Woodcarvings: a West Country Study* (Newton Abbot, 1969).

K. D. M. Snell, 'Parish registration and the study of labour mobility', *Local Population Studies*, 33 (1984).

Annals of the Labouring Poor: Social Change and Agrarian England, 1660–1900 (Cambridge, 1985).

Church and Chapel in the North Midlands: Religious Observance in the Nineteenth Century (Leicester, 1991).

'Deferential bitterness: the social outlook of the rural proletariat in eighteenth- and nineteenth-century England and Wales', in M. L. Bush (ed.), *Social Orders and Social Classes in Europe since 1500: Studies in Social Stratification* (1992).

'Settlement, poor law and the rural historian: new approaches and opportunities', *Rural History*, 3 (1992).

The Bibliography of Regional Fiction in Britain and Ireland, 1800–2000 (forthcoming).

Parish and Belonging in England and Wales, 1660–1914 (forthcoming).

K. D. M. Snell (ed.), *The Whistler at the Plough*, by A. Somerville (Manchester, 1852, 1989 edn).

Letters from Ireland During the Famine of 1847, by A. Somerville (Dublin, 1994).

The Regional Novel in Britain and Ireland, 1800–1990 (Cambridge, 1998).

R. A. Soloway, *Prelates and People: Ecclesiastical Social Thought in England, 1783–1852* (1969).

'Church and society; recent trends in nineteenth-century religious history', *Journal of British Studies*, 11 (1972).

R. Southey, *Letters from England* (1807, Gloucester, 1984 edn).

G. F. R. Spenceley, 'The origins of the English pillow lace industry', *Agricultural History Review*, 21 (1973)

M. Spufford, 'The dissenting churches in Cambridgeshire from 1660–1700', *Proceedings of the Cambridgeshire Antiquarian Society*, 61 (1968), 67–95.

Contrasting Communities: English Villagers in the Sixteenth and Seventeenth Centuries (Cambridge, 1974).

M. Spufford (ed.), *The World of Rural Dissenters, 1520–1725* (Cambridge, 1995).

R. Stanes, 'The Compton census for the Diocese of Exeter, 1676', *Devon Historian*, 9 (1974), pp. 14–27, and 10 (1975), pp. 4–16.

E. D. Steele, 'The Irish presence in the north of England, 1850–1914', *Northern History*, 12 (1976).

Palmerston and Liberalism, 1855–1865 (Cambridge, 1991).

C. Stell, *An Inventory of Nonconformist Chapels and Meeting-houses in Central England* (1986).

W. B. Stephens, 'A seventeenth century census', *Devon and Cornwall Notes and Queries*, 29 (1958).

Education, Literacy and Society, 1830–1870: the Geography of Diversity in Provincial England (Manchester, 1986).

J. Stratford, *Robert Raikes and Others: the Founders of Sunday Schools* (1880).

H. E. Strickland, *A General View of the Agriculture of the East Riding of Yorkshire* (1812).

R. Swift and S. Gilley, *The Irish Presence in the Victorian City* (1985).

J. Sykes, *The Quakers* (1958).

A. J. Tansley, 'On the straw plait trade', *Journal of the Society of Arts*, 9 (21 December 1860).

W. E. Tate, *The Parish Chest* (1946, Cambridge, 1960 edn).

C. Taylor, *Dorset* (1970).

The Cambridgeshire Landscape: Cambridgeshire and the Southern Fens (1973).

P. A. M. Taylor, *Expectations Westward: the Mormons and the Emigration of their British Converts in the Nineteenth Century* (1965).

A. Temple Patterson, *Radical Leicester: a History of Leicester, 1780–1850* (Leicester, 1975).

J. Thirsk, 'Industries in the countryside', in F. J. Fisher (ed.), *Essays in the Economic and Social History of Tudor and Stuart England* (Cambridge, 1961).

J. Thirsk (ed.), *Land, Church and People: Essays Presented to Professor H. P. R. Finberg* (Reading, 1970).

J. G. Thomas, 'The middle borderland', in E. G. Bowen (ed.), *Wales: a Physical, Historical and Regional Geography* (1957).

D. Thompson, *The Chartists: Popular Politics in the Industrial Revolution* (Aldershot, 1984).

D. M. Thompson, 'The 1851 Religious Census: problems and possibilities', *Victorian Studies*, 11 (1967).

'The churches and society in nineteenth-century England: a rural perspective', in G. J. Cuming and D. Baker (eds.), *Studies in Church History: Popular Belief and Practice* (Cambridge, 1972).

'The Religious Census of 1851', in R. Lawton (ed.), *The Census and Social Structure: an Interpretative Guide to Nineteenth-Century Censuses for England and Wales* (1978).

E. P. Thompson, *The Making of the English Working Class* (1963, Harmondsworth, 1975 edn).

'Time, work-discipline and industrial capitalism', in M. W. Flinn and T. C. Smout (eds.), *Essays in Social History* (Oxford, 1974).

F. Thompson, *Lark Rise to Candleford* (1939, Harmondsworth, 1976 edn).

F. M. L. Thompson, *English Landed Society in the Nineteenth Century* (1963).

D. Thomson, 'Charities in Rutland' (unpub. MA dissertation, Dept. of English Local History, University of Leicester, 1999).

A. Thwaite, *Edmund Gosse: a Literary Landscape, 1849–1928* (Oxford, 1985).

K. Tiller (ed.), *Church and Chapel in Oxfordshire, 1851*, Oxfordshire Record Society, 55 (1987).

F. Tillyard, 'The distribution of the Free Churches in England', *Sociological Review*, 27 (1935).

R. Tittler, 'Seats of honor, seats of power: the symbolism of public seating in the English urban community, c.1560–1620', *Albion*, 24 (1992).

M. Tranter, 'Landlords, labourers, local preachers: rural nonconformity in Derbyshire, 1772–1851', *Derbyshire Archaeological Journal*, 101 (1981).

'"Many and diverse dissenters": the 1829 religious returns for Derbyshire', *The Local Historian*, 18 (1988).

M. Tranter (ed.), *The Derbyshire Returns to the 1851 Religious Census*, Derbyshire Record Society, vol. 23 (Chesterfield, 1995).

J. L. G. Tucker, 'Mount St Bernard's Reformatory, 1856–81: a correction', *Recusant History*, 15 (1979–81).

M. E. Turner, *English Parliamentary Enclosure* (Folkestone, 1980).

Enclosures in Britain, 1750–1830 (1984).

M. Tylecote, *The Mechanics Institutes of Lancashire and Yorkshire before 1851* (1957).

A. C. Underwood, *A History of the English Baptists* (1947).

G. Unwin, *Samuel Oldknow and the Arkwrights: the Industrial Revolution at Stockport and Marple* (1924).

A. M. Urdank, *Religion and Society in a Cotswold Vale: Nailsworth, Gloucestershire, 1780–1865* (Berkeley, 1990).

D. M. Valenze, *Prophetic Sons and Daughters: Female Preaching and Popular Religion in Industrial England* (Princeton, 1985).

C. Vancouver, *A General View of the Agriculture of the County of Cambridge* (1794).

R. T. Vann, 'Quakerism and the social structure in the Interregnum', *Past and Present*, 43 (1969).

The Social Development of Early Quakerism, 1655–1755 (Cambridge, Mass., 1969).

R. T. Vann and D. Eversley, *Friends in Life and Death; the British and Irish Quakers in the Demographic Transition* (Cambridge, 1992).

J. A. Vickers (ed.), *The Religious Census of Hampshire, 1851* (Hampshire Record Series, Winchester, 1993).

J. Vincent, *Pollbooks: How Victorians Voted* (Cambridge, 1967).

'The effect of the Second Reform Act in Lancashire', *Historical Journal*, 11 (1968).

P. Virgin, *The Church in an Age of Negligence* (1988).

M. Vovelle, *Ideologies and Mentalities* (Cambridge, 1990).

A. P. Wadsworth, 'The first Manchester Sunday Schools', in M. W. Flinn and T. C. Smout (eds.), *Essays in Social History* (Oxford, 1974).

K. D. Wald, *Crosses on the Ballot: Patterns of British Voter Alignment since 1885* (Princeton, 1983).

J. Walsh, 'Methodism and the mob in the eighteenth century', in G. J. Cuming and D. Baker (eds.), *Studies in Church History: Popular Belief and Practice* (Cambridge, 1972).

J. K. Walton, 'The north-west', in F. M. L. Thompson (ed.), *The Cambridge Social History of Britain, 1750–1950, vol. 1, Regions and Communities* (Cambridge, 1990).

J. Walvin, *The Quakers: Money and Morals* (1997).

D. Wardle, *English Popular Education, 1780–1970* (Cambridge, 1970).

A. Warne, *Church and Society in Eighteenth-century Devon* (Newton Abbot, 1969).

M. Waterson, *The Servants' Hall: a Domestic History of Erddig* (1980).

E. I. Watkin, *Roman Catholicism in England from the Reformation to 1950* (1957).

R. Watson, *A Biblical and Theological Dictionary* (1832).

M. R. Watts, *The Dissenters. Vol. 1: From the Reformation to the French Revolution* (Oxford, 1978).

R. Watts, *Gender, Power and the Unitarians in England, 1760–1860* (1998).

S. and B. Webb, *English Local Government, vol. 5: The Story of the King's Highway* (1913, 1963 edn).

A. Weinberg, *Portsmouth Jewry* (Portsmouth, 1985).

J. S. Werner, *The Primitive Methodist Connexion: its Background and Early History* (1984).

Revd J. Wesley, 'Rules for a helper' (1744), in *The Works of the Rev. John Wesley*, 6 (1810).

J. Wesley Bready, *Lord Shaftesbury and Social-Industrial Progress* (1926).

E. G. West, *Education and the Industrial Revolution* (1975).

W. White, *History, Gazetteer, and Directory of Leicestershire* (Sheffield, 1846).

History, Gazetteer and Directory of Devonshire (Sheffield, 1850).

A. Whiteman, 'The Compton Census of 1676', in K. Schurer and T. Arkell (eds.), *Surveying the People* (Oxford, 1992).

A. Whiteman (ed.), *The Compton Census of 1676: a Critical Edition* (Oxford, 1986).

A. Whiteman and M. Clapinson, 'The use of the Compton Census for demographic purposes', *Local Population Studies*, 50 (1993).

W. T. Whitley, *A History of British Baptists* (1923).

M. J. L. Wickes, *Devon in the Religious Census of 1851: a Transcript of the Devon Section of the 1851 Church Census* (1990).

E. R. Wickham, *Church and People in an Industrial City* (1957, 1969 edn).

M. J. Wiener, *English Culture and the Decline of the Industrial Spirit, 1850–1980* (Cambridge, 1981).

O. Wilkinson, *The Agricultural Revolution in the East Riding of Yorkshire* (York, 1956).

G. Williams, *The Making of Manchester Jewry, 1740–1875* (Manchester, 1976).

G. A. Williams, *When Was Wales? A History of the Welsh* (Harmondsworth, 1985).

G. J. Williams, *The Welsh Tradition of Gwent* (Cardiff, n.d.).

R. Williams, *The Long Revolution* (1961, Harmondsworth, 1971 edn).

'Are we becoming more divided?', *Radical Wales*, 23 (Autumn, 1989).

T. Williamson and L. Bellamy, *Property and Landscape: a Social History of Land Ownership and the English Countryside* (1987).

J. M. Wilson, *The Imperial Gazetteer of Scotland; or, Dictionary of Scottish Topography, Compiled from the Most Recent Authorities, and Forming a Complete Body of Scottish Geography, Physical, Statistical, and Historical* (London, 1868), 2 volumes.

The Imperial Gazetteer of England and Wales, 6 volumes (Edinburgh, n.d., c.1870–2).

Revd H. Woodcock, *Piety among the Peasantry: being Sketches of Primitive Methodism in the Yorkshire Wolds* (1889).

C. Woodham-Smith, *The Great Hunger: Ireland, 1845–1849* (1962).

Sir L. Woodward, *The Age of Reform, 1815–1870* (1938, Oxford, 1962).

Wright's Directory of Leicestershire and Rutland (Leicester, 1896).

P. Wright, *The Village That Died for England: the Strange Story of Tyneham* (1995, 1996 edn).

S. Wright, 'Easter books and parish rate books: a new source for the urban historian', *Urban History Yearbook* (1985).

'A guide to Easter books and related parish listings', *Local Population Studies*, part 1, 42 (1989), 18–32; and part 2, 43 (1989), 13–28.

S. Wright, *Friends in York: the Dynamics of Quaker Revival, 1780–1860* (Keele, 1995).

T. Wright, *Some Habits and Customs of the Working Classes by a Journeyman Engineer* (1867, New York, 1967 edn).

E. A. Wrigley 'Men on the land and men in the countryside', in L. Bonfield, R. M. Smith and K. Wrightson (eds.), *The World We Have Gained: Histories of Population and Social Structure* (Oxford, 1986).

E. A. Wrigley, R. S. Davies, J. E. Oeppen and R. S. Schofield, *English Population History from Family Reconstitution, 1580–1837* (Cambridge, 1997).

E. A. Wrigley and R. S. Schofield, *The Population History of England, 1541–1871: a Reconstruction* (1981).

D. Wykes, 'A reappraisal of the reliability of the 1676 "Compton Census" with respect to Leicester', *Transactions of the Leicestershire*

Archaeological and Historical Society, 60 (1980).

N. Yates, 'Urban church attendance and the use of statistical evidence, 1850–1900', in D. Baker (ed.), *Studies in Church History, 16: the Church in Town and Countryside* (Oxford, 1979).

N. Yates, R. Hume and P. Hastings, *Religion and Society in Kent, 1640–1914* (Woodbridge, 1994).

M. Zell, *Industry in the Countryside: Wealden Society in the Sixteenth Century* (Cambridge, 1994).

Index

This index covers textual entries, and does not include religious denominations and place-names where they are listed in tables.

Aber, 203
Aberayron, 116
Aberdare, 116
Abergavenny, 58, 248, 249, 442
Aberystwyth, 99, 147, 166
agriculture, 41, 48, 45, 141, 170, 203, 206, 209, 210, 212, 213, 214, 215, 217, 218, 219–20, 221–2, 227, 228–9, 318, 353, 382, 389–92, 411
Ahlstrom, Sydney, 276
Aldeburgh, 214
Aldershot, 324
Alnwick, 64
Alston, 137
Alton Locke, 213
Ambler, R., 45
Amersham, 112
Amlwch, 204, 205
Ampthill, 215
Amsterdam, 103
Anglesey, 11, 86, 155, 201, 203–5, 224, 231, 235, 239, 240, 246, 297, 302, 346, 382, 442, 443
Anglican Church *see* Church of England
Anti-State Church Association, 27, 78
Appleby Magna, 329, 333, 335, 340, 447
Arch, Joseph, 142, 322–3, 324, 357, 359
ARC/VIEW, 438
Arden, Forest of, 133
Ardington, 365
Arnesby, 273
Ashbourne, 442
Ashburnham, 365
Ashby-de-la-Zouch, 217
Ashby Folville, 251
Ashover, 218
Ashton, T. S., 80
Ashton-under-Lyne, 116, 180, 219, 402
Askrigg, 111
Aston, 411
Atherstone, 160
Aveling, J. C. H., 258
Axbridge, 147
Aylesbury, Vale of, 58
Aylsham, 149

Baggrave, 336
Baines, Edward, 38, 52, 171, 450, 452
Bakewell, 218
Bala, 155, 167, 279
Baltonsborough, 334
Bamborough, 221
Bamford, Samuel, 283
Bangor, 167, 204, 205
Baptists, 74, 93, 94, 95, 102–8, 114, 116, 118, 143, 157, 186, 191, 192, 193, 213, 215, 217, 218, 240, 269
  attendances, 43
  index of attendances measure, 104–5, 229
  occupancy measure, 106
  seating, 341–2, 346, 349, 352, 354, 355, 356, 359
  Sunday schools, 297, 299, 305, 312
  see also General Baptists; New Connexion General Baptists; Particular Baptists
Barford, 322
Barker, Joseph, 283
Barking, 214

Barnsley, 62, 133, 180
Barton-upon-Irwell, 180
Bassaleg, 224
Bath, 60
Beaminster, 210
Bebb, E. D., 106
Bebbington, D. W., 172
Bedford, Vale of, 215
Bedfordshire, 11, 106, 127, 201, 214–16, 223, 224, 228, 229, 231, 235, 239, 240, 243, 289, 290, 302, 346, 368, 382, 383, 443
Bedminster, 147
Bedwas, 207
Bedwelty, 157, 280
Beeston, 178
Belford, 64, 97
Bellingham, 65, 97, 127, 222
Belper, 149, 218
Belsay, 221, 365
Belvoir, Vale of, 384
Bennett, Arnold, 282
Berington, Joseph, 175, 177
Berkshire, 55, 65, 107, 120, 137, 139, 144, 164, 335, 365, 382
Bermondsey, 178, 179, 180
Berrington, 258
Berwick-upon-Tweed, 64, 97
Beverley, 220, 256
Bible Christians, 4, 123, 143, 151–4, 167, 170, 194
  attendances, 49
  index of attendances measure, 151–4
  seating, 49, 349
  Sunday schools, 299
  urbanisation, 398
  see also Methodism
Bicester, 180
Biggleswade, 215
Biggs, John, 115
Biggs, William, 115
Billericay, 127, 179
Billesdon, 62, 338
Binbrook, 383
Birmingham, 57, 60, 62, 65, 66, 67, 69, 111, 115, 116, 127, 130, 139, 147, 162, 164, 178, 283, 402, 411
Bishop Burton, 220
Blaby, 341
Blackburn, 177, 219, 278, 284
Black County, 57, 66, 67, 69, 101, 115, 124, 126, 130, 139, 169, 396, 411
Blaenavon, 208
Blaise Hamlet, 368
Blake, R., 25–6
Blanchland, 368
Blandford, 210
Bodmin, 144
Bolton, 116, 162, 219, 278, 284, 402
Bontgoch, 206
Book of Mormon, 163
Bootle, 58
Bossy, J., 257
Boston, 179
Bourn, 179
Bourne, Hugh, 135–6
Bournemouth, 118
Bowdler, John, 82
Boynton, 220
Bradford, 60, 97, 178, 180
Bradford-on-Avon, 60
Brandon, P., 212
Breadalbane, Marquess of, 40
Brecklands, 101
Brecknock, 157
Breedon-on-the-Hill, 327, 447
Brethren, 349, 350, 398
Bridgnorth, 57
Bridgwater, 334
Bridlington, 220, 442
Bridport, 116, 211
Brierley, Benjamin, 283
Briggs, Asa, 279, 283
Brighton, 60, 101, 116, 118, 212, 399
Bristol, 64, 65, 71, 108, 116, 126, 166, 169, 207
Bristol Channel, 126, 153
Brocklesby, 365
Bromsgrove, 67
Brontë, Patrick Branwell, 285
Brotherly Society of Birmingham, 283
Brougham, Lord Henry, 30–1, 288
Broughton Astley, 260
Brown, C. G., 396
Browne, Robert, 98
Bryanites *see* Bible Christians

Buckerell, 334, 336
Buckinghamshire, 104, 106, 112, 118, 127, 289, 290, 292
Bugthorpe, 220
Bunting, Jabez, 147, 281
Burley-on-the-Hill, 216, 335
Burslem, 136, 141
Burton Bradstock, 210
Bury, 116, 162, 219, 278, 284
Bury St Edmunds, 67, 74, 214
Buxton, 218

Caernarvon, 205
Caernarvonshire, 11, 87, 201, 203–5, 223, 224, 235, 239, 243, 246, 297, 346, 368, 369, 381, 442, 443
Caird, James, 213, 221–2, 382
Calvinistic Methodists *see* Countess of Huntingdon's Connexion
Cambo, 221
Cambridge, 60, 166
Cambridge Group for the History of Population and Social Structure, 4–5
Cambridgeshire, 11, 58, 104, 106, 127, 139, 201, 212–13, 214, 219, 222, 224, 228, 229, 235, 239, 242, 243, 246, 257, 269, 297, 302, 336, 346, 368, 382, 383, 443
Camelford, 146
Campsall, 326
Canford Magna, 368
Canterbury, Diocese of, 57
Canterbury, Province of, 102
Capability Brown, 211
Capheaton, 221
Captain Swing, 143
Cardiff, 107, 115, 427
Cardigan, 206
Cardiganshire, 11, 87, 201, 205–7, 227, 228, 229, 231, 235, 239, 280, 297, 346, 381, 442, 443
Carlisle, 146
Carmarthen, 107, 157
cartography, 438–9
Castle Acre, 369, 383
Castle Ward, 149
Catcott, 334
Catherington, 55
Catholic and Apostolic Church, 349
Catholic Relief Act (1791), 247, 258
Catholics *see* Roman Catholics
Cecil, Lord Robert, 449
Census of Population, 11, 41
Census of Religious Worship, 7, 8, 9, 12, 15, 16, 237, 266, 371, 394, 404, 449–52
  attendances, 39–45, 46–51, 245–6, 247, 286, 303, 431–3, 434
  correction, 425–30
  derived measures, 431–7
  enumeration form, 37, 38, 39, 44
  historiography, 35–46, 431, 438
  seating, 39, 45–51, 321–63, 433–4
  source, 23–35, 232, 234, 268, 269–70, 286–7, 395, 396–8
Cerne Abbas, 210
Channel Islands, 153
Chardstock, 210
Charles, Thomas, 279, 280
Charnwood, 253, 260
Chartism, 116, 208, 217
Cheadle, 178
Chelmondiston, 214
Chelmsford, 179, 180
Chepstow, 157, 207, 249
Cheshire, 45, 64, 69, 97, 104, 115, 116, 118, 124, 133, 137, 146, 157, 164, 177, 333, 411, 415
Chester, 204
Chester, Diocese of, 174
Chesterfield, 133, 442
Chester-le-Street, 67
Cheviot hills, 221
Chichester, 180
Chichester, Diocese of, 55, 84
child labour, 290–3, 294, 295, 296, 302, 312, 313, 316, 319, 383
Chilterns, 104, 107
Chippenham, 213, 286, 368
Chipping Norton, 180
Chorley, 177
Chorlton, 62, 177
Christchurch, 58, 183
Christ Church, Timperley, 333
Christian Remembrancer, 52

Church Building Acts, 26, 337, 338, 339, 357, 399
Church of England, 1, 54–92, 121, 204, 205, 211, 212, 213, 214, 215, 216, 236, 376, 377, 378, 387, 404, 418, 419, 438, 449–52
absenteeism, 84–7, 89, 214, 380
attendances, 42–4, 48, 49, 50–1
church size measure, 65–6
Compton Census and, 236, 237, 238–9, 261–2, 265–6, 269
core area, 71, 73–4, 407
demography, 65–8, 83–4
enumeration, 38, 40
income, 31, 40, 54, 77–8, 79, 83, 84, 87–90, 91, 92, 207, 227, 228, 309–10, 354, 384–5, 416, 440, 448
index of attendances measure, 54, 67–71, 72, 229, 357–8, 373, 418
index of sittings measure, 67–71, 72, 373, 405–7
industrialisation, 4, 54, 60, 64, 188
landownership, 54, 77, 83–4, 304–5, 307–8, 351–2, 365, 373–4, 388–9
occupancy measure, 66–7, 83, 101, 359
parochial structure, 5, 54, 55, 78–82, 83–4, 91, 102, 183, 188, 212, 219, 222, 227, 371–2, 373
people per place of worship measure, 62–4
place of worship density measure, 59–62
politics, 25–6, 74–7, 78, 171
proportion share measures, 55–9, 357
relations to Nonconformity, 5, 120, 123, 127, 129–31, 146, 153, 154, 155, 159, 167, 170, 185–94, 197, 217, 221, 287, 288, 437
religious census returns, 11, 31, 35
settlement patterns, 58, 60–2, 79–82, 83, 91, 158, 212
seating, 9, 14, 41, 48, 49, 218, 329–40, 341, 344–6, 349–52, 354, 356, 357–8, 359, 360, 361, 433
Sunday schools, 278, 286, 297–302, 303, 304–5, 307–8, 313, 315, 317, 319–20
Church Pastoral Aid Society, 88
Church Reform Act, 26
Church of Scotland, 93, 97–8
attendances, 49
occupancy measure, 97, 359
seating, 49, 349, 350, 359
urbanisation, 398
see also Presbyterians
Church Stretton, 57
Cirencester, 57
City of London, 60
Civil War, English, 95, 99, 103, 108, 211
Clayworth, 235
Cleobury-Mortimer, 57, 139
Clergy List, 37
Cliff, P. B., 286
Clitheroe, 177
'close' parishes, 84, 91, 143, 216, 220, 221, 224, 264, 304, 307, 315–16, 351–2, 353, 365–94, 419, 441, 442–4, 447
see also landownership
Clovelly, 334
Clowes, John, 162
Clowes, William, 135–6, 141
Clun, 137
Clytha, 249
Cobbett, William, 48
Coffin, Walter, 116
Colchester, 67, 162
Coleman, B. I., 52, 187
Compton Census (1676), 8, 11, 12, 16, 102, 196, 232–73, 394
Conformists *see* Church of England
Congregational Union of England and Wales, 99
Congregationalists *see* Independents
Conservative Party, 74, 171, 177, 217, 249
Conventicles Return (1669), 271
Cooper, Thomas, 217, 283
Corbridge, 221
Cornwall, 58, 60, 64, 67, 69, 71, 77, 83, 101, 104, 111, 118, 126, 129, 130, 135, 139, 146, 151, 153, 154, 164, 167, 405, 407
Cosby, 262
Cotswolds, 57
Cottesmore, 216
cotton, 65, 113
Countess of Huntingdon's Connexion,

155, 159–60, 161, 299, 303, 312, 358, 398
see also Methodism
Covent Garden, 336
Coventry, 57, 60, 64, 65, 164
Coxe, William, 208
Cranborne, 211
Cranoe, 224
Crickhowell, 58
Crockett, Alasdair, 16–17, 357, 376, 394, 418, 436
Croft, 327
Cromford, 218
Cross, F. L., 98
Crossley, Frank, 39, 52
Croxdale, 182
Croxton, 213
Croxton Kerrial, 326
Cumberland, 58, 60, 64, 69, 74, 87, 111, 113, 133, 146, 164, 175, 411, 415
Currie, R., 135, 150, 160, 186–7, 189, 190, 192, 317
Cwm, 249

Dalton in Furness, 279
Darlington, 111, 178, 180
Dartford, 180
Dean, Forest of, 153, 207
Dee Estuary, 55
demography, 4–5, 25, 48, 65–6, 78, 83, 126, 143, 188, 206, 207, 208, 215, 216, 217, 219, 222–3, 227, 234, 263–4, 286, 311–12, 353, 354, 372, 387, 398–9
Denbighshire, 204, 315
Derby, 60, 65, 67, 126, 162, 178, 218
Derbyshire, 11, 58, 60, 80, 87, 101, 104, 115, 124, 129, 133, 137, 141, 149, 150, 167, 201, 217, 218–19, 224, 227, 229, 231, 235, 239, 243, 246, 257, 278, 289, 292, 298, 302, 327, 333, 335, 365, 368, 382, 443
Devon, 57, 60, 67, 71, 101, 104, 107, 115, 126, 139, 149, 151, 153, 154, 334, 336
Dewsbury, 60
Didcot, 141
Dissent *see* New Dissent; Nonconformity; Old Dissent
Docking, 149
Doncaster, 180
Donington Park, 103
Dorchester, 87, 210
Dorking, 111
Dorset, 11, 48, 57, 58, 66, 67, 71, 101, 102, 127, 139, 144, 146, 179, 201, 209–11, 221, 224, 227, 228, 229, 289, 297, 302, 368, 382, 383, 405, 407, 443
Dover, 166
Dow, Lorenzo, 136
Downs, south, 55, 212
Driffield, 220
Dudley, 116, 402
Dulverton, 153
Dunn, Samuel, 147, 150
Dunsfold, 327
Dunstable, 215
Dunton Bassett, 262
Durham, 67, 178, 180, 182
Durham, County, 64, 65, 69, 137, 141, 164, 167, 178, 181, 221, 411

Earl of Shaftesbury (Seventh), 324
Easingwold, 180
East Anglia *see* Eastern Division
Eastbourne, 126
Easter books, 235
Eastern Division, 59, 64, 66, 69, 71, 101, 102, 103, 113, 116, 133, 139, 141, 142, 144, 194, 195, 407
East London, 60
East Riding, 11, 87, 118, 137, 139, 141, 144, 169, 201, 219–20, 227, 229, 231, 235, 239, 240, 241, 242, 246, 254–7, 262, 263, 297, 302, 346, 382, 405, 442, 443
see also Yorkshire
Eastry, 180
East Stonehouse, 179
Eastwell, 251, 263
Eccles, 219
Eccleshall-Bierlow, 133
economic history, 4
Edensor, 368
Edmondesham, 211
Education Act (1870), 281, 289
Edwards, George, 283
elections, religion and, 2–3, 10, 18, 27

Eliot, George, v, 1, 2, 6, 417
Ellingham, 257
Elsdon, 221
enclosure, 77, 87, 90, 130, 215, 217, 219, 224, 416
Enderby, 447
Engels, F., 177, 219
English Church Census (1989), 17
English–Welsh border, 58, 405, 414–18
Erddig, 315
Erpingham, 149
Escrick, 220
Essex, 59, 74, 99, 101, 102, 106, 107, 111, 118, 127, 129, 139, 164, 179, 180, 196, 214, 405, 407
Established Church *see* Church of England
estate villages *see* 'close' parishes
Evangelical Revival, 25
Evans, Eric, 90
Evans list (1715), 17, 232, 272
Everett, James, 147, 150
Everingham, 254, 258, 263, 273
Everitt, Alan, 188–9, 223, 364, 370
Evesham, Vale of, 129
Exe estuary, 57
Exeter, 60, 126
Exton, 216

Factory Bill (1843), 288
Falmouth, 127, 135, 183
Falstone, 221
Farnborough, Surrey, 57
Farnborough, Warwickshire, 333
Farningham, Marianne, 283
Felden, 57
Felton, 182
Female Union Society for the Promotion of Sabbath-Schools, 283
Fens, 60, 67, 101, 126, 149, 213
Festiniog, 157
Fitzwilliam, Earl, 40
Flintshire, 64, 204
Ford, 221
Fordington, 210
Foston, 224
Fox, George, 108–9, 113
Fox, William, 282
France, 3–4, 258
Free Church of Scotland, 453
French Protestants, 424

Gaddesby, 326
Garbett, Cyril, 324–5
Garthorpe, 262
Gateshead, 60, 133, 411
Gay, J. D., 2, 84, 99, 113, 116, 130, 131, 153–4, 166, 175
General Baptists, 93, 94, 103–4, 115, 240, 242
  attendances,
  seating, 349, 358
  Sunday schools, 303
  see also Baptists
General Baptists of the New Connexion *see* New Connexion General Baptists
German Catholics, 424
German Protestant Reformers, 424
Gilbert, A. D., 91, 93, 187–8, 189, 245, 317
GIMMS, 438
Gladstone, W. E., 451, 452
Glamorgan, 80, 107, 179, 207, 208
Glastonbury, 334
Glendale, 64, 97, 221
Glenn Magna, 447
Glossop, 218, 278
Gloucester, 281–2
Gloucestershire, 57, 60, 65, 101, 102, 107, 118, 126, 149, 289, 318, 368
Godstone, 57
Gorleston, 214
Gosse, Edmund, 283
Gough, Richard, 321
Gower, 414
Grace Dieu, 253
Graham, George, 28–9
Graham, Sir James, 288
Grantham, 149
Granville, Earl, 40
Gravesend, 180
Great Boughton, 180
Great Eastwick, 163
Great Eversden, 269
Great Yarmouth *see* Yarmouth
Greek Church, 424

Grey, George, 31
Griffith, William, 147, 150
Grimston, 251
Guildford, 180
Gwennap, 124

Halévy, E., 3
Hall, Robert, 273
Hall, Thomas, 333
Hallaton, 335
Haltwhistle, 221, 222
Hampshire, 55, 57, 60, 66, 67, 71, 126, 127, 137, 139, 144, 146, 151, 153, 324
Hanley, 315
Hardy, Thomas, 210–11
Harewood, 368
Harris, Howel, 154, 419
Harrison, J. F. C., 28, 164
Hartley, Thomas, 162
Haslingden, 116, 162
Hastings, 60, 212
Hathersage, 273
Haverfordwest, 157
Haworth, 285
Hayfield, 133
Hay-on-Wye, 104
Hearth Tax returns, 235, 236
Hedon, 256
Helston, 146, 151
Hemphill, Dom B. 178, 257
Hemsworth, 111
Hereford, 180
Hereford, Diocese of, 58, 84
Herefordshire, 57, 60, 65, 71, 101, 104, 249, 290, 411, 415
Herries, Lord, 254
Hertfordshire, 104, 118, 127, 164, 216
Hesleyside, 182
Hexham, 182
Hinckley, 217, 251, 253, 260, 341
Hirst, M., 76
History of Myddle, 321
Hobsbawm, Eric, 3, 170
Holbeach, 104, 149
Holborn, 60
Holderness, 67
Holderness, B. A., 367
Holland *see* Netherlands, The
Holme-on-Spalding-Moor, 254, 256
Holsworthy, 151
Holyhead, 204–5
Holyoak, George, 283
Horsley, L., 317
Hose, 261
Hoskins, W. G., 64, 216, 217
Houghton on the Hill, 261
Howden, 255
Huddersfield, 133
Hull, 62, 65, 115, 126, 166, 219, 220, 257
Humphreys, M., 330
Hungarton, 336
Hunslet, 60
Huntingdonshire, 104, 106, 127
Husbands Bosworth, 251, 253, 338

Ifton, 207
Ilam, 368
Illinois, 163
Ilston on the Hill, 261
Imperial Gazetteer, The, 11, 86, 88, 203, 223, 304, 351, 369, 370–1, 383, 440–8
Incorporated Church Building Society, 337, 338
Independent Methodists, 123, 132, 159, 160, 303, 349, 398
  see also Methodism
Independents, 74, 93, 94, 95, 98–102, 103, 104, 114, 115, 116, 117, 118, 157, 159, 186, 191, 192, 193, 211, 213, 217, 218, 240, 242, 269
  attendances, 43,
  index of attendances measure, 99–100, 229
  occupancy measure 101–2
  seating, 340, 341, 352, 353, 354, 355, 356, 359, 360
  Sunday schools, 298, 300, 302, 303, 305, 312, 315, 318
industry, 3, 25, 48, 54, 78, 81, 107, 130, 131, 157, 188, 207, 208, 210, 213, 214, 215–16, 217, 218, 219, 220, 221, 224, 227, 229, 251, 290–3, 296, 316, 318–19, 381, 389–92, 415–16
Ingoldsby, 336
Ipswich, 116, 147, 214

Ireland, 29, 78, 253
famine, 48, 109, 173–4, 180, 182–3, 272, 318
immigration, 48–9, 83, 95, 98, 173, 177, 182–3, 184, 208, 209, 219, 249, 250, 251, 253, 257, 263, 264–5, 270
Isle of Wight, 57, 64, 151, 153, 179
Islington, 65, 179, 180
Isolated Congregations, 404, 424
Italian Reformers, 424

Jenkins, Philip, 280
Jews, 15–16, 81
Johnson, Matthew, 144
Jones, Ieuan Gwynedd, 91–2, 205, 206
Jones, Revd Griffith, 279
Joyce, Patrick, 284, 316
Juniper Hill, 333

Kay, J. P., 177
Keighley, 284
Kendall, 177
Kendall, Revd H. B., 141, 142, 306
Kensington, 179
Kent, 57, 60, 71, 101, 104, 106, 111, 118, 126, 127, 139, 151, 153, 164, 179, 271, 290, 411
Kessingland, 214
Ketton, 216
Kidderminster, 116
Kilham, Alexander, 132
Kilsby, 332
Kingsley, Charles, 213
King's Lynn, 67, 126, 149
King's Norton, 261
Kingston, 180
Kingswood, 124
Kirkley, 214
Knossington, 335, 339

Labour Party, 172
Lady Huntingdon, 419
Lady Huntingdon's Connexion *see* Countess of Huntingdon's Connexion
Lake District, 188
Lampeter, 99, 116
Lancashire, 11, 45, 58, 60, 62, 65, 66, 67, 69, 74, 80, 98, 101, 104, 107, 108, 111, 113, 115, 116, 118, 126, 133, 139, 146, 149, 157, 160, 162, 164, 169, 172, 177, 180, 182, 201, 207, 215, 218–19, 222, 224, 227, 229, 257, 275, 278, 280, 284, 289, 290, 302, 314, 315, 381, 405, 409, 411, 416, 443
Lancaster, 219
landownership, 9, 211, 212, 216, 219, 223–4, 257–9, 264–5, 270, 272, 303–9, 313, 314, 315, 351–2, 364–94, 416, 440–8
see also 'open' parishes, 'close' parishes
Land Tax Returns, 370, 378, 441, 443, 444–8
Langton, 220
language, 417
Cornish, 146
Gaelic, 10
Welsh, 10, 32, 92, 102, 107, 114, 158, 159, 201–2, 205, 208–9, 280, 302, 317, 380, 414
Laqueur, T. W., 283–4, 285–6, 297, 314, 315
Laslett, Peter, 271
Latter Day Saints, 162–6, 318
index of attendances measure, 164–6
index of sittings measure, 164
seating, 349, 358
urbanisation, 398
Laud, Archbishop, 329
Ledbury, 57
Leeds, 60, 62, 124, 144, 278, 450, 452
Lees, L. H., 184
Leicester, 45, 60, 65, 66, 67, 71, 108, 111, 116, 126, 147, 217, 218, 252, 253, 260, 261, 273, 278, 341
Leicestershire, 11, 45, 48, 49–50, 60, 65, 85, 101, 106, 107, 108, 118, 124, 149, 167, 169, 201, 217–18, 224, 227, 235, 238, 239, 240, 241, 242, 243, 246, 250–3, 259–62, 263, 271, 292, 297, 302, 326, 327, 329, 335, 336, 338, 341, 370, 378, 382, 405, 433, 441, 443, 444–8
Leighton Buzzard, 169
Leiston, 214
Lewes, G. J., 159
Lewis, G. C., 177

Lewis, George, 451
Liberal Party, 74–7, 78, 115, 171–2, 388–9, 452
Liberation Society, 78
Limerick, County, 450, 452
Lincoln, 103, 112
Lincolnshire, 58, 59, 60, 64, 65, 66, 67, 69, 84, 90, 101, 104, 106, 111, 118, 124, 130, 137, 144, 149, 167, 169, 179, 326, 336, 365, 382, 383, 405, 407, 443
Lindisfarne, Archdeacon of, 98
Liskeard, 450, 452
Liverpool, 60, 62, 65, 115, 116, 157, 163, 166, 177, 180, 183, 219, 278, 293, 402
Llanarth, 249, 250, 263, 273
Llanbadarn Fawr, 205, 206, 280
Llanberis, 204
Llandewi-Brefi, 205, 206
Llandudno, 204, 236
Llandysilio, 204
Llanfaethly, 205
Llanfihangel Geneu'r Glyn, 205, 206
Llanfihangel y Creuddyn, 205
Llanfihangel yng Ngwynfa, 327
Llanfoist, 249
Llangeitho, 206
Llangorwen, 207
Llangranog, 206
Llanrhystud, 206
Llanrwst, 157, 167
Llanvihangel by Usk, 250
Llanwern, 224
Lleyn, 203
Lobley, J., 338
Lockinge, 365
London, 57, 60, 62, 64, 65, 67, 69, 71, 83, 97, 98, 101, 107, 108, 111, 116, 118, 120, 123, 126, 127, 135, 139, 146, 147, 149, 153, 157, 162, 164, 169, 174, 175, 177, 178, 180, 182, 183, 184, 194, 206, 212, 215, 278, 396, 402, 403, 404, 405, 407, 409, 411, 414, 415, 416, 417
Lord and Peasant in Nineteenth Century Britain, 364
Loughborough, 178, 217, 251, 253, 260
Lovett, William, 283
Lowestoft, 214
Luckcock, James, 283
Lutherans, 424
Luton, 169, 215
Lutterworth, 260
Lyme Regis, 210
Lymington, 126
Lytchett-Minster, 211

Macclesfield, 293
Machen, 208
Machin, G. I. T., 131
Machynlleth, 167
Madeley, 57
Madingley, 213
Malthus, Thomas, 275
Malton, 180
Manchester, 60, 62, 65, 97, 115, 116, 162, 177, 180, 219, 278, 315, 369, 402
Manchester, Diocese of, 26, 79
Manchester, New York, 163
Mann, Horace, v, 24–5, 29–30, 31, 32, 34, 35, 36, 37, 41–2, 44, 51–2, 98–9, 103, 124, 131, 142, 155, 174, 323–4, 325, 344–5, 349, 350, 360, 395, 404, 411, 425–6, 428–9, 431
Market Harborough, 260
Marriage Act, 26
Martinsthorpe, 224
Marylebone, 179, 180
Matfen, 221
Matlock, 218
Medway, 153, 180
Melton Mowbray, 217, 251, 261
Mendips, 282
Merthyr Tydfil, 58, 71, 116, 293
Methodism, 18, 25, 74, 77, 83, 84, 90, 93, 94, 104, 107, 114, 170–1, 185–98, 206, 211, 218, 229, 249, 265, 280, 287, 293, 296, 305, 312, 313, 315, 322, 356, 384, 407–9, 420
see also Bible Christians; Countess of Huntingdon's Connexion; Independent Methodists; Methodist New Connexion; Primitive Methodists; Welsh Calvinistic Methodists; Wesleyan Methodist Association; Wesleyan Methodist Original Connexion; Wesleyan Reformers

Methodist Committee of Privileges, 26
Methodist New Connexion, 121, 132–5
  index of attendances measure, 133–5
  Sunday schools, 299, 303, 312, 318
  urbanisation, 398
  see also Methodism
Miall, Edward, 27
Middle Barton, 383
Middle Rasen, 383
Middlesborough, 279
Middlesex, 180, 290
Midhurst, 180
migration, 10, 78, 81, 83, 95, 98, 142, 157, 163, 166, 173–4, 177, 180, 182–3, 184, 201–3, 206, 208, 209, 219, 249, 250, 253, 263, 264–5, 270, 414, 417
Milbanke Pew, 327
Milburn, G. E., 52–3
Million Act (1818), 82
Mills, Dennis, 364
Milton Abbas, 211, 368
mining, 57, 58, 141, 170–1, 203–4, 206, 207, 208, 209, 217, 218, 221, 251, 293, 296
Minsteracres, 182
Missouri, 163
Misterton, 260
Mitford, 149
Monks Kirby, 251, 260, 335
Monkswood, 224
Monmouth, 157, 248, 249
Monmouthshire, 11, 80, 87, 107, 153, 157, 179, 182, 201, 207–9, 222, 224, 227, 229, 235, 239, 240, 241, 243, 246, 247, 248–50, 263, 280, 297, 381, 442, 443
Monmouthshire Merlin, 208–9
Monsell, W., 450
Montgomeryshire, 327, 330
Moorman, J. R. H., 87
Moravians, 299, 349
Morcott, 216
More, Hannah, 282
Mormons *see* Latter Day Saints
Morning Chronicle, 275, 278, 292–3
Morpeth, 139, 182
Motcombe, 211
Mothering Sunday, 44–5
Moulton, 326
Mount Melleray, 253

Nantwich, 146
Narbeth, 157
National Agricultural Labourers' Union, 323
Nauvoo, 163, 166
Neath, 58
Nether Broughton, 262, 447
Netherbury, 210
Netherlands, The, 99, 102, 103
Netherseal, 333, 335
Netherwitton, 257
Neville Holt, 252
Newburn, 221
Newbury, 180
Newbury, Deanery of, 39
Newcastle-in-Emlyn, 99, 116, 157
Newcastle-under-Lyme, 315
Newcastle upon Tyne, 60, 67, 111, 126, 139, 162, 178, 333, 411
New Church, 160, 162, 299, 318, 398
  attendances, 49
  seating, 49
New Connexion General Baptists, 93, 103–4, 106
  attendances, 48
  seating, 48
  Sunday schools, 299
  see also Baptists
New dissent, 12, 13, 93, 120, 121–72, 185–98, 214, 399
  see also Methodism
New Forest, 60, 64, 69, 118, 147, 169
New Houghton, 368
New Parishes Acts, 337, 399
Newport, Monmouth, 58, 157, 166, 183, 208, 249
Newport, East Riding, 220
Newtown, 104
Nonconformity, 1, 4–5, 25, 31–2, 37, 74–6, 77, 80, 83, 205, 209, 211, 217, 222, 286, 288, 293–4, 319, 339, 357, 359, 365–6, 375–8, 389, 449–52
  attendances, 50, 376
  enumeration, 38, 40
  seating, 50, 340–3, 376, 407

see also New dissent, Old dissent
Norfolk, 60, 64, 65, 67, 101, 104, 118, 126, 129, 137, 139, 141, 144, 149, 150, 167, 169, 196, 213, 266, 330, 335, 341, 368, 369, 383, 405, 407
Norfolk, Duke of, 181
Norman, E., 183
Normanton, 216
Northamptonshire, 60, 101, 104, 118, 169, 332, 405
Northern Division, 58, 101, 102, 106, 133, 147
Northleach, 57
North Midland Division, 57, 129, 141, 144, 191, 415
North Riding, 64, 65, 69, 101, 111, 118, 126, 129, 133, 137, 139, 164, 182, 327, 405
see also Yorkshire
Northumberland, 11, 60, 64, 65, 69, 97, 98, 101, 111, 124, 126, 127, 137, 139, 146, 149, 164, 167, 169, 178, 181, 201, 220–2, 224, 227, 229, 231, 257, 298, 365, 368, 381, 411, 415, 443
North West Division, 58, 126, 147, 407, 414, 415
North Witchford, 149
North York Moors, 67
Norwich, 74, 87, 99, 102, 111, 126, 162, 164, 182
Nottingham, 45, 65, 126, 147, 150, 162, 178
Nottinghamshire, 60, 65, 101, 104, 118, 129, 133, 135, 137, 146, 149, 289, 292
Nuneaton Courtenay, 368

Oadby, 85
Oakham, 57, 149
Obelkevich, James, 364
O'Bryan, William, 150, 151
occupations, 3, 4, 310–13, 352, 353, 389–93
Oldcastle, 224
Old dissent, 12, 13, 92–120, 121, 123, 126, 185–98, 212, 214, 217–18
attendances, 48
Compton Census and, 237, 238–4, 245, 246, 259–63, 265–9, 271–2
index of attendances measure, 118, 229, 407
percentage share measures, 239–40, 246
seating, 48, 356
Sunday schools, 305, 312, 313
urbanisation, 399
Oldham, 293
Old Warden, 368
'open' parishes, 84, 143, 304, 308, 352, 365–94, 419, 441, 444, 447
see also landownership
Ordnance Survey, 41, 438
Ormskirk, 177
Osborne, Bernal, 450
Other Isolated Congregations *see* Isolated Congregations
Overseal, 335, 336
Oxford, 57
Oxford Movement, 25, 399
Oxfordshire, 111, 127, 129, 333, 368, 382, 383

Pakefield, 214
Palmerston, Lord Henry, 450–1
Papism, 236, 237, 238–44, 245, 246–59, 263–70, 272
see also Roman Catholics
parish registers, 5
Parnham, 211
Particular Baptists, 93, 94, 103–4, 106–7, 240, 242, 378
Sunday schools, 299, 303
see also Baptists
Parys Mountain, 204
Pattern of Rural Dissent, The, 364
Peak district, 218
Peasenhall, 214
Peatling Parva, 262
Peel, Robert, 26, 76
Pelling, H., 98, 107, 131
Pembroke, 157
Pembrokeshire, 102, 382, 414
Penkridge, 178
Pennines, 67, 175
Penthurst, 365
Penzance, 111, 151
Pershore, 57
Perthir, 249

Petersfield, 57
Peto, Sir Morton, 52
Petworth, 55
Pevsner, N., 254
Phillimore Atlas and Index of Parish Registers, 438
Phillips, J. A., 74
Phillips, Peter, 160
Pickering, 137
Pickering, W. S. F., 38, 45,
Pickwell, 262
Piers Plowman, 326
Pinners Hall, 103
Plymouth, 65, 151, 179, 183
Plynlimon, 206
Pontrhydygroes, 206
Pontypool, 157
Poole, 101, 183, 210, 211
Poole Harbour, 127
Poor Law Amendment Act (1834), 78, 143, 213
Poor Law Commissioners' Reports, 11
Poplar, 180
Port Dinorwic, 205
Porter, G. R., 28
Portland, 209, 211
Port Penrhyn, 205
Portscuett, 224
Portsea Island, 57, 60, 151
Portsmouth, 183
Potteries, the, 65, 137, 141
Presbyterian Church in England, 93, 97–8, 240, 312, 349, 359, 398
  see also Presbyterians
Presbyterians, 74, 83, 94, 95–8, 115, 116, 118, 186, 211, 221, 269
  see also Church of Scotland; Presbyterian Church in England; United Presbyterian Church
Prescot, 219
Preston, 163, 177, 219
Prestwich, 219, 278
Priestley, Joseph, 115
Primitive Methodists, 4, 101, 122, 131, 132, 135–44, 149, 151, 153, 154, 155, 169, 170, 191–2, 193, 194, 197, 211, 217, 218, 219, 378, 384
  attendances, 49
  church size measure, 137–9
  index of attendances measure, 137,138, 141, 229
  occupancy index, 139–41
  percentage share measures, 137, 139
  seating, 49, 346, 349, 352, 354, 356, 358, 360
  Sunday schools, 298, 299, 302, 306, 308, 312, 318
  urbanisation, 398
  see also Methodism
Proclamation Society, 282
Progress of the Nation, 28
Protestant Methodists, 144
  see also Wesleyan Methodist Association
Protestant Society for the Protection of Religious Liberty, 26
Protestation returns (1641–2), 235
Pugin, A. W. N., 64
Purbeck, 127, 209
Puritanism, 118
Pwllheli, 66, 155, 167
Pryce, W. T. R., 158

Quakers, 32, 93, 94–5, 108–14, 118, 217, 240, 242, 269, 272
  attendances, 48, 95, 108, 111
  enumeration, 48
  index of attendances measure, 109–12
  index of sittings measure, 111
  occupancy measure, 95, 112
  seating, 48, 95, 111, 349, 350, 433
  Sunday schools, 299, 318
  urbanisation, 398
Queen Anne's Bounty, 84, 88
Quenby, 336

Raglan, 249
Raikes, Robert, 281, 315, 318–19
Rawding, C., 25
Reach, Angus Bethune, 177, 275
Reading, 60, 64, 65
Rebecca riots, 91, 206
Redesdale, 221
Redruth, 126
Reeth, 126

Reform Act (1832), 26, 76
Reformed Church of the Netherlands, 424
Reformed Irish Presbyterians, 424
regional fiction, 10
Religion and Respectability, 283–4
Religious Worship Act Amendment Bill (1857), 324
Return of the Native, 210–11
returns of non-Anglican places of worship (1829), 8, 11, 12, 49–50, 196, 232, 259–60, 268
returns of papists (1767), (1780), 232
Rhayader, 104
Rheidol, 206
Rhiwabon coalfield, 158
Ribble, 163
Rickinghall Superior, 326
Ringwood, 116
Ripley, 150
Ripon, Diocese of, 26, 79
Risca, 208
Rochdale, 146, 219, 278
Rockfield, 249
Roman Catholics, 4, 12, 13, 74, 81, 83, 113, 121, 173–84, 192, 196, 219, 250, 272, 273, 452
  attendances, 40–1, 48, 174
  Compton Census and, 240–4, 247–59, 263–5, 266–8, 270
  index of attendances measure, 175–9, 184, 229
  occupancy measure, 174, 179–82, 184
  percentage share measures, 239–40, 246, 247–9, 263
  seating, 38, 48, 174, 349, 359
  Sunday schools, 299, 303, 318
  urbanisation, 398
Rothbury, 60, 97, 178, 182
Rowland, Daniel, 419
Runcorn, 180
Rural Rides, 48
Ruthin, 155
Rutland, 11, 48, 133, 149, 201, 216–17, 221, 222, 224, 227, 228, 229, 235, 239, 246, 297, 335, 381, 383, 405, 407, 442, 443
Rye, 212
Saddington, 262
Salford, 177, 180
Salisbury, 66
Salisbury, Bishop of, 40
Salisbury, Diocese of, 84
Salt Lake City, 163
Samford, 57
Sancton, 256
Sandemanians, 424
Sandy, 215
Sawston, 273
Saxelby, 251
Scilly Isles, 153, 167
Scotch Baptists, 424
Scotland, 8, 33–4, 36, 77, 83, 95, 97, 98, 221, 450
Scraptoft, 261
secularisation, 3, 9, 14, 16–17, 25, 229–31, 289, 296, 394, 395–420, 434
Sedbergh, 109
Selby, 178
Select Committee on Settlement and Poor Removal, 382
Settlement Act (1662), 78
settlement patterns, 14, 58, 79–80, 102, 129, 146, 219, 221
Seventh-Day Baptists, 424
Severn, River, 111, 118, 178
Shaftesbury, 210, 211, 286
Shaftesbury, Lord, 210
Shangton, 261
Shaw, James, 331, 332
Shaw, T., 153
Sheffield, 65, 116, 124, 135, 149, 332, 340, 396, 402
Shepshed, 251, 260
Sherborne, 210, 211
Shibbear, 150
Shoreham, 212
Short, Brian, 212, 364, 370
Shrewsbury, 57, 60, 67, 164
Shropshire, 57, 60, 64, 71, 101, 104, 137, 139, 141, 383, 411, 415
Sidmouth, Lord, 26
Sigston, James, 144
Silas Marner, v, 1, 6, 417
Simonburn, 221
Skenfrith, 249

Skipton, 146
Skirbeck, 326
slavery, 26, 109
Sledmere, 220
Smith, Adam, 275
Smith, Frank, 275, 276–7
Smith, Joseph, 162, 163
Society for Promoting the Enlargement, Building and Repair of Anglican Churches and Chapels, 82–3
Society of Friends *see* Quakers
Solent, 67, 120, 146, 151
Somerleyton, 368
Somerset, 57, 60, 67, 71, 104, 106, 107, 115, 126, 139, 149, 151, 153, 334
Southampton, 64, 151, 166
South Carlton, 336
South East Division, 133, 139, 144, 147, 194
Southey, Robert, 319
South Midland Division, 87, 118, 127, 144, 407, 417
South Shields, 411
South West Division, 139, 143, 160, 164, 194
Southwold, 214
Soutter, Francis, 283
Spaldington, 255
Spufford, Margaret, 364, 372
St Columb, Cornwall, 151
St David, Diocese of, 58
St George, London, 178, 179
St George in the East, London, 180
St Giles, London, 179, 180
St James, London, 60, 97
St Luke, London, 62, 65
St Margaret's, Leicester, 278
St Martin-in-the-Fields, London, 97
St Mary's, Leicester, 252
St Mary's, Whitby, 338
St Maughan's, Monmouthshire, 249
St Nicholas's, Newcastle upon Tyne, 333
St Olave, London, 178, 180
St Paul's, Covent Garden, 336
St Peter's, Netherseal, 333
St Pierre with Runstone, Monmouthshire, 224
St Woollos, Monmouthshire, 249
Stafford, 178
Staffordshire, 57, 80, 104, 129, 133, 135–6, 137, 141, 149, 178, 289, 368
Stalbridge, 211
Stamford, 57, 449
Statistical Society, 51
Staunton Harrold, 447
Stepney, 179, 180
Steyning, 55
Stockport, 293, 315
Stockton, 111, 178
Stoke Abbot, 211
Stoke Dry, 224
Stoke-on-Trent, 60, 64
Stour Provost, 211
Stow on the Wold, 57
Strand, 60, 178, 179, 180
Sturminster Marshall, 211
Sudbury, 57, 365, 368
Suffolk, 11, 48, 57, 60, 65, 99, 101, 102, 104, 106, 107, 118, 139, 164, 196, 201, 212, 214, 227, 228, 229, 235, 239, 242, 243, 297, 302, 327, 346, 382, 405, 443
Sunday scholars *see* Sunday schools
Sunday schools, 9, 13–14, 41–2, 114, 205, 216, 274–320, 333–4, 355, 380, 399, 416, 431, 432
Sunday School Society, 281
Sunday School Union, 281
Sunderland, 60, 180
surnames, 10
Surrey, 55, 57, 71, 111, 118, 139, 290, 327, 411
Sussex, 11, 55, 71, 87, 104, 106, 111, 118–19, 126, 129, 139, 151, 164, 201, 212, 223, 224, 227, 229, 231, 235, 239, 241, 243, 290, 297, 330, 365, 382, 383, 411, 443
Sutcliffe, Frank Meadow, 338
Sutton, 336
Swanage, 211
Swansea, 104
Swedenborg, Emanuel, 160, 162
Swedenborgians *see* New Church
Swindon, 141
Swine, 254, 256
Sydling St Nicholas, 211

Tadcaster, 178
Tamworth, 178
Tealby, 383
Teesdale, 178, 182
Tees, River, 118, 146
Tenterden, 116
Test and Corporation Acts, 26, 74, 181
Tetworth, 213
textile industry, 60, 102, 107
Thakeham, 55
Thames marshes, 71
Thames valley, 69
Thanet, Isle of, 64, 179, 180
Theddingworth, 260
Thingoe, 57
Thirsk, 383
Thompson, David, 37, 45, 53
Thompson, E. P., 3, 133, 170, 283
Thompson, Flora, 333
Thompson list (1772), 17
Thornton, 447
Thurnby, 261
Thurning, 330, 335
Tillett, Ben, 283
Tillyard, F., 185, 186, 189, 190, 192
Tillyard Thesis, 12, 185–6, 196
Times, The, 18
Timperley, 334
Tintern, 207
Tintinhull, 334
Tisbury, 179
tithes, 89–90, 91, 109, 130
Tiverton, 151
Toddington, 215
Toleration Act, 26, 77, 114
Tolpuddle, 210
Tonge, 447
Tongham, 324
Tregaron, 155
Tremadoc, 368
Trent valley, 64, 141, 218
Tre'rddol
Trevecca, 154, 159
Trevethin, 208, 280
Troedyraur, 206
Truro, 126
Tunbridge, 180
Tunstall, 136
Twycross, 262
Tynemouth, 133, 149, 411
Tyne, River, 146, 221
Tyneside, 60, 62, 65, 66, 67, 108, 124, 133, 147, 166, 183

Ulverstone, 58, 74
Underwood, A. C., 107
Uniformity, Act of (1662), 95, 99, 211, 328
Unitarians, 74, 93, 95, 114–17, 157, 240, 273, 303, 312
  attendances, 116
  index of attendances measure, 116–17
  seating, 341, 358
  urbanisation, 398
United Presbyterian Church, 93, 96–8, 303, 359
  see also Presbyterians
United States of America, 2, 17, 162, 163, 166, 276, 283
Unwin, George, 276
urbanisation, 395–420
Utah, 163

visitation returns, 17
voting patterns, 74–7

Wadsworth, A. P., 276
Wakefield, 149
Wakerley, 224
Wald, Kenneth, 50
Wales, 18–19, 74, 77, 78, 83, 88, 91–2, 99, 102, 104, 107, 111, 113–14, 116, 118, 126, 127, 129, 130, 133, 139, 141, 144, 147, 149, 153, 157, 158, 160, 164, 167, 169, 170, 171, 175, 179, 192–3, 201–3, 208, 209, 227, 229, 231, 239, 240, 241, 249, 279–80, 289, 290, 297, 305, 306–7, 308, 310, 312, 313–14, 361, 376, 378, 379–80, 382, 383, 396, 398, 402, 404, 407, 414, 417, 418
Walsall, 178, 411
Walsingham, 149
Walton, 221
Wanlip, 262
Wareham, 210, 211
Warren, Samuel, 144
Warter, 220

Warwickshire, 57, 64, 101, 111, 238, 322, 336, 382
Warwickshire coalfield, 57
Wash, the, 55, 58, 64, 66, 69, 71, 83, 102, 104, 106, 118, 126, 127, 149, 153
Waterless, 262
Weald, 60, 64, 66, 69, 71, 107, 212, 411
Weardale, 137
Wellington, 57
Welsh Calvinistic Methodists, 83, 122–3, 127, 143, 150, 154–9, 160, 167, 170, 172, 192–3, 205, 206, 207, 309, 376, 377, 379–80, 418, 427, 437
  attendances, 49
  index of attendances measure, 155–8, 229
  percentage share measures, 155
  seating, 49, 346, 349, 352, 353, 354, 355, 356, 358, 359, 360
  Sunday schools, 297, 299, 302, 303, 305, 306–7, 313, 317–18, 355
  urbanisation, 398
  see also Methodism
Welsh Division, 58, 60, 62, 64, 65, 66, 67, 69, 106, 154, 155
Welsh Marches, 64, 102
Welwick, 256
Weobly, 57
Werry, Mary Ann, 153
Wesley, John, 123, 124, 130, 169, 197, 275, 419–20
Wesleyan Methodist Association, 122, 132, 133, 144–7, 149
  attendances, 49
  index of attendances measure, 144–7
  percentage share measures, 146
  seating, 49, 358
  Sunday schools, 303, 306, 312
  urbanisation, 398
  see also Methodism
Wesleyan Methodist New Connexion *see* Methodist New Connexion
Wesleyan Methodist Original Connexion, 4, 101, 114, 121, 122, 123–32, 133, 135, 136, 137, 139, 141, 143, 144, 146, 147, 149, 150, 151, 154, 155, 157, 167, 169, 170, 191–3, 194, 206, 215, 217, 219, 378, 384, 450
  attendances, 49
  index of attendances measure, 124–6, 229
  index of sittings measure, 126
  occupancy measure, 124, 127–9
  percentage share measures, 126
  relations with Church of England, 185, 191
  seating, 49, 346, 350, 352, 354, 356, 358, 359, 360
  Sunday schools, 298, 299, 302, 303, 312, 317
  see also Methodism
Wesleyan Methodists *see* Wesleyan Methodist Original Connexion
Wesleyan Reformers, 121, 132, 133, 144, 147–50
  attendances, 49
  index of attendances measure, 147–9
  seating, 49, 349, 358
  Sunday schools, 303
  urbanisation, 398
  see also Methodism
Westbourne, 55
West Derby, 60, 177
West Grinstead, 330
West Ham, 180
Westhampnett, 55, 60
West Leake, 224
West London, 60
West Midland Division, 118, 126, 129, 133, 141, 144, 147, 178, 183, 411, 414, 415
Westminster, 60
Westmorland, 69, 74, 111, 133, 164, 411
Weston on Trent, 327
West Riding, 62, 65, 67, 83, 98, 104, 107, 109–10, 115, 116, 118, 126, 127, 131, 133, 135, 137, 146, 149, 162, 289, 290, 405, 409, 411
  see also Yorkshire
West Ward, 74
West Woodhay, 335
Weymouth, 58, 60, 129
Whaley Bridge, 315
Whalley, 219
Whetstone, 260
Whitby, 183, 338
Whitechapel, 180

Whitefield, George, 159, 419
Whitehaven, 74, 180
Whiteman, Anne, 232, 237, 238, 239, 268, 269
Whiteside, J., 451
Whitfield, 221
Whitley, W. T., 107, 108
Whitwick, 251, 253
Wickes, M. J. L., 153
Wickham, E. R., 337
Wigan, 177, 219, 278
Wigton, 111
Wilberforce, Bishop of Oxford, 39, 40, 42–3, 52
Williams, Gwyn, 92
Willoughby, 262
Wilson, 447
Wilson, John, 283
Wiltshire, 65, 102, 106, 107, 127, 139, 144, 146, 151, 179, 289
Wimpole, 213
Winchester, 182
Winchester, Diocese of, 55, 84
Windsor, 180
Winwick, 162
Wirral, 97, 177
Wisbech, 149
Witchampton, 210
Witham, 111
Wolstanton, 60
Wolverhampton, 65, 178, 402, 411
Wonastow, 249
Woodbridge, 147, 214
Woodhouse Moor, 278
wool, 66, 118, 206
Worcester, 57, 67, 111, 160, 182
Worcester, Diocese of, 84
Worcestershire, 57, 60, 71, 101, 382, 411
working class, 25, 32, 75, 136, 154, 166, 284–5, 298, 308, 309, 314, 315, 317, 322–5, 361
Worthing, 180
Worthington, 447
Wortley, 133
Wright, Thomas, 323, 324
Wye, River, 207, 208
Wymondham, 341

Y Gweithiwr, 116
Yarmouth, 57, 67, 133
Yeovil, 210, 334
Yetminster, 210
York, 87, 182, 220
Yorkshire, 58, 60, 64, 65, 66, 69, 80, 101, 104, 129, 130, 131, 133, 146, 160, 164, 167, 178, 181, 219, 235, 326, 368, 383, 407
  see also East Riding; North Riding; West Riding
Young, Brigham, 163
Yspyty Ystwyth, 206
Ystumtuen, 206